MILITARY EFFECTIVENESS
VOLUME I:
THE FIRST WORLD WAR

Titles of related interest

The Birth of Independent Air Power
British Air Policy in the First World War
Malcolm Cooper

British Strategy and War Aims, 1914–1916
David French

Fire-Power
British Army Weapons and Theatres of War, 1904–1945
Shelford Bidwell and Dominick Graham

The Naval War in the Mediterranean, 1914–1918
Paul G. Halpern

The War Plans of the Great Powers, 1880–1914
Edited by Paul Kennedy

The Navy and German Power Politics, 1862–1914
Ivo Nikolai Lambi

'The Origins of the Second World War' Reconsidered:
The A. J. P. Taylor Debate after Twenty-five Years
Edited by Gordon Martel

Warfare in the Twentieth Century
Theory and Practice
Edited by Colin McInnes and G. D. Sheffield

European Armies and the Conduct of War
Hew Strachan

In Defence of Naval Supremacy
Finance, Technology, and British Naval Policy 1889–1914
Jon Tetsuro Sumida

The Killing Ground
The British Army, the Western Front and the Emergence of Warfare, 1900–1918
T. H. E. Travers

MILITARY EFFECTIVENESS

VOLUME I: THE FIRST WORLD WAR

Edited by

Allan R. Millett and Williamson Murray

Mershon Center, The Ohio State University

Series on Defense and Foreign Policy

Boston
UNWIN HYMAN
London Sydney Wellington

This volume was prepared, proofed and passed for press by the editors and contributors.

Unwin Hyman Inc.
955 Massachusetts Avenue, Cambridge, MA 02139, USA

Published by the Academic Division of
Unwin Hyman Ltd
15/17 Broadwick Street, London W1V 1FP, UK

Allen & Unwin (Australia) Ltd
8 Napier Street, North Sydney, NSW 2060, Australia

Allen & Unwin (New Zealand) Ltd
in association with the Port Nicholson Press Ltd
Compusales Building, 75 Ghuznee Street, Wellington 1, New Zealand

First published in 1988
Paperback edition first published 1989
Second impression 1990

Library of Congress Cataloging-in-Publication Data

Military effectiveness.
Includes bibliographies and indexes.
Contents: v. 1. The First World War — v. 2. The interwar period — v.3. The Second World War.
1. Military art and science—History—20th century.
2. Military history, Modern—20th century. 3. Armed Forces—History—20th century. I. Millett, Allan Reed.
II. Murray, Williamson.
U42.M55 1987 355'.009'04 87-15284
ISBN 0–04–445053–2 (v. 1: alk. paper)
ISBN 0–04–445578–X PBK

British Library Cataloguing in Publication Data

Military effectiveness.
1. Armed forces—History—20th century
2. Military history, Modern—20th century
I. Millett, Allan, R. II. Murray, Williamson
ISBN 0–04–445053–2 v. 1 ISBN 0 04–445578–X Pbk
ISBN 0–04–445054–0 v. 2
ISBN 0–04–445055–9 v. 3

Printed in Great Britain at the
University Press, Cambridge

Table of Contents

Preface

We began this study on the effectiveness of military institutions in the belief that historians have an obligation to examine the issues involved in why some military forces succeed, while others fail. If we have not succeeded fully in our goal, we believe that the essays in this volume have at least suggested the dimensions of the issues. There are *no* easy answers, *no* quick fixes, *no* simple formulas for the achievement of military effectiveness. While one of the authors of the summarizing essays in Volume 3 suggests that 'one can doubt whether any other profession [than the military] in these seven nations during the same period would have received such poor ratings by similarly competent outside observers,' these studies also suggest how intractable, complex, and resistant to analysis and calculation are the problems roused by war.

This study involves seven nations over three distinct time periods: the First World War (Volume 1), the interwar period (Volume 2), and the Second World War (Volume 3). We have asked each one of the historians examining these twenty-one case studies to follow the direction provided in a guidance essay (the first chapter in Volume 1). That essay asked our historians to examine what we believe to be the four distinct levels of war: the political, the strategic, the operational, and the tactical from the point of view of their national case study. Thus, there are consistent themes running through all of the essays. In addition, we asked three of the scholars in the project to write summarizing essays on each of the distinct time periods, looking for common themes and common problems. These essays appear as the final chapters in each volume. Finally, in Volume 3 we have asked an eminent military historian and a senior retired US Army general to comment on the whole study.

There have been numerous individuals involved in the working up of these volumes. Therefore, we can thank only a very few of them. We would particularly like to thank Mr. Andrew Marshall, Director of the Office of Net Assessment, for the funding and for his consistently intelligent guidance. Mr. Richard Perle, Assistant Secretary of Defense, provided funding and support in the creation of this project. At Ohio State, Kenneth Watman, Charles Munnell, and Don Lair have provided the administrative support and footwork necessary to keep the project running smoothly. The Program in International Security and Military Affairs at the Mershon Center provided a solid base for the administration of the project. Joni Wood-Ward and Allison Hoffman provided the typing support and administrative backup required. Finally, we would like to thank our wives, Marjorie Murray and Martha Farley-Millett, for their help and understanding throughout the four years needed to complete this project.

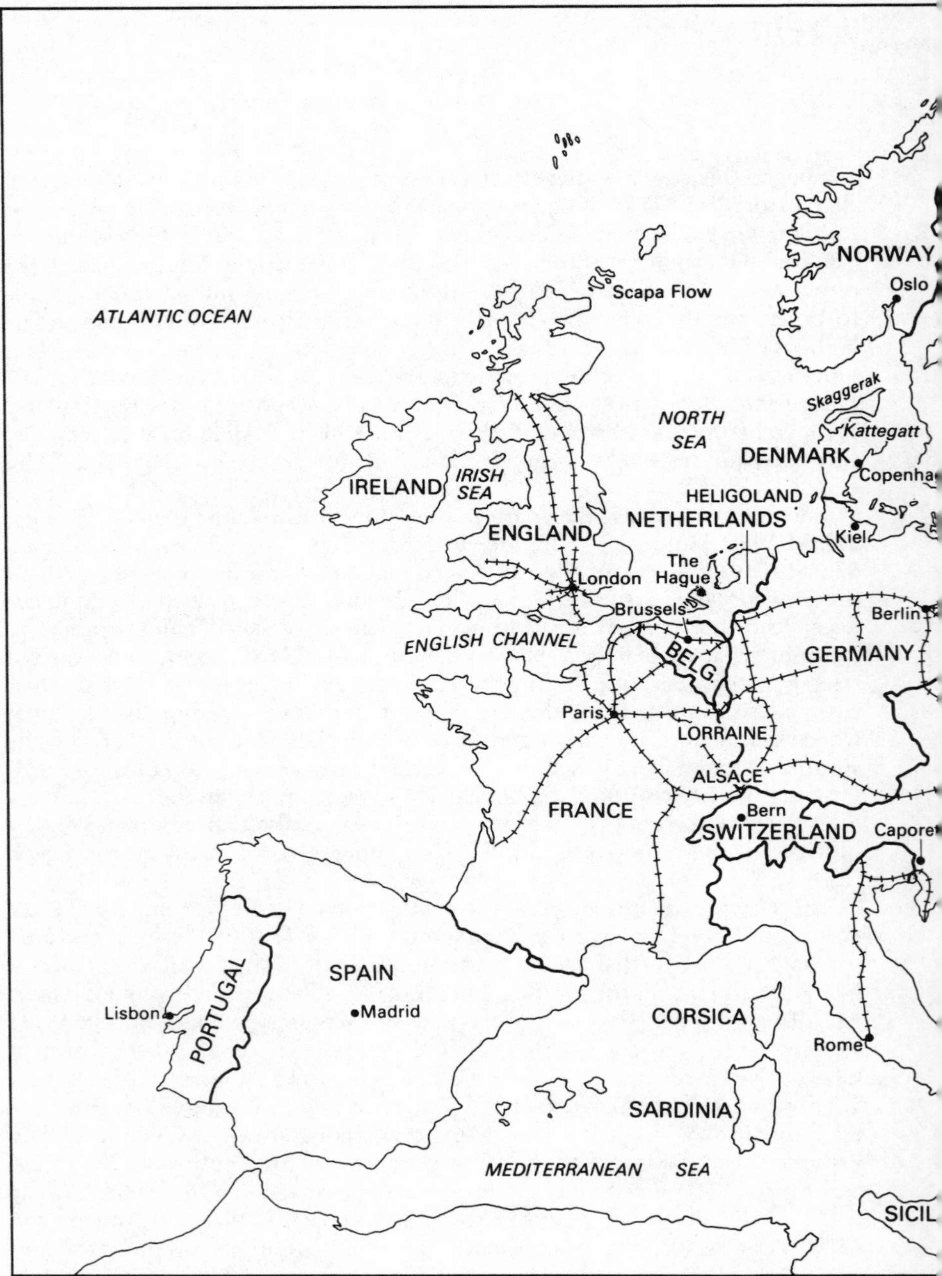

Map 1.1 Europe, 1914

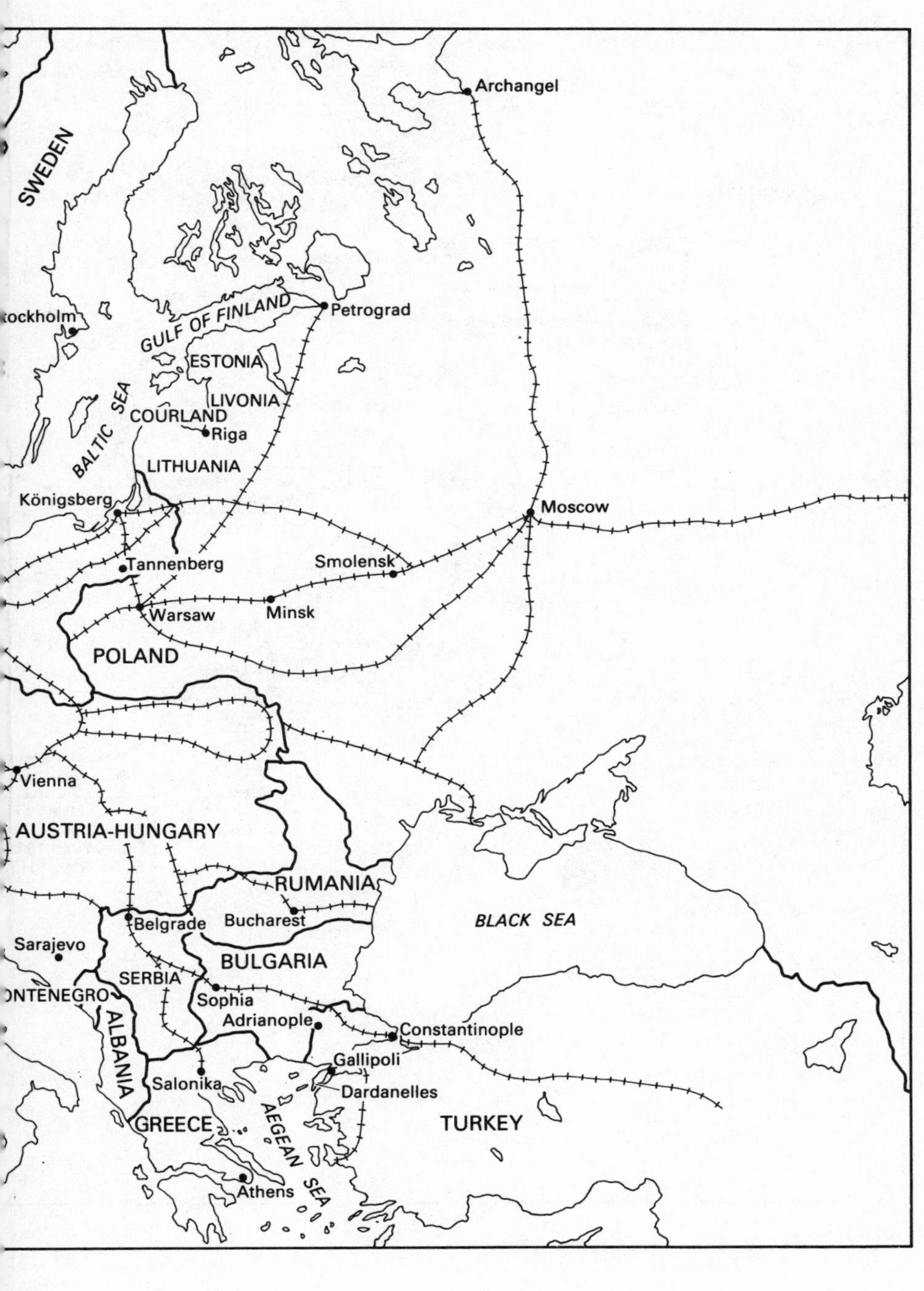
SWEDEN
Archangel
ockholm
GULF OF FINLAND
Petrograd
ESTONIA
LIVONIA
BALTIC SEA
COURLAND
Riga
LITHUANIA
Königsberg
Moscow
Tannenberg
Smolensk
Warsaw
Minsk
POLAND
Vienna
AUSTRIA-HUNGARY
RUMANIA
Belgrade
Bucharest
BLACK SEA
Sarajevo
BULGARIA
SERBIA
ONTENEGRO
Sophia
ALBANIA
Adrianople
Constantinople
Gallipoli
Salonika
Dardanelles
GREECE
AEGEAN SEA
TURKEY
Athens

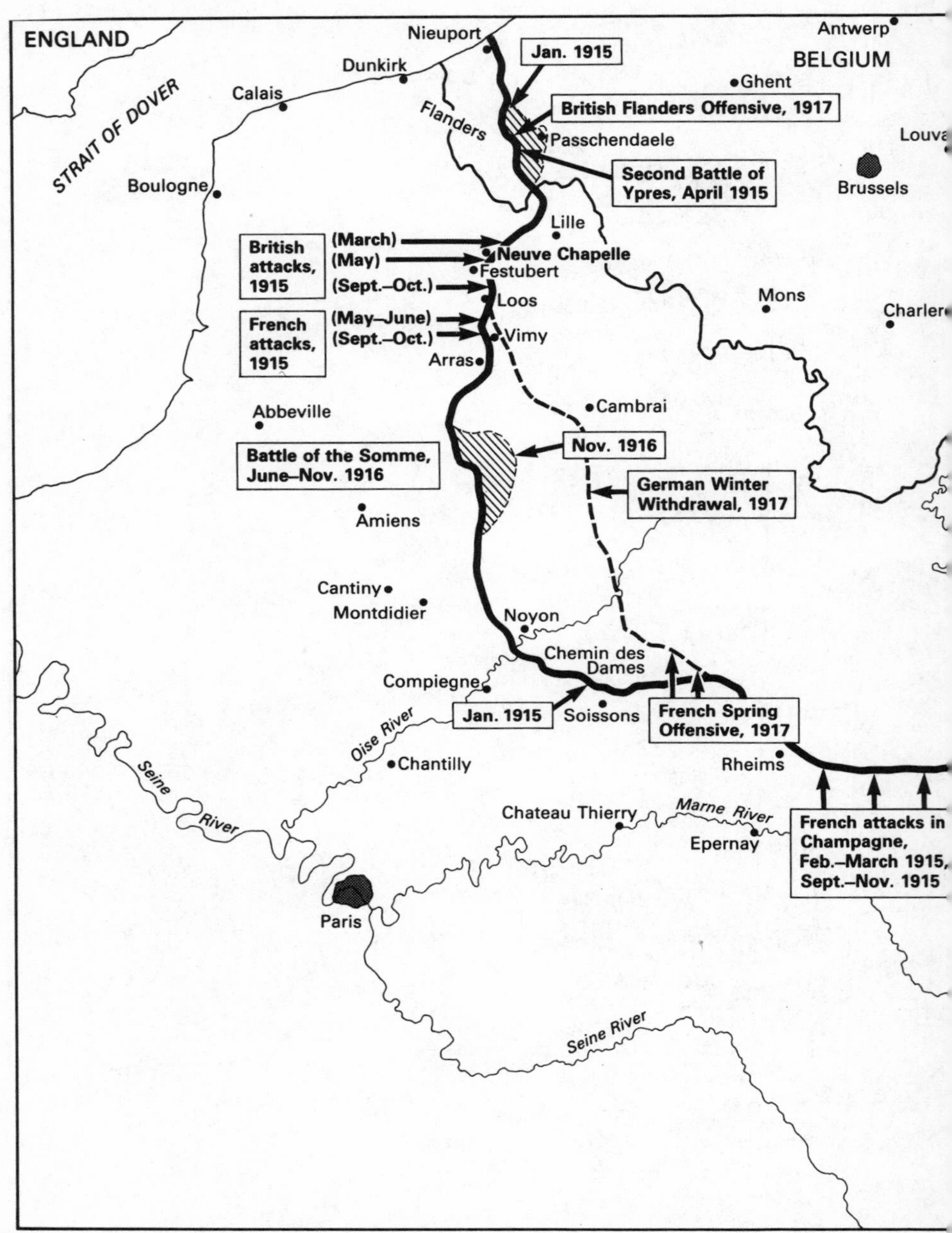

Map 1.2 The Western Front, 1914–17

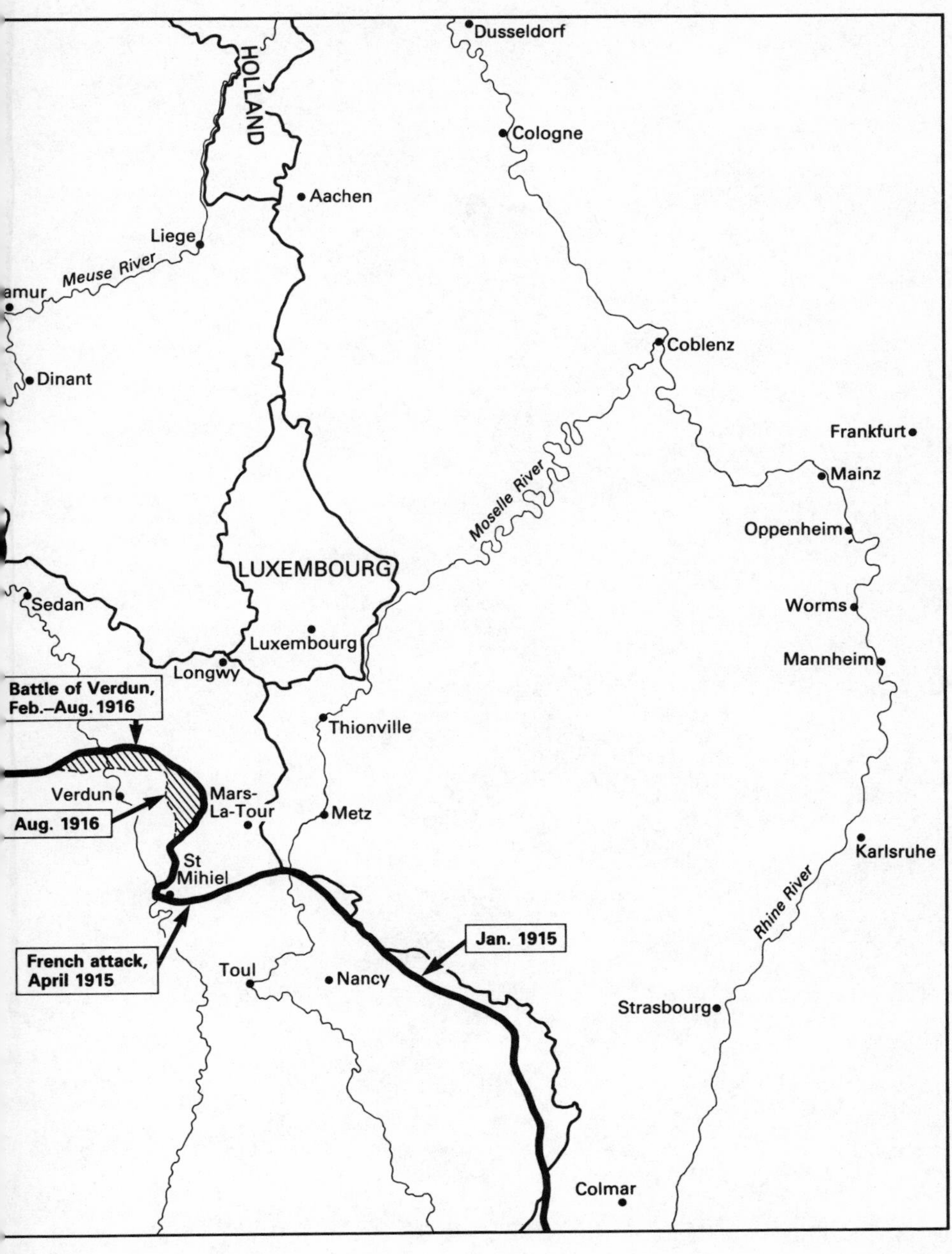

Dusseldorf
HOLLAND
Cologne
Aachen
Liege
Meuse River
amur
Dinant
Coblenz
Frankfurt
Mainz
Moselle River
Oppenheim
LUXEMBOURG
Sedan
Worms
Luxembourg
Longwy
Mannheim
Battle of Verdun, Feb.–Aug. 1916
Thionville
Verdun
Mars-La-Tour
Metz
Aug. 1916
Karlsruhe
St Mihiel
Rhine River
Jan. 1915
French attack, April 1915
Toul
Nancy
Strasbourg
Colmar

MILITARY EFFECTIVENESS

VOLUME I:

THE FIRST WORLD WAR

[1]

The Effectiveness of Military Organizations

ALLAN R. MILLETT, WILLIAMSON MURRAY, and KENNETH H. WATMAN
Mershon Center, The Ohio State University

Introduction

The interrelated issue of military structure and effectiveness confronts planners and commanders with some of the most intractable intellectual issues associated with organizational behavior. The realities of preparing forces to kill and to face death in the service of the state create problems with no analogues in other forms of social interaction. It is easier to define the behaviors one wishes to discourage in individuals – cowardice, flight, and non-cooperation – than to define the positive performance of complex organizations, which all armed forces inevitably become. 'The primary object of organization,' wrote General Sir Ian Hamilton, 'is to shield people from unexpected calls upon their powers of adaptability, judgment, and decision.'[1] Yet other commanders have observed that individual and organizational flexibility is essential to military success.

Despite a sizeable theoretical literature on organizational efficiency, military effectiveness remains an ill-defined concept. For some civilian and military analysts, effectiveness is tied to the social structure of military organizations. The sociological approach focuses on factors such as unit cohesion, group solidarity, small-unit leadership, and *Kameradschaft*. Similar research seeks to link effectiveness to non-material factors like esprit, staying power, and the will-to-fight. Outside of the small-unit focus, the sociological focus – regardless of whether the methodology is quantitative or descriptive – may provide special insights into the likely performance of large-scale military organizations, since it focuses on such problems as the normative aspects of officership, recruitment, military socialization, morale and political attitudes, and troop trainability.[2]

The operational approach emphasizes the importance of doctrines and tactical systems and their proper utilization on the battlefield. By implication, this concept is also sensitive to companion issues such as training and leadership, but pays special attention to weapons utilization. The analysis may flow from various types of wargames, a mainstay of military education for almost two hundred years, or from field exercises. It may also be developed from combat experience, distilled from post-combat interviews, or analyzed in the quantitative reconstruction of a series of engagements. Operational analysis pays special attention to the physical environment in which military events occur, and it may even attempt to introduce such mathematical rigor that it allows the prediction or at least the establishment of probable outcomes. Most comparisons of modern armed forces utilize such approaches. While operational analysis employs quantitative techniques for the prediction of combat results between various forces, it has also been transformed into another variant, systems analysis, which produces cost-benefit comparisons of functionally similar forces in order to aid in the building of strategic theory, the clarifying of weapons procurement, and the assessing of logistical efficiency.[3]

These modes of analysis, however valid, provide only partial answers to organizational effectiveness. Military activity is extraordinarily heterogeneous, and the existing measures of effectiveness fail to capture the full complexities of military organizations and their missions. Military activity has both vertical and horizontal dimensions. The vertical dimension involves the preparation for and conduct of war at the political, strategic, operational, and tactical levels. Taken together, these categories form a hierarchy of actions which military organizations must coordinate from the highest policy levels to tactical execution. The horizontal dimension consists in the numerous, simultaneous, and interdependent tasks that military organizations must execute at each hierarchical level with differing levels of intensity in order to perform with proficiency. These tasks include manpower procurement, planning, training, logistics, intelligence, and technical adaptation as well as combat. An adequate definition of military effectiveness must include all these aspects of military activity. Similarly, the determination of overall military effectiveness requires assessments across the horizontal and vertical range of military activities. In addition, a true assessment of effectiveness should examine the likely barriers to purposeful change as well as the opportunities for reform. Aggregating the estimated effectiveness of hundreds of small units is not the same as evaluating overall organizational performance.

Definitions and General Points

Military effectiveness is the process by which armed forces convert resources into fighting power. A fully effective military is one that derives maximum combat power from the resources physically and politically available. Effectiveness thus incorporates some notion of efficiency. Combat power is the ability to destroy the enemy while limiting the damage that he can inflict in return. The precise amount of necessary damage depends on the goals of the war and the physical characteristics of armed forces committed to its prosecution. Resources represent the spectrum of assets important to military organizations: human and natural resources, money, technical prowess, industrial base, governmental structure, sociological characteristics, political capital, the intellectual qualities of military leaders, and morale. The constraints under which military organizations labor are both natural and political. Natural constraints include such things as geography, natural resources, the economic system, population, time, and weather. Political constraints refer to national political and diplomatic objectives, popular attitudes toward the military, the conditions of engagement, and civilian morale.

Obviously, no precise calculation of the aggregate military effects of such disparate elements is possible. But it is essential to reach a judgment about the possibilities open to a particular military organization in a given situation. Only then can one compare national armed forces, possessing vastly different characteristics, problems, and enemies, in a fashion that can explain their relative effectiveness.

Some relationship exists between military effectiveness and victory. If 'victory' were the sole criterion of effectiveness, however, one would conclude that the Russians were more effective than the Finns in the 'Winter War' of 1939–40 and the Germans in the 1941–45 war. However, a detailed examination of those struggles suggests that this was simply not so. Rather the Finns and Germans functioned more effectively at the operational level with limited resources than did their opponents. Victory is an outcome of battle; it is not what a military organization does in battle. Victory is not a characteristic of an organization but rather a result of organizational activity. Judgments on effectiveness should retain some sense of proportional cost and organizational process.

Military activity takes place at four different levels: political, strategic, operational, and tactical. Each category overlaps others, but each is characterized by different actions, procedures, and goals. Therefore, one must assess military effectiveness separately at each level of activity. It is doubtful whether any military organization is completely effective at all four levels simultaneously. No doubt this results from human limitations, but it also reflects the fact that the prerequisites for effectiveness at one level may conflict with those at another. For example, American military forces in South Vietnam might have increased their effectiveness at the tactical level by a greater willingness to close with the enemy instead of relying so much on indirect fire power. However, the price would likely have been higher casualties and therefore reduced political effectiveness.[4] When such conflicts occur, the organization may have to make deliberate choices to diminish effectiveness at one level in order to enhance effectiveness at other levels.

The basic characteristics of military effectiveness cannot be measured with precision. Instead, any examination must rely on more concrete indicators of effectiveness at the political, strategic, operational, and tactical levels. Therefore, we have divided the remainder of this chapter into four sections. Each begins with a general description of a level of military activity and then examines various aspects of effectiveness for that particular level. The answers provided aim at focusing attention on the various facets of military effectiveness at that level and at determining precisely where and in what ways organizations have or have not been effective. The goal is to identify those characteristics of military organizations useful to planners interested in assessing the effectiveness of potential adversaries or allies.

Political Effectiveness

For a military organization to act strategically, operationally, or tactically, it must consistently secure the resources required to maintain, expand, and reconstitute itself. Almost always, this requires the military to obtain the cooperation of the national political elite. Hence, the effort to obtain resources for military activity and the proficiency in acquiring those resources constitute political effectiveness. Resources consist of reliable access to financial support, a sufficient military-industrial base, a sufficient quantity and quality of manpower, and control over the conversion of those resources into military capabilities. The process through which modern military organizations obtain resources follows a general pattern. Military leaders assess potential adversaries and calculate the variety and level of the threat posed to national security. On the basis of those conclusions, they present arguments to the political leadership for a share of resources over some period of time to meet the threats to national security. Depending upon the regime and circumstances, military services will face objections from civilian departments that other needs are more crucial to national welfare. In a limited sense, a military organization's political effectiveness depends on an ability to articulate its needs more persuasively than its competitors can articulate theirs.

A critical element in the ability to persuade or coerce involves the degree to which the political elite regards military activity as legitimate and officership as a distinct profession requiring extended education and special expertise. If the political leadership perceives military skills as largely intuitive and undifferentiated from civilian occupations, military arguments for a large share of the nation's resources are not likely to carry much weight. However, to the extent that officers are viewed as experts in a specialized and demanding function not mastered without long preparation, military assessments of the threat confronting a nation and recommendations for a particular response are much less likely to be directly contested. Military claims on resources may still not be granted *in toto*, but the credibility of the military's arguments for resources will usually not be the primary issue in dispute. Without political effectiveness, all other types of effectiveness are endangered. The following are various measures for evaluating the political effectiveness of a military organization.

To What Extent Can Military Organizations Assure Themselves a Regular Share of the National Budget Sufficient to Meet Their Major Needs?

Obviously armed forces need financial and economic support. The mechanisms through which they satisfy their requirements vary from nation to nation, but in each the essence of the process is similar: the armed forces must compete both among themselves and with others for scarce resources. They accomplish this by convincing the political leadership that their needs are of greater importance than those of others. There are various cases to be made, but usually the military must educate or persuade budgetary authorities that the nation will face increased risk and dangers without the desired funding. This case is usually made by assessing the capabilities of potential adversaries and by using that analysis to extrapolate possible intentions. Armed forces persuasive enough to secure steady, predictable, and high levels of support must rate highly in terms of political effectiveness.

Both the British Army and the French Air Force during the interwar period provide examples of political ineffectiveness as measured by their ability to secure resources. In the former case, the British Army was underfunded in almost every category of budgetary support. Admittedly, factors outside the army's control, such as the popular revulsion over the slaughter on the Western Front and the political denial of the strategic necessity for a continental commitment, contributed to this state of affairs. Nevertheless, the army generally failed to convey its strategic vision to those in power. Similarly the French Air Force failed in the same period to articulate the importance of its mission to the politicians of the Third Republic. Only in 1938, when the mismatch between French and German air strength had reached catastrophic proportions, was the French Air Force able to influence its government, and then the desperate scramble to make up what the French 'locust years' had lost occurred too late.[5]

To What Extent Do Military Organizations Have Access to the Industrial and Technological Resources Necessary to Produce the Equipment Needed?

Even with an ample budget, armed services still must convert financial support into equipment. They can do this either by depending upon national industries or by importing arms from abroad. Almost all military organizations need to do some of both, but, as a general rule, more advanced forces generally rely on internal sources of supply. To the degree armed forces acquire their equipment from domestic sources, they must assess their nation's industrial, technical, and research and developmental capabilities, communicate their requirements, supervise and monitor production of those items, and test the end products. In a market economy they must consider the relationship of investment risk to price. To operate such a system requires technologists capable of dealing with such concerns in the language of business, engineering, and science. Military organizations dependent on foreign suppliers may not need such elaborate arrangements, but they do require an ability to assess products and to enter into intelligent commercial relationships with suppliers. A military organization that cannot or does not exploit either domestic or foreign industrial and scientific communities limits its effectiveness.

In the 1920s and 1930s, despite considerable internal difficulties, the Soviet military was able to make good use of foreign technology as well as its own engineering and production capabilities. One example of domestic exploitation of foreign design was arguably the finest tank of the Second World War – the T-34. In the 1920s the Soviets imported the Christie tank suspension system and incorporated it into their tank designs.[6] In the 1930s, building on their past experiences, they utilized their own engineering and industrial capabilities, including even naval architects, to design a series of vehicles that culminated in the T-34. They then put their design into production with relative dispatch, so that the T-34 was available for the 1941 battles and in increasing numbers thereafter. It proved one of the nastiest surprises of the war for German armored forces. On the other hand, the Italian military forces, despite the allocation of considerable resources and financial support (outspending the French in the 1935–1938 period), failed to utilize the capabilities of Italian industry.[7] Among other items, the Whitehead firm of Fiume developed an aerial torpedo in the late 1930s; the Italian services showed no interest despite its obvious applicability to the Mediterranean theater, and the weapon was eventually sold to the Germans.[8] Such blindness to the importance of available technology, foreign as well as domestic, in general characterized the Italian military in the interwar period. The former case suggests an effective use of national industrial and technological resources; the latter, the opposite.

To What Extent Do Military Organizations Have Access to Manpower in the Required Quantity and Quality?

Access to manpower involves not only legal power, but also moral and practical legitimacy. For example, the military may possess the legal right to universal conscription, but coercion alone cannot provide the personnel, if the society, or an elite within it, desires to circumvent the legal structure. The history of various American drafts illustrates that societal resistance or support can influence the effectiveness not only of conscription, but also of combat power.[9] Especially important for military organizations is the willing cooperation and service of the educated and skilled middle and upper classes. Without their participation, military skills, particularly in the officer corps, cannot be maintained at a sufficiently high level of expertise. In addition, the absence from military service of the most politically active and influential segments of society will serve to isolate and alienate the military from the nation they protect. The citizenry will then lose the sense that defense is a legitimate activity. Effectiveness by this measure requires that the nation not stigmatize its armed forces. Furthermore, officership must be regarded by both the officer corps and civil society at large as a distinct profession incorporating a body of specialized knowledge and a code of self-regulation.[10]

Strategic Effectiveness

The strategic level of military activity refers to the employment of national armed forces to secure by force national goals defined by political leadership.

Strategic activity consists of plans specifying time, geography, mission, and objectives and the execution of those plans. Subsumed within the definition are the analysis and selection of strategic objectives and the linkage of those objectives to national goals through the mechanism of campaign or contingency plans. A campaign is a sustained operation designed to defeat enemy forces in a specified space and time with simultaneous and sequential battles. Usually several campaigns are required to achieve strategic objectives. An example would be the decision by US Army Air Forces in 1941 that airpower could be most effectively used in attacks on Germany to destroy its ability and will to make war. Another example would be the decision by American forces in the Pacific to launch an island-hopping campaign in order to bring air and sea power within range of the Japanese home islands.[11]

One must not confuse this military activity with the analysis and designation of national goals by the political leadership. Germany's total defeat was the primary political goal of the United States in the European theater; bombing German industry represented a strategic decision intended to secure that goal. However, political and military decisions at these levels do overlap and are made iteratively; a purely linear conception that political goals always drive strategic decisions is simplistic. Political goals no doubt should inform strategy, but the strategic alternatives, enunciated by the military, may simultaneously shape those goals. The analysis of strategic effectiveness should aim at capturing this reciprocity.

To What Degree Would Achievement of the Organization's Strategic Objectives Result in Securing the Political Goals of the Nation?

The need for consistency between strategic means and political ends has become a truism – especially since the 'rediscovery' of Clausewitz. Therefore a test of that means-ends relationship must be a fundamental measure of strategic effectiveness. The Japanese decision to attack the United States in the Pacific is an interesting case. Why did the Japanese believe that even a complete initial strategic success in the Pacific would result in a victorious peace with the United States?[12] An analysis demands more than the reason why the Japanese adopted their course of action. It must also assess the process of Japanese strategic decision-making. Since effectiveness has a normative component, the critique must provide a well-supported judgment about the fit between the available strategic alternatives and Japanese national goals. The applicable normative standard would be the consistency or inconsistency between means and ends. A gap between means and ends beyond prudent risk would suggest ineffectiveness at the strategic level.

To What Degree Are the Risks Entailed in the Desired Strategic Objectives Consistent with the Stakes Involved and the Consequences of Failure?

A strategic objective or course of action may fit desired political goals but still not be prudent if the risks and costs of failure are sufficiently great. Therefore, an analysis must assess the chances and consequences of failure of available strategic alternatives. It must then compare these with the benefits of success and the costs of tolerating the status quo. Again, the analysis must emphasize the normative aspect of effectiveness, and it requires a critique of those cultural or psychological impediments to strategic effectiveness in each particular case. To return to the Second World War Pacific case, one can argue reasonably that Japan's assumption that America lacked the will to fight simultaneously on two fronts (Pacific and European) constituted a key element in the Japanese decision for war. The analysis must evaluate this assessment both in terms of what the Japanese knew at the time and *what they should and could be reasonably expected to have known*. For example, was it intelligent for the Japanese to base their entire campaign against the United States upon an evaluation of national political will, a type of judgment that has historically proven notoriously unreliable? Did the Japanese impute too much rationality to their adversaries? Was it reasonable to devise a strategic plan that contained the possibility of catastrophic failure, if the predicted enemy behavior proved incorrect? To the extent that the answers are negative, an analysis would judge the Japanese strategically ineffective.

To What Degree Were the Leaders of the Military Organization Able to Communicate with and Influence the Political Leadership to Seek Militarily Logical National Goals?

The process of selecting national political goals and strategic objectives should be interactive. Strategic objectives chosen in a political vacuum possess no meaning. Political goals chosen without reference to what is strategically possible are futile at best and disastrous at worst. The military must communicate effectively to political leadership what is militarily possible and thereby influence the choice of national goals. A military that performs this task badly is strategically ineffective. Obviously, such strategic effectiveness requires certain skills within the military leadership, including the ability to persuade with candor when required and to obfuscate when necessary. Practical prowess in bureaucratic maneuvering and coalition building is essential. An interesting example is whether the American military were strategically effective in communicating their limits to the civilian leadership during the Vietnam war. General William C. Westmoreland has argued that he made clear that the level of available American ground forces in Vietnam required the South Vietnamese to take over most pacification tasks. This meant, argues Westmoreland, that progress toward American political objectives in Vietnam would be far slower than with more American troops. On the other hand, Colonel Harry G. Summers, Jr., asserts that the American military failed to inform President Johnson and his advisors about what was and was not militarily possible with the prescribed goals, forces, and rules of engagement.[13] If Westmoreland's view obtains, one would have to rate the strategic effectiveness of the American military more highly than if Summers' assessment prevails.

One must also note that there have been times in the twentieth century when military organizations have shown enormous political effectiveness in persuading the national leadership to accept *illogical* national goals. Wilhelmine Germany represents the most clear-cut example. From Tirpitz's 'risk fleet' theory to Ludendorff's and Hindenburg's arguments for overambitious strategic and political goals in 1917–18 in both the East and the West, the German military indicated political effectiveness – but an effectiveness that resulted in the most catastrophic consequences.[14]

To What Degree Are Strategic Goals and Courses of Action Consistent With Force Size and Structure?

Although a military organization may possess limited power over the ultimate fit between strategic decisions and national goals, it usually has more control over the extent to which its force structure is appropriate to its anticipated uses. Accordingly, the military's level of accountability in this area ought to be high. Force size, of course, refers to numbers, force structure to the internal organization and the composition of forces.

The Russo-German war provides significant examples of strategic ineffectiveness arising from a poor relationship between available forces and strategic objectives. Even in 1941 German forces were undoubtedly too small, too ill-equipped, and too badly supported for many of their strategic tasks. Above all they lacked an effective logistics structure to accommodate the distances and weather of the theater. Few infantry formations were mechanized. Strategic planning was careless and often incomplete, and the Germans generally refused to face the problems inherent in conquering a country of continental proportions. Similarly, in 1942 the *Luftwaffe*'s assessment of its size, force structure, and the potential threat was so faulty that its continued emphasis on bomber production and other decisions lost air superiority over the Mediterranean and Eastern fronts by late summer 1943 and over all of Europe by spring 1944.[15]

One can contrast these cases with the American naval forces in the prewar Pacific. Both the navy and the marine corps anticipated the nature of amphibious warfare and the requirement for naval air superiority with considerable accuracy in the 1920s and 30s. While force numbers were still low in the late 1930s, especially in aircraft carriers and amphibious shipping, the force structure of the two organizations was fundamentally sound for the strategic tasks they faced. Therefore, the strategic effectiveness of these two military organizations was high.[16]

To What Degree Are the Military's Strategic Objectives Consistent with Their Logistical Infrastructure and the National Industrial and Technical Base? Included in the Industrial Base Are Manufacturing Capabilities and Rates, Reserve Capacities, Sophistication, Vulnerability, and Access to Raw Materials.

Clearly, different strategic objectives require diverse supporting organizations and industrial foundations. For example, Anglo-American strategy in the Second World War faced enormous logistical problems in waging war far from the centers of Allied power, in fighting a massive aerial campaign to break German industrial power, and in mounting and supporting great amphibious efforts on coastlines where well-entrenched, highly motivated forces awaited Allied landings. An industrial-technical base that did not possess enormous productive potential and that did not have access to large, secure sources of raw materials would have rendered Anglo-American strategy difficult, if not impossible to implement. Likewise, the Anglo-American strategy that heavily emphasized the air arm required a foundation of continuous technological innovation and the ability to translate those refinements into mass production. In addition, it demanded large numbers of highly skilled support personnel for the large infrastructure of bases, maintenance and repair facilities, transportation systems, and storage-distribution installations. Without those things, a sophisticated and effective strategic air campaign was unthinkable, however well conceived in military terms.

The German case in the Second World War makes an interesting comparison. As a result of their victories in the spring of 1940, the Germans had acquired access to virtually the entire manufacturing capacity of Europe. In terms of available raw materials, the Germans could cover their needs in every area except for petroleum and a narrow band of specialized metals. At the same time, German strategic thought clearly began to turn to the problems involved in realizing the Führer's grandiose dreams of destroying the Soviet Union and dealing with the United States.[17] Throughout the period between the fall of France and the opening of massive military operations against Russia, German leaders underestimated the capacity of Soviet industry and the massive potential of the United States for industrial mobilization and production. In a limited sense Hitler perceived the dimensions of the problem. In the summer of 1940 he suggested that German industry increase the number of tanks produced from a hundred to a thousand a month. The army's ordnance authorities persuaded the Führer against implementing that decision with the argument that such a production level would overstrain the German economy.[18] Generally, the German military echoed the sentiments of Göring that American industry could only produce radios and refrigerators, and they shared Hitler's optimistic belief that when one kicked in the Soviet door the whole regime would collapse like a house of cards.[19] Not until late 1941 or early 1942, with the disaster in Russia and Hitler's declaration of war on the United States, did the Germans begin to mobilize fully the industrial and technological resources available to them – a year and a half too late and the direct result of the military's strategic incompetence.

To What Degree Are Military Organizations Successful at Integrating Their Strategic Objectives with Those of Their Allies and/or Persuading Them to Adopt Consistent Strategic Objectives?

Historically – and certainly in this century – coalitions have conducted a significant percentage of wars. Coalition warfare carries with it the problems of deriving full benefit from the partnership through the integration and coordination of individual contributions into a joint effort. The First and

Second World Wars offer several interesting cases of both effectiveness and ineffectiveness in this strategic dimension.

The relations between the British and French armies during the First World War fall somewhere in the middle of this measure for strategic effectiveness. Initial relations between the British Expeditionary Force (BEF) and its French counterpart were marked in 1914 and 1915 by considerable formality and coldness, if not a general failure of understanding. Matters improved under Field Marshal Sir Douglas Haig, who supported his French colleagues. Nevertheless, there was no combined staff, no centralized planning, and little sharing of operational concepts. The disastrous impact of Germany's March 1918 offensive finally forced the two allies to create a supreme allied commander who could articulate and guide overall strategy for the allies.[20]

On the other hand, the Axis alliance between Germany and Italy possessed virtually none of the characteristics of a serious alliance. Mussolini characterized the Italian effort in 1940 as a 'parallel war.'[21] The failures in coordination, the lack of a grand strategy, and the arrogant disregard of overall alliance strategy culminated in the ill-considered and disastrous Italian invasion of Greece in October 1940. In a real sense the combination of Fascist Italy and Nazi Germany represented an alliance where the whole was less than the sum of its parts.

The best example of strategically effective coalition warfare is the behavior of British and American military forces in the Second World War. Consultation and active coordination began early in the war and before American belligerency. Both sides hammered out strategic objectives in a series of conferences at which top political and military leaders and staffs communicated freely. These consultations led to the early creation of combined staffs and eventually combined commands for most deployed forces, at least at the theater level. The two allies often held significantly different views on Allied strategy. Yet they were almost always able to bridge potential divisions so that actual military operations, once decided upon, were neither impaired nor weakened. To the extent that the British and American military organizations were responsible for this integration and cooperation, one must judge them as strategically effective.[22]

To What Degree Do the Strategic Plans and Objectives Place the Strengths of Military Organizations against the Critical Weaknesses of Their Adversary?

Ideally, the best strategic course should aim to place strength against critical weakness. Admittedly, this is not always possible since the strengths and weaknesses of opponents are often not sufficiently complementary or clearly recognized. Therefore, in practice, a strategically effective military organization may have to be satisfied with a strategic course that at least would allow it to exploit fully its own strengths.

Germany's strategy at the beginning of 1916, cast by Chief of the General Staff Erich von Falkenhayn, reflected a general ineffectiveness in this category. In a strategic memorandum written for the Kaiser in December 1915,

Falkenhayn argued that Germany faced a mighty coalition that possessed enormous numerical advantages in resources, population, and industrial potential. As the war continued, Allied military power would continue to wax while Germany's power could only wane. England, continued Falkenhayn, was Germany's principal enemy. The chief of staff then proceeded to argue that Germany should fight a great battle of attrition against the French Army in 1916 as a means of destroying Britain's most formidable ally on the Continent. Indeed, the German high command insured that the German forces in front of Verdun could not launch a quick, decisive thrust at the French fortress city, but rather possessed only enough strength to embroil both French and German troops in a massive killing battle of attrition – a disastrous commitment of the German Army against the Allies' greatest strengths, mobilized manpower and material.[23]

In the same war, the Royal Navy understood quite well the strategic advantages that accrued to Britain by geography, trade patterns, and the navy's clear numerical superiority. The distant blockade, while keeping the fleet concentrated and avoiding needless risks, accurately reflected the strategic realities that obtained between the two nations. It forced Germany to take the offensive to break the deadlock by seeking a major fleet engagement. At Jutland, Admiral Jellicoe fully understood that the annihilation of the High Seas Fleet was desirable, but that decisive fleet action was not necessary for accomplishing his primary strategic objective. This understanding explains his often criticized reluctance to press home his advantages on the evening of May 31, 1916. Whatever the operational failings of the Royal Navy, its strategic effectiveness throughout the war was enormous.[24]

Operational Effectiveness

The operational level of military activity refers to the analysis, selection, and development of institutional concepts or doctrines for employing major forces to achieve strategic objectives within a theater of war. Operational military activity involves the analysis, planning, preparation, and conduct of the various facets of a specific campaign. Within the scope of operational matters lie the disposition and marshalling of military units, the selection of theater objectives, the arrangement of logistical support, and the direction of ground, air, and sea forces. A combination of military concerns shape these operational-level decisions: the mission, the nature of the enemy and his probable objectives, terrain, logistics, the available allied and national forces, and the time available for mission accomplishment. An example of activities at the operational level was the choice by US Army Air Forces in the Second World War to use massed, daylight, high-altitude precision bombing raids against industrial targets for the strategic objective of reducing or eliminating the enemy's ability to wage war. Another is the development and application of the ship-to-shore amphibious assault doctrine as a guide for employing landing forces in the Pacific to bring concentrated air and sea power to bear on Japan. Measures or indicators of operational effectiveness must reflect this doctrinal focus.

To What Extent Do the Military Organizations of a Nation Possess a Professional Ethos and Integrity That Allows Them to Deal with Operational Problems in a Realistic Fashion?

The military organizations of the major powers have in the past century come to view the position of officership as that of a profession, demanding ethical sensibility and considerable intellectual attainments.[25] The staff and war colleges founded in the nineteenth century attest to a growing belief that only serious study could prepare officers for the most senior positions of military leadership. Yet there remains some doubt about how fully all officer corps have accepted this particular attribute of the definition of professionalism. As MacGregor Knox has noted about the Italian military in the past half century:

> The Duce's problems . . . lay in what one might term the Italian general staff tradition: Custoza, Lissa, Adua, Caporetto. On those occasions the military, as yet uncontaminated by contact with fascism, distinguished itself by the lack of the sort of diligent study, careful planning, and scrupulous attention to detail which characterized the Germans, and by a tendency to confusion of responsibilities and of incessant intrigue among senior officers.[26]

The degree to which the officer corps of a nation accepts the concept of professionalism is going to influence its ability to perform its mission in the operational and tactical spheres.

Similarly the issue of integrity between the different levels of command represents an important attribute of a serious professional force. Without trust and honesty, information that is critical to the evaluation not only of enemy capabilities, but of one's own as well, will either become distorted or in some cases entirely false as it moves between levels of command. In this case the exceptional critical self-analysis of the German Army after its victory in Poland especially deserves attention. In spite of a massive victory over its opponents, the army's high command was dissatisfied by the performance of combat units. Moreover, the German system allowed subordinate commanders full freedom to discuss the weakness of their own forces in terms of equipment, manpower, and training. The result was that the General Staff was able to evaluate the army's strengths and weaknesses in realistic fashion and to design a realistic training program to correct its defects. Victory over France in May and June of 1940 was due in no small measure to that process.[27]

To What Degree Are the Military Organization's Operational Methods Integrated? To What Degree Do Organizations Attempt to Combine Combat Arms to Take Full Advantage of Their Strengths While Covering Their Weaknesses?

The history of warfare has been marked by an accelerating growth in the variety of weapons, combat arms, operational transportation, and specialized units. Each weapon, unit, and technique possesses a unique set of capabilities and vulnerabilities. Taking full advantage of these military assets increases the likelihood that an armed force will fulfill its mission. Taken in aggregate, the operationally effective military organization is one that derives maximum benefit from its components and assets by linking them together for mutual support. Not only does this require complete utilization of combat branches within and between military services, but also the exploitation of weather, terrain, time, surprise, morale, training, and the physical capabilities of troops. The greater the integration of these disparate elements, the better will a military organization generate combat power from its available resources.

In this area, German military forces in the first several years of the Second World War exhibited a high level of effectiveness, particularly with regard to the evolution of operational concepts dealing with armored warfare. German armored doctrine as developed by its pioneers, generals Lutz and Guderian, gave heavy emphasis to developing an all-arms approach to armored warfare. Consequently, German armored divisions consisted of motorized artillery, infantry, and combat engineers as well as armored components. With the addition of Stukas from the *Luftwaffe*'s specialized *Fliegerkorps VIII*, the Germans were able to test and refine an all-arms doctrine of enormous effectiveness in the campaigns against Poland and France.[28]

The Israeli ground forces in the Yom Kippur War provide an interesting contrast. After the 1967 victory, Israeli operational planners gradually de-emphasized combined arms in favor of an almost pure armor-aircraft combat doctrine. They essentially relegated artillery and infantry to a secondary status. This decision left Israeli forces vulnerable to weapons against which artillery and mechanized infantry would have been effective. It was only after battlefield reverses in the first week of combat in 1973 that they relearned the basic need for a combined arms doctrine. Ultimately, the reintegrated Israeli ground forces breached Egyptian air defenses, and this, in turn, allowed Israeli aircraft to function with their full lethal force. In terms of integration, the Israelis were at first operationally ineffective, but through rapid adaptation recovered their high level of effectiveness.[29]

Operational effectiveness has a distinct human element. The professional and personal relationships between officers of different branches within the same service as well as between different services provide the institutional and psychological underpinnings for integrated action. The personnel and training policies of military organizations determine in large part these relationships. Attendance at a service military academy can provide a common foundation of trust and experience that may endure between classmates who have gone into different combat branches. Likewise, personnel policies, as in the German case, that rotate staff officers through various branches and assignments between line and staff may have the same effect. The practice of assigning officers to a regiment for the duration of their career may have a positive impact on unit cohesion, but it may also create narrow professional and psychological perspectives. The result of a parochial personnel policy may be the creation of officers with an intense 'us-them' feeling that discourages their full integration into an all-arms concept. If poorly controlled by the leadership, the conflicting perspectives held by personnel from different services, amplified by interservice competitiveness, can hamper combined efforts.

To What Extent Are the Military Organizations Mobile and Flexible at the Operational Level? Can the Organization Move Rapidly Both Intellectually and Physically in Either Anticipated or Unanticipated Directions?

Existing technical conditions, of course, limit mobility. At the most obvious level, mobility means being able to move units in a flexible, timely fashion. This requires an infrastructure to support them as well as to move them. At a deeper level, mobility and flexibility depend at least as much, if not more, on an appropriate command and control network and on staff elements that permit military units to remain cohesive, distinctive organizations while they maneuver.

There is in fact no single military organization that provides an example of both mobility and flexibility in all their implied meanings. The British and Americans in the Second World War had superb mobility and flexibility between theaters of war. Within theaters these forces also possessed excellent mobility. However, it is arguable whether British and American forces demonstrated the flexibility at the operational level necessary to seize the fleeting opportunities that their mobility presented. By contrast, German forces were physically less mobile; much of the army consisted of non-mechanized units, while force structure and size severely limited *Luftwaffe* airlift capabilities. However, the Germans had an unparalleled operational flexibility that allowed them to react rapidly with their numerically inferior forces to great effect. German flexibility highlights the importance of command and control as well as staff work to operational effectiveness. For many reasons, the use of mission tactics not the least important, German commanders and staffs possessed both the desire and the ability to shift, recombine, and redirect forces as the situation demanded. American and British forces always possessed the technical and physical ability to do so, for Allied communications, mechanization, and motorization were far superior to those possessed by the Germans. However, the Allies seldom showed the organizational abilities and flexible habits of mind to make full use of those great resources. In this respect, the Allies were less effective than their German opponent.[30]

To What Extent Are a Military Organization's Operational Concepts and Decisions Consistent with Available Technology?

This measure searches for the relationship between technical innovation and operational effectiveness, a subject that has endlessly occupied military historians and analysts. It is still not clear to what extent technology drives operations or the reverse. What is certain is that each has powerfully influenced the other and that the exploitation of technology by military organizations has been of increasing significance. Therefore, an armed service's adeptness at identifying, encouraging, and assimilating useful technologies is an important measure of operational effectiveness.[31]

Examples of gross failures to exploit available technology abound in the nineteenth century; military organizations from the early twentieth century have become more receptive to technical innovation and their failures in this area have become less dramatic. Perhaps the most famous as well as one of the most effective utilizations of technology came in the 1930s and early 1940s in Great Britain. The head of the RAF's research and development establishment, Air Vice Marshal Sir Hugh Dowding, played a major role in encouraging the first experimentation with what was to be known as radar. At the same time he was negotiating the original contracts that resulted in two single-engine air superiority fighters, the Hurricane and the Spitfire. Then, under his leadership, Fighter Command incorporated these new technological advances, designed an effective operational air defense system for defending Britain's air space, and finally, in the Battle of Britain, met the *Luftwaffe* with the technology and the operational doctrine designed to utilize the RAF's strengths. The resulting triumph represented a true marriage of technology and operational doctrine.[32]

There are many reasons why military organizations may reject new weapons. Frequently, insufficient funding by political authorities may not permit the development of new and untested devices. Obviously, the budget is something over which military organizations often exercise incomplete control. Rejection may result from the military leadership's judgment that a new technology is unreliable or not significantly superior to present equipment and therefore would not enhance fighting power. Paradoxically, the military may recognize a new technology's merit and still reject it if another technical innovation seems to possess even greater potential. If done often enough, the desire to wait for the 'best' weapon can stifle technological improvement of military organizations. An analysis must examine military evaluations of technology for reasonableness and accuracy in the light of existing knowledge. Military organizations may slowly adopt a new technology only if its application is uncertain. The US Navy's tepid interest in early submarines was in part the result of these considerations.[33] Finally, a new technology that might increase combat power may still be rejected because it threatens either the status of existing organizations or the social environment of a military organization. Such was the case with the tank, the airplane, the aircraft carrier, and the submarine in the armed services of many nations. Since military organizations generally aim to increase their combat power, the rejection of new weapon systems for sociological reasons is a strong indication of operational ineffectiveness.

To What Extent Are Supporting Activities Well Integrated with the Operational Concepts of the Military Organization? Do the Military Organizations Have the Capability to Support Their Operational Practices with the Required Intelligence, Supply, Communications, Medical, and Transportation Systems?

The most potent and ingenious operational capabilities are worthless unless a network of supporting activities buttresses them. An example or two can illustrate this point.

The German invasion of the Soviet Union in the summer of 1941 is an interesting case in point. Military historians have rightly given due credit to the awesome operational capabilities of the invading forces. What has not received adequate notice is the fact that the underpinnings of that invading force, from logistical capabilities through to basic intelligence on the Soviet order-of-battle, were completely inadequate. The expansion of the German armored force between the Battle of France and Barbarossa saw a doubling in the number of armored divisions through a halving in the number of tanks in each division. Even more harmful, and rarely noted in the Anglo-American literature, is the fact that the Germans were only able to equip these divisions with a hodgepodge of supporting vehicles drawn from every nation in Europe.[34] Not only were the vehicles generally unsuited for their logistical tasks on the primitive roads of the Soviet Union, but the very multiplicity of supporting vehicles created a logistic nightmare in terms of parts and maintenance. German operational planning had foreseen a rapid drive to Smolensk and a pause to refit as the rail system back to Brest-Litovsk was repaired by railroad engineers. The repair units, however, were given the lowest priority of all army units moving forward into the depths of Russia.[35] It is no wonder then that the army's logisticians had to warn the high command in October that the supply system could provide *either* a build-up to meet the coming conditions of winter in Russia *or* the fuel and ammunition for a drive on Moscow. The army leadership, reflecting its general disdain about logistics, drove on towards Moscow, and the winter catastrophe was a direct result.[36]

If the logistical support for the *Wehrmacht*'s awesome operational capabilities was inadequate, its intelligence support was even less impressive. From its estimation of Russian equipment to its forecast of what the Soviet Union could mobilize, the Reich's military intelligence services proved catastrophically wrong. Those miscalculations are best summed up by Halder's complaint of August 11, 1941:

> The whole situation shows more and more clearly that we have underestimated the colossus of Russia – a Russia that had consciously prepared for the coming war with the whole unrestrained power of which a totalitarian state is capable.
>
> This conclusion is shown both on the organizational as well as on the economic levels, in the transportation, and above all, clearly in infantry divisions. We have already identified 360. These divisions are admittedly not armed and equipped in our sense, and when we destroy a dozen, the Russians simply establish another dozen.[37]

It is worth contrasting the German experience in Russia with the Allied (British, Canadian, and American) effort in the Battle of the Atlantic during the Second World War.[38] Not only did that sustained campaign depend on a secure logistical base of immense proportions, but the use of intelligence, especially the deciphering of German messages to their U-boats, was important in winning the battle over German submarines. At least in the last half of 1941, 'Ultra' alone was almost solely responsible for blunting the terrible threat posed by the rising numbers and effectiveness of Dönitz's forces.[39]

That intelligence success may be one of the few times in the twentieth century when intelligence by itself was of decisive importance.

The importance of the integration of intelligence and operational activity is equally clear in another example: aircraft carrier operations in the Pacific. Successful carrier air strikes at other ships depend upon precise and timely intelligence. Given the vastness of the Pacific, inaccurate force direction resulted in failure with no accompanying 'bonus damage,' which often resulted when land bombers missed their original targets. In addition, given aircraft carrier vulnerability, timely intelligence on an adversary's location was of supreme importance. These lessons were replayed many times in the Pacific, and naval intelligence in that theater was an effective part of fleet operations. Diverse information sources (e.g., MAGIC, RDF, coast watchers, submarine pickets, and air patrols) produced data for centralized analysis, which naval intelligence staffs were rapidly able to provide to operating units. The extent of this dissemination, required by the size of the Pacific and the rapid pace of naval warfare, increased the risk of compromise, but resulted in a series of crucial American successes.[40]

To What Extent Is the Military Organization's Operational Concept Consistent with the Strategic Objectives Assigned to It?

Clearly certain methods of employing military organizations are totally unsuited to particular types of strategic objectives. Yet, an age-old problem is the employment of military forces to achieve objectives for which they are largely unsuited.

In this category the evaluation must look for more than just the problem of whether an organization's operational concepts are consistent with the strategic objectives assigned to it. Given the difficulty in estimating enemy capabilities as well as the doctrinal adaptation that enemy forces go through, the real problem in this area may not emerge in the initial battles of a campaign. Rather, the problem may lie in how well a military organization recognizes the obstacles that the enemy, its own technological capabilities, and its operational weaknesses in combat stand in the way of achieving its strategic goal.

Thus, with the difficulties in training a vast new army and the technological problems (largely unsolved) that accompanied the introduction of rapid-fire, long-range infantry weapons and artillery, it is not hard to see why the British Army had such a difficult time on the Somme.[41] Where Haig and his generals on the Western Front are particularly open to criticism, however, is the fact that the same operational concepts that had proved so unrealistic in 1916 were once again employed in Flanders in 1917. The pursuit of largely unrealistic strategic objectives with inadequate operational conceptions led to the blood bath of Paschendaele. Similarly, in the Second World War it is not entirely clear that the first great bomber attack on Schweinfurt was a mistake, given what was known about the overall situation.[42] What was inexcusable was that the Eighth Air Force continued to send massive unaccompanied bomber formations into the Reich until the second attack on Schweinfurt underlined in blood the inadequacies of its operational concepts. The strategic objective, the destruction of the German ball bearing industry, remained well beyond reach.

To What Degree Does the Operational Doctrine of Military Organizations Place Their Strengths against Their Adversary's Weaknesses?

The conduct of Bomber Command's operations in the Battle of Berlin from December 1943 through March 1944 may best represent operational ineffectiveness in this category. Determined to prove that his command could replicate its successes of summer 1943 on a far heavier and more extensive scale, Air Marshal Arthur T. Harris set as Bomber Command's strategic goal the complete destruction of Berlin and victory over the Reich before Allied armies landed on the coast of France. Berlin, however, lay far from Bomber Command's bases and thus required an extended flight that exposed British bombers to the maximum German air defense effort. Moreover, winter weather was so bad that it was doubtful whether Pathfinder crews could find and mark a sufficiently clear object on the ground to achieve the necessary bombing concentrations. The result was that Bomber Command did not place its strengths against German weaknesses. Rather, it placed strength against strength and a terrible battle of attrition culminated in the disastrous raid against Nuremberg in March 1944. Harris came close to wrecking his command without achieving his goals.[43]

The German campaign against France and the Low Countries in 1940 stands out in strong contrast to the Berlin air campaign. By taking considerable risks, the Germans placed their armored forces where they were most likely to utilize operational maneuverability and flexibility. Because the French high command had placed virtually all its motorized and mechanized forces on the left wing, it did not possess forces in the area that could meet the operational capabilities of German forces. Once the German armored forces had broken out into the open behind the Meuse River, the French did not have the reserves available in the area to react effectively. In this campaign the Germans must be judged effective in pitting strength against weakness.[44]

Tactical Effectiveness

The tactical level of military activity refers to the specific techniques used by combat units to fight engagements in order to secure operational objectives. Tactical activity involves the movement of forces on the battlefield against the enemy, the provision of destructive fire upon enemy forces or targets, and the arrangement of logistical support directly applicable to engagements.

During the Second World War strategic bombing, the non-evasive flying by American heavy bombers, was a tactical activity designed to provide a more stable platform for defensive machine gun fire and more accurate bombing. Likewise, the use of wingmen in fighter combat is a tactical activity; so too are attacks by fighters out of the sun and from a higher altitude. The increased reliance by the US Marine Corps on flame throwers and demolitions to deal with Japanese fortifications is another example. The line between the operational and tactical levels is often blurred, and analysts may disagree over the classification of particular military actions. It is important to distinguish tactical practices since they may provide a clearer focus for comparing military organizations of different nationalities in different eras. Some of the characteristics of tactical effectiveness resemble those for operational activity. Others are quite different.

To What Extent Are Military Organizations' Tactical Approaches Consistent with Their Strategic Objectives?

The adoption of particular tactical systems can hamper military organizations in their pursuit of strategic objectives. For example, suppose that American bomber pilots in the Second World War had found that violent evasion greatly increased their chances for survival against flak and enemy interceptors. The effect most likely would have been a significant loss in bombing accuracy with accompanying injury to organizational strategic purposes, although with a lower attrition rate. It is not always clear that disharmony between strategic objectives and tactical methods indicates tactical ineffectiveness. Ideally, what is tactically feasible should shape the selection of strategic objectives and plans. Therefore, conflict between strategy and tactics may suggest strategic rather than tactical ineffectiveness.

To What Extent Are Tactical Concepts Consistent with Operational Capabilities?

Here too dysfunctions can occur that pose interesting problems for the evaluation of tactical effectiveness. Consider the case of the French Army in the opening weeks of the First World War.[45] The dubious doctrine of the Du Picq-Grandmaison school constituted French operational doctrine. The tactical system was accordingly based on the infantryman's ability to move rapidly in close order across the artillery and machine gun killing zone to engage the enemy in close combat, preferably with the bayonet. The French saw little need for large numbers of machine guns or heavy artillery, and relied for close support on light, rapid-firing 75-mm cannon. These tactics proved so unsuited to combat realities that French infantry essentially imposed a new tactical system on their military leadership: trench warfare.

The dysfunction between operational concepts and tactical capabilities haunted the First World War armies for the remainder of the conflict. Staffs and generals on the Western Front persisted in thinking of operational movement on a Napoleonic scale. As late as the battle of Paschendaele in 1917, Haig was thinking in terms of a great breakthrough followed by a cavalry pursuit of the beaten enemy.[46] At the same time, Allied commanders frequently neglected the immediate tactical problem of how to get through the killing zone of the enemy's firepower. In the BEF, some argued that the British Army should approach the problem of the Western Front as if it were a seige and thus cut down its operational plans to fit more realistically with available tactical conceptions.[47] Interestingly, the solution – the use of firepower with flexible maneuver – seems to have come from the front-line soldiers. In 1915 Captain André Laffargue of the French Army saw very clearly the full dimensions of the problem as well as the possible solutions. Unfortunately, it was the Germans who built on Laffargue's tactical conceptions. In 1916 Ludendorff drew not only on the French doctrinal concepts but, for the first time, forced the General Staff to seek out the combat experiences of those in the trenches in order to create realistic combat tactics. Only then were the Germans in a position to bring tactics in line with operational conceptions; the result was the return of maneuver to warfare.[48]

To What Extent Does the Military Organization's Tactical System Emphasize Integration of All Arms?

This measure of tactical effectiveness closely resembles that of its counterpart at the operational level. However, tactical effectiveness requires that the principle of integration and combined arms not be strictly weapons-centered, but rather be applied to all the factors affecting combat power. Besides weapons, these include such things as terrain, training, qualities of the troops, morale, and weather. A tactical system that does not deliberately consider these and other important military variables will cause serious problems.

The examples of Finnish ground forces during the Winter War and the British Army during much of the First World War provide a useful contrast. The Finnish tactical system melded the characteristics of Arctic terrain and weather with the skills, small size, and light equipment of the Finnish Army.[49] Consequently, they were able to engage the Red Army in depth by utilizing ski troops and deep raids to fragment and destroy enemy columns. The Finns avoided set-piece combat situations in which the more ponderous and numerous Soviet forces could utilize their strengths. So long as the battlefield remained fluid, the Finnish tactical system generated considerable fighting power from relatively few resources. The Soviets were not successful until they pinned the Finns in prepared, static defenses.

The tactical system of the British Army during the First World War, on the other hand, was deficient in integration in a variety of ways on both offense and defense.[50] On the attack, the British depended almost entirely on a clumsy integration of artillery and infantry armed with rifles. The British were slow to utilize small unit attacking formations, to use natural cover and concealment, to exploit the forward employment of light machine guns and mortars, and to use adjusted artillery fire. The result of this poorly integrated tactical system was essentially offensive impotence for much of the war. The defensive capabilities of the British Army in the war also suggest interesting issues. In 1914, the integration of army and artillery was generally good, although because of a lack of communication systems the artillery often had to support the infantry by remaining within sight. While effective in the defensive battles of 1914, the cooperation proved very costly to Royal Artillery batteries that operated in the open, directly exposed to German counterbattery fire.

In 1918 the British were fully aware that the Germans were about to strike in the west. Haig's headquarters, in fact, used captured German manuals and combat experience from the 1917 Flanders battles to draw up an effective scheme of defense in depth that relied on close cooperation between infantry and artillery. Unfortunately, the British found it difficult to implement the new doctrine, and Gough's Fifth Army, which almost collapsed in March 1918, seems to have done almost nothing to implement the new concepts. The disaster of March 1918 provided a real spur to integrating the army's capabilities.[51]

To What Extent Do a Military Organization's Tactical Conceptions Emphasize Surprise and a Rapid Exploitation of Opportunities?

Historically, surprise has been a potent multiplier of combat power. It is difficult to find a military that rejects surprise as an advantageous condition. There are, however, tactical systems with attributes that make surprise difficult to achieve. There are many sorts of surprise. Tactical surprise involves where an attack will take place, the axes of the attack and its exploitation, and the timing and the weight of the attack. Tactical surprise differs from strategic surprise (e.g., the general geographical area where an attack will take place) and technical surprise (e.g., the qualities of the weapons being used), both of which may be possible in principle regardless of the tactical system.

The British Army in both world wars provides interesting examples of relative ineffectiveness in tactical surprise and exploitation. Lloyd George's memoirs contain an entry pertaining to Field Marshal Haig's unwillingness to pay attention to the element of surprise in the conduct of their operations: 'Germans accustomed to [Haig's] heavyfooted movements.'[52] The massive artillery bombardments of great length and severity only served to disclose to the Germans where the next great British 'battle of material' would occur. It enabled them, well before the British infantry attacks began, to redeploy reserves of artillery and other forces to meet the threat. Only after the bloodletting of Paschendaele had exhausted his army for a second time in two years did Haig allow his artillery and tanks to launch a raid, almost entirely based on surprise, against the German position at Cambrai. The subsequent success of British tank and artillery forces suggests what a more enterprising use of surprise might have achieved in 1916 and 1917.[53]

Although different from surprise, rapid exploitation requires similar capabilities and attributes. Effectiveness in this category involves the utilization of a wide variety of opportunities created by the almost random fluidity of mechanized warfare. These opportunities usually appear and disappear suddenly. Therefore, a tactical system that utilizes decentralized decision making, rapid movement, small-unit initiative, and imagination are basic if a military organization is to convert these fleeting advantages into battlefield success. By contrast, tactical systems that stress set-piece battles, rigid schedules for reaching objectives, and tight central control do not create the conditions necessary for timely exploitation.

In the Second World War the British Army paid more attention to the element of surprise. Certainly Montgomery is justly remembered for his set-piece battles. Nevertheless, even Montgomery attempted to include surprise as a basic element in his plans. 'Market Garden' did not fail because of a neglect of surprise as a basic element in warfare. Rather that failure reflected a considerable British unwillingness (with the possible exception of O'Connor's operations against the Italians) to exploit tactical and operational advantages to the full extent possible. Consequently, the real British blunder in September 1944 came not with 'Market Garden' but rather with the unwillingness to exploit fully the capture of Antwerp and the operational and tactical disarray of German military forces streaming back toward the Reich.[54] That British desire for a 'tidy' battlefield and the deliberateness of tactical concepts resulted in the loss of unexpected tactical opportunities.

To What Extent Is the Military Organization's Tactical System Consistent with Its Approach to Morale, Unit Cohesion, and Relations between Officers, NCOs, and the Enlisted Ranks?

There have been several high-quality studies as well as much historical and anecdotal evidence pointing to the value of close relationships between soldiers within combat units.[55] Though *any* tactical system requires a military organization to pay attention to these issues, some systems require unusually strong and resilient bonds with military units. Military organizations that neglect this prerequisite of combat power pay a price in terms of tactical effectiveness.

The relative performance of the Egyptian and Israeli armies in the wars of 1948, 1956, and 1967 are cases in point. Obviously there are a number of causes for the striking differences in the social ethos of these armies, but there is strong evidence that in many Egyptian units, the relationship between officers and men reduced cohesion and morale. Apparently, many Egyptian line officers were corrupt and exploited their units in various ways. There was minimal sharing of hardships and risks, front-line troops had little contact with their commanders, and few officers led from the front. Most officers individually and the organization as a whole demonstrated a lack of even minimal sensitivity in such things as leave policy, regular pay, living conditions, and bonds among other unit members. Indeed, officers frequently did not hide their feelings of social superiority from their subordinates. The Egyptians attempted to ameliorate these problems, and their relative successes in 1973 may have been an indicator of progress.[56]

The Italian Army in both world wars presents a picture quite similar to that of the Egyptians.[57] In its early First World War battles against the Austrians, an army quite similar in every fashion, the Italians put up a respectable showing, at least in terms of the casualties that they suffered. When, however, the Italians faced the pressures of combat against the Germans at Caporetto and against Anglo-American and Soviet units in the Second World War, their military structure shattered. While not entirely responsible, the relationship between the Italian officer corps and its men and the almost complete absence of a professional NCO corps to provide additional unit cohesion played a major role in Italian battlefield ineffectiveness. Italian officers by and large ignored their men, refused to share front-line hardships, and generally led from the rear. The result was an almost complete lack of trust. The Italian case may well suggest a paradigm for Third World military forces: certainly the performance of the Argentinian ground forces in the Falklands suggests a similar lack of cohesion between different levels within units, with the same result.[58] To the extent that military organizations are responsible for these shortcomings, they risk tactical ineffectiveness.

There are some tactical systems that require an especially high level of trust between officers and men if they are to function. Any tactical approach that stresses initiative, independent action, day and night operations out of contact with headquarters or flanking units, and rapid movement depends upon front-line leadership and an uncommon level of unit cohesion. To develop these characteristics, military organizations must pursue deliberate policies. These include stable unit affiliations and small-unit memberships, timely and accurate recognition of skills and actions by promotion and awards, and an officer and NCO corps constituted from men with outstanding martial and intellectual qualities, particularly moral and physical courage.

To What Extent Is the Military Organization's Approach to Training Consistent with Its Tactical System?

It is possible for a military organization to fail to train its personnel to perform the tasks prescribed by its tactical system. When this occurs, tactical effectiveness obviously will be reduced. This sort of disjunction can appear when tactical doctrine and training are managed by different, semi-autonomous bureaucracies with little intercommunication or when tactical doctrine has been changed suddenly and training has not yet adjusted.

The separation of training and doctrine is a common problem for military organizations. The German Army's response to its victory over the Poles in 1939 suggests a high level of effectiveness in this category as well as the importance of this index to battlefield performance.[59] The *Oberkommando des Herres* (*OKH*) took a close look at how well its doctrinal concepts had held up under the combat conditions of the Polish campaign. It then made an across-the-board effort to insure that training and retraining programs throughout the army reflected the lessons learned from Poland. In fact, *OKH* spent the next six months insuring that the training program, closely integrated with its doctrinal conceptions, brought the army up to a high level of capability. It is also worth noting that the actual training programs in the German Army, including basic training, remained largely decentralized, with the division and regiments maintaining training cadres, both at home and, in some cases, close to the front to integrate soldiers directly into combat units. The system was probably not cost effective in terms of the number of front-line officers and NCOs detailed to training duties at any given time, but it did insure that German soldiers trained in a realistic environment that not only reflected current doctrinal practices but front-line conditions as well.

The US Army's efforts to train newly arriving soldiers in Vietnam through specialized in-country centers served a similar purpose. While those combat divisions had little control over the nature of the training that replacements received in the United States, they tried to prepare the soldier for the realities of combat in Vietnam and current divisional combat practices. The training reduced the casualties usually suffered by 'green' troops with little knowledge of conditions in the front-line, at least in comparison to Second World War standards.[60]

The British example in North Africa presents an interesting contrast to the German and US cases. In 1940 the performance of British armored forces trained by Hobart and led by O'Connor suggests a high concurrence between a realistic doctrine and effective training. Thereafter, serious problems arose. The British do not seem to have developed a mechanism for transferring combat experience gained in the desert back to the training establishment in Britain. Consequently, the troops that arrived in the desert theater from the British Isles varied widely in their doctrinal concepts and the effectiveness with which their training had prepared them for combat against Rommel. Only with Montgomery's arrival was a more consistent doctrinal approach articulated and then incorporated into training the Eighth Army. The consequent improvement in British battlefield performance was directly attributable to Montgomery's efforts in this area.[61]

To What Extent Are Military Organizations' Tactical Systems Consistent with Support Capabilities?

It is not uncommon for a tactical system to require greater support than a military organization can actually provide. This problem is frequently most acute in the area of sustainability. Characteristically, military organizations underestimate requirements for transport fuels, ammunition, spare parts, and support personnel. A related problem is the tendency to underestimate the demands that a tactical system may place on troops, e.g., sustained periods of combat, the amount of time without rest, and the impact of casualties. The result of such errors is usually an inability to maintain combat operations at the tempo required by the tactical system. Therefore, military organizations that exhibit this problem would be considered less tactically effective than those whose tactical systems or support capabilities were more realistic.

The archetypal case is the October War of 1973. All the contestants underestimated the logistical requirements for tactical systems incorporating large numbers of automatic weapons, precision-guided munitions, and tanks. Within a short period, the Israelis had to ration ammunition and antitank missiles, a condition not alleviated until a massive American airlift of material had begun.

To What Extent Do Tactical Systems Place the Strengths of Military Organizations against Their Adversary's Weaknesses?

Strengths and weaknesses refer to the range of weapons and human characteristics that affect combat power. For example, an armed force based on a large national population and a backward industrial base would obviously be in error if it adopted tactical systems that required small forces equipped with sophisticated weapons. Faced with a similar mixture of strengths and weaknesses, the People's Republic of China has employed a tactical system emphasizing a lightly armed mass army trained to meet an invasion with protracted territorial defense. Only nuclear weapons vitiated the concept and then only to the extent that the PRC needs to retain its cities. The armed forces of a society whose population is small and/or that values the individual as much as the common good would logically avoid tactical systems likely to produce high casualties.

Ideally, a military organization should seek tactical systems designed not only to use national strengths, but also to pit those strengths against the crucial weaknesses of its likely adversaries. The Israeli case illustrates this point. The Israeli tactical system attempts to minimize casualties and to utilize its national technical base and highly educated population to confront Arab forces with combat situations in which the Israelis can exploit Arab weaknesses, e.g., situations requiring improvisation, rapid decision making, and independent action by small units. The Arabs' inability to deal effectively with such problems is a function of larger social and national characteristics that are difficult to change, especially in combat. On the other hand, Arab military organizations have attempted a tactical response that exploits their larger populations by enmeshing the Israelis in battlefield conditions resulting in high levels of attrition and minimizing their personnel and technical superiority.[62]

The extent to which military organizations place their tactical strengths against enemy weaknesses – or at least maximize their strengths and minimize their own weaknesses – is one measure of tactical effectiveness.

Conclusion

A common thread unites the measures of military effectiveness proposed in this chapter. They all describe various aspects of effectiveness, not as absolutes but in terms of different means-ends relationships. However, the attempt to address the question, 'What is military effectiveness and how can it be measured?' poses a new and equally important question: 'What kinds of military effectiveness are most important and in what conditions?' For example, to what extent can tactical or operational effectiveness offset strategic ineffectiveness? While the concept of military effectiveness is not often clearly articulated, many combat officers believe it is synonymous with tactical effectiveness. They rightly argue that strategic effectiveness is useless unless a military force can operate successfully on the battlefield once it has made contact with the enemy.

On the other hand, the German experience in the Second World War suggests other conclusions. The *Wehrmacht* was a superb tactical instrument. Yet it was frequently launched in strategic and operational directions that nullified numerous battlefield successes. This pattern occurred repeatedly in the first two years of the Russian campaign, 1941 and 1942. Under some conditions, strategic ineffectiveness can render tactical effectiveness less relevant or counterproductive; under other conditions, the reverse is true. The key task is to determine what these conditions are and when they are likely to occur.

Similarly, within the strategic, operational, and tactical categories, what types of effectiveness are most important and in what conditions? For example, what contributes most to overall tactical effectiveness – technological sophistication or unit cohesion? Obviously both are crucial, but which counts for more and under what circumstances? There is a growing sense based on the experience of the Vietnam war, the Falklands campaign, and the wars in the Middle East that unit cohesion may be the key to tactical effectiveness. On the other hand, no amount of unit cohesion can outweigh an extreme disparity in technical sophistication, as the Zulus learned in the 1870s.

Similarly, what contributes more to operational effectiveness, mobility or integration? During much of the campaign in North Africa, air power and superiority in supplies of vehicles and gasoline gave the British forces greater overall mobility than their opponent. The Germans, on the other hand, integrated their forces, especially armor and artillery, into a potent anti-tank defense, offset the British advantages in material, defeated poorly integrated British armored attacks, and then exploited their advantage into significant operational successes.

In any event, one cannot limit the judging of military effectiveness to non-dynamic assessments of tactical units. One must include in the analysis non-quantifiable organizational attitudes, behaviors, and relationships that span a military organization's full activities at the political, strategic, operational, and tactical levels. A more limited method of assessment only provides equally limited conclusions.

Notes

1 Gen. Sir Ian Hamilton, *The Soul and Body of an Army* (London, 1921), p. iv.

2 Charles Moskos, Jr., 'The Military,' in *Annual Review of Sociology*, vol. 2 (1976), pp. 55–77; Morris Janowitz with Roger Little, *Sociology and the Military Establishment*, 3rd ed. (Beverly Hills, Calif., 1974); Charles H. Coates and Roland J. Pelligrin, *Military Sociology* (University Park, Md., 1965); Maury D. Feld, *The Structure of Violence: Armed Forces as Social Systems* (Beverly Hills, Calif., 1977); John Downey, *Management in the Armed Forces* (London, 1977); Sam C. Sarkesian (ed.), *Combat Effectiveness* (Beverly Hills, Calif., 1980); W. Darryl Henderson, *Cohesion: The Human Element in Combat* (Washington, D.C., 1985).

3 S. L. A. Marshall, *Men Against Fire* (Washington, D.C., 1947); Martin Van Creveld, *Fighting Power: German and U.S. Army Performance, 1939–1945* (Westport, Conn., 1982); T. N. Dupuy, *Numbers, Predictions and War* (Indianapolis, Ind., 1979); E. S. Quade and W. I. Boucher (eds.), *Systems Analysis and Policy Planning* (New York, 1968); James F. Dunnigan, *How to Make War* (New York, 1982); Robert E. Harkavy and Stephanie G. Newman, *The Lessons of Recent Wars in the Third World* (Lexington, Mass., 1985); George Quester, *Offense and Defense in the International Systems* (New York, 1977); Lt. Col. Barry D. Watts, *The Foundations of U. S. Air Doctrine: The Problem of Friction in War* (Maxwell AFB, Ala., 1984).

4 Dave R. Palmer, *Summons of the Trumpet* (San Rafael, Calif., 1978); Bruce Palmer, Jr., *The 25-Year War: America's Military Role in Vietnam* (Lexington, Ky., 1984); Shelby L. Stanton, *The Rise and Fall of an American Army: U.S. Ground Forces in Vietnam, 1965–1973* (Novato, Calif., 1985).

5 For the best discussion of the British Army and its funding difficulties, see Brian Bond, *British Military Policy between the Two World Wars* (Oxford, 1980); on the failure to make a Continental commitment, see Michael Howard, *The Continental Commitment* (London, 1972).

6 Albert Seaton, *The Russo-German War, 1941–45* (New York, 1970), p. 93.

7 See the tables in Appendix 2, MacGregor Knox, *Mussolini Unleashed, 1939–41; Politics and Strategy in Fascist Italy's Last War* (Cambridge, 1982), pp. 292–6.

8 Ibid., pp. 24–5.

9 Marvin A. Kreidberg and Merton G. Henry, *History of Military Mobilization in the United States Army, 1775–1945* (Washington, D.C., 1955).

10 Morris Janowitz, *The Professional Soldier* (Glenco, Ill., 1960); Bengt Abrahamsson, *Military Professionalism and Political Power* (Beverly Hills, Calif., 1972); Allan R. Millett, *Military Professionalism and Officership in America* (Columbus, Ohio, 1977).

11 Thomas A. Fabyanic (1973), 'A Critique of United States Air War Planning, 1941–1944,' Ph.D. dissertation, St. Louis University; W. F. Craven and J. L. Cate (eds.), *The Army Air Forces in World War II*, Vol. 1, *Plans and Early Operations, January 1939 to August 1942* (Chicago, 1948); Haywood S. Hansell, Jr., *The Air Plan That Defeated Hitler* (Atlanta, Ga., 1972).

12 For an analysis of Japanese strategic thinking both before and during the early months of the Second World War, see H. P. Willmott, *Empires in the Balance, Japanese and Allied Pacific Strategies to April 1942* (Annapolis, Md., 1982), and *The Barrier and the Javelin, Japanese and Allied Pacific Strategies, February to June 1942* (Annapolis, Md., 1983). See also Saburo Ienaga, *The Pacific War* (New York, 1978).

13 William C. Westmoreland, *A Soldier Reports* (Garden City, N.Y., 1976); Harry G. Summers, Jr., *On Strategy: A Critical Analysis of the Vietnam War* (Novato, Calif., 1982); Leslie H. Gelb with Richard K. Betts, *The Irony of Vietnam: The System Worked* (Washington, 1979).

14 See the critique by Gerhard Ritter in *The Sword and Scepter, The Problem of Militarism in Germany*, Vol. 3, *The Tragedy of Statesmanship: Bethmann Hollweg as War Chancellor (1914–1917)*, and Vol. 4, *The Reign of German Militarism and the Disaster of 1918* (Miami, Fla., 1973).

15 Horst Boog, Jürgen Förster, Joachim Hoffmann, Ernst Klink, Rolf-Dieter Müller, and Gerd R. Ueberschär, *Das Deutsche Reich und der Zweite Weltkrieg*, Vol. 4, *Der Angriff auf die Sowjetunion* (Stuttgart, 1983); Williamson Murray, *Luftwaffe* (Annapolis, Md., 1985), pp. 92–104.

16 Jeter A. Isely and Philip A. Crowl, *The U.S. Marines and Amphibious War* (Princeton, N.J., 1951) pp. 14–71; Clark G. Reynolds, *The Fast Carriers: The Forging of an Air Navy* (New York, 1968), pp. 1–22.

17 Boog, *et al.*, *Das Deutsche Reich und der Zweite Weltkrieg*, Vol. 1.

18 Heinz Guderian, *Panzer Leader* (New York, 1957), p. 114.

19 Murray, *Luftwaffe*, p. 82.

20 Barrie Pitt, *1918, The Last Act* (New York, 1963), pp. 98–102; John Terraine, *To Win a War: 1918, The Year of Victory* (Garden City, N.Y., 1981).

21 Knox, *Mussolini Unleashed*, pp. 116–33.

22 Maurice Matloff and Edwin M. Snell, *Strategic Planning for Coalition Warfare: 1941–1942* (Washington, 1953); and Maurice Matloff, *Strategic Planning for Coalition Warfare: 1943–1944* (Washington, D.C., 1959), both in Office of the Chief of

Military History, U.S. Army, *United States Army in World War II*; J. R. M. Butler, *et.al.*, *Grand Strategy: 1939–1945*, 6 vols. to date (London, 1956–1976), in the series, *History of the Second World War*; Kent Roberts Greenfield, *American Strategy in World War II: A Reconsideration* (Baltimore, Md., 1963).

23 Alistair Horne, *The Price of Glory* (New York, 1963), pp. 27–55.

24 Holger Herwig, *'Luxury' Fleet: The Imperial German Navy 1888–1918* (London, 1980), ch. 8. For the best short analysis of the leadership at Jutland, see Arthur Marder, *From Dreadnought to Scapa Flow*, Vol. 3, *Jutland and After, May 1916-December 1916* (London, 1966), pp. 180–87.

25 Gen. Sir John Winthrop Hackett, *The Profession of Arms* (Lee Knowles lectures at Trinity College, Cambridge University, 1962), reprinted as Department of the Army Pamphlet 302–360.

26 Bernard MacGregor Knox (1976), '1940: Italy's 'Parallel War'', Ph.D. dissertation, Yale University, p. 27.

27 Williamson Murray, 'German Response to Victory in Poland: A Case Study in Professionalism,' *Armed Forces and Society*, Vol. 7, no. 2 (Winter 1981), pp. 285–98.

28 Williamson Murray, *The Change in the European Balance of Power*, (Princeton, N.J., 1984) p. 35; Heinz Guderian, *Panzer Leader* (London, 1952), app. 24.

29 Chaim Herzog, *The War of Atonement, October, 1973* (Boston, 1975).

30 Russell F. Weigley, *Eisenhower's Lieutenants: The Campaigns of France and Germany, 1944–1945* (Bloomington, Ind., 1981); Field Marshal Lord Carver, *The Apostles of Mobility* (New York, 1979), pp. 55–86; Kenneth Macksey, *Tank Warfare* (New York, 1971), pp. 178–244; Max Hastings, *Overland, D-Day and the Battle for Normandy* (New York, 1984), pp. 58–68.

31 William H. McNeill, *The Pursuit of Power: Technology, Armed Force, and Society since AD 1000* (Chicago, 1982); Bernard and Fawn M. Brodie, *From Crossbow to H-Bomb* (Bloomington, Ind., 1973); Trevor N. Dupuy, *The Evolution of Weapons and Warfare* (Fairfax, Va., 1984).

32 Murray, *The Change in the European Balance of Power*, pp. 81–2; Len Deighton, *Fighter* (New York, 1978).

33 Richard K. Morris, *John P. Holland, 1841–1914* (Annapolis, Md., 1966); Ernest Andrade, Jr., 'Submarine Policy in the United States Navy, 1919–1941,' *Military Affairs*, Vol. 35 (April 1971), pp. 50–6; Edward P. Stafford, *The Far and the Deep* (Philadelphia, 1967).

34 Horst Boog, *Das Deutsche Reich und der Zweite Weltkrieg*, Vol. 4, pp. 186–7.

35 For German logistical preparations for Barbarossa, see either Martin van Creveld, *Supplying War* (Cambridge, 1977); or Klaus Reinhardt, *Die Wende vor Moskau, Das Scheitern der Strategie Hitlers in Winter 1941/1942* (Stuttgart, 1972).

36 Reinhardt, *Die Wende vor Moskau*, pp. 57, 126–33, 140–1.

37 Franz Halder, *Kriegstagebuch*, Vol. 3 (Stuttgart, 1964), p. 170.

38 Donald Macintyre, *The Battle of the Atlantic* (London, 1961); Alfred Price, *Aircraft versus Submarines* (Annapolis, Md., 1973); Ladislas Farago, *The Tenth Fleet* (New York, 1962).

39 Patrick Beesley, *Very Special Intelligence: The Story of the Admiralty's Operational Intelligence Centre, 1939–1945* (Garden City, N.Y., 1978), pp. 92–106.

40 Samuel Eliot Morison, *The Two-Ocean War* (Boston, 1963); Ronald Lewin, *The American Magic: Codes, Ciphers, and the Defeat of Japan* (New York, 1982).

41 For an intriguing analysis of the complex problems that the First World War posed, see Shelford Bidwell and Dominick Graham, *Firepower, British Army Weapons and Theories of War, 1909–1945* (London, 1982), pp. 61–148.

42 Anthony Verrier, *The Bomber Offensive* (New York, 1968), p. 170; Craven and Cate, *U.S. Army Air Forces in World War II*, pp. 681–7.

43 For a thorough discussion of Harris's failure in the Battle of Berlin, see Sir Charles Webster and Noble Frankland, *The Strategic Air Offensive Against Germany*, Vol. 2, *Endeavour* (London, 1961), pp. 190–213. See also Max Hastings, *Bomber Command* (London, 1979), pp. 306–63; Martin Middlebrook, *The Nuremberg Raid, March 1944* (New York, 1974), pp. 30–1; and Lee Kennett, *A History of Strategic Bombing* (New York, 1982), pp. 125–62.

44 For the best accounts of the 1940 campaign, see Telford Taylor, *The March of Conquest* (New York, 1958); Alistair Horne, *To Lose a Battle, France 1940* (London, 1969); and Hans-Adolf Jacobsen, *Fall Gelb, Der Kampf um den deutschen Operationsplan zur Westoffensive 1940* (Wiesbaden, 1957).

45 Barbara Tuchman, *The Guns of August* (New York, 1962), pp. 28–43.

46 For a description of the gulf between strategic arms and operational capabilities, see Leon Wolff, *In Flanders Fields: The 1917 Campaign* (New York, 1963), pp. 103–29.

47 Bidwell and Graham, *Firepower*, p. 71.

48 Timothy Lupfer, *The Dynamics of Doctrine: The Changes in German Tactical Doctrine During the First World War* (Leavenworth, Kans., 1981), pp. 11–23.

49 Carl Mannerheim, *The Memoirs of Marshal Mannerheim* (New York, 1954); Allen F. Chew, *The White Death: Epic of the Soviet-Finnish War* (East Lansing, Mich., 1971).

50 Bidwell and Graham, *Firepower*, pp. 61–148.

51 Martin Middlebrook, *The Kaiser's Battle, 21 March 1918: The First Day of the German Spring Offensive*, (London, 1978), pp. 74–82.

52 David Lloyd George, *Memoirs*, Vol. 6 (London, 1939), p. 3474.

53 Bidwell and Graham, *Firepower*, pp. 129; Winston S. Churchill, *The World Crisis* (Toronto, 1931), pp. 741–4.

54 Murray, *Luftwaffe*, pp. 274–76.

55 F. M. Richardson, *Fighting Spirit* (New York, 1978); Anthony Kellett, *Combat Motivation* (Boston, 1982); J. C. M. Baynes, *Morale* (London, 1967); William L. Hauser, 'The Will to Fight,' in Sam C. Sarkesian (ed.), *Combat Effectiveness* (Beverly Hills, Calif., 1980) pp. 186–211.

56 Edgar O'Ballance, *No Victor, No Vanquished: The Yom Kippur War* (San Rafael, Calif., 1978); Saad El Shazly, *The Crossing of the Suez* (San Francisco, 1980); G. P. Armstrong, 'Egypt,' in Richard A. Gabriel (ed.), *Fighting Armies* (Westport, Conn., 1983), pp. 147–65; Trevor N. Dupuy, *Elusive Victories: The Arab-Israeli Wars, 1947–1974* (New York, 1978).

57 See Knox, *Mussolini Unleashed*, pp. 25–30.

58 Max Hastings and Simon Jenkins, *The Battle for the Falklands* (New York, 1983).

59 Murray, 'German Response to Victory in Poland.'

60 Albert N. Garland (ed.), *A Distant Challenge: The U.S. Infantryman in Vietnam, 1967–1972* (Nashville, Tenn., 1983); Julian J. Ewell and Ira A. Hunt, Jr., *Sharpening the Combat Edge: The Use of Analysis to Reinforce Military Judgment* (Washington, D.C., 1974); Stanton, *The Rise and Fall of an American Army, passim.*; Charles Moskos, Jr., *The American Enlisted Man*, (New York, 1970).

61 Correlli Barnett, *The Desert Generals* (New York, 1960).

62 Herzog, *The War of Atonement, passim.*

[2]

Britain in the First World War

PAUL KENNEDY
Yale University

Introduction

The performance of Great Britain and its fighting services during the 1914–18 conflict offers an excellent example of the various categories by which military effectiveness can be assessed, and of the marked discrepancies which may exist in a nation's ability to be effective at all levels. As many historians have pointed out, a country such as twentieth-century Germany was able to produce a military system which was extremely flexible, resourceful, and therefore very effective in operational and tactical terms, but all this was vitiated by persistent failures at the political and strategical level.[1] By contrast, as the following essay will seek to show, the British were not particularly effective at the 'sharp end' of battle fighting, and (at least in the First World War) were slow to discover ways of improving their operational performance. Yet they were much better at the level of grand strategy, having evolved a politico-strategic process which could exploit the country's natural advantages, take into account the larger purposes of this complex and geographically disparate war, and try to balance means against ends.

The strong points of the British system could, therefore, help to mitigate the weaknesses which were being exposed at the operational and tactical level; but they could not of course eliminate those weaknesses, since no amount of political wisdom or strategic finesse can secure victory if a country's armed forces are ineffective on the battlefield. Furthermore, the very technical nature of the problem of achieving greater operational-tactical effectiveness along the Western Front trenches or in the North Sea – together with the gap which existed between the civilian and military branches of the British government – meant that only the army and navy authorities themselves could evolve newer means if they were going to achieve operational victories. Yet, as we shall see, the structure of command and assessment within the armed forces did not encourage a re-evaluation of the basic pre-

1914 assumptions about the nature of land and sea warfare, and thus the process of improving British military effectiveness at battlefield level was painfully slow and expensive – in turn provoking tensions with the political leadership and angry debates about British strategy as a whole.

Generally, this chapter will show that the tendency was for a gradual improvement in military and naval effectiveness. This is perhaps not surprising because, like other combatants in the First World War, the British in 1914 were not very well prepared for the actual conditions of battle; and since Britain and its empire had the strategic and economic capacity to endure a lengthy war, it had the chance to learn from experience and to improve its fighting machine. The real issue, then, is not so much the actual enhancement in British military effectiveness – no one would deny that the army and navy of August 1918 was better than that of August 1914 – as the question of why it took so long to improve operational performance. To answer this, it will be necessary to discuss cultural and psychological factors as well as command structures, technology, training, and so on.

One final preliminary remark may be called for here. When the British armed services entered the First World War, they were forced by geographical and, to a certain extent, historical circumstances to campaign in four major areas:

(1) the surface war in the North Sea,
(2) the war against the U-boats in the Atlantic and Mediterranean,
(3) the war in the Western Front trenches, and
(4) the 'easterners" war in Gallipoli, the Middle East, German colonies, and so on.

This means that assessments of British military effectiveness need to be made not only according to the differing levels (strategic and tactical) but also according to the particular campaign and the constellation of political, organizational, and other features which it alone possessed. While this survey of a four-campaign war makes the analysis more complex – producing many more exceptions to, as well as confirmations of, almost every general statement – nonetheless it still seems valid to argue that the overall tendency was for an improvement in Britain's military effectiveness. Whether that improvement was enough, or could have come earlier, will be discussed below in terms of individual services and campaigns.

Political Effectiveness

Although the politics of war in Britain was extremely heated and controversial on occasions, producing the most serious disagreements over civil–military relations in the country's twentieth-century history, there was never much doubt of the broad political will to commit national resources until the enemy was defeated. The actual decision to intervene in 1914 was a popular one, supported by the opposition Conservative Party and by most of the small Labour Party as well as by the great majority of the ruling Liberal Party.[2] While public support for the war would be slowly eroded by the heavy losses and by the lack of a military breakthrough, there was no wavering among the political leadership in Parliament. (The 1915 and 1916 changes in ministries were attempts to produce a more determined and effective national leadership, rather than one which would reduce support for the war effort.) With the exception of minority political groups like the Union of Democratic Control and the Independent Labour Party, there was no question but that civilian opinion would provide the funds deemed necessary by the military organizations. In consequence, the Treasury, which made strong efforts to control military-naval spending before 1914 and was to make even more determined efforts to reassert that control after 1919, lost its traditional role; its job now was simply to provide the money for the war. Thus the outlay upon the armed forces, which had been about \$438 million (29.9% of total government expenditures) in 1913, rose to about \$3439 million (74.8%) in 1915, and to a staggering \$9388 million (80.6%) in 1918.[3]

Political will, however, was only half the problem. It was also necessary to possess the financial resources required for total war. In this respect, too, there were few obstacles. Britain was an immensely wealthy country, with vast amounts of internal resources and stupendously large (around \$19 billion) overseas investments. London was the center of the world's financial network and could provide large sums of money on credit. There were serious questions of a technical nature (e.g., avoiding gross inflation, preserving the productive base, and ensuring continued credit) about how to pay for the war, just as there were important debates of a political nature (e.g., direct versus indirect taxation, taxing war profiteers, and pacifying Labour), but there was less of a threat that resources would run dry.[4]

Perhaps the only large-scale problem to note in this area was the growing trade imbalance between Britain and the USA due to the increasing flow of foodstuffs, munitions, ships, and so on, which American farmers and factories produced to meet the British demand. Since British exports to the USA, the sale of British-owned overseas assets, or gold transfers could not, even combined, pay for these enormous war orders, the UK Treasury was increasingly forced to borrow on the New York and Chicago markets, and this led to an unnerving degree of dependence upon another nation. In October 1916, in fact, the Chancellor of the Exchequer warned the Cabinet that 'by next June or earlier, the President of the American Republic will be in a position, if he wishes, to dictate his own terms to us.'[5] As it happened, the slightly later American entry into the war and its commitment to fight in western Europe both meant that this financial dependency did not impinge upon British military effectiveness, although it increased Whitehall's desire to finish the war as soon as possible, and it affected political, diplomatic, and naval negotiations during and after the armistice.[6]

Getting access to the industrial and technological resources needed to produce the right military equipment was an altogether more difficult area for the British, although the story is one of steady improvement after the initial failures. One of the problems was that the equipment needed soon changed according to the experiences of conflict: small escort vessels became more important than new battleships for the war at sea; machine guns, trucks, tanks, and howitzers became absolutely essential for the war on land; and aircraft were needed, in fast-growing numbers, for the first time in combat. Yet until the military and naval staffs had themselves defined what new weaponry was required, and in what numbers, British industry could not itself anticipate that demand. Still, the greatest problem – for Britain as for all the other combatants – was the completely unforeseen quantitative needs of the armed services when it was realized that this was going to be a long, drawn-out, 'total' war. Quick-firing guns were using up shells four, six, and even ten times faster than they could be replaced.[7] Moreover, while other countries at least had the advantage that they had always planned the deployment of mass armies, the lack of a fixed British military commitment to fight in France before August 1914, and the country's traditional strategic preference for 'limited liability,' meant that the miniscule British Expeditionary Force (BEF) of 6 divisions needed to be multiplied in size as soon as possible, and those new armies would all need to be equipped.

The sheer number of areas in which British industry was found incapable of supplying the vastly increased demands of the armed services was very large – heavy guns, high explosives, fuses, trucks, gun sights, aero-engines, light machine guns, barbed wire – and each could fairly receive a detailed scrutiny.[8] Given the limitations of space, it may be appropriate to refer here to the most controversial item of all – the famous 'shell scandal' of May 1915, when *The Times* made public Sir John French's bitter complaints about the lack of high-explosive shells and in so doing precipitated a government crisis. The wealth of literature upon this topic points to the following conclusions:[9] First, while the British munitions manufacturers could and did produce both guns and shells in excess of the targets set in prewar plans, they could in no way meet the highly inflated demands made by the extended mass warfare along the Western Front. Only a totally new system could solve this crisis.

Secondly, the chief fault was not that of the armaments industry, which did its best to meet the (often preposterous) demands which worried generals and optimistic politicians forced upon it in 1914–15. The chief culprits were the chronically bad method of military contracting, the running-down of the government's own ordnance factories prior to the war, and the reliance upon private industry to close any gap – without, however, taking preparations to ensure that there was spare capacity to meet emergency demands. In consequence, as the historian of this sorry episode has pointed out, 'Ammunition firms capable of turning out 3m rounds per week for the Lee Enfield rifle found themselves by the end of August 1914 confronting an expeditionary force with an immediate need for 176m rounds.'[10] The worst fact of all was that exactly the same sorts of problems had occurred in the first year of the Boer War (1899–1902), and yet no efficient remedies had been devised.

Finally, no amount of detailed investigations into these inadequate industrial and technological resources can leave aside two larger questions. The first is, how viable was this British policy of 'limited liability' (requiring no great armies and munitions) before 1914, when the government also reserved the option to intervene militarily, if necessary, to defend France and Belgium from German attack?[11] Secondly, how necessary – and useful – was the operational strategy of generals like French and Haig in blasting a potential

Table 2.1 UK Munitions Production, 1914–18

	1914	*1915*	*1916*	*1917*	*1918*
Guns	91	3,390	4,314	5,137	8,039
Tanks	–	–	150	1,110	1,359
Machine guns (in thousands)	0.3	6.1	33.5	79.7	120.9
Aircraft (in thousands)	0.2	1.9	6.1	14.7	32.0
Aero-engines (in thousands)	0.1	1.7	5.4	11.8	22.1
Rifles (in millions)	0.1	0.6	1.0	1.2	1.1
Shells (in millions)	0.5	6.0	45.7	76.2	67.3
Powder and explosives (in thousands of tons)	5.0	24.0	76.0	186.0	118.0

Source: Hardach, *The First World War, 1914–1918* (London, 1977), p. 87

breakthrough area with millions of shells? These are issues which will be dealt with elsewhere in this chapter; at this point it is necessary only to recall that material resources alone do not win wars.

What is indisputable is that inadequacies in equipment and supply did affect British military effectiveness. At the beginning of the war, Britain had 'an army almost without heavy guns,'[12] and it had preferred shrapnel to high-explosive shells because of its prewar belief in the swift infantry offensive. Thus, in February 1915 French's forces had only enough shells to allow the expenditure of ten per gun per day; at Festubert, on May 9th, the position was even worse. The failure of the BEF's attack around Loos in September 1915 was also attributed in part to the lack of guns and shells. Only with the coming of the Ministry of Munitions was this critical weakness slowly remedied; the overall figures show the enormous expansion in munitions output from 1915–16 onwards (see Table 2.1).[13]

The Royal Navy, by contrast, already rested upon an extensive industrial and technological base, since the British shipbuilding industry was by far the largest in the world. Moreover, the fleet had been steadily expanded over the preceding three decades, and it possessed a good (and increasing) superiority in battleships over the German Navy. It also appeared to have been adequately stocked in terms of fuel, munitions, and other supplies. Its difficulties lay elsewhere: in the poor quality of its shells, torpedoes, mines, fire-control, and anti-flash systems, and in intelligence and battle tactics, all of which are dealt with later.[14]

The two British air forces, the Royal Flying Corps (RFC) and the Royal Naval Air Service (RNAS), were virtually created from nothing; the RFC, for example, had only 67 planes at the outset of war, and British officials had to rush over to France to buy every airframe and aero-engine they could lay their hands upon.[15] It inevitably took years to produce equipment to the quantity and quality desired, and until 1917–18 the RFC in particular felt the lack of good aircraft. Nevertheless, there was an adequate potential industrial base in Britain, given the time to mobilize it. By the last year of the war, when the Royal Air Force possessed some 22,000 aircraft (not all by any means front-line), the shortage lay elsewhere, in trained pilots.

The military's access to adequate manpower was also more a question of organizing resources properly, and in the desired time, than of an inherent lack of suitable stock.[16] The manpower stock in Britain suitable for military service was at least 5 million men (in fact, 5.7 million actually joined the services); and the empire, especially the self-governing Dominions and India, provided another 3 million. However, to switch from a small, professional army of 200,000 men to a mass force of millions was quite beyond the capacity of the existing machinery of August 1914. By the end of the next month, for example, over 760,000 recruits had responded to Kitchener's call for men and by the end of 1914 nearly 1,200,000 had joined up. This was in one way splendid, in another hopeless, for there were not enough barracks, rifles, boots, or uniforms for them. Since Kitchener also declined (for reasons peculiar to himself) to use the reserve Territorial Army framework and instead chose to create 'New Armies,' horrendous bottlenecks and overlaps in training were inevitable. In addition, the large number of volunteers from key industries (munitions, metals, and shipbuilding) threatened the armaments build-up, and by the summer of 1915 those industries had lost between 16 per cent and 24 per cent of their workforce.[17] Britain's manpower policy during the first six to twelve months of the war has therefore been described as 'anarchic' and 'so ill-thought-out.'[18]

Britain was fortunate in one sense, however, in that the far larger French Army could take the brunt of the German military pressure in the west until the expected British forces were ready; only in early 1916, it should be noted, did Haig possess more than 1 million men under his command. His 38 infantry and 5 cavalry divisions were to be joined by another 19 divisions by midsummer, making this by far the largest army ever assembled by the British Empire.

And yet, as is well known, these numbers were never enough for the military. By 1916, after a bitter political battle, conscription had been introduced in the UK, which itself was a sign that recruitment was falling off and that controls over manpower were now to replace the voluntarist and *laissez-faire* order. Yet despite the regular 'combing-out' of more workers in industry and commerce (and their replacement by 1.5 million females), the flow of numbers steadied and then began to dry up. For much of 1917 and 1918 Haig and his fellow generals pleaded for reinforcements, either to aid their own offensives or to sustain their desperate defense against Ludendorff's great attack of March–June 1918, during which the British Empire's forces were outnumbered and, in fact, slightly smaller than in early 1917.[19]

This manpower shortage on the Western Front reflected, however, certain political, economic, and strategic priorities as much as – and perhaps more than – demographic constraints. By the last years of the war (as also in 1943–45), few extra able-bodied men could be drafted into the army without affecting armaments production. Furthermore, there were the other two armed services to consider, for by 1918 the Royal Navy had swollen to 438,000 men and the newly formed Royal Air Force to 290,000 men. Early in 1918, the Manpower Committee of the War Cabinet gave priority first to the navy and the air force, then to the merchant marine, shipbuilding, coalmining and timber industries, and then to armaments and food production: the army came at the bottom of the list. Furthermore, as Haig and Robertson often pointed out, there were vast numbers of British and imperial troops located in regions far away from the Western Front where the decisive battle was being fought; over 750,000 imperial troops (including 12 British divisions) were serving in the Middle East and Salonika; and although it was not true that Lloyd George and the War Cabinet had deliberately kept some 600,000 men in the UK to prevent Haig from wasting them in another offensive, it was the case that the maximum possible number of troops was denied to the 'westerners.' In consequence, reinforcements had to be swiftly shipped from home, from Italy, from Egypt, and elsewhere once the true size of Ludendorff's offensive became clear.[20]

In his own defense, Lloyd George could argue that Haig's army would have been far stronger had he not pursued the fruitless frontal assaults of the Somme (where British casualties were well over 400,000 men) and Passchendaele (at least 250,000 casualties); and the 'easterners' could also point out that the forces deployed outside the Western Front were at least making significant territorial and strategical gains. But that, once again, takes the question from manpower *per se* to strategy and politics.

The quality issue can be discussed more briefly. There is little evidence that the quality of the Royal Navy's personnel was other than good. The only weakness identified was the unimaginative and sometimes simple-minded nature of a disturbingly large array of the senior naval officers in the first two years of the war. By contrast, the junior officers, like the long-service ratings, gunners, and petty officers, were of high caliber.[21] And the air services, benefiting from the attractions of novelty and romance, also had relatively few difficulties over personnel – except, of course, in the vital issue of trained pilots during the great aerial battles over the Western Front. However, in this latter respect, the British case was no different from that of any other nation (or from its 1939–43 shortages of experienced pilots), since demand for capable fliers was always in excess of supply.

The biggest problem the British faced was in finding qualified manpower for the army. As will be detailed later in this chapter, it simply had been expanded far too quickly to allow the service's own undermanned training departments to do a decent job.

Strategic Effectiveness

The political goals (that is, the war aims) of Britain and its empire slowly changed during the conflict. During the late nineteenth and early twentieth centuries, Britain had seen itself, rightly or wrongly, as an essentially satisfied power, wanting peace with all other nations and the enjoyment and development of the territorial and economic gains acquired throughout the world over the preceding three hundred years. This cozy position had been subjected to many challenges by countries less satisfied with the status quo, but none of the international crises since the 1870s had led Britain into a large-scale war – until 1914 itself. Now, the overriding strategic objective was the defeat of Germany and of that country's perceived threat to British interests, both at sea (to preserve British naval supremacy) and on land (to preserve France's independence and the general European equilibrium). In addition, the German invasion of Belgium – guaranteed neutral by the 1839 treaty – gave a legal and idealistic motive to containing German power in Europe. Yet it was difficult to see how Germany's latent capacity to upset the European balance could be satisfactorily contained unless by total defeat, occupation, and possible partitioning (as would happen in 1945), which conflicted with prevailing beliefs in national self-determination. Still, because the British government held that 'Prussian militarism' was behind Germany's aggressive policies, the political aim of forcing internal constitutional reforms upon the German elite was increasingly advocated, in addition to defeat in the field.[22] It ought to be noted, however, that Haig and his generals showed no interest in 'democratizing' Germany; all they wished to do was to win a military victory.[23]

It should be noted also that both in July–August 1914 and in 1918–19 there was concern in some quarters that the total elimination of Germany would leave the British Empire exposed in the future to the renewed ambitions of France and (especially) of Russia. Such an anxiety was never the central preoccupation of the British government, but it does help to explain why the strategic objective of defeating Germany totally did not always seem to Lloyd George, Milner, Smuts, and others to guarantee the long-term political goals of the British nation.[24]

The unease over a possible dichotomy between strategic objectives and political goals was, if anything, reinforced by the ambivalent British attitude towards Austria-Hungary. Despite some ideological disapproval of the Habsburg monarchy, the British had no direct quarrel with Vienna and many felt that a strong and independent Austria-Hungary would block Berlin's *Drang nach Osten*; hence the secret diplomatic efforts during the war to detach the Austrians from the Dual Alliance. Only when those efforts failed did the British slowly accept the political goal of supporting self-determination for the subject nationalities within the Habsburg Empire and thus agree to its disintegration.[25]

It therefore followed that, since the defeat of Austria-Hungary was not a central British strategic objective, no great risks (i.e., military campaigns) were taken to defeat the Habsburg monarchy, and British strategy was essentially supportive and defensive. On land, it would send aid to allies such as Serbia, Rumania, and Italy, which were directly fighting Austro-Hungarian forces; at sea, it would help the Franco-Italian navies in retaining command of the Mediterranean. It is true that if Italy had collapsed after Caporetto, London believed the consequences might have been very great; hence the Franco-British decision to rush reinforcements to that theater, despite Haig's protests and Robertson's suspicions.

The strategic objective of defeating Turkey would, the British government felt, unequivocally secure certain political goals. In the first place, it would permit the West to re-establish contact with Russia – broken off, at least via the Straits, since November 1914 – and help to sustain that country's vital task of engaging the German forces in the east. Secondly, the coming of war with Turkey allowed British strategists and imperial enthusiasts to argue that, with the defeat of this new enemy, territorial gains could be made which would enhance the British Empire's security in the Middle East and Persian Gulf for the future. The same sort of arguments were used by the British Dominions to justify the seizure and possession of Germany's overseas colonies in Africa and the Pacific. The existence of those Turkish and German territories was not a cause of the war, but once the conflict began, their acquisition became another political goal which would be secured by the defeat of the Central Powers.[26]

The risks entailed in pursuing the defeat of Turkey also seemed consistent with the stakes involved and the consequences of failure. Although it is an open question whether Russia would have avoided military collapse and revolution had the Dardanelles operation succeeded, the possible gains certainly justified that venture.[27] Furthermore, given the sheer size of British imperial interests in the eastern Mediterranean, Suez Canal, and Persian Gulf regions, the strategic objective of driving Turkey from those parts was a logical one. If the 'easterners" campaigns involved considerable expenditure of men and matériel, the benefits were also considerable – and the risk of utter defeat was very small.

In the naval war against Germany, there was also both consistency and logic in British policy.[28] The defeat of the High Seas Fleet's attempt to challenge the Royal Navy's control of the North Sea was vital for Britain's own strategic and economic independence, and was the chief justification for the expensive battleship-building program prior to 1914. In the same way, the very large investment of resources involved in beating off the German U-boat threat to Allied shipping was absolutely logical: had the transatlantic flow of supplies been interrupted, as it very nearly was in 1917, the Allied cause would have been lost. Precisely how the High Seas Fleet was contained and how the U-boats were defeated are operational matters that will be examined below. All accepted that command of the sea had to be preserved.

The land struggle against Germany, however, because of its tactical and operational nature, involved enormous costs, which (at least in the minds of some Britons at the time, and many commentators later) called into question the entire strategy of hoping to defeat Germany in the field. The issue was, and still is, central to all questions of British military effectiveness in the First World War, but it is not possible to address it at one level alone, for the reasons brilliantly given by Michael Howard some years ago:

> If we are to condemn [the total commitment of British resources to the Western Front], we must distinguish three elements in it: operational, strategic, and political. One may accept its necessity on strategic and political grounds without endorsing the manner in which the operations to which it led were actually conducted. By autumn 1915 the original highly trained British Expeditionary Force had disappeared, and in the New Armies which replaced it all ranks from the Commander in Chief to private soldiers were learning, from the beginning and at hideous cost, a new kind of war which baffled even experienced continental armies. It was only in 1918 that even the Germans developed effective techniques of attack under conditions of trench warfare. The strategic argument, that

> more effective support could have been given to Britain's allies at less cost by intervention on other fronts in other parts of Europe is superficially attractive; yet it has never been conclusively shown that the terrain of South or South-East Europe – that famous 'soft underbelly' – offered battlefields which German troops could not have reached as quickly and defended as stubbornly as they did their lines on the Western Front, and where the inexperienced British armies could have attacked with any greater chance of success. As for the political argument, it is seldom explicitly raised, but it is this: would it have mattered to Britain if Germany *had* defeated France and Russia and established a new Napoleonic Empire? Was not seven hundred thousand dead too high a price to pay to prevent a German hegemony in Europe?[29]

Because this issue can be dealt with only at several levels, it is further discussed below. This writer's belief is precisely that, to quote Howard again, 'One may accept its necessity on strategic and political grounds without endorsing the manner in which the operations to which it led were actually conducted.'

In theory, the hammering out of a grand strategy which both reflected Britain's political aims and accorded with the capacities and needs of the armed services ought to have been relatively easy. The British politico-military system prior to 1914 was, compared with those of most other powers, an excellent one, evolved through the Cabinet and Committee of Imperial Defence (CID) structures and possessing different levels of communication between the military and civilian branches of government.[30] At the outset of the war, however, this system almost (but not quite) broke down. Many individual officers on the Imperial General Staff moved across to France with the BEF, and the early wartime Chiefs of the Imperial General Staff (CIGS) (Douglas, Archie Murray, and Wolfe-Murray) were ineffectual. The Committee of Imperial Defence staff under Hankey was almost disbanded on the false assumption that its planning roles had ended and that decision making and assessment were solely for the Cabinet and/or the services themselves. Yet the Cabinet *per se* was far too large a group of men to work efficiently, both on a day-to-day basis and in considering longer term issues of grand strategy. Moreover, precisely because certain key strategic decisions (like the Continental commitment, or withdrawal of the Mediterranean battlefleet) involved contentious political issues, Asquith's pre-1914 administration had avoided making firm choices and preferred instead to let things drift; and this habit of mind continued after August 1914.

In the early stages of the war, then, the prevailing assumption in the Liberal Cabinet was to let the service ministries (and especially the formidable Kitchener, who had been brought in as War Minister) get on with the fighting while the nation mobilized itself to provide the required resources. This was basically satisfactory to the navy, waiting in the North Sea to crush the High Seas Fleet, and to the army, gearing up for offensives in Flanders once the trench lines had been established. It was not satisfactory – because there was insufficient detailed scrutiny by either politicians or military – when it came to an ambitious new wartime venture like the Dardanelles operation, requiring close cooperation between the two services, and a careful assessment of means versus ends; the result was misunderstanding, confusion, and ultimately disaster. It was not satisfactory in dealing with economic strategy (war production, blockade, and cooperation with the Allies), where coordination between departments was also essential. Finally, it was not satisfactory in controlling individual Cabinet ministers who felt themselves entitled to have a voice in operational strategy. As Henry Wilson recalled:

> It thus came about by the end of 1914 that while the Secretary of State for War was aiming at decisive results on the Western Front, the First Lord of the Admiralty was advocating the seizure of the Dardanelles and Constantinople; the Secretary of State for the Colonies was concerned with operations in various parts of Africa; and the Chancellor of the Exchequer was impressing upon his Cabinet colleagues the strategical advantages to be gained by transferring the main British military effort from the Western Front to the Balkan Peninsula and Syria.[31]

The various *ad hoc* measures to the end of 1915 – special subcommittees, the Dardanelles Committee, the War Committee – had still not solved the key problem of synthesizing political control, strategic deliberation, and executive authority.

Only with the further changes of 1915 and 1916 did the structure really improve. New 'super' ministries of munitions, blockade, shipping, and so on, coordinated efforts in those areas, and left the half-dozen senior politicians of Lloyd George's War Cabinet free to discuss strategy, to call in and listen to the military advisors, and to make personal visits to various campaign theaters to talk with the officers in charge. By that time, too, the Chief of the Imperial General Staff had had his status redefined so that he could tender advice to the government on military affairs as a whole. When the occasion called for it, the Prime Minister (or another War Cabinet member) would travel to France with the CIGS to discuss matters with Haig; or the latter, like Admiral Jellicoe, would be asked to a War Cabinet session. The system was small-scale, flexible, and in theory effective, since it gave the military clear channels for communicating their wishes to the political leadership.

Yet the real issue in British policy by then was not the degree to which generals and admirals could influence politicians to seek militarily logical national goals, but rather the degree to which the political leadership could influence the military to achieve strategic goals by practicable means.[32] Because the First World War produced profound disagreements over operational means, there was repeated tension between 'frocks' and 'brass hats.' There are two great examples here: first, the pressures exerted by Lloyd George and others upon a very reluctant British Admiralty in 1917 to introduce a convoy system in the light of the merchant ship losses to German U-boats; and, secondly, the repeated attempts by Lloyd George, Milner, and others to moderate Haig's strategy of launching costly offensives along the Western Front. To be sure, Haig's supporters would argue that the leaders of the military organization were not able successfully to communicate with and influence the political leadership to seek 'militarily logical national goals'; but that opens again the whole issue of whether Haig's *methods* as well as his *aims* were sensible ones. What can be said is that the channels for communication did exist, and were often used, although Haig himself was never very keen to explain things to the War Cabinet.

In the extra-European theaters of war, there seems to have been less tension between the political and military leadership about the pursuit of national goals, even if the early stages of the Mesopotamian campaign revealed an appallingly complex overlap of political and military authorities in London, Simla-Dehli, and Basra. When the question arose of sending further divisions to Mesopotamia, both the army in France and the Indian authorities opposed the transfer of troops from their area. It was only the 'breathing space' afforded by the ending of the Somme campaign, together with the widespread humiliation felt at the Kut disaster, which permitted the British to assemble the adequate means to capture Baghdad at last.[33]

The fact was that, despite the British traditions of imperial and naval campaigning, little in the way of adequate force size and structure was ready early in the war for extra-European operations. Von Spee's squadron, for example, could only be dealt with by the prompt but quite *ad hoc* dispatch of Sturdee's battlecruisers (which reduced the Grand Fleet's numerical superiority to virtually its lowest level). Some consideration of overseas operations had been done by the CID prior to 1914, and there did exist a string of British, British-Indian, and Dominion bases across the globe; by contrast, the Germans had made little provision for the defense of their widely scattered colonies.[34] Nonetheless, where the Germans resisted (e.g., in East Africa under Lettow-Vorbeck), they soon exposed some glaring British inadequacies; the disastrous attack on Tanga in November 1914 showed, among other things, a quite inadequate force structure for the operation in question.[35]

The British (and, in some cases, the French) also persistently underestimated the defensive capacity of the Turks, and this was clearly shown in the force size for the Euphrates campaign of 1915–16. In the Gallipoli venture, the size of the Allied forces – and of the later reinforcing units – was never enough to give a clear superiority; and the confused structure of the forces involved was a classic example of how not to run a combined operation.[36] The Salonika operation also lacked adequate size to achieve its end.[37] Only by 1917, when the British had heavily invested resources into their Middle Eastern campaigns (and especially into Allenby's command), was the force size sufficient. The overall chain of command in the Middle East was always complex (and made more so by the relations with Lawrence and the Arabs, and pressures from India, Egypt, and the French), but Allenby's own force structure for the advance upon Jerusalem and Damascus was satisfactory enough, with a good balance between infantry and cavalry, and a handsome advantage in artillery and aircraft.[38]

In the surface war in the North Sea, the force size and structure was consistent with the defined strategic goals and courses of action.[39] Whatever the particular deficiencies of the Royal Navy's Grand Fleet in, say, imaginative leadership or antiflash provision, its very existence, its size, and its deployment area all reflected the essential aim of defeating the High Seas Fleet should it ever emerge to dispute command of the sea. To have moved the Grand Fleet elsewhere would have been rash; to have divided it into smaller fleets would have played into German hands; and to have reconstructed it along the lines suggested by radicals like Percy Scott (submarines, aircraft, and cruisers, rather than battleships) might have worked, but it would have seemed too risky an experiment while the German Navy itself gave preference to the battlefleet.

On the other hand, the Royal Navy's force size and structure in 1914 was definitely not consistent with the goal of defeating the U-boat challenge, which had not been properly anticipated. The readjustment was only slowly made, both psychologically (in admitting that this was more of a real threat than the High Seas Fleet) and in material terms (in devising new countermeasures, in withdrawing destroyers from the Grand Fleet for Atlantic convoy protection, in the control of merchant shipping, etc.). By 1918, though, things were much improved.

The militarily logical national goal of defeating the German Army in the field may or may not have been sensible politically, and may or may not have been pursued by faulty operational-tactical means. What does seem clear was that the size of the British forces in France was never enough to achieve that goal during the first three years of the war – though it might be argued, perhaps a little perversely, that by 1917 Haig's force was too large (in that it fired too many shells, and tried to send forward too many men, so that the offensives 'stuck' rather than broke through). Only in August–September 1918, when a better trained and reinforced British Army, together with French and American forces, all combined to put pressure upon Ludendorff's weary troops, could the aim of defeating the formidable German Army in France be achieved.

So far as one can tell from the literature, no one has argued that significant changes in the overall force structure would alone, or substantially, have allowed Haig's troops to be more successful in the field. The structural problems which did arise – e.g., the difficulties which the central strategic decision makers in Whitehall had in exercising control over Haig, and the problems which the Commander-in-Chief faced when troops were withdrawn to Italy – were caused essentially by disagreements over strategy. Moreover, the problems caused by the distancing of the GHQ staff from the actual front-line fighting conditions could only have been remedied by changes of mind and habit, rather than of the structure of the British Army in France.[40]

Behind the force structures themselves lay the larger logistical infrastructure, and the national industrial-technical base. As was stated above, with a few exceptions this base existed – but it took a long time to mobilize it fully for wartime purposes. When the conflict began, neither the logistical infrastructure nor the industrial-technical base was prepared for a total war involving millions of troops. Recruiting offices, barracks, training grounds, uniforms, weapons, munitions, signals equipment – everything was in short supply. With no reserve capacity, the private armaments industry could not respond to the enormous and sudden demand. Moreover, Britain was dependent upon imports of such strategically vital items as machine tools, ball bearings, magnetos, aircraft engines, precision instruments of all sorts, dyestuffs, explosives, and other matériel. These deficiencies were only remedied by the most prodigious reorganization of British industry under the direction of the Ministry of Munitions, building hundreds of new factories, creating virtually new industries, and engaging in comprehensive industrial planning with civil servants, managers, and trades unionists. The result has been described as a 'wartime industrial revolution'[41] – but it all took time, and this largely explains the relatively small role played by the British Army in France until mid-June 1916.

The expansion of the Royal Navy's supporting infrastructure during the war was in no way as rapid, simply because the pre-1914 naval races had already created a large shipbuilding industry and a considerable logistical and fleet-base structure. Facilities at the Scapa Flow anchorage and fleet base had to be enormously extended during the war, if only because the provision of bases for the Royal Navy in the North Sea area was 'shocking,' even as late as 1914;[42] neither Scapa, Cromarty, nor Rosyth, nor any of the smaller east coast bases like Harwich, were on a par with Kiel and Wilhelmshaven, simply because history and geography had caused the Royal Navy's main fleet bases to be developed along the south coast. In the same way, a large-scale development of facilities at Queenstown had to take place when the Battle of the Atlantic began in earnest.[43]

Given the size of the British shipbuilding industry, it could continue to complete the recently ordered fast battleships and battlecruisers even in wartime, and deal with other demands. Over time, however, it did have to turn more of its resources to ship repair work and small-vessel construction – and this is precisely why the Admiralty began to get alarmed after 1916 at the reports of increased American and Japanese battleship building. The same remarks about sufficient potential can be made about Britain's scientific base. It was, admittedly, not organized for total war in August 1914; but there was a reservoir of scientists, engineers, entrepreneurs, and manufacturers who could be mobilized. In the campaign against the U-boats, for example, naval officers and scientists combined to produce far more efficient depth-charges, horned mines, mine nets and barriers, hydrophones laid on the sea bottom, paravanes, and finally detection equipment. However, all this took time, and was not too well organized by a traditionalist Admiralty staff;[44] and none of these individual advances in design and equipment were as important in defeating the U-boats as the operational decision to adopt the convoy system.

Before the war, there was virtually no British airframe or aero-engine industry; it had to be constructed from scratch, under Ministry of Munitions guidance. Once again, the key problem was organization. For example, even when the go-ahead was given for large expansion programs, there were inevitable bottlenecks and overlaps – at one stage, some forty types of aero-engine were under construction, before the number was whittled down to eight. Similarly, when the Royal Naval Air Service was given the responsibility for aerial defense over Britain (because the Royal Flying Corps had left for France), it hardly had any supporting facilities at all – and the national shock at the Zeppelin and (especially) Gotha bomber raids almost overwhelmed the Cabinet at one stage. Not surprisingly, the government resolved to pour even more financial and technical resources into the air forces, and this is why the Royal Air Force could claim to be the biggest in the world by 1918. However, for the preceding three or more years, its inadequacies were all too evident.[45]

The expansion of the logistical infrastructure of the British Army in France has been examined in a number of studies. Within two years, a vast organization had grown up behind the British front lines and extending all the way back to the great depots at Le Havre, Boulogne, and Rouen: bakeries, engineering workshops, rest areas and training grounds, ammunition depots, new railhead-depots, hospitals (fifty-eight by 1916 alone), facilities for the tens of thousands of trucks and motorcars, canteens, ordnance works, and so on. 'Thus the British army in France by 1916 was the largest, most complicated, and most comprehensive single organization ever evolved by the British nation.'[46]

Provided Britain retained command of the sea, access to raw materials was not a major problem. Large stocks of most produce existed within the empire and could be bought from overseas suppliers (especially the USA); but all this again emphasized the importance of winning the battle against the U-boats. What was required – and implemented – was a careful survey and exploitation of empire resources, a rigorous organization of sea transport (to cut down on shipping space and costs), and a utilization of products from the sterling area as much as possible. Significant industrialization occurred in Canada and Australia during the war, but the empire's contribution came much more in the form of men and raw materials than in 'industrial-technical base.' One might also note the very successful development of British agriculture during the war, compared with the disasters which hit Germany, Austria, France, and Russia.[47] By the later stages of the war, British shipping formed the largest part of an Allied 'pool,' to ensure that troops, foodstuffs, and raw materials needed by the coalition were transported in the most efficient manner.

Nevertheless, integrating shipping resources, and even having British troops located in France and (later) Italy in large numbers, did not necessarily mean that Britain's strategic objectives were fully integrated with those of its major allies. It is true that the strategy of the war at sea was understood by all the coalition partners, and integration was relatively easily achieved. In the Mediterranean, Royal Navy forces worked with the Italians to ensure the continued 'bottling-up' of the Austro-Hungarian battlefleet and to try to check the U-boat attacks against Allied lines of communication. After Japan entered the war, it was persuaded to patrol the maritime routes in the Pacific, then in the Indian Ocean; later, it even sent destroyers to the Mediterranean. The USA's entry into the conflict brought cooperation over Atlantic convoys, and later the dispatch of a powerful battleship squadron to join the Grand Fleet. Although there would be disagreements and complaints at the lower, operational level (e.g., over demarcation zones for convoying in the Mediterranean), there was no disagreement over strategy. The same could be said about military operations outside Europe. Most of those, except for the Anglo-French move against Togoland and the Cameroons, did not involve integrated forces; in the Pacific, for example, Japan seized German possessions north of the equator, whereas those to the south fell into Australian and New Zealand hands. Nearer home, the British and French readily cooperated in agreeing to the Russian request to seize the Dardanelles and Constantinople, the strategic rationale for which seemed obvious. The Salonika expedition was much more of a French affair (with, appropriately, a French instead of a British commander) and only with reluctance did the British agree to keep their forces in the area after 1916.

The real issue, in negotiating with Allies over strategic objectives, was the degree to which British resources should be concentrated along the Western Front. Indeed, the heated debate between 'westerners' and 'easterners' was the strategic controversy of the First World War, so far as Britain was concerned – and the quarrel has hardly lessened in intensity since then.[48] Probably no one favored a complete British pull-out from France and Belgium, but on the whole the Dominions (which can be counted here as 'allies of a kind') stressed such extra-European strategic objectives as the German colonies and the Middle East, and were supported in this by the imperialists within Lloyd George's War Cabinet and by all those who came increasingly to doubt whether any breakthroughs were possible on the Western Front. By contrast, Britain's major allies of France and Russia, facing the massed might of the Central Powers, were overwhelmingly concerned about the defeat of Germany in Europe. This did not necessarily mean Franco-Russian insistence that Britain concentrate all its efforts on the Western Front. Both Paris and St. Petersburg encouraged the 1915 attempt upon Gallipoli; France strongly pressed for a British contingent in the Salonika operation, and opposed its withdrawal (and the winding-down of the entire venture) when people like Robertson preferred to use those troops in Flanders; and both France and Britain felt it necessary to rush reinforcements to Italy after the defeat at Caporetto. These appeals for British aid to Serbia, Russia, Italy, and Greece interacted with the desires of Lloyd George and other Cabinet ministers to avoid offensives on the Western Front, to which Haig, Robertson, and most of the other generals were so attached. At other times, however, French (and, after him, Haig) could join with Joffre in denouncing all such diversions from the Western Front. And the French government and General Staff was never in favor of British troops leaving Flanders to operate in Mesopotamia and Palestine, which the British imperialists fancied.

This already complicated situation was exacerbated by two other factors. The first was the bitter opposition from Haig and the 'military organization' to all of Lloyd George's attempts to put the British Army in France under the strategic control of Nivelle, or Foch, since this was (correctly) seen as an attempt to hobble Haig.[49] In addition, British GHQ in France not infrequently quarrelled with their French opposite numbers about how many miles of front each should defend, about the timing of their respective offensives, and in general about whether their partner was fully pulling his weight. Perhaps naturally, such tensions were most in evidence when the

Franco-British armies along the Western Front were under strain (September 1914, Joffre's 1915 offensive, just before the Somme offensive, and especially in spring 1918). The many *bouleversements* of early 1918 – for example, of Haig's desperate urging of a 'General Reserve' for the Allied armies, after months of resisting that idea, simply because of the pressures Ludendorff was applying on the British front; or of Lloyd George's alarmed withdrawal of British troops from Italy, Salonika, Egypt, and Palestine to reinforce the Western Front, only a short while after the War Cabinet had decided to fight 'easterner' campaigns – shows how difficult it is to generalize about strategic integration and cooperation between Britain and its allies.

Strategic integration with Russia was for the most part impossible, due to geographical constraints. Still, it has recently been argued that both the political and the military leadership in Britain saw the importance of maintaining Russia, since the Eastern Front would absorb millions of German and Austro-Hungarian troops which would otherwise be dispatched to the West, or to Turkey.[50] Although there were attempts at cooperative campaigns (e.g., the 1916 agreement that offensives be mounted at about the same time on the Western, Eastern, and Italian fronts; or the early 1917 Anglo-Russian agreement to put pressure upon Turkey from three regions, the Caucasus, Mesopotamia, and Palestine), the chief strategic function of the British was to provide Russia with the munitions and raw materials necessary for the continuance of the war on the Eastern Front; in this regard, British and other supplies were simply inadequate to meet the enormous Russian demand. Hence the tangled quarrels, in 1915 especially, about how best to support Russia: by seizing Constantinople, as Churchill, Hankey, and (sometimes) Kitchener advocated; by operations in the Balkans, as the French suggested; by taking munitions destined for the British armies and letting Russia have them, as the Russians, and also some British officials, proposed; or by renewed offensives on the Western Front, which was the only solution considered by Sir John French and Joffre. None of these, as it turned out, could stop the Russian collapse by 1917.

Strategic cooperation with Japan was never so important; perhaps for that reason, it was generally harmonious, although there were British political suspicions about Tokyo's intentions in China. There were also political differences over war aims, annexations, and freedom of the seas between Britain and the USA, but that did not affect the basic strategic consensus to defeat the German Army in the field and to maintain control of the sea routes; hence the integration of the US battleship squadron at Scapa Flow, and of the US Army along the Western Front.[51]

All these organizational and preparatory steps would be useless, however, if the British and their allies did not hit upon a strategy of damaging their foes without being more badly hurt themselves. In this respect, it seems clear that the strategy of the Royal Navy in the surface war in the North Sea was essentially correct and effective. Geographical position, and the Grand Fleet's own numerical superiority, meant that the British retained command of the sea routes even when adopting a 'waiting' strategy; Jellicoe, and even more, Beatty after him, knew that they did not have to steam into dangerous waters to accomplish their primary strategic objective. Nor did they need to take unnecessary risks when the rare fleet action occurred – even if the 'turn-away' of the Grand Fleet to avoid enemy torpedoes at Jutland was much criticized at the time and afterwards. Although an inglorious action, it was sensible strategy.

This could not be said, however, of the navy's trade-protection strategy, at least until the convoy system was introduced in 1917. None of the reasons given against convoy (e.g., the great differences of speed between fast and slow merchantmen in the age of steam, economic costings, diversion of warships, etc.) obviated the central strategic point which was as true in the 1914–18 and 1939–45 battles of the Atlantic as it had been in checking the *guerres de course* of the Dutch Wars or the Napoleonic contest: namely, that the overriding objective was to get merchantmen safely across the sea, and not to hunt enemy raiders and U-boats by instituting cruiser patrols or sending out 'hunter-killer' groups; and secondly, that by far the most efficacious way to find (and then try to sink) enemy raiders was to compel them to attack a well-protected convoy. Only after 1917, therefore, did the Royal Navy place its strengths against the enemy's weaknesses in the U-boat war.[52]

Command of the sea, and general control of the extra-European world, gave Britain, its allies, and its empire enormous advantages of flexibility in their operations against the German colonies and the outlying parts of the Turkish Empire. In all these campaigns, British strengths were placed against the weaknesses of their foes; and even in operations which failed (Kut, Tanga, Second Gaza, and arguably also Gallipoli), the British possessed the strategic strengths but were unable to execute the design effectively.

However, the war along the Western Front did not normally conform to this ideal of setting strengths against weaknesses. Following its initial gains in the west, the German Army rested upon high ground and built up a defense in depth. British GHQ under both French and Haig preferred an offensive which would bludgeon its way through the enemy lines by sheer weight of shell and manpower. The result was to forgo the advantage of surprise most of the time, to churn up the landscape across which the attacking troops were to advance, and to give the Germans plenty of time to choose between reinforcing the front or pulling back to prepared second lines. A breakthrough did become possible in 1918, partly because of changed operational methods, and partly because of the renewed Anglo-American-French pressures; but the basic point remains that throughout the entire Western Front campaign the British Army usually placed its strengths against an even more formidable German strength.

Throughout the war, opponents of the 'Western Front first' strategy repeatedly sought to place what they perceived as Britain's military strengths against what they held to be the adversaries' weaknesses. But all attempts at an alternative strategy (Gallipoli, Salonika) failed in their execution, and the other proposals were all flawed: a Baltic landing was technologically impossible; the Italian front was unpromising and even more bloody (in terms of relative numbers) than Flanders; joining up with Russia was geographically and logistically impossible; and most of these alternative strategies avoided the critical question of how one was to bring down German power in Europe.[53] One suspects that these alternatives would not have been so frequently considered had it not been for the repeated disasters which were occurring at the operational level in western Europe itself, and which now require more analysis.

Operational Effectiveness

At the operational level, the British Army and Navy fought their own wars (as they had planned to do long before 1914), and there was little interservice cooperation with regard to military campaigning. This became all too clear during the Dardanelles campaign, which in its early stages was a purely naval action, and, when that had failed, became an overwhelmingly military operation, with the navy increasingly resentful of the use of its warships, support vessels, and crews for a secondary role. Apart from small-scale actions like the Zeebrugge Raid, combined operations in both theory and practice were not part of the British experience in the First World War.

Both services got increasing use out of their air forces, at first for reconnaissance purposes only, then for control of the skies above the trenches (or fleet), and then as a close or distant support for military operations. However, the process was a very slow one, and the Royal Navy in particular failed to exploit this new weapon. At Jutland, for example, the carrier *Campania* was left in port, the seaplane carrier *Engadine* and its craft were ineffectual in their reconnaissance roles, and Jellicoe was acutely conscious of shadowing Zeppelins. Despite the building of proper aircraft carriers and experimentation with torpedo drops, the Royal Navy did not really exploit offensive air power at sea. This was not simply due to the many technical problems which had to be overcome, but was also caused by the RNAS's diversion of attention to the aerial campaigns over France and Germany, and, in Marder's view, to 'the cramping influences displayed by anti-airminded senior naval officers and, particularly in the first two years of the war and more, by the Sea Lords of the Admiralty and the War Staff.'[54] On the other hand, the Admiralty did successfully learn to employ aircraft later to patrol the 'protected lanes' of convoys approaching British ports, significantly reducing the number of U-boat attacks in those zones.[55]

The best use of aircraft was made by the Royal Artillery, whose striking power was much enhanced by counter-battery observations done by airmen using wireless; by 1917, 90 per cent of artillery work was being done in conjunction with aerial reconnaissance.[56] Obviously, whoever had command of the air over the trenches possessed enormous operational advantages: hence the seesaw struggle by the fighter squadrons of each side. From Neuve Chapelle onwards, RFC and RNAS squadrons were also used in each major campaign on the Western Front to attack railway tracks and stations – although the chief function of those raids was often to seek to draw off enemy fighters from the front lines.

Aircraft were also used for strafing; all available planes were thrown in, as soon as the weather cleared, to aid Gough's hard-pressed Fifth Army during Ludendorff's great offensive of March 1918. In the important advance of August 8th to 11th, 1918, British squadrons were used in conjunction with tank attacks, and were particularly useful when they could bomb and strafe German anti-tank guns (a role which the RAF was quickly to forget after the war). The greatest attention was given to aerial attacks on the nearby Somme bridges. This was understandable enough, argued Slessor (who conducted an analysis of this campaign), but was less help to the British Army's offensive than interdicting more distant railway-road targets and thus preventing the arrival of those German reinforcements which eventually stabilized the line.[57]

Allenby, perhaps predictably, made superb use of aerial power. On appointment, he had insisted upon receiving modern machines, which soon gained total command of the air and thereby allowed him to carry out surprise moves with his troops which might otherwise have been detected. During the Megiddo battle, his aircraft bombed the main Turkish telegraph-telephone exchanges, cutting off von Sanders from the collapsing front; and they then bombed and strafed the Seventh and Ninth Turkish Armies, turning a retreat into a rout.[58]

Within the two main services, it seems evident that it took a very long time before combined arms and integrated operational methods were used effectively. This was partly to do with the existing state of technology; thus, even when the convoy system was introduced in 1917, it was probably closer to the Napoleonic War methods of trade protection than to the combined arms (close escort vessels, light carriers, long-range aircraft patrols, supporting 'hunter-killer' groups) which had been developed by mid-1943 in the Battle of the Atlantic. Arguably the greatest weakness was that the navy devoted little time to systematic operational thought and practice. This statement may seem belied by the fact that the integration of all of the parts of Jellicoe's Grand Fleet (the battlecruiser squadron ahead, cruisers scouting on the wings, main battlefleet escorted by destroyer squadrons) had been practiced in frequent naval maneuvers; but the relationship of those different parts to each other had not been properly worked out, even after the Dogger Bank experience, and the Jutland encounter once again revealed many deficiencies.[59] Here, as elsewhere, the lack of a powerful and efficient naval staff at the Admiralty showed through.

During the first three years of warfare on the Western Front, the integration of the British Army's operational methods and its ideas about combined arms were generally crude and simplistic. When the prewar notions of rapid cavalry and infantry movements, supported by shrapnel-firing artillery, had foundered on the enemy's trench-cum-barbed-wire systems, the call arose for greater fire power. Sir John French put this at its crudest when, in January 1915, he declared: 'Breaking through the lines is largely a question of expenditure of high explosive ammunition. If sufficient ammunition is forthcoming, a way out can be blasted through the line.'[60] From that time until Passchendaele whimpered to a close, the pattern was set: artillery had to blast away, often for days; then the infantry would go 'over the top,' with the cavalry waiting hopefully to follow through. Even this level of integration was vitiated by the defects which existed at GHQ. Although French, Haig, and their senior staffs called for more artillery, they had little appreciation of what it could and could not do; and even when senior artillery officers were seconded to the General Staff, they were often regarded as second-class citizens. In the (pre-Somme) GHQ publication *Training of Divisions for Offensive Action*, the role of artillery and of artillery-infantry cooperation was hardly mentioned. Add to this Haig, Kiggell, and Rawlinson's confusion over shrapnel versus HE (heavy explosive) shell, and the even more serious confusion between Haig and Rawlinson over whether the Somme operation was to achieve 'attrition' or a 'breakthrough,'[61] and it is not surprising that the British performance in combined arms on the battlefield was poor. This will become even clearer when tactical aspects are examined, but the greatest reason for these deficiencies obviously lay in GHQ's inability to formulate an integrated operational doctrine.

In 1917–18, however, a whole variety of reforms occurred which – if generally applied – promised much greater military effectiveness. As mentioned above, reconnaissance aircraft were linked with artillery to improve bombardment techniques. Generals Maxse, Monash, and other innovators trained small units to operate with a variety of weapons – grenades and Lewis guns as well as rifles – and to move across the ground swiftly (not in regular waves), harmonizing their advance with artillery fire. When Cambrai (November 1917) showed the potentialities of the tank for initiating a surprise breakthrough of enemy lines, the problems of infantry-tank-artillery-aircraft cooperation were also studied; by now, wireless could link up all four.[62]

It ought to be noted, however, that these advances in combined arms theory were often vitiated by breakdowns in communication during actual battles, by technical failures of the tanks, by infantry failing to keep up with the tanks, and so on. Furthermore, as will be seen when tactical effectiveness is discussed below, much of this reformism was generated at the divisional level, and was not fully noticed (or perhaps even understood) at the top. Haig was quite amenable to some of these ideas (e.g., tanks and the surprise use of gas), provided they did not affect his overall battle plan. In the view of Dominic Graham, Haig did not help the application of combined arms by creating the right sort of battle – despite the fact that most of the major engagements with the enemy were those of his own choosing.[63] The reforms detailed above were, in consequence, piecemeal rather than uniform, and applied only late in the war.

Given this backwardness with respect to combined arms, it is not surprising that British military organizations did not have a very good record in terms of operational mobility and flexibility. For example, Britain and the Allies had command of the sea, but while this gave the Royal Navy general strategic flexibility (e.g., sending Sturdee's battlecruisers to the Falklands in 1914), the service rarely seemed to display much initiative at the operational level. Beatty himself emphasized – and displayed – initiative and flexibility at the Dogger Bank and Jutland, although it could be said that the Battlecruiser Squadron was specifically and uniquely established to emphasize those qualities. This was also true, in part, of Evan-Thomas's Fifth Battle Squadron at Jutland. By contrast, the other battle squadrons under Jellicoe were tied to synchronized movements *en masse* (as in the eighteenth-century 'line'), and seem not to have been organized for fighting as individual squadrons or in unusual conditions. Again, the whole story of the Admiralty's attitude to convoys hardly suggests an interest in operational flexibility. By contrast, Tyrwhitt's Harwich Force, or the ships of the 'Dover Patrol,' were much readier for the unforeseen, for night fighting against German destroyers, or for cooperation with the main battlefleet. Mobility was usually found in smaller units with independent commands and leaders of drive and initiative.[64]

These remarks are also true of British Army operations. Under French and Haig, the army was not usually on the defensive or subjected to surprise enemy thrusts; when the latter did occur, the military organization was not very well prepared to meet them. The German counterattack, just ten days after the British tank breakthrough at Cambrai, so exposed those traditional weaknesses that it led to a War Cabinet enquiry; but even when, in February 1918, General Maxse circulated a brilliantly accurate forecast of the impending 'Storm Trooper' attack, there was little evidence – to quote from one analyst – 'that his defensive teaching bore any fruit on this occasion.'[65] Many observers noted that the British, unlike the Germans and the French, had a large proportion of their men in the first line of trenches – which not only exposed them to a surprise bombardment and attack, but also left fewer troops for a mobile reserve. It is fair to recall that the British efforts to resist the German offensive of March–April 1918 depended very much upon the balance of troop and weaponry strength on each area of the front, and that Gough's Fifth Army was massively outnumbered day after day. However, had there been better training and preparation for defensive fighting under pressure, the British line might have withdrawn without so much of the confusion, nervousness about being outflanked, and general breakdown of communications which did occur in late March 1918. From the very top (i.e., Haig's failure to appreciate the seriousness of the German attack on the southern part of the British lines) to the smallest units (where the confusion in some companies reached panic levels), there were too many instances of a failure to react to the unexpected.[66]

Since we are discussing operational flexibility and mobility, it may be as well at this point to go just a little deeper into this debate upon the failure of British generalship on the Western Front.[67] The traditional defenders of Haig and his staff argue that formidable obstacles – political constraints, an untried mass army, shortages of matériel and reserves, and the unprecedented nature of modern industrialized war – meant that easy successes were impossible; there was no other way but a long, hard grind.[68] Many critics of the generals, from Lloyd George and Liddell Hart to later writers on 'military incompetence' and 'the donkeys,'[69] assert that the blind repetition of set-piece assaults which never succeeded reveals the unimaginative and callous nature of the senior officers. More subtly, scholars such as T. H. E. Travers have demonstrated that the Edwardian army 'was locked into a traditional nineteenth-century set of ideas and a traditional, hierarchical method of decision-making.'[70] The officer corps was very much like an extended family or tribe; personal contacts were all-important, and promotions depended upon finding a patron to advance one's career. Criticism of one's seniors (especially to outsiders like politicians) was disloyal; junior officers should be deferential, not 'clever.' While the traditional military qualities of discipline, courage, optimism, and high morale were stressed, there was a strong dislike for theory and for open argumentation. There was also a profound suspicion of the city-bred masses who were recruited in their millions into Kitchener's New Armies.

The consequences of these attitudes in the unprecedented battle conditions of 1915 and 1916 were, Travers shows, disastrous. Although admitting that there had been a 'firepower revolution,' senior staff officers reacted in two contradictory ways: first, by calling for ever heavier artillery, which would demoralize and kill the enemy; and secondly, by still insisting upon orderly advances by lines of infantry across the battlefield, with the argument that if their morale and 'keenness' were high enough, they would succeed despite the heavy losses. Traditional values would thus triumph over mere technology; if failures should occur, they would be remedied next time by greater artillery bombardments and greater displays of battlefield solidarity. There were, to be sure, some exceptions to this pattern of fighting; but it was the norm, as testified to by Britons and amazed Germans alike. What was more, there was no real method for protesting against this system in favor of a full and open discussion among the commanders of alternative tactics, or for a reassessment of basic assumptions. Officers who did object to futile attacks were regarded as suspect by their superiors, and were frequently 'de-gummed' (that is, dismissed); a *low* casualty rate was taken as evidence that a regiment was shirking, and also led to dismissals.

Perhaps this widespread system could have been altered from the top downwards, but the sad fact was that Douglas Haig personified much of what was wrong with the British Army. Austere, aloof, and disciplined, Haig avoided free-ranging discussions and discouraged criticism. The senior-level conferences which did occur were large, formal meetings at which he, as Commander-in-Chief, told the generals what they must do. Many of the latter admitted that they were scared of Haig, and feared his reprimands. Loyalty and obedience were stressed above all other virtues, and the more particularly when Haig became worried that Lloyd George was out to 'get' him. All this was compounded by the fact that Haig rarely visited the front-line battlefields to see the actual conditions of fighting.[71] Physically as well as mentally distanced from the trenches, GHQ could do little other than call upon the politicians to provide more guns and men, and call upon the corps and divisional commanders to provide ever greater displays of gallantry.

This hierarchical system did not necessarily mean that GHQ took a full part in the detailed planning of operations. On the contrary, Haig seems to have believed that, while he should not be criticized by his subordinates, he in turn ought to let army commanders get on with their own plans (although they would, of course, discuss them with him). While this did mean that certain armies had a different battle style – Plumer was the more cautious and meticulous, Gough the more pugnacious, and so on – this ought not to be taken too far. The overall tone of the army remained a conservative one, which discouraged any questioning of the basic assumption that war was a personal, moral struggle, not a technical-operational contest. This again implies that, while changes in operational and tactical methods could be tried out, they would be on a piecemeal basis, and that the army as a whole did not encourage open discussion and reassessment, since that would have threatened the service's cultural norms of loyalty, deference, and unthinking courage.

It is true that part of the difficulty which the British (and all other) military organizations faced after 1914 was that their operational concepts were not matched by the appropriate technology: either the scheme was not complemented by the right weapons, or the newer weapons had emerged but the military and naval leaders had not worked out how to handle them. The record of the Royal Navy in this respect is a mixed one. As is well known, the pre-1914 naval races had been 'forcing-houses' for new technology and improved weapons systems. Given the Grand Fleet's operational concept of retaining command of the sea by crushing the High Seas Fleet in battle, the available technology (e.g., large, fast *Queen Elizabeth*-class battleships) was consistent. However, faulty shells and an inadequate fire-control system reduced the Royal Navy's prospects of inflicting decisive damage upon the well-constructed German battleships. Protective armor and anti-flash arrangements on the British battlecruisers were not good, thus undermining their role as fast scouts which could also engage enemy capital ships. Instead of being invulnerable – as a combination of their high speed, big guns, and Pollen fire-control had suggested prior to the war – they were in fact all too vulnerable.[72] Wireless proved itself as vital for communication between ships as it was to army commanders in the 'fog of battle'; but the wireless range of many of the scouting destroyers in the North Sea was less than fifty miles. The same was true of British submarines' wireless sets. British mines were hopeless, being weak and subject to drifting; Marder writes that they 'were more dangerous to the navy than to the enemy.' The mine-nets and other barrages laid across the Channel to stop the U-boats operating from the Belgian ports were also pretty useless. Mine-sweeping techniques were poor (see Gallipoli), and there were far too few vessels, which is why vast numbers of trawlers had to be employed. Torpedoes were weak and erratic.[73] Although Fisher raged at all these defects, his critics pointed out that much of the trouble may have stemmed from his own emphasis upon big-gun ships, and upon scrapping dozens of smaller vessels whose uses in wartime were all too apparent. Finally, until the very closing stages of the war, and the development of Asdic, the British found no real means of detecting the U-boats.

The British air forces' operational concept soon evolved from simple reconnaissance flights to a struggle for command of the air above the trenches, and bombing attacks beyond. Yet at critical periods in the war, the British aircraft were technologically inferior to their German rivals – except (interestingly enough) in the Royal Naval Air Service's sector, where the agile Sopwith Triplane held its own. Not until late 1917, with the advent of the SE5 and Sopwith Camel types, could the Royal Flying Corps compete successfully for command of the air.[74]

The operational concept of long-range strategic bombing was developed a considerable time before machines were ready to carry out such deep penetration missions. Only in 1918 were the Handley-Page bombers being constructed that would be able to attack Berlin and other distant German cities. Before then (i.e., June–November 1918), the Independent Force under Trenchard carried out 239 raids, chiefly against German aerodromes, but also against industrial targets. Since the total weight of bombs dropped was a mere 550 tons, the campaign had 'no more than a nuisance value.'[75]

In the land war, the technology for a breakthrough offensive was not available until after 1917, although this also involved tactical changes (see below) and may also have required the steady weakening of the German Army over the preceding three years. Even when the new weaponry of tanks, mobile machine guns, and aircraft all worked to help punch a hole in the enemy's lines, the technical and logistical means for a swift, expanding follow-up of that blow were not really available. Fuller's ideas of wide-ranging, destructive tank operations were too far ahead of the technology of even 1918–19, and an all-tank offensive would have been difficult to sustain across the fields, forests, and rivers of northwest Europe against a tough German defense. By contrast, Allenby's forces did by that time have the technology (armored cars, aircraft, mobile troops, plus cavalry) for sustained advances through the more open desert conditions.

On the other hand, while it is true that the newer technology had first to be created, it was also clear that there was considerable ignorance and distrust of anything that represented a threat to traditional ways of fighting. It was Haig rather than Rawlinson who pressed for the use of tanks at the Somme, since the Commander-in-Chief still entertained hopes of a breakthrough; but his own interest in tanks later declined, and GHQ's continued belief in the value of cavalry reveals its true state of mind. More important still, a number of commentators felt that neither Haig nor his entourage – nor many of his corps commanders – properly understood artillery, how important counter-battery work was, or how little damage the guns could do to enemy bunkers.

To be fair, in the early part of the war the overriding concern of British Army commanders was simply to get their hands on more men, guns, and ammunition, with little or no time left over to think of newer weapons technology. The unprecedented nature of trench warfare for the British Army meant that it was deficient in almost every aspect of supporting activities, at least until 1916. By that time, massive improvements had been made in transportation, supply, and medical services. Given that the basic operational concept by the middle of the war was to employ a massive artillery barrage to disrupt the enemy's lines, that element of supporting activity had been well established – as the statistics show:

> The preliminary bombardment of the battle of Hooge, in May 1915, required 18,000 shells, that for the first battle of the Somme, from 24 June to 1 July 1916, 2,000,000 and for the third battle of Ypres 16 to 31 July 1917, 4,300,000. The expense of this method of warfare was commensurate. The last-named bombardment lasted nineteen days, used 321 trains for transporting the shells to the front and represented the output of 55,000 workers for one year. The total cost of approximately 22 million pounds was only just short of the total costs of the home army in 1914.[76]

Despite this sort of matériel increase, British military operations were hampered by flaws in intelligence and communications. Given the somewhat rudimentary state of British intelligence prior to 1914, and the immensity of the task of building up an organization to monitor the German Army from Belgium to the Dardanelles, it is perhaps remarkable that so much was achieved. By 1915, for example, the various intelligence branches (at GHQ as well as the Secret Service) had networks of agents across western Europe who were reporting upon enemy troop movements. The German deployment of forces to the Eastern Front in the early summer of 1915 was swiftly detected, for example, and played a considerable role in the Anglo-French staff decision to launch their offensive soon. In the same way, the coming of war swiftly transformed the very small aerial reconnaissance section of the Royal Flying Corps into a much larger and more sophisticated organization, using the modern techniques of photography and wireless telegraph to spot enemy troop movements, direct artillery fire, and so on.[77] Although much here depended upon which side had control of the air over the Western Front – thus integrating the fate of the land battles with the aerial struggles as never before – the 'eye in the sky' gave GHQ much more information about the enemy's lines than any previous generation of staff officers had been able to enjoy.

Nonetheless, real problems remained. One of them was, as always, that of interpreting the raw evidence from different sources. Did agents' reports of German troop trains heading westwards mean an attack was planned in Flanders, or in Champagne? Did the state of the aerial war, not to mention the unpredictable weather, allow for confirmation by aircraft? (Ludendorff's March 1918 offensive was purposefully launched under heavy cloud.) Perhaps the greatest problem was that, since Germany normally stood on the defensive in the west, intelligence really needed to be coordinated to the requirements of the Allied offensive campaigns, and here it was less successful. Distant agents could not report on front-line battlefield operations, and aerial reconnaissance could say little about changes in German defensive tactics, or how many men were in deep bunkers. Raids could be launched to garner information and prisoners, but poor staffing work often failed to draw the proper conclusions. Some of the pre-Somme offensive raids discovered that the German deep dug-outs were untouched by Allied artillery; other raids failed because of the masses of uncut enemy wire, even after earlier shelling. Both of these alarming facts ought to have caused Rawlinson and his staff to revise their assumptions, but apparently they did not, nor was this information picked up by anyone at GHQ. In general, there was too little communication between the various levels of command in the British Army in France. Haig's own distancing from the front did not help, but it is amazing to learn that during the Passchendaele operation he simply was not told of the swampy areas which had made the deployment of tanks and other vehicles quite impossible.[78]

Another remark to be made about British military intelligence on the Western Front was that it concentrated far too much of its attention upon the (pretty well impossible) task of guessing when the enemy would 'crack' – feeding overoptimistic assessments about German casualties and reserves to GHQ and to London, and encouraging both in their false belief that the enemy would collapse after one more offensive. In this respect, at least, the early intelligence officers such as MacDonagh and Kirke were little different from Haig's chief of intelligence, Charteris, who notoriously fed his superior with rosy assessments and who was actually sacked, by Cabinet demand, in 1918. Even then, instances of poor intelligence estimating were to occur; Haig believed that Ludendorff would launch his forthcoming offensive against Arras in March 1918, which is one reason why the assault on Gough's Fifth Army was so successful in its initial stages.[79] There were occasional bright spots – the seizure of German tactical handbooks late in 1917 and (a great gain) the capture of plans of the entire Hindenburg Line defenses in the summer of 1918 – but they were few and far between.

The Gallipoli venture was perhaps the classic instance of an operation being carried out without adequate supporting facilities. When Hamilton was appointed to this command, there was no intelligence backup at all; there were no maps of the area, and (astonishingly) no awareness of the strategic inquiry of 1907 which showed how difficult, even hopeless, such an operation might be! The navy's mine-sweeping resources were inadequate; and the bombarding squadron – whose very actions alerted the Turks to the impending campaign – lacked trained spotter pilots and, indeed, aerial reconnaissance in general. Hamilton's troops were a veritable *mélange* of ill-prepared units. Artillery was well below standard issue, and ammunition stocks were far too small. For the trench warfare which actually occurred, the landing force possessed neither mortars, nor grenades, nor periscopes. Water supplies and containers – absolutely vital in that heat – were dreadfully low; medical facilities were insufficient. Whatever additions and improvements were made (proper landing ships, balloons and aircraft, and howitzers) were negated by the reinforcements to the Turkish side and by tactical failings.[80]

The Royal Navy was in a far better position than the army in respect to supporting facilities (bases, supplies, shipyards, etc.). Of course, much work still had to be done at Scapa Flow, Harwich, and in the Channel ports to accommodate the various fleets at wartime levels of operation, and to improve their defenses; but the basic difference – as Trebilcock nicely points out[81] – was that the navy had been planning to be ready for the 'big' battle for years before the war, whereas the creation and mobilization of a mass army meant that it was not ready for large-scale conflict until two years after the war began.

As detailed investigations of the Battle of Jutland have shown, however there were serious deficiencies both in British naval communications, and in the exploitation of Room 40's intelligence, which certainly reduced the chances of a decisive British victory.[82] Admiral Oliver's refusal to delegate, and his lack of comprehension about how Room 40 (which he never visited) actually worked, vitiated many of the brilliant breakthroughs in deciphering and intelligence by Hall's staff. In a rather similar way, Room 40's deciphering of how the U-boat traffic passed through the Channel Barrage was of little use when the Royal Navy's ships possessed inadequate means of detecting and attacking underwater craft. Intelligence, communications, matériel, and technique all needed to be integrated but, largely because of the Fisher legacy, the navy did not have a really good staff organization, either at the Admiralty or with the fleet commands. This also meant that, even when a number of deficiencies in operational practice, signals, and matériel revealed themselves during the first year of the surface war, many of them remained to reduce the Grand Fleet's effectiveness at Jutland.[83] To put it bluntly, poor mines, poor torpedoes, and poor shells were not helpful to a navy dedicated to the 'decisive' battle.

The war in the air, and the war against the U-boats in the Atlantic and the Mediterranean, and the military operations under Allenby in the Middle East, all required a substantial investment in 'supporting activities,' indeed, in basic infrastructure, before the operational concepts of those campaigns could in any way be implemented. In all three cases, it was not until 1917–18 that an adequate system of support was ready. Given the compelling need on the part of the British military organizations to grapple with the new conditions and technology of warfare, it might be supposed that they would have had little time to relate operational concepts to strategic objectives, and to ensure that they placed their operational strengths against the adversary's weaknesses. In actual fact, the British record here is a mixed one, being as much influenced by geography as by any other factor. Thus, the Royal Navy's operational concept of bringing the High Seas Fleet to battle was consistent with the strategic objective of maintaining command of the sea. It would not seek to give battle in such operationally hazardous waters as the Heligoland Bight; but it would do so in the central North Sea, should the enemy fleet come out that far. Despite the disappointments produced by the confused battle at Jutland, the operational concept was correct. Perhaps the only questionable part of it was the use of the battlecruiser force in its hybrid 'scouting-cum-fighting' (cruiser-cum-battleship) role – ingenious in theory, like many of Fisher's operational ideas, but marred by defects in the vessels themselves.

On the other hand, the operational concept of defeating the U-boat menace by patrolling the trade routes, and sending ships to hunt for the elusive submarines was wasteful in the extreme. Winton gives one of many examples of this misuse of resources:

> In one week of September 1916 three U-boats operated in the Channel between Beachy Head and the Eddystone Light, an area patrolled by forty-nine destroyers, forty-eight torpedo boats, seven Q-ships, and 468 armed auxiliaries – some *572* anti-submarine vessels in all, not counting aircraft. Shipping in the Channel was held up or diverted. The U-boats were hunted. They sank thirty ships, and were entirely unscathed themselves.[84]

His observation about the Admiralty's claim that there were insufficient escorts to permit a full convoy system is also worth quoting:

> There was no shortage of escorts in early 1917. The only blockages were mental ones. There were available, and ready to start on convoy duties, 350 destroyers and sixty sloops, with sixty old cruisers and twenty-four old battleships. This was a truly staggering total of *very nearly 500 ships*. But large numbers of destroyers and cruisers were still used in patrolling empty ocean wastes, or escorting single troopships.[85]

As soon as the Royal Navy switched to convoy protection policies in the

Atlantic, it placed its defensive strengths against the U-boats' weaknesses, compelling the latter to attack defended targets.

The operational concept of the first Gallipoli attacks (i.e., by naval forces alone) was extremely unsound – and not consistent with the strategic objectives of seizing Constantinople, knocking Turkey out of the war, relieving Russia, and so on. It ignored the general technological trends (minefields, mobile shore batteries, and torpedoes) that had rendered hazardous close-in operations by battlefleets in hostile waters; it ignored the specific assessments made prior to 1914 about the Royal Navy's chances of taking the Straits; and it ignored the doubts expressed in 1915 by senior officers at the Admiralty itself. Strategically it might have seemed that Britain and France were using their strengths (derived from the flexibility of sea power) to attack a weak member of the enemy coalition; but operationally the deployment of warships against shore batteries, and steaming in unknown waters, was bound to place their forces against the adversary's strengths.

From the very beginning of the British Army's campaigning in France and Belgium, it had found itself placed against the enemy's general strategic strength, simply because the early German advance had allowed it to occupy a good defensive position from the Swiss Alps to the Channel. With the failure of the 'Russian steamroller' to crush the German military machine, British (and French) generals were faced with the problem of trying to defeat the formidable German Army in the field or of advising their political leaders that pressure should be applied elsewhere (the Balkans, Italy, etc.). For all sorts of reasons, some sensible and some not, the general staffs insisted upon a breakthrough victory on the Western Front.

Yet the ending of mobile warfare in September 1914 and the coming of static, well-defended trench lines meant that the army faced quite unforeseen operational conditions. To effect a breakthrough seemed to require ever more men, and ever more guns – but even when both were forthcoming in large numbers, the German lines still withstood the repeated assaults. This problem was exacerbated to a large degree by the British Army's general failure until late in the conflict to think through new tactics that would be better suited for trench warfare. While leaving the tactical issues until later in this chapter, it ought to be noted here that by 1916 some British commanders, such as Rawlinson, had given up hopes of achieving a major breakthrough and thought simply in terms of 'attrition' warfare, that is, seizing a limited area of enemy-held soil and forcing him to wear himself out trying to recapture it. By contrast, Haig still hoped for a breakthrough, both in 1916 and in 1917; hence his willingness to use tanks, or gas, to speed up the battle, and also his dislike of a too lengthy bombardment at the Somme (which, however, an 'attrition' policy required). This failure to settle which operational aim was the real one caused misunderstandings during that battle,[86] and may also help to explain some of the instances where British commanders were content to occupy new positions, but not to push ahead and exploit things.

The second major weakness was an even more serious one: namely, that the same operational concept which had shown itself unfeasible on the Somme in 1916 was still being used by Haig under similar operational conditions in 1917 (and probably would have been used again in early 1918, had he possessed enough troops). Even the most devout Haig followers find that difficult to justify.[87]

Tactical Effectiveness

As the introduction to this chapter suggested, it was at the 'sharp end' of war, the actual conditions of battle, that the British appeared to have found it most difficult to be militarily effective. Since this obviously needs a reasonably detailed analysis which makes allowance for the differing requirements of land, sea, and aerial warfare, the following discussion of tactical effectiveness will be structured on a service-by-service basis.

The war in the air may be given only a brief analysis here, for an obvious reason. The tactical approaches needed to gain command of the air – aircraft working in small groups, diving out of the sun, going into a loop, and coming out of a spin – in the dogfights over the Western Front were readily appreciated by all air forces. The key issue for the Royal Flying Corps was not the tactical positioning of an aircraft in the skies, or the flying formations used, but whether the corps possessed planes fast enough and maneuverable enough to take on the German *Albatros*.[88]

This plain fact centrally affected the issue of training for RFC and RNAS pilots, who essentially had to learn on the job. The School of Special Flying at Gosport under Major Smith-Barry offered an excellent course;[89] but the demand for new pilots was so great that many were sent to the Western Front with a minimum number of hours of training. Novices were 'easy meat' to Richthofen's Flying Circus; and those who survived had something more than good training – intuition, flying genius, and sheer good luck.

Because of the novelty, the romance, and the small-unit nature of both the RFC and the RNAS, however, morale stayed high; and the chief combatants were, after all, officer class. The high casualty rate among RFC pilots over the Western Front in 1916 and 1917 did depress spirits – but there was little that could be done about it in tactical or organizational terms: what was needed was better aircraft! When they arrived, the problem was essentially solved.

The Royal Navy's tactical record during the 1914–18 war was neither disastrous nor distinguished; but it improved over time. The tactical-operational policy of sending out patrols to hunt for U-boats was uneconomic and hopeless, and examples have been given above of the dichotomy between resources used and gains secured. Convoys altered that. The tactical problem which the creation of convoys presented to an attacker (especially in an age before the Germans could use wireless intercepts or aerial reconnaissance) was nicely described by a U-boat captain whose vessel was sunk in the attempt in October 1918. His name, incidentally, was Karl Dönitz.

> The oceans at once became bare and empty; for long periods at a time the U-boats, operating individually, would see nothing at all; then suddenly up would loom a huge concourse of ships, thirty or forty of them, surrounded by a strong escort of warships of all types. The solitary

U-boat, which most probably had sighted the convoy purely by chance, would then attack, thrusting again and again and persisting, if the commander had strong nerves, for perhaps several days and nights, until physical exhaustion of both commander and crew called a halt. The lone U-boat might well sink one or two ships, or even several; but that was only a poor percentage of the whole. The convoy would steam on. In most cases no other German U-boat would catch sight of it, and it would reach Britain, bringing a rich cargo of foodstuffs and raw materials safely to port.[90]

In other words, in the war against the U-boats, the convoy system now placed British strengths, both operationally and tactically, against the weaknesses of the attacking submarines. Whether on the surface or under it, U-boats ran considerable risks in approaching a convoy protected by patrolling aircraft, depth-charge-firing escorts, and auxiliary cruisers.

Since the tactics of convoy protection had to be worked out from scratch, much training was required so that the frigates and sloops would be advantageously positioned around the merchantmen, know how to react to a U-boat attack, and know how to integrate the new technology of wireless, aircraft, depth-charges, and ultimately Asdic. Some of this training could be done out of Portsmouth or Queenstown; the greater part, once again, had to be acquired from combat experiences. Since the operational concept was a sound one, and the correct technology was becoming available, tactical effectiveness was acquired – although it ought to be stressed once again that the prime aim was to preserve the merchant ships, and sinking U-boats was a secondary consideration.

In the surface war in the North Sea, the British objective of maintaining command of the sea could usually be achieved by a waiting policy; but if the High Seas Fleet did emerge, the intention was to engage it and defeat it. For those naval officers – and there were many – who believed that victory in battle was the strategic objective, the desire to come to grips with the enemy was even more keenly felt. Yet, as a number of studies have pointed out, tactical weaknesses were going to make success in battle less likely. In this area, the Heligoland Bight and Dogger Bank operations (although successful in terms of losses inflicted upon the enemy) anticipated many of the failures which would occur at Jutland: cruisers and other scouting vessels – not to mention the Admiralty itself – failing to relay vital information to the Commander-in-Chief; signals from the flagship being ambiguous, misread, or simply not noticed; squadrons of vessels being steadily separated during a prolonged chase; lack of initiative by many of the divisional commanders; and lack of practice in night-fighting techniques.[91] For all these practical reasons, therefore, what looked like a commendable emphasis in Royal Navy doctrine upon the integration of all arms of the fleet was rarely achieved in actual fighting. As Jutland revealed, coordinating the many different parts of the Grand Fleet was extraordinarily difficult to carry out across broad expanses of sea when visibility was poor and wireless communication restricted.

Most probably, it was in anticipation of such confusion that the Grand

Fleet's tactical system was very tight, and surprise was not emphasized enough at the tactical level. Given the sheer number of battleships and escorts, and the fact that they were steaming at 20 to 25 knots (compared with 3 or 4 knots in the age of sail), the need to have each vessel knowing its place and turning according to the prearranged patterns was understandable. Smaller divisions, like the Battlecruiser Force or the Harwich Force, had much more flexibility, which in theory permitted the exploitation of opportunities (though the Dogger Bank battle showed how rigidly even the Battlecruiser Force adhered to line tactics). At the Battle of the Falklands, Sturdee virtually allowed a general chase – which might be contrasted with Troubridge's overcautious reading of orders in his pursuit of the *Goeben* and *Breslau*. In the Channel fighting carried out by the Dover Patrol, frequent attempts were made to surprise the German destroyer squadrons operating out of Zeebrugge, but these were not always successful.[92] The actual Zeebrugge Raid by Keyes and his assault force did emphasize – and require – surprise; but that action, like the new army tactics, came very late in the war. By that stage, too, Beatty had come to stress the importance of flexibility and surprise in the Grand Fleet; to his great chagrin, however, he was never able to see these improvements demonstrated in a fleet encounter.

For much of the war, the Royal Navy's approach to tactical training still reflected its prewar conceptions of battle. Frequent battle maneuvers, working out the relationship between the destroyers and the main fleet, practicing line formations, signalling drills, and firing exercises were the order of the day – after 1914 as before. However, there was no substitute for battle experience, which the navy (in contrast to the army) got all too rarely once the war began. Nicely worked-out ideal scenarios for fleet actions which had been done in formal training became impractical when the enemy disappeared into the mist, when the battlecruiser flagship was badly hit and the admiral (Beatty) had transferred to a destroyer, or when sightings and other messages were contradictory and confused.[93]

Although it is difficult to generalize about Royal Navy morale in so short a space, the overall impression is that it was easier to achieve unit cohesion and maintain morale in smaller commands like the Harwich Force or the Dover Patrol, both because they were less formal and because the prospects of action were greater. Morale among the Royal Navy's 'lower deck' remained high until 1916, and was then somewhat eroded by the months of tedious waiting in Scapa Flow, Rosyth, and Portsmouth. Fisher and Churchill had introduced significant improvements in lower-deck conditions prior to 1914, but their impact was weakened by rising prices in wartime, prolonged absence from home, and so on.[94] The sheer size of a battleship's crew meant that there was little real contact between officers and men. A hierarchy existed, reflected in the separate messes; orders were mediated downwards by petty officers; marines enforced discipline; and the reports of most flag officers about lower-deck complaints suggest a considerable lack of sympathy and political acumen. Shore facilities at Scapa were vastly improved during the war, but improvements took time, and the climate and isolation of that main base were not appealing. Still, despite murmurs of discontent, the crews of the Grand Fleet seemed to be as eager as Beatty for action; it was boredom which was the chief enemy to morale.

By far the most controversial aspect of British tactical effectiveness remains the army's performance on the Western Front. Repeated failures here not only threatened to undermine British grand strategy in a more strictly military sense, but they also seemed to be bleeding to death most of the able-bodied male population of the British Isles and the white Dominions. It was from this lack of success in the field, and the bloody costs involved, that the heated debates between 'easterners' and 'westerners,' the problems of civilian versus military control, and the later images of the futility and waste of modern, industrialized warfare, all have their origin. Quite apart from these repercussions in the non-tactical field, the issue is also complicated by the fact that, after nearly four years of failure, the British Army (along with its allies) did manage to achieve a breakthrough in the summer of 1918.

The tactical problem itself, at least by the end of 1914, was nicely defined by someone who served throughout the war on the Western Front: it was, briefly,

> how to surprise, overrun, and penetrate a well-sited defence system some four miles deep, the front edge of which was only a short distance from one's own, protected by massive wire entanglements and covered by the flanking fire of machine-guns and a wall of fire from artillery and mortars of all calibres sited in depth.[95]

To which one might add the reminder that, generally, the Germans held the higher ground along the Western Front, and thus looked down upon the approaching Allied armies.

Given these unpromising circumstances, it could plausibly be argued that there was no other way, no soft underbelly, no easy solution. The strategic objective was to break German military power in the field, and both geographical and technological constraints meant that that could only be done by unrelenting pressure (i.e., offensives) to bleed the enemy's strength. Extremely heavy artillery bombardments and large-scale troop assaults were of the essence; and the justification came in 1918, when the German Army at last cracked.[96]

By contrast, it has been argued that the British and French manpower losses were so severe because of the repeated use of the wrong tactical approach that this might well have undermined their entire war effort and forced them into a compromise peace. It has further been pointed out that by the later stages of the conflict, officers in various national staffs (Bruechmüller, Laffargue, Maxse, and Fuller) had come to see that the prevailing tactics were crude, uneconomic, and often hopeless, and that more flexible tactical actions – using surprise, and restoring mobility to the battlefield – were possible. This was, inevitably, a *Lernprozess*; but the charge against Haig and his fellow generals is that they took too long to learn, and persisted with tactics which had already failed when ordering fresh offensives.[97]

Which of these viewpoints comes closest to the truth? As has been pointed out in the discussion on operational effectiveness above, British generals and military commmentators before 1914 had been aware to some degree of the 'fire power revolution' created by quick-firing rifles, machine guns and artillery; and they had also been made aware – by studying the Russo-Japanese War – of the possibility that armies might adopt trench warfare on the battlefield itself. Yet these twin and related obstacles to the tactical concept of the swift infantry-cavalry offensive were countered by the assertion that moral courage, willpower, and physical and mental stamina would carry the day.[98] When those fond illusions were shattered, the emphasis switched to heavy, prolonged bombardments to punch a hole through the enemy's lines. Thus, the shell-shattered Germans would not be in any position to resist the advancing lines of British infantry (not to mention the ever hopeful cavalry, consuming vast amounts of forage in the rear as it waited for its chance to shine).

However, this idea in turn was flawed by a large array of tactical weaknesses. Perhaps the best way to understand such deficiencies is to examine the first day on the Somme, where the British Army suffered more casualties in twenty-four hours than in any similar period before or since.[99] As many analysts have pointed out, the enormous and lengthy bombardment threw away all chance to surprise the enemy and allowed him to move reinforcements to the area. The bombardment did not wipe out the German forces holding the line in question, since many of them had had time to retreat to deep bunkers, from which they emerged to man their machine guns when the British infantry assault began. (The bombardment did cause heavy German casualties in the early stages – but that prompted the Prussian General Staff to switch the main body of defenders from the first to the second or third trench lines in future engagements, and thus made the problem for the attackers even more difficult.)

The bombardment churned up the ground across which the attacking troops moved, and in rainy weather (at the Somme, and even more so later at Passchendaele) turned everything into mud. It did not destroy many of the enemy's barbed-wire entanglements, but it did make the ground more confusing than ever for the aerial 'spotters,' and in some instances the landmarks were so broken up that the front-line forces could not relate them to their instructions and maps.

On the first day of the Somme, the troops were sent forward in daytime – actually, in clear sunshine. They advanced in formal lines (as if nothing had changed in the realm of fire power since Waterloo); and they carried an enormous amount of equipment, often 60 or 70 pounds in weight, but did not carry much mobile fire power with them. The 'creeping barrage' did not really cover them. They were, therefore, sitting ducks, and were slaughtered accordingly.

This was not, alas, a unique experience. In British Army assaults before and after the Somme – and, most particularly, in the futile Passchendaele campaign of 1917 – troops were sent forward in waves once again to pick their way through churned-up mud and uncut wire in attacks upon well-held enemy positions. Infantry coordination with the artillery was flawed; all too often, the barrage would stop as much as ten minutes before the time the troops were scheduled to go 'over the top,' which appalled Gallipoli veterans, who knew what the consequences would be. Assaults were made at predictable times, and against difficult objectives (such as an enemy-held wood); they were all too often made in formal lines, offering easy targets to German machine-gunners.

Obviously, then, British Army tactics rarely emphasized surprise; and for all the stress upon 'exploitation of opportunities,' this usually meant that the cavalry was kept waiting for the breakthrough which never occurred.

Surprise was achieved on a number of occasions, but rarely exploited. Neuve Chapelle (March 1915) was carefully prepared beforehand, and after a sudden and intense bombardment the troops advanced rapidly, gaining all their early objectives from the surprised foe. As soon as the front deepened and widened, however, the artillery support became inadequate, and breakdowns in communication delayed further attacks until it was too late.[100] At Loos, Scottish battalions made very good progress, almost compelling the German commander to order a retreat; but there were no reinforcements to follow up this advantage, and Falkenhayn managed to stabilize the line.[101] In the second stage of the Somme campaign, on July 14th, 1916, Rawlinson used surprise – a short, heavy bombardment, troops advancing at night, and then a creeping barrage – and broke through two lines; but the British troops were by then exhausted, while reinforcements stiffened the German positions. Before the Passchendaele operation, Plumer's much praised attack on the Ypres salient (7th June, 1917) was successful because it used a vast stock of simultaneously detonated mines to stun the enemy and achieve surprise, and then deployed troops to seize a limited objective; *no* exploitation was planned, and none attempted. The use of tanks at Cambrai, achieving great surprise and bursting right through the German lines, was not followed up; it had been conceived of as a 'disorganizing raid,' and no fresh troops were made ready to exploit this blow. Even in the advance of August 1918, there was a general reluctance on the part of many units to drive ahead as far as possible – perhaps because of the grim experience of the useless battering against German lines over the preceding three years.

In partial defense of these failures, it was often claimed that the British Army was tactically disadvantaged in possessing neither the necessary support facilities nor the trained men to achieve victory against a foe who was well equipped in both areas. This may have been true in respect of weapons and ammunition in the first part of the war (see above), but it could also be argued that after 1915 the British Army under French and Haig emphasized support facilities to the detriment of many other (at least equally important) factors. The belief that the only feasible policy was to batter a hole through the enemy's front line placed a great stress upon the quantity of men and guns to achieve the desired result. Yet despite Haig's complaints about inadequate numbers of troops and artillery, it is difficult to believe that, for example, another five or ten divisions could have done much more in the appalling mud swamps of Passchendaele. The weaponry itself, that is, the Lee–Enfield rifle, heavy machine guns, well-designed mortars, and long-range artillery, was by then not a great problem. On the other hand, when the tactical concept was changed and the British made the occasional surprise breakthrough, as at Cambrai, it is true that the facilities were not on hand to permit the exploitation of that advantage. Even the much touted 'wonder weapon' of the tank was by itself no proper solution. Tanks still broke down easily, got stuck in wide ditches, and were very vulnerable to flank fire: thus, of the 400 British tanks used in the advance of August 8th, 1918, only 6 were still functioning by August 12th.[102] In terms of support facilities as well as tactics, it may be said that by 1918 the British Army at last knew how to break in, but not yet how to break out.

In terms of securing adequate personnel and of training them up to battlefield level, however, it is clear that the army faced a problem of far greater magnitude than any of the other services did. Simply because the country had not contemplated being involved in a mass, continental struggle prior to 1914, the military organization found that it had simultaneously to adjust itself to the new type of warfare along the Western Front and to train hastily a mass of willing but ignorant civilians (not usually reservists) for battle as soon as possible. The consequence was that the army never had the chance to provide itself with a solid structure of trained officers and NCOs on the German model, and had a far higher proportion of untrained troops. Dealing with the vast expansion of Kitchener's New Armies was an administrative nightmare:

> One battalion (and it was among the more fortunate) had just three 'trained' officers: a pre-Boer War commanding officer aged sixty-three, a regular subaltern with a badly broken leg, and a stone-deaf quartermaster who had retired in 1907. The junior officers and non-commissioned-officers were often virtually devoid of any kind of military knowledge or experience. Trained staff-officers to man formation headquarters – essential to the complex mass operations of war – were absolutely lacking.[103]

Before the battles of the Somme and even Passchendaele, therefore, Haig and his generals were regularly complaining that the men were not trained; and one of the justifications for the tactic of advancing in straight lines across the battlefield was that these new recruits could not be expected to do anything more sophisticated.

As critics have pointed out, however, until late in the war the British Army generally did not try to instill more sophisticated tactics into the men, and was not good at delegating authority and encouraging initiative. Maxse was a good commander because he took the training of his division seriously; Monash, with the Australian Corps, also tried to have his troops well prepared, and was willing to work out new tactics. When Haig put Maxse in charge of training, and the various preparations were made for the summer 1918 offensive, the response of the troops was mixed. Some units willingly turned to the newer, more flexible tactics. Others followed the new guidelines in practice training but found it difficult, say, to keep up with the 'Whippet' tanks in actual battle when enemy shells were exploding all around. Some junior officers and NCOs, who had become used to the crude tactical system of advancing in waves, with the officers leading and the

NCOs behind (to push the slower troops forward), were uneasy at the idea of these looser formations.[104]

In the light of the appalling conditions and casualties suffered by the troops, it is surprising that army morale held up so well, although there were some obvious reasons for this. The 'regular,' long-service regiments which were recruited prior to 1914 may not have all enjoyed the 'atmosphere of a family' so lovingly depicted in retrospect by their colonels; but they did offer a nexus of relationships, familiar faces, and existing loyalties which stood up well under stress. Moreover, the New Armies recruited by Kitchener were organized along local (Tyneside Irish, London Rifle Brigade) or even occupational (London Clerks, North-East Railway Battalion, Forest of Dean Pioneers) lines.[105] Class divisions were much more blurred in the New Armies, and the same was obviously true of the Dominion troops. Normally, officers led the assaults. Furthermore, however many hundreds of thousands of troops were involved in a big offensive, the fog of war soon reduced everything to a series of small-unit engagements. After the battle, and behind the lines, there lay a considerable array of supporting services, from the chaplain to the cinema, the rest billet to the soccer field; a great deal of British working-class popular culture was transferred to the rear areas of the army in France. By contrast with these positive elements, there was the frightening prospect of execution in the event that a soldier was found guilty of desertion, cowardice, mutiny, or other offenses.[106]

Despite all this, the tactical policy of frontal assaults across minefields and barbed wire, against well-held enemy positions, inevitably eroded morale, simply because of its enormous casualties and evident fruitlessness. The connection between battle losses and morale was a pretty direct one; Gallipoli, as James records it, was an early example of that.[107] After being needlessly sacrificed (in their view) on the Somme, the surviving Australian troops' comments about their generals were unprintable. The most significant, if small-scale, mutiny in the British Army occurred during Passchendaele – at Etaples, in September 1917 – although that was chiefly due to 'a particularly obnoxious training programme.'[108] If the British Army along the Western Front did not crack as openly as the French after Nivelle's offensive, or the Russians in 1917, nonetheless the cases of self-inflicted wounds, desertion, hiding in shell holes, and refusal to obey orders all signified this sagging of morale. The number of men executed by capital courts-martial in France and Belgium for desertion was never large, but it did rise over time: from three in 1914, to forty-five in 1915, and seventy-one in 1916.[109] The brutal and clumsy response by some officers – shackling men to wagons, drum-head courts-martial, filthy military prisons – merely intensified resentments, although the greatest venom was reserved for visiting staff officers rather than regimental or battalion commanders, many of whom were very popular.

These symptoms of low morale were less in evidence among specialist units – mining sappers, or Royal Artillery battalions, or the experimental combined-arms platoons devised in 1917–18, since the latter restored a sense of rationality and purpose to fighting that Loos, the Somme, and Passchendaele had almost destroyed. It also has to be remembered that the constant inflow of fresh troops (especially, perhaps, from the Dominions) brought new reserves of morale and regional-national patriotism and self-confidence. For all the criticisms of Gough's Fifth Army, which buckled under the stupendous German offensive of March 1918, the facts were that the divisions in that area were heavily outnumbered; they occupied a section of line (recently taken over from the French) which was not well prepared to withstand a large attack; and considerable numbers of them did not panic. A few months later, many of the same units were part of the August–September counteroffensive. Ludendorff himself thought that the British troops were tough, phlegmatic, and not easily frightened, even if they were unimaginative and did not exploit all available opportunities when they moved from defensive to offensive.

Two final points are worth making. There was no proven relationship between troop unrest and poor fighting capacity. Indeed, just as a good many of the individual court-martial cases of desertion and cowardice occurred with soldiers who had become overstrained and mentally broken by hard fighting, so the broader unrest was most likely to occur among units which had acted with valor, and been asked to do the impossible. A good example of this was provided by the Australian Corps during the summer 1918 offensive. On September 14th, officers and men briefly mutinied when denied a night's rest after a week's continuous fighting, and within another three weeks the Australian government had insisted that the entire corps be withdrawn to rest. When the Australians finally handed over to the Americans on October 5th, they had been almost continuously in action since August 8th. They had 'fought their way forward for 37 miles, liberated 116 villages and towns, captured 610 officers and 22,000 soldiers from 30 different divisions, and 332 guns.'[110] The Germans repeatedly declared that the Australian and Canadian troops were their toughest, most ferocious opponents. In the light of that record, the unrest on September 14th was simply a sign of very natural exhaustion.

Secondly, it seems worth arguing that the widespread disillusionment and sense of futility at the war were much more frequently a post-1919 experience, as the masses of ex-combatants began to wonder whether the so-called victory had been worth the appalling costs, and also began to wonder what had happened to the politicians' promises to create 'a land fit for heroes.'[111]

If the discussion so far of the British Army's tactical weaknesses along the Western Front presents a gloomy picture, then it needs to be stressed that by 1917 things were beginning to change. Just how this transformation came about has not been studied in depth, but it does not seem as if it were due to a rethinking at GHQ, where Haig's performance until the bitter end of the Passchendaele campaign showed the same incomprehension of the realities of front-line conflict as before. Furthermore, as was noted above, the British Army at the center did not possess that system for thorough reassessments of operational practices, and for circulating new ideas to a wide number of involved officers, which was one of those habits that made the Prussian General Staff so formidable an enemy at battlefield level.[112] On the other hand, perhaps precisely because the British Army in France had grown so large, and because GHQ exercised only a distant control over its army commanders (and they in turn over corps and divisional staffs), there did emerge a growing number of officers who began to rethink the tactical problem of breaking through an enemy trench system. Before examining this development further, however, it is important to emphasize again that this was not a sudden break, and that there had been some earlier precedents. Examples of certain surprise attacks with careful planning (in Plumer's case at Messines, down to battalion level) have already been given above. In the battle of the Somme, to give another case, the divisions of XIII Corps in the south moved forward under a creeping barrage, they had good observation of the enemy ground, and the artillery provided fine counterbattery fire. However, the success achieved was too isolated, and was not exploited by the Fourth Army command. Given the sheer extent of the German lines, a successful breakthrough would only occur when improved tactics were carried out at many points along the front. This is what happened in 1918.

There are some obvious reasons for that transformation. In the first place, the Passchendaele operation had shown the sheer futility of set-piece, mass-bombardment offensives. By this stage, moreover, a considerable number of middle to senior officers who were decidedly not 'donkeys' (among others, Fuller, Haldane, Harington, Maxse, Monash, Munro, plus Birch and Uniacke for the artillery) were devoting their intellectual energies to improving British military effectiveness. Some of them were beginning to get an idea, chiefly from captured documents and manuals, of the rethinking which was going on in German staff circles about both 'flexible defense' and 'storm-trooper' attacks; others were in contact with French tactical innovators. Again, many of these officers were excited by the possibility of using new weapons, such as the tank, to achieve a breakthrough; and most of them were advocates of much closer infantry-artillery coordination, using new techniques for communication. By this time, the artillery had evolved into a very powerful and forward-looking arm, capable of excellent counterbattery work and of carefully planned creeping barrages.[113] In addition, the aerial war over the trenches was swinging in the direction of the Allies, and this not only enhanced the artillery's capabilities, but also allowed for the deployment of aircraft for tactical purposes, bombing and strafing enemy troops.

All these background factors coincided with a very marked improvement in tactical doctrine and training for the infantry. Individual commanders were training their men for combined-arms work: for sudden artillery bombardments on a quiet front, then small units going forward armed with a variety of weapons (machine guns, Lewis guns, and grenades), and going around – rather than frontally attacking – German strong points. There was also training to use infantry more effectively in conjunction with tank assaults.[114]

These preparations for more flexible and innovative offensive tactics were, of course, massively disrupted by Ludendorff's own great strike against the Western Front in March 1918, the thrust of which took GHQ by surprise and showed up many British weaknesses in conducting a tactical defensive. Once the line was stabilized in early summer, however, the British Army could combine with its French and American allies to increase the pressure once again upon the now overextended German forces. In such circumstances, the time had come to put the new offensive tactics into play. Once again, it needs to be stressed that only certain British units were now capable of combined-arms work, though many of the Australian and Canadian contingents were. To give but two examples: in the victory at Hamel (July 4th, 1918), Monash had carefully worked out tactics with both the artillery and the Tank Corps staff. Sporadic, harassing fire of a rather normal kind covered the noise of the approaching tanks; then six hundred guns blasted the German front for four minutes, by which time the tanks and accompanying infantry were moving onto the German lines. In the far larger assault of August 8th, 1918, Leigh-Mallory's No. 8 Squadron RAF worked hand in hand with the tanks, dropping messages to them, swooping down on enemy field guns, and driving away German reconnaissance aircraft. On some occasions, aircraft noise was used to mask the noise of tanks approaching German positions. While there were still many flaws in the execution of this combined-arms warfare, it was scarcely surprising that the reformers believed they had at last found the key to unlock the battlefield stalemate.[115]

The summer 1918 victories have also been claimed by Haig's supporters as evidence of his great leadership, but that claim needs considerable qualification. What is true is that Haig was one of the first to see that a breakthrough was under way, and he was very active in urging on those who were inclined to stop; the newer, more open conditions of warfare showed him to better advantage than the earlier circumstances had done. On the other hand, it is worth noting that as late as February 1918, GHQ informed Fuller that it was planning to reduce the Tank Corps by 33 per cent, and to deploy the vehicles behind the British lines as strong points. Furthermore, when the great tank-cum-infantry attacks of August 1918 achieved breakthroughs south of the Somme, GHQ insisted on sending forward the 3rd Cavalry Division – which promptly ran ahead of all the other arms until it encountered enemy machine gun nests, from which it was rescued by the slower moving tanks and Australian infantry.[116] To repeat: there was a revolution in British tactics, but it came late, was piecemeal, and was not directed from the top.

The overall conclusion must be, therefore, that the British tactical record along the Western Front was not a good one – although it must again be said that the German Army *in situ* showed few obvious weaknesses between 1914 and 1918 to be exploited. Even if the revised British tactics of summer 1918 did at last produce a breakthrough, it cannot be conclusively proved that the adoption of such tactics, say, two years earlier would have led to an equally decisive victory, since (and here Haig's defenders have a valid point) the German Army of 1918 was weaker, and much more overextended, than it had been at the time of the Somme campaign. Regardless of those arguments, the fact remains that in general the British system placed strength against strength, and suffered accordingly.

Only a few remarks will be made here about the tactical aspects of British campaigning away from the Western Front. What is clear is that a belief in the straightforward assault permeated the entire British officer corps and was not to be seen in Flanders alone. Frontal attacks were also the norm at Gallipoli (though the Turks were, if anything, even more rash). It was also a frontal assault – against alerted and reinforced enemy positions – that led to the repulse of 'Second Gaza.' At Tanga (November 2nd-3rd, 1914), General Aitken's orders were simplicity itself: 'The town of Tanga is to be seized tonight.' Accordingly, the British–Indian forces advanced up the road to Tanga, in clear light, and were then machine-gunned down by the *Schutztruppe*. The main assault was also a frontal one, though it involved marching in line abreast through the jungle, and then being machine-gunned.[117]

By contrast, Allenby's exploitation of the element of surprise in the battle of Megiddo – of lulling the Turks into false expectations of where and when he would strike – has long been regarded as one of the classical instances of the unexpected, the indirect approach, and the rapid, wide-ranging exploitation of opportunities. Obviously, the terrain was much more open – and the Turkish defenders far fewer – than along the Western Front; but Allenby's force was equipped to be mobile, and this was one of the few campaigns where cavalry could be used to good effect.[118]

This, in turn, brings us to the question of supply and support facilities. Given the strong traditions of colonial soldiering in the British Army, the possession of numerous bases, ports, and garrisons in the tropics, and the pre-1914 strategy of having an expeditionary force ready to go to an 'Eastern theater,'[119] one might have expected that the military organization would have been better equipped for the various overseas campaigns fought during the war. Yet, in the important Mesopotamian operation, Townshend's bold strike up the Tigris as far as Aziziya in 1915 far outran the primitive supply system available; there was inadequate river transport, too few oxen and mules, no plans for aerial reconnaissance, and shrinking food and medical stocks. Even when the force fell back on Kut, it was too isolated from Basra; and three attempts at the relief of the beleaguered Kut garrison were also hampered by the severe lack of river transport, inadequate artillery, and dwindling supplies of food even for the relieving troops. One consequence of this shortfall was that the 1916–17 advance upon Baghdad by Maude's army was made only after many months of reorganization and logistical preparation. Another consequence was that the British force took few risks, moved slowly, and missed opportunities of destroying the Turkish Army – even if it successfully occupied Baghdad by March 1917. It was understandable that those whose reputations had suffered following the Kut disaster felt that they, too, might have achieved victory had Townshend's 30,000 men been Maude's 147,000; and had the 6 steamers and 8 tugs available in 1915 actually been the 446 steamer tugs and steam launches, 774 barges, and 414 motorboats that accompanied the later advance up the river.[120] Maude played slow but sure. The contrast with Allenby's much more decisive strike from Jaffa to Damascus in 1918, covering 350 miles and capturing 75,000 prisoners, shows what could be done when logistical support and operational boldness were combined.[121] Unfortunately, that combination was only rarely in evidence.

One other remark needs to be made about military operations outside of Flanders. In theory (that is, according to the advocates of a 'peripheral' strategy, such as Fisher, Esher, and Hankey), the enemy's weakest areas were away from the Western Front – in the Balkans, the Straits, or even the Baltic. Yet since the British evolved no operational-tactical organizations for amphibious landings, and since Gallipoli had been such a disaster, there were no developments in this area. There was, for example, no Special Boat Service, no Long-Range Desert Group, no Commandos, no Chindits, as were produced in the Second World War when the tactics of surprise and indirect approach were also advocated. That more along these lines might have been done is suggested by the Zeebrugge Raid of April 1918. The force was trained for weeks beforehand in the Thames Estuary; special ships were requisitioned, or old ones reconstructed; special smoke shells and other effects were produced; monitors with heavy guns were to give artillery support; and the landing party consisted of 'picked companies of marines . . . armed with the paraphernalia of trench warfare, howitzers, stokes-mortars, flame-throwers, and machine-guns.'[122] Still, this was only a belated effort at the creation of special forces, and was soon forgotten after 1919. No doubt much of this neglect was due to the very obvious fact that the War Office and the General Staff disliked any idea of combined operations, and that there was no one in power (like Churchill between 1940 and 1945) to push its case. However, it does remind us that alternative strategies are unlikely to get off the ground – or, if they do, are unlikely to succeed – unless considerable technical and tactical preparation is made for the operations which are being proposed.

Conclusion

Britain enjoyed certain very important strategic advantages during the First World War. Together with its allies, it possessed a superiority in economic and industrial resources.[123] With command of the sea, it prevented the Central Powers from getting access to overseas supplies. With an established array of Dominions, colonies, and bases, it was not seriously challenged outside Europe. Britain's own geographical position cramped the prospects of a strategic breakthrough by the High Seas Fleet, and the Royal Navy's 1914 numerical superiority made a German battlefleet victory unlikely. On the other hand, Germany possessed strategic advantages in the land campaigns, since it had swiftly occupied defensible ground, could use its excellent internal transport system to switch military pressures (and reinforcements) from one front to another, and benefited from military-technological developments that gave defensive warfare the edge over offensive. Any campaign to dislodge the German Army – let alone to defeat the formidable German nation – was going to be a hard one.

Such a victory was harder still for the British because of their military ineffectiveness in certain key areas. In the few battles with the High Seas Fleet, the Royal Navy's performance revealed weaknesses in matériel, command, communications, and tactics. In the desperate struggle against the U-boats, the Admiralty was slow to adopt the correct countermeasures. In the bloody and exhausting war along the Western Front, the generals repeatedly sent troops forward in unfavorable circumstances, and only belatedly and partially agreed to newer, more flexible tactics. Yet much of the campaigning away from the Western Front was also inept. All this was exacerbated by tensions between soldiers and civilians, and by institutional structures that (at least in the early stages) did not allow for a full assessment of strategic possibilities at the top and did not (throughout the war) produce swift and useful feedback from the military and naval front lines. In many areas, a rigidity of mind and a certain lack of imagination were all too evident.

These strictures should not cause one to forget the campaigns in which the British were extremely successful – the war in the air, the post-1917 defeat of the U-boats, Allenby's drive through the Middle East, and the penetration of the Hindenburg Line. They should not obscure the considerable strengths of the British military organization – the regimental system, morale-building services, Room 40's intelligence breakthroughs, the Royal Artillery, and the technological inventiveness behind the newer weapons of the tank, aircraft, and Asdic. Finally, they should not hide the point made above, that geography and technology were going to make the defeat of the Central Powers a lengthy, hard, and bloody business in any case. All these facts, and that of ultimate victory, are vital aspects in any summary of Britain's performance during the First World War.

However, at the end of the day, and with some of that wisdom of retrospect that rightly annoys those who had to grapple with the pressing task of fighting a formidable enemy, it is difficult to avoid the conclusion that British military effectiveness between 1914 and 1918 was only moderately good. Not possessing an adequate system for analyzing the operational and tactical conditions thrown up by modern warfare and new technology, or for encouraging initiative and imagination below, the British unwittingly retarded the prospects of solving some of the problems with which they were confronted. While they prevailed in the end, it seems fair to say that they might have done better.

Notes

I should like to acknowledge the kind and useful comments made by Brian Bond and Williamson Murray upon the first draft of this essay. I also benefited greatly from being able to read the manuscript of Tim Travers' forthcoming book, *The Killing Ground: The British Army, the Western Front, and the Emergence of Modern Warfare, 1900–1918*.

1 See the chapters on German military effectiveness in these volumes.

2 For general works on Britain in the First World War, see L. Woodward, *Great Britain and the War of 1914–1918* (London, 1967); A. J. P. Taylor, *English History 1914–1945* (Oxford, 1965), pp. 1–125; and A. Marwick, *The Deluge* (Harmondsworth, Mddsx., 1967). British politics during the war are covered in Taylor, *English History, passim*; P. Guinn, *British Strategy and Politics 1914–1918* (Oxford, 1965); D. R. Woodward, *Lloyd George and the Generals* (Newark, N.J., 1983); M. Pugh, *The Making of Modern British Politics, 1867–1939* (Oxford, 1982); C. Hazlehurst, *Politicians at War*, Vol. 1 (London, 1971).

3 Figures from A. T. Peacock and J. Wiseman, *The Growth of Public Expenditure in the United Kingdom* (London, 1967). There is an excellent synopsis of the Treasury's role in K. Burk, 'The Treasury: From Impotence to Power,' in Burk (ed.), *War and the State: The Transformation of British Government, 1914–1918* (London/Boston, 1982), pp. 82–107; but see also E. V. Morgan, *Studies in British Financial Policy, 1914–1925* (London, 1952). S. Pollard, *The Development of the British*

Economy, 1914–1967, 2nd ed. (London, 1969), shows how Britain was able to finance the war internationally.

4 Pollard, Taylor, and Marwick are best here.

5 M. Beloff, *Imperial Sunset*, Vol. 1, *Britain's Liberal Empire, 1897–1921* (London, 1969), p. 235.

6 K. Burk, *Britain, America, and the Sinews of War, 1914–1918* (London and Boston, 1984); Beloff, *Imperial Sunset*, pp. 229 ff.

7 For general discussions of this problem, see H. Strachan, *European Armies and the Conduct of War* (London/Boston, 1983), chs. 8 and 9; M. Pearton, *The Knowledgeable State: Diplomacy, War, and Technology since 1830* (London, 1982); and W. H. McNeill, *The Pursuit of Power: Technology, Armed Force and Society since A. D. 1000* (Oxford, 1983), ch. 9.

8 C. Barnett, *The Collapse of British Power* (New York, 1972), ch. 2; G. Hardach, *The First World War, 1914–1918* (London, 1977), pp. 77 ff.; R. J. Q. Adams, *Arms and the Wizard: Lloyd George and the Ministry of Munitions* (London, 1978).

9 D. French, *British Economic and Strategic Planning, 1905–1915* (London and Boston, 1982), esp. chs. 7–9; C. Trebilcock, 'War and the Failure of Industrialization: 1899 and 1914,' in J. M. Winter (ed.) *War and Economic Development* (Cambridge, 1975), pp. 139–64, which are altogether more understanding of the practical difficulties than Lloyd George's *War Memoirs*.

10 Trebilcock, 'War and the Failure of Industrialization,' p. 156.

11 This contradiction is discussed in innumerable works. For a sample, see M. Howard, *The Continental Commitment* (London, 1972), chs. 2 and 3; N. J. D'Ombrain, *War Machinery and High Politics* (Oxford, 1973), *passim*; P. M. Kennedy, *The Rise and Fall of British Naval Mastery* (London and New York, 1976), chs. 8 and 9. For the longer term dimensions to it, see the useful review-essay by H. Strachan, 'The British Way in Warfare Revisited,' *Historical Journal*, vol. 26, no. 2 (1983), pp. 447–61.

12 J. D. Scott, *Vickers, a History* (London, 1962), p. 99, as cited in Trebilcock, 'War and the Failure of Industrialization,' p. 151.

13 See Adams, *Arms and the Wizard*, *passim*; and C. Wrigley, 'The Ministry of Munitions: An Innovatory Department,' in Burk (ed.), *War and the State*, pp. 32–56.

14 McNeill, *The Pursuit of Power*, pp. 269 ff.; A. J. Marder, *From the Dreadnought to Scapa Flow*, Vol. 1, *The Road to War* (Oxford, 1961), ch. 13; J. Sumida, 'British Capital Ships and Fire Control in the *Dreadnought* Era: Sir John Fisher, Arthur Hungerford Pollen and the Battle Cruiser,' *Journal of Modern History*, vol. 51 (1979), pp. 205–30.

15 Pearton, *The Knowledgeable State*, p. 170; B. D. Powers, *Strategy without Sliderule: British Air Strategy, 1914–1939* (London, 1976), chs. 1 and 2. See also the massive detail in W. Raleigh and H. A. Jones, *The War in the Air*, 6 vols. (Oxford, 1922–37).

16 Pollard, *Development of the British Economy*, ch. 2; Woodward, *Great Britain and the War of 1914–1918*, pp. 486 ff.; French, *British Economic and Strategic Planning*, p. 124 ff.

17 Hardach, *The First World War*, p. 79.

18 French, *British Economic and Strategic Planning*, pp. 130 ff.

19 According to at least one of the ways of calculating the figures: D. R. Woodward, *Lloyd George and the Generals*, chs. 10–12, is the most up-to-date analysis of the manpower crisis/Maurice Debate of 1918.

20 Ibid., *passim*; Guinn, *British Strategy and Politics*, pp. 279 ff; Woodward, *Great Britain and the War of 1914–1918*, pp. 320–2.

21 Marder, *Dreadnought to Scapa Flow, passim*; and J. Goldrick, *The King's Ships Were at Sea: The War in the North Sea, August 1914-February 1915* (Annapolis, Md., 1984), esp. chs. 2 and 13.

22 Apart from Guinn and Woodward, see also V. H. Rothwell, *British War Aims and Peace Diplomacy, 1914–1918* (Oxford, 1971), *passim*; P. Kennedy, *The Realities behind Diplomacy: Background Influences on British External Policy, 1865–1980* (London, 1981), pp. 199 ff.; and the commentary in Beloff's *Imperial Sunset.*

23 Guinn, *British Strategy*, p. 183.

24 Beloff, *Imperial Sunset, passim*; Kennedy, *Realities behind Diplomacy*, pp. 203 ff.; J. Gooch, 'Soldiers, Strategy and War Aims in Britain 1914–18,' in B. Hunt and A. Preston (eds.), *War Aims and Strategic Policy in the Great War* (London, 1977), pp. 21–40. For a more extreme argument about British fears of Russia, see K. M. Wilson, *The Policy of the Entente* (Cambridge, 1985).

25 W. Fest, *Peace or Partition: The Habsburg Monarchy and British Policy, 1914–1918* (London, 1978).

26 W. R. Louis, *Great Britain and Germany's Lost Colonies, 1914–1919* (Oxford, 1967), *passim*; V. H. Rothwell, 'Mesopotamia in British War Aims, 1914–1918,' *Historical Journal*, vol. 13, no. 2 (1970), pp. 273–94; M. Kent, 'Great Britain and the End of the Ottoman Empire,' in Kent (ed.), *The Great Powers and the End of the Ottoman Empire* (London and Boston, 1984), pp. 172–205; Beloff, *Imperial Sunset*, pp. 254 ff.

27 A. J. P. Taylor, *The Struggle for Mastery in Europe, 1848–1918* (Oxford, 1954), pp. 542 ff.; T. Higgins, *Winston Churchill and the Dardanelles* (London, 1963), *passim.* The British inability to produce enough munitions and other supplies for Russia hardly suggests that a great flow of goods would have been sent through the Straits even if Constantinople had been seized; see K. Neilson, *Strategy and Supply: The Anglo-Russian Alliance, 1914–17* (London and Boston, 1984).

28 For a brief summary, see Kennedy, *The Rise and Fall of British Naval Mastery*, ch. 9; for fuller details, see Marder, *Dreadnought to Scapa Flow, passim.*

29 Howard, *The Continental Commitment*, pp. 57–8. For a brief summary of the debate, see Strachan, 'The British Way in Warfare Revisited,' *passim.*

30 For what follows, see J. Ehrman, *Cabinet Government and War, 1890–1940* (Cambridge, 1958), chs. 2 and 3; J. Turner, 'Cabinets, Committees and Secretariats: The Higher Direction of War,' in Burk (ed.), *War and the State*, pp. 57–83; M. P. A. Hankey, *The Supreme Command*, 2 vols. (London, 1961); and Woodward, *Lloyd George and the Generals, passim.*

31 Robertson concluded: 'A more deplorable state of affairs can surely never have existed in the conduct of any war,' which seems a bold claim. See Sir William Robertson, *Soldiers and Statesmen, 1914–1918,* (New York, 1926), Vol. 1, p. 160. This view of the vast diversity of opinions is strongly confirmed in K. Neilson, 'Kitchener: A Reputation Refurbished?' *Canadian Journal of History*, vol. 15, no. 2 (1980), pp. 207–27. For the later improvements, see Ehrman, *Cabinet Government and War*, ch. 3.

32 The two works by Guinn and D. R. Woodward are the best accounts here; but see also the summary in D. R. Woodward, 'Britain in a Continental War: The Civil-Military Debate over the Strategical Direction of the War of 1914–1918,' *Albion,* vol. 12 (1980), pp. 37–65.

33 For details, see A. J. Barker, *The Neglected War: Mesopotamia, 1914–1918* (London, 1967); and J. S. Galbraith, 'No Man's Child: The Campaign in Mesopotamia, 1914–1916,' *The International History Review*, vol. 6, no. 3 (1984), pp. 358–85.

34 See Louis, *Britain and Germany's Lost Colonies;* and, for pre-1914 considerations of

overseas operations generally, see J. Gooch, *The Plans of War: The General Staff and British Military Strategy c.1900–1916* (London, 1974).

35 L. Mosley, *Duel for Kilimanjaro* (London, 1963), ch. 3.

36 The best study is R. R. James, *Gallipoli* (New York, 1965), but there is also an excellent analysis in Marder, *Dreadnought to Scapa Flow*, Vol. 2; and a succinct coverage in B. E. Schmitt and H. C. Vedeler, *The World in the Crucible, 1914–1919* (New York, 1984), pp. 105 ff.

37 See the comments upon the Salonika operation in Woodward, *Great Britain and the War of 1914–1918*, and Guinn, *British Strategy and Politics*.

38 Allenby's campaigns are covered in B. H. Liddell Hart, *History of the First World War* (London, 1970); A. P. Wavell, *The Palestine Campaigns* (London, 1928); C. Falls, *Military Operations: Egypt and Palestine*, Vol. 2 (London, 1928). The British tendency to underestimate the Turks is nicely commented on in D. French, 'The Origins of the Dardanelles Campaign Reconsidered,' *History*, vol. 68 (1983), pp. 210–24.

39 Apart from Marder, one might also consult the relevant parts of S. W. Roskill, *The Strategy of Sea Power* (London, 1962), and G. S. Graham, *The Politics of Naval Supremacy* (Cambridge, 1965).

40 See the very good analysis of these points in Travers' forthcoming book, *The Killing Ground*.

41 Barnett, *The Collapse of British Power*, p. 113. See also, Hardach, *The First World War*, pp. 77 ff.

42 Marder, *Dreadnought to Scapa Flow*, Vol. 1, p. 426.

43 Especially since, after 1917, the base was also used by US destroyers.

44 J. K. Gusewelle, 'Science and the Admiralty during World War I: The Case of the Board of Invention and Research,' in G. Jordan (ed.), *Naval Warfare in the Twentieth Century* (London, 1977), pp. 105–17.

45 Powers, *Strategy without Sliderule*, chs. 1–3; M. Dean, *The Royal Air Force and Two World Wars* (London, 1979), ch. 2.

46 C. Barnett, *Britain and Her Army 1509–1970: A Military, Political and Social Survey* (London, 1970), pp. 392–3.

47 Barnett, *The Collapse of British Power*, ch. 2, covers a lot of these reforms. See also the details in Woodward, *Great Britain and the War of 1914–1918*; Pollard, *The Development of the British Economy*; and McNeill, *The Pursuit of Power*.

48 Woodward, *Lloyd George and the Generals*, and Strachan, 'The British Way in Warfare Revisited,' are good introductions to the debate. The pro-Haig school is still strongly represented by, *inter alia*, J. Marshall-Cornwall, *Haig as Military Commander* (London, 1973), and the innumerable works of John Terraine. Guinn, *British Strategy and Politics*, *passim*, and the innumerable works of Liddell Hart, provide an antithesis.

49 See the details in Guinn, *British Strategy and Politics*, pt. 3, and Woodward, *Lloyd George and the Generals*, esp. chs. 6, 10–11.

50 Neilson, *Strategy and Supply*, *passim*.

51 Kennedy, *The Rise and Fall of British Naval Mastery*, pp. 261–4; I. Nish, *Alliance in Decline: A Study in Anglo-Japanese Relations, 1908–1923* (London, 1972); Marder, *Dreadnought to Scapa Flow*, Vol. 5, pp. 224 ff.

52 Apart from Marder's volumes, the best analysis is J. Winton, *Convoy: The Defence of Sea Trade, 1890–1990* (London, 1983).

53 Howard, *The Continental Commitment*, ch. 3; Kennedy, *The Rise and Fall of British Naval Mastery*, ch. 9.

54 Marder, *Dreadnought to Scapa Flow*, Vol. 4, p. 23.

55 Woodward, *Great Britain and the War of 1914–1918*, p. 369.

56 S. Bidwell and D. Graham, *Firepower: British Army Weapons and Theories of War, 1904–1945* (London and Boston, 1982), p. 143. See also the very good analysis in P. Mead, *The Eye in the Air: History of Air Observation and Reconnaissance for the Army, 1785–1945* (London, 1983), pp. 51 ff.
57 Bidwell and Graham, *Firepower*, pp. 143–5; Mead, *The Eye in the Air*, p. 137; J. C. Slessor, *Air Power and Armies* (London, 1936), pp. 148–99.
58 Ibid., pp. 11–12, 97, 102; Mead, *The Eye in the Air*, pp. 117–20.
59 See the analysis of these weaknesses in Goldrick, *The King's Ships, passim.*
60 As quoted in Strachan, *European Armies and the Conduct of War*, p. 138.
61 Travers, *The Killing Ground*, ch. 5, thoroughly covers these points.
62 There is a good discussion of the improved tactics of 1917–18 in Bidwell and Graham, *Firepower*; and compare with the folly of the line advance as described in A. Clark, *The Donkeys* (London, 1961).
63 D. Graham, 'Observations on the Dialectics of British Army Tactics, 1904–1945,' paper given to the Eleventh Military History Symposium, Royal Military College of Canada, Kingston, Ontario, March 23, 1984.
64 See the analyses in Marder, *Dreadnought to Scapa Flow*, Vols. 3–5; and Goldrick, *The King's Ships, passim.* For the activities of the Harwich Force and the Dover Patrol, see P. Kennedy and O. Eckert, 'The Channel War,' *History of the First World War*, vol. 4, no. 14, pp. 1728–35; Kennedy, 'Dover Patrol,' ibid., vol. 6, no. 3, pp. 2301–5.
65 E. K. G. Sixsmith, *British Generalship in the Twentieth Century* (London, 1970), pp. 130–2.
66 For details of the 1918 campaigns, see H. Essame, *The Battle for Europe, 1918* (New York, 1972); B. Pitt, *1918 – the Last Act* (New York, 1962); J. Toland, *No Man's Land: The Story of 1918* (London, 1980).
67 For what follows, I am again indebted to the writings of Graham and Bidwell, and especially those of Professor Travers.
68 Marshall-Cornwall, *Haig as Military Commander*, and J. Terraine, *Douglas Haig* (London, 1963), are good examples of this. See also Terraine's recent study, *The Smoke and the Fire* (London, 1980).
69 N. Dixon, *On the Psychology of Military Incompetence* (New York, 1976); Clark, *The Donkeys*.
70 T. H. E. Travers, 'Learning and Decision-Making on the Western Front, 1915–1916: The British Example,' *Canadian Journal of History*, vol. 18, no. 1 (1983), pp. 87–97.
71 Travers, *The Killing Ground*, chs. 4 and 5.
72 Sumida, 'British Capital Ships and Fire-Control,' *passim*; and A. Pollen, *The Great Gunnery Scandal* (London, 1981), *passim.*
73 Apart from the analyses by Marder and Goldrick, there is also an excellent commentary upon the matériel and staff weaknesses of the Royal Navy in S. Roskill, *Admiral of the Fleet Earl Beatty: The Last Naval Hero* (London, 1980).
74 There is a good brief discussion of both tactics and aircraft types in A. Clark, *Aces High: The War in the Air over the Western Front, 1914–18* (New York, 1973).
75 H. Montgomery Hyde, *British Air Policy between the Wars, 1918–1939* (London, 1976), p. 46; C. Webster and N. Frankland, *The Strategic Air Offensive against Germany, 1939–1945*, 3 vols. (London, 1961), Vol. 1, pp. 34–51; N. Jones, *The Origins of Strategic Bombing* (London, 1973).
76 Pearton, *The Knowledgeable State*, p. 156.
77 Mead, *The Eye in the Air, passim.*
78 The pre-1914 state of British military intelligence is thoroughly covered in T. G. Fergusson, *British Military Intelligence, 1870–1914* (Frederick, Md., 1984). The

wartime developments are analyzed in J. Haswell, *British Military Intelligence* (London, 1973), pp. 106 ff., and D. French, 'Sir John French's Secret Service on the Western Front, 1914–15,' *The Journal of Strategic Studies*, vol. 7, no. 4 (1984), pp. 423–40. For Haig's ignorance of the Passchendaele conditions, see B. Bond, 'The First World War,' in C. L. Mowat, (ed.) *The New Cambridge Modern History*, Vol. 12, *The Shifting Balance of World Forces, 1898–1945*, 2nd ed., (Cambridge, 1968), p. 196.

79 B. H. Liddell Hart, *The Tanks,* 2 vols. (London, 1959), Vol. 1, p. 159.

80 James, *Gallipoli, passim*; Schmitt and Vedeler, *The World in the Crucible*, pp. 105 ff.; A. J. Marder, *From the Dardanelles to Oran* (London, 1974), ch. 1, 'The Dardanelles Revisited,' *passim*.

81 Trebilcock, 'War and the Failure of Industrialization,' p. 160.

82 The most thorough study of British naval intelligence is now P. Beesly, *Room 40: British Naval Intelligence, 1914–1918* (London, 1982), but there are useful comments about its role at Jutland in Marder, *Dreadnought to Scapa Flow*, Vol. 3, *passim*, and Roskill, *Beatty*, pp. 152–4.

83 See the compelling evidence on these weaknesses in Marder, *Dreadnought to Scapa Flow, passim*; Roskill, *Beatty*, chs. 5–12; and Goldrick, *The King's Ships, passim*.

84 Winton, *Convoy*, p. 40.

85 Ibid., p. 70.

86 Travers, *The Killing Ground*, chs. 6 and 7.

87 But see the efforts by Terraine, *Douglas Haig*, and by Marshall-Cornwall, *Haig as Military Commander*, in their respective discussions of Passchendaele.

88 Clark, *Aces High*, chs. 2–3, 6–7.

89 Dean, *The Royal Air Force and Two World Wars*, p. 12.

90 Quoted in Winton, *Convoy*, p. 100.

91 See again the analyses in Marder, Goldrick, and Roskill.

92 Kennedy, 'Dover Patrol,' *passim*. There is a good discussion in Marder, *Dreadnought to Scapa Flow*, vols. 2–5, and Goldrick, *The King's Ships, passim*, of British fleet tactics and their failings.

93 See Goldrick *The King's Ships Were at Sea*, ch. 11, for an analysis of the breakdown of communications during the Dogger Bank battle.

94 A. Carew, *The Lower Deck of the Royal Navy 1900–1939: Invergordon in Perspective* (Manchester, 1981) is very useful here.

95 This definition comes from Major-General R. C. Money: see Sixsmith, *British Generalship*, p. 157, n. 9.

96 Marshall-Cornwall, *Haig as Military Commander*; J. Terraine, 'History and the 'Indirect Approach,'' *Journal of the Royal United Services Institute for Defence Studies*, vol. 116 (1971).

97 Liddell Hart, *History of the First World War* and *The Tanks* provide good examples of this criticism, as does his article 'The Basic Truths of Passchendaele,' *Journal of the Royal United Services Institute for Defence Studies,* vol. 104 (1959). Bond, 'The First World War,' and Sixsmith, *British Generalship*, provide balanced overviews.

98 M. Howard, 'Men against Fire: Expectations of War in 1914,' *International Security*, vol. 9, no. 1 (1984), pp. 41–57; T. H. E. Travers, 'The Offensive and the Problem of Innovation in British Military Thought, 1870–1915,' *Journal of Contemporary History*, vol. 13, no. 3 (1978), pp. 531–53; idem., 'Technology, Tactics and Morale: Jean de Bloch, the Boer War, and British Military Theory, 1900–1914,' *Journal of Modern History*, vol. 51, no. 2 (1979), pp. 264–86.

99 Liddell Hart, *History of the First World War*, pp. 303 ff.; J. Keegan, *The Face of Battle* (Harmondsworth, Mddsx., 1978), ch. 4; A. H. Farrar-Hockley, *The Somme* (London, 1964); and M. Middlebrook, *The First Day on the Somme* (London,

1971), provide good details. There is also an excellent analysis in Travers, *The Killing Ground*, chs. 6 and 7.

100 Sixsmith, *British Generalship*, p. 81.

101 Liddell Hart, *History of the First World War*, p. 263.

102 Strachan, *European Armies and the Conduct of War*, p. 143; Liddell Hart, *The Tanks*, Vol. 1, pp. 177–84.

103 Barnett, *Britain and Her Army*, p. 379.

104 Sixsmith, *British Generalship*, p. 132. This volume is also useful in describing Maxse's various reform proposals.

105 There is a good discussion of this in Keegan, *The Face of Battle*, pp. 219 ff. For more detail on the social composition of the British Army, the state of morale, its 'home entertainments,' etc., see the valuable collection by I. F. W. Becket and K. Simpson (eds.), *A Nation in Arms: A Social Study of the British Army in the First World War* (Manchester, 1985).

106 See A. Babington, *For the Sake of Example: Capital Courts-Martial, 1914–1920* (London, 1983).

107 James, *Gallipoli*, esp. chs. 12 and 13.

108 K. Robbins, *The First World War* (Oxford, 1984), p. 154. For further details, see D. Gill and G. Dallas, 'Mutiny at Etaples base, 1917,' *Past and Present*, no. 69 (1975), pp. 88–112.

109 Babington, *For the Sake of Example*, app.

110 G. St. John Barclay, *The Empire is Marching* (London, 1976), pp. 77–8; Essame, *The Battle for Europe, 1918*, p. 191.

111 See the comments in Barnett, *The Collapse of British Power*; Robbins, *The First World War* ch. 6; and the very good discussion in Pugh, *The Making of Modern British Politics*, pp. 189 ff. D. Englander and J. Osborne, 'Jack, Tommy, and Henry Dubb: the Armed Forces and the Working Class,' *Historical Journal*, vol. 21 (1978), pp. 593–621; P. Abrams, 'The Failure of Social Reform,' *Past and Present*, no. 24 (1963), pp. 43–64; and P. B. Johnston, *Land Fit for Heroes* (London, 1968), are all important here in discussing *what* the war was supposed to achieve.

112 T. T. Lupfer, 'The Dynamics of Doctrine: The Changes in German Tactical Doctrine during the First World War,' *Leavenworth Papers*, no. 4 (July 1981), *passim*. There is a succinct survey of changes in tactical thought in Strachan, *European Armies and the Conduct of War*, pp. 140 ff., and in P. Griffith, *Forward into Battle: Fighting Tactics from Waterloo to Vietnam* (Chichester, Sussex, 1981), ch. 4 (see esp. the charts on pp. 78–79.)

113 See again the works by Bidwell and Graham, Sixsmith, Essame, and Strachan.

114 Bidwell and Graham, *Firepower*, chs. 4–8.

115 Liddell Hart, *The Tanks*, Vol. 1, pp. 171–6; Essame, *Battle for Europe,* 1918, pp. 116 ff.

116 Liddell Hart, *The Tanks*, Vol. 1, pp. 161.

117 Mosley, *Duel for Kilimanjaro*, ch. 3.

118 Perhaps because it is a good example of the indirect approach, it is given much attention in Liddell Hart, *Strategy*, 2nd ed. (New York, 1974), pp. 181 ff.

119 See Gooch, *The Plans of War, passim*.

120 Galbraith, 'The Campaign in Mesopotamia,' pp. 384–5.

121 Liddell Hart, *History of the First World War*, pp. 208–9, 351 ff., 553 ff.

122 C. R. M. Cruttwell, *A History of the Great War, 1914–1918* (London and New York, 1982), pp. 537 ff. For the failure to develop combined operations, see Marder, *From the Dardanelles to Oran*, p. 52; and B. Fergusson, *The Watery Maze: The Story of Combined Operations* (London, 1961).

123 For an analysis of the economic balances, see P. Kennedy, 'The First World War and the International Power System,' *International Security*, vol. 9, no. 1 (1984), pp. 7–40.

[3]

The Dynamics of Necessity: German Military Policy during the First World War

Holger H. Herwig
Vanderbilt University

Introduction

This is a rather traditional historical account. The reader will scan what follows in vain for trendy sociological categorizations.[1] These lie beyond my limited talents. Rather, this chapter seeks to analyze the military activity of Imperial Germany before and during the First World War at the political, strategic, operational, and tactical levels. It wishes neither to eulogize nor to condemn.[2] Both the passage of time and the disappearance of anything remotely resembling the Royal Prussian Army or the Imperial German Navy leave little room for rancor or glorification. This paper will detail to what degree the German military operated efficiently within that strange federal composite called Imperial Germany; 'the best administered, worst governed country in Europe.'[3]

One should note at the outset that the discussion of army matters must come from published documents, memoirs, handbooks, official histories, and secondary accounts – due to the virtually total destruction of the erstwhile Prussian-German Army archives at Potsdam during Allied air raids in February 1942 and April 1945. Moreover, this chapter will deal primarily with the Prussian Army and its Great General Staff, rather than with the various federal contingents of Bavaria, Saxony, and Württemberg that comprised the peacetime German land forces. For in time of peace the Prussian king–German emperor possessed the right of 'inspection' over these troops; and in time of war overall command of them devolved upon him and was largely exercised in his name through the Chief of the General Staff. The navy, on the other hand, was in peace and remained in war a federal German institution directly under the emperor.

Political Effectiveness

> The common soldiers form the foundations; the colonels and other senior officers are the pillars of a perfect military rotunda; they support the massive cupola; they also carry – if need be – a hollow Hercules, perched on top of the cupola into the rains and the thunderstorms.[4]
>
> Georg Heinrich von Berenhorst, 1805

The command structure of Germany's armed forces was a nightmare – the contentions of Anglo-Saxon military historians concerning the efficacy of the German military notwithstanding. The truth is that the Reich never possessed an overall military planning capability between the 'cupola' and the 'hollow Hercules.' The constitution of 1871 had dictated decentralization by accepting the Prussian Army's hallowed division between a 'command' and an 'administrative' domain: the former, pertaining to the organization, training, discipline, and disposition of forces, remained exclusively with the emperor; the latter, revolving around budgetary items such as the size, recruitment, and equipping of forces, required the emperor to seek the countersignature of the Imperial Chancellor or the Prussian War Minister as well as the consent of Parliament (Reichstag). Obviously, the dividing line between command and administrative domains was often blurred and generally favored the command side of the equation.[5]

Military command itself lay among three major bureaus: the Prussian War Ministry, the Military Cabinet, and the General Staff, all responsible to the king-emperor. The war minister in particular held an impossible position entailing great yet dual responsibility and little power. As an active officer of the Prussian Army he was directly responsible to the Prussian king for the combat readiness of the Prussian Army – but not the armies of Bavaria, Saxony, or Württemberg; concurrently, he was a plenipotentiary to the Federal Chamber (Bundesrat), and as such the chancellor's deputy before the Reichstag, where he had to answer for all federal armies – save the Bavarian. Moreover, as War Minister of the Prussian Army, he had to account to both houses of Parliament in that state for the effectiveness of the army. In case of conflict among these various agencies, the Prussian War Minister's only constitutional recourse lay in resignation. By 1914, his office employed between six hundred and seven hundred officers and civil servants. The Military Cabinet by 1914, on the other hand, was a small bureau of about ten officers and an equal number of civil servants, and was responsible for the army's personnel. It answered only to the emperor and was widely denounced – then as well as later – as an irresponsible shadow military government. In truth, its very existence attested to the *Kommandogewalt* of the emperor and it would have required a constitutional revision to alter its central role as Wilhelm II's major advisory body.

The Chief of the General Staff enjoyed great power and prestige by tradition and example, but virtually no responsibility save to the king-emperor. Constitutionally, he was but 'the first advisor of the Imperial Supreme Commander,' Wilhelm II, possessing no legal or constitutional power to impose his will even upon other agencies of the Prussian Army. Only in the Byzantine world of German military administration could such an officer in time of war exercise *de facto* command over all the land forces of the Reich as well as over much of its military and industrial establishment. By the outbreak of the First World War, the General Staff consisted of about 650 officers. Finally, there was the office of the Imperial Chancellor. As the only true *Reichsminister* – he was aided by a number of state secretaries – he was ultimately responsible for all governmental affairs other than the military *Kommandogewalt*. The emperor's orders required his signature and he presented the military budget to Parliament. He was responsible only to the emperor. Yet, by and large, the chancellor traditionally did not take an active role in strategic planning.[6] At least in theory, all differences of opinion or policy among the War Ministry, Military Cabinet, General Staff, and Chancery fell to the king-emperor to solve.

The latter sought to screen his military from the scrutiny of the Reichstag as best he could. To this end, Wilhelm II in July 1888 had gathered his aides into a 'headquarters' or *maison militaire* – soon expanded into an 'imperial headquarters' – with no clear-cut functions whatsoever. In addition, Wilhelm II jealously guarded his right to make *all* military appointments, from the lowest lieutenant to the Chief of the General Staff. This *Ernennungsrecht*, exercised through the Military Cabinet, lay outside of parliamentary control. Finally, the emperor accorded no less than forty army and eight naval officers the right of direct audience (*Immediatstellung*).[7] It requires no great imagination to gâuge whether this system of direct access to an impressionable and volatile monarch by nearly fifty senior officers – not counting department heads – enhanced military effectiveness.

Worse yet, Wilhelm II proved utterly incapable of coordinating joint services planning – with the one exception of conducting combined army–navy maneuvers in the Baltic region in 1904. Already in 1897 he had dissolved the joint services Home Defense Commission (*Landesverteidigungskommission*), composed of admirals and generals entrusted with the coordination of joint defense policies. It was never replaced with an analogous organization, something along the lines of the British Committee of Imperial Defence.[8]

The emperor's centrality of function manifested itself in many ways. On the surface, there were the countless uniform changes and special service regulations. More seriously, Wilhelm's insistence on exercising his *Kommandogewalt* reduced the annual maneuvers to static set pieces, which usually ended in glorious cavalry charges led by the monarch. Not only did such theatrics enhance the role of the cavalry in an age of mass armies and massive small-arms fire power, but, as Wilhelm Deist has noted, they 'corrupted the intellectual development of senior military officers.'[9] Officers with independence of thought and action became so-called maneuver victims. New methods of combat and modern forms of transport were ignored. There simply was no room in the Prussian Army for the notion of long-term peoples' wars as expounded by generals Colmar von der Goltz and August Keim. Nor was there room for the establishment of an 'economic general staff' as advocated by Heinrich Class. As early as 1894, Wilhelm II had decreed that officers who opposed official doctrine in print or word were to be summarily dealt with through the army's courts of military honor.[10] In the final analysis, the army remained first and foremost the guarantor of the existing social order.

At the heart of that order stood the officer corps, the 'first estate in the realm.' It did not represent the nation at large; rather, the landed aristocracy, if not numerically then at least in tone and outlook, dominated it. Jews and Social Democrats were effectively, if indirectly, barred from the active officer corps.[11] Bourgeois aspirants found themselves attached to the less prestigious supply, logistics, artillery, engineering, and medical corps. Nor did the army share contemporary society's affinity for higher education. It preferred good lineage and domestic upbringing; until 1919 the Prussian Army successfully rejected attempts to require high school graduation with university admission (*Abitur*) – as had been the case in Bavaria since 1872. Moreover, the emperor frequently gave candidates from 'good' families dispensation from entrance examinations as well as from high school graduation with general curricula (*Primareife*). And few army or navy officers, usually no more than 2 or 3 per cent, attended the Technical University. Indeed, when General von der Goltz at the turn of the century recommended enhanced technical training for officers and the creation of a special engineering staff, both the War Ministry and the General Staff vetoed the proposal. Nor should one overlook the fact that the General Staff did not represent the Prussian officer corps as a whole. Its members had been carefully culled from the 30,000-man officer corps for intellect and represented an elite brain trust of the gifted and the eccentric; it was a safety valve of talent in a corps largely known for its homogeneity and singularity of outlook. The members of the General Staff were products of the prestigious *Kriegsakademie*, which placed a heavy emphasis upon 'technical' subjects such as tactics (four hours), mathematics (four hours), military history, weapons, fortifications, and staff work (each three hours). The curricula of the *Kriegsakademie* entirely omitted such topics as foreign affairs, economics, and domestic politics; at no time did the Reich develop institutions analogous to the British Imperial Defence College or the French Centre des Hautes Etudes Militaires. What some have called the resulting 'arrogant *Fachidiotie*' and 'blinkered professionalism of specialists' conversely accounted for the high degree of competence in operational and tactical matters.[12]

Both army and navy did possess adequate access to the required quantities of military manpower. The bulk of the army, of course, consisted of NCOs and enlisted men or draftees. Every fit male citizen owed seven years' service to the army; after the reforms of 1893, two years with the active army and five years in the reserve. Thereafter, he served a further five years in the militia (*Landwehr I*). In the case of the navy, recruits were on active duty for three years, followed by four years in the reserve, and finally by enrollment in the naval militia (*Seewehr*). However, there existed a wide gap between universal military obligation and universal military service: it is estimated that in 1914, of a potential 10.4 million men between the service ages of twenty and forty-five (forty trained age groups), almost 5.4 million had escaped military training.[13] The peacetime strength of the army stood at 800,000; that of the navy under 70,000 (a total of about 1.4 per cent of the population).

In addition, the military managed to assure itself of a regular share of the nation's budget sufficient to fund its major programs. Army and navy independently submitted their fiscal requests through the War Minister and the Navy Office to the chancellor. The army budget was determined after 1894 for five-year periods (*Quinquennat*) according to a complicated formula that granted funds according to the number of men serving at any given time. The navy, for its part, did not enjoy the luxury of such an automatic funding system, but rather submitted its fiscal demands to the Reichstag as national security and expansion programs demanded. Only replacement of ships every twenty years (after 1908) was decreed by the Reichstag. At no time does it appear that army and navy planners coordinated their budgetary strategies, with the result that *overall* defense needs were never seriously debated in committee.

On the whole, Germany's armed forces also had ample access to the industrial and technological resources necessary to produce the equipment needed. The Reich was a semi-authoritarian state, and the government saw to it that its armories and shipyards as well as private purveyors fulfilled the weapons needs of its armed forces. By the turn of the century, this was accomplished in equal proportions by state and by private industry. Tactics naturally dictated needs. The army trained mainly for attack – though not to the extremes of the French *élan vital*, and the Service Regulations of 1888 and 1906 stressed the magazine rifle ('Rifle 98') as a modern assault weapon. On the other hand, it introduced machine guns only slowly owing to their great weight, tendency to jam, and high consumption of ammunition. A cabinet order of 1901 integrated them into the infantry on a regular basis, and a modified Maxim gun 'MG 08' had entered service by 1913 at the rate of one machine gun company of six guns per brigade.[14]

Artillery, which caused the greatest number of casualties (70 per cent) during the First World War, had posed a number of problems. Tactically, it was heavy, slow, and cumbersome and could not easily move forward to support assault troops. Communications through telephones connected by wire were vulnerable to hostile fire. And the massive quantities of shells required for a sustained barrage presented considerable problems to a logistic system based on man and beast. More importantly, the firm of F. A. Krupp in Essen attained a virtual monopoly over artillery due to its special relationship to Wilhelm II. Competitors were either bought out or driven from the market. Technological innovations, such as the light-weight recoil cannon developed by the Rheinische Metallwaren-Maschinenfabrik (Ehrhardt) in 1896, were often ignored. As Eckart Kehr stated: 'The will of the Krupp firm determined the makeup of Prussian artillery.' And while Krupp in the process accorded the Prussian Army a steady supply of weapons, it also sold about one-half of its products overseas, including its advanced nickel-steel cannons, thereby giving the Reich's potential adversaries access to its latest technology.[15]

Generally speaking, the Prussian Army was not a great innovator in the technological aspect of war planning. General Helmuth von Moltke as late as 1910 thought that use of the airplane to drop bombs was 'for the present unimportant.' A colleague (General von Lyncker) one year later still rated aircraft inferior to dirigibles for reconnaissance. War Minister Erich von Falkenhayn in January 1914 again deemed the airplane of little use in a long war, and the General Staff fully turned to the potential of air power only three months later. These views combined with the inadequacy of the German air industry in 1912 to give the French Army a clear superiority of 390 to 100 aircraft, and 234 to 90 pilots.[16]

Trucks were not accorded sufficient attention either. Moltke had been instrumental in introducing motor transport companies after 1906, but the 'technics' of warfare were generally looked down upon in Imperial Germany. Thus, it would have taken about 14,000 more trucks than Germany possessed in 1914 to transport the combat units of the right wing of the Schlieffen plan alone; and fully 60 per cent of available trucks broke down as the Battle of the Marne raged in September 1914.[17] Neither in aircraft nor in truck production did the Reich attain a substantial degree of standardization. The situation with regard to the navy was also dominated by a lack of competition and failure to standardize. Admiral Alfred von Tirpitz, State Secretary of the Navy Office, gave Krupp and Dillinger-Hüttenwerke a monopoly over armor-plate production. Turbine development, however, rested in the hands of no less than seven major builders, resulting in great duplication of effort and funds; indeed, the navy did not manage to complete a single class of battleships powered with turbines. Submarines were likewise left with Krupp, and the navy entered the war with only two shipyards actively developing them. By and large, Tirpitz left technological innovation in the hands of the private sector.[18]

Finally, special cultural factors were at work to give the German situation a unique development. The elections of 1912 brought the Social Democrats (SPD) to the fore as the largest single party with 110 seats, and concomitantly the number of Jewish Reichstag delegates doubled to eighteen. As a result, nearly 40 per cent of the electorate belonged to circles not acceptable to the armed forces. In fact, the army had been most active for years in combatting the spread of social democracy, both directly through regulations forbidding SPD influence in the barracks, and indirectly through the powerful veterans' organizations (*Kriegervereine*).[19] With Social Democrats too unreliable to draft into the ranks, and Jews unacceptable as active officers, a crisis developed by 1912–13. The General Staff, largely at the urging of Colonel Erich Ludendorff, attempted to increase the army's peacetime strength by three army corps, or about 300,000 men (personnel-intensive armament). The Prussian War Ministry opposed such expansion, fearing that it would undermine the social cohesion and political reliability of the officer corps. Instead, it recommended increases in artillery, military aircraft, and machine gun companies (material-intensive armament). In the end, a compromise was reached in 1913 with the addition of 135,000 officers and men.[20] In the process, two quite distinct visions of the future army emerged between General Staff and War Ministry: while the former was willing to accept the new concept of an industrial war of the masses, the latter was unwilling to see Prussia-Germany transformed into a nation in arms.

What united the various antipodal groups in Wilhelmian Germany was fear of Russia and hatred of France. Demotic slogans such as the 'inevitable showdown between Slavs and Teutons' combined with patriotic anti-French sentiment to rally Germans from Jews to Socialists behind the proclaimed *Burgfrieden* of 1914. At least for the first few months of the war, domestic strife was set aside in favor of the great national cause. Only the long duration of the war and the emergence of a 'silent dictatorship' on the part of the General Staff eventually were to shatter the delicate domestic fabric engineered in 1914.

Strategic Effectiveness

> Germany dare not hope to free itself in a short time from the one enemy by a quick and successful offensive in the west, in order thereafter to turn against another [enemy in the east].[21]
>
> Helmuth von Moltke, 1871

Moltke's words leave no doubt that Germany's most successful soldier eyed a future two-front war even as he led his victorious armies back from France. He realized fully that Germany had only attained semi-hegemony on the Continent in 1871, and that the recently defeated opponent could renew the struggle only through an alliance with Russia. For the next two decades, Moltke wrestled with the problems of a two-front war. The French citizen armies of Léon Gambetta had shown that future conflagrations would be Seven or even Thirty Years Wars. In the end, Moltke's strategy – the Germans in fact preferred the term operations – dictated an active defense in the west along the axis Metz-Strassburg, while the main offensive would come in the east, where a common flat-land border of 500 miles with Russia ruled out a defensive posture. Indeed, Russian Poland seemed ideal for a coordinated German-Austro-Hungarian pincer movement designed to encircle tsarist forces. Above all, Moltke rejected the notion that future wars could be decided by single engagements; even the most successful outcome of his strategy would require cabinet diplomacy to bring about peace.[22]

Alfred von Schlieffen totally rejected this concept. He had closely studied the battles of Cannae (216 BC) and Leuthen (AD 1757), and firmly believed that protracted war was a 'luxury' that modern industrial states could ill afford. Schlieffen believed that France constituted the most immediate danger and, with this in mind, produced the panacea of a quick 'knockout' blow against France by a massive sweep through Dutch Limburg via Luxembourg and Belgium to Dunkirk and finally into the Seine basin. Such a bold concept followed the teachings of Clausewitz and Moltke concerning the need to concentrate all available forces at the decisive point. Moreover, it would lead to a strategic encirclement of the main enemy, strike him in the flank, bar his escape to the west, and crush his remaining forces between the hammer of the advancing armies around Paris and the anvil of the German troops in Lorraine. Thereafter, forces could be shuttled east to meet the slowly advancing Russian 'steamroller.' Schlieffen's thaumaturgic strategy, put to paper in December 1905 and refined up to December 1912, ruled out major Habsburg actions; the dual monarchy's fate would be decided not along the Bug but the Seine River.[23] German grand strategy, in short, was reduced to a single battle in the west.

This is not the place to rehash the so-called Schlieffen plan, or to address its later critics. Its main tenets are sufficiently well known. What remains is to examine how the plan was conceived, how extensively it was debated in German councils, the degree to which it was coordinated with naval strategy, and how it related not only to Austro-Hungarian plans but also to German potential.

On the whole, there was no attempt to integrate military strategy with the Viennese ally, nor was Schlieffen able to communicate with and influence the political leadership to seek coordinated, national goals. Quite the contrary! Schlieffen preferred to draft what he termed his 'purely military' plan in December 1905 almost in isolation. He did not consult Germany's Habsburg ally: in fact, Schlieffen so distrusted the Austro-Hungarian military that after 1896–7 he virtually ended all contacts with it. Only with this in mind can one understand how Franz Conrad von Hötzendorf, the Austro-Hungarian Chief of the General Staff, as late as the summer of 1908 had drawn up an operations plan that called for massive German thrusts against Russia.[24] Although he must have realized that any future conflagration would entail a coalition war, Schlieffen, as well as his successor, never once before 1914 discussed with Conrad the matter of a unified military command;[25] nor is it at all certain that the Schlieffen plan was ever taken up with other Prussian Army planners. We have seen in the preceding section that the War Ministry and the General Staff failed to coordinate manpower and material needs before the war. Gerhard Ritter asserts in addition that the War Ministry in Berlin was kept ignorant of Schlieffen's plans – which since 1897 had envisaged a march through neutral Belgium – probably until December 1912.[26]

And what about the navy? While the Admiralty Staff probably was aware of the planned violation of the neutrality of Belgium and the Netherlands by 1905, there seems to have been no direct planning between the two services. To be sure, General Staff and Admiralty Staff officers had been exchanged between 1900 and 1905, but both agencies had kept their operations plans secret from such visitors.[27] Schlieffen did not raise the possibility that the fleet might interrupt British cross-Channel troop transports either in 1905, or 1906, or 1912; in fact, his study of 1905 failed to mention the British at all, while the revision of 1906 simply stated that a potential British force of 100,000 men would be 'shut up' in Antwerp along with the regular Belgian Army.[28] His successor, Moltke, argued in January 1913 that the German fleet's expansion would probably force the British to land at Dunkirk rather than at Antwerp. But like Schlieffen, Moltke declined to raise the prospect of naval action against these forces. The navy, for its part, at times refused the General Staff's request to exchange intelligence data.[29]

On the other hand, it seems likely that three successive chancellors (Hohenlohe-Schillingsfürst, Bülow, and Bethmann Hollweg) as well as the Foreign Office's *éminence grise*, Friedrich von Holstein, were knowledgeable at least of the basic tenets of the Schlieffen plan.[30] Indeed, Holstein met regularly with Schlieffen and allowed the general routinely to read Foreign Office correspondence. We also know that Bethmann Hollweg on December 21, 1912, received a detailed memorandum concerning the planned

Westaufmarsch from the General Staff.[31] In fact, the considerations behind the Schlieffen plan lucidly reveal the difficult position of the chancellor in military matters. On the one hand, Bethmann Hollweg consistently argued that it was not his 'business' to comment on German strategy, yet on the other, he lamented that 'there never took place during my entire period in office a sort of war council at which politics were brought into the military for and against "considerations"'.[32] And Admiral von Tirpitz's bitter postwar complaint that the chancellor had failed to bring him in on the crucial stages of the Schlieffen plan and especially the proposed march through Belgium is misleading and unjust.[33] Such civilian handling of a 'purely military' operations plan was inconceivable in Imperial Germany. The fateful decentralization of army and navy commands, the division of military affairs into command and administrative domains, and the overcentralized role of the Imperial Supreme Commander – taken up in the first section – militated against coordinated planning.[34] Only under this system could a theoretical study by the Chief of the General Staff become dogma almost overnight and without thorough airing. In short, there was precious little consistency between strategic means and national political goals.

On another level, the Schlieffen plan was not in line with the military's force structure, size, or resources. The plan sought through a General Staff brain center to dictate not only the opening moves of the campaign, but also all subsequent operations of millions of men in a foreign land. Not only would this deny front commanders initiative, but the slightest disruption of communications threatened to unravel the overall timing of the advance. Jettisoned from the start was the elder Moltke's admonition that 'no plan of operations can look with any certainty beyond the first meeting with the major forces of the enemy.'[35]

Once underway, any number of factors could inhibit the offensive: the narrowness of the terrain could hinder the deployment of millions of men; enemy destruction of railroads, tunnels, and bridges could slow the advance; the all-decisive right wing, despite a projected seven-to-one advantage over the opponent, could be subject to flanking attacks; the giant fortress of Paris might not, as even Schlieffen conceded, be taken without major reinforcement of the field armies; and available rail lines favored the French and denied rapid resupply to the Germans.[36]

To be sure, the younger Moltke was well aware of some of the problems inherent in his predecessor's 'knockout' formula. In memoranda of 1911 and 1913, he sought to include not only the British (132,000 men) but also the Belgians (150,000 men) in his calculations. Politically, Moltke cancelled the proposed march through the Maastricht Appendix, preferring to keep the Netherlands as a neutral 'windpipe' for possible maritime succor. French expansion of forts in the south since 1905 prompted him to deploy major forces there, thus weakening the right wing to a ratio of only three to one.[37] In the end, the problem of Belgian neutrality remained insurmountable: not even Foreign Secretary Gottlieb von Jagow's plea in 1913 to alter the plan because an attack on Belgium was sure to bring the British into the war could alter General Staff thinking.[38] The emperor's exclusive *Ernennungsrecht*, which had resulted in Moltke's appointment against the advice of the Military Cabinet, the War Ministry, and the Chancery, thus became evident. Like General James Longstreet at Gettysburg, Helmuth von Moltke at the Marne executed a plan in which he had less than absolute confidence.

Was there a strategic alternative? The General Staff under Schlieffen had annually put together an operations plan for the east. There were apparent advantages. Fears concerning unreliable Polish elements, Ukrainian independence aspirations, and possible social revolution as a result of protracted national emergency might force the Russians to accept a decisive battle soon after the onset of hostilities. General Ludwig Beck in 1941 claimed that Germany should have assumed an 'active defensive' posture in both the east and the west in order 'to exploit the interior lines in accordance with a coordinated plan.' In the end, Moltke rejected an *Ostaufmarsch* because he feared that the Russians might, as against Napoleon, have refused battle and opted for a strategic retreat; hence, a German advance in the east would have been akin to a 'gust of air' (*Luftstoss*).[39] Moltke believed that the Franco-Russian military alliance of 1892 had rendered such an eastern strategy unrealistic, and he ordered his staff to halt contingency planning for the east in 1913.[40] Above all, any eastern strategy would have necessitated the closest planning between Berlin and Vienna.

To be sure, relations between army staffs in Berlin and Vienna improved dramatically under Moltke, with frequent exchanges of letters and personal meetings with Conrad von Hötzendorf, but neither staff was willing to coordinate planning fully. Each man pursued his own war plan doggedly. In May 1914, Conrad asked Moltke at Karlsbad what he intended to do in the event that he was denied a quick victory in the west. Moltke's evasive reply, 'Well, I will do what I can. We are not superior to the French,' laid bare the German dilemma after the failure at the Marne.[41] Finally, it is almost incomprehensible that the two allies made absolutely no concrete plans about how they would coordinate their war strategies. That the German military attaché in Vienna, Karl von Kageneck, on August 1, 1914, could cable Moltke's deputy, Georg von Waldersee, 'It is high time that the two general staffs consult now with absolute frankness with respect to mobilization, jump-off time, areas of assembly, and precise troop strength,' speaks volumes for the lack of planning between Berlin and Vienna before 1914.[42]

To sum up: Germany's strategy in 1914, as in 1941, was tied to a *Blitzkrieg* designed to overwhelm numerically superior adversaries. This 'short-war' concept reflected not only German personnel and armaments decisions before 1914, but also the semi-absolutist nature of Imperial Germany. Total mobilization of the nation had been ruled out as too dangerous to its social fabric – in Wilhelmian Germany as well as later in the Third Reich. Alone Schlieffen's strategy of gambling all on a single roll of the dice along the Seine River seemed to be consistent with the Reich's logistic infrastructure, its industrial-technical base, and its supplies of reserves and raw materials before 1914. A war of attrition had to be avoided at all costs. And when the great gamble failed at the Marne, all that remained was a so-called strategy of the diagonal, that is, one much like Frederick the Great's during the Seven Years War, to meet the enemy's thrusts as they developed with as much force and for as long as possible. Obviously, the risk entailed in the single strategic objective in the west was inconsistent with the stakes involved and the consequences of failure.

As early as 1898, General Alfred von Waldersee, the elder Moltke's successor as Chief of the General Staff, had mused: 'What does the navy propose to do if the army is defeated, be it in the west or in the east?'[43] It was a reasonable inquiry, especially since the junior service's budget grew from 20 per cent of the army's outlays in 1898 to 53 per cent by 1911.

Germany's naval strategy was as rigid though less complex than the Schlieffen plan: to annihilate the British fleet in the North Sea within about a hundred nautical miles of Helgoland Island. In his famous 'Memorandum IX' of 1894 – as well as in previous tracts of 1888 and 1891 – Tirpitz had banked all on a single decisive naval battle (*Entscheidungsschlacht*) in the south-central North Sea. Paul Kennedy states that Tirpitz 'saw his battlefleet in the form of a sharp knife, held gleaming and ready only a few inches away from the jugular vein of Germany's most likely enemy.'[44] Tirpitz equated sea power with battleships and placed the battle at the center of his strategy. 'In a war at sea, destruction of the enemy rather than territorial gain [*Geländegewinn*] is the only goal.'[45] While the admiral therewith recognized the primary objective of land strategy, he missed the lesson that control of major maritime arteries constitutes true sea power.

Sea power, in a word, consists of fleet and position: one is useless without the other.[46] Tirpitz either ignored or never grasped Alfred Thayer Mahan's unwritten presupposition that unfettered access to the world's oceans was the cardinal prerequisite for sea power. Given that Britain was Germany's primary potential opponent, a brief glance at the map would have confirmed the obvious: the British could bottle up the German fleet, based either on Kiel or Wilhelmshaven, in the North Sea if they chose to close the Straits of Dover and the waters between Scotland and Norway. Despite this, Tirpitz failed to develop an alternative strategy. Rear Admiral Magnus von Levetzow stated that at no time did Tirpitz ever assess the possibility of basing the fleet on French Channel and Atlantic ports in the event that the Schlieffen plan succeeded and France came under German control.[47]

It is symptomatic of the tangled web of German military organization that the navy's highest *administrative* officer, Tirpitz as head of the Navy Office, should have dictated *strategy* to the fleet. It was only the admiral's great influence with the emperor that permitted this state of affairs to exist. Tirpitz preferred organizational decentralization in order to prevent the emergence of a possible rival; he probably hoped that in time of war the Imperial Supreme Commander would entrust him with command of the fleet.

There was never a council to hammer out naval strategy. Like Schlieffen, Tirpitz imposed his personal views upon the service. The Admiralty Staff, which was charged with developing strategy at sea, was kept powerless by Tirpitz. There were no less than seven different heads of this organization between 1899 and 1915.[48] The fact of the matter is that Tirpitz feared the evolution of the Admiralty Staff into a central planning agency akin to the General Staff. In 1903, for example, he brusquely rejected Vice Admiral Wilhelm Büchsel's proposal to dispatch one *Admiralstab* officer per year for two months to the General Staff, and another naval officer to the army's fortress inspectorate.[49] Four years later, Tirpitz persuaded Wilhelm II to veto a proposal to send one-half of the Naval Academy graduates to the Admiralty Staff for three years, because he saw therein an undesirable enhancement of service with the Admiralty Staff.[50] He even objected for similar reasons to Admiralty Staff officers wearing distinctive pants stripes like their General Staff counterparts.

Likewise, army and navy failed to coordinate their strategies. Schlieffen had since 1892 realized that the German fleet was too small to assume the offensive in the North Sea, against either Britain *or* France, and would have to concentrate instead on maintaining the Baltic sea lanes. The Admiralty Staff in 1904 first broached the subject of war against Britain *and* France with Schlieffen; the general replied that in this case he would simply leave it up to the navy to do what it could.[51] Not satisfied, Admiral Büchsel that same month pushed for a strategy council of army and navy leaders, to be chaired by the emperor and to include the chancellor, in order to analyze in detail the case of war with the two western powers. His bold bid was rejected out of hand.[52] The lack of a central planning agency since 1897, when Wilhelm II had dissolved the Home Defense Commission, once more became painfully clear.

Again, it is indicative of the state of German planning that the Navy Office in June 1909 decided to base the fleet on Helgoland rather than in the Kattegat in case of war; neither the Admiralty Staff, nor the General Staff, nor even the fleet command was ever given the plan for its information, much less its critique.[53] Naval strategy was to remain with Tirpitz at the Leipzigerplatz.

To be sure, critics of the Tirpitzean master plan were not lacking. As early as 1908, Vice Admiral Friedrich von Baudissin of the Admiralty Staff had warned that the British might not, as Tirpitz confidently predicted, descend into the Helgoland Bight at the outbreak of war. One year later, Baudissin's successor, Admiral Max von Fischel, raised the central issue of naval strategy: 'We are fighting for access to the ocean, whose entrances on that side of the North Sea are in England's hands.' Fischel implied that only an aggressive German sortie could turn the tide: 'We are therefore basically the attacker, who is disputing the enemy's possessions.'[54] Moreover, others argued that Tirpitz was incorrect in concentrating on battleships at the expense of overseas cruisers and submarines. Such critics (Galster, Maltzahn, Persius, and Schleinitz) were relegated to the ranks of the retired – much like the army's 'maneuver victims.' Nor did Tirpitz tolerate civilian critics of naval strategy as did Britain (Brassey, Corbett, Dilke, Jane, and White).

Not even the British decision of 1912 to replace the 'close' blockade with a looser 'observation' blockade, nor the final turn in early 1914 to the 'distant' blockade, altered Tirpitz's strategy. He merely changed his reasoning, arguing that national character, pride, tradition, and history would never permit the Royal Navy to eschew a 'second Trafalgar.' The British would simply have to come. His question in May 1914 to the fleet chief, Vice Admiral Friedrich von Ingenohl, 'What will you do if they do not come?,'[55] speaks volumes for the failure of Tirpitz's maritime strategy. It was the counterpart to Conrad's inquiry to Moltke in May 1914 concerning Germany's options in case of failure to defeat the French armies quickly.

Yet, Tirpitz carried the day on August 5, 1914: Operations Order No. 1 sent the fleet out of Wilhelmshaven with decks cleared for action (*klarschiff zum Gefecht*) in order to repel an attack by the entire British Grand Fleet.[56] In the meantime, Britain safely shuttled eight army divisions across the Channel to France. In fact, the Royal Navy's refusal in 1914 to play the role accorded it by Tirpitz effectively ended naval *strategy* for Germany during the First World War. Subsequent 'tip-and-run' operations by the fleet against the British Isles, unrestricted submarine warfare, and torpedo-boat raids into the Baltic Sea were but *ad hoc* tactical maneuvers designed to overcome the strategic impasse at sea. The North Sea became a 'dead sea' owing to the British distant blockade. Admiral John Jellicoe chose not to risk losing the war in a single day, and the chance meeting of the two battlefleets at Jutland in May–June 1916 failed to alter the strategic balance of the naval war. The Germans, like the French after Trafalgar, merely turned the *guerre de course* out of a sense of frustration.[57]

The basic flaw in Tirpitz's maritime strategy was laid bare in the summer of 1915 by Lieutenant Commander Wolfgang Wegener, an Admiralty Staff officer with the High Sea Fleet. In a memorandum that was circulated to most naval commands, Wegener challenged Tirpitz's notion that the destruction of enemy forces was the primary objective at sea; rather, it was 'to a certain degree an incidental goal.' Above all, Wegener realized that Britain's maritime geographical position as well as its crushing superiority in floating material effectively denied the Reich sea power. Territorial expansion on a grand scale was required in order to outflank Britain: the Flanders coast as well as the French Channel ports; Denmark and the Skagerrak; the Faeroe Islands; and ultimately, the Portuguese Atlantic islands, the Azores, and the Cape Verde Islands.[58] Here, in a nutshell, was maritime *strategy*. Wegener's memorandum was basically endorsed in April 1917 by Rear Admiral Adolf von Trotha, the fleet's chief of operations, and partially accounted for the various contingency plans developed at about the same time against especially Denmark (Case J) and Norway (Case N). In short, there developed a growing awareness that access to the Atlantic Ocean alone could provide sea power.[59]

In brief: Germany was denied strategic effectiveness. Apart from the blatantly obvious, namely, losing the war, neither admirals nor generals achieved their strategic objectives: destruction of the British fleet and the French armies. Neither army nor navy coordinated its strategy with the other service. Neither apparently sought out the political leadership in order to bring foreign policy in line with military objectives. Neither Schlieffen nor Tirpitz involved other service agencies in their deliberations. Neither coordinated policy with the Habsburg ally. The plans of both Schlieffen and Tirpitz soon became dogma, inviolate and unchallengeable. Both ignored the east in favor of the west. Both sought total annihilation of the enemy. Both experienced strategic bankruptcy early in 1914.

Operational Effectiveness

> A strategy of attrition will not do if the maintenance of millions [of men] requires billions [of marks].[60]
>
> Alfred von Schlieffen, 1909

The greatest single military operation of the war, designed to achieve by combat a strategic objective within a theater of the war, was the German 'wheel' through Belgium and northern France in 1914. It revealed the logistic and technological problems that were to plague the Reich's land forces throughout the war. We have already seen that the operational methods of the army were not integrated with those of the navy, and that the plan was neither mobile nor flexible at the operational level. In addition, the plan placed German weakness (lack of motor transport) against enemy strength (interior rail lines). It remains to be seen whether the plan was consistent with strategic objectives as well as with the technology available, and whether it took account of existing supply, communications, and transport.

In a nutshell, the German Army in 1914 prepared for a traditional advance on foot and horse in a campaign that demanded mechanization and mobility. Even Moltke's 'small wheel' turn-in around Brussels, which ran counter to Schlieffen's strategic objective, still meant that the troops would have to march 300 miles to the Marne. Each of the roughly 30 corps would consume about 130 tons of food and fodder per day, occupy nearly 20 miles of road, and require a full day to resupply – while standing still! Indeed, General Alexander von Kluck's First Army required 2 million pounds of fodder per day for its 84,000 horses. Moreover, ammunition tables were 40 years old, with the result that inadequate transport was available for the quantities of guns and shells that needed to be moved across Belgium. Destruction of vital rail links by the Belgians fully taxed all of the 26,000 repairmen of the German Army at the onset of hostilities. The upshot was that on the eve of the Battle of the Marne, key railheads for the German First, Second, and Third Armies were between 85 and 105 miles behind the front. Schlieffen's admonition that the troops live off the land and his 'ostrich-like refusal' to address the 'technical side' of his plan guaranteed exhaustion rather than victory. As Martin van Creveld put it, 'the sheer size and weight of the German Army in 1914 proved wholly out of proportion to the means of tactical transportation at its disposal.'[61]

Moreover, what Clausewitz termed 'friction of war' soon set in. Troops simply could not sustain an advance of 15 miles per day for three weeks without pause and defeat two major enemies. Field kitchens fell behind. Horses slowed owing to utter exhaustion. Motor transport broke down. The horse-drawn artillery lagged ever farther behind the advancing infantry. By September 4, both the First and the Third armies reported the exhaustion of their troops. Finally, the German force size was inadequate for the great 'shoulder-to-shoulder' sweep from Verdun to Dunkirk and onto Paris; gaps in the line had to appear, and eventually did so between the First and Second armies.[62]

Problems raised in the preceding section were fully revealed in August–September 1914. Overcentralization of staff planning brought about Colonel

Richard Hentsch's hasty tour of the front and his momentous decision on September 9 to retreat behind the Marne. Placement of General Staff headquarters far behind the advancing armies, first at Koblenz and then at Luxembourg, had put Moltke out of reach of his commanders. Reliable communications to army commanders were nonexistent; no exchange of information or orders took place between Moltke and his army leaders from September 5 to 9. Moreover, the fateful placement of two armies in Lorraine, the strategically inadvisable assault against Toul-Epinal in the south, and the untimely transfer of two army corps from the right wing to the east at the decisive stage of the battle effectively denied the Germans superior strength at the decisive point.[63] The sacking in 1914 in the west of thirty-three generals, including two army commanders, fully attests to the failure of Germany's land strategy.[64]

If anything, the demand for transport and resupply only increased during the great *Materialschlachten* of 1916 and 1917. Colonel Albrecht von Thaer noted in April 1917 that his army group of 140,000 men *daily* expended 6 or 7 train loads of heavy shells – an amount that required no less than 26,000 horses just to haul it the 50 to 70 kilometers from the railhead to the front.[65] This was a war of machines and material that Germany had neither envisioned nor prepared for. Especially after the United States entered the war in April 1917, it pitted the enemies' strength against the Reich's weakness.

Experiences at other fronts corroborated these findings. The breakthrough at Caporetto in October 1917, which the Germans delivered in rain and snow after only a brief artillery and gas bombardment, could not be fully exploited owing to the lack of motor transport and armored vehicles. 'Friction' again set in as communication and supply lines quickly fell behind the troops rushing across the Tagliamento. And finally, foreshadowing events in France the next spring, German troops at Caporetto raided captured supply depots rather than pursuing the enemy.[66]

At no time did Germany erase the material disadvantage in the west. Lack of standardization among truck producers (Benz, Daimler, Hansa-Lloyd, Büssing, and Opel) kept production well below that of a single Italian manufacturer, Fiat. German motor transport in the west in 1918, set at about 30,000 vehicles that ran mostly on steel or wooden tires, faced an Allied fleet of roughly 100,000 trucks, mostly on rubber tires. Attempts to offset this by laying light (60 cm) rail lines to the front came too late and brought little relief. Horses by then were not available in sufficient numbers to haul even heavy machine guns or light trench mortars.[67] Against the Allies' 800 tanks, the Reich never managed to produce an effective counterpart: neither the initial use of 200 20-mm anti-aircraft guns nor the development of a special 13-mm anti-tank gun proved sufficient. In fact, the Reich had given the tank a low priority until 1918, and even then could only produce about 20 new A7V tanks. The latter proved so defective that the series was scrapped and the available frames used for trucks. The American invention of caterpillar tracks had not found favor with the General Staff, which as late as 1918 still thought tanks 'more suitable as armored ammunition carriers than as potential armored and mobile field batteries or nests of machine guns.' In short, the Germans ignored technical innovation and mass production in favor of the hallowed concept of 'bravery in battle.'[68] In the process, they denied themselves mobility and flexibility at the operational level.

How, then, did the General Staff attempt to enhance operational effectiveness after the debacle at the Marne? To be sure, there was no change in the strategic military objective. General von Falkenhayn, in line with the German Field Regulations of 1906, opted not only to hold every inch of territory gained, but also to reconquer every inch lost, regardless of the cost.[69] Moreover, he declined to shift the fulcrum of the war to the east and perhaps deal the Russians a decisive blow on both sides of the Vistula River. Instead he expended great quantities of men and material in a war of attrition in Flanders. Again, early in 1916, Falkenhayn dismissed operations in Russia as 'adventures'; the decision would have to come before Verdun, where he hoped 'to deal the enemy a severe blow at a decisive point.'[70] There was no clear operational goal. Even the official German history of the war states that operations had been fully abandoned in favor of tactics. The failure to 'bleed the enemy white' and the resulting German losses – 282,000 at Verdun, 500,000 at the Somme, and 350,000 in the east in 1916 – prompted the army to invent the new term *abgekämpft* (exhausted) for its troops.[71] It was a situation that cost Falkenhayn his position later that year.

The Third Army Supreme Command (OHL) of Erich Ludendorff and Paul von Hindenburg, realizing that 'the core of the old infantry still trained in peacetime had been bled to death' in 1916, at once set out to reassess the war and to incorporate intelligence reports along with battle experience into a new system of strategic defense.[72] Already in January 1915 at Soissons, Colonel Hans von Seeckt had revised operational procedures: defensive artillery and infantry pinned down the attacking enemy, thereby preventing his resupply and reinforcement, and morally destroying the assault; thereafter, German infantry counterattacked a demoralized adversary.[73] Four months later, the Germans captured a French document at La Ville-aus-Bois detailing a new elastic defense-in-depth consisting not of a rigid line but rather of an outpost zone, a battle zone, and a rearward zone. The new defense aimed at forcing the enemy to expend himself against several echelons of forces arranged in depth; counterattack infantry units would supply the resiliency or elasticity of the system. Moreover, units would deploy on reverse slopes wherever possible; artillery would be incorporated into the defense and commanded at the divisional level; and all combat arms would be fully integrated into the defense units. In December 1916, a Bavarian captain, Hermann Geyer, published these findings in 'The Principles of Command for the Defensive Battle in Position Warfare.' Timothy Lupfer has argued that the new method resulted from a collective General Staff effort, headed by colonels Max Bauer and Fritz von Lossberg, Major Georg Wetzell, and Geyer.[74] In addition, Colonel Georg Bruchmüller in the east contributed the notion of an accurate creeping artillery barrage (*Feuerwalze*) to the German operational doctrine; it was later incorporated into the Western Front as well. In place of prolonged artillery bombardments, which denied the attacker the element of surprise, Bruchmüller at Tarnopol in the summer of 1916 had surprised the Russians with a hurricane-like brief bombardment that pitted accurate artillery fire against previously identified targets. Bruchmüller used aerial photographs to select the targets and a 'highly centralized' firing command instructed each battery throughout the bombardment.[75] Finally, to enhance organizational effectiveness, the Germans in September 1916 officially revamped their forces into army groups.

The new defensive operations were consistent with the technology available. The Germans had been quick in 1914 to introduce trenches with parallels, saps, communication posts, dug-outs, barbed wire, sand bags, and camouflage. Soon to be added were steel-cored bullets designed to pierce parapets and sand bags as well as incendiary bullets for use against observation balloons. Next came hand grenades and, at Malancourt forest in February 1915, flamethrowers. Steel helmets for the infantry appeared in the autumn of 1916, and trench mortars followed early in 1917.[76] Asphyxiating gas was tried at Langemarck on April 22, 1915, by Fritz Haber with the Fourth Army; a lack of infantry reserves resulted in a complete failure to utilize this technological innovation.[77] The greatest tool of the war, of course, was the machine gun. Especially the introduction early in 1917 of the light 'MG 08–15' at the rate of eighteen per regiment – later raised by Ludendorff to thirty-six – greatly enhanced fire power. Overall, the number of machine gun companies rose from 323 with six guns each in 1914, to 2,500 with twelve guns each in 1918.[78]

Ludendorff also tried to integrate the air arm into his forces. In June 1917, he ordered monthly production of 2,000 aircraft and 2,500 motors for the following year. It was an unrealistic figure; over the four years of the war, Germany managed to build only 47,637 airplanes of more than 150 different types. Operationally, the Germans eschewed bomber production in favor of pursuit planes (44 per cent) and observation planes (49 per cent). German intelligence managed to capture and adapt the French (Roland Garros) method of having the machine gun synchronized with the propeller in 1915. But generally speaking, the Germans preferred to use their aircraft in squadrons of covering and fighter planes, flying low, and supporting the infantry's advance or strafing enemy positions. The navy, for its part, remained firmly wedded to the dirigible as the 'eyes of the fleet.'[79]

The new defensive principles and machines were combined early in 1917 in the so-called Hindenburg or Siegfried line.[80] After evacuating the Noyon salient (Operation *Alberich*), the Germans dug in at their new positions: a frontal zone 8,000 yards deep, with an outpost trench on the skyline, followed 600 yards back by the main line of defense consisting of three trench lines. The men were underground and wire entanglements 100 yards deep were placed in front of the trenches, while concrete emplacements housed the machine guns both before and behind the trenches. The potential battle zone was hidden from the enemy wherever possible on reverse slopes 1,500 to 3,000 yards behind the first trench line, and the entire zone was dominated by new artillery placements.[81]

Thus Ludendorff and his advisors had drastically reevaluated the nature of warfare. Emphasis now lay, as the official German history put it, on 'war machines' rather than on 'men and horses.'[82] Soldiers became the 'workers' of war (Ernst Jünger). The principle of territorial gain yielded to that of available reserves of men and material *vis-à-vis* those of the enemy. Technological enhancement (material-intensive armament) triumphed. And while the attack remained a distant 'future ideal,' for the moment accent was placed upon 'superior deployment in the defensive battle.' General Wilhelm Groener later termed the withdrawal to the Siegfried line as 'masterful' and as Ludendorff's 'greatest achievement.'[83]

But the enhanced operational effectiveness of the army was purchased at a price. The General Staff now became *de facto* if not *de jure* the nerve center of the entire German war effort. It attempted, especially under Ludendorff and Bauer, nothing less than the total mobilization of Germany in the firm belief that in time of war the army, not the government, represented the nation. On the last day of August 1916, Hindenburg presented the Prussian War Ministry utterly Utopian goals for enhanced war production – the so-called Hindenburg Program – which called for doubling the production of ammunition and heavy artillery, and tripling that of machine guns within six months. Michael Geyer has argued that this 'symbiosis between military and industry' effectively removed control over wartime production from the War Ministry and placed it with industry.[84]

While the Chancellor as well as the war minister had serious reservations about the feasibility of the Hindenburg Program, the Army Supreme Command in October created a special Weapons and Munitions Procurement Office ('Wumba') – a direct copy of the British Ministry of Munitions under David Lloyd George. When this office failed to meet its expectations, the Army Supreme Command in November replaced it with a 'War Office' under General Groener within the Prussian War Ministry to centralize in one office the entire war effort. Moreover, in December 1916, it promulgated the so-called Auxiliary Service Law, designed to rally all able-bodied males between the ages of 15 and 60 to the war effort; females were exempted.[85] Finally, the army initiated the so-called patriotic instruction (*Vaterländischer Unterricht*) in July 1917 in an attempt to uplift the morale of both the fighting troops and the home front.[86] In the end, these measures served mainly to cement the growing power of the Army Supreme Command, for their military effectiveness was minimal.[87]

And yet, the new central position of the Army Supreme Command adversely affected operational effectiveness over time. Quite apart from Ludendorff's attempts to usurp the powers of the chancellor and the Foreign Office especially in the matter of German war aims – which go beyond the scope of this paper – there was a growing inclination on the part of the Army Supreme Command to gather all decisions into its own hands.[88] The staff system became rigid and dogmatic. Army commanders were ignored as their staff officers reported directly to Ludendorff. The telephones hummed constantly to all units with orders and counter-orders. Staff chiefs were changed according to Ludendorff's whims: in 1918, the Ninth Army received three different staff chiefs in as many weeks. A bureaucratic 'war of ink' threatened to engulf army commanders. In the process, the Imperial Supreme Commander was shunted aside by the General Staff; decrees were issued under Hindenburg's name, thereby further minimizing Wilhelm's role. Crown Prince Rupprecht lamented Ludendorff's penchant 'to decide all details himself.'[89] In the end, Ludendorff wore himself out as he sought 'to combine everything in his person: not only the conduct of all military operations, but also domestic as well as foreign policies, the national food supply, raw materials acquisition, and transportation.' The general's complete exhaustion came as little surprise to many members of his staff.[90]

Ludendorff also placed considerable hope in the German navy. By and large, it was denied operational effectiveness during the First World War. Its decision in August 1914 not to attempt to interdict British cross-Channel shipping to France combined with the British 'distant' blockade to reduce the High Sea Fleet to a mere 'fleet-in-being.' It spent much of the war in port. The emperor as well as some of his naval paladins even sought to preserve the fleet as a bargaining chip to be used at a future peace conference.[91] 'Tip-and-run' operations against the eastern coast of the British Isles in December 1914, January 1915, and April, August, and October 1916, were undertaken in the hope that the British would disperse their fleet among the various ports, where the Germans might surprise and annihilate inferior units. Admiral Jellicoe's concentration of the Grand Fleet at Scapa Flow – with David Beatty's battlecruisers in the Firth of Forth – effectively negated such hopes. The German sortie into the Skagerrak in May–June 1916 has previously been taken up; a subsequent raid in April 1918 to the coast of Norway brought only the breakdown of the *Moltke*. Indeed, it is interesting to note that the situation with regard to army–navy cooperation in the spring of 1918 was similar to that of August 1914: on March 21, as the army launched its great final offensive in France, the navy remained idle – with the exception of a minor torpedo-boat raid that morning against Dunkirk, Bray-Dunes, and La Panne.[92] Once more, Britain was permitted to shuttle large quantities of men and supplies across the Channel with impunity in order to bolster General Douglas Haig's defense. Worse yet, a desperate 'suicide sortie' (Operations Plan No. 19) planned in October 1918 against the combined Anglo-American surface fleets not only died in port but was the signal for the revolution.[93]

Moreover, neither the intelligence nor the logistics of these operations were planned particularly well. The German navy's reliance upon dirigibles left the fleet constantly at the mercy of fog, wind, sleet, and snow, with regard to reconnaissance. Shore command never appreciated that the British not only routinely intercepted their signals to the fleet, but that they expeditiously deciphered them in Room 40 at the Admiralty, with the result that the Grand Fleet was often out to sea before the High Sea Fleet had hoisted anchors.[94] Both in the summer of 1917 and in October 1918, the German fleet command grossly miscalculated the depressed morale of the sailors; the first instance resulted in food riots, the second in open rebellion.[95]

Operations in the Baltic Sea were of secondary importance, given that the Russian fleet remained in port and thus never threatened deliveries of Swedish iron ore to Germany. A raid into the Baltic in October 1917 by two squadrons of the High Sea Fleet was a classic case of overkill, designed in the main to raise the morale of the crews after the recent unrest.[96]

As stated in the preceding section, after January 1917 the Reich sought operational effectiveness primarily from its submarine force. The political risk – bringing the United States into the shooting war – was out of proportion to the mental gymnastics that promised victory over Britain in six months if an average of 600,000 tons per month of shipping could be destroyed, a 'final and irreplaceable loss.'[97] It was also based upon insufficient force. Given Tirpitz's aversion to submarine building and Krupp's virtual prewar monopoly over their development, it is little wonder that early in 1915 the Reich possessed a mere twenty-eight units, of which fully one-half were elderly petrol boats. By January 1917, when the decision for unrestricted submarine warfare was made at Pless, the Reich had about a hundred U-boats available. If one keeps in mind that the navy throughout 1917 never managed to keep more than one-third of these boats on patrol off the British Isles – the rest were either en route to stations, heading home, or undergoing refit and repair – then it is not unfair to state that resources were grossly out of proportion to expectations.[98]

The submarine flotillas did not appreciate greatly in strength either. Between January 1917 and January 1918, the entire force gained only about a dozen units; in the interim, eighty-seven boats had been built and seventy-eight lost. Organization was diffused among High Sea Fleet, Admiralty Staff, front commands, and even the Austro-Hungarian ally. No systematic procedure for managing construction was devised until December 1917 (U-Boat Office), when the campaign had failed. And a highly publicized effort in September 1918 to increase submarine production from thirteen per month to thirty-six per month by late 1919 was largely a tonic designed to uplift sagging morale. Touted as the Scheer Program – an obvious parallel to the army's Hindenburg Program – it failed to address pressing problems such as procurement of raw materials, labor, housing, and food for the workers, or trained crews for the new boats.[99]

Finally, it should not be overlooked that the submarine offensive greatly strained the internal cohesion of the naval officer corps. Many of the best junior officers transferred from the idle fleet to the U-boats, all too often to be replaced with cadets or reservists. In addition, this 'war of lieutenants' troubled senior officers as submarines required few flag-rank officers. In the very month that Germany decided to risk all on the U-boat gamble, Admiral Eduard von Capelle, Tirpitz's successor at the Navy Office, warned that emphasis on submarine building would endanger the long-term capital-ship program and called for the creation of a special 'submarine cemetery' after the war.[100] Three months later, he asked the Reichstag to cogitate upon 'how organization and promotion will function in a navy which has replaced its capital ships with dirigibles and submarines.'[101] This was a portent of a similar rift between the proponents of *Grosskrieg* and those of *Kleinkrieg* that would trouble the Germany navy by 1942–3.

Tactical Effectiveness

> I object to the word 'operation.' We will punch a hole into [their line]. For the rest, we shall see. We also did it this way in Russia![102]
>
> Erich Ludendorff, spring 1918

Some military historians and most Ludendorff admirers will object to handling the great *Michael* offensives in France in the spring of 1918 under the rubric 'tactics.' Yet, these assaults were dominated by tactical rather than operational – much less strategic – considerations.[103] Moreover, Ludendorff was guided in his decision more by political goals (war aims) than by purely military considerations. Although the new German tactical system devised late in 1917 was consistent with its training methods and emphasized the total integration of all combat arms (save the tank and motor transport), it was not consistent with its support capabilities and did not emphasize surprise in the attack. Above all, it was not consistent in evaluating unit morale and cohesion.

It should be noted first and foremost that the solipsistic Ludendorff reached the decision to gamble on a strategic offensive rather than to remain with the strategic defensive in the west solely by himself as early as April 1917, and that he defended his decision against all critics from October 1917 through the winter of 1917–18.[104] As had been the case with the Schlieffen plan, there was never a basic discussion of German strategy for 1918 among General Staff, emperor, chancellor, and the Austro-Hungarian ally (which deployed four divisions in the west in 1918).[105] In fact, Ludendorff and his staff denuded especially the southeastern front of troops, with the result that the German presence in Turkey – which had been of minimal *overall* importance throughout the war – was virtually curtailed.[106] On the other hand, Ludendorff's megalomania over the issue of the vast postwar annexations in the east, which he felt alone could uphold the Prussian-German monarchy, meant that thirty-four German divisions remained in Russia at the height of *Michael*![107] Indeed, his tart comment to a doubting Colonel Albrecht von Thaer in the spring of 1918, 'What is the purpose of your croaking? . . . Am I now to conclude peace at any price?,' reveals much about the general's political reasoning behind *Michael*.[108]

In terms of men and materials, both sides could muster about 5 million men each in the west in March 1918. Of course, the growing American presence in France – up about 1 million men between April and July 1918 – would work against a prolonged campaign. Moreover, Germany was outnumbered in 'war machines' by the Allied and Associated Powers: 14,000 to 18,500 artillery pieces, 3,670 to 4,500 aircraft, and 10 to 800 armored vehicles.

Ludendorff and his paladins sought to offset this material disadvantage with superior training and tactics. Timothy Lupfer has suggested that the German Army early in 1918 developed one of the most modern operational concepts for land warfare.[109] Once again, the new tactics came about as a result of past experience, astute intelligence gathering, and detailed collective staff work, especially by Captain Geyer, the principal author in January 1918 of the treatise 'The Attack in Position Warfare.'

In the early summer of 1916, the Germans had captured a French document entitled 'The Attack in Trench Warfare.' Unlike the British, they translated it; unlike the French, they adopted it. Its author, Captain André Laffargue, called for new infiltration tactics by *groupes de tirailleurs* for an in-depth attack designed to disrupt the enemy, to destroy only his main centers of resistance, and to infiltrate his defensive zone as deeply as possible. Special assault troops would lead the charge. Artillery bombardment would be sudden and cover the full depth of the field.[110] Indeed, the Germans first practiced principles similar to these at Riga in the east in September 1917, at Caporetto in October 1917, and at Cambrai in November 1917. Their greatest application, however, would come in France in March 1918.

The major German contribution to the new assault tactics – which combined a hurricane-like bombardment, a rapid assault spearheaded by troops armed with semi-automatic weapons, and supporting reserve to clear up centers of bypassed resistance – was the development and training of *Stosstrupps*. These 'storm troops' of ten- or eleven-man units armed with light machine guns, trench mortars, grenades, and flamethrowers, had first appeared in August 1915 under Captain Willy Rohr; both Colonel Bauer and General von Falkenhayn had been impressed with their effectiveness, and Ludendorff began to organize them in October 1916 up to battalion strength. Their task was to infiltrate (*durchfressen*) enemy lines as rapidly as possible, and to exploit any advantage gained thereby. Schlieffen's encirclement panacea was thus effectively shelved in favor of infiltration tactics.[111]

Above all, Ludendorff placed great emphasis upon retraining both officers and men. As early as September 1916, he had started one-month instruction courses for company and battery commanders in the art of the elastic defense-in-depth. These *Feld-Kriegsschulen* were initially held just behind the front, but early in 1917 they moved to more permanent quarters in Germany. While it is not possible to gauge how many combatants attended the courses, it is estimated that Army Group Crown Prince Wilhelm alone sent 100 officers and 100 noncommissioned officers through the five- to six-week courses late in 1916.[112]

By February 1917, special training courses for General Staff officers and front commanders were offered at Solesmes, with eighty officers above the rank of regimental commander attending the first class. The need to train especially company commanders and staff officers who had not attended the *Kriegsakademie* in peacetime brought further three-week courses of instruction at new training centers at Sedan and Valenciennes. No less than nine special artillery schools offered instruction in Colonel Bruchmüller's hurricane-like artillery bombardment.[113] Finally, Ludendorff organized the best available units into about seventy attack divisions (*Mob. Divisionen*) for the express purpose of breaching the enemy line according to the treatise 'The Attack in Position Warfare.' After Christmas 1917, the *Mob. Divisionen* were pulled out of the line, given special three- to four-week instruction at Sedan and Valenciennes, and ordered out on maneuvers to practice the new tactics. Officers again were the first to undergo retraining. Generally speaking, the new attack divisions received the best equipment, but their mobility was curtailed by the fact that only one-half of the machine gun units were horse-drawn owing to a lack of animals.[114] Not surprisingly, the regular and more poorly equipped *Stellungsdivisionen* resented the preferential treatment given the attack divisions.[115] At Mons it was decided on November 11, 1917, to launch the great offensive in France early in 1918. General Max Hoffmann, the German commander in the east, noted that Ludendorff's tactics were 'to test various positions' in the west 'one after another in order to ascertain where one encountered the enemy's weakness,' against which 'one would have to press the attack with all possible force.'[116]

The *Michael* offensives began on March 21, 1918, with 52 attack divisions and 11 *Stellungsdivisionen*, 6,263 guns, and 2,840 ammunition trains.[117] After some spectacular initial gains – which, incidentally, bloodied virtually every *Mob. Division* and lengthened the German front by 90 to 150 kilometers – the assaults ground to a halt. Allied counterattacks on July 18 at Villers-Cotterêts, spearheaded by the new light Renault, Berliet, and Schneider tanks, turned the tide in the war – despite the nearly 50 per cent losses suffered by the tanks. Thereafter, German strategy was reduced to one of evasion.[118]

How does one account for this failure of the most advanced assault tactics devised during the First World War? One obvious cause was that Ludendorff had gravely underestimated enemy strength. In addition, simple fatigue set in: especially the reserves were exhausted, and great disappointment came quickly after *Michael* had failed to end the war.[119] Numerous units abandoned the attack in order to raid plentiful Allied food and wine depots.[120] Others mutinied and greeted reserves coming up to the front with cries of 'strike breakers.'[121] Still others deserted either en route from the east, at home, or at the front.[122] The army had obviously reached the end of its physical and psychological capacities – as had Ludendorff, although he refused to admit it, and instead retreated into his world of petty staff work, mentally broken.[123] But his staff realized that the last reserve of 637,000 men (those born in 1899–1900) was insufficient to pursue the war.[124]

In addition, lack of sufficient technology had hampered the assault. The German official history of the war attributes failure to lack of anti-tank weapons, lack of tanks, lack of trucks, and lack of railroads to the front – despite the innovative use of wooden travelways for artillery.[125] The dearth of motor transport not only slowed the advance, but also forced many *Mob. Divisionen* to leave their heavy machine guns and light mortars behind. Communications were rapidly outstripped, and many attack divisions waited at the front for orders that never came; the rigid staff system thus proved a hindrance to mobile warfare.[126]

Above all, the German Army's tactical system was consistent neither with its strategic objective nor with its operational concept. Ludendorff's decision to probe the enemy line repeatedly for signs of weakness led to the wearing down of both the attack divisions and their supply systems. His hasty decision on March 29 to switch the main attack from the British to the French – which reminded one staff officer of the debacle at the Marne in 1914 – brought lack of direction to the front.[127] Moreover, Ludendorff had from the start jettisoned the element of surprise: on January 30, 1918, he had informed General Hermann von Kuhl that he considered 'a painstaking preparation of the attack more important than its surprising execution.'[128]

The memoirs of several senior German officers attest to these observations. General Groener later claimed that *Michael* violated the basic tenet of strategy to be strong at the decisive point, which in this case, would have been the right wing. Groener instead spoke of an 'unraveled operation,' one that had turned 'the tactical victory . . . into a strategic defeat.' Ludendorff, he asserted, had pursued 'success for the sake of success, without [possessing] a clear operational goal.'[129] Crown Prince Rupprecht went so far as to describe the early successes of *Michael* as 'to a degree Pyrrhic victories.'[130] Ludendorff's plan simply to punch a hole into the enemy lines in effect meant that tactics would have to pave the way for operational effectiveness, which in turn *might* lead to strategic results. Even the emperor noted in February that *Michael* would bring no 'operational breakthrough,' but rather a series of attacks designed to 'damage' the enemy.[131] In the end, Rupprecht attributed to the General Staff an obsession with gaining ground: 'I get the impression as if the OHL is living from hand to mouth without acknowledging definite operational designs.' By November, he spoke of Germany's 'military bankruptcy.'[132]

Colonel Wilhelm Ritter von Leeb concurred. In March 1918, he accused Ludendorff of tailoring his tactics 'to the size of territorial gain, rather than according to operational' effectiveness: 'According to Ludendorff, we are to conduct *operations* wherever a tactical victory has been achieved; in other words, the OHL utterly lacks a definite plan of operations.' One month later, he again lamented the lack of overall direction: 'We had absolutely no operational goal! That was the trouble.'[133] Colonel von Lossberg was of similar opinion and accused Ludendorff of seeking 'operational breakthroughs' wherever 'tactical breakthroughs' had been achieved.[134] Later, Colonel von Thaer added his name to the list of critics, seeing in *Michael* 'our last card,' and generally 'little in the way of strategy.'[135]

Yet, in all fairness, it should not be overlooked that the German tactical accomplishments of 1918 were quite remarkable, especially given the horrendous loss of trained officers and men in the *Materialschlachten* of 1916 and 1917. The new tactics pitted German strengths (infiltration and pursuit) especially against British weaknesses (heavily manned forward lines of trenches). However, against the French elastic defense – especially in the *Friedenssturm* against Rheims – these tactics brought little gain owing to lack of mobility and flexibility. In the end, Ludendorff had to realize that Clausewitz had been correct in attributing the advantage to the defender – in the case of trench warfare, by a ratio perhaps as high as six to one.[136] Attrition worked to the advantage of the Allies, not to that of the Reich. It was a lesson that Berlin's U-boat force also had to learn in 1917 and 1918.

The euphoria over early sinkings in the submarine offensive in the waters surrounding the British Isles – 841,118 tons in April 1917 – dissipated by late summer 1917, when the U-boats bagged only about 350,000 tons per month. This decline notwithstanding, Admiral Henning von Holtzendorff, Chief of the Admiralty Staff, confidently predicted victory over 'perfidious Albion' before the end of October 1917, which drew from Crown Prince Rupprecht the caustic comment: 'The gentlemen of the navy are dangerous optimists.'[137]

In fact, the submarine offensive proved to be consistent neither with the strategic objective (throttling Britain's maritime support system) nor with the operational concept (destruction of isolated ships bound for Britain by isolated U-boats). The Allies, urged on by Prime Minister David Lloyd George (and President Woodrow Wilson) had in May 1917 experimented with convoying shipping and escorting the convoys with fast surface vessels.

By 1918, the loss rate among convoys had fallen to 0.98 per cent, and that of submarines had risen to 7.4 per cent. As a result, the Germans desperately sought to upgrade their tactical system. U-boat crews were trained in the art of attacking convoys at Eckernförde. Submarines were ordered to concentrate on convoys near shore where the escorts generally left them. The egress and return of the undersea craft were protected by units of the High Sea Fleet. And the U-boat force attempted to improve its intelligence gathering with regard to ship arrivals and departures.[138]

The Germans also attempted to make use of the latest communications technology; as wireless range increased to almost 1,000 nautical miles in 1918, the Admiralty Staff toyed with the notion of using the larger U-cruisers as information stations off Britain to coordinate attacks on convoys. More specifically, the idea of hunting convoys with 'packs' of submarines surfaced in 1916, and received support from Wilhelm II by June–July 1917.[139] The leader of U-boats, Captain Andreas Michelsen, tried throughout 1917 and 1918 to gain permission to experiment with 'wolf packs,' but Holtzendorff remained adamant in his belief that by covering all approaches to Britain, he would force the enemy convoys to disperse their escort craft.[140] Karl Dönitz later claimed that there was not one successful joint operation of even two U-boats during the First World War; he regarded the future *Rudeltaktik* to have been the major lesson of the war at sea.[141] It is highly indicative of the emperor's otiose 'command' role during the war that his recommendations for 'wolf-pack' tactics were never enacted.

Finally, the German navy attempted to integrate its surface and underwater forces. The High Sea Fleet undertook several sorties into the North Sea in order to force the Allies to scatter their escort craft.[142] In October 1917, the cruisers *Bremse* and *Brummer* intercepted an Allied convoy of ten freighters and two destroyers between Norway and Britain; two months later, four German torpedo-boats and a light cruiser successfully attacked another convoy. While Wilhelm II toasted the success with champagne, the British reacted by assigning heavier surface units to convoy duty, and by reducing the number of convoys at sea.[143] Not a single troop transport bound for Europe was destroyed by U-boats.[144] Finally, the failure of the German navy to press on with seaplane and seaplane-carrier development left it late in 1918 without reliable reconnaissance and facing a British enemy that, in June 1918, unleashed the first carrier-launched strike from the flying-off deck of the *Furious* against the German airship base at Tondern.[145]

The mounting losses of U-boats – up from nineteen in 1915 to sixty-nine in 1918 – attest to the tactical ineffectiveness of the submarines against convoys as well as to the adversary's efficacy in anti-submarine warfare. In terms of size of forces, tactics, technology, and communications, the U-boats simply were not consistent with the high expectations placed upon them by naval leaders.

Conclusion

> Warfare is the highest expression of the national 'will to live,' and politics must, therefore, be subservient to the conduct of war.[146]
>
> Erich Ludendorff, post-1918

The historian of the military in time of war has a simple test of effectiveness:

victory or defeat. Germany set out in 1914 to attain victory on the battlefield, be it to maintain the semi-hegemony created by Otto von Bismarck in 1871, be it to establish hegemony over the Continent, or be it for a *Griff nach der Weltmacht.*[147] It failed. Defeat and revolution denied it military effectiveness at the most obvious level.

Given the standard dictionary definition of effectiveness as that which is 'adequate to accomplish a purpose; producing the intended or expected result,' Germany again must be judged ineffective, especially in the areas of politics and strategy. In a nutshell, German military policy both before and during the First World War was inconsistent with the demands placed upon it. Political effectiveness was severely hampered by a highly fractured command structure and a lack of coordinated national policy making. Coalition warfare was never developed and relations with the ally in Vienna remained at best correct, at worst strained, before and after 1914. Organizational effectiveness was sharply curtailed because army and navy bureaus worked without central direction before the war; the breakdown of the Imperial Supreme Commander's pivotal 'command' role in the First World War merely underlined the existing chaos.

Strategic effectiveness was greatly limited by the adherence to two rigid plans: Schlieffen's encirclement panacea, and Tirpitz's maritime annihilation obsession; neither service developed viable alternative strategies. For the army, the initial strategy of encirclement yielded to a 'strategy of the diagonal,' of meeting the enemies' blows wherever they developed with as much force and for as long as possible; Falkenhayn's attrition warfare gave way to Ludendorff's infiltration and exploitation doctrine, and finally to simple evasion. For the navy, the absence of a Cannae at sea in 1914 left it without an overall strategic objective: like the French after Trafalgar, it could only turn to *guerre de course* in the form of the submarine campaign.

On the other hand, the Germans were much more effective in the areas of operations and tactics. Officers were drilled on *Taktik* at cadet schools, in the War Academy, and in the General Staff, while the ranks were inculcated with tactics through the German Field Regulations; both routinely tested operations and tactics in the annual *Kriegsspiele*. After 1914, operational effectiveness was achieved by superb retraining of both officers and men in the art of 'The Attack in Position Warfare' at about a dozen infantry and artillery schools in France and Germany. Yet, operational effectiveness was hampered by the very nature of the war – that is, by Germany's acceptance of a war of attrition, which pitted its weaknesses (small reserves of manpower and materials) against the adversaries' strengths (numerical and logistical superiority). Finally, the decision to accord all available manpower and material resources under the Hindenburg Program to conventional artillery and machine gun enhancement forced an effectiveness trade-off upon the Army Supreme Command insofar as the development of tanks and even anti-tank weapons was denied priority.

Above all, the Army Supreme Command in 1917–18 sought to enhance tactical efficiency through the evolution of a modern operational concept of land warfare via the collective staff efforts of men such as Bauer, Bruchmüller, Geyer, Lossberg, Ludendorff, and Wetzell. Especially the development of *Stosstrupps*, consisting of attack battalions with fully integrated arms and of so-called attack divisions (*Mob. Divisionen*), greatly enhanced the tactical effectiveness of the exhausted German Army of 1917–18. Yet even the new tactical system was flawed because it was inconsistent with available technology and support systems. The lack of motorized transport and armored vehicles plagued German planners from Schlieffen to Ludendorff. They simply could not conduct a mobile, flexible, mechanized war with technology and logistics that stemmed from the nineteenth century. In addition, to the best of my knowledge not a single German planner of the First World War ever devised a bold integration of aerial bombing, armored spearheads, and infantry infiltration tactics as put forth in France by Colonel Marie-Victor Duval. Ironically, twenty years later it was the Germans rather than the French who remembered Duval's concept.

Finally, attention must be given to the cultural factors, to the values, traditions, and unique attitudes that accorded a special development to the distinctly German society before 1914. These greatly affected military performance in what one could term 'the German way of war.' At the top, there was the continued Frederican notion of the *roi connétable*, of the Imperial Supreme Commander actively exercising a command role. Given the great victories of 1864 to 1871, there was an idolization of the General Staff as well as a tendency to overestimate one's own potential. Wilhelm Deist has termed this a 'permanent self-deception' that led directly to an inability to evaluate one's own position in sober and critical terms.[148] In addition, there existed a very special view of the officer corps as the first order in the realm; corps homogeneity and exclusiveness not only kept certain social groups from serving the nation, but in 1912–13 prevented the expansion of the peacetime army by three army corps. Imperial Germany rejected total mobilization of the nation as being too dangerous to its social fabric. During the First World War, many officers believed that only a victorious war with annexations and indemnities could preserve the peculiar Prussian-German monarchy; Ludendorff's unwillingness to accept defeat in July 1918 is in part attributable to this belief.

Above all, the twin visions of 1912–13, that is, of the General Staff with its principle of manpower enhancement (personnel-intensive armament) and the War Ministry with its formula of technological enhancement (material-intensive armament), continued to plague German planners. While Michael Geyer has argued that these twin visions were 'explosively fused' by Ludendorff through a 'new symbiosis between army and industry,' the record would suggest instead that friction and discord continued to exist among General Staff, War Ministry, captains of industry, and labor throughout the First World War.[149] To be sure, what I have termed 'the dynamics of necessity' brought change: officers were transformed from 'gentlemen' to 'specialists' as social origin yielded to technical expertise, troops became the new workers of war, and machines came to the forefront of combat. Wilhelm Groener especially realized that a sustained war effort was difficult without the workers, and impossible against them. Walter Rathenau brilliantly addressed the need for some sort of 'economic general staff,' a notion repeatedly rejected by the German Army before 1914. And the Hindenburg

Program, the Auxiliary Service Law, and patriotic instruction in 1916–17 were undertaken by the Army Supreme Command in an attempt to catapult the German military into the twentieth century and industrialized society. Nevertheless, as Manfred Messerschmidt has pointed out, Germany proved incapable (or unwilling) fully to comprehend and to adjust to the new industrial war of the masses, either before or after 1914. The shouts of 'strike breakers' that greeted the reserves moving up to the front late in 1918 clearly indicated that large segments of the troops now regarded war as an industrial undertaking. And while the severe limitations placed upon the German military by the Treaty of Versailles for a time permitted army leaders to shelve this development, it would nevertheless reemerge fullblown during rearmament in the mid-1930s.[150]

Notes

1 Compare with the chapter headings in Norman Dixon, *On the Psychology of Military Incompetence* (New York, 1976).
2 See Alfred Vagts, *A History of Militarism* (London, 1959), p. 25; and 'Zielsetzung und Methode der Militärgeschichtsschreibung,' *Militärgeschichtliche Mitteilungen*, vol. 20, pp. 9–19.
3 Friedrich Stampfer, cited in David Schoenbaum, *Zabern 1913: Consensus Politics in Imperial Germany* (London, 1982), p. 180.
4 Cited in Wilhelm Deist, 'Kaiser Wilhelm II in the Context of His Military and Naval Entourage,' in John C. G. Röhl and Nicolaus Sombart (eds.), *Kaiser Wilhelm II: New Interpretations* (Cambridge, 1982), p. 187.
5 See Wiegand Schmidt-Richberg, 'Die Regierungszeit Wilhelms II.,' *Handbuch zur deutschen Militärgeschichte 1648–1939*, Vol. 3 (Munich, 1979), p. 62; Ernst Rudolf Huber, *Deutsche Verfassungsgeschichte seit 1789*, Vol. 3 (Stuttgart, 1963), pp. 76–8, 1000–4; and Manfred Messerschmidt, *Militär und Politik in der Bismarckzeit und im wilhelminischen Deutschland* (Darmstadt, 1975).
6 *Handbuch zur deutschen Militärgeschichte*, Vol. 3, pp. 63–72, 74–5; Germany Reichsarchiv, *Kriegsrüstung und Kriegswirtschaft*, Vol. 1 (Berlin, 1930), pp. 7–8, n. 6. In January 1881, Wilhelm II pompously announced his intention to keep the General Staff merely as 'a kind of amanuensis to me.' H. O. Meisner (ed.), *Denkwürdigkeiten des General-Feldmarschalls Alfred Grafen von Waldersee*, Vol. 2 (Stuttgart-Berlin, 1922), p. 179.
7 *Handbuch zur deutschen Militärgeschichte*, Vol. 3, p. 62; Holger H. Herwig, *The German Naval Officer Corps: A Social and Political History, 1890–1918* (Oxford, 1973), p. 26.
8 *Handbuch zur deutschen Militärgeschichte*, Vol. 3, pp. 60–1.
9 Deist, 'Kaiser Wilhelm II,' pp. 179–81. For examples of the corruption engendered by the 'Kaiser maneuvers,' see Robert Zedlitz-Trützschler, *Zwölf Jahre am deutschen Kaiserhofe* (Stuttgart, 1925), pp. 37–8, 42–3, 83–4.
10 *Handbuch zur deutschen Militärgeschichte*, Vol. 3, p. 81; Walter Görlitz, *Der deutsche Generalstab: Geschichte und Gestalt 1657–1945* (Frankfurt, 1950), p. 204; and Karl Demeter, *Das deutsche Offizierkorps in Gesellschaft und Staat 1650–1945* (Frankfurt, 1965), p. 164.
11 See Demeter, *Das deutsche Offizierkorps*, pp. 29–30, 33–4; Herwig, *German Naval Officer Corps*, pp. 42–3, 76–9; Karl Bosl (ed.), *Bayern im Umbruch: Die Revolution von 1918, ihre Voraussetzungen, ihr Verlauf und ihre Folgen* (Munich, 1969), p. 148; Hermann Rumschöttel, *Das bayerische Offizierkorps 1866–1914* (Berlin, 1973), pp.

63–4; and Holger H. Herwig, 'Die Frage der sozialen Herkunft und wissenschaftlicher Vorbildung in der kaiserlichen Marine vor 1914,' *Militärgeschichtliche Mitteilungen*, vol. 10, pp. 81–111.

12 Manfred Messerschmidt, 'Die preussische Armee,' *Handbuch zur deutschen Militärgeschichte*, Vol. 2, pp. 120–1; David Schoenbaum, 'The Art of the Impossible: German Military Policy Between the Wars,' in R. J. Bullen, H. Pogge von Strandmann, and A. B. Polonsky (eds.), *Ideas into Politics: Aspects of European History, 1880–1950* (London and Sydney, 1984), p. 103; Edward Mead Earle (ed.), *Makers of Modern Strategy: Military Thought from Machiavelli to Hitler* (Princeton, 1944), p. 313; Demeter, *Das deutsche Offizierkorps*, pp. 93 ff.

13 *Handbuch zur deutschen Militärgeschichte*, Vol. 3, pp. 55–8; Rolf Güth, 'Die Organisation der deutschen Marine in Krieg und Frieden 1913–1933,' ibid., Vol. 4, pp. 282–3; *Kriegsrüstung und Kriegswirtschaft*, Vol. 1, pp. 2 ff.

14 *Handbuch zur deutschen Militärgeschichte*, Vol. 3, p. 166; *Kriegsrüstung und Kriegswirtschaft*, Vol. 1, pp. 224–31, and *Anlageband*, pp. 389–91; and Bernd F. Schulte, *Die deutsche Armee 1900–1914: Zwischen Beharren und Verändern* (Düsseldorf, 1977), pp. 368–80.

15 *Handbuch zur deutschen Militärgeschichte*, Vol. 2, p. 376; *Kriegsrüstung und Kriegswirtschaft*, Vol. 1, p. 239; Eckart Kehr, 'Krieg und Geld im Zeitalter der Maschinenrevolution. Fragmente,' in Hans-Ulrich Wehler (ed.), *Primat der Innenpolitik: Gesammelte Ausfsätze zur preussisch-deutschen Sozialgeschichte im 19. und 20. Jahrhundert* (Berlin, 1965), p. 227. See also the naval estimates of Krupp production in Bundesarchiv-Militärarchiv (hereafter BA-MA), Freiburg, F 7631, Nachlass Dähnhardt, Vol. 4, 1912–13; *Handbuch zur deutschen Militärgeschichte*, Vol. 3, p. 376.

16 Schulte, *Die deutsche Armee*, pp. 353–6; Earle, *Makers of Modern Strategy*, p. 312; *Kriegsrüstung und Kriegswirtschaft*, Vol. 1, pp. 272–3, and *Anlageband*, p. 413; and John H. Morrow, Jr., *German Air Power in World War I* (Lincoln, Nebraska, 1982), pp. 6–8.

17 Martin van Creveld, *Supplying War: Logistics from Wallenstein to Patton* (Cambridge, 1977), pp. 126, 137, 138; *Kriegsrüstung und Kriegswirtschaft*, Vol. 1, pp. 282–5, and *Anlageband*, pp. 414–15.

18 See Holger H. Herwig, *'Luxury' Fleet: The Imperial German Navy 1888–1918* (London, 1980), *passim*; Gary E. Weir, 'The Imperial Naval Office and the Problems of Armor Prices in Germany, 1897–1914,' *Military Affairs*, Vol. 48 (April 1984), pp. 62–5.

19 See Werner T. Angress, 'The Impact of the 'Judenwahlen' of 1912 on the Jewish Question,' *Leo Baeck Institute Year Book*, Vol.28 (1983), pp. 381–2; Roger Chickering, 'Der 'Deutsche Wehrverein' und die Reform der deutschen Armee 1912–1914,' *Militärgeschichtliche Mitteilungen*, Vol. 25, pp. 7–33; Klaus Saul, 'Der 'Deutsche Kriegerbund'. Zur innenpolitischen Funktion eines 'nationalen' Verbandes im kaiserlichen Deutschland,' *Militärgeschichtliche Mitteilungen*, Vol. 6, pp. 95–114.

20 See Gerhard Ritter, *Staatskunst und Kriegshandwerk: Das Problem des 'Militarismus' in Deutschland*, Vol. 2 (Munich, 1965), pp. 262, 279; Hermann von Kuhl, *Der deutsche Generalstab in Vorbereitung und Durchführung des Weltkrieges* (Berlin, 1920), pp. 110–11. See the fears concerning a possible 'democratization' of the officer corps by War Minister Karl von Einem to Alfred von Schlieffen, April 19, 1904, and War Minister Josias von Heeringen to Helmuth von Moltke, January 20, 1913, in *Kriegsrüstung und Kriegswirtschaft*, *Anlageband*, pp. 91, 180 and Vol. 1, pp. 172–89; and above all, in Michael Geyer, *Deutsche Rüstungspolitik 1860–1980* (Frankfurt, 1984), pp. 83 ff.

21 Cited in Ritter, *Staatskunst und Kriegshandwerk*, Vol. 2, p. 244.

22 Gerhard Ritter, *Der Schlieffenplan: Kritik eines Mythos* (Munich, 1956), pp. 14–17; Helmuth von Moltke, *Die deutschen Aufmarschpläne 1871–1890*, F. von Schmerfeld (ed.) (Berlin, 1929), pp. 65 ff; *Kriegsrüstung und Kriegswirtschaft, Anlageband*, p. 44, citing Moltke's last Reichstag speech of May 14, 1890, wherein he warned of a future seven or thirty years war. '*Wehe dem, der Europa in Brand steckt.*'

23 *Kriegsrüstung und Kriegswirtschaft, Anlageband*, pp. 73–6; Ritter, *Schlieffenplan*, pp. 30, 141–60.

24 Franz Conrad von Hötzendorf, *Aus Meiner Dienstzeit 1906–1918*, Vol. 1 (Vienna-Leipzig-Munich, 1925), p. 377, memorandum of summer 1908; Ritter, *Staatskunst und Kriegshandwerk*, Vol. 2, p. 299.

25 Conrad von Hötzendorf, *Aus Meiner Dienstzeit*, Vol. 4 (Vienna-Leipzig-Munich, 1923), p. 259, states: 'The matter of a common supreme command was never brought up before the war.'

26 Moltke to Heeringen, December 21, 1912, cited in *Kriegsrüstung und Kriegswirtschaft, Anlageband*, pp. 156–7; Ritter, *Ştaatskunst und Kriegshandwerk*, Vol. 2, p. 261.

27 Friedrich-Christian Stahl, 'Der Grosse Generalstab, seine Beziehungen zum Admiralstab und seine Gedanken zu den Operationsplänen der Marine,' *Wehrkunde*, Vol. 12 (January 1963), pp. 7, 10.

28 Ritter, *Schlieffenplan*, pp. 176, 182–92.

29 Ibid., pp. 71–2, n. 50; Görlitz, *Der deutsche Generalstab*, p. 210; Holger H. Herwig, 'Imperial Germany,' in Ernest R. May (ed.), *Knowing One's Enemies: Intelligence Assessment Before the Two World Wars* (Princeton, 1984) pp. 65 ff.

30 Stahl, 'Der Grosse Generalstab,' p. 7; Ritter, *Staatskunst und Kriegshandwerk*, Vol. 2, pp. 240–1; Theobald von Bethmann Hollweg, *Betrachtungen zum Weltkriege*, Vol. 1 (Berlin, 1919), p. 166, and Vol. 2 (Berlin, 1921), p. 8.

31 Kuhl, *Der deutsche Generalstab*, p. 108.

32 Bethmann Hollweg, *Betrachtungen zum Weltkriege*, Vol. 1, p. 167, and Vol. 2, p. 7. See also Kuhl, *Der deutsche Generalstab*, p. 177.

33 Alfred von Tirpitz, *Erinnerungen* (Leipzig, 1920), p. 228. The German leaders apparently forgot Clausewitz's dictum: 'It is absurd to bring the military into the process of war planning so that they can decide *purely militarily* what the Cabinets must do; but it is even more absurd for theoreticians to demand that available war resources be turned over to the military commander so that he can make a military war plan accordingly.' *Vom Kriege* (Leck, Schleswig, 1963), p. 219.

34 'The political leadership was not involved in the creation of the war plan. Nor in the changes which the Schlieffen plan underwent long before the outbreak of the war.' Bethmann Hollweg, *Betrachtungen zum Weltkriege*, Vol. 2, p. 7.

35 Cited in Earle, *Makers of Modern Strategy*, p. 179.

36 See Ritter, *Schieffenplan*, ch. 2, *passim*.

37 Ibid., pp. 71–2, n. 50; 179–80; Heinz-Ludger Borgert, 'Grundzüge der Landkriegführung von Schlieffen bis Guderian,' in *Handbuch zur deutschen Militärgeschicte*, Vol. 5 (Munich, 1979), p. 494.

38 See Jagow's position of February 1913 in *Deutscher Offiziersbund*, Vol. 23 (1927), p. 966.

39 Fritz von Lossberg, *Meine Tätigkeit im Weltkriege 1914–1918* (Berlin, 1939), pp. 173, 175; Erich Ludendorff, *Kriegführung und Politik* (Berlin, 1923); Ludwig Beck, *Studien*, ed. Hans Speidel (Stuttgart, 1955), p. 173; and Dennis E. Showalter, 'The Eastern Front and German Military Planning, 1871–1914–Some Observations,' *East European Quarterly*, Vol. 15 (June 1981), pp. 163–76.

40 *Kriegsrüstung und Kriegswirtschaft*, Vol. 1, p. 17; Ritter, *Schlieffenplan*, pp. 31–5.

41 Conrad von Hötzendorf, *Aus Meiner Dienstzeit*, Vol. 3 (Vienna-Leipzig-Munich,

1922), p. 669. Discussion of May 12, 1914. The Central Powers in 1914 were outnumbered by the Entente 238 million to 110 million in population, and 5.8 million to 3.8 million in mobilized troops.

42 Cited in Gordon A. Craig, 'The World War I Alliance of the Central Powers in Retrospect: The Military Cohesion of the Alliance,' *Journal of Modern History*, Vol. 37 (September 1965), pp. 337–8.

43 Cited in Hans Mohs (ed.), *General-Feldmarschall Alfred Graf von Waldersee in seinem militärischen Wirken*, Vol. 2 (Berlin, 1929), p. 388; entry dated January 25, 1898.

44 Paul M. Kennedy, 'Tirpitz, England and the Second Navy Law of 1900: A Strategical Critique,' *Militärgeschichtliche Mitteilungen*, Vol. 8, p. 38.

45 Tirpitz, Erinnerungen, p. 112.

46 Edward Wegener, 'Die Tirpitzsche Seestrategie,' in Herbert Schottelius and Wilhelm Deist (eds.), *Marine und Marinepolitik im kaiserlichen Deutschland 1871–1914* (Düsseldorf, 1972), p. 241.

47 Memorandum of October 12, 1930, cited in ibid., p. 249. See also BA-MA, Nachlass Levetzow, N 239, box 54.

48 Herwig, *'Luxury' Fleet*, p. 261.

49 BA-MA, Nachlass Levetzow, N 239, box 2, band 1. 'Ausbildung der Offiziere im Admiralstabe zu Berlin,' October 7, 1903.

50 BA-MA, F 3343-PG 66913 Marine-Kabinett. Kommandierungen zum Besuch der Marine Akademie, Vol. 1. Tirpitz to Müller, June 8, 1907; Müller to Tirpitz, July 2, 1907.

51 Stahl, 'Der Grosse Generalstab,' pp. 9–10.

52 Ibid., pp. 11–12. See also Wolfgang Foerster, *Aus der Gedankenwerkstatt des deutschen Generalstabes* (Berlin, 1931), pp. 62, 67.

53 Walther Hubatsch, *Der Admiralstab und die obersten Marinebehörden in Deutschland 1848–1945* (Frankfurt, 1958), p. 143.

54 Cited in Herwig, *'Luxury' Fleet*, p. 190.

55 Cited in Albert Hopman, *Das Logbuch eines deutschen Seeoffiziers* (Berlin, 1924), p. 393.

56 Otto Groos (ed.), *Der Krieg in der Nordsee*, Vol. 1 (Berlin, 1920), p. 251. This is the first volume of the official naval history: Marine-Archiv, *Der Krieg zur See 1914–1918*, ed. Eberhard von Mantey.

57 Admiral Reinhard Scheer, the fleet chief, stated in his report to Wilhelm II on July 4, 1917, that 'there can be no doubt that even the most successful outcome of a fleet action in the war will not *force* England to make peace in *this* war.' He pointed to the Reich's 'disadvantageous military-geographical position,' and returned to a theme he had already aired in December 1914: 'the defeat of British economic life – that is, by using the U-boats against British trade.' BA-MA, Nachlass Levetzow, N 239, box 19, band 2.

58 Wolfgang Wegener, *Die Seestrategie des Weltkrieges* (Berlin, 1929), pp. 9–10; Herwig, *'Luxury' Fleet*, p. 191.

59 See Trotha's memorandum, 'Welche Stellung an der See braucht Deutschland für seine nationale Entwicklung,' April 21, 1917, in BA-MA, Nachlass Tirpitz, N 253, Vol. 178, p. 119. For the Scandinavian contingency plans of 1916–17, see Carl-Axel Gemzell, *Organization, Conflict, and Innovation: A Study of German Naval Strategic Planning, 1888–1940* (Lund, 1973), pp. 167–74; and Ivo Nikolai Lambi, *The Navy and German Power Politics, 1862–1914* (Boston, 1984), *passim*.

60 Alfred von Schlieffen, 'Der Krieg in der Gegenwart,' in Hugo von Freytag-Loringhoven (ed.), *Cannae* (Berlin, 1925), p. 280. Originally published in *Deutsche Revue* (January 1909).

61 Creveld, *Supplying War*, pp. 140–1.

62 Ibid., pp. 113–35; Hew Strachan, *European Armies and the Conduct of War* (London, 1983), pp. 132, 137.
63 Kuhl, *Der deutsche Generalstab*, p. 183; Lossberg, *Meine Tätigkeit im Weltkriege*, pp. 77–9, 127–8.
64 Moltke's successor, Prussian War Minister Erich von Falkenhayn, on September 5, 1914, sarcastically commented: 'Our General Staff has completely lost its head. Schlieffen's notes do not help any further, and so Moltke's wits come to an end.' Cited in Basil Liddell Hart, *Reputations: Ten Years After* (Boston, 1928), p. 52.
65 Albrecht von Thaer, *Generalstabsdienst an der Front und in der O.H.L. Aus Briefen und Tagebuchaufzeichnungen 1915–1919* (Göttingen, 1958), pp. 114, 116. The official German history of the war states that the army fired 10 million artillery shells in May 1917, killing or wounding 100,000 enemy soldiers: it deemed the shell–kill ratio of 100 to 1 as inefficient. Germany Reichsarchiv, *Der Weltkrieg 1914 bis 1918*, Vol. 12 (Berlin, 1939), p. 408.
66 Ibid., Vol. 13 (Berlin, 1942), pp. 145, 230 ff., 340. See also, Cyril Falls, *The Great War* (New York, 1959), pp. 308–9; B. H. Liddell Hart, *The Real War 1914–1918* (Boston, 1930), pp. 356–64.
67 See Hans C. von Seherr-Thoss, *Die deutsche Automobilindustrie* (Stuttgart, 1974), p. 60; James Laux (ed.), *The Automobile Revolution* (Chapel Hill, 1982); James A. Huston, *The Sinews of War: Army Logistics, 1775–1953* (Washington, 1966), p. 379.
68 Von einem Generalstäbler, *Kritik des Weltkrieges* (Leipzig, 1920). The failure to develop the tank weapon is well documented: Seherr-Thoss, *Deutsche Automobilindustrie*, pp. 42, 62; M. Schwarte (ed.), *Die Technik im Weltkrieg* (Berlin, 1920), pp. 208–19; *Der Weltkrieg 1914 bis 1918*, Vol. 14 (Berlin, 1944), pp. 33–4, 525; Thaer, *Generalstabsdienst*, pp. 104–5, 111, 113, 140, 220–1, 239; Crown Prince Rupprecht of Bavaria, *Mein Kriegstagebuch*, ed. Eugen von Frauenholz, Vol. 2 (Munich, 1929), pp. 292, 375; and Edgar Graf von Matuschka, 'Organisationsgeschichte des Heeres 1890 bis 1918,' in *Handbuch zur deutschen Militärgeschichte*, Vol. 3, p. 264.
69 *Handbuch zur deutschen Militärgeschichte*, Vol. 5, p. 505.
70 Lossberg, *Meine Tätigkeit im Weltkriege*, pp. 122–3, 159, 203, 206, 212.
71 *Der Weltkrieg 1914 bis 1918*, Vol. 11 (Berlin, 1938), pp. 186, 481.
72 Ibid., p. 105.
73 *Handbuch zur deutschen Militärgeschichte*, Vol. 5, p. 507.
74 Ibid., p. 512; Timothy T. Lupfer, *The Dynamics of Doctrine: The Changes in German Tactical Doctrine During the First World War* (Fort Leavenworth, 1981), pp. 12 ff.; *Der Weltkrieg 1914 bis 1918*, Vol. 11, pp. 107–9.
75 Lossberg, *Meine Tätigkeit im Weltkriege*, pp. 275–6; Lupfer, *Dynamics of Doctrine*, p. 45; G. C. Wynne, *If Germany Attacks: The Battle in Depth in the West* (London, 1940), p. 294; *Handbuch zur deutschen Militärgeschichte*, Vol. 3, p. 223; *Der Weltkrieg 1914 bis 1918*, Vol. 12, p. 490.
76 Marc Ferro, *The Great War, 1914–1918* (Boston, 1973), pp. 83–8; *Handbuch zur deutschen Militärgeschichte*, Vol. 3, pp. 232–3, 255; and Crown Prince Rupprecht, *Mein Kriegstagebuch*, Vol. 2, p. 11.
77 *Handbuch zur deutschen Militärgeschichte*, Vol. 3, p. 253, and Vol. 5, p. 508; *Der Weltkrieg 1914 bis 1918*, Vol. 13, pp. 29–30. See also Ulrich Trumpener, 'The Road to Ypres: The Beginnings of Gas Warfare in World War I,' *Journal of Modern History*, Vol. 47 (September 1975), pp. 460–80.
78 *Handbuch zur deutschen Militärgeschichte*, Vol. 3, p. 258, and Vol. 5, p. 512; Lossberg, *Meine Tätigkeit im Weltkriege*, p. 276; Thaer, *Generalstabsdienst*, p. 99; Crown Prince Rupprecht, *Mein Kriegstagebuch*, Vol. 2, p. 63. *Der Weltkrieg 1914 bis 1918*, Vol. 14, p. 33, lists the following delivery rates: 7,200 machine guns in 1915,

21,600 in 1916, and 104,000 in 1917. Lord H. H. Kitchener, Britain's Secretary for War, in 1914 believed that 4 machine guns per battalion were adequate, to which David Lloyd George replied: 'Take Kitchener's figure. Square it. Multiply by two. Then double again for good luck.' Cited in Holger H. Herwig and Neil M. Heyman (eds.), *Biographical Dictionary of World War I* (Westport and London, 1982), p. 15.

79 Erich Ludendorff, *Urkunden der Obersten Heeresleitung über ihre Tätigkeit 1916/18* (Berlin, 1921), p. 162; Ferro, *The Great War*, pp. 94–5; *Handbuch zur deutschen Militärgeschichte*, Vol. 3, p. 292; *Der Weltkrieg 1914 bis 1918*, Vol. 12, pp. 17–18; and Morrow, *German Air Power, passim.*

80 The German elastic defense is in Lossberg, *Meine Tätigkeit im Weltkriege*, pp. 223–4, 237, 295–304; Thaer, *Generalstabsdienst*, p. 89; Crown Prince Rupprecht, *Mein Kriegstagebuch*, Vol. 2, pp. 30–1; Ludendorff, *Urkunden der Obersten Heeresleitung*, pp. 592 ff. The retreat to the Siegfried line is in *Der Weltkrieg 1914 bis 1918*, Vol. 11, pp. 514 ff., and Vol. 12, pp. 40 ff., 45 ff., 130 ff.

81 Wynne, *If Germany Attacks*, pp. 138–9; Strachan, *European Armies*, p. 141; Kuhl, *Der deutsche Generalstab*, p. 196.

82 *Der Weltkrieg 1914 bis 1918*, Vol. 11, pp. 32 ff.

83 Wilhelm Groener, *Lebenserinnerungen: Jugend. Generalstab. Weltkrieg* (Göttingen, 1957), p. 420; Crown Prince Ruppprecht, *Mein Kriegstagebuch*, Vol. 2, p. 65; Geyer, *Deutsche Rüstungspolitik*, pp. 100–1.

84 Geyer, *Deutsche Rüstungspolitik*, pp. 102–9. See also Ludendorff, *Urkunden der Obersten Heeresleitung*, pp. 63 ff.; *Der Weltkrieg 1914 bis 1918*, Vol. 11, pp. 32–5; and Gerald F. Feldman, *Army, Industry, and Labor in Germany 1914–1918* (Princeton, 1966), pp. 149 ff.

85 *Der Weltkrieg 1914 bis 1918*, Vol. 11, pp. 36–40; *Handbuch zur deutschen Militärgeschichte*, Vol. 3, pp. 138, 143.

86 *Der Weltkrieg 1914 bis 1918*, Vol. 13, pp. 23–4; Ludendorff, *Urkunden der Obersten Heeresleitung*, pp. 271 ff.

87 Walter Rathenau's efforts in behalf of German war production, which foreshadowed those of Fritz Todt and Albert Speer, should not be underestimated, however. See Gerhard Hecker, *Walter Rathenau und sein Verhältnis zu Militär und Krieg* (Boppard, 1983), pp. 357–72.

88 The official German history, *Der Weltkrieg 1914 bis 1918*, Vol. 14, pp. 690–1, fully recognizes this.

89 See, for example, the entries in Crown Prince Rupprecht, *Mein Kriegstagebuch*, Vol. 2, pp. 130–1, 171, 301, 396, 435, 443.

90 Ibid., Vol. 2, p. 211, entry dated July 2, 1917. Leeb, *Tagebuchaufzeichnungen*, p. 142, entry for October 6, 1918, comes to the same conclusion.

91 See especially Wilhelm's terse order of September 7, 1915, instructing fleet officers desirous of greater operational freedom to stifle their comments and to subordinate their views to those of the Imperial Supreme Commander. BA-MA, F 7162-PG 68818 Reichs-Marine-Amt, Allerhöchste Kabinetts-Ordres, Vol. 129.

92 Julian S. Corbett and Henry Newbolt (eds.), *History of the Great War, Naval Operations* (London, 1931), Vol. 5, p. 227.

93 See the pioneering study by Wilhelm Deist, 'Die Politik der Seekriegsleitung und die Rebellion der Flotte Ende Oktober 1918,' *Vierteljahrshefte für Zeitgeschichte*, Vol. 14 (October 1966), pp. 341–68.

94 Herwig, *'Luxury' Fleet*, p. 150.

95 Herwig, *German Naval Officer Corps*, pp. 196 ff., 240 ff; and Wilhelm Deist, 'Die Unruhen in der Marine 1917–18,' *Marine-Rundschau*, vol. 168 (June 1971), pp. 325–43.

96 Vice Admiral Albert Hopman, chief naval staff officer in the Baltic, described the military value of the operation as 'nonsense.' He informed Tirpitz: 'It brings a fresh breath of air into the fleet, whose spirit, as far as the ratings are concerned, is in even more dire straits than Your Excellency suggested some time ago.' BA-MA, Nachlass Tirpitz, N 253, Vol. 181. Hopman to Tirpitz, October 4, 1917.

97 Corbett and Newbolt (eds.), *History of the Great War, Naval Operations*, Vol. 4, p. 345.

98 See Bernd Stegemann, *Die deutsche Marinepolitik 1916–1918* (Berlin, 1970), pp. 76 ff.; Karl Galster, *England, Deutsche Flotte und Weltkrieg* (Kiel, 1925), p. 144; Andreas H. Michelsen, *Der U-Bootskrieg 1914–1918* (Leipzig, 1925), p. 125; Arno Spindler, *Der Handelskrieg mit U-Booten* (Berlin, 1941), Vol. 4, p. 1; Robert M. Grant, *U-Boats Destroyed: The Effect of Anti-Submarine Warfare, 1914–1918* (London, 1964), p. 41; Ludendorff, *Urkunden der Obersten Heeresleitung*, pp. 322–4.

99 Grant, *U-Boats Destroyed*, p. 72; Michelsen, *Der U-Bootskrieg*, pp. 128–30; Herwig, *German Naval Officer Corps*, pp. 237–9; Reinhard Scheer, *Germany's High Sea Fleet in the World War* (London, 1920), p. 328; BA-MA, Nachlass Behncke, N 173, Vol. 11, pp. 20–1, and Vol. 12, pp. 10–18; BA-MA, Nachlass Keyserlingk, N 161, Vol. 19, p. 138.

100 *Das Werk des Untersuchungsausschusses der Verfassunggebenden Deutschen Nationalversammlung und des Deutschen Reichstages 1919–1928. Vierte Reihe. Die Ursachen des Deutschen Zusammenbruches im Jahre 1918. Zweite Abteilung, Der innere Zusammenbruch* (Berlin, 1919–1928), Vol. 10, pt. 1, p. 128.

101 Hauptstaatsarchiv Stuttgart, ü 130 I. Staatsministerium, *'Niederschriften über Sitzungen von Reichstagsausschüssen 1915–1918,'* Fasc. III, *146. Sitzung des Ausschusses für den Reichshaushalt*, April 26, 1917.

102 Cited in Crown Prince Rupprecht, *Mein Kriegstagebuch*, Vol. 2, p. 372 note. See also the entry for January 21, 1918, in ibid., p. 322.

103 The official German history, *Der Weltkrieg 1914 bis 1918*, Vol. 14, p. 258, acknowledged the absence of an overall *Schwerpunkt* in Ludendorff's strategy.

104 Ibid., Vol. 13, pp. 330, 337; Lossberg, *Meine Tätigkeit im Weltkriege*, p. 315.

105 *Handbuch zur deutschen Militärgeschichte*, Vol. 3, p. 150. It might be noted that an agreement between Berlin and Vienna in September 1916 to give overall military command to the German emperor was never fully developed; it ended with the coronation of Emperor Charles I in November 1916.

106 Ulrich Trumpener, *Germany and the Ottoman Empire, 1914–1918* (Princeton, 1968), pp. 104–7, claims that the influence of the various German commanders in Turkey (Otto Liman von Sanders, Colmar von der Goltz, Erich von Falkenhayn, and Friedrich Kress von Kressenstein) and the 25,000 men under their command amounted to 'virtually nil.' *Der Weltkrieg 1914 bis 1918*, Vol. 13, pp. 442–6, concurs with this assessment.

107 *Der Weltkrieg 1914 bis 1918*, Vol. 13, p. 398.

108 Thaer, *Generalstabsdienst*, pp. 196–7, entry for May 1, 1918. Thaer on May 17, 1917, had already noted that a peace without annexations would be 'against monarchy and army, and for democrats and Marxists.' Ibid., pp. 122–3. General Groener, *Lebenserinnerungen*, p. 421, later spoke of Ludendorff's 'shocking egocentricity' in military as well as political matters.

109 Lupfer, *Dynamics of Doctrine*, pp. 57–8.

110 *Der Weltkrieg 1914 bis 1918*, Vol. 14, pp. 46–50; Ludendorff, *Urkunden der Obersten Heeresleitung*, pp. 594 ff.; *Handbuch zur deutschen Militärgeschichte*, Vol. 5,

p. 520; Strachan, *European Armies*, pp. 144–5; Wynne, *If Germany Attacks*, p. 58; Lupfer, *Dynamics of Doctrine*, pp. 38–9.

111 See *Der Weltkrieg 1914 bis 1918*, Vol. 11, p. 113, and Vol. 12, p. 60; *Handbuch zur deutschen Militärgeschichte*, Vol. 3, p. 236, and Vol. 5, pp. 516, 520, 524; Wynne, *If Germany Attacks*, pp. 294–5; Lupfer, *Dynamics of Doctrine*, pp. 28, 46.

112 *Der Weltkrieg 1914 bis 1918*, Vol. 12, pp. 53–4.

113 Ibid., p. 59. See also Crown Prince Rupprecht, *Mein Kriegstagebuch*, Vol. 2, p. 46; Wynne, *If Germany Attacks*, p. 162; Lupfer, *Dynamics of Doctrine*, p. 24.

114 *Der Weltkrieg 1914 bis 1918*, Vol. 14, p. 41.

115 Ibid., p. 42. See also, Kuhl, *Der deutsche Generalstab*, p. 209; Thaer, *Generalstabsdienst*, p. 156.

116 Cited in *Handbuch zur deutschen Militärgeschichte*, Vol. 5, p. 525.

117 Thaer, *Generalstabsdienst*, p. 170; *Der Weltkrieg 1914 bis 1918*, Vol. 14, pp. 52 ff., for Operation *Michael*.

118 *Der Weltkrieg 1914 bis 1918*, Vol. 14, pp. 254–5, claims the average loss of the attack divisions stood at 2,000 men. Crown Prince Rupprecht, *Mein Kriegstagebuch*, Vol. 2, p. 451, spoke of a *Strategie des Ausweichens*.

119 See Lossberg, *Meine Tätigkeit im Weltkriege*, p. 314; Thaer, *Generalstabsdienst*, p. 182.

120 Thaer, *Generalstabsdienst*, pp. 183 (n. 106), 198; Crown Prince Rupprecht, *Mein Kriegstagebuch*, Vol. 2, p. 387, and Vol. 3, p. 326, where he spoke about creating special *Beutekommandos* to liberate the rich supply depots in an orderly fashion.

121 Lossberg, *Meine Tätigkeit im Weltkriege*, p. 356; *Der Weltkrieg 1914 bis 1918*, Vol. 14, p. 622; Thaer, *Generalstabsdienst*, p. 234. It is interesting to note that Thaer's observations pertained to the privileged attack divisions; they might also have included one of the prestigious *Garde* divisions on August 8, 1918.

122 Lossberg, *Meine Tätigkeit im Weltkriege*; p. 349; Thaer, *Generalstabsdienst*, p. 188; Crown Prince Rupprecht, *Mein Kriegstagebuch*, Vol. 2, pp. 281, 402. The official *Der Weltkrieg 1914 bis 1918*, Vol. 14, p. 760, sets the number of 'deserters' at home at anywhere between 200,000 and 1.5 million!

123 Ludendorff's 'broken nerves' were observed especially by Crown Prince Rupprecht, *Mein Kriegstagebuch*, Vol. 2, p. 451; and Lossberg, *Meine Tätigkeit im Weltkriege*, pp. 344–5, 351.

124 *Der Weltkrieg 1914 bis 1918*, Vol. 14, p. 666; Ludendorff, *Urkunden der Obersten Heeresleitung*, pp. 560 ff.; Crown Prince Rupprecht, *Mein Kriegstagebuch*, Vol. 2, pp. 242, 463; Leeb, *Tagebuchaufzeichnungen*, p. 146, simply recorded: 'Das ist alles.'

125 *Der Weltkrieg 1914 bis 1918*, Vol. 14, pp. 525, 681.

126 Lupfer, *Dynamics of Doctrine*, p. 53; Crown Prince Rupprecht, *Mein Kriegstagebuch*, Vol. 2, pp. 305–7, 383.

127 Crown Prince Rupprecht, *Mein Kriegstagebuch*, Vol. 2, p. 364.

128 Cited in ibid., p. 326.

129 Groener, *Lebenserinnerungen*, pp. 429–31.

130 Crown Prince Rupprecht, *Mein Kriegstagebuch*, Vol. 3, p. 321. Entry dated May 8, 1918.

131 Ibid., pp. 285, 331, 374, 436. Groener, *Lebenserinnerungen*, p. 433, also spoke of Ludendorff's penchant for 'victorious hammer blows' devoid of 'operational effectiveness.'

132 Crown Prince Rupprecht, *Mein Kriegstagebuch*, Vol. 2, pp. 372, 472.

133 Leeb, *Tagebuchaufzeichnungen*, pp. 111, 112, 115.

134 Lossberg, *Meine Tätigkeit im Weltkriege*, p. 321. Lossberg also reprimanded Ludendorff for his rigid and often arrogant staff system; ibid., pp. 326–7.

135 Thaer, *Generalstabsdienst*, pp. 28, 149, 151, 163, 164.
136 *Handbuch zur deutschen Militärgeschichte*, Vol. 3, p. 153.
137 Crown Prince Rupprecht, *Mein Kriegstagebuch*, Vol. 2, p. 248. Entry dated August 20, 1917.
138 See Spindler, *Handelskrieg mit U-Booten*, Vol. 4, pp. 396, 399–400; R. H. Gibson and Maurice Prendergast, *The German Submarine War, 1914–1918* (London, 1931), pp. 186, 191.
139 See BA-MA, Nachlass Levetzow, N 239, box 19, band 2; BA-MA, F 2022/PG 65983 Admiralstab der Marine, Immediatvorträge, Vol. 30, p. 77; and BA-MA, F 4055/PG 64726 Anlage zum K.T.B. Seekriegsleitung.
140 Herwig, *'Luxury' Fleet*, pp. 228–9.
141 Karl Dönitz, *40 Fragen an Karl Dönitz* (Munich, 1979), p. 15.
142 See Kurt Assmann, *Deutsche Seestrategie in zwei Weltkriegen* (Heidelberg, 1957), pp. 52–3; Scheer, *Germany's High Sea Fleet*, p. 310.
143 Walter Görlitz (ed.), *The Kaiser and His Court: The Diaries, Note Books and Letters of Admiral Georg Alexander von Müller, Chief of the Naval Cabinet, 1914–1918* (New York, 1961), p. 318, entry for December 14, 1917. On the raids of October and December, see Galster, *England, Deutsche Flotte und Weltkrieg*, p. 121; and Otto Groos, *Seekriegslehren im Lichte des Weltkrieges* (Berlin, 1929), p. 93.
144 David F. Trask, *Captains and Cabinets: Anglo-American Naval Relations, 1917–1918* (Columbia, Mo., 1972), p. 223.
145 Herwig, *'Luxury' Fleet*, p. 211.
146 Cited in Strachan, *European Armies*, p. 148. War Minister Werner von Blomberg in May 1934 argued that the 'thinking of both our troops and National Socialism springs from the same source, our experience in the Great War.' Cited in Manfred Messerschmidt, 'The Wehrmacht and the Volksgemeinschaft,' *Journal of Contemporary History*, Vol. 18 (1983), p. 731.
147 The most recent evaluation of the literature concerning Germany's decision to accept war in July–August 1914 is Wolfgang Jäger, *Historische Forschung und politische Kultur in Deutschland: Die Debatte 1914–1980 über den Ausbruch des Ersten Weltkrieges* (Göttingen, 1984).
148 I am greatly indebted to Dr. Deist for his acute observations on the German military in the First World War, which he has unselfishly shared with me. These have now appeared: Der militärische Zusammenbruch des Kaiserreiches,' in Ursula Büttner (ed.), *Das Unrechtsregime: Internationale Forschung über den Nationalsozialismus. Festschrift für Werner Jochmann zum 65. Geburtstag* (Hamburg, 1986), 2 vols..
149 Geyer, *Deutsche Rüstungspolitik*, pp. 92, 105.
150 See Michael Geyer, *Aufrüstung oder Sicherheit: Die Reichswehr in der Krise der Machtpolitik 1924–1936* (Wiesbaden, 1980); and *Das Deutsche Reich und der Zweite Weltkrieg: Ursachen und Voraussetzungen der Deutschen Kriegspolitik* (Stuttgart, 1979).

[4]

American Military Effectiveness in the First World War

TIMOTHY K. NENNINGER

Introduction

During the First World War the US Army grew from a constabulary force of about 100,000 professionals to a conscript army of four million. The Navy changed in an equally rapid fashion, from a force built around a few powerful battleships to one consisting of hundreds of smaller craft for combatting submarines. The American military effort was immense, and in some respects unique – supporting a 2 million man expeditionary force 3,000 miles from home, fighting a war with allies for the first time since 1783, and attempting to mobilize the entire industrial economy to prosecute the war. To a considerable extent traditional practices, in Russell Weigley's terms 'the American way of war,' shaped wartime performance at all levels – political, strategic, operational, and tactical. American effectiveness in each of these spheres depended on how readily the military adapted its past experience to the demands of the world war situation. A few key issues, including how to use US combat troops overseas, shipping shortages, and the difficulties of industrial mobilization, had an impact on military effectiveness at all levels. Perhaps the most significant limitation on American effectiveness, especially operationally and tactically, was the short time the United States was an active belligerent. The Americans, despite a massive war effort, had little opportunity, because they had so little time, to learn from their experience and improve effectiveness.

Political Effectiveness

Several factors influenced the political effectiveness of the American military during the era of the First World War, with the military itself having more control over some factors than others. Political leaders were more receptive to military advice after the declaration of war on Germany, April 6, 1917, than in the period of nonbelligerency. Neither the army nor the navy had mature, well-functioning mechanisms to analyze defense problems, on the one hand, and systematically convey that analysis to civilian leadership with recommendations for military needs, on the other. As a result, some of the military assessments of foreign threats and military requirements were strategically unrealistic and politically naive.

If the policy-formulating entities within the services were weak, the mechanisms for interdepartmental coordination of military policy were even weaker. The Joint Army-Navy Board, established in 1903, was supposed to coordinate planning between the two departments. Never especially effective, the Joint Board played an even smaller role during the Wilson administration, which frequently denigrated the need for long-range military planning. Henry Breckinridge, Assistant Secretary of War from 1913 to 1916, indicated its importance to the political leadership: 'This was a board I fooled with on hot summer afternoons when there was nothing else to do.'[1]

Political–military cooperation was even more haphazard. With no organizational structure such cooperation was heavily dependent on the personalities involved. Wilson's first secretary of state, William Jennings Bryan, was a pacifist who on one occasion thundered that military officers 'could not be trusted to say what we should or should not do, till we actually got into war.'[2] At the Navy Department, the near-pacifist secretary, Josephus Daniels, perpetually feuded with the General Board and many of the other senior officers. Robert Lansing, who in 1915 succeeded Bryan at State, on the other hand, met nearly daily with officers from the navy's General Board and the army's General Staff. Relations between Newton D. Baker, Secretary of War from 1916 to 1921, and more senior army leaders were also good.

The American tradition in civil–military relations, and particularly Woodrow Wilson's strict interpretation of that tradition, was perhaps the crucial limitation of the military's political effectiveness in the pre-belligerency period. Civil authority was always to be dominant and unless in an actual state of war the military was to remain as inconspicuous as possible. Wilson demonstrated his inflexibility on the subject, as well as his misunderstanding of the need for military contingency planning prior to hostilities in the fall of 1915. He brought to the attention of Henry Breckinridge, then Acting Secretary of War, an article in the Baltimore *Sun* which stated that the General Staff was preparing plans in case of war with Germany. Wilson instructed Breckinridge to determine the accuracy of the story, and, if true, 'to relieve at once every officer of the General Staff and order him out of Washington.'[3] So long as he thought war with Germany was avoidable Wilson wanted no military action that increased the chance of a clash and was thus generally unreceptive to military advice.

During early 1917, as war seemed increasingly likely, the President and the military leaders found some common ground. Wilson still opposed intervention in the European war and wanted to avoid overt actions, but he gradually recognized the necessity for some military preparations. By mid-February, the General Staff had prepared a plan for conscripting, equipping, and training a 4 million man army – a plan Wilson endorsed. In late March he dispatched Rear Admiral William S. Sims to London to coordinate plans with the British in the event of American intervention. But even at this late hour, Wilson thought any American participation in the European war would be limited to loans, merchant shipping, and possibly moral support. Neither he nor the military leadership foresaw the dispatch of a large expeditionary force to France.

After the declaration of war there was still vacillation among the political leadership on how to prosecute the war. Wilson did not provide clear direction on the type or scale of American intervention. As late as September 1917 he still raised questions about a massive intervention in France. But increasingly, especially beginning in the fall of 1917, the administration let the military prosecute the war. The overseas commanders, Pershing and Sims, had extraordinary powers to deal unilaterally with the Allied governments. At home, Wilson seldom interfered with Baker's running of the War Department or Daniels' of the Navy Department.

During 1916–17 Congress and the military, especially the army, were not on good terms, further limiting military preparations. As one observer has noted, the General Staff program for military preparedness from 1915 to 1917 'showed an extraordinary insensitivity to the limitations and requirements of public policy.'[4] General Staff planners ignored the National Guard as the principal resource for increased military manpower during this period and emphasized compulsory universal service – both were anathema to large segments of Congress. Consequently, Congress, like the administration, would not act decisively in early 1917. As late as mid-February, after resumption of unrestricted submarine warfare by the Germans, after Germany and the US broke diplomatic relations, and only six weeks before the declaration of war, the House Military Affairs Committee unanimously concluded that it should undertake no radical changes in the country's military policy.[5]

The actions of the military planners themselves also limited their ultimate effectiveness. Before early 1917 few talked openly of the possibility of intervention in the European war and the requirements that would entail for building up the army and navy. Rather, most military planners and civilian preparedness advocates spoke in terms of preparing the army and navy for a defensive war to repulse an invasion of the United States and its possessions by foreign powers in the wake of the European war. Like many of their countrymen, the military planners doubted the US could be drawn into the European war, believed in the ultimate victory of the Allies, considered the Atlantic Ocean a 3,000-mile strategic cushion, and, even when intervention seemed more likely, considered the dispatch of a large expeditionary force unwise.[6] Although this task avoided some immediate political problems, it distorted long-range military planning and inhibited mobilization once war was declared.

Only after the diplomatic break with Germany in February 1917 did the American military clearly focus on intervention in the European war. And only after the declaration of war in April 1917, when the enemy and American military needs became clearer, would budget authorities in the administration and Congress consider funding the military's proposed expansion program; even then some reluctance remained.

The fate of budget requests for the Ordnance Department is indicative of the process. On April 5, 1917, the Chief of Ordnance submitted a $3 billion estimate for initial arms purchases to support a 1 million man army. Because the request was not itemized, the House Military Affairs Committee rejected it. A second ordnance request included the proviso that 10 per cent of the amount appropriated under any particular heading could be spent for any purpose the Secretary of War thought necessary. Congress also rejected this submission. Ultimately, Congress appropriated the full $3 billion initially requested, but it took until June 5, 1917, to do so. An additional request for $3.7 billion to arm the second million men inducted did not pass until October 6, 1917. After that time, however, largely because the requirements had become clearer, the budgeting process did not inhibit the ordnance program.[7]

Despite such initial faltering, the American military generally received adequate budgetary support for its program during the First World War. To support the war effort, Congress increased most taxes and also issued loans, thus passing a major portion of the cost on to future generations. Of the total war expenditures, nearly $33 billion, over $21 billion came from borrowing and the remainder from taxation. Significantly, the four Liberty Loans and a final Victory Loan at the end of the war were all oversubscribed.[8] The American people enthusiastically supported the war effort by their purchase of the bonds. Yet this enthusiasm was undoubtedly directed more to support of American war aims in general than to the military's program in particular.

In order to prosecute the war, the military had to convert the nation's financial resources into militarily useful matériel. This required the assistance of scientists, engineers, and businessmen. Throughout much of the nineteenth and early twentieth centuries elements of the American military had maintained some relationships with these groups. During the First World War the previous connections proved useful but were not sufficiently strong or sophisticated enough to overcome structural weaknesses in the system of military procurement and economic and scientific mobilization.

From 1915 to 1917 scientists, engineers, businessmen, and their organized associations were among the most active participants in the preparedness movement. George Ellery Hale, a spokesman for the National Academy of Sciences, promoted the academy as a potential coordinator of the nation's entire scientific effort in the event of war. Secretary of the Navy Daniels brought scientists and engineers into even closer cooperation with his service when in July 1915 he appointed a Naval Consulting Board, with Thomas A. Edison as chairman. Experts from the Society of Automotive Engineers and the National Automobile Chamber of Commerce worked with the Quartermaster Corps during the war to modernize a fleet of standard truck models.[9]

But the more traditional relationship between the military and American business had been entrepreneurial, with inventors attempting to peddle original ideas and business trying to sell goods and services. The military services sometimes advanced money for a pilot model, but usually the inventor produced the model himself and the department tested it. For most businesses, this was risky, especially since the purchasing bureaus within the services decided by competitive bidding who would get most production contracts. Additionally, prior to the First World War the services expected government-run arsenals and foundries to produce most of the small arms and heavy ordnance they required. In 1917 only Springfield Armory, of the five principal Ordnance Department establishments, could handle mass production.[10] Because there had been no regular, large-scale demand for arms and military equipment, government arsenals and private industry had only a limited capacity for immediate expansion to meet war requirements. To be effective that expansion had to be well organized and well managed. It was not.

Before the war, the individual War Department bureaus handled their own procurement without regard for an integrated departmental program. The system survived because it was never severely tested by shortages, competing interests, or a need for immediate results. The navy's supply system, largely centralized in the Bureau of Supplies and Accounts, was somewhat more efficient. But the war brought on a frenzy of procurement that the existing organizational structure proved unable to bear.

In the early days of the war, War Department bureau chiefs went on a spending spree. They succeeded to the extent that most of the supplies secured from American sources before the armistice had been contracted during the first six months of the war. The Quartermaster Corps bought uniforms and contracted for the construction of training camps; the Ordnance Department purchased small arms and other munitions; and the Adjutant General tried to corner the market on typewriters. But they were working at cross purposes with no centralized planning, no setting of priorities, and no ultimate authority. The frenzied activity of the bureaus absorbed a great portion of the nation's industrial capacity, created shortages, and contributed to a near paralysis of industry and transportation by the end of 1917.

Within the War Department, Secretary Baker, under considerable pressure, took steps to bring army supply under control. Increasingly he concentrated authority for procurement in the hands of Major General George W. Goethals, first as Quartermaster General and later as Director of Purchase, Storage, and Traffic. The appointment of Peyton C. March as chief of staff in February in 1918 resulted in further emphasis that the General Staff, not the individual bureaus, should direct the supply program. By the end of the war Goethals virtually controlled military supply procurement in the United States.

Mobilization of the private sector, to a large extent out of control during the early days of the war, remained chaotic to the end. The General Munitions Board (created April 1917) and its successor, the War Industries Board (WIB, created July 1917), superficially represented an effort to centralize economic mobilization. But the War Department, with Baker's approval, often ignored the WIB and continued to deal directly with its civilian suppliers. In March 1918 the situation improved when Wilson appointed Bernard Baruch chairman of the WIB and gave him authority to settle conflicts between departments, to follow up on contracts and deliveries, and to anticipate future military requirements. But Baruch did not become a supply tsar, merely the symbol for unified industrial mobilization. To a limited extent he coordinated the efforts of the military services, other government agencies, and industry. Yet many businesses continued to deal in their traditional way, directly with the services, bypassing the WIB.

However great American industrial capacity was, it could not adjust overnight to many specialized military requirements. A military aviation industry could not be created in just eighteen months, for example. As in other areas, industrial production and the smooth functioning of the mechanisms for economic mobilization did not become fully developed during the limited period of American participation in the war.

The effort to meet French and British production needs, in addition to American, further impeded economic mobilization. American industry had accepted large orders for munitions and other war goods from the Allied powers that between 1914 and 1917 accounted for $2.2 billion. The expertise gained in filling these orders provided a small technical base on which American industrial expansion later built. Yet to a far greater extent production for Allied needs complicated American production. In early April 1917 the Ordnance Department decided not to interfere with orders already placed for the Allies. This considerably limited the plants available for American ordnance production, thereby contributing to matériel shortages that plagued US troops to the end of the war. While the United States continued to meet Allied needs for some important war commodities, it was Allied, not American, production that largely supplied the American Expeditionary Forces (AEF) in 1918.[11]

American industry did produce prodigious quantities of war matériel. It made more rifles than either Great Britain or France during the same period; it produced more machine guns and automatic rifles than Great Britain, though not as many as France; and it turned out nearly as much smokeless powder as Britain and France combined. Quantities of munitions aside, in 1918 the United States was not the 'arsenal of democracy' it would become by 1940. Organizational weakness inhibited war production at many levels. Fewer than 3 per cent of the Ordnance contracts let before December 1917 had been completed by the time of the Armistice. Much of the production program, especially of ordnance, was out of balance. Although American industry produced 30.6 million 75-mm shell primers and 26.8 million shell cases, it made only 12 million fuses, 13.9 million shell bodies, and 10.9 million shell boosters. The AEF fought in France only because the French and British were able to furnish much of its supplies and equipment. American troops were especially dependent on foreign sources for artillery, ammunition, tanks, airplanes, and machine guns. The scale of this dependency was great; the AEF purchased 10 million tons of supplies and equipment in Europe during the war and received only 7 million tons shipped from the United States.[12]

The American military was effective in gaining access to the industrial and technological sources required to produce the equipment needed for the forces being created in 1917–18. They effectively exploited previous contacts with the business and scientific communities to gain such access. They were woefully ineffective, however, in managing the overall effort, especially in setting priorities, establishing realistic needs, and getting the arms and equipment to the AEF in France.

Through most of the First World War the American military had adequate qualitative and quantitative manpower resources. Resistance to military service generally was limited to socialist, pacifist, and religious groups, and had little significant impact on the military's requirements. Much of the success of military manpower policies had a basis in developments prior to the declaration of war.

Preparedness advocates, military reformers, and General Staff planners in 1916 and early 1917 debated the merits of some form of peacetime universal training and wartime conscription to meet military manpower needs. On several occasions in 1916, Hugh Scott, the chief of staff, testified in favor of compulsory military training for all able-bodied 18- to 21-year-olds as a means to raise 3 million men. At this early time Secretary Baker and the Wilson administration disassociated themselves from Scott's proposals. During late 1916 and early 1917, however, there was growing public sentiment in favor of some form of universal training. Baker, opposing peacetime universal military training (UMT), did believe that in the event of war some type of selective conscription would be necessary. By March 1917, Baker and Scott had also convinced President Wilson that for the duration of the war selective service was the most effective means to mobilize the nation. It not only would allocate men for military needs, but would provide for industrial and agricultural manpower as well.[13]

The Wilson administration and military planners resorted to conscription within six weeks of the declaration of war partially in response to earlier British experience. Great Britain did not adopt conscription until 1916, in the process demonstrating that indiscriminate volunteerism was a poor way to mobilize a nation for war. In particular British war production suffered from shortages of skilled labor in some key industries as many workers volunteered for military service. Wilson agreed to conscription less as a way to field a large force in France than as a way 'to keep the right men in the right jobs at home.' The Selective Service Act itself provided for occupational deferments and furloughs for servicemen to return to civilian jobs if production needs required it. Some 800,000 men received industrial and agricultural deferments (of 18 million classified) and a few thousand got furloughs in the summer of 1918. Although there were some occupational shortages, principally in shipping, shipbuilding, railroads, and the coal mines, manpower mobilization during the war was generally consistent with industrial mobilization.[14]

The prewar debates, particularly the support for UMT among influential segments of the population, went far to establish in the minds of most Americans the legitimacy of military service. The General Staff reinforced this by the careful framing of what became the Selective Service Act of 1917. There would be no bounties, no substitutes, and no purchased exemptions. All male citizens and resident aliens, from age 21 to 30 (later extended to 18 to 35), had to register with the local boards that actually administered the draft. The concept of local administration was politically astute and helped further support for and compliance with the system, which most perceived to be essentially fair.

Between May 1917 and the armistice, conscription was the principal means of raising men for the military services. While the draft directly supplied over two-thirds of military personnel during the war, indirectly it also spurred voluntary enlistments. Local boards registered nearly 24 million men, inducted almost 3 million, and forced millions of others into vital war industries. Given its size, the selective service system worked remarkably well in furnishing the services, largely the army, with the numbers of men needed.

One French officer told an American colleague late in 1918 that recruiting and conscripting over 3 million men in nineteen months was 'very good but not so difficult.' But it was 'astonishing,' if not 'impossible,' that in the same time the United States was able to commission 200,000 officers, most of them competent. Officer Training Camps (OTCs) of 90-day duration, first established in 1917 and an outgrowth of the prewar Plattsburg training camps, were the source of these officers. Because they were supplying the leadership cadres for the wartime army, the OTCs had had to open, screen, and train candidates and provide commissioned junior officers quickly, before the first draft calls began sending conscripts to the induction centers. The first series of OTCs admitted 43,000 officer candidates on May 16, 1917, just five weeks after the declaration of war. Their opening was an administrative disaster but a triumph of political effectiveness for the army. With neither the manpower nor the organization to work out the details of establishing the camps, the War Department accepted the assistance offered by the Military Training Camps Association (MTCA) – the Plattsburgers. Throughout the war the MTCA helped the army recruit for the officer corps and the technical services. It even provided the War Department with its card files of potential candidates and with clerical assistance. The MTCA also assisted the War Department in identifying and inducting men with specialized skills. When the AEF needed 7,000 men to work in its ordnance depots, MTCA recruiters enlisted the needed mechanics in three weeks. Connections between the War Department and the MTCA not only produced tangible results, but also assured support for the military by a significant segment of upper-middle-class American society.[15]

With some exceptions, the quality and quantity of available manpower remained adequate throughout the war. All newly commissioned officers of the line (infantry, cavalry, and artillery) were graduates of the OTCs. Only those who demonstrated ability – somewhat over 50 per cent of the candidates – received commissions on completing the course, thus assuring some consistency in the quality of the officer corps. Unlike the Second World War, when large numbers of the best qualified officer material went to the army air forces, the navy, or other specialized organizations, there was considerably less competition from other arms in the First World War, thus assuring the army combat branches of a large pool from which to draw junior leaders.

The principal shortcoming of the First World War personnel system occurred late in the war when combat divisions in the AEF faced significant shortages of trained replacements. But the shortages occurred because the

AEF expanded more rapidly than planned, casualties were heavier than expected, and the management of the replacement system was poor. In general, the military was effective in securing the manpower it needed.

Strategic Effectiveness

Allied decisions and actions were significant factors in limiting American strategic alternatives during the First World War, particularly since the United States was the junior partner in the coalition and entered the war late – after many of the important strategic decisions had been made. Prewar American strategic plans had little relevance in the war of 1917–18. Black, the plan for war with Germany, envisaged German intervention in the Western Hemisphere. None of the plans included the contingency of an American force being sent to Europe. American strategy during the war evolved largely from decisions and events after the diplomatic break with Germany in February 1917.

By mid-February the General Staff had developed plans for raising, equipping, and training an army of 4 million men. Also before the declaration of war, proposals surfaced in the War Department on potential theaters of war for American forces. Some American political and military leaders were reluctant to join the Allies in the bloody battles underway on the Western Front. Even after the declaration of war many assumed the United States would furnish the Entente with supplies, financial aid, and shipping and naval support but not put a large army in the field in France. President Wilson was among those who were unsure that the Western Front was where an American army should be committed in force. As late as November 1917 Wilson was still asking Secretary Baker for alternatives. The army however, had virtually settled the issue between May and July 1917.[16]

British and French missions visited the United States in late April to initiate military cooperation. The British wanted support troops and raised the sensitive question of using individual American replacements in their units. The French requested service troops and at least one combat division to show the flag and boost French morale. During May the administration agreed to send immediately a token expeditionary force to France. Wilson, on Secretary Baker's recommendation, selected Major General John J. Pershing to command the AEF. Baker delegated considerable authority to Pershing, who was to cooperate with the Allies in operations against the Germans but in so doing was to preserve the identity of American forces as a 'separate and distinct component.'[17] The maintenance of a separate American army, resisting Allied efforts to amalgamate American manpower into the French and British armies, remained a key element in US ground strategy for the rest of the war.

By the end of May 1917 Baker, Bliss, Pershing, and the planners on the General Staff had agreed that France was the decisive theater. Expeditions to other areas could influence the ultimate outcome but in themselves would not be decisive. Details of the ultimate size of the American commitment, how the US Army would cooperate with the Allies, and the area in France in which it would operate were all Pershing's responsibility.

Shortly after arriving in France, Pershing began to press for a much larger American contingent. The General Organization Project, completed by his General Headquarters (GHQ) staff on July 10, 1917, called for 1 million men by 1918 organized in 20 combat divisions, with an ultimate force level of 3 million in 1919. Over the course of the war the planning targets for force levels changed from 30, to 80, to eventually 100 divisions with GHQ of the AEF in France and the War Department General Staff in Washington often disagreeing. From the early summer of 1917 on, the US Army planned to send more than simply a token force to France.

Even before arriving in France, Pershing's staff began considering where on the Western Front to employ the force. The French wanted the AEF to occupy a sector on the eastern end of the front that ran from Toul in Lorraine to the Swiss border. Because the Lorraine front had been generally inactive for several years the Americans could train there and eventually release French divisions for more active sectors. Pershing believed that Lorraine provided good terrain that might allow the AEF to operate in the open and break the trench stalemate. The logistical arguments were most compelling, however. The base ports along the southwestern French coast and the railroad network south of Paris provided direct access to Lorraine. They were less congested than the facilities further north, which would have to be used if the AEF operated with the British or in a sector between the British and French armies.[18]

On September 25, 1917, the operations section at GHQ provided Pershing with 'A Strategical Study on the Employment of the AEF against the Imperial German Government,' which shaped much of what the AEF planned for and did over the next year. The study concluded that the AEF could not mount a major offensive in 1918, but established Metz as the objective for a decisive 1919 offensive. Pershing used the Metz offensive as justification for creation of an independent American army, for his refusal to turn US troops over to Allied commanders other than for training or temporary emergencies, and in his insistence on training the AEF for open warfare. Despite its importance to American strategic planning, the AEF never launched its Metz offensive.

The success of American ground strategy depended on cooperation with the British in combatting German submarine attacks on merchant shipping in the Atlantic. In 1916 the country had adopted a naval building program to create a fleet of sixty capital ships by 1925. Such a fleet was inappropriate to American naval needs in the Atlantic after April 1917. Admiral William S. Sims, sent to London to determine naval requirements and eventually the American naval commander in Europe, realized that German submarines posed a deadly threat to the French and British and to any American attempt to send men and material to Europe. Although other naval leaders wanted to continue the 1916 program, Sims advocated meeting the immediate submarine threat by concentrating on the construction of anti-submarine craft and merchant shipping. The Administration accepted Sims' recommendations and postponed the capital ship construction. American naval strategy was as much a response to peculiar wartime conditions as was the ground strategy.

American strategy in 1917–18 was both consistent with the political goals of the Wilson administration and militarily sound for hastening the defeat of the German armed forces. Key elements of that strategy, concentration in France, insistence on an independent American army, and cooperation with the Royal Navy in the anti-submarine effort, could all be justified politically and militarily.

When Woodrow Wilson led the United States into the European war his ultimate war aim was to influence the peace making following the war. To achieve that objective the United States had to maintain political and diplomatic flexibility, yet also make a major military contribution to winning the war. Creation of an independent American army and concentrating that force for offensive operations on the Western Front contributed to both. Alternatives to concentration in France had been tried by the Allies already, at Gallipoli and in Salonika, with not very successful results. An American sideshow was unlikely to be any more decisive, particularly given the limits on manpower and material immediately available. If the United States did not join in the effort on the Western Front, it would have contributed little to winning the war, might have even contributed to losing it, and would have been able to exercise far less moral and political leadership in the ensuing peace negotiations.

Similarly a policy of amalgamation might have obscured the American contribution to victory, whereas the effort of an independent American army was more discernible, more obvious. Wilson and Baker explicitly told Pershing that they wanted to maintain the separate identity of American forces, but considered that secondary to meeting any critical situations. In other words, if Pershing thought it was necessary to divert troops to help the French and British prevent a German breakthrough he should do so. Pershing and his staff thought amalgamation would disperse American strength; thus they persisted in building an independent American force. A recurring argument in their effort was the political effect it would have on Wilson's ultimate role as peace maker: 'when the war ends our position will be stronger if our army acting as such will have played a distinct and definite part.'[19]

The psychological impact of a separate American army, positive for the Allies, especially the French, and negative for the Germans, is difficult to gauge. But there is some reason to believe that an independent expeditionary force had more of an effect on both sides than amalgamated reinforcements would have had. Neither the Allies nor the Germans anticipated the speed and impact of the American build-up in France, nor the ability of US forces once on the battlefield. Ludendorff, after the war, lamented: 'I admit that the German General Staff did not perceive, right from the start, the speed and full scope of this American achievement.' Although Ludendorff admitted to some surprise at Pershing's eventually exercising independent command of an American army at St. Mihiel, he declared that for reasons of prestige and national self-esteem, Pershing 'simply had to take such a course.'[20]

Naval strategists also faced limited options. Yet when it became obvious that the big-fleet, capital-ship navy envisaged prior to the war by the General Board was not adequate for the immediate threat facing the US Navy, the strategy was changed. Destroyers, escorts, and merchant ships, to combat the German U-boats, became the focus of the naval build-up.

One historian has described the effectiveness of American First World War strategy, both politically and militarily, in the following terms: 'Rarely had a great nation followed a course so consistently and seemingly achieved its ends so fully. During 1918 the United States had gained its military goal – the provisional acceptance of President Wilson's plans for the post-war world.'[21] American strategy during the war had been congruent – securing the nation's political goals and reducing Germany's ability to resist.

There were risks inherent in that strategy, however. Wilson based his decisions to break relations with Germany in February 1917 and to declare war in April of that year on the belief that the United States had reached a point from which it could not turn back. Only by entering the war could the country shape a peace settlement that averted future wars and preserved a world in which American values could thrive. He did not believe that in early 1917 any European power directly menaced the physical security of the United States. But he could not acquiesce in the sacrifice of American prestige and moral influence, particularly for what he conceived such a sacrifice would mean in terms of affecting a postwar settlement.[22] For Wilson, war with Germany entailed fewer risks than did the loss of American moral suasion and influence if the country had ignored the German submarine threat.

The United States became a belligerent late in the First World War. At the time German submarines were sinking thousands of tons of merchant shipping each month while Allied offensives on the Western Front gained little ground, led to virtually no decisive results, and expended as much French and British manpower as German. In this situation the greatest risk for American strategy makers was that the war might be lost before US forces could be engaged in strength. It was obviously a risk shared by the Allies, for whom the consequences of failure were more severe than for the Americans.

The deliberate pace of American mobilization, imposed by the desire to create an independent, self-sufficient expeditionary force, had concerned the Allies for much of 1917. With the military and political situation deteriorating late in that year, and with an awareness that the Germans were building forces for a major offensive early in 1918, Allied concern was heightened. American reinforcements would be needed to stop the German offensive. Yet Pershing, with the support of Baker and Wilson, opposed any proposal to amalgamate American units in French and British organizations. When the crisis came in the spring of 1918 Pershing continued to resist. But Bliss and House, working through the Supreme War Council, forced some modifications in Pershing's position. In exchange for additional British shipping for American infantry reinforcements, but not for the support personnel needed to create the balanced independent force he wanted, Pershing agreed to allow US troops to serve temporarily with the British Expeditionary Force. When the crisis passed in mid-summer 1918, the Allied demand for amalgamation also passed.

In August 1918, Pershing organized his separate American army, but it was hardly independent for it relied on the Allies for much of its artillery, air, and logistical support. Pershing's unbending resistance to any form of amalgamation, particularly in the face of the German attacks of the spring and summer of 1918, involved grave risks. In the end he was correct: the Allies did not need as many individual American reinforcements as fast as they claimed. Pershing's success came with a political price, for the amalgamation controversy was the one issue that threatened Allied unity in the last year of the war. A less rigid American attitude on the question might have better preserved that unity, met immediate manpower needs in the 1918 crisis, and still have resulted in creation of an independent US force.

American naval strategy offers an interesting contrast. Although the General Board never completely renounced its desire to complete the 1916 capital-ship building program, it quickly recognized that the Germans might win the war before full American power could be brought to bear. Given that risk the naval strategists were more willing to cut back capital-ship construction in favor of the more urgently needed anti-submarine craft. There was thus greater consistency between risks and goals in American naval strategy during the war than in its military strategy.

During the First World War the United States had few formal mechanisms to integrate political and strategic planning. There was no National Security Council or Joint Chiefs of Staff. The existing interservice planning staff, the Joint Army-Navy Board, was largely ignored and played no significant role in framing American strategy. With no regularized means by which to receive information and recommendations, the political leadership sometimes made decisions in ignorance of the military consequences.

Wilson eventually tired of armed neutrality and opted for war out of a mistaken estimate of what war would require. Principally, he wanted to fight German submarines and defend American rights at sea. Additionally, the United States would supply the Allies with arms, supplies, and money. Although aware of General Staff plans for a 500,000-man expeditionary force, most of whom were to be regulars or other volunteers, he probably could not have envisaged in April 1917 the nearly 2 million man AEF that was in France in November 1918. Closer coordination between military planners and the administration might have avoided such situations, especially in the period just prior to the declaration of war.

After April 1917 Wilson exhibited little interest in and seldom interfered with the military aspects of the war. He ratified Pershing's selection as commander of the AEF, wanted US troops to fight as organized units in France, but was principally concerned with wartime diplomacy and with congressional efforts to reduce presidential authority for administering the war effort. Political access for military leaders was constrained. Between April and December 1917 Wilson met only once with Pershing and never with Bliss. The president exercised control over the army indirectly through Secretary Baker. This lack of direct political access made some senior officers uneasy. In December 1917 one General Staff officer recommended that the chief of staff seek to gain 'a direct constant voice on his own initiative in the councils of the Chief Executive.'[23] But when Baker left the country for an extended trip to Europe, Wilson began dealing directly with the new chief of staff, Peyton C. March. For the remainder of the war March had somewhat more access to the president than had earlier been the case. Additionally, several issues arose during 1918 that had major military and political components and that bore on aspects directly related to Wilson's war aims. These included amalgamation, intervention in Russia, and the armistice.[24]

Although lacking formal means to communicate regularly with the political leadership, the military did influence civilian policy makers over the course of the war. Most military leaders understood the political objectives of the administration. They knew that Wilson wanted to maintain political flexibility during the war and avoid too many commitments in order to have maximum influence at the peace conference. In fact, when it suited their purposes, as in the effort to create and maintain an independent American army, they used these political arguments to support their military objectives. Finally, the military leadership were universally able and politically attuned officers. Bliss and Pershing in particular had long civil-military experience. One reason Baker recommended Pershing for the AEF command, after all, was because he had willingly carried out Wilson's orders during the Mexican Punitive Expedition, even though he did not completely agree with the administration's position.

Although the military eventually was able to communicate its views to civilian policy makers and despite politically able military leaders, civil-military relations during the war were marked by the initial failure to inform Wilson of the military consequences of his actions in April 1917. Yet overall, American political and strategic goals proved logical.

On the other hand, America's strategic goals during the First World War were nearly totally inconsistent with the military force size and structure available in early 1917. The basic American war effort was to try to build an army and navy to meet the demands required by the strategic goals set between April and June 1917.

In 1917 the navy consisted of some 64,000 officers and men manning 130 shore stations and 300 ships. Battleships were the dominant force in the fleet and their strategic and operational employment dominated naval thinking. But the immediate need in the sea war was some means to counter the growing success of the German submarine campaign; in April 1917, coincidently, U-boats sank more merchant ships than in any other month of the war. Battleships were not a viable means to counter the submarines. Initially the navy had just 70 destroyers, only 44 modern oil burners, to use as escorts and in anti-submarine patrols. About half of these were sent in July 1917 to reinforce the British. As naval construction shifted to producing ships suitable for the anti-submarine war, American industry proved very adept at rapidly completing destroyers and other anti-submarine warfare (ASW) craft. Shipyards reduced the completion time for destroyers from over a year to two to three months. At the end of the war 248 destroyers, 60 large subchasers, and 116 small subchasers were built or being built for the US Navy and many more for the Allies.[25] By November 1918 over 80,000 American sailors were operating 47 bases and 370 ships in European waters alone. Over 200 were destroyers, subchasers, and other craft directly involved in ASW. The navy had also contributed to the ASW effort aviation squadrons and a mine-laying force that sowed a belt of mines 230 miles long and 15 to 35 miles wide. In eighteen months the Navy adjusted its force size and structure to meet the strategic requirements of its new anti-submarine mission.

The army had a more difficult and less successful time adjusting to its strategic requirements. Prior to the declaration of war the regular army consisted of something over 100,000 officers and men. Essentially it was a constabulary force whose principal missions included defending the coasts from seaborne attack and policing the Mexican border and America's insular possessions. It was not suited for the sort of war being waged in Europe. About one-third of its strength was in cavalry and fixed defense coast artillery troops. Only six of its fifty-two line regiments were field artillery; machine gun strength was equally inadequate. With the regular army small and ill-fitted for sustained combat on the Western Front, and with no reliable reserve component available, clearly the Western Front was not consistent with the resources at hand.

The amalgamation debate was essentially over whether the United States could create quickly enough an army consistent with its strategy. From the first the French and British did not think so. In particular they believed the US Army did not have enough competent, experienced commanders and staffs to run an independent army. Most estimates predicted that no significant US formations would reach France until 1919. With some important qualifications, the estimates proved wrong. By the time of the armistice, and well ahead of most projections, the United States had raised nearly 4 million men, with 2 million in France and over 1 million seeing combat. By contrast, it took the British three years to put 2 million men on the Continent – a task the Americans did in eighteen months. And the Americans did organize an independent army – two field armies, in fact, by November 1918. Forty-two American divisions reached France, of which twenty-nine saw combat.

However impressive the statistics, there was a price. Because the initial force size and structure were inconsistent with strategic objectives, a number of expedients were necessary to assure that American troops reached France in time to have an effect. Most divisions reached France and entered combat without completing their training regimen, and components of one division often had to fight with elements of another division with which they had never trained. American divisions were also nearly twice the size of similar Allied formations. This reduced requirements for staff officers and senior commanders but made the divisions unwieldly to maneuver and difficult to supply. Most of the machine guns, artillery, tanks, and aircraft that the AEF used had to be supplied by the Allies. Because no well-functioning replacement system existed, other divisions were skeletonized to obtain fillers for infantry units hard hit by casualties. Some of the expedients adopted in an effort to overcome the inconsistencies between force structure and size and strategic goals reduced the potential fighting power, endurance, and overall effectiveness of the AEF during its 1918 battles.

Although American strategy was consistent with the nation's industrial-technical base, planning of the overall economic mobilization was weak, as was the logistical infrastructure of the military.

The strategic decisions made in the spring and early summer of 1917, to field an independent American army on the Western Front and to shift naval construction from producing capital ships to large numbers of ships more suitable for anti-submarine warfare, were based in part on the assumption that the country's industrial base could shift rapidly from a peacetime to a wartime footing and that it could sustain the necessary rates of production to produce the specialized tools of war required. Potentially, it could. The United States possessed essential raw materials; a large output of iron, steel, and coal; and an expanding manufacturing base.

American industry did produce prodigious quantities of war material during 1917–18, increasing production significantly from prewar levels. For instance, in 1915 shipyards in the United States completed 325,413 tons of merchant shipping. By 1918 the total had increased to 2,080,262 tons, which represented about half of the total tonnage completed worldwide.[26] But inadequate overall planning for industrial mobilization, some production programs that were too ambitious, and unfortunate timing all plagued the American war effort. For tanks, aircraft, artillery, and machine guns, the AEF was nearly totally dependent on the Allies.

In some instances this was the result of conscious decisions. Artillery production facilities in the United States were limited. The Ordnance Department therefore concluded that existing capacity should be refit to produce French artillery pieces. Whatever the converted American plants could not furnish then could be made up from French stocks. Under the circumstances this was undoubtedly the correct decision. The conversion, unfortunately, was more difficult than anticipated. Only a small number of guns of American manufacture arrived in AEF hands before the armistice.[27] Overambition also plagued American war production. One three-year plan for military aviation proposed completing 23,000 aircraft and 45,000 engines at a cost of $640 million – this despite the example of a three-year French effort that produced only 4,700 planes and despite a virtually nonexistent American aircraft industry.[28] Unfortunate timing and poor allocation of available resources also plagued the American logistical effort. During the spring of 1918, when overseas transportation was in short supply and first priority was given to combat troops, Pershing recommended suspending shipment of horses and mules. By October 1918 he was paying the price in chronic shortages throughout the AEF of all means of ground transport – motor vehicles, railroads, mules, and horses.

At least some of the logistical chaos late in the war resulted from the AEF's having to make its major effort months in advance of the projected 1919 campaign. Had the effort been postponed to 1919 some of the potential war production might have been realized. Organizational changes in civilian economic agencies and the War Department, made early in 1918, had not had sufficient time to take full effect prior to the armistice. Although the military's initial strategic objectives were consistent with the nation's industrial-technical base, the management of the logistical infrastructure within the services, particularly the army, and the overall management of the war economy were ineffective.

Because the United States entered into belligerency late and joined the coalition as the junior partner, American strategists aligned their objectives with those already established by the Allies. They recognized that the strategic alternatives available in 1917 were limited and followed the Allies largely out of necessity.

Having attempted operations against the Central Powers in theaters other than the Western Front with limited success, the Allies concluded that a campaign of attrition against the German Army in France and Belgium was the only means by which a decision could be won. The Americans, recognizing that they were unlikely to change Allied strategy significantly and lacking a viable alternative strategy, reluctantly agreed. Similarly, the Americans conformed to the essential principles of already established Allied (largely British) naval strategy, namely containment of the German High Seas Fleet and defensive measures against attacks on merchant shipping.

While the Americans accepted the strategic assumptions of the Allies, it could not be said that their strategic objectives were completely integrated. President Wilson believed a decisive military victory over Germany was a necessary prelude for a postwar settlement that would create a stable world order. He made clear, however, that there were limits on how closely the United States would cooperate with the Entente powers. Military cooperation on the Western Front would be as complete as possible, but Wilson wanted to avoid political entanglements that could complicate the postwar peace making. The fight against amalgamation and for a separate American army was one aspect of the limits on cooperation.

The Allied command structure during the war put other limits on how closely the war aims and strategic objectives of the belligerents could be integrated. Until late in the war Allied armies in the field operated nearly independently, taking their strategic direction from their own governments. There was little coordination and no central direction of the strategic effort. When the United States entered the war it exchanged a series of missions with the French and British to work out the minimal means of cooperation. With the collapse of the Italian Front, the withdrawal of Russia from the war, and the threat of a German offensive, late in 1917 the Allies established the Supreme War Council (SWC) to provide additional coordination. For the discussion of some political and strategic issues the SWC was useful. Gradually it became the medium through which the amalgamation controversy was resolved. Bliss, the American representative on the SWC, was more willing than Pershing to compromise on the question of amalgamation. The Wilson administration, also not as completely opposed to amalgamation as Pershing, gradually gave Bliss more responsibility for settling the issue.

The SWC was an improvement over the previous arrangement and it was a useful forum for debate. But the Allied effort still had no central focus until April 1918, when the Allied governments entrusted Foch with the strategic direction of military operations. Because the respective army commanders-in-chief retained tactical employment of the forces, as well as the right to appeal Foch's decision to their governments, the Generalissimo had limited power. The command arrangement for the last six months of the war in no way resembled General Dwight Eisenhower's headquarters (SHAEF) twenty-five years later. Haig, Pershing, and sometimes even Pétain 'disputed almost every issue with Foch and obeyed his orders with reservation and when it suited them to do so.'[29] With the creation of the SWC, however, and the appointment of Foch, the Allies made some effort to coordinate strategic planning, concentrate their operational efforts, and give a minimum overall operational direction to the war.

Necessity, more than any original strategic designs, forced the Americans to integrate their overall military objectives with those of the Allies. This was true despite differences in political goals among the Allies. The United States used the SWC effectively as a means to protect its ultimate political interests while cooperating with the Allies militarily.

The naval war and the ground war fought by American forces in 1917–18 offer interesting contrasts in terms of putting strategic strengths against German weaknesses. In the Western Front strategy, the decision to create an independent American army, and even in the conception of the Metz offensive, army strategists were pitting strength against strength. On the other hand, naval strategists, particularly Admiral Sims, recognized vulnerabilities in the German naval campaign that the Allies could exploit.

A remarkably small German force carried the submarine war. As of February 1917 just over a hundred U-boats were in operation, generally with less than half at sea at any time. Given the strategic importance of the U-boat campaign, the German navy underemphasized its submarine-building program. Although clearly making a major strategic contribution to the German war effort in early 1917, the U-boat campaign was also vulnerable.

Within weeks of the declaration of war, Sims made several recommendations to the Navy Department on measures to combat the German submarine offensive: 'At present our battleships can serve no useful purpose in this area'; 'Maximum number of destroyers to be sent, accompanied by small anti-submarine craft'; and 'the critical area in which the war's decision will be made is in the eastern Atlantic at the focus of all lines of communication.'[30] Sims recognized that the Germans had only a limited number of U-boats and those had a limited range of operation; thus the ASW effort should concentrate on attacking them in the critical transatlantic sea lanes where they were most vulnerable.

American ground strategy in the First World War, emphasizing concentration of effort on the Western Front, pitted a potential strength, US manpower, against existing strength, the main force of the German Army. But the decision was not illogical. The Allies had already determined that France was the decisive theater; sideshows had not been particularly successful; and importantly, in the war of attrition waged between the Allied and German armies, American manpower represented an untapped and possibly decisive force. However sanguinary the prospects for a war of attrition on the Western Front, such a strategy nonetheless was consistent with prewar American strategic thought, which emphasized that victory would be won only by confronting, head-on if necessary, the enemy's main force.

American military leaders pursued the strategy of concentration in France consistently, although sometimes political considerations mitigated against it, e.g., intervention in Russia. In the end they were successful. During 1918 American manpower did make a quantitative and qualitative difference on the Western Front. As German manpower was worn down, particularly after the spring and summer offensives, American troops held larger and larger sections of the front. By November 11, 1918, the AEF held a slightly larger portion of the front than the BEF. A German general, Herman J. Von Kuhl, put the American contribution in perspective. Fresh, strong-nerved, though inexperienced, US troops in 1918 faced an exhausted German Army: 'In this and in the great numerical reinforcements which the Americans brought to our opponents at the decisive moment lies the importance of American intervention.'[31]

Operational Effectiveness

The US Army of 1916–17 was campaign experienced, many officers and enlisted men having fought against Moro bands in the Philippines and Villa's irregulars along the Mexican border. The principal combat arms were all tactically proficient. It was a small army more suited for constabulary duties than for mounting a major campaign against experienced European opponents.

But the US Army did possess a coherent, codified, and generally relevant operational doctrine. In 1905 the General Staff had adopted German regulations to American organization and produced the first US Army edition of *Field Service Regulations (FSR)*. Subsequent, revised editions appeared in 1910, 1914, and 1918. In both general principles and specific details the *FSR* governed the administrative, tactical, and operational employment of the army in the field. Above all they emphasized offensive operations by mobile field forces as the means to achieve decisive results.

The *FSR* were the basic organizational and operational doctrine followed by the AEF in 1918. Nonetheless, even the July 1918 revised regulations had important shortcomings and omissions. They did not take into account the use of aviation, tanks, or gas, and they underemphasized machine guns, field artillery, and motor transport. Doctrine for employment of new weapons systems and the integration of new technology with traditional means was not, therefore, completely codified but evolved during 1917–18 through use.

The US Army also possessed a small cadre of experienced, trained officers capable of implementing its operational doctrine. From 1903 through 1916 the Army War College, Staff College, and School of the Line had emphasized the operational realm in their curriculum. When the United States entered the war graduates of these schools, by age, grade, and experience, were destined to become the key staff officers and brigade and regimental commanders in the AEF. (Many of the division, corps, and army commanders had been too senior to attend the schools.) At the schools these officers had studied the workings of general staffs in war games, practiced moving armies to battle, sharpened their tactical decision making in map maneuvers, and in general prepared themselves intellectually for managing mass armies at war. The greatest shortcoming of the schools was the small number of officers who attended; about four hundred graduates were available in 1917.[32]

The course of the war and the pace of the American build-up in France necessitated a piecemeal commitment of US units. GHQ AEF did not organize its ultimate operational objective, a separate field army, until August 10, 1918. Thus the AEF did not fully enter the operational realm until eighteen months after the United States had declared war and only three months before the armistice. This limited the time in which commanders, staffs, and troops could learn from their experience and improve their performance.

Other factors beyond the control of the AEF also limited its operational effectiveness. Allied strategy assumed the United States could not play a major role until 1919; American organization and training projected such a timetable as well. With the Allied defensive and offensive successes from June through August 1918, Foch and Haig saw the prospect of defeating the Germans before the end of the year if the British, French, and American armies all pushed hard. Foch wanted the principal US effort along the southern flank of the attack pushing north between the Argonne Forest and the Meuse River toward Sedan. Pershing wanted to follow the AEF's original strategy of launching an attack on St. Mihiel-Metz, 60 miles south of where Foch wanted the US effort. The compromise, a limited First Army attack on St. Mihiel followed two weeks later by a major effort in the Meuse–Argonne, put severe operational strains on the AEF. Within two weeks the First Army would mount two major attacks 60 miles apart, in the process shifting its axis of advance 90 degrees. The terrain in the region between the Argonne and the Meuse, where Foch wanted the American attack, was rough, wooded, and clearly favored the defense. It was not a region conducive to attack by an inexperienced army. Because of the forces assigned to the St. Mihiel attack, Pershing had few experienced divisions for use in the Meuse–Argonne. Of the nine assault divisions, five had little battle experience, three were worn from the summer campaigns, and only one was a sound, veteran unit.[33] Given these difficulties, it is not surprising that the AEF was in a number of respects operationally ineffective.

Despite obvious problems with performance, American operational doctrine in the First World War was basically sound. It stressed integration of the combat arms and combat support units to conduct offensive operations. Both the current *Field Service Regulations* and pronouncements from GHQ AEF emphasized that all arms, especially the artillery, had to support the infantry in gaining fire superiority and fulfilling the organization's mission.

To some extent the selection of key personnel also fostered operational integration in the AEF. Pershing made good use of the small number of regular army officers that had any previous training in operational planning and execution such as the service schools at Fort Leavenworth provided. When he initially formed his headquarters staff, twenty-four of the twenty-seven officers he requested were Leavenworth men. Throughout the war, of the twelve officers who served at GHQ as chief of staff, deputy chief of staff, and heads of the five staff sections, nine had been to Leavenworth. The pattern continued in the operational commands, where the chiefs of staff of both field armies and nine of the ten officers who were chiefs of staff of the seven AEF army corps were Leavenworth men, as were most of the heads of the operations sections of the corps. Only three of the twenty-nine US divisions that saw combat did not have Leavenworth graduates as chiefs of staff. The common background of the Leavenworth men provided some unity and consistency to the AEF's operational performance. One AEF staff officer remembered meeting with three corps chiefs of staff in October 1918 to plan an attack: 'Except for an ominous rumble to the north of us, I might have thought that we were back at Leavenworth. It seemed just like a Staff College conference between the phases of one of the old map maneuvers. The technique and the talk were just the same.'[34]

The Leavenworth-trained staff officers were not omniscient. Some had difficulty dealing with older officers who had not attended the schools and who were often the division and corps commanders. Leavenworth men were in part responsible for some of the AEF's major operational breakdowns – the delay in taking Montfaucon, the stalled Meuse–Argonne offensive, and the race to Sedan. But they did contribute a unity of purpose to AEF operations that would otherwise have been sorely lacking. To the extent that Pershing utilized this trained group of officers throughout the combat elements of the AEF to assure the integration of operational doctrine with performance, he enhanced the organization's operational effectiveness.

In its two operational efforts, St. Mihiel and the Meuse–Argonne, the AEF attempted to follow doctrine and utilize combined arms to support the main infantry advance. Several factors hindered performance. For instance, only a small number of tanks, less than a quarter of what the planners thought necessary, was available for either action. In both offensives the limited tank resources permitted support to only two divisions on a small portion of the front.[35] Despite poor tank–infantry liaison, the tanks assisted the infantry advance in the sectors where they were employed but had little impact on the overall objectives of the operations.

In preparing for the two offensives in the fall of 1918 American operational commanders were cognizant of factors that could enhance the fighting power of their units – namely, exploitation of weather, terrain, and surprise. Because Foch, not the AEF, had established the objectives and the basic timetable for the fall offensives, American commanders were unable to utilize the weather or the terrain to their advantage. Terrain in the Meuse–Argonne region, in fact, worked to their considerable disadvantage. Yet in both attacks, they had some success in achieving initial operational surprise. They masked the concentration of troops for the attacks by limiting most road movements to the night; they held artillery registration and radio messages in the concentration area to a minimum; and they attempted a number of ruses to convince the Germans that French troops were still occupying positions in what were supposedly quiet sections of the front. The First Army achieved some surprise in the initial stages of both operations.

As with the integration of forces to enhance combat power, American experience with mobility and flexibility was also mixed. The technology during the First World War imposed limits on mobility in the AEF; application of that technology imposed others. Although the AEF used great numbers of motorized vehicles, motor transport was little more than a supplement to horses and wagons for local transportation and a substitute for railroads for longer hauls. The AEF never had more than half of the vehicles prescribed in tables of organization. More importantly, because this was the

US Army's first large-scale use of motorized equipment, there was uncertainty as to how accurately the organization tables represented real needs.

In order to overcome its transportation shortages and limited mobility, the AEF resorted to expedients, particularly in the last months of the war. During the first week of August 1918 the 89th Division moved by truck to the front near Toul. It was the first large-scale movement of an American division conducted by an American organization entirely in American trucks. To accomplish the move of just this single division, however, required trucks 'from all over the AEF.' The division itself had to plan, organize, and coordinate the move at the last minute.[36] On the one hand, this incident illustrates the limited operational mobility of the AEF. On the other, it indicates that the organization was sufficiently flexible to overcome some of the limits on its mobility, if only in a limited area.

The United States demonstrated its greatest feat of mobility and flexibility in transporting troops to the theater of war. Shipping was perhaps the most difficult, intractable problem faced by the United States in the war. It affected American participation at all levels. Losses in merchantmen to U-boats in early 1917 were serious, but the difficulty was more fundamental. In 1917 the US merchant fleet was 'more legend than reality'; American ships carried less than 10 per cent of US foreign commerce. Early in the war Wilson recognized the inadequacy of the merchant marine and wanted legislation to help expand it. Congressional opponents, fearing government intervention in international commerce, expansion of presidential power, and possible friction with the British, put off action for two years. The Shipping Act of September 1916 did lay the basis for the effort in 1918 that permitted the rapid movement of a large portion of the AEF to France. But it was several years late in passage and months slow in implementation. Inadequate American shipping resources led to great dependence on the Allies for transatlantic transport. The Allies exacted political and strategic concessions from the Americans; shipping shortages also had a negative impact on the operational and tactical effectiveness of the AEF.[37]

By end of 1917 fewer than 200,000 US troops were in France, largely because the shipping available to the army was only one-fourth that needed to meet the goal of putting and maintaining 1 million men in France by the end of June 1918. Between March and August 1918 an additional 124 ships went into service transporting US troops and supplies to Europe. Most of the additional tonnage was British, diverted from other use. However, German merchant ships and passenger liners, interned in American ports since the outbreak of the war, provided another 300,000 tons of shipping capacity. When the United States declared war the German crews of these ships wrecked the engines and other machinery. Naval shipyards quickly repaired these ships, much to the surprise of the Germans, who believed many of the vessels were permanently disabled. The former German ships carried over 500,000 American troops to France in 1918. The overall movement of manpower to France in the months following the March 1918 German offensive was remarkable; 1.5 million men in the last six months of the war. The German high command had not expected such an achievement; even Ludendorff considered the effort skillfully and energetically undertaken.[38]

In demonstrating intellectual flexibility in command and control, American forces were only partially effective. The St. Mihiel and Meuse–Argonne campaigns offer examples of both operational effectiveness and ineffectiveness in this regard. Within two weeks in September 1918, the First Army launched two major offensives on battlefields 60 miles apart connected by only three usable roads. The staff work alone needed to extricate the First Army from one battle and ready it for another would have strained the staffs of any of the Western Front belligerents in 1918. That the relatively inexperienced First Army staff on very short notice mastered the operational and logistical details was testament to its 'outstanding flexibility of mind.'[39]

Unfortunately the flexibility demonstrated by the First Army staff in planning and massing forces for the Meuse–Argonne offensive was not often carried over to the actual conduct of operations. Operations orders in the AEF normally prescribed in great detail division and corps boundaries, phase lines, and objectives. For the initial attack in the Meuse–Argonne the planners believed that such precise, detailed orders were essential to facilitate the movement of the large numbers of inexperienced troops engaged. The close adherence to the prescribed orders that the planners thought necessary for control, however, dampened whatever initiative the commanders on the ground might have exercised. Too often units halted on their initial objective, within their unit boundaries, to await progress by units on their flanks, even when they had the opportunity to seize additional key objectives. A German observer of the St. Mihiel offensive described this inflexibility: '. . . the plan of attack was too schematic. An attack on a large scale does not run like clock-work . . . This was not taken into consideration in the American plan of attack.'[40] At St. Mihiel the First Army plan succeeded beyond all expectation with the army objectives being reached, in some places, within the first few hours. But this was not followed up. The American command needed to liberate itself from previous preparations and make new decisions. This they did not do.

The Americans were also slow to adapt new technology to battlefield operations during the war. In 1917 the United States possessed few combat aircraft, no tanks, and no offensive or defensive gas warfare capability. By November 1918 American industry had produced few of these weapons for use by the AEF, and no clearly codified doctrine for their employment had been developed. Yet at the operational level the AEF did employ aircraft, tanks, and gas. With respect to new weapons the principal American failure was one of organization and production, a reflection of the general disorganization of the War Department for most of the first year of the war.

The AEF from its earliest organization projects in the summer of 1917 planned to use these new weapons. Far more than the War Department, Pershing recognized the advantages of providing an organizational base to oversee the doctrinal development and employment of new weapons. At GHQ AEF he established chiefs of the air service in May, of the chemical warfare service in September, and of the tank corps in December 1917; at the War Department those services did not get an institutional basis until May, June, and April 1918 respectively. One careful student of technology and doctrine has postulated that the greatest stumbling block to the revision of doctrine and the integration of new technology with existing operational concepts is the absence of a system, or institutional base, to analyze the new weapons and their relation to prevailing practices.[41] Yet Pershing's effort at the operational level could not overcome the dispersion of effort in the United States in development and production.

The American experience with chemical warfare was indicative of the process. By April 1917 the Bureau of Mines at the Interior Department, which had been testing masks and respirators, had done more to prepare for gas warfare than had any element of the War Department. Following the declaration of war, the medical department of the army developed and procured gas masks (functions later turned over to the Engineers); the ordnance department developed offensive chemical weapons; and the General Staff formulated offensive and defensive doctrine and supervised chemical warfare training. All this stateside activity had virtually no effect on the AEF.

In August 1917 Pershing organized a gas service in the theater of operations that in many respects paralleled or duplicated the gas activity in the War Department. However, AEF division commanders and staffs were unwilling to sacrifice training time from more traditional military skills for a new, unfamiliar weapon. As a result, between one-quarter and one-third of all combat casualties suffered by the AEF were from gas, although fatalities were relatively few.[42] The AEF made minimal offensive use of gas as well. Early in the Meuse–Argonne, corps and division commanders, with no training, experience, or doctrine to follow, seldom resorted to gas to neutralize enemy batteries and strong points. As the First Army artillery commander noted: 'offensive use of gas does not seem to be understood.' Over the course of the campaign, subjected to often incessant gas attacks by the Germans, AEF commanders gradually recognized the necessity of using it themselves. By the November 1 attack the AEF had gained confidence in the use of gas and used it to good effect.[43]

American experience with gas warfare during the First World War was basically one of learning by doing. There was no systematic effort beforehand to assess the new weapon, determine needs, develop a doctrine, and train troops and commanders in its use. To some extent the same situation obtained with tanks and military aviation. There was a general recognition of the importance of technology and the new means of warfare. But there was a critical lack of coordination between the AEF and the War Department. As a result no American doctrine for their employment developed. American production of these weapons faltered, making the AEF dependent on the Allies for material; and actual operational employment was poor. The United States did not make effective use of the weapons technology available.

Support and logistical activities were major operational weaknesses of the AEF. In part the problems were spatial, material, and doctrinal. Never before had the United States (or any nation) attempted to support a 2 million man force 3,000 miles from its industrial base; the sheer magnitude and unique character of the situation caused problems. There were also material shortages that had an adverse impact on American operational performance.

Finally, although *Field Service Regulations* provided some doctrinal basis for the administration and support of an army in the field, few officers in the prewar US Army had seriously studied battlefield logistics. Before the war Leavenworth had included separate field engineer, signal, and field medical schools, but never a separate supply school. Instructors at Leavenworth recognized that while their curriculum did not completely ignore logistical support of operations, it was heavily weighted to purely tactical and operational considerations. Thus while the AEF had many competent officers in supply billets, regular army quartermasters or recently commissioned civilians with business backgrounds, there was no cadre of logisticians trained in all aspects of supply operations.

The AEF classified supplies (classes 1–4) for distribution to combat divisions according to recurring requirements. Class 1, for instance, included all items of daily automatic supply – rations, fuel, gasoline, oil, and forage. The distribution of the other classes of supplies was dependent on requisitions from supply officers based on use, need, or other variables. Regulating officers and regulating stations at the railheads, innovations adopted from the French, governed the flow of supplies between the depots and the divisions. It was a well-conceived scheme that recognized operational performance depended on a regular, automatic flow of supplies to the combat elements.

The Meuse–Argonne offensive put severe strains on the system. Transportation of troops, supplies, and casualties was the principal problem. The poor roads in the region could not support the heavy traffic needed to sustain a major offensive – fresh troops and supplies moving in one direction with casualties and exhausted units travelling the other. Traffic, heavy bombardment, and years of neglect eventually broke the surfaces of the three main roads leading into the area. Large numbers of engineer and pioneer troops spent the remainder of the war keeping the roads minimally passable. Shortages of trucks, horses, and mules intensified the transportation problem. Shipping priorities the previous spring, which emphasized infantrymen but not the service troops and equipment (including animals) needed to support large formations, had come home to haunt the AEF. The number of casualties sustained in the last weeks of the war also began to tax the evacuation and hospital system to its limits. Although the AEF had a well-conceived logistics system, problems in implementation, particularly transportation shortages, hampered its effective support of offensive operations.[44]

Despite the relatively slow pace of First World War operations, the AEF faced a persistent problem of communications. Numerous other means of communications were tried, including visual lamp and flag signals, carrier pigeons, and buzzer codes sent over telephone lines; all had serious limitations. So did field radios, which were immobile, unreliable, and tended to give away friendly positions to enemy intercept operators. Runners and field telephones, both vulnerable to enemy fire, were the principal means of communication within the AEF. As a result, operational commanders frequently lacked timely information on which to base their decisions and had no rapid, dependable means to convey decisions, once made, to subordinate units.[45]

The AEF developed an extensive intelligence apparatus that utilized agent reports, prisoner-of-war interrogations, interception of enemy communications, and analysis of German press reports. But this effort had little positive effect at the operational level. Few of the messages intercepted and decoded by the Radio Intelligence Service (G-2-A-6) had immediate operational relevance in the two American offensives, although radio traffic analysis helped clarify the extent of the enemy withdrawal and order of battle in the latter stages of the Meuse–Argonne campaign. At the beginning of that campaign, insufficient intelligence contributed to the overambitious attack plan. Although American order-of-battle information on the German units in the zone of operations was accurate, the assessment of the morale and staying power of the enemy was not. In part because he had been led to believe that the German units had low morale, Pershing risked using inexperienced assault divisions in the unsuccessful effort to overwhelm them.[46]

In several respects, the AEF's offensively oriented operational doctrine was not sufficiently supported by its logistical system. In particular, the AEF experienced difficulties in keeping troops at the front adequately provisioned. During the last two months of the war the rough terrain and poor road network in the Meuse–Argonne region exacerbated existing weaknesses in the AEF's logistical and transportation infrastructure. Other shortcomings in communications and intelligence further eroded American operational effectiveness.

American operational doctrine and practice during the First World War were generally consistent with the country's strategic objectives. The navy's principal strategic mission was to assist the Royal Navy in defeating the German U-boat campaign and to protect merchant ship and troop convoys destined for Europe. Although the main operating units of the US fleet, the battle line, were inappropriate for the anti-submarine campaign, the navy rapidly adjusted its forces and operational doctrine to meet the U-boat threat. The immediate dispatch of available destroyers for escort duty in European waters, the shift in the naval building program to construction of anti-submarine craft, and the adoption of the convoy system all furthered the strategic objective of defeating the submarines. The convoy system in particular proved effective. Convoys employed light cruisers and armed merchantmen as escorts for commercial shipping on the high seas. Destroyers and other light escort craft provided protection when a convoy passed through the most dangerous U-boat zones, generally in the mid-Atlantic. Because the escorts made the convoys more difficult and dangerous to attack, the U-boats began to operate in narrower waters where other ASW measures (mines, depth charges, aircraft, and nets) were more effective. The ASW campaign adopted in 1917 ultimately defeated the U-boats and permitted the rapid build-up of American forces in France during the spring and summer of 1918.

American army operational doctrine emphasized offensive action by combined arms to engage the main force of the enemy army, head on if necessary. This approach, basically attritional, was consistent with Allied strategy and with the strategic and political objectives of the Wilson administration. The administration wanted a visible, viable American presence that would affect the military outcome of the war in such a way as to increase American political influence during the peace making. An American army conducting offensive operations against the Germans on the Western Front was one means of demonstrating the military and political power of the United States. Alternative operational employment of American forces, such as amalgamating them into French and British formations, would have diminished the strategic and political impact.

The operational doctrine implemented by the AEF pitted American strength against German strength. The operational realm, in this respect, reflected the strategic. However, by the late summer of 1918, when the AEF first began functioning at the operational level, the relative strengths of the two forces were rapidly changing. The AEF could afford to wage an attrition campaign much more than the German Army could sustain one.

Pershing did not rush to implement his operational concepts. Early AEF planning foresaw no significant operational role for US forces until 1919. Pershing recognized that through much of 1918 his troops were inexperienced and his tactical units undertrained or untrained for the operations he wanted to undertake. Even after the First Army was operational Pershing wanted to limit its deployment. At one point in early September 1918, he argued with Foch that the First Army should carry out the St. Mihiel assault and then withdraw from active operations to train throughout the winter of 1918–19 for an offensive in early 1919 against Metz.

Allied strategic imperatives in the face of the deteriorating German position, however, demanded the full-scale commitment of the First Army after St. Mihiel. In the Meuse–Argonne campaign Pershing utilized his growing operational strengths – fire power and manpower. The American zone of operations afforded little opportunity for maneuver, but then American doctrine placed little stress on it anyway. The First Army plan combined strong air support by over a thousand planes and massive fire support by 2,700 guns with overwhelming infantry superiority; the assault troops would outnumber the German defenders by eight to one. After some initial success the Meuse–Argonne attack came to a halt. Logistical and operational failures by the Americans and fierce German resistance, magnified by the terrain and prepared defensive positions, all contributed. Pershing continued to press his commanders and his troops to the attack. The last six weeks of the war for the AEF were very much a battle of attrition.

Once engaged in the Meuse–Argonne attack, Pershing never doubted the operational strengths of the AEF nor the superiority of his troops over those of his Allies or the Germans. He believed they would triumph. As one British historian put it: 'In the end, and at a cost which the United States could well afford, he would be right.'[47] But American operational doctrine had evolved in a vacuum; the US Army was preparing to fight no particular enemy, least of all the German Army. Thus it was fortunate that the AEF's operational strengths, its manpower and fire power, were increasing at the moment it became heavily engaged with the German Army, whose combat power was then on the wane.

Tactical Effectiveness

Tactical performance in the AEF did not completely match tactical pronouncements and intentions. American commanders, particularly Pershing, believed that three years of trench warfare had eroded the offensive spirit of the French and British and led them to accept a defensive attitude, which resulted in an indecisive war of attrition. Pershing concluded that if his troops adopted the trench warfare tactics of the Allies, their offensive spirit would also wane. He wanted aggressive American troops capable of driving the Germans out of their trenches and of defeating them in a war of movement and pursuit. Pershing continually stressed the importance of the infantry rifleman: 'The rifle and the bayonet are the principal weapons of the infantry soldier. He will be trained to a high degree of skill as a marksman both on the target range and in field firing. An aggressive spirit must be developed until the soldier feels himself, as a bayonet fighter, invincible in battle.'[48]

Despite Pershing's faith that the American rifleman was the key to success on the Western Front, other aspects of AEF planning took into account the effects of modern weapons on warfare. In July 1917 the Operations Section (G-3) at GHQ rejected recommendations that the AEF adopt light, mobile howitzers for its artillery regiments. Choosing fire power over mobility, the G-3 determined the AEF should use heavy French weapons, 75-mm and 155-mm guns. The size and organization of American infantry divisions also indicated that the AEF expected battles of attrition against German defenses organized in depth. AEF divisions were twice as large as European, were rich in infantry, and had a full artillery brigade for fire support. In May 1918 GHQ AEF rejected a smaller three-regiment division organization that had advantages in mobile, flexible maneuver operations. The staff concluded that the square division of four regiments-two brigades of infantry was more suited for Western Front combat.[49]

AEF doctrine stressed that commanders should press an aggressive offensive using flexible formations that made use of the terrain and supporting arms. Particularly in frontal assaults, fire superiority and formations in depth were required to carry the enemy position. Conventional wisdom in the AEF deemed that such assaults could be successful if conducted in strength on a sufficiently narrow front. Early experience in offensive operations, however, did not go according to doctrine. During the summer of 1918 a German intelligence officer suprisingly reported of the Americans: 'Apparently little stress is laid on marksmanship.'[50] There had also been little noticeable command influence, particularly in coordinating the action of infantry and artillery.

Americans were equally critical of themselves. The training section (G-5) at GHQ analyzed combat performance and pointed out shortcomings. In early September 1918 a G-5 publication noted: 'The principles enunciated [regarding offensive combat] are not yet receiving due application.'[51] Assault formations had been too dense and lacked flexibility; scouts were seldom used; supporting arms were improperly employed; and junior officers displayed little initiative. After St. Mihiel and the first week of the Argonne, the G-5 had seen improvements, but noted that some troops lacked aggressiveness and that brigade and division headquarters were too far in the rear.[52] By the time of the armistice, American units were becoming more tactically proficient: 'Rapid progress in the art of war was everywhere to be seen. Divisions were more mobile, formations less dense; suitable maneuvers in the attack were more often seen; and vastly better advantage was taken of cover. Commanders and staffs were generally more confident, and worked with greater sureness and dispatch.'[53] Clearly the AEF learned to fight by fighting, as much as by Pershing's insistence on open warfare.

American tactics, emphasizing offensive combat and open warfare, were consistent with the country's political, strategic, and operational objectives. The political leaders wanted a visible, prominent American military presence overseas that would maximize political influence during the postwar peace making. Strategically this entailed organizing an independent field army capable of conducting offensive operations against main-force German units in France. Operational doctrine similarly stressed the attack: 'Decisive results are obtained only by the offensive. Aggressiveness wins battles.'[54]

From shortly after Pershing arrived in France in June 1917, the AEF based its planning, organization, and training on an offensive role for US troops, with the main effort to come in 1919 by an independent US field army. It took time and assistance from battle-experienced Allies to create the sort of force that the Americans wanted and to train it in offensive tactics. While open warfare was the ultimate tactical goal, all American divisions received extensive training in trench warfare. In fact, most US troops first saw action occupying trench positions, on the defensive, usually closely supervised by the French or British.

Indeed, some in the AEF believed the Allies exerted too much influence on American tactical development. One staff officer in July 1918 articulated a commonly held view among AEF professionals: 'Berlin cannot be taken by the French or the British. . . It can only be taken by a thoroughly trained, entirely homogeneous American army, in which the sense of initiative and self-reliance upon the part of all officers and men has been developed to the very highest degree.'[55] American insistence on its own tactical methods and doctrine was consistent with the objective of emphasizing a unique US contribution to the war effort for political and strategic purposes.

Besides political considerations and national pride, there were valid tactical reasons why the AEF opposed amalgamation of small units (companies and battalions) as the Allies had requested. After four years of war Allied interoperability was far from perfected. At the tactical level, the French and British remained remarkably ignorant of each other's language, doctrine, organization, and methods. There was little reason to suppose the Americans would have any more success in such matters, especially with the French. The language problem frequently proved insurmountable between French company officers and the Americans who trained with them, served with them in quiet sectors, and sometimes relieved them at the front. American experience with French staff work and command methods during the defensive and counteroffensive operations of June–July 1918 was sometimes exasperating and costly. French commanders repeatedly changed orders, often with little advanced warning, and paid little attention to the logistics needs of the American units serving under them. For instance, on three occasions during the Aisne–Marne counteroffensive, on the Marne, on the Ourcq, and at Fismette, units of the 28th Infantry Division, while attached to French divisions, suffered heavy casualties directly as a result of faulty French tactics.

The experience of the 28th Division made Allied criticism of American training, tactics, and competence all the more difficult for Pershing and his subordinates to accept. It reinforced their opinion of American methods and their opposition to amalgamation.[56]

Doctrinally, American offensive tactics emphasized the close integration of infantry with supporting arms and the need for infantry to use fire and maneuver when attacking hostile positions. Performance was inconsistent, with most divisions seldom achieving the level of tactical proficiency Pershing expected. Rigid plans of attack, lines of infantry advancing over open ground without regard for concealment or cover, little use of fire and maneuver, and improper employment of infantry supporting arms were typical of American infantry in the offensives of the summer and fall of 1918.

Artillery support was most effective when controlled by observers with the front-line infantry who could communicate with the gun batteries to adjust the fire directly on identified targets. Although the requirement was understood, it proved nearly impossible for most American units to achieve. Reliable communications linking the front-line observers with the guns did not exist. Radios were not yet portable enough and telephone wire linking the gunners to the observers was easily and often cut by fire and vehicular traffic. American artillery relied more on map firing, saturating a preselected area with shells, than on observed fire, which was more efficient for infantry close support.[57]

Infantry attacks on the Western Front could seldom carry beyond the limit of the range of the field artillery. Thus any army contemplating offensive-oriented tactics needed to find a means to extend the range of artillery support. Most simply, this required firing batteries to displace forward as the infantry advanced. Because guns on the move could not fire and were vulnerable to counter battery fire, especially the closer they got to the front, the process required planning, training, and coordination. Some batteries had to remain in place to continue fire support for the infantry while others were on the move. Engineers had to make roads passable so the guns would have unhindered, rapid movement to their new firing positions. And the infantry had to stay in touch with the gunners so the advance would not be deprived of maximum support at critical moments. Few American divisions trained to accomplish such complicated movements. Division artillery, in fact, normally trained separately from the other combat elements. Furthermore, divisions in the latter stages of the war had artillery regiments from other divisions attached, rather than their organic units. Tactical effectiveness suffered because the AEF did not take steps to maximize coordination and integration of the infantry and artillery within combat divisions.

American tactics in the First World War also underemphasized surprise and the rapid exploitation of opportunities. The only specific mention of surprise in *Field Service Regulations* was in a defensive context: 'To be surprised is never justifiable in warfare.'[58] Doctrinal statements from the G-5 section of the AEF also virtually ignored tactical surprise and exploitation. The necessity for subordinate infantry commanders to exercise 'a high degree of initiative' while handling local tactical situations was addressed by G-5 only after the armistice and largely as recognition of tactical shortcomings in the last stages of the war.[59]

Far more than with surprise and exploitation, American tactical doctrine was concerned with careful planning, with preparing precisely drafted operations orders according to a fixed format, with developing fire support, and with maintaining correct formations and troop frontages. In short, the Americans fought set-piece battles. American commanders recognized some of the shortcomings of the AEF and believed that these required closely controlled operations. The shortcomings included deficient small-unit leadership, too few trained staff officers to support a system of decentralized leadership, and inexperienced troops that did not always recognize the opportunities presented to them.

The closely controlled tactical dispositions in the AEF resulted in numerous missed opportunities. Perhaps most significant was the failure to take Montfaucon, the dominant German position, early in the Meuse–Argonne attack. Montfaucon was the first day's objective for the 79th Division. Early in the attack, the 4th Division, facing less opposition than the 79th, had the opportunity to flank and possibly encircle the town. The corps chief of staff prevented the movement of the 4th Division into the 79th's zone of action because operations orders did not specify such a movement and it would have complicated control. The Germans were given time to consolidate their hold on Montfaucon, which did not fall for several days. This contributed to the early stalling of the entire Meuse–Argonne attack. Exploitation, in this and other situations, was forsaken for control.

Despite the absence of doctrinal guidance, in some situations units in the AEF did attempt, sometimes successfully, to achieve tactical surprise. Artillery fired smoke barrages to mask the movements of attacking infantry. Night movements and, in the last phase of the Meuse–Argonne, night attacks were attempted. Some commanders also tried to adjust the patterns of attacks so that preliminary artillery barrages would not always signal an assault. Surprise and exploitation of opportunities, although not completely ignored in practice, were underemphasized in American tactical doctrine. Thus overall the AEF proved ineffective by this measure of tactical performance.

A tactical system that relied on offensive combat by combined arms in open warfare should have put a premium on junior officer leadership, unit cohesion, and morale. Heavy dependence on inexperienced infantry made such requirements even more necessary. Personnel policies in the US Army, however, did not give sufficient attention to the needs of the tactical units. In a few cases procedures in the AEF were actually destructive of the required results.

The quantity and quality of manpower from which the army drew its small-unit leadership was generally adequate, possibly of an even higher quality than was available to it during the Second World War. While even the harshest critics considered most American junior officers 'gallant and brave,' many platoon leaders lacked tactical skill, 'could not hold their units together,' or generally proved unable to maintain discipline.[60] Part of the problem was training and accountability. Instruction at the Officer Training Camps, from which most of the platoon leaders had been commissioned, had in some cases been too rudimentary. Equipment shortages, inadequate housing, and not enough instructors experienced in dealing with civilians plagued the OTCs. As a result officer training too closely resembled recruit training without sufficient development of leadership qualities and tactical skills.[61]

Other personnel policies did not compensate for the shortcomings of the officer corps. Unlike some European armies, for instance, the US Army tended to undervalue the importance of its noncommissioned officers (NCOs). They were not a class apart from other enlisted ranks, with distinct privileges, duties, responsibilities, and prestige. Such distinctions would have enhanced their role as small-unit leaders, especially in combat. Promotion to noncommissioned rank was often a causal affair – easily won and easily taken away. This likewise eroded their potential value in fostering unit cohesion. Wartime NCO training tended to be on the job and stressed the vocational aspects of an NCO's duties. The training neglected the leadership role of noncommissioned officers and their status in the hierarchy of command. This is not to say that some American NCOs did not rise to the occasion when required by circumstance of battle, even assuming command of platoons and companies when the officers became casualties.[62] But the system of NCO selection, training, and promotion neither emphasized nor inculcated such performance.

Particularly destructive to unit cohesion in the AEF was the practice of relieving officers from their commands for detached service, often to attend army schools, on the eve of major operations. Several divisions were nearly decimated as a result. Long after the war George Marshall complained that just before the Meuse–Argonne attack several of the inexperienced assault divisions 'were absolutely scalped . . . in order that the next class at Langres [the AEF Staff College] might start on scheduled time. The amount of confusion and mismanagement resulting from this was tremendous.'[63] The staff at AEF GHQ, specifically the Training Section, was principally responsible for these practices. Thus that element of the command structure that should have been most cognizant of troop needs and unit cohesion was fostering practices destructive of them.

The replacement system also created personnel turbulence and was not conducive to fostering unit cohesion. Because the War Department wanted to ship full-strength units to France, it broke up established organizations to provide fillers and replacements for divisions ready to embark for overseas. Many units were cannibalized in this manner, some more than once; morale and unit esprit could hardly develop under such circumstances. A similar situation obtained later in France when the AEF broke up some of the newly arrived combat divisions in an effort to replace casualties and maintain experienced divisions at near fighting strength. But even this fell short of needs as the number of replacements was sufficient for American divisions to stay in action but at strengths considerably below tables of organization. Replacement shortages occurred early in 1918 and persisted until the armistice. In February 1918 the system was operating so badly that the four combat divisions of the I Corps were short 8,500 officers and men. The 41st Division, responsible for furnishing replacements to the corps, was itself short 4,500 men. By October AEF combat units needed 80,000 replacements but only 45,000 were available. Combat divisions reduced their strength by 4,000 men in that period, mostly infantrymen.[64]

Generally the deleterious aspects of American personnel practices were more evident during the last two months of the war than during the fighting in the summer of 1918. The divisions that bore the brunt of the summer fighting (1st, 2nd, 3rd, 4th, 26th, 32nd, and 42nd, for example) in most cases had served for at least a few weeks in less active sectors, thus allowing an opportunity to develop some unit cohesion under fire prior to involvement in full-scale offensive combat. These units also tended to have a larger percentage of experienced regular army (or marine) personnel in key leadership positions. By the late summer that leadership pool had been diluted by casualties and transfers to other newly created divisions.

Late in the war, particularly in the Meuse–Argonne, evidence became clearer of the weak personnel practices. After the armistice an AEF inspector reported: 'Discipline as shown by inattention and carelessness in saluting, straggling, lack of proper measures in sanitation, carelessness in observance of traffic regulations, etc., seemed to grow more lax as the offensive went on.' Straggling was an especially pernicious problem, sapping combat strength and effectiveness. It was evident in some divisions more than others. One division in the Meuse–Argonne had reported an effective front-line strength of only 1,600 men. Yet when the division came out of the line and arrived in its rest area, the infantry regiments alone had over 8,400 men.[65] The AEF used expedients such as straggler posts of military police to keep the troops moving toward the front. But these had only limited effect and did not address the root causes of the problem.

During the First World War the US Army organized a system of training that dwarfed all its previous efforts. Most of the 1.4 million soldiers who actually fought in France passed through a progression from individual, to small-unit, to division training. Officers and specialists attended schools that covered a range of subjects from general staff duties to proper use of the Stokes mortar. Although the magnitude of the training effort was considerable, a number of problems hampered the overall effectiveness of the program.

Neither the training branch of the War Department General Staff nor the training section of the AEF staff had full responsibility or authority for training. Both organizations, in fact, published some training literature, supervised some aspects of individual training, and issued unit training schedules. Because of the rapid and hurried shipment of US troops to France after April 1918, some individual replacements had marksmanship training at camps in the United States while others learned under French instructors overseas. Some units began one part of their training cycle under War Department supervision but completed it in France under the AEF. Neither the training branch nor G-5 supervised all American troops in any single aspect of the training cycle. Although there was some liaison between the training branch in Washington and G-5 in France, neither had the resources required to supervise closely individual and unit training in their areas of responsibility. Many departmental, camp, and unit commanders consequently exercised their own initiative in carrying out various training functions. That most American units upon reaching Europe initially trained and served in quiet sectors under French and British supervision only exacerbated the diffusion of responsibility.

The doctrinal ambiguity between trench warfare and open warfare tactics was a second major area that prevented implementation of a coherent training regime. Pershing pushed an open warfare doctrine based on infantry marksmen, yet approved of the heavy, square division more suited for attritional warfare. War Department and AEF training publications stressed trench warfare as much as open warfare, often reprinting French and British documents on the subject. Most US units first saw combat in trenches, on the defensive, at a quiet sector.

The original AEF training plan anticipated complete divisions arriving in France on a regular basis. After arrival each infantry division was to have three months of training before commitment to combat. The three one-month phases included preliminary small-unit training; integration of US battalions into quiet defensive sectors with French or British units 'to harden and accustom them to all sorts of fire'; and finally regimental, brigade, and division maneuvers in the attack. The German 1918 spring offensives, necessitating early commitment of American units, curtailed the divisional training program. After April 1918 few divisions had a full four weeks in any phase; for some the entire cycle was only a month.[66]

Because of the demands of offensive combat on the Western Front it was especially important that infantry and artillery developed as a combined arms team. Infantry could not advance without artillery fire support. Joint training was essential to develop the liaison and coordination necessary to assure that support. Field artillery brigades were supposed to have a four-phase training program – technical artillery instruction, brief service at the front under French or British supervision, tactical training with the remainder of the division, and schooling for higher commanders and staffs. No brigade ever completed all four phases; only two or three finished the third; less than half completed the second, although most finished the first.[67] AEF artillery training, therefore, was weakest in the most crucial area of infantry-artillery liaison.

The necessity to speed troops to the front likewise affected individual training. Many untrained replacements, for example, reported to combat divisions in the latter stages of the war. In late September 1918 the 77th Division received 2,100 replacements. Over half lacked rudimentary infantry skills. Many had not been issued weapons prior to reporting to the division and did not know how to care for or use a rifle. The day after receiving these replacements the division jumped off at daylight as part of the Meuse–Argonne attack.[68]

Many in the AEF recognized the shortcomings of the training system. The G-5 section in particular tried, though unsuccessfully, to inculcate doctrinal uniformity on American units and troops. To that end, and to compensate for the obvious lack of combat experience, G-5 had observers with nearly all front-line divisions during combat. Based on their observations, G-5 produced a series of 'lessons learned' for dissemination throughout the AEF. Units not yet in combat could adjust their training regimens and gain some benefit from the experience of veteran outfits. Seasoned units too, after their periods in the line, withdrew to rest areas where they resumed training. After its hard battles in June and July 1918 the 2nd Division, one of the best in the AEF, practiced 'open order warfare' in its rest area in Lorraine eight hours a day through most of August. The training emphasized small-unit tactics with one squad of a platoon utilizing maximum fire power from rifles, grenades, and automatic rifles to attack an enemy position while the other squads used cover and maneuvered against the flanks.[69]

Given time, veteran AEF units could profit from their combat experience, conduct realistic training based on that experience, and improve overall tactical effectiveness. For most units, however, the rapid expansion and early commitment of the AEF prevented the orderly training required.

In the tactical realm the AEF had other serious problems with the human and material aspects of combat support and sustainability. Failures of leadership, inadequate organization, lack of resources, and simple inexperience all accounted for the problems. Although some of the weaknesses were apparent even before US troops entered combat, the sustained fighting in the last two months of the war magnified them. The large, 28,000-man American divisions did not meet the expectations of AEF planners for staying power in battle. Moreover the divisions proved difficult to supply, transport, and manage. They had difficulty getting into battle and once engaged had difficulty distributing food, ammunition, and other supplies.

Division transport depended on primitive motor trucks and especially on horse- and mule-drawn wagons, all road bound. Because shipment of animals from the United States to France was considerably reduced in the spring of 1918 to make room for infantry replacements, severe shortages of transport animals occurred later. Without proper fodder and care the animals quickly broke down. By the end of the war, the condition of horses and mules in many divisions was very poor, contributing to the already difficult transport and supply distribution problems. Besides shortages of vehicles and animals, congestion within division areas was a greater hindrance. The movement of trucks and wagons was triple that of French divisions, prompting an observer to characterize the automobile traffic in one area as 'fantastic.' Traffic conditions throughout the First Army during much of the Meuse–Argonne offensive 'became a severe impediment' to movement. Division engineers worked almost solely on repair and construction of roads over shelled areas. It took three to five trains daily just to bring in materials to maintain the existing road system. The AEF clearly underestimated the difficulties of transporting troops and supplies in close proximity to the battlefront.[70]

Availability of supplies for combat units also became a problem late in the war. Again, a contributing factor was the shipping schedules during the spring and fall. To sustain the high rate of troop shipments, automatic supply was cut from 50 pounds per man per day, to 40, and then to 30. By the fall some commodities were in short supply. Distribution was the main difficulty, however. In the first phase of the Meuse–Argonne many division supply officers were content with waiting for the automatic supplies to reach them or with submitting requisitions to army depots and waiting for deliveries. As divisions moved, supplies frequently failed to reach the units on time. With experience, supply officers became more aggressive in locating depots and personally supervising delivery of supplies. Some troops went hungry in the first weeks of the Meuse–Argonne. After they finished the two days of iron rations they carried, they could get little resupply. Field kitchens could not get so far forward and carrying parties had difficulty getting over the rough, shell-pocked terrain to ration dumps in the rear. One platoon leader described a ration dump in the 2nd Division sector as 'just what the name implies – a dump.' Ration wagons had deposited great heaps of bread and canned goods into a huge hole caused by the collapse of a dugout. There was no system, no issue – anyone could carry away what he wanted.[71]

Despite the huge size of its infantry divisions the AEF did not have sufficient service troops to carry rations, bury the dead, evacuate casualties, and perform other direct combat support functions. Too often the infantry, already strained and exhausted from combat, had to do these tasks. Commanders sometimes did not appreciate the effects that sustained combat had on individual troops. The weaknesses of the AEF's combat support and sustainability became manifest in the Meuse–Argonne. As one eminent American historian put it: 'The 'staying' power of a division often was reduced to replacing exhausted troops who had suffered casualties with exhausted troops who had not.'[72]

Much like American operational doctrine, the tactical system emphasized by the AEF placed American strengths against German strengths. The German Army, employing innovative infiltration tactics by combined arms teams in its 1918 spring offensives and elastic, flexible, deep defense tactics in the face of the Allied counteroffensives, demonstrated its tactical prowess. The US Army had neither the experience, training, nor ability to match the Germans in the tactical realm. Against the skill of the Germans the United States pitted inexperienced, often undertrained troops. In 1918 the untapped pool of American manpower, however, was one potentially decisive resource recognized by the Allies and the enemy alike. From the battles of the early summer 1918 to the end of the war, numerous French, British, and German observers commented on the aggressiveness of US troops, particularly while attacking. This aggressiveness continued and the morale of US troops remained generally high until the Meuse–Argonne offensive bogged down in early October 1918.

Pershing was inspired by the right idea. In order to break the Western Front stalemate, the AEF had to adopt aggressive, offensive, open warfare tactics. He wanted to capitalize on what he perceived as the inherent strengths, the individualism, aggressiveness, and high morale, of his principal asset – American manpower. If properly led and thoroughly trained in open warfare tactics, in late 1918 US troops could have achieved as important a tactical innovation as the Germans had earlier in the year. But Pershing put too much faith in the ability of individual infantrymen to overcome the fire power of modern weaponry. Pershing correctly wanted to drive the Germans into the open and defeat them in a war of maneuver, but concluded that only the rifle could accomplish that. He demanded men schooled in individual marksmanship. Unfortunately, the stress on the individualistic rifleman diluted the needed emphasis on combining infantry fire power and maneuver with heavy artillery, machine gun, and tank support.

The tactical system employed by the AEF did try to exploit the quantitative and qualitative manpower strengths of the United States. But it also placed those strengths against German strengths. The strain on the Americans was even greater because of the difficulty of forming the cohesive units needed to conduct offensive combat from untrained, inexperienced personnel.

Conclusion

In general, the American military of the First World War was more effective in the political and strategic realms than the operational and tactical. But there were some weaknesses at the political and strategic levels and several positive aspects to operational and tactical performance. More significantly, important operational and tactical failings were directly attributable to decisions made at the political and strategic level.

Prior to the declaration of war in April 1917 the American military was not effective in assessing the military situation, analyzing requirements, and convincing the civilian political leadership of military needs. Traditional American attitudes toward military advice during peacetime and the Wilson Administration's desire to remain strictly neutral in the European war further inhibited contingency planning. With the commencement of hostilities, however, the military was considerably more successful in gaining access to the financial, industrial, technological, and manpower resources required to prosecute the war. Organizational weaknesses within the military establishment, between military and civilian policy-making entities, and between the government and the business community, continued to limit the efficiency with which these resources were mobilized.

Because it was the junior partner in the coalition and because it entered the war well after the other major belligerents, the United States faced limited strategic alternatives after April 1917. Yet the strategy pursued – concentration on the Western Front, organization of a separate American field army in France, and cooperation with the Royal Navy in the anti-U-boat campaign – was consistent with the Wilson administration's political objectives and with the nation's industrial bases. To a large extent all elements of the strategy had been achieved by November 1918. This perhaps was more a function of the limited options available and the material support of the Allies than of the logic of the strategic objectives.

American operational doctrine in the First World War stressed integration of all arms to conduct offensive operations and relied on one important American asset – a large, untapped manpower pool. Besides a sound doctrine, the AEF utilized to good effect the small cadre of Leavenworth-trained staff officers and commanders for important operational billets. In some cases the AEF exhibited an intellectual and physical flexibility to adjust to changing battlefield conditions. But in more instances insistence on rigid adherence to orders, inadequate combat support capability, and limited utilization of technology hindered operational effectiveness. Besides, American forces functioned at the operational level for less than six months; divisions and corps did not enter large-scale offensive operations until the summer of 1918. The American had little opportunity, therefore, to learn from their initial mistakes and improve operational performance over time. The overall assessment of American operational effectiveness must be low, but as the fighting in early November 1918 demonstrated, the AEF gradually became more operationally proficient, however slowly.

Although the American tactical approach, exemplified by Pershing's advocacy of open warfare, was consistent with the country's strategic objectives and operational doctrine, it often failed miserably because personnel practices did little to enhance the unit stability, cohesion, and training required to employ such tactics. Neither the War Department nor GHQ AEF had complete responsibility for supervising individual and unit training. Virtually none of the AEF divisions completed their full training cycles, while many individual replacements went into combat with only rudimentary fighting skills. Unit tactics emphasized correct frontages, depth, and alignment, rather than surprise, flexibility, and maneuver. By the armistice only a handful of American divisions had become skilled, reliable offensive formations.

In the First World War American experience, there were clear relationships between military effectiveness at one level and performance at other levels. Most notably, decisions made to improve political and strategic effectiveness, or in pursuit of political and strategic goals, inhibited performance in the operational and tactical realms. This was true despite the basic logic and consistency of American policies among the four levels. For instance, even though open warfare tactics were consistent with American operational, strategic, and political objectives, decisions made at the political and strategic levels made the pursuit of such tactics less likely to succeed.

For a valid political reason – to maximize flexibility in postwar peace making – the Wilson administration wanted to avoid too close a military attachment to the Allies. Military strategists, especially Pershing, used this to insist on forming a separate American field army, rather than amalgamating US troops with Allies, and on developing American tactics that were perceived to be different from previous French and British practices. The decision to create oversize US divisions stemmed from these political and strategic considerations. This in turn complicated supply, training, and battlefield employment; there were few compensating enhancements at the operational and tactical level to overcome these problems. Personnel practices, creating considerable turbulence, in fact intensified the difficulties.

The principal trade-offs among the four levels of participation flowed from the political and strategic to the operational and the tactical. Political and strategic objectives were held paramount, despite the operational and tactical problems this attitude might have created. Put another way, political decisions drove tactical practices and performance, not the reverse. The First World War was thus very much in the traditional 'American way of war.'

Notes

1 Edward M. Coffman, 'The American Military and Strategic Policy in World War I,' in Barry Hunt and Adrian Preston (eds.), *War Aims and Strategic Policy in the Great War* (London, 1977), p. 68.
2 Ernest R. May, 'The Development of Political-Military Consultation in the United States,' *Political Science Quarterly*, June 1955, p. 166.
3 Frederick Palmer, *Bliss, Peacemaker: The Life and Times of Tasker Howard Bliss* (New York, 1934), pp. 106–7.
4 Paul Y. Hammond, *Organizing for Defense: The American Military Establishment in the Twentieth Century* (Princeton, N.J., 1961), p. 33.
5 John Patrick Finnegan, *Against the Specter of a Dragon: The Campaign for Military Preparedness, 1914–1917* (Westport, Conn., 1981), p. 186.
6 James L. Abrahamson, *America Arms for a New Century: The Making of a Great Military Power* (New York, 1981), pp. 167–8, 171–3.
7 Harvey A. DeWeerd, *President Wilson Fights His War: World War I and the American Intervention* (New York, 1968), p. 222.
8 Leon H. Canfield, *The Presidency of Woodrow Wilson: Prelude to a World in Crisis* (Rutherford, N.J., 1966), p. 108.
9 Robert D. Cuff, *The War Industries Board* (Baltimore, 1963), pp. 14–16; Daniel R. Beaver, 'Politics and Policy: The War Department Motorization and Standardization Program for Wheeled Transport Vehicles, 1920–1940,' *Military Affairs*, October 1983, p. 102.
10 Merritt Roe Smith, 'Military Arsenals and Industry Before World War I,' in B. Franklin Cooling (ed.), *War, Business, and American Society* (Port Washington, N.Y., 1977), p. 41.
11 James A. Huston, *The Sinews of War: Army Logistics, 1775–1953* (Washington, D.C., 1966), p. 302; DeWeerd, *President Wilson Fights His War*, p. 222.
12 Leonard P. Ayres, *The War with Germany: A Statistical Summary* (Washington, D.C., 1919), p. 145; Daniel R. Beaver, 'The Problem of American Military Supply, 1890–1920,' in Cooling (ed.), *War, Business, and American Society*, p. 88; DeWeerd, President Wilson Fights His War, p. 208.
13 Finnegan, *Against the Specter of a Dragon*, p. 177; John Garry Clifford, *The Citizen Soldiers: The Plattsburg Training Camp Movement, 1913–1920* (Lexington, Ky., 1972), pp. 223–5.
14 David M. Kennedy, *Over Here: The First World War and American Society* (New York, 1980), pp. 147–8; Marvin A. Kreidberg and Merton G. Henry, *History of Military Mobilization in the United States Army, 1775–1945*, (Washington, D.C., 1955), pp. 271–2.
15 Clifford, *The Citizen Soldiers*, pp. 228, 229, 248.
16 Daniel R. Beaver, *Newton D. Baker and the American War Effort, 1917–1919* (Lincoln, Nebr., 1966), pp. 46–8.
17 John J. Pershing, *My Experiences in the World War*, Vol. 1 (New York, 1931), pp. 38–9.
18 Coffman, 'American Military and Strategic Policy'; Allan R. Millett, 'Over Where? The AEF and American Strategy for Victory on the Western Front, 1917–1918,' unpublished paper in author's possession, 1979.
19 Pershing, quoted in David F. Trask, *The United States in the Supreme War Council: American War Aims and Inter-Allied Strategy, 1917–1918* (Middletown, Conn., 1961), p. 74.
20 Ludendorff, quoted in George S. Viereck, *As They Saw Us: Foch, Ludendorff, and Other War Leaders Write Our War History* (Garden City, N.Y., 1929), pp. 24–5, 29.
21 Trask, *Supreme War Council*, p. 172.

22 Ernest R. May, *The World War and American Isolation, 1914–1917* (Cambridge, 1959), pp. 425–8.
23 Beaver, *Baker*, p. 180.
24 Edward M. Coffman, *The Hilt of the Sword: The Career of Peyton C. March* (Madison, Wisc., 1966), pp. 97–103.
25 Russell F. Weigley, *The American Way of War: A History of United States Military Strategy and Policy* (New York, 1973), pp. 193–4.
26 William S. Sims, *The Victory at Sea* (New York, 1929), p. 401.
27 Harvey A. DeWeerd, 'American Adoption of French Artillery,' *Journal of the American Military Institute*, Summer 1939, pp. 104–16.
28 Edward M. Coffman, *The War to End All Wars: The American Military Experience in World War I* (New York, 1968), pp. 190–2.
29 H. Essame, *The Battle for Europe* (New York, 1972), pp. 141–2.
30 Sims, *Victory at Sea*, pp. 375, 379.
31 Kuhl, quoted in DeWeerd, *President Wilson Fights His War*, pp. 392–3.
32 Timothy K. Nenninger, *The Leavenworth Schools and the Old Army: Education, Professionalism, and the Officer Corps of the U.S. Army, 1881–1918* (Westport, Conn., 1978), pp. 157–8, 142.
33 Allan R. Millett, *The General: Robert L. Bullard and Officership in the United States Army, 1881–1925* (Westport, Conn., 1975), p. 397.
34 John M. Palmer, *Washington, Lincoln, and Wilson: Three War Leaders* (Garden City, N.Y., 1930), p. 340.
35 Timothy K. Nenninger, 'The Development of American Armor, 1917–1940,' MA thesis, University of Wisconsin, 1968, pp. 44–9.
36 George H. English, *History of the 89th Division, U.S.A.* (Denver, Colo., 1920), pp. 53–5.
37 Kriedberg and Henry, *Military Mobilization*, pp. 324–36; Coffman, *War to End All Wars*, p. 16.
38 Thomas G. Frothingham, *The Naval History of the World War: The United States in the War, 1917–1918* (Cambridge, 1927), pp. 152–5, Ludendorf quoted in Viereck, *As They Saw Us*, p. 25.
39 Essame, *Battle for Europe*, p. 160.
40 Lt. Col. Herman von Giehrl, 'The Fight for St. Mihiel,' January 9, 1922, File 801–18.2, German World War I Records (GWWIR), Record Group (RG) 165, National Archives (NA).
41 I. B. Holley, Jr., *Ideas and Weapons* (New Haven, Conn., 1953), p. 15.
42 Charles E. Heller, *Chemical Warfare in World War I: The American Experience* (Fort Leavenworth, Kans., 1984), pp. 35–59.
43 Rexford C. Cochrane, 'The Use of Gas in the Meuse–Argonne Campaign, September–November 1918,' Gas Warfare in World War I, study no. 10 (US Army Chemical Corps, 1958).
44 Huston, *Sinews of War*, pp. 386–7.
45 Allan R. Millet, 'Cantigny, 28–31 May 1918,' unpublished manuscript in author's possession, 1981, pp. 20–1.
46 Essame, *Battle for Europe*, p. 172; Elliott J. Johnson, 'The Military Experiences of Hugh A. Drum from 1898–1918,' PhD Dissertation, University of Wisconsin, 1975, p. 325.
47 Essame, *Battle for Europe*, p. 168.
48 Pershing, quoted in Maj. Harold B. Fiske, 'Training in the AEF,' April 21, 1920, Army War College Lecture, RG 165, NA.
49 James W. Rainey, 'Ambivalent Warfare: The Tactical Doctrine of the AEF in World War I,' *Parameters*, September 1983, pp. 38–40.

50 Section for Foreign Armies, 'Report on American Training,' July 31, 1918, file 801–21.8, GWWIR, RG 165, NA.
51 'Combat Instructions,' September 5, 1918, G-5 Document 1348, GHQ AEF, RG 120, NA.
52 'Notes on Recent Operations: No. 3,' October 12, 1918, G-5 Document 1376, GHQ AEF, RG 120, NA.
53 'Notes on Recent Operations: No. 4,' November 22, 1918, G-5 Document 1417, GHQ AEF, RG 120, NA.
54 Office of the Chief of Staff, *Field Service Regulations: 1914: Corrected to July 31, 1918* (Washington, D.C., 1918), p. 73.
55 Col. Harold B. Fiske to Chief of Staff AEF, July 4, 1918, 'Training,' AEF AG File 16875–5, RG 120, NA.
56 Essame, *Battle for Europe*, p. 97; Louis Felix Ranlett, *Let's Go!* (New York, 1927), pp. 86–7; John Kennedy Ohl, 'The Keystone Division in the Great War,' *Prologue*, Summer 1971, pp. 83–99.
57 Millet, 'Cantigny,' pp. 53–4; Richard Lee Pierce, 'A Maximum of Support: The Development of US Army Field Artillery Doctrine in World War I,' MA thesis, Ohio State University, 1983.
58 *Field Service Regulations: 1918*, p. 88.
59 'Notes on Recent Operations: No. 4,' November 22, 1918, RG 120, NA.
60 Brig. Gen. M. G. Spinks to Chief of Staff AEF, 'Notes Made By the Inspector General AEF,' December 11, 1918, folder 1115-A, G-3 correspondence, RG 120, NA.
61 Clifford, *Citizen Soldiers*, p. 256.
62 Ernest F. Fisher, 'The American Noncommissioned Officer in World War I,' Center of Military History draft paper in author's possession, 1984.
63 Marshall to Pershing, October 24, 1930, in Larry I. Bland (ed.), *The Papers of George Catlett Marshall* (Baltimore, Md., 1981), Vol. 1, p. 360.
64 Leonard L. Lerwill, *The Personnel Replacement System in the United States Army* (Washington, D.C., 1954), pp. 180, 212.
65 Spinks to Chief of Staff AEF, December 11, 1918, G-3 folder 1115-A, RG 120, NA.
66 Brig. Gen. Harold B. Fiske, 'Report of G-5 GHQ AEF,' June 30, 1919, folder 215, Commander-In-Chief Reports, RG 120, NA.
67 Pierce, 'Maximum of Support,' p. 30.
68 Spinks to Chief of Staff AEF, December 11, 1918, G-3 folder 1115-A, RG 120, NA.
69 Ranlett, *Let's Go!*, p. 162.
70 Millett, *The General*, p. 347; Huston, *Sinews of War*, p. 383.
71 Coffman, *Hilt of the Sword*, p. 87; Spinks to Chief of Staff AEF, December 11, 1918, G-3 folder 1115-A, RG 120, NA; Ranlett, *Let's Go!*, p. 280.
72 Millett, *The General*, p. 347.

[5]

Italy during the First World War

JOHN GOOCH
University of Lancaster

Political Effectiveness

When Archduke Franz Ferdinand, heir to the throne of Austria-Hungary, was assassinated at Sarajevo on 28 June 1914, Italy's political leaders detected a chance to attain territorial goals within Europe which would complete the *Risorgimento* and also ease the naval situation in the Adriatic, where Austrian bases on the Dalmatian coast posed a standing threat to Italy. Although it was formally a partner of Vienna and Berlin as a member of the Triple Alliance, Italy had already made it clear that it did not regard itself as bound to come to the aid of either party in an aggressive war – and the letter of the treaty backed it in taking this stance. Accordingly, in mid-July and before he realized how far Vienna intended to go, the Italian foreign minister Di San Giuliano took his stand on Article VII of the Triple Alliance treaty and insisted that Italy must have adequate territorial compensation for any Austrian advance.[1] Concrete goals were not difficult to identify. The outbursts of irredentism which had intermittently imperilled relations with Austria-Hungary for forty years pointed inexorably at the Trentino and Trieste; a well-established Italian interest in Albania could be further strengthened; and the government was fully aware of the views of the navy on the strategic significance of the eastern coast of the Adriatic.[2]

When the terms of the Austrian ultimatum were read out to Di San Giuliano on 24 July and it became apparent that a third Balkan war might shortly occur, the Italian foreign minister stuck to his established policy, regarding Italian involvement in a war as 'possible, but not likely.'[3] Italian neutrality was formally announced on 2 August. In the weeks which followed Di San Giuliano and his premier, Antonio Salandra, acted on the premise that Italy might achieve its goals without ever having to use force and that alongside the possibility of being bribed to fight there existed the opportunity of being bribed not to fight. The precariousness of Italy's strategic position, vulnerable as it was to the exercise of British and French sea power, was matched by the delicacy of its international position. If Germany and Austria-Hungary were victorious, Italy would then be reduced to servitude, but if the Triple Entente won it would be subject once more to Anglo-French suzerainty over the Mediterranean and elsewhere. The successful achievement of Italy's political goals therefore depended chiefly not upon the successful application of Italian military power – although this was of course an important component in Italy's array of bargaining counters – but upon an impossible outcome; for as Di San Giuliano remarked on 12 September 1914, 'the ideal situation for us would be if Austria and France were both beaten.'[4] Between August 1914 and April 1915 Di San Giuliano and his successor as foreign minister, Sidney Sonnino, bargained with both sides. On 26 April 1915 Italy signed the Treaty of London, which offered it gratification of its European desires, and joined the Entente.[5] There was at this time no serious consideration of territorial acquisitions outside Europe.

Once it had become a belligerent, Italy fought a parallel war alongside its allies. The prewar staff conversations and diplomatic understandings which had bound Britain to France and France to Russia had no counterpart as far as Rome was concerned, so that it was distanced from its partners by more than mere geography. This political fact, for which no remedy was sought until after the defeat of Caporetto in October 1917 and which was never satisfactorily resolved, placed yet another obstacle in the way of the achievement of Italian ambitions. Excluded from full coalition warfare by its own wish, Italy closed off the option of contributing troops to the main front in north-west Europe and reaping the rewards from a subsequent peace conference. Instead it sought to inflict a decisive defeat upon its opponent, Austria-Hungary, more or less alone. Two considerations determined that it would adopt this means of achieving its goals. Conventional military wisdom, as propounded by the government's chief military adviser, General Luigi Cadorna, dictated the search for a decisive victory in the field. And successful offensive action was no less a priority if, as left-wing historians maintain, two of the main motives which caused Italy to enter the war were a desire to consolidate the hegemony of the ruling right-wing political alliance (the so-called *blocco prussiano*) and a determination to break the advancing tide of the workers' movement.[6]

In contemplating the use of force to gain political goals, most Italian politicians felt some reservations about the capacity of their armed forces to bring hostilities to a satisfactory conclusion. This was not entirely unjustified as both services bore the incubus of historic defeats which engendered doubts. Lissa, Custoza and Adua were episodes which any force would have found it hard to live down and even success in the Libyan war of 1911–12 did not counterbalance a poor reputation, for some politicians firmly believed that an incompetent military had allowed that war to drag on far too long.[7] Moreover, whenever the two services met in a common forum, which happened only rarely, they showed a marked tendency to be at odds with themselves as well as with one another. This was certainly Giolitti's experience when, as premier, he chaired meetings of the Supreme Defense Commission in 1908 and 1913 at which quite striking divergencies of view on matters of strategy, fortification, and armaments policy were revealed.[8] During the 1913 sessions the then war minister became so worried at the dissension that he sought to get the army's leaders together to thrash out a common policy before it reconvened.[9]. This never happened, and the differences remained as wide as ever.

Salandra's experience during August 1914, when his chief of staff urged general mobilization and his war minister vehemently resisted it, can only have confirmed in his mind the picture of a military riven with disagreements; and the revelations he heard in mid-September from General Adolfo Tettoni, head of logistical and administrative services, about the ineptitude of the war minister probably did nothing to encourage a change of heart. The war minister, Grandi, was soon dismissed and his successor, Zupelli, showed an encouraging and energetic sense of purpose. At first Zupelli and Cadorna worked well as a team but by February 1916 they had fallen out. At this stage in the war generals were still predominant in the military politics of Britain and France as well as of Italy, and it is therefore unsurprising that Cadorna was able to sack Zupelli and replace him with his own nominee.

Giolitti, who had a pronouncedly cynical view of the Italian Army, remarked in May 1915 that although the regular officers were as brave as any and technically prepared for war, 'the generals are worth little, they came up from the ranks at a time when families sent their most stupid sons into the army because they did not know what to do with them.'[10] Writing after the First World War, and with his own reputation to defend, Salandra contributed to the view that Italian politicians placed no faith in their army by suggesting that his awareness of military weaknesses was the main factor in accounting for Italy's delayed entry into the fray. However it seems that this was never anything more than a secondary consideration, overshadowed by the diplomatic maneuvering necessary to get the promises of territorial gain which Italy wanted. At the time most politicians seem to have been prepared to allow the armed forces a considerable degree of functional integrity and – in common with almost all the rest of Europe's political leaders – to regard their leaders as expert custodians of the secrets of applied military science who would be able to apply the means necessary to gain the desired ends when the time came.

Civil-military relations in pre-1914 Europe were often imperfect, with the result that politicians took decisions based on little in the way of considered military advice. Italy numbers high among the victims of this situation. By the time that the First World War broke out, tradition and practice together dictated that decisions for war or peace were taken by a small and closed group of politicians – usually only the premier and foreign minister – without their having consulted the soldiers or the sailors about any facet of the relationship between military power and political goals.[11] This had been so in September 1911 at the time of the outbreak of the Libyan war and again in May 1913 during the Balkan crisis; and the aims of the African war of 1886–96 had never been clearly apparent to anyone, except perhaps Francesco Crispi. This phenomenon was in part caused and in part compounded by an inadequate bureaucratic machinery for consultation over defense issues which, in its turn, owed a great deal to the constitutional power of the crown.

The king, who became titular commander-in-chief in wartime and spent much of his time at or near the front, exercised a powerful role on military affairs behind the scenes, and any attempt to tighten the links between soldiers and politicians would have been regarded as an inexcusable act of *lèse-majesté*.

In the light of Italian practice in civil-military relations and of the guiding principles of Italian politics it is scarcely surprising that the military exercised no influence in the process which culminated on 31 July 1914 in a cabinet decision for neutrality. Indeed, the gap between those in uniform and those in frock coats was so great that on the very day when the cabinet opted for neutrality the new chief of the Italian general staff, Cadorna, was despatching a memorandum to the king in which he outlined his plans to send all the forces which were not strictly necessary for the defense of Italy and Libya to fight alongside Germany on the French front, in accordance with prewar military agreements.[12] The king approved Cadorna's scheme on the day that Italian neutrality was announced. Once aware of the politicians' view that Italy was not bound by the terms of the Triple Alliance to support Vienna, Cadorna spent the whole of August trying to persuade the foreign minister that Italy should mobilize and attack Austria. Di San Giuliano stubbornly resisted. As well as being entirely clear minded about diplomatic goals, the foreign minister recognized that Italy lacked the capacity to sustain a long war and was acutely skeptical of the argument that the addition of Italian military power might decisively tilt the European military balance.

The role of the military in the negotiations which preceded Italy's formal entry into the war on 26 April 1915 was a very limited one. The war minister, Zupelli, who took office on 11 October 1914, imparted a clearer direction and greater energy to the process of re-equipping the army. The new foreign minister, Sidney Sonnino, who took office shortly afterwards, knew that his actions were circumscribed by the unavoidable reality that the army would not be ready to fight until the following spring. The navy was prepared to take the sea, but its capacity to act was much less crucial to Italy's future in the event of war. Its indirect influence on the formation of policy was, however, of considerable importance, for the anxiety of Italian naval chiefs at the prospect of Russia establishing itself at Ragusa or Cattaro after the war – for which Italian possession of the Austrian naval base at Pola would not be sufficient compensation – was clearly put to Sonnino and was reflected in political goals.[13]

The Treaty of London was never officially communicated to the chief of the Italian general staff, and Cadorna only found out on 2 May that his government had decided to enter the war on 26 May, one month after the signing of the agreement.[14] Ever since the previous September he had been kept more or less in the dark on political and diplomatic events and had never been asked for his advice. Whether this was a consequence of lack of method rather than lack of regard, as has been claimed, is debatable.[15] However once the fighting began Cadorna showed no disposition to break a mold which now cast him as the dominant figure. Strategic control of the war remained firmly in his grasp and in 1916 he successfully fought off a threat to change the pattern of civil-military relations and diminish his influence by setting up a defense council. He was also successful in shaking off the watch-dog shackled to him in the shape of a government representative at the *Comando Supremo*, calling at the same time for an end to all government missions save those with limited and well-defined purposes, so that the direction of the war might be left to the High Command and the war minister.[16] Only after the defeat of Caporetto, when Cadorna was replaced as effective commander-in-chief by General Armando Diaz, were the civilians able to exercise much influence over the military.

Caporetto created the opportunity – and revealed the necessity – for innovation in the structure of civil-military relations. On 15 December 1917 a war committee was established, comprising the premier and six ministers along with the chiefs of staff of the army and the navy, who both attended in a consultative capacity.[17] However, although contacts between military and politicians were now closer, it was clear to all that Italy must wage a defensive war, and the importance of diplomacy was correspondingly heightened as matters such as the emergence of Yugoslavia threatened Italy's goals in the Balkans. At bottom the military remained masters of the front and only at the end of September 1918 did pressure come from political circles for an offensive in order to prevent a compromise peace or to forestall a dissolution of Austria- Hungary in which Italy had not participated and which would therefore jeopardize the attainment of its goals. The Austro-Hungarian Empire was already disintegrating when, in mid-October, the *Comando supremo* gave the orders which culminated in the battle of Vittorio Veneto.[18]

Whatever reservations successive generations of Italian politicians may have felt about the capacity of their soldiers and sailors, they were never such as to lead to a parsimony with state funds. Historically the Italian armed forces experienced no difficulty in gaining control over a substantial quota of general state expenditure: between 1862 and 1912–13 the army took 17.4 per cent of state spending and the navy 6.3 per cent. The army's share had built up steadily in the decade before the First World War from 25 per cent of state expenditure in 1907 to 47 per cent in 1912–13 – the latter figure being a direct consequence of the Libyan war. In 1913–14 military spending had totalled 650 million lire; in the same year 150 million had been allocated to public education. Although such levels could not be sustained, and in 1914 the government was in the process of a drastic cutting-back exercise, the armed forces could not complain on the eve of war that they had been kept short of cash.[19]

However, the armed forces were not as well off as the bald figures might at first suggest. For one thing, in relative terms these sums were not as huge as they appeared. In 1914 the army budget appeared to be settling at a figure of some 350 million lire a year, then equivalent only to £13 million.[20] More importantly perhaps, the conversion of money into equipment posed a much greater problem than did the acquisition of financial resources. Neither the state nor the private sectors of the arms industry were sufficiently advanced to be able to undertake the modernization of matériel which had become imperative by the end of the nineteenth century. In 1898 the Italian Army had begun to search for a new quick-firing field gun and had quickly been seduced by Krupps. After fourteen years of delay and maladministration it was finally decided in 1912 to copy the French Deport 75. Twenty-seven Italian firms formed a consortium to make it but quickly ran into technical difficulties which proved difficult to overcome, so that the gun was only just entering service when the army went to war in May 1915. Similar delays were experienced in the prewar years with mountain guns, howitzers, and machine guns. This poor procurement record partly reflected the backwardness of the domestic arms industry, but it was also partly the consequence of a clumsy bureaucratic machinery which hinged on a series of autonomous specialist committees and a complete imperviousness to outside advice.[21]

The navy's procurement record was if anything worse, for rather than favoring foreign manufacturers it had consorted too closely with domestic industry. In April 1903 the incoming navy minister, Admiral Giovanni Bettolo, was accused by *Avanti!* of being in collusion with the Terni state shipyard, and when the results of a parliamentary enquiry were published exactly three years later they revealed grave irregularities. Among other things the examining commission discovered that payments had been made for supplies which did not exist.[22] Giolitti skillfully brushed the mess under the carpet, but both services had revealed procurement policies which were at best weak and at worst corrupt.

Beyond these organizational difficulties lay the inescapable fact of Italy's economic weakness. Its domestic manufacturing capacity was very limited, although certain elements within it such as automobile manufacture were relatively advanced, and was irremediably hindered by the fact that it produced only 90,000 tons of steel a year, whereas Austria-Hungary and Germany produced over 20 million tons. Italy lacked raw materials and was heavily dependent upon imported metals. It also lacked coal – 87 per cent of its requirements being met by Great Britain. And it suffered from a shortage of food as harvests failed in 1914 and again in 1915; indeed, in the latter year Italy had to import 22,522,000 quintals of grain, a record amount and one only surpassed twice in the Fascist years.[23] The closure of the Dardanelles cut Italy off from its traditional sources of grain, Russia and Rumania, and exacerbated its wartime problems by increasing its dependence upon Britain and America. The fact that three-quarters of all prewar Italian imports and exports had been sea-borne emphasizes the difficulties Italy faced in obtaining the necessary supplies to sustain the war.[24]

Utilization of raw materials in the manufacture of weapons and munitions was gravely disadvantaged by the small size of the arms producing sector of heavy industry, and in some cases, such as machine guns, capacity had to be built up from scratch. The consequence of this and of poor procurement policies was that Italy entered the war grossly deficient in almost every material respect. In May 1915 it possessed a total of only 112 heavy field guns – a weapon for the supply of which it relied upon the Allies throughout the war. By June 1917 it had only amassed a total of 2,731 medium and heavy guns.[25] Initially capable of manufacturing some 14,000 rounds of artillery ammunition a day – or seven rounds per gun – Italy had raised this by May 1916 to 50,000 rounds a day.[26] It was drastically short of machine guns, rifles, bayonets, and rifle ammunition but by the end of 1916 most of the problems in these categories had been solved, largely due to the improved output of state factories and to the cooperation of a few private companies.[27] The position with regard to aircraft procurement was rather better: 382 planes were built in 1915, 1,255 in 1916, 3,861 in 1917, and 6,523 in 1918 – figures which reflected a more than twenty-fold increase in the number of firms making aeroplanes from three in 1915 to sixty-two by the war's end.[28]

As with Walther Rathenau in Germany and David Lloyd George in Britain, the machinery necessary to co-ordinate demand and supply in arms manufacture was the creation of a single individual, General Alfredo Dallolio. In a minute to the war minister of 28 February 1915 Dallolio pointed out Italy's shortage of raw materials and also highlighted the problem of retaining specialized labor for industrial purposes at a time of large-scale conscription. In identifying the problems Dallolio had effectively selected himself as the man to resolve them. Early in June he was appointed under secretary for arms and munitions and two months later, on 12 September 1915, he set up the Central Committee for Industrial Mobilization. The war ministry identified and took over private companies which were producing goods for the war or were capable of doing so, and the Central Committee for Industrial Mobilization, working through eleven regional committees, shared out the work and resolved disputes by means of joint committees containing representatives of workers, employers, and the military. Although the auxiliary factories were slow to get going this was due less to flaws in their conception than to a lack of funds and shortage of the necessary technical skills. The numbers of auxiliary factories rose from 221 in December 1915 to 998 in December 1916, 1,708 in December 1917, and 1,976 by the end of the war.[29]

Dallolio's design can be counted one of the successes of the Italian war effort, and its central importance was recognized in June 1917 when Arms and Munitions was given independent ministerial status, with Dallolio as its first head. Labor relations improved markedly under the consultative system, and the auxiliary factories were a major factor in enabling Italy to replace the artillery it lost at Caporetto with remarkable speed. However, although resource acquisition and utilization was maximized under the new industrial system, fundamental weaknesses in Italy's manufacturing base could never be eradicated. In August 1918 General Delme-Radcliffe reported Diaz's disappointment on hearing that he would not be getting 30 tons of Yprite (mustard gas) and twenty-five light tanks which he had requested from the Allies, and recorded without comment the fact that French factories produced ten tons of Yprite a day and 600 light tanks a month.[30]

The Italian war ministry made matters somewhat more difficult for the government by grossly underestimating the cost of the war. In June 1915 General Zupelli optimistically forecast munitions expenditure of 1 billion lire for the army and 50 million lire for the navy; by September 1915 the premier was forced to announce to the cabinet that the military alone would require 6 billion to see out the first year of the war and a further 3 billion to the end of September 1916.[31] Loans – both internal and external – could only bridge a part of the gap and so for this and other reasons Cadorna was forced from this time on to limit the use of artillery, with adverse effects on operations.

Another factor hampering Italy in its attempts to achieve its political goals through war was the poverty of inter-service co-ordination and co-operation. Institutional arrangements for the interchange of ideas and plans between army and navy before 1914 were skeletal, and when the two services came together in a joint forum the usual result was the highlighting of their differences. At the first meeting of the Supreme Commission for the Defense of the State in 1899 the navy revealed that it would not be able to safeguard mobilization and could not accept any obligation to protect the great maritime cities, anchoring its position in the contemporary orthodoxy of naval strategy which required that the fleet be kept together to contest the inevitable attempt by the enemy to gain command of the sea.[32] The customary division of responsibility whereby the army defended the coasts and frontiers whilst the navy prepared to try to gain command of the sea was re-confirmed, after some confusion, at another meeting of the commission in 1908 and again in 1913. Other than on these set-piece occasions, there was no formalized opportunity for cooperative planning of policy or strategy, although on occasion a form of pragmatic collaboration did occur. In 1909, as a consequence of the Bosnian crisis, joint military and naval regulations were drawn up for an amphibious operation involving the transportation of 40,000 men, and they were the basis for the transportation of Italian forces to Libya two years later.[33]

Once neutrality had been decided upon in 1914, joint discussions began between the services on how best the navy might assist the army in a field campaign against Austria-Hungary. Naval authorities saw no value whatsoever in amphibious operations to land troops on the Adriatic coast and warned that heavy naval guns could not be expected to dislodge an enemy from prepared trench lines. Cadorna, who was looking to naval artillery to provide enfilading fire and possibly to destroy enemy defensive lines, was prepared to accept help from destroyers and light craft but rejected the only positive naval suggestion – that it should land small parties on the enemy coastline which would then destroy road and rail communications.[34] In April 1915 Cadorna renewed his request for fleet cooperation in the army's advance along the coast to Trieste, requesting active naval assistance against enemy trenches and defences and protection against the fire of enemy ships.[35] The navy had already withdrawn a promise of assistance given to Cadorna earlier, although it was prepared to contemplate using old ships instead of modern units.[36] It now informed Cadorna that he could not rely on naval help in the land campaign, which would depend upon the circumstances of the moment, and in reply to a request from the chief of the Army General Staff about what help he could expect from light craft – protection which he regarded as absolutely necessary for the Italian advance – he was told that even this depended on relative command of the sea by the Italian fleet since it would require the prolonged presence of torpedo boats and since the enemy could sweep any protective minefields.[37] This exchange apparently marked the end of attempts at inter-service cooperation; and naval intransigence determined that Italy's armies would be locked in a bitter and costly land campaign on the Isonzo River rather than having the opportunity to undertake a more imaginative amphibious strategy.

Italian naval policy was entirely governed by the fear of exposing all or part of the fleet in a major action in the northern Adriatic on unfavorable terms. Italian strategy for the decisive naval encounter – which never occurred – was to control the Austro-Hungarian fleet in Pola from the middle and lower Adriatic and confront it if it left port, or to attempt a decisive encounter in the north in conjunction with an army push on Trieste if it never came out.[38] Whether natural caution would ever have been sufficiently overcome to undertake the latter operation is questionable. In the event, the army remained wedged in the Isonzo valley and never got fleet support for a drive along the coast.

Italy's political goals in war were set without any reference to its military capacity to attain them. Those goals were not determined by the aggressive action of another power, as was the case for France, Great Britain, Russia, and later the United States. Rather they were the product of dispassionate calculation. For this reason Italian intervention has appeared as opportunistic – which it undeniably was. Where Italian politicians can be faulted is not in pursuing their national interests but in delaying too long before throwing Italian military power onto the scales; what turned out to be a marginal factor in May 1915 might very well have been of much greater weight both physically and psychologically in August and September 1914. Once in the war, Italy took steps to maximize its industrial output but suffered from the inability – or unwillingness – of politicians to interfere in strategic affairs. Up to 1917 British and French politicians were as much in the hands of their military as were Italians; in 1918 Lloyd George and Clemenceau won back overall control and exerted political authority to the full. In Italy this never happened, due to the strength of the established pattern of civil-military relations.

Strategic Effectiveness

It is not necessary to go along with left-wing interpretations of Italian military history in their entirety to accept the truth of Rochat's contention that in 1915 Italy had to wage an offensive war because it sought imperialist goals.[39] To gain those goals a military defeat had to be inflicted upon Vienna of such dimensions as to force it to accept the loss of what it regarded as integral parts of its empire. In planning the campaign which was to attain the political goals, a single military objective was identified as the only one of sufficient weight and importance to embody the heart of the enemy's will to resist: the city of Vienna itself. This decision both limited Italy's strategic options and determined how it would attempt to apply force to seek its ends. It also put Italy in an extremely difficult position from the outset, for its topographical situation relative to Austria-Hungary was weak.[40]

Before 1914 Italian planning for a war with Austria-Hungary had been wholly defensive. Now only a strategy of deep penetration would allow Italy to gain its objective. Accordingly, by 21 December 1914 Cadorna had entirely re-cast Italian strategy, sketching the outlines of a plan of campaign in which the first major battle would take place within a fortnight after the start of operations and two or three days' march inside the Austrian frontier, to be followed by a second great battle at twice that distance within forty-five days. This would bring Italian troops onto the Lubljana plain, from where they would launch a drive on Vienna.[41] This plan appeared to unite military objectives with political goals. In April 1915, with the Russians apparently poised to fall on the plain of Hungary from the north, it appeared also to conform to the shape of the war.

Appearances were, however, deceptive. Thinking in a Jominian rather than a Clausewitzian frame of reference, and therefore placing predominance upon a physical objective rather than upon defeat of the enemy's will to resist, Cadorna closed off alternative strategic options which might have better suited Italy: a Dardanelles-type operation away from the central front, or a Balkan strategy. Operations in support of Serbia might have enabled Italian troops to force the Austro-Hungarian fleet out of its bases from the land; and a campaign against European Turkey could have unlocked much-needed supplies of Russian grain. Neither option conformed to Cadorna's narrow strategic vision. Cadorna's plan also assumed that tactics on the north-eastern front would not be fettered by the combination of factors which was producing static trench warfare in the west by spring 1915. It assumed concentric – if not co-ordinated – operations against Austria-Hungary by the Allies. It was based on the supposition that Vienna would not be in a position to release troops from its eastern front which, after defeating Russia at Gorlice, it was able to do.[42] Finally, and because of the obsession with gaining the Lubljana gap and threatening Vienna, once the initial design had failed Cadorna could see no other way than attrition to achieve his military objective.[43]

Having already paused for ten months before entering the fighting in May 1915, Italy had at least to act quickly. This it did not do, and in numerous instances a slow advance by corps commanders gave the enemy time to seize and fortify key positions which could have been taken without loss.[44] Once the war on the Isonzo had revealed its horrible similarity to that being waged in Flanders, Cadorna saw himself as left with no choice but to launch a series of costly hammer-blows in an attempt to break the enemy line. He was also determined that his armies should never abandon an inch of hard-won ground. Both these facts multiplied the costs Italy was forced to pay by its preferred strategic plan, and both were the consequence of a process of formulating goals which made no provision for flexibility.

The pre-eminence of the Isonzo and the predominance of Cadorna in the process of translating political goals into military objectives was cemented by the failure of the one attempt to undertake an alternative strategy with a high political input. Sonnino was keen to undertake an operation in Albania and, backed by the war minister, beat down Cadorna's objections that it would be difficult, dangerous, and of little use in gaining the ends for which the war was being fought. An Italian force was accordingly landed at Durazzo in December 1915 but was quickly cut off by an Austrian advance into northern Albania and had to be rescued by the navy on 26 February 1916 with much loss of equipment. Thereafter, although a small Italian contingent did fight on the Western Front in 1918, Italian efforts focused on the Corso and Gorizia. At no point did any leading soldier or politician suggest that Italy abandon its initial strategy in the light of its patent failure and deploy troops elsewhere.

The chief instrument by which Italy hoped to win victory, its army, displayed to an exaggerated degree the characteristics of all other European armies save that of Great Britain. Its preponderant power lay in mass infantry formations: in 1914 Italy could mobilize 1,250,000 men. However the training of the reserves had frequently been abbreviated for financial reasons, and that of the territorial militia was often non-existent. Its weakest point was its shortage of medium and heavy artillery. Given the military thinking of the day, there appeared to be no inconsistencies whatever between the shape of Italy's army and the goals it was to be employed to achieve. But as the war ground on Italy's inability to make up its deficiencies became ever more apparent. The major technological novelty of the war – the tank – offered no solution to the problem of unlocking Austrian defensive positions, and military leaders settled down too readily to using the army simply as a battering ram; not until the summer of 1918 were serious attempts made to copy the techniques of penetration first practiced by the Russian armies under Brusilov in 1916.

The Italian Navy had fallen behind the Austro-Hungarian fleet in terms of matériel in 1912 and was only catching up in Dreadnoughts two years later. In any case it regarded itself as in a strategically inferior position because of the natural defensive line of islands along the eastern Adriatic which masked the bases of Pola and Cattaro, from which the Austrian Navy could sally forth at its own choice of time and place.[45] Awareness – one might reasonably say exaggeration – of Italy's weaknesses in force structure led the chief of the Italian naval staff, Admiral Thaon di Revel, to base his negotiating position for a joint naval convention with France and Britain in 1915 on a demand that he be given six battleships capable of 17 knots plus, twenty-four destroyers capable of 30 knots, and considerable numbers of mine-sweepers and torpedo craft. When the convention was signed in mid-May 1915 Thaon got much of what he wanted, including four British battleships and twelve French destroyers.[46] Although he continued to regard his force levels as inadequate, strategic paralysis at sea was later compensated for by imaginative operational and tactical developments.

Like almost everyone else, Italian politicians and soldiers were unable to conceive of a war as lasting any great length of time. In August 1915 Cadorna expected that the fighting would continue through 1916 as big operations could not begin until then, but by January 1916 he was wondering: 'Who would have imagined a catastrophe of this kind and lasting so long?'[47] Sixteen months later, in May 1917, the Duke of Aosta, commanding the Third Army, could see no military way out of the attrition which characterized the Italian front and believed that the war would still be going on ten years hence.[48]

It was soon evident that a campaign in the north-east would put great strain on Italy's logistical capacity. Prewar planners had based their defensive strategy in part upon the poor railroad connections to the region where the war was now being fought, in contrast to Austrian lines with approximately twice as much carrying capacity. The nature of the front along the Isonzo and on the *altoplano* of the Trentino exacerbated these difficulties: the upland terrain was frequently so rugged that the only way to move supplies and ammunition was on men's backs, and in many places even this was impossible. Italian ingenuity produced the *teleferiche* – cable-ways up which supplies were transported and down which, very occasionally, seriously wounded men were carried – but logistical obstacles remained immense. Narrow-gauge railways compensated for deficiencies in the national rail network, particularly after the retreat to the Piave in the winter of 1917; but maintaining the road network was always burdensome, requiring three to four men per kilometer and thus cutting into manpower resources.

Italy's industrial capacity proved increasingly incapable of sustaining the burdens of a war of attrition. As well as a shortage of plants it suffered from shortages of raw materials – greatly exacerbated after the German declaration of unrestricted submarine warfare in 1917 – and of power. Coal imports were cut in half between 1911 and 1917 and although domestic lignite production was boosted it could only be used for heating and cooking. Hydro-electric power filled only a part of the gap between supply and demand of power, with knock-on effects throughout the war effort; in January 1918 coal consumption by the railways was down to only 25,000 tons.[49] By the latter stages of the war, and thanks in large part to Dallolio, Italian industry was responding more effectively to the country's war needs. At Caporetto 3,152 guns were lost out of a total stock of 7,138, but within six months 4,000 replacements had been manufactured, largely by ceasing certain categories of production.[50] Otherwise, to fill the gap between what it had and what it needed, Italy turned to the Allies for loans and for gifts of materiel in the earlier stages of the war and for manpower after Caporetto. Italy's underestimation of its likely needs, revealed in the fact that it asked for a loan of only £50 million to underpin the Treaty of London, suggests that it did not intend to rely so heavily at the outset upon its wartime allies.[51] Those allies did help Italy to cover vital needs; though by the same token other calls upon allied capacity meant that enough could never be spared to mass an overwhelming superiority of men or guns on the Isonzo front.

Until the disaster of Caporetto changed things, Italy fought its war with the minimum of strategic integration with its allies. Failure to foresee the importance of this sphere was apparent from the outset: the Italo-Russian military convention of 21 May 1915 had no effect, Serbian promises of aid never materialized, and Rumanian support was never enlisted. In consequence, the Italian Army found itself alone as it launched its attack on Austria in late May 1915, thus depriving itself of one of the essential preconditions for the success of Cadorna's plan.

Some co-ordination in the timing of Italian attacks to chime in with Allied needs was achieved. Following Verdun and in line with an inter-allied agreement to take the offensive in the event of major attacks by the enemy, Cadorna launched the fifth battle of the Isonzo in March 1916. However, the disjointed nature of Allied military action was clearly demonstrated in a sequence of events which saw the Italian attack quickly run out of steam, the great Austrian *Strafexpedition* begin on 15 May but itself run out of impetus by early June, and the Brussilov offensive begin on 4 June. Cadorna's unleashing of the eleventh battle of the Isonzo on 18 August 1917 in response to an Allied request to ease the position on the Russian front demonstrates the central fact of Allied military relations at this time: while there was genuine co-operation, there was no real co-ordination. Without this there could be no real integration of strategic objectives. After Caporetto Diaz adopted a different style of strategy, but his willingness to spend Italian blood on his allies' behalf was less than that of his predecessor; the *Comando Supremo* twice turned down requests by Foch for an offensive, once in May 1918 and again later in the summer.

The waging of parallel war was perhaps even more apparent at sea than on land. Among the numerous reefs which threatened to shipwreck the Anglo-French-Italian naval convention in 1915, one of the most substantial was the understandable view taken by the Italian Navy that the Adriatic was the main theater of war and the equally understandable view taken by the French that this theater was the Mediterranean. The agreement which was reached over the division of command demonstrates the degree to which the Allies were to keep one another at arm's length on the sea: Italians got command of the First Allied Fleet based in the southern Adriatic, including some French light ships, but the French got command of the Second Allied Fleet in the eastern Mediterranean and kept their battleships out of the clutches of the Italians. Among the thorny but vital questions which were carefully left to one side was the issue of which commander would prevail if both fleets entered the Adriatic.[52]

Divided control, and its consequences, remained a feature of the naval war for its duration. The Italian Navy took little or no part in allied convoys but merely protected its own coastal shipping, whilst its capital fleet stayed in port. An Allied Naval Council was set up in November 1917 in an attempt to overcome this fundamental problem but it failed to make any impact; 'to obtain real disinterested cooperation appears as an ideal impossible of attainment' wrote the assistant chief of British naval staff on 28 January 1918.[53] A last-ditch attempt to improve matters by creating an *admiralissimo* to command all naval forces in the Mediterranean, Adriatic, and Aegean – and a thoughtful British offer to provide the man – failed when Italy refused to contemplate putting its fleet under foreign control. National sensitivity was and remained a fundamental barrier to strategic integration.

One way in which Italian strategy might have been most effectively implemented would have been by juxtaposing domestic strength against enemy weakness. Even with the benefit of hindsight – which makes such calculations very much easier than they were for contemporaries – it is difficult to identify significant Italian strengths which might have been deployed against detectable Austrian weaknesses; indeed, in many respects the two powers might be said to have been more or less evenly matched, with Vienna perhaps having a slight edge. However, attainment of Italian objectives meant defeat not merely of Austria-Hungary, from whose empire Italy's territorial objectives were to be torn, but of Germany also. Italian politicians failed to comprehend the extent to which German support for Austria-Hungary was unconditional and unlimited, and Italian soldiers failed to perceive the likely military consequences of this. Even though Italy did not formally declare war against Germany until 1916, the content of the prewar military conversations of the Triple Alliance ought to have provided some indication of how closely Berlin and Vienna were bound together.

In at least one respect Italian participation in the war was of decisive importance, for without it Russia would probably have collapsed much earlier. But in terms of securing victory rather than of preventing defeat the addition of Italian strength on the Allied side in 1915 seems more of a marginal factor. Had Italy fought beside Germany on the Rhine in 1914, as provided for in the prewar plans, the Schlieffen plan might have been successful. Had it attacked Austria-Hungary, then the outcome of the first Russian encounters with the German Army might have been different. By 1915 Italian arms were insufficient to tilt the balance decisively in the Allies' favor. The achievement of Italy's goals required the defeat of Austria-Hungary, and this Italy could not bring about unaided. To optimize its strategic effectiveness, it should therefore have been an active participant in an Allied strategy. Instead Italy fought its own battles and clung doggedly to a military design which doomed it to attrition.

Operational Effectiveness

In one respect at least the Italian Army ought to have been well prepared for the situation it faced on the Isonzo, for its prewar chiefs of staff had concentrated on the problems of defense in mountainous regions. Summing up the lessons of a staff ride in 1911 the then Chief of the General Staff, Alberto Pollio, had remarked: 'Given the state of development of every country's fixed defenses it is to be expected that any war will begin with repeated attacks upon and defense of reinforced positions around a central point which will have been prepared, or perhaps only studied, in peacetime.'[54] Infantry tactics evolved before the war had included some advice on mountain warfare; but the Italian general staff had concentrated its efforts on the location of defensive fortifications at the most suitable geographical points and had come to regard attacking French or Austrian defences as an impossible task. More importantly, the Italian Army had not developed an articulated operational doctrine by 1915, and Cadorna did nothing to remedy this deficiency.

Prewar military thought had scarcely created the most fertile soil in which to nurture an agreed operational doctrine. *The Regulations for the Tactical Employment of Major Units in War* issued in 1903 laid heavy weight on flexibility and emphasized that the application of norms was not to become automatic, and the 1910 edition stressed the importance of the commander's intuition and his ability to size up the situation confronting him as more important than any regulations.[55] When Cadorna took command of Italy's armies his attitude toward operational doctrine and concepts did nothing to remedy the situation.

In the months before Italy's entry into the war Cadorna saw the need to prepare the army for war entirely in terms of the provision of manpower, arms, and matériel. His initial operational ideas were extremely simple: he proposed merely to attack with large masses of infantry supported by an enormous artillery barrage.[56] By January 1916 he had come to the conclusion that trenches and barbed wire had annulled maneuver and that long-range indirect artillery fire had made the holding of positions impossible, and believed that the only way to overcome the situation was by gradual attrition. If sufficient stress had been laid on training for the new style warfare an operational doctrine might have evolved, but thanks to Cadorna's mental rigidity this basic precondition was missing; he saw no need for an intermediate phase between theoretical studies and the moment of action, remarking that 'it is enough that at the right moment the decisions are taken quickly.'[57]

The Italian method of holding the front, which remained largely unchanged for the better part of three years, was to mass almost every available man and gun in the front line with no reserve or supports. The idea that infantry might be used more flexibly, in smaller waves and in attacks which were not pressed home with ever-mounting momentum, was one which developed only very slowly and then proved difficult to disseminate throughout the army. That this was so was partly due to deficiencies in the command structure and partly to a failure to learn lessons, but it was also due to gross internal contradictions of command style which obstructed the development and diffusion of a coherent operational doctrine. Thus while Cadorna warned his commanders in September 1916 not to press attacks beyond the culminating point so as to avoid unnecessary slaughter, his command system was penalizing those who did not show exemplary aggressiveness.[58]

Operational successes came from the vision and ability of individual commanders rather than from the acceptance and adoption of any of the stream of orders, circulars, and advice which flowed down the hierarchical chain from Cadorna's headquarters. During 1917 Badoglio developed an effective operational design to break up enemy attacks which relied on artillery fire and hidden machine guns – although it availed him nought at Caporetto. The same technique, fired in the furnace of experience, was well used by General Giardino in checking the Austrian offensive on the Piave in June 1918.[59] Perhaps most striking of all was the concept of the defensive battle developed before Caporetto by General Luigi Capello. At a conference called on 17 September 1917 he analyzed the problems of halting an enemy offensive and then undertaking a counter-offensive, emphasizing the need for second line defences, mutual support, maneuver in the trenches (which he believed still possible), and automatic intervention by the artillery.[60] Capello's stress on the viability of the offensive rested on intelligent analysis.

The First World War was an artillerist's war and the employment of the artillery arm represents perhaps the greatest failure of Italian operational doctrine. Guiding principles were in a state of continual confusion. In 1916 inadequate supplies of ammunition meant that artillery could not be used to cut gaps in the enemy's wire; instead it was to be used for counter-battery fire and then to seal off the assault area and prevent the enemy from bringing up reinforcements.[61] Shortly afterwards artillery was ordered to concentrate on paralyzing enemy command systems and batteries in its offensive capacity.[62] In defense the guns were to gain maximum effect by not unleashing their fire until the enemy neared Italian wire.[63] Commanders who were having to tailor their firing to the ammunition shortage must have found Cadorna's instructions in June 1916 – that the enemy's defensive lines were to be subjected to a very heavy bombardment before the attack in order to create openings in them – somewhat confusing.[64]

Only in March 1917 did the notion of 'creeping barrages' begin to enter the Italian mind. Regulations for the offensive use of artillery – which now demanded a long period of preparatory fire where the previous year they had urged a brief one – put forward the idea of breaking enemy defenses in attack zones and of infantry advances under a moving curtain of fire.[65] At the same time defensive artillery was to concentrate on what was in effect a doctrine of counter-preparation, locating the zone in which the enemy attack was massing in order to crack it. In June 1917, following the success of the Austrian attack on the Asiago plateau which had been preceded only by a brief but violent bombardment, the Italian artillery abandoned multi-day preliminary shelling and switched back to very brief bombardments. In the same month Cadorna changed artillery doctrine yet again, ordering only limited counter-battery fire and abandoning destructive fire directed against enemy trenches in order to concentrate on interdiction fire, which would seal off the target of an infantry attack from sources of reinforcement.[66]

The consequences of doctrinal confusion were fully visible during the battle of Caporetto and help to account for the Italian defeat. When the Austrian bombardment began at 2:00 a.m. on 24 October 1917, there was no methodical Italian counter-fire. Although arrangements for automatic artillery intervention did exist, most battery commanders waited for direct orders which never reached them, or which they took as no more than suggestions if they did receive them. Once in action the artillery shifted from counter-preparation to interdiction fire and back again; there was no counter-battery fire to speak of. And, as a reflection of the procurement weakness, at least one commander withheld fire because of his concern about the shortage of ammunition.[67]

A successful process of learning and applying the lessons of others, as well as of absorbing and analyzing experiences on the Italian fronts, might have led to the development of a more coherent and apposite operational doctrine. No such thing took place. The explanation for this deficiency is not to be found in a belief that happenings on other fronts and in other theaters were irrelevant to Italian experience; in 1915 and 1916 a mass of circulars about French, German, and Austro-Hungarian practice emanated from headquarters.[68] Rather it lies in the Italian conception of staff work, which was more concerned with active operations than with longer-term intellectual analysis. In consequence there existed no specialized lesson-drawing organ; in its place, Cadorna and his personal assistant Colonel Bencivenga selected what they thought relevant or interesting. The result was a body of generalized and abstract circulars from which commanders could pick whatever they liked.[69]

Finally, in the summer of 1918 – and under a new commander – this defective system changed for the better. On 4 July 1918 headquarters issued a critical analysis of the fighting on the Piave the previous month, in which an Austrian attack had been successfully beaten off, entitled *Experiences of the Recent Battle*. For the first time this explored and demonstrated the new way of attack – violent, rapid, directed against distant targets and weak spots. Operating on new tactical principles, selected infantry backed by mobile artillery launched the initial attack, to be followed by an enveloping assault by the main body.[70] This tiger was but a paper one, however, for at that time the specialized units needed to mount such assaults did not exist.

To the French naval attaché, writing in December 1913, one of the most distinctive features of the Italian Navy was that it appeared to have no operational doctrine at all. This was perhaps not altogether surprising since there then existed no *Scuola superiore*, but the consequence was that Italian sailors tended to attribute more importance to secondary operations such as landings than to naval combat.[71] Although the Italian Navy had developed plans for its war in the Adriatic, those plans stressed the avoidance of battle by the battleships under unfavorable circumstances; it is therefore not surprising that battle doctrine came low down on their list of priorities. Only in one area did Italy develop an effective naval doctrine – and then more tactical than operational: for the employment of MAS torpedo boats.

Air doctrine was in its infancy in 1915, but Italy had profited from early and important experience in the operational use of aircraft during the Libyan War of 1911–12. This clearly showed that air power could most valuably be used in observation of enemy movements. For this reason, and also because of the technical limitations of machines, little importance was attached to aerial bombardment during the first stages of the war. By 1916, however, and despite considerable problems with bad weather over the mountains, the Italian Air Force was developing bombing techniques and perfecting its combat techniques against enemy fighters.[72] A combination of flexibility in response to immediate needs and some freedom from the constricting coils of the Army High Command produced further operational advances during 1918; in the attack across the Piave in November 1918, which culminated in the battle of Vittorio Veneto, the Air Force successfully re-supplied four Italian divisions which had been cut off by floods from their magazines and used ground-attack techniques to support the advance.

One reason for the operational deficiencies displayed by the Italian armies until the closing stages of the First World War was the fact that operational practice and *mentalité* generally pulled in the opposite direction from what was required. The hallmark of Italian operational posture was caution. This led the Austrian official historian to remark of the three battles of the Isonzo which took place in September, October, and November 1916 that 'the success of the Italians bore no relation to the mighty expenditure in men and material which it cost' and to conclude that failure to achieve more was due 'mainly to the caution of the Italian Supreme Command, who would not venture to throw in the last reserves which might have secured victory.'[73] Repeated plaints by British admirals suggest that the same characteristic was manifest in Italy's conduct of the war at sea.

Cadorna for one found the trench warfare in which he was engaged *antipaticissima*.[74] This may have been a contributory factor in formulating his style of command, which further separated the strategic from the operational. Issuing orders for the fifth battle of the Isonzo, he merely told his army commanders that they could attack whatever objective they liked as long as they contributed 'directly or indirectly' to the first objective in the move east – the entrenched enemy camps of Gorizia and Tolmino.[75] Closer control might have produced a more effective use of Italian arms, although it would have required a change of attitude on Cadorna's part. It was claimed of his successor, Diaz, that his approach abandoned the idea of uniform pressure over the whole front varied by a series of hammer-blows and consciously reached back to the pre-1914 style of maneuver warfare.[76] However, since Diaz simply had to hold the line of the Piave, and until the eve of Vittorio Veneto did not envisage major offensive operations that year, it seems unlikely that in this respect there was any significant change in style in the *Comando Supremo*.

One of the main aims of the Italian Navy was to maintain in being as large a fleet as possible so as to be in the most advantageous position with respect to France after the war ended. This far-sighted strategic goal contributed a great deal to the formulation of an operational concept which expressed itself in the policy of keeping the major fleet units in Taranto harbor, out of harm's way. However, Italy's naval situation was in truth a difficult one: like the Grand Fleet, the Austro-Hungarian Navy might keep to its bases all the time and still be a decisive factor. Further, the mine and the torpedo posed such great dangers to expensive capital ships that all the major navies found it difficult to resolve the problem of reconciling the strategic goal of gaining command of the sea with the operational deterrents to aggressive action.

When Sir William Robertson visited the Italian front in March 1917 he found 'no system of cooperation between the artillery and infantry in attack, in fact the relations between the two arms seemed strained.'[77] This was an accurate observation, and one which reflected the continuation into wartime of a water-tight compartmentalization, which had been one of the features of the pre-1915 army. In action artillery commanders operated by firing-plans instead of co-ordinating with the advancing infantry, and on occasion fire ceased before the infantry ever reached the enemy wire – with disastrous results.[78] While there were improvements under Allied tuition after Caporetto, fundamental deficiencies still remained, particularly as regarded artillery. Lord Cavan reported to Sir Henry Wilson in June 1918: 'I can tell you privately that they simply will not go in for the scientific side of accurate shooting.'[79] The command system was never alert enough, and perhaps in any case lacked the power, to break down the barriers between arms.

Air–ground co-operation was at first hindered by the practice of retaining independent control of the air weapon from headquarters, but in June 1917 planes were allotted to individual army corps for tactical reconnaissance and for use in artillery spotting.[80] When he took over command in the autumn of 1917, Diaz drew up a plan for a force of some 1,600 planes; of these the largest number were to be for reconnaissance and pursuit, with bombardment squadrons relegated to third place – an order of priorities which confirms that air-ground co-operation still commanded only a lowly priority. The plan was scheduled for completion in two stages by 1 August and 31 December 1918 and therefore had only small effect by the war's end.[81]

Much of the blame for the ineffectiveness of Italian military effort can be laid at the door of poor command, control, and co-ordination and weak staff work, especially in the area of intelligence. To a large extent, these deficiencies were the direct consequence of Cadorna's style of command and resulted from his 'egocentric authoritarianism.'[82] In the first place, Cadorna's headquarters were located too far away from the front, a habit which he maintained during the retreat from Caporetto and one which loosened his hold on the operational command of his forces. The habit of distancing command from troops on the ground, which resulted in a lack of grip on operations, was further replicated at lower levels. The Third Army was reported to be a 'co-operative' in which the Duke of Aosta failed to exercise his role as commander properly; one of its corps commanders, General Pecori Giraldi, never came down from his villa to headquarters during the winter of 1916–17, but sent cars twice a day to collect his staff officers for meals.[83] Central control was further weakened by Cadorna's failure to acknowledge the need for army group commanders to be interposed between headquarters and the four active armies.[84] Isolation from the body of the army reinforced an historical trait and led the *Comando Supremo* to regard the army as a machine and not as an aggregate of human beings.[85]

At Cadorna's headquarters the deputy chief of staff and chief of operations were reduced to office workers and their tasks handed over to the head of Cadorna's secretariat. He counted for little to the army commanders, who went their own way and frequently disregarded Cadorna's operational intentions. A structure based on extreme authoritarianism thus had the paradoxical result of diminishing Cadorna's control over his forces to a dangerous degree.

Command isolation was magnified by Cadorna's almost complete lack of effort to get to know anyone outside his own immediate circle. That small group of staff officers effectively controlled promotions, and the favoritism that resulted led to a widespread belief within the army in the existence of a *camorra* and to questions being raised in the Chamber of Deputies in June 1917 about the fragmentation of the army from the rank of lieutenant colonel upwards which had resulted from the knowledge that advancement often depended on a single recommendation from an influential staff officer.

General Fayolle's report of 26 December 1917 – independently confirmed in its essentials the following month by General Lord Plumer – found the Italian staff to be energetic but noted two major defects: a lack of organizing capacity and an inability to adapt to the circumstances of the war. Among the operational and tactical consequences which followed from this were a lack of any proper system of reliefs, imperfect artillery liaison with the infantry, late delivery of local counter-attacks, and hasty delivery of methodical counter-offensives.[86] The staff thought in terms of paper-work rather than of mission assignments, presuming that an order issued was an order carried out. The consequences of this state of affairs were again most clearly visible after Caporetto: during the retreat the *Comando Supremo* failed to issue appropriate orders and to ensure that they were obeyed, to control traffic, and to regulate the distribution of supplies.

In default of an articulated chain of command, Cadorna exercised control over his armies by the crudest of means. Officers at all levels down to battalion commanders were dismissed before and during as well as after combat, generally for supposed lack of offensive spirit. The technique, which started at the top, was also adopted by at least one of Cadorna's army commanders. Superficially the policy of rigorously weeding out incompetents may seem to have been a beneficial one; Joffre's reputation rests not least upon the *limogés* whom he ruthlessly sacked during the summer of 1914. However, as some British generals had to be reminded during the Second World War, the supply of commanders or potential commanders is never limitless. Also, continuous sackings will have an adverse effect upon morale – particularly when carried out with the capriciousness manifested by Cadorna. Many stories abound to bear this out. In the midst of battle General Carignani of the VIII Corps was reported to have said to one of his brigadiers: 'I know I have enemies; I know I may fall; and if I do, so will a lot of other people, so remember that.'[87] In all, 217 generals, 255 colonels, and 335 battalion commanders had been sacked by October 1917; throughout the remainder of the war a further 176 officers followed them.[88]

Failures in the Italian command system were both partially caused and magnified by weaknesses in intelligence and counter-intelligence. Headquarters leaked like a sieve. As soon as an operation was planned the military hierarchy passed down general details of it to corps level and below, while Cadorna's secretariat told foreign ministers exactly what operational intentions and orders were.[89] In the circumstances, it is scarcely surprising that the enemy was often well informed about Italian plans. Incoming intelligence was imperfectly processed or dismissed. Again Caporetto provides the outstanding illustration of this. Italian intelligence got wind of Austrian preparations a month before the attack by a combination of direct observation, interrogation of prisoners, and secret service information, but Cadorna refused to believe that the enemy would unleash an offensive just before winter or in the mountain zone. Final confirmation came on the eve of the attack, when two Rumanian deserters gave away the fire plan, but still Cadorna refused to react. After Caporetto there seems to have been an improvement in the quality of incoming Italian intelligence, due in large part to the practice of parachuting officers behind enemy lines into former Italian territory, where they were sheltered by the local inhabitants.[90]

In one obvious respect Italy ought to have been able to improve its operational effectiveness, for by May 1915 the impact of defensive technology on traditional concepts of military operations was being clearly displayed on the Western Front. Cadorna was doubly well placed to take account of this, for he was well briefed by his military attachés on the configurations of trench warfare by the time that Italy entered the fray. Reports from Lieutenant Colonel Breganze in Paris in December 1914 and February 1915 stressed the strength of the defensive, the importance of artillery and fortifications in the new warfare, the heavy losses suffered by both attack and defense, and the high rates of ammunition consumption. Breganze concluded his second report by stating that it appeared to be impossible to reach a decision at the front in the circumstances currently prevailing.[91]

At the end of March 1915 Cadorna received confirmation of Breganze's warnings in the shape of a brilliantly perceptive report from Colonel

Bongiovanni in Berlin. The military attaché pinpointed the central problem posed by static warfare: 'An attack, provided that it is carefully prepared and well conducted, can carry the fire zone between the point of departure and the enemy's line without excessive losses; the really great difficulty is the barbed wire entanglement. If it is thick, deep and defended by riflemen well supplied with ammunition it is an almost insuperable obstacle.'[92] Bongiovanni described in detail all the main characteristics of trench warfare: the dominant role of artillery, especially howitzers, and the need for advanced posts, artillery observers, and support lines of trenches, and for hand grenades, periscopes, and all the other paraphernalia necessary to sustain the new style of fighting.

Cadorna disregarded these timely and perceptive warnings about the impact of technology on military operations. In the foreward to a pamphlet of French techniques he remarked that the nature of the terrain on the Italian front and the character of Italian operations made it 'improbable' that Italian troops would have to resort to such action.[93] To have changed Italian operational and tactical doctrine in order to accommodate the new landscape of war would have meant reversing a major trend toward the attack. It would also have injected a considerable degree of dissonance into the relationship between political goals and military strategy, since Cadorna would have had to acknowledge that his armies could not in current circumstances create the successes which would lead to victory. Instead he chose to believe that with greater effort all obstacles could be overcome: 'Everyone must persuade themselves that trench warfare can and must end and that this will depend on their energy, their tenacity, and their conviction of their own material and moral superiority.'[94] Rather than analyze how greater effort might be applied to the problem of attack, Cadorna's staff followed their master's lead.

In respect of support activities at least, Italy experienced no major difficulties. The static character of the war from May 1915 to October 1917 allowed a territorialization of supply services, with fixed magazines and advanced depots for ammunition and stores. The elements of the system were connected by trunk railways, narrow-gauge railways, electric lines, and *teleferiche*. The system worked adequately, constraints being rather more on supply than on transport, until the crisis at Caporetto, when large amounts of stocks were lost during the retreat. The Grappa-Piave line on which the Italians eventually made their stand lacked stations and sidings as well as the more complex apparatus of distribution, and these had to be slowly built up.[95] In general, the support system was never as great a constraint upon Italian military effectiveness as was supply or command.

Tactical Effectiveness

Cadorna's advocacy of offensive tactics conformed to both his own strategic plan and prewar patterns of thought, for both his predecessors had put their names to offensive tactics. The difference was only one of degree. In the *Regulations for Tactical Employment of Major Units in War* published in 1903, Saletta had recommended combining frontal and flank attacks, and in the revised edition of 1910, Pollio had stated that the offensive spirit was the essence of war but had cautioned that improvised offensives must be avoided at all costs. The *Combat Regulations* of 1913 openly acknowledged the effectiveness of fire power but argued that it favored the attack rather than the defense 'because the employment of new means, especially modern portable arms, is affected more than ever before by the state of mind of those carrying them, that is of whoever can better make his own material and moral superiority count.'[96] The regulations proposed staged attacks which alternated movement with fire power, the latter being provided by rifles with artillery in support; machine guns were to be held back for action when artillery weakened or fell silent.

Cadorna's edition of collective instructions for tactical action, which was issued in August 1914, merely put more stress on frontal attacks, claiming that they were less difficult than they had been made to appear. In his *Regulations on Frontal Attack*, published in February 1915, Cadorna developed his own theory to explain both how and why offensive tactics could succeed. The technique was to make the defender expose himself to the fire of the attacker, and this was to be achieved by means of the forward threatening movement of the infantry. In Cadorna's scheme artillery protected the advancing infantry rather than preparing the way for the assault.[97] His ideas may well have been entirely out of tune with modern war;[98] but they were broadly in tune both with prewar Italian tactical doctrine and with that of other European armies of the day.

Once the Italian high command had been disabused of the notion that static warfare was not going to obtain on their front, neither offensive nor defensive tactics were revised to husband manpower for decisive action. Offensive tactics continued to stress mass infantry assaults in 1917, by which time perceptive observers were already pointing out that small attacks which enabled success to be followed up were the most effective form of tactical action. At the same time defensive tactics still stressed the need to mass troops and artillery in the front line in order to contain the enemy when it was apparent that a more effective technique was to hold the front line thinly and keep the main body in reserve for local counter-attacks.[99] Underpinning Italian tactics by this time was the conviction that maneuver was an essential component of the offensive and an irrelevance to the defensive. As simple articles of faith, both assumptions were incorrect. Offensive maneuver was a costly blunder until such time as the infantryman could be equipped with heavy weapons and used in more subtle tactics rather than being employed as a battering-ram; and defensive maneuver, as Capello realized, was a necessary tactic to prepare the way for the counter-attack. These lessons were only applied in the closing months of the war.

The failure to reconcile offensive operational objectives with defensive tactical reality was apparent in the slowness with which Italy adapted to trench warfare. Not until December 1915 was it proposed that parallels be dug to advance towards enemy lines before attacking across open lines, and the first footways, huts, and shelters were constructed to improve the lines of trenches.[100] Thereafter improvements were slow. A report by Plumer's staff officers in December 1917 found that Italian trenches were too shallow, machine guns were poorly sited on 'pulpits' on top of the parapets, barbed-wire entanglements were too close to the trenches, and communication trenches, were non-existent.[101] After the retreat from the Piave, Diaz revised defensive doctrine, locating artillery according to its range rather than simply positioning it forward, holding front lines more thinly, and extending the defense to cover three separate zones rather than one. To bring about such changes in established patterns of thought had required a military disaster of almost overwhelming proportions, a fact which speaks volumes about the rigidity of Italian military practice.

The high command frequently complained that offensive tactics were being practiced with undue hesitation. In August 1917 the Third Army chided its troops for not pressing the attack beyond the enemy's first line and for showing an excessive concern with keeping in contact with flanking units, and sought to encourage troops to outpace one another – which might well be regarded as the height of military unwisdom.[102] At the same time more cautious tactics were being adopted, consisting of attacking enemy trenches from two sides and then mopping them up. As was the case at the operational level, there was no unified tactical doctrine.

The most successful marrying of tactical and operational concepts was undoubtedly the navy's development of MAS torpedo boats. The notion that torpedo boats were particularly well adapted for warfare in the Adriatic had been around for some years before the war.[103] Early French setbacks helped to stimulate the development of the new vessels; the *Jean Bart* was torpedoed on 21 December 1914 while detached for blockade duties with the French squadron in the eastern Mediterranean, and the cruiser *Leon Gambetta* was torpedoed and sunk on 26 April 1915. The operational concept of a main fleet action which dictated the husbanding of Italian battleships can only have worked to encourage those who scented a tactical opportunity.

The first MAS raid of consequence took place on 6–7 June 1916, when two boats penetrated the harbor at Durazzo and sank the *Lokrum*. Further successes followed that year, but during it fewer vessels were built: while Italy possessed 45 MAS boats in 1916, it had only 35 in 1917, of which 6 were lost. However the combination of new weapon and new tactics produced a dramatic success on 9–10 December 1917, when Commander Rizzo sank the cruiser *Wien*. The following June Rizzo sank the Austrian battleship *Svent Istvan*, forcing Admiral Horthy to abandon an attempt to force the allied barrier at Otranto. Finally, on 1 November 1918, two Italian frogmen using a self-propelled torpedo penetrated the defenses of Pola harbor and sank the battleship *Viribus Unitis*.[104] The MAS campaign and the action of Italian frogmen had shown ingenuity, courage, and skill and had won significant gains at very low cost.

As with inter-service co-operation, the record with all-arms integration was poor. The failure to concert the action of artillery and infantry is clearly illustrated in the initial phase of the battle of Vittorio Veneto, which began on 24 October 1918. Artillery preparation for the attack was inadequate, and Italian troops were soon involved in yet another battle of attrition of the type fought along the Isonzo for three and a half years. After four days, three small bridgeheads had been established across the Piave. The accelerating collapse of the enemy's rear on 27–28 October was the event which transformed the battle into an Italian victory of sizeable proportions.[105]

Tactical support for attacking infantry was limited as much by dogma as by technical limitations; using artillery in a more mobile manner – one of the keys which eventually helped to unlock the front – was as much as anything a matter of changing patterns of use. In common with all other armies, the Italians suffered most from the lack of an adequate means of signaling through which attacking units could indicate the extent of their progress and communicate with headquarters in order to summon support. The infantry carried colored disks which they were supposed to display for aerial observers but these were frequently difficult to see. In consequence local tactical successes were on occasion nullified or reversed through failure to provide adequate support fast enough.

Strategic surprise could be achieved by Italian forces in their own theater in two ways. One was to shift the geographical focus by landing troops at some point on the enemy's coastline. Two factors ruled this out. Cadorna was never willing to release more than a few battalions from the Isonzo; and the navy was quite unwilling to hazard its ships in such a risky operation. A second route to strategic surprise was via tactical surprise. Operational or tactical surprise was fully possible; the Austrians achieved it both with the *Strafexpedition* and at Caporetto. To achieve it required the adoption of new techniques of assault, the concealed massing of men and munitions, safeguarding the plan of attack from the enemy, and – most importantly of all – an articulated attack doctrine.

The first step towards a new tactical system came in 1917 with the creation of small assault units of picked men – the *Arditi*. Their hallmark was a complete fearlessness in attack, and their successes were largely due to their eagerness to get to close quarters and use the knife, club, or grenade. Their brutal attitude caused at least one member of Cadorna's headquarters staff to ponder what they would do in peacetime – 'these people who no longer know the value of human life.'[106] During 1918 the *Arditi* were given a larger role in attacks, but their use alone did not modify the clumsy and mechanical nature of Italian assaults and they did not achieve the same type of penetration as did the Germans during the offensive of March 1918 on the Western Front.[107] However, *Arditi* units could help turn setback into success by their sheer fearlessness. An example of this came at an early point in the battle of Vittorio Veneto, when *Arditi* units played a central role in taking a vital bridge by attacking it with bombs.

The steps towards an articulated assault doctrine were gradual ones. Assault units were first attached to regiments, then formed into separate battalions and finally in 1918 into assault divisions – an important recognition of the specialized nature of their task. In September 1918, following their experience at the Piave three months earlier, the Italian authorities experimented with T battalions: no larger in size than conventional battalions, they were much more heavily armed with automatic rifles, light and heavy machine guns, 37-mm cannon, and mortars and included *Arditi* platoons armed with flamethrowers. At the same time the *Alpini* were provided with heavier arms, including the Stokes mortar.[108] These advances all came slowly and were all essentially imitative. In general, the Italians waited to see how others would react to the tactical problems posed by war before cautiously introducing their own reforms. The one outstanding exception to this was the MAS torpedo boat.

The effectiveness with which weapons are used and tactics adopted depends upon the manpower qualities of the armies which operate them. In the Italian case, military effectiveness was severely constrained by the manpower problem, and further exacerbated by the techniques adopted to overcome it. Resources could be supplied by allies; deficiencies in Italian manufacturing capacity and technology could to some extent be made up by recourse to the same source; but the nature of the human machine with which Italy had to fight was the foundation upon which all else had to be built.

The mass of manpower which made up the Italian armies could not rest on any quiet sense of legitimacy of the military as a government activity critical to the welfare of society. Quite the opposite was true. From the moment that compulsory military service was first introduced in 1854 a system of lotteries and exemptions encouraged Italians to think of it as an unwelcome intrusion which was to be evaded or avoided if at all possible, and to regard the system of examining potential draftees as a duel between the individual and the state.[109] This attitude of mind continued throughout the rest of the century and beyond; the level of absenteeism in the draft of 1914 was 10.44 per cent, just short of the all-time record set in 1863.[110] Many Italians donned their uniforms only with great reluctance.

If the raw material of Italy's army was unwilling, then the pool from which it would be drawn was unpromising. Commenting on the failure of the Risorgimento, H. Stuart Hughes remarked that 'if the solutions they [the rulers] devised were mostly rather mediocre, so was the physical and political material with which they had to work.'[111] No denigration of the Italian character is necessary to justify this generalization. On the eve of war, the level of education of the peasant masses was abysmally low. Under the Legge Copino of 1877 education was obligatory only up to the age of 9, and in 1901–2 only 4.6 in every 1,000 children of an age to attend secondary schools did so. The problems this posed were immense. In the first place, the peacetime army had had to spend considerable time remedying that illiteracy at the cost of training. Secondly, it made propagandizing the troops a very much harder task. During the war a heavy propaganda campaign was directed at the industrial labor force to convince them of their integral role in the defense of Italy, apparently with considerable success.[112] No such campaign could be launched at the mass of uniformed peasants. Thirdly, high levels of illiteracy made it doubly difficult to re-construct Italian patriotism, which was first local, then provincial, and only finally – if at all – national. An illiterate peasant army could be motivated by religion or by loyalty to their monarch. Neither force operated in the Italian context.

In these circumstances a much greater weight was thrown onto the officer corps, and it was unable to compensate for the cultural deficiencies which detracted from Italian military effectiveness. In part this was due to the small size of the pool of educated upper class and *borghesia* from which officer candidates could be drawn. Of this already small pool – perhaps 10 to 15 per cent of the population – the most promising chose civil careers and the dullest entered the army.[113] Although the army made some attempt to remedy the deficiency by opening one quarter of officers' commissions to rankers, the supply was simply not enough. When war broke out and general mobilization began in August 1914, the army was short of 13,500 officers.[114] The Italian ratio of officers to men was approximately one to twenty-five. The relative scarcity of officers at the front must have diminished the fighting potential of the troops. The charge that the high command deliberately restricted the number of officers in order to benefit from a high proportion of the budget in the shape of salaries must remain at present not proven.[115]

Quality matters in an officer corps as much as, and probably more than, quantity. The evidence suggests that junior officers of the regular army took a high-handed attitude towards the men, exercising control not through natural authority or professional competence but by virtue of their epaulettes. Commenting on the treatment handed out to veterans of the Libyan War who were recalled to the colors in September 1914, the British military attaché remarked that 'the younger officers especially are wanting in tact, and do not seem to realize the difference between a reservist, who is a fully trained soldier, and a recruit.'[116] Wartime officers were clearly distrusted by the regulars at headquarters because of their supposed lack of ideals, other than a devotion to material well-being. Their quality seems to have been better than many allowed at the time, or have allowed since. Capello, an acute critic of his service, was firmly of the opinion that a large proportion of the wartime officers were superior to their counterparts in the permanent army, who showed signs of 'habitual laziness.'[117] But they were too few in number.

To make matters worse, the Italian Army lacked a solid body of well-trained non-commissioned officers to fill what is always an important slot in any army. Potential NCOs were few in number, partly as a result of the educational policies of the state, and the opportunity to step up to commissioned rank meant that as many as 90 per cent of those attending sergeants' courses saw them as a stepping stone to a commission or to a job in the state bureaucracy.[118] Under a law of 1883 non-commissioned officers had a right to a government post after twelve years' service, but since places were not reserved for them – as the law had required – aspirant civilians stayed in the army. The war ministry was unwilling or unable to find enough money to offer incentives to them to retire early, and so the disenchanted stayed on, with results which may readily be imagined.

In peacetime the Italian Army followed a system of regional recruitment, combining together men from two different regions and posting them in a third. This system is generally assumed to have failed to overcome regional differences and cement Italians together into a homogeneous military force. However, it cannot safely be used to explain deficiencies in Italian military effectiveness for two reasons. First, as far as reserves were concerned it was abandoned in 1892; thereafter recruits who were recalled to the colors after having completed their military service joined their local regimental depot and fought alongside their neighbors and acquaintances. Secondly, although there are reports that locally recruited wartime units such as the *Alpini* and the

Brigata Sassari fought well, while mixed units such as the *Brigata Ancona* and *Brigata Valtellina* did not, they are balanced by accounts of *Alpini* units on occasion fleeing 'like rabbits.' As Cadorna remarked in February 1918, there were many units which were sometimes good and sometimes bad.[119]

The nature of Italian political culture and the structure of Italian society produced an army whose potential effectiveness was drastically restricted, so much so that it has caused one leading Italian military historian to conclude recently that even if Cadorna had had a greater elasticity of ideas, the instrument at his disposal would not have produced very different results.[120] However, even without considering his capacity for tactical and strategic innovation, Cadorna's attitude towards maintaining morale and unit cohesion diminished Italian military effectiveness rather than enhancing it. Italian generals traditionally displayed a low regard for their troops' capabilities, and their commander was no exception. He believed the Italian nation to be fundamentally undisciplined and made it clear from the outset that he intended to use on all back-sliders 'the usual discipline of persuasion which is needed in Italy.'[121] He applied it rigorously. During the course of the war some 350,000 soldiers, or 6 per cent of those under arms, were tried for military crimes, of whom 4,028 were condemned to death. Of the 1,061 actually available for punishment, 750 were shot.[122] In addition, there were untold summary executions and decimations of units deemed to have failed in attack or defense.

Excessive punishment was accompanied by a policy of minimal leave, which was frequently suspended altogether. This was the case during the winter of 1916–17, particularly for Sicilians, and by June 1917 some troops had gone seventeen months without any relief from the lines at all.[123] When serious mutinies broke out in the *Brigata* Ravenna in March 1917 and in the *Brigata* Catanzaro in July, Cadorna immediately blamed them on socialists and defeatists and accused the interior minister of being too soft behind the lines. In fact the troubles were spontaneous reactions to the excessively harsh disciplinary policy and the hardships of war. Despite the efforts of Marxists to explain it as a failed uprising by the disenchanted masses, Caporetto was essentially a military defeat, and the army's recovery at the Piave disproved Cadorna's theories about the penetration of socialist pacifism into the ranks.

Considering that its commander-in-chief employed policies best calculated to break morale and to sever the troops from those in authority, the rank and file of the Italian Army stood up to the hardships of war astonishingly well. Regionally recruited units often did well, and the success of the *Brigata* Aosta, which was largely Sicilian, disproved prewar beliefs that southerners did not fight as well as northerners and that Sicilians were inferior to the *Calabresi* of the mainland. The general staff's failure to recognize the importance of keeping formations intact and its policy of detaching troops from divisions or brigades for service elsewhere did nothing to improve unit cohesion, and the unenlightened policies pursued by the high command in respect to morale until almost the last moments of the war represented the least effective way to underpin a tactical system which relied heavily on infantry attacks.

Tactical effectiveness was further diminished due to the small amount of attention paid to troop training.[124] Training schools for all arms were only introduced at British instigation at the start of 1918, and in April of that year a special mission sent by the British Chief of the Imperial General Staff reported that the Italians 'are not playing up too well as they don't take up all the vacancies allotted.'[125] The hard school of experience counted for much more than theoretical instruction. In the aftermath of Caporetto Badoglio introduced a wide range of tactical reforms, modeling assault units on those used by the Germans, echeloning defenses in depth and hinging them on a combination of strong points and counter-attacks, improving infantry–artillery coordination, and relaxing the principle of hanging onto every inch of ground.[126] Where Cadorna embodied the deficiencies of Italian military thought, Capello and Badoglio demonstrated its strengths; but they were subordinates, not commanders-in-chief.

Conclusion

The potential military effectiveness of Italy during the First World War was limited partly by physical factors which disadvantaged it: its exposed geographical position, its shortage of raw materials, its restricted manufacturing capacity. It was also threatened by culture-specific factors which posed special obstacles. Social attitudes and political culture combined to produce a manpower force which lacked any common and unifying moral focus on which to base a war effort. The inadequacies of the officer corps, partly a consequence of these same factors and partly also the product of a well-ingrained tradition, exacerbated these problems rather than ameliorating them. Nevertheless Italian troops often fought bravely and stubbornly. Had command style taken account of the specific cultural factors shaping the army, better results might have been achieved.

Partly for this reason and partly as a consequence of the unique political circumstances surrounding and shaping Italy's war, Italy displayed marked defects in both vertical and horizontal integration. Although having an individual character, the vertical deficiencies seem to have been shared in varying degrees by all the other powers. For example, where political goals dictated an offensive operational plan, battlefield conditions and state-of-the-art technology demanded a more cautious and defensive approach to combat until new attack techniques could be devised. This is to say no more than that to defend is easier than to attack. But Italian experience suggests that the attack highlights integrational dissonances particularly strongly.

Horizontal ineffectiveness was manifest at all levels of the Italian war effort. This is largely to be explained by tradition and by the historical development of a particular pattern of intra-military relationships. At the level of operational doctrine horizontal dissonance is readily observable in the cases of artillery doctrine and of co-operation between arms. This happened because the peacetime army put inadequate emphasis on higher training for war and because the corps of general officers was the legatee of an historical development which fragmented it. Different army commanders therefore issued their own instructions about doctrine and operations; sometimes they conformed to those of the commander-in-chief, but at other times they did not. Rank structures further hindered horizontal integration. During the war the highest effective military rank in use was that of lieutenant general. In the absence of indisputable hierarchical authority, generals turned readily to seniority tables to justify complaints and disagreements.

As well as being less than optimally effective for culture-specific reasons, the Italian forces displayed during the First World War a spectrum of general deficiencies which was also shared by others. They, like others, underestimated their needs in terms of heavy artillery, ammunition, and reserves; they followed a policy with regard to leave and rest periods which detracted from the natural or potential effectiveness of their troops. At least as far as the First World War is concerned, it seems reasonable to conclude that 'war-specific' or 'time-specific' factors were working independently of national circumstances – although of course their effect was incremental.

No two powers have the same aims or control the same means with which to fulfil them. But the problems posed by Italy's membership in an alliance are worth remarking. Although not as effective a partner in the alliance as it might have been, Italy was not alone in its unwillingness to sacrifice its own interests to those of the common cause. The reason is not far to seek, as the events of March 1918 and their consequences demonstrate. The threat was not great enough to overcome national *amour-propre* and to allow Italy to sink its individuality to the degree necessary to maximize its potential military effectiveness within an alliance.

In the fifty-five years since the capture of Rome had inserted the capstone in the creation of the Italian state, no power had ever seriously threatened to use military force against Italy in order to force it to make a significant shift in policy. On those grounds its military effectiveness in 1915 might be deemed to have been high. Yet the test of war is a very different matter, and here Italy was found wanting. Ultimately the effectiveness of any armed force must be measured by the degree to which it successfully supports its country's foreign policy up to and beyond the point of war. The fact that Italy's armed forces did relatively well in peacetime and less well in war is a good guide to their general effectiveness. Military ineffectiveness, in Italy's case as in others, was no less the responsibility of politicians than of generals and admirals.

Notes

1 *Documenti diplomatici italiani*, 4th series, Vol. 12, Di Sangiuliano to Bollati, 14 July 1914, no. 225. See also R. J. B. Bosworth, *Italy, the Least of the Great Powers: Italian Foreign Policy before the First World War* (Cambridge, 1980), p. 389.

2 Ufficio Storico della Marina [hereafter USM]. Coste istriane e dalmate ed isole prospicienti nei riguardi bellici, 13 October 1914. Cartella 323/7.

3 Di San Giuliano to Vittorio Emanuele III, 24 July 1914, quoted in A. Salandra, *La neutralità italiana (1914): ricordi e pensieri* (Milan, 1928), pp. 78–80.

4 Olindo Malagodi, *Conversazioni della guerra* (Milan-Naples, 1960), Vol. 1, p. 20.

5 The process may be followed in W. A. Renzi, 'Italy's Neutrality and Entrance into the Great War: A Re-examination,' *American Historical Review*, vol. 72 (1968), pp. 1414–32; C. J. Lowe, 'Britain and Italian Intervention, 1914–1915,' *Historical*

Journal, vol. 12 (1969), pp. 533–48; A. Monticone, 'Sonnino e Salandra verso la decisione dell'intervento,' in AA. VV., *Gli italiani in uniforme*, (Bari, 1972), pp. 57–87; J. Whittam, 'War Aims and Strategy: The Italian Government and High Command 1914–1919,' in B. Hunt & A. Preston, *War Aims and Strategic Policy in the Great War*, (London, 1977), pp. 85–104; Richard Bosworth, *Italy and the Approach of the First World War* (London, 1983).

6 Giorgio Rochat, *L'Italia nella prima guerra mondiale* (Milan, 1976), pp. 60–1, 78.

7 Archivio Centrale di Stato [hereafter ACS]. Carte Brusati. Spingardi to Brusati, 20 November 1911. Scatola 10, VI-4–36/319; Sidney Sonnino, *Diario 1866–1912* (Bari, 1972), pp. 504–5 (26 November 1911).

8 John Gooch, *Army, State, and Society in Italy 1870–1915* (Macmillan, forthcoming), chs. 7 and 8.

9 ACS. Carte Brusati. Spingardi to Brusati, 22 May 1913. Scatola 10, VII-3–43/492.

10 Malagodi, Vol. 1, p. 58 (9 May 1915).

11 John Gooch, 'Italy before 1915: The Quandary of the Vulnerable,' in E. R. May (ed.), *Knowing One's Enemies: Intelligence Assessment before the Two World Wars* (Princeton, N.J., 1984), pp. 207–9.

12 Luigi Cadorna, *Altre pagine sulla grande guerra* (Milan, 1925), pp. 15–23, 26.

13 Thaon di Revel to Sonnino, 14 April 1915, quoted in Sidney Sonnino, *Carteggio 1914–1916* (Bari, 1972), pp. 386–8.

14 Lucio Ceva, *Le forze armate* (Turin, 1981), pp. 118, 161.

15 Aldo Valori, *La condotta politica della guerra* (Milan, 1934), p. 245.

16 Cadorna to Boselli, 7 August 1916, quoted in Carlo De Biase, *L'Aquila d'Oro – Storia dello stato maggiore italiano (1861–1945)* (Milan, 1969), p. 24.

17 Ceva, p. 174.

18 Giorgio Candeloro, *Storia dell'Italia moderna*, VIII: *La prima guerra mondiale, il dopoguerra, l'avvento del fascismo* (Milan, 1978), pp. 219–20.

19 Giorgio Rochat and Giulio Massobrio, *Breve storia dell'esercito italiano dal 1861 al 1943* (Turin, 1978), pp. 66, 71, 163.

20 Great Britain, with a much smaller, non-conscript army and having abandoned the expensive policy of fortification, managed under Haldane on an annual budget of approximately £8 million.

21 Gooch, *Army, State and Society in Italy*, ch. 7.

22 Giorgio Candeloro, *Storia dell'Italia moderna*, Vol. 7, *La crisi di fine secolo e l'età giolittiana* (Milan, 1974), pp. 152, 223.

23 In 1921 and 1927: Candeloro, Vol. 8, p. 69; Ceva, p. 157.

24 Massimo Mazzetti, *L'industria italiana nella grande guerra* (Rome, 1979), p. 169.

25 Ministero dell Guerra – Comando del Corpo di Stato Maggiore – Ufficio Storico, *L'Esercito italiano della grande guerra (1915–1918)* (Rome, 1931) [hereafter Official History], Vol. 4, tomo 2, p. 171. As always, no two sets of figures agree. Ceva gives stocks for 1917 as 3,828 light guns, 2,933 medium guns, 157 heavy guns, and 2,402 bombards. During that year 34 million rounds of artillery ammunition were available, of which 21 million were fired. Ceva, p. 127.

26 Official History, Vol. 3, tomo 1, pp. 28, 50.

27 Official History, Vol. 3, tomo 1, pp. 98–103. Normally highly discreet, the official history goes so far as to name one company – Toschi & Castelli – which was contracted to supply rifles but which by mid-June 1916 had failed to provide a single one.

28 Mazzetti, p. 47.

29 Ibid., p. 18.

30 Imperial War Museum [hereafter IWM]. Delmé-Radcliffe to Wilson, 1 August 1918, Wilson MSS, 73/1/11/14.

31 Ferdinando Martini, *Diario 1914–1918* (Milan, 1966), pp. 442, 536 (5 June and 18 September 1915).
32 Ufficio Storico dello Stato Maggiore dell'Esercito [hereafter SME]. Commissione suprema per la difesa dello Stato: verbali delle sedute tenute in Ottobre-Novembre 1899, p. 17 (30 October 1899). *Carteggio commissioni di difesa*, busta 1.
33 USM. Progetti di imbarco per spedizioni oltremare ipotesi A, 8 July 1909; Nicastro to Pollio, 17 September 1909. Cartella 199/7.
34 USM. Vice Admiral Borea to Thaon di Revel, 16 October 1914; Cadorna to Thaon di Revel, 29 October 1914. Cartella 323/6.
35 USM. Relazione a S.E. il Ministro circa la prepararzione dei principali elementi di efficienze militare marittima Parte Seconda: Preparazione ed impiego delle forze navale – Preparazione strategica della campagna in Adriatico e sua condotta fino ai primi di Ottobre 1915, n.d. (quoting Cadorna to Thaon di Revel, 5 April 1915). Cartella 351/4.
36 USM. Di Revel to Zuccari, 29 March 1915. Cartella 444/3.
37 USM. Viale to Vice Admiral Garelli, 13 April 1915. Cartella 444/3.
38 Mariano Gabriele and Giu Friz, *La politica navale italiana dal 1885 al 1915* (Rome, 1982), pp. 258–9.
39 Rochat, *L'Italia nella prima guerra mondiale*, p. 98.
40 Brig. Gen. Sir James E. Edmonds, *Military Operations, Italy 1915–1918* (London, 1949), p. 10.
41 Giorgio Rochat, 'L'esercito italiano nell'estate 1914,' *Nuova Rivista Storica*, vol. 45 (1961), p. 332, n. 2.
42 Malagodi, Vol. 1, p. 67.
43 Angelo Gatti, *Caporetto. Dal diario di guerra inedito (maggio-dicembre 1917)* (Bologna, 1964), p. 92.
44 Piero Pieri and Giorgio Rochat, *Badoglio* (Turin, 1974), pp. 58–9.
45 Paul G. Halpern, *The Mediterranean Naval Situation, 1912–1914* (Cambridge, Mass., 1971), pp. 191–3, 208.
46 Paul G. Halpern, 'The Anglo-French-Italian Naval Convention of 1915,' *Historical Journal*, Vol. 13 (1970), pp. 106–29.
47 Cadorna to Maria Cadorna, 17 January 1916, quoted in Raffaele Cadorna, *Lettere famigliari* (Milan, 1967), p. 135.
48 Gatti, p. 40 (26 May 1917).
49 Mazzetti, p. 33.
50 Ibid., p. 43.
51 Candeloro, Vol. 8, pp. 126–7.
52 Gabriele and Friz, pp. 262–3.
53 Arthur J. Marder, *From the Dreadnought to Scapa Flow*, Vol. 5, *1918–1919: Victory and Aftermath* (Oxford, 1970), p. 20.
54 SME. Relazione del viaggio dei generali 1911, p. 119. *Carteggio Campi, Esercitazioni, Manovre*, raccoglitore 44.
55 Filippo Stefani, *La storia della dottrina e degli ordinamenti dell'esercito italiano* (Rome, 1984), Vol. 1, pp. 418, 446.
56 Cadorna to Raffaele Cadorna, 8 June 1915, quoted in *Lettere famigliari*, pp. 106–7.
57 Malagodi, Vol. 1, p. 117 (29 March 1917).
58 Pieri and Rochat, p. 178.
59 Malagodi, Vol. 1, p. 366 (3 July 1918).
60 Pieri and Rochat, pp. 252–60.
61 'Operazioni offensivi methodiche,' 17 January 1916, quoted in Official History, Vol. 3, tomo 1 bis, pp. 136–8.

62 'Memoria di base per l'impiego dell'artiglieria in fase offensiva,' 26 April 1916, quoted in Pieri and Rochat, pp. 111–13.
63 'Criteri d'impiego dell'artiglieria,' April 1916, quoted in Official History, Vol. 3 tomo 2, p. 123, n. 1.
64 Cadorna to Duke of Aosta, 16 June 1916, quoted in Pieri and Rochat, p. 107.
65 'Impiego dell'artiglieria nelle azioni offensive. Schieramento e dipendenza delle artiglierie,' 11 March 1917, quoted in Official History, Vol. 4, tomo 2 bis, pp. 95–9; Pieri and Rochat, pp. 249–50.
66 'Predisposizioni concrete per la ripresa offensiva,' 29 June 1917, quoted in Official History, Vol. 4, tomo 2 bis, pp. 350–1.
67 Pieri and Rochat, pp. 319–25, 351–2.
68 Stefani, Vol. 1, pp. 636–8, 670.
69 Gatti, p. 75 (6 June 1916).
70 Stefani, Vol. 1, p. 662.
71 Report of French naval attaché, 30 December 1913, quoted in Gabriele and Friz, p. 233.
72 Official History, Vol. 3, tomo 2, pp. 117–18.
73 Quoted in Edmonds, p. 23.
74 Pieri and Rochat, pp. 62–63.
75 'Ripresa offensiva sulla fronte dell'Isonzo,' 16 March 1916, quoted in Official History, Vol. 3, tomo 1 bis, p. 172.
76 Alberto Baldini, *Diaz, duca della Vittoria* (London, 1935), p. 165.
77 Edmonds, p. 28.
78 Gatti, p. 131 (25 May 1917).
79 IWM. Cavan to Wilson, 10 June (1918). Wilson MSS, 73/1/12/20. Italics in original.
80 'Mezzi aeronautici dell'Armata nell'azione difensiva uno,' 4 June 1917, quoted in Official History, Vol. 4, tomo 2 bis, p. 129.
81 Baldini, pp. 76–9.
82 Candeloro, Vol. 8, p. 125.
83 Gatti, pp. 16, 39 (19 and 26 May 1917).
84 General Luigi Capello, one of the ablest army commanders, levelled these criticisms at Cadorna in a memorandum dated 14 February 1917; see Pieri and Rochat, pp. 173–4.
85 Gatti, esp. pp. 66, 131; see also pp. 65, 73.
86 Edmonds, p. 144.
87 Gatti, p. 64 (3 June 1917).
88 Edmonds, p. 14; Ceva, p. 145.
89 Gatti, p. 18 (21 May 1917); Ceva, p. 130.
90 Pieri and Rochat, p. 431.
91 Giorgio Rochat, 'La preparazione dell'esercito italiano nell'inverno 1914–1915 in relazione alle informazioni disponibili sulla guerra di posizione,' *Risorgimento*, Vol 13 (1961), pp. 17–22.
92 SME. Guerra di posizione, 30 March 1915, p. 45. *Addetti Militari: Berlino*, busta 166.
93 De Biase, pp. 284–6.
94 Quoted in Stefani, Vol. 1, p. 516.
95 Baldini, pp. 25–7.
96 Quoted in Stefani, Vol. 1, pp. 458–9.
97 Ibid., p. 515.
98 Peiro Melograni, *Storia politica della Grande Guerra, 1915/1918*, (Bari, 1969), pp. 84–5.

99 Gatti, pp. 80, 133–4, 137–8 (6 and 23 June 1917).
100 Pieri and Rochat, pp. 91–3; Official History, Vol. 3, tomo 1, p. 150.
101 Edmonds, p. 116.
102 'Raccolta di norme tattiche,' 8 August 1917, quoted in Official History, Vol. 4 tomo 2 bis, pp. 500–1.
103 Gabriele and Friz, p. 248.
104 USM. Alcune considerazioni sulla grande guerra navale in Adriatico – Il contributo della Marina all'Esercito del giugno all'ottobre 1915: Argomento Vsos – Le incursioni nei porti nemici, n.d. Cartella 336/12.
105 Pieri and Rochat, pp. 443–6.
106 Gatti, pp. 229–30 (6 September 1917).
107 Ceva, pp. 145, 153.
108 Stefani, Vol. 1, pp. 681, 696–7, 703, 712.
109 Bernardino Farolfi, 'Dall'antropometria militare alla storia del corpo,' *Quaderni storici*, vol. 42 (1979), pp. 1067–8.
110 Piero del Negro, *Esercito, stato, società* (Bologna, 1979), p. 231.
111 H. Stuart Hughes, 'The Aftermath of the Risorgimento in Four Successive Interpretations,' *American Historical Review*, vol 41 (1955), p. 76.
112 Mazzetti, p. 97.
113 F. de Chaurand de Saint Eustache, *como l'esercito italiano entrò in guerra* (Milan, 1929), p. 132; 'Gli ufficiali in Italia e fuori,' *L'esercito italiano*, 3/4 August 1899. The class analysis of the officer corps given in Rochat and Massobrio, pp. 97–9, although impressionistic, is the best available.
114 Official History, Vol. 1, p. 68.
115 In the absence of any official figures it is difficult to answer this question with any pretence at accuracy. However in 1907 the Italian army consisted of 141 generals earning an average salary of L.10,000, 1,780 colonels and majors earning an average salary of L. 8,300, and 11,782 officers of captain rank or below earning an average salary of L.4,000. (Source: *L'Esercito italiano*, 7 November 1907.) Thus the total salary bill would amount to L.63,382,500, or some two-ninths of the sum spent during the financial year 1907/8 by the war ministry, L.273.900.000.
116 Public Record Office, Granet to Rodd, 21 September 1914, W.O. 106/749.
117 Luigi Capello, *Caporetto perché* (Turin, 1967), p. 209.
118 'Il reclutamento dei sottufficiali,' *L'esercito italiano*, 7 March 1900. By May 1915 Cadorna had made good the officer deficiency to the extent of 9,412 new subalterns, but as many of these had come through accelerated NCO courses this merely exacerbated the NCO problem.
119 Ceva, pp. 172–3; Malagodi, Vol. 1, pp. 184, 192, 289 (6 and 13 November 1917; 25 February 1918).
120 Ceva, p. 166.
121 Cadorna to Ninetta Cadorna, 19 August 1915, quoted in *Lettere famigliari*, p. 123.
122 Enzo Forcella and Alberto Monticone, *Plotone di esecuzione: I processi della lsas guerra mondiale* (Bari, 1968), pp. 334–43.
123 Gatti, pp. 87, 106–7 (7 and 14 June 1917).
124 Edmonds, p. 134.
125 IWM, Delmé-Radcliffe to Wilson, 7 January 1918; Price-Davies to Wilson, 30 April 1918. Wilson MSS, 73/1/11/2,8.
126 Pieri and Rochat, pp. 429–30.

[6]

The French Army in the First World War

DOUGLAS PORCH
The Citadel

Introduction

The First World War has cast a long shadow across the history of modern France. The campaign on the Western Front, the war's critical theater, soon settled down into a narrow belt of congealed horror running from Switzerland to the North Sea. The concentrated destruction, the staggering numbers of young men expended to reclaim a few acres of blood-drenched mud, the eerie, lunar landscape of the combat zone were images etched on the minds of generations of French men and women. Indeed, so frightful was the experience of millions of men, who faced each other across a narrow killing ground, and who were driven to nervous exhaustion by the constant danger, filth, wetness, noise, death of comrades, and anticipation of one's own demise that, for many years, the First World War was dismissed as an aberration, an alpine failure of human intelligence and imagination.

There can be no denying that intelligence and imagination often seemed on short ration between 1914 and 1918. But it must not be forgotten that the Western Front was not a product of cynical minds, a plot by committees of military Machiavellis eager to raise the status of their profession by multiplying war's destructiveness. Trench warfare did not come about by design. Digging was simply the natural response of massed soldiers forced to coexist with the enemy on a small patch of disputed terrain. But herein lay the crux of the problem – the generals were blamed, first, because they had failed to foresee the nature of modern war, and, secondly, because once confronted with it, they wasted the lives of a generation of Frenchmen in a *guerre d'usure* which lent to the word *victory* an empty and sinister ring. Indeed, as early as 1915, the French deputy Abel Ferry had recognized that *'la guerre d'usure se fait contre nous.'*[1]

In the desire to find a scapegoat for the 'pyrrhic' victory of 1918, *esprit militaire* has perhaps achieved an unmerited prominence both in the popular mind and in the view of many historians. Once German resistance was exhausted in 1918, the professional soldiers were excoriated for the bloody offensives, faulty tactical doctrine, inadequate armament, unimaginative leadership, and a steadily deteriorating climate of civil-military relations. One of the effects of the First World War in France was to deepen the chasm of distrust between soldiers and politicians, which was to make effective cooperation between Parliament and the high command so problematic in the interwar years.[2]

That French soldiers made many miscalculations on the strategic, tactical, and technical levels cannot be in doubt. However, to denounce them simply as incompetent or, worse, as men who placed professional ambition above the lives of their troops or the long-term interests of France leaves too many questions begging. The irrationality of the war was all of a piece. If no one was prepared to ask, 'Is the price of victory too high?' then soldiers should be required to shoulder no more than their fair share of the blame for the bloody futility of the war. French soldiers did not fight the war in a vacuum. Therefore, the performance of the French Army must be placed in the political context in which the war was fought.[3] It must also be compared to the performance of the other belligerents, especially of the German Army. The failings of the French Army were failures of degree. Casualty rates for all armies on the Western Front were unacceptably high. However, in France, where concern with the plunging birthrate had reached almost hysterical proportions by 1914, critics were especially harsh – and justifiably so – in condemning the cavalier disregard for human life sometimes exhibited by the high command.

Nor must it be forgotten that French soldiers achieved some notable successes during the First World War, most especially in the development of aviation, artillery tactics, and motorized transport – *'C'est la voiture qui a sauvée Verdun!'* In many, perhaps most, respects, French generals proved more imaginative and adaptable than their British colleagues. However, despite appearances often to the contrary, it was Germany rather than Great Britain that was France's major enemy. The fact remains that French commanders, even the best ones, lagged behind their German foe in developing the training, tactics, and staff work, not to mention a credible overall strategic view of the war, which might have saved many French lives. The institutional failings of the French Army, therefore, must also be analyzed.

The difficulties faced by the French high command must not be underestimated. On the technical level, they were called upon to manage an unwieldy, bureaucratic machine, and to force it to adapt to new and unforeseen conditions of modern war. To these were added political pressures which increased as the inability of the generals to deliver victory despite elaborate and costly offensives became more apparent. Anti-militarism had a long and venerable history in France, and one which had been only temporarily submerged by the *union sacrée* of August 1914 – the political truce among all parties which was meant to last the duration of the war. Hardly was the conflict 4 months old when the first disagreements between politicians and generals over the conduct of the war began to surface. From the very beginning, therefore, the

French war effort was to be pummelled and shaped to a great degree by politics.

Political Effectiveness

The great problem faced by French soldiers on the eve of the First World War was that they served a politically divided society. This made it difficult to establish a defense policy based on the actual tactical and strategic needs of the country. The intrusion of politics into defense questions became a constant feature of political life in the Third Republic, especially as war approached. Anti-militarism, as opposed to pacifism, had always been a salient feature of the French left. Their Jacobin patriotism, combined with the all too obvious vulnerability of France's northern frontier to German invasion, meant that almost everyone in France recognized the need for a defense policy. But they disagreed violently on how that policy should be implemented. France, of course, invented the citizen soldier. An army of short-service conscripts, even a militia, was favored by the left because it was believed (quite wrongly) that the national guard had saved the French Revolution. Furthermore, a broadly-based army of citizen soldiers which reflected the political opinions of the population would never allow itself to be used as a tool of imperialistic expansion or of domestic repression by despotic rulers.

The right, on the other hand, surveying France's turbulent history of revolutions, argued (quite wrongly) that a small, professional force offered the best guarantee of internal stability. For politicians, as well as for some intellectuals, the history of the French Army since the Revolution was seen as a constant struggle between the professional army and the 'nation in arms,' between career officers and citizen soldiers.[4] This pseudo-historical perspective, especially on the part of the left before 1914, led to a denigration of professional values and skills at the very time when the German Army was perfecting the education and training of its officers and NCOs, and increasing the power of its armaments and the efficiency of its organization. The vote against the military budget joined the pilgrimage to the Mur des Fédérés as part of the annual ritual of the left.

The conflict between the republic and its professional soldiers, which achieved its apogee with the climax of the Dreyfus affair in 1899, began to lose some of its bitterness as the war approached. The reason for this was simple – the Agadir crisis of 1911 served to convince many, including former Dreyfusards, of the growing German menace. The result of this shift in attitude was the Nationalist Revival, the renewal of patriotism which occurred before 1914. Recent historians have questioned the extent and influence of the Nationalist Revival in the country at large, as well as its practical effects within the army. However, without this renewal of interest in defense questions, the three-year service law would certainly not have been voted by Parliament in 1913.[5]

With the outbreak of war, the pendulum of power swung wildly back to the soldiers. For the first two months of war, France virtually had a military dictatorship. The general belief that the war would be a short one was based not only upon the military view that 'the first battles will be decisive,' but also on the widely shared belief that complex urban societies could not feed and supply themselves during a prolonged conflict. Consequently, the government merely reserved to itself the political conduct of the war, while soldiers were given *carte blanche* to direct operations.[6]

By 1915, the shortcomings of this division of labor between soldiers and politicians had become obvious. France had to organize its resources, both industrial and human, for a long war. The burden of this reorganization would fall upon the government. Furthermore, it soon became apparent that the conduct of operations would also raise political controversy, that war was not something which could be delegated to soldiers while the politicians waited at home, like company stock-holders, for news of profit or loss. Consequently, deputies struggled to regain political direction of the war from the commander-in-chief. They were ill placed to do this for several reasons. First, the French Parliament had never seen its primary role as one of government, but rather of arbitrating disputes between the bureaucracy and the citizen, and of resisting the power of the state.[7] Therefore, they were inadequately prepared to direct policy. Rather they concentrated on their traditional role of investigating abuses and exposing scandal.

A second factor which inhibited firm parliamentary control of the war effort was that, until the arrival of Clemenceau as Prime Minister in December 1917, no French war lord existed to enforce the smack of firm government. Ministries tended to be unstable coalitions which stood or fell largely on the success of the military chiefs. Therefore, General Joseph Joffre, the French commander-in-chief who had acquired enormous prestige as the victor of the Marne, was largely immune from effective criticism for the first two years of the war, lest the mere suggestion of doubt on the part of the ministers bring the fragile edifice of government collapsing around them. The ephemeral nature of parliamentary alliances meant that ministers had to take account of the large number of politicians who supported the generals. These deputies, led by War Minister Alexandre Millerand, were mindful of the prewar days when political interference in military affairs had lowered the efficiency of French forces. Consequently, they resisted parliamentary attempts to monitor military operations, often by supporting the brutal and insensitive restrictions placed by soldiers on visits to the front, or access to military information by deputies.[8]

Lastly, the French, in common with the other belligerents, had no experience of directing and organizing a long war. In the Second World War, governments could draw upon a vast amount of accumulated knowledge in mobilizing the war economies and in directing operations. However, in the First World War, politicians, *fonctionnaires*, and soldiers could only procede piecemeal, improvising rather than applying a master economic or strategic plan. As a consequence, political direction of the war on the French side was haphazard, often fraught with intrigue and suspicion. This must be kept in mind when assessing the political, strategic, operational, and tactical effectiveness of the French Army in the First World War.

As French politicians were frequently at pains to point out before 1914, France spent a far greater portion of its budget on national defense than did

Germany.[9] However, this fact in itself did not guarantee adequate resources for many military programs, especially armaments. That this was so was due to several factors. First, and perhaps most importantly, the bureaucratic structure of the French Army before 1914 and the lack of clearly defined paths of authority, meant that the military budget was determined in a piecemeal fashion after consultation with the various *directions* in the war ministry. Money tended to be allocated on the basis of the bargaining talents of the section chief or branch director, usually a colonel or brigadier general, rather than according to an overall scheme of army needs. The commander-in-chief, when he was appointed after 1911, the army chief of staff, and the *conseil supérieur de la guerre* were seldom consulted on important matters like armaments, even by the sympathetic politicians of the Nationalist Revival.[10]

Since the early days of the Third Republic, politicians had proved reluctant to organize a high command which could wield real power in peacetime. This sprang from a fear virtually ingrained on the republican left that a unified and homogeneous force under a single chief might be tempted to intervene in the political arena. This politically inspired arrangement was to have far-reaching consequences for the military organization, for seldom did the army speak with a single voice in deciding important questions which affected its efficiency. Rather, the chief of the general staff, the *conseil supérieur de la guerre*, the various military committees, the ministry *directions* and the war college often offered a babble of contradictory opinions. On no subject was this more true than on the question of armaments. The debate over heavy artillery in the prewar years was especially long and bitter. However, no one with sufficient expertise, authority, and force of personality existed who could settle the argument and present Parliament with an agreed shopping list.[11]

The army's budgetary difficulties were merely symptomatic of the delicate state of civil-military relations in prewar France. The four-year period immediately preceding the declaration of war was particularly tense, for at least two reasons. First, politicians of the left-leaning Radical Party, which had supplied most of the ministers since 1899, increasingly were forced to reconcile their basic anti-militarism with their growing recognition of the German menace, their fears for the safety of the republic with those for the safety of France. The second reason flowed at least in part from the first – these four years witnessed a period of great parliamentary instability at a time when military questions had taken the center stage. France seemed torn between the deep desire to avoid conflict with Germany, and the growing realization that this might be impossible. The result was a series of unsatisfactory and politically motivated compromises which did little to improve military efficiency. On the right, the affirmation of a desire to stand up to the kaiser became more important than a thorough and effective overhauling of the military machine. On the left, the extreme reluctance to vote money for military needs had become a conditioned reflex. And then there was the almost legendary parsimony of the parliamentary finance committee, which cut military requests to the bone. Military reform became a political issue, with questions of substance sacrificed to the need to score points on the opposition. An example is the three-year service law of 1913. In many respects, this was a very useful piece of legislation. But this bill came about, not at the request of the high command, but was initiated by center-right politicians eager to demonstrate to the kaiser and to the French left their support for the army. This law had at least one bad side effect – the debates had so embittered feelings both inside and outside of Parliament, that deputies, even on the right, felt that, despite the well-publicized German superiority in matériel, the moment was not propitious to ask for yet more credits for heavy artillery.[12]

Parliamentary instability also hindered the establishment of sound armaments policies. On several occasions prior to 1914, financial programs painstakingly hammered out between the war ministry and the government disappeared with the fall of the cabinet. Drawing up a military budget in pre-1914 France was the work of Sisyphus. The continual difficulties and disappointments of establishing a budget served to diffuse any sense of urgency in the military bureaucracy: 'The divergencies of opinion among the experts were only a pretext for those who did not know or did not want to take any decision whose utility they did not believe in, and also for those who preferred to put off the expenses which they believed inconvenient,' wrote General Banquet, 'director' of the artillery during the war.[13]

The situation changed dramatically with the outbreak of the war. The awesome power of German artillery combined with the shortage of French shells forced War Minister Millerand to call a historic meeting on September 20, 1914, to assess army needs. However, neither the high command nor Parliament was to play a major role in the massive expansion of the French armaments industry after 1914. This task fell to middle-level functionaries and staff officers in the ministries of commerce and war. Their efforts were coordinated by socialist deputy Albert Thomas, first as under secretary of war for armaments in May 1915, and finally as the autonomous minister of armaments from December 1916 to September 1917. The organization of the French war effort by Thomas was a remarkable achievement. By mobilizing the resources of private industry, the French were able not only to supply their own army but also to furnish the American Expeditionary Force with artillery, trucks, and aircraft. According to American historian Robert Paxton, the French produced more weaponry and ammunition than did Great Britain, which had a far larger industrial base and more raw materials.[14] Production of 75-mm shells was increased from 10,000 to 300,000 per day by May 1917; machine gun production was multiplied 170-fold and rifle production 290-fold in the same period. By the end of the war, France was producing 30 tanks a day, as well as trucks, cars, and airplanes, despite labor shortages and the fact that almost half of its coal- and iron-producing facilities were occupied by the enemy.[15] After 1914, the army had no need to fight to obtain equipment.

However, economic mobilization did not proceed without difficulties. France's economic effort was all the more surprising given the fact that its prewar economy was generally regarded as backward or retarded. This view must be clarified. Certainly in overall production, French industry seemed to be in relative decline before the war. In 1880, French industry produced 9 per cent of the world's industrial goods, but by 1914, its share had dropped to a mere 6 per cent. In terms of brute production figures, Germany outstripped France, and by a wide margin, before the war. France produced 3.3 million tons of steel annually to 13 million in Germany; the French chemical industry produced neither the ammonia nor the nitric acid necessary for explosives, while the German chemical industry dominated Europe; and no French electrical firm could match the Allgemeine Elektrische Gessellschaft in stature or technical capacity. Of course, France had an enormous pool of investment capital (it was the second greatest financial power in the world on the eve of war). But even this bore testimony to the stagnation of the French demographic growth and the 'mediocrity' of French industry.[16]

Nevertheless, this dour prognosis masked some surprising economic strengths. The first thing which must be realized is that the French market, then as now, was largely a quality market rather than one geared to mass-produced goods. This was to lead to problems of rationalization in wartime. But the apparent lack of 'dynamism' in the industrial sector obscured the fact that several industries had achieved a high level of technical proficiency. The quality of French armaments, especially of light and medium artillery, placed that industry among the world's leading exporters after 1897. The French automobile industry was dispersed, largely in the hands of small businessmen and tinkerers, which meant that France only produced 45,000 cars in 1913. But in terms of innovative design, the French products were considered superior, so that firms like Bréguet, Renault, and Peugeot had a strong tradition of technical excellence to draw upon when they turned to mass production. The same situation prevailed in the air industry, and the Nieuports and Spads were considered at least the equal of the redoutable Fokkers and Albatrosses during the war. However, inefficient production techniques, especially of motors, and the demands of allies meant that the French seldom had these aircraft in sufficient numbers until late in the war, when the British ceased to rely on French production and developed an aircraft industry of their own. The level of technical competence in the French iron and steel industries was considered very high, while the French aluminum industry, which was to prove its importance in the war, was among the strongest in Europe.[17]

Therefore, the skills and the industrial base which made the wartime expansion possible existed in prewar France. However, before the war, soldiers preferred to deal with state arsenals supervised by graduates of the Ecole Polytechnique while a small number of private manufacturers, like Schneider, supplemented state production. This caused problems. The arsenals had been run down after construction of the 75-mm cannon at the turn of the century, so that many of the best technical officers were lured away to more lucrative jobs in industry.[18] The arsenals were also desperately short of skilled manpower in the years immediately preceding the war.[19] This, the general staff pointed out, would complicate the production of heavy artillery; nor did private industry appear eager to fill the gap. Creusot did not have the productive capacity to fill artillery orders rapidly, nor did it seem willing to expand its armaments section before 1914. In 1911, War Minister Adolphe Messimy attempted to speed up the selection of heavy and medium-range artillery pieces by throwing competition open to private industry. But this did nothing to settle the artillery debate in France.[20]

That French war stocks would be insufficient was readily apparent after the first battles. To the original shortage of arms, munitions, and coal were added others, especially petroleum. French problems were further multiplied by the fact that many of its most productive industrial areas had been overrun, and because 63 per cent of the male labor force had been conscripted. The French response to these problems was very much *ad hoc*. Not knowing that resources were actually available to it, the government was forced to rely for help on the employers' organizations. Robert Pinot, General Secretary of the Comité des forges (the French employers' union), virtually became the unofficial minister of munitions, for only he knew the capacity of each producer. For these reasons, the French war effort on the industrial front soon became a jungle of boards, committees, and commissions (291 of them by the end of the war), often with vague or duplicative functions. Although some order was brought to the process by 1917, this proved an inefficient and expensive way of making war. Yet it did not hinder production, for French producers proved that they possessed the capital, technical knowledge, and skill to expand rapidly once they realized that there were profits to be made.[21]

All of these requirements required enormous industrial expansion and the production in France of many things which before had been imported. The chemical and aluminum industries burgeoned, while the production of hydroelectric power doubled. But one should not exaggerate the scope of the wartime industrial revolution. Many areas, like the aircraft industry, found it difficult to rationalize production procedures. Moreover, while some industries grew, it was at the expense of those less important to the wartime economy, like textiles, construction, and agriculture; nor were the long-term results of the expansion of industry all beneficial. Rather than increase taxes, France relied on loans and inflation to pay for wartime production, with the result that, by the end of the war, France's external debt had run to 19 billion francs.[22]

Like armaments, manpower, or the lack of it, was a constant concern for the French Army. The growing disparity between the French and German birthrates by the end of the century meant that French anxiety over its stagnating population was profound by 1914. Universal male conscription had been introduced following the Franco-Prussian War of 1870–71. However, soldiers and politicians disagreed over service time. The staff solution to the shortfall in soldiers was to keep them longer under arms. The left, with its historical commitment to a militia, believed that young men should be retained just long enough to acquire the basics of the military art. In fact, the length of service became a political issue over which left and right battled throughout the Third Republic. In 1905, service was reduced from three to two years. However, it was again raised to three years in 1913 after acrimonious debate, to match the 1912 expansion of the German Army.

Conscripts did not look forward to their time in uniform with great enthusiasm. It would have been surprising if they had. However, apart from an insignificant number of pacifists, both the left and the right accepted the need for conscription, both as necessary for French defense and as a civic experience which could give young provincials a stronger sense of national community. This is not to say that the army had complete control over the allocation of manpower resources. It employed far too many men in administrative and other support posts. Pressures, both official and unofficial, to have a conscript serve close to home or in soft jobs were difficult to resist, especially in the southwest, where the ruling Radical Party was strong. According to official estimates, France conscripted a higher percentage of young men than did Germany in peacetime. Too often, however, these men were not utilized to best advantage; nor could France match the German Army in sheer numbers of men, which meant critical shortages in areas like the artillery.[23]

The alacrity and enthusiasm with which Frenchmen answered the call to arms in 1914 came as a great relief to pessimists, who had feared that the ravages of pacificism and the anti-war pressures of the trade unions might produce a general strike which would sabotage mobilization. Only 1.5 per cent of reservists failed to report for duty in 1914. Of all the belligerent countries in the First World War, only Serbia surpassed France in the percentage of its male population put into uniform. As manpower continued to be a critical problem throughout the war, more the pity that the French high command squandered so many lives in futile offensives. The main tug of war over manpower during the war occurred between the army and industry. The wholesale call-up of 1914 caught up in the military net many skilled workers vital to the war industries. When the shell shortage became critical in early September 1914, a number of *afféctes spéciaux* were returned to their workbenches. Thomas increased the numbers of men snatched from the front lines for war production. After the critical losses at Verdun in 1916, Pétain pushed to recover 800,000 men occupied behind the lines. In this he was supported by Parliament, which reflected growing discontent about the numbers of *embusqués* lounging behind the lines in jobs where the life expectancy was somewhat longer than in the trenches. In April 1918, Clemenceau returned 200,000 of these men to the front.[24] Their places in the war industries were occupied in part by women, and by men drawn from the colonies.

One of the surprising things about the French war effort, especially given French concern over stagnating population growth, was how long it took France to begin to tap its enormous potential reserves of manpower in Africa and Indochina. In 1910, in a book which he called *La force noire*, Colonel (later General) Charles Mangin argued that the colonies offered the obvious solution to France's manpower shortages. His views were echoed by Adolphe Messimy, Radical Party defense spokesman and twice war minister before 1914. Regiments of native *tirailleurs* had been organized in Algeria and Senegal, and later in Indochina and Madagascar. Under the leadership of officers from the *armée d'Afrique* and the French marines, these troops had provided the bulk of the forces used for the conquest and maintenance of France's colonial empire. By 1914, there were 30,000 *tirailleurs sénégalais* and 35,000 Algerians under arms.[25]

Despite the obvious advantages offered to France by the expansion of the colonial army, resistance came from several sources. The left, which in general was unsympathetic to imperialism, denounced native troops as mercenaries and feared that they might be employed by the government to break strikes. They also argued that workers imported from the colonies would depress industrial wages. Metropolitan soldiers were also skeptical of the value of native troops in a European war. While many were willing to concede that North Africans made adequate trench fighters, their opinion of black soldiers was less enthusiastic. 'Senegalese' (a term applied to all West African troops) had first been used at Gallipoli in 1915, and from 1916 were introduced in substantial numbers on the Western Front. Their performance was, at best, uneven. While many officers complimented their courage, they commented unfavourably on their training, fire discipline, and leadership. However, this was not altogether their fault. Many had been conscripted against their will or even by fraudulent methods, and given only the most summary instructions before being tossed into battle. They also suffered horribly from the cold. During the Nivelle offensive of 1917, their casualty rates were catastrophic – two to three times that of white units – and not surprisingly, some of the black units broke and ran. After this, most of the black troops were withdrawn from the front lines and the high command dropped any idea of further large-scale use.

Opposition to the use of colonial troops was not confined to Europe. Settlers, especially in Algeria, and colonial administrators pointed out that demobilized native troops would demand jobs or political rights in return for having defended France. Also, they feared that the political upheaval which the implementation of conscription caused in parts of Algeria and West Africa in 1916 would spread to the entire empire.[26]

In the end, it was Georges Clemenceau, ironically the man who for years had opposed colonial expansion as a waste of resources, who ordered the high command to step up conscription in the colonies. Despite the fears of administrators, the call-up of 1918 went smoothly, producing another 50,000 Algerians and 72,000 West Africans for the army without a shiver of rebellion. In all, the empire produced 600,000 soldiers for the war effort and sent 184,000 workers to French industry.[27] Colonial soldiers like Mangin complained that these numbers could have been trebled, but even they allowed the stereotypes developed over the decades to determine how these soldiers would be employed: Indochinese troops, thought intelligent, were assigned almost exclusively to armaments and aviation factories; the Hovas of Madagascar were sent to the ambulance corps, but also to the artillery; North African and Senegalese infantry were thrown into almost all of the major offensives, but even Mangin divided his black troops into 'warrior races' – those from the savannah – and the rest, who were employed as workers or replacements. North Africans were sent to the front in regiments, but the high command preferred to intersperse battalions of blacks and whites because, until the final offensives of 1918, they continued to suspect the solidity of the Senegalese.[28]

Furthermore, the French Army could not match that of Germany in the numbers and quality of its cadres. The cloud of official disfavor which had drifted over the army with the Dreyfus affair was reflected, at least in part, in a decreasing number of applicants for Saint-Cyr and in the resignations of many career officers, especially ex-polytechnicians in the artillery and engineers. The absence of good men was soon felt in the *Ecole supérieure de la guerre*, which supplied men for the general staff. This helped to undermine the quality of the officer corps in the early years of the twentieth century, at the very time when France was to face its most serious challenge.[29]

The quality of French NCOs had always been uneven. Most French NCOs were recruited among peasants who lacked the education or skills to stake out a career in civilian life. The best of these men were commissioned into the officer corps – fully one-half of the officers in the pre-1914 French Army were ex-NCOs – or found their way into more comfortable administrative positions, so that there was a constant hemorrhage of the best men out of the NCO class. What remained was too often men who lacked a true military vocation, but who sought to escape the dull, back-breaking tedium of rural life by securing a minor civil service post which became their due after fifteen years' service. This is one reason why short service was such a divisive issue in France. While two years was certainly enough time to train a soldier, the two-year service law of 1905 also lowered the calibre of NCOs by removing from the army conscripts who, in their third year of service, had performed valuable duty as sergeants. The absence of quality cadres lowered the tactical efficiency of the French Army during the war, and lessened the adaptability of the French to the unexpected conditions of trench warfare.[30]

Strategic Effectiveness

Despite the relative weakness of the French Army *vis-à-vis* its German opponent, or rather because of it, the French adopted an offensive strategy in August 1914. This decision almost cost them the war, before the situation could be redressed in the nick of time on the Marne in September. In the first place, a defensive strategy would have been a more prudent option for an army which was neither as strong numerically, as tactically efficient, nor as well endowed with heavy guns as was the German Army. This was certainly the option recommended by Clausewitz, of whom Foch and others claimed to be disciples. Secondly, the decision to strike at Germany posed the problem of Belgian neutrality. While on a military level, Belgium offered the best strategic path for an offensive, its premature invasion by France would almost certainly have forfeited the prospect of British assistance. Therefore, Joffre opted to strike into Alsace and Lorraine. Not only did his troops run up against prepared German defenses, but the northeastern axis of the French advance meant that Joffre was ill placed to parry the main German thrust through Belgium. If a French offensive through Belgium offered poor prospects for success, at least it would have placed France in a better position to counter the Schlieffen Plan. As Professor S. R. Williamson writes, 'If Joffre bears the final responsibility for succumbing to the madness of the offensive *à outrance*, the elusive prospect of British help, or, more precisely, the ambiguous entente, shares the responsibility for creating the framework in which Plan XVII was elaborated.'[31]

Lastly, the final French war plan, known as Plan XVII, was based upon a misreading of German intentions. While Joffre had suspected the German offensive through Belgium, he had foreseen neither its magnitude nor its direction. Joffre's attack into Lorraine had a superficial military logic in that it was meant to unhinge the German right wing. But he chose his country badly, and overlooked the fact that his army simply did not have the muscle to make the breakthrough. Only then would his strategy have achieved the political end of making Germany, rather than France, into the main battleground of the First World War. As it was, Plan XVII offered only the negative political advantage of not alienating the British.

Once the war settled into a trench deadlock, 'strategic goals,' at least on the Western Front, became academic. It is often said that the Allies selected strategic goals for their offensives but did not have tactical skills to achieve those goals. In contrast, the Germans were by far the most tactically sophisticated army in the Great War, but failed too often because they did not set strategic goals: the Schlieffen Plan was 'conceived in a strategic vacuum,' while, in 1918, Ludendorff simply chose to 're-enforce success' rather than guide his offensives toward strategic targets. There may be an element of truth in this, especially for the opening and closing months of the war when the battle lines were relatively fluid. But it is difficult to see how in between the seizing of certain 'strategic targets' like Ypres or Verdun, or even of Amiens in August 1918, it would have done more than shift the front a few miles in either direction. For most of its four years, the First World War was a struggle for tactical advantage. The strategic goals were only gradually formulated as the war progressed in the form of war aims. For France, the primary war aim was the avoidance of defeat, followed by the pursuit of victory over Germany.[32] Increasingly it appeared that these would be achieved not by a brilliant strategic thrust, but only when one side or the other collapsed from exhaustion.

Possibly the only opportunity to achieve a strategic coup occurred in the east. Whether or not the Dardanelles operation might have succeeded with better planning is a subject worthy of endless debate. In the final analysis, however, the operation was a fiasco and subsequent attempts to attack through the Balkans were pressed more for reasons connected with domestic French politics rather than because of any strategic advantages which might have been achieved there.[33]

When, following the failure of the Nivelle offensive of 1917, Pétain was named to command the French Army, he set himself three strategic priorities: first, to preserve the French Army by limiting wasteful offensives; secondly, to maintain the pre-eminent position of the French Army in the alliance despite declining French strength; and, lastly, to shift the axis of the war toward Alsace–Lorraine which, he feared, might be signed away at the peace table if the French made no serious attempt to recover it. These were sensible strategic goals. Yet even in the pessimistic days following the 1917 mutinies which had exposed the fragile morale of the French Army, they earned for Pétain the reputation as an overly cautious, even timorous, commander and placed considerable strains on his relationship with the mercurial and aggressive Foch.[34] Nevertheless, Pétain was one of the few

French generals capable of taking the long strategic view, who realized that there was no facile formula for victory, and who was not obsessed with throwing the quick knock-out punch. Without him, France would have seen its powerful position in the alliance eroded to the advantage of the British, and it might even have lost the war.

Germany capitulated only hours before Pétain was able to implement his plan for a strategic sweep through Alsace and into the German heartland. Whether or not this would have produced the resounding success predicted by Pétain cannot, of course, be known with any degree of certainty. However, given the progressive disintegration of the German forces and the fact that Alsace was held by second-echelon and territorial units, the auguries were good.[35] In one sense, the plan proved unnecessary as France achieved the political goal of recovering Alsace–Lorraine without the need to shed blood there. However, with the luxury of hindsight, a successful strategic breakthrough into the Ruhr would have scotched once and for all the myth of the 'stab in the back' so successfully exploited by Hitler in the interwar years.

Even before the war began, French soldiers appeared unable to evolve a balanced view of France's strategic interests. Joffre's decision to carry out an offensive in Lorraine in August 1914, had a certain – albeit tenuous – military logic. As the consequences of its failure were nearly catastrophic for France, however, it may be said that Joffre was like a gambler prepared to bet the family fortune on a single throw of the dice. Had he bothered to calculate the odds against success, had he possessed the most elemental notions of the superiority of defensive fire power over the attack, he most certainly would have selected a more prudent maneuver. Why he did not is an interesting and complex question, but one which is tied up with notions of relative French weakness *vis-à-vis* Germany, and with the political tensions of the post-Dreyfus years, tensions which often focused on the army. The stagnating French birthrate gave the German Army a numerical superiority which was backed by an advantage in weaponry. In August 1914, Germany counted 4,500 machine guns to 2,500 in France, 6,000 77-mm cannons to 3,800 French 75s, and an almost total monopoly in heavy artillery. Such an obvious disadvantage in manpower and matériel sent France in search of allies to offset its deficiencies. In the long term, of course, France was to be successful. But at the time, there was nothing which guaranteed effective help from either Russia or Great Britain which might have helped ease the sense of insecurity in France. French strategists obviously hoped for Russian assistance, but they could not count on it. And even if it came, Russian mobilization was so slow that France would have to bear the full weight of the German Army in the initial stages of the conflict. The British Army, though small, was highly regarded by the French; but Paris calculated that the British government was distracted by the Irish question and reluctant to mortgage its policies to French action. Therefore, French planners did not include British forces in their line of battle.[36]

Political confusion was added to the matériel disarray of the army. The conviction in 1894 of Captain Alfred Dreyfus on charges of espionage, on the basis of flimsy and even perjured evidence, inaugurated a campaign for revision which eventually overturned the political balance of power in the

Third Republic. The formation of the Waldeck-Rousseau government of 1899 with the slogan 'no enemies to our left,' meant that the army, like the church, was singled out for special retribution by the politicians in power. Army morale plummeted as many of the best men resigned to seek careers elsewhere. Applications for Saint-Cyr declined by about two-thirds. Confusion spread into the high command, which lost confidence in itself and seemed unable to provide the army with a coherent doctrine based on the realities of French strength.[37]

The spectacle of a politically divided France and a demoralized army was especially agonizing to colonial soldiers. Under the leadership of men like Gallieni and Lyautey, colonial officers had come to see imperialism as a way to reforge French confidence, to heal the political divisions which separated Frenchmen, and to infuse a dose of 'moral force' and 'offensive spirit' into an army which had become bureaucratic and lethargic.[38]

In the final analysis, 'moral force' and 'offensive spirit' seemed an excellent cure for all of the ills which afflicted the army – deficiencies in armaments, political divisions, and lack of a doctrine. An offensive attitude was something upon which all Frenchmen could agree. Professional soldiers could point to the military tradition of the *arme blanche* and the *furia francese* upon which France's past glories had been won. In the divisive atmosphere of the Dreyfus years, 'moral force' and 'offensive spirit' offered a rallying point for an army at odds with important groups in French society, and one at odds with itself. For the right, it was a source summoned up from the depths of *vielle France*, part of the Gallic genius which stood in contrast to the slow-witted Hun. For the left, the offensive was bound up with the patriotic *élan* of the French Revolution, when national guardsmen, fortified with revolutionary zeal, had charged boldly to scatter the professional armies of despotic Europe. For the colonial army, it was a unique contribution to the spiritual reconstruction of France born of confidence and a sense of mission spawned by imperial service. 'Moral force' and 'offensive spirit' were ideas which divided Frenchmen the least, uniting left and right, Dreyfusard and anti-Dreyfusard, colonial and metropolitan. In the conditions of prewar France, a defensive strategy would simply have been too divisive, as was proved in 1911 when General Michel attempted to convince the *conseil supérieur de guerre* to adopt one.[39]

From 1915, the great dilemma for Joffre was that he could not remain inactive. The demands of his Russian allies and pressures from the government and public opinion eager that something must be done to cast the Germans out of France cancelled that option. On the other hand, he simply did not have the power to break through the German position. But this, in itself, only added to Joffre's problems. The defensive, strong in 1914, was growing stronger with the addition of trenches, machine guns, heavy artillery with registered targets, and defense in depth which precluded counter-battery fire and made it impossible for French artillery to spread destruction over the entire German position. This caused French soldiers to rush events in 1915, pressing the offensive in the realization that, by waiting, they would make the task of the breakthrough more difficult.[40] Joffre's solution was the least practical: he continued a series of offensives which wasted his strength, thereby bringing the strategic goals of the Germans, rather than the French, one step closer.

The French suffered also from a bad case of strategic tunnel vision; that is, they failed to see their strategic situation in global terms. It did not occur to Joffre, for instance, to await the day when Great Britain would be fully mobilized before undertaking his lonely, and extremely costly, attacks. However, lack of imagination and a Euro-centric vision of the war was not confined to Joffre, or even to the army. The attitude of French politicians and soldiers to the American declaration of war on Germany may perhaps best be described as ambivalent. Initially, the French did not envisage, or even encourage, the organization of the American Expeditionary Forces (AEF). They believed the Americans irretrievably backward in military matters. France distrusted the diplomatic ambitions of Wilson and sought to give the impression of a strong nation. What it desired from America was the continuation and extension of material aid, in particular loans. Only gradually did America's potential contribution to the military effort percolate through official circles, and then principally because it was believed that French power and prestige would be increased by tying the US Army closely to that of France.[41]

Traditionally, the navy had never loomed large in French strategic thinking. This is hardly surprising given France's fixation with its vulnerable northwestern frontier with Germany. While French sailors had been responsible for some of the more enterprising technical innovations of the nineteenth century, their fleet lagged far behind that of Great Britain in size and quality. The major role of the navy had been in supporting colonial conquests in Africa and Indochina, conquests which many, even on the right, believed to be nothing more than adventures, a waste of resources which could have been spent more profitably on the army. It was a singular misfortune for the French Navy that the Dreyfus affair coincided with the massive German naval build-up. Radical naval minister Camille Pelletan appeared to be more concerned to *épater la bourgeoisie navale* with his Bohemian life style than to remedy glaring deficiencies in his service – disorder in the dockyards, the leisurely pace of shipbuilding, small and ill-designed warships which maneuvered badly, used too much coal, and were armed with a multiplicity of guns which often shot badly due to poor-quality powder. By 1905, the French Navy had declined to a 'poor third' among European navies, and England's First Sea Lord, Admiral Fisher, seemed reluctant to bind Britain to an ally of such dubious value.[42]

However, as the war approached, the two powers were pushed inexorably closer. The Agadir crisis of 1911 served to convince many in Britain and in France that war with Germany was near. At the same time, the rise of Austrian and Italian naval power in the Mediterranean posed a potential threat to Britain's communications with its empire. Fisher's response was to call for an expansion of the British Navy to make it strong in all seas. But his retirement in 1912 removed a major obstacle to closer Franco-British cooperation, as did the resurgence of the French Navy after 1909 under the guiding hand of Vice Admiral Boué de Lapeyière. Franco-British naval talks resumed in the spring of 1912, and in September, the Brest fleet was moved to Toulon.

Although both Churchill and Asquith were keen that the naval agreements not tie Britain's hands, France felt that it had elicited a moral commitment from Britain to prevent a German attack on the French north coast.[43]

In strategic terms, the Anglo-French naval convention of 6 August, 1914, made perfect sense. The Royal Navy assumed responsibility for the North Sea and Dover Straits, while the French patrolled the western Channel and most of the Mediterranean. The French Navy's primary task at the beginning of the war was to assure the link with Algeria, bringing troops of the XIX corps to Europe. However, the entry of Turkey and Italy into the war, and the effective U-boat campaign in the Mediterranean, complicated matters to the point that a sound strategic decision was too often poorly applied in practice. The division of the Mediterranean into zones of national responsibility was an open invitation to misunderstanding and confusion. Ships were not distributed according to any rational plan because national sensibilities made everyone reluctant to give over command of craft to Allied admirals. Each navy operated independently, so that by the end of 1915, the Allies held forty battleships in the Mediterranean to oppose twelve of the enemy.[44] The French and Italian battlefleets obligingly concentrated in the Adriatic to bottle up the diminutive Austrian Navy, allowing U-boats to ravage shipping in the rest of the Mediterranean. The main burden of anti-submarine warfare fell upon the British, but as the Admiralty regarded the Mediterranean as a backwater, they never had sufficient destroyers and light craft to sink more than a handful of German boats. The fear in 1917 that the Germans might take over the Russian Black Sea fleet and break out into the Mediterranean forced the convening of an Allied Naval Council in November. However, it proved to be little more than a talk shop.[45]

Moreover, the naval dimension of the war was never fully appreciated by the French. Their attitude to the British naval blockade of Germany is perhaps best encapsulated by Clemenceau who, when told that the British fleet would destroy the German Navy if it ventured into the North Sea, replied to the effect that 'that would make a nice hole in the water' but could hardly win the war.[46] The Mediterranean theater impinged little on the collective Allied conscience. Therefore, the navy, whether French or British, received little consideration in French strategic planning. This is not entirely surprising, for to have done so, the generals must have possessed a vision of war as a struggle of peoples and of rival economies, rather than merely as a military duel in which victory was measured in terms of casualties inflicted, guns captured, and ground gained. Yet if the French can be taken to task for this strategic oversight, Haig can be blamed even more, for he of all generals should have been able to integrate the navy into his calculations.

In the formation of militarily logical goals, the 1914–18 war constitutes a category apart. In a real sense, rationality became the first battlefield casualty in 1914. Twice, in 1905 and 1911, France had backed down in the face of German threats over Morocco, because its generals had stated categorically that it did not possess the '70 per cent chance of victory' which Napoleon had considered the prudent margin before accepting battle. By 1914, however, the time for rational decision making had passed. Germany wanted war, it was felt, and to refuse to grant the kaiser's wish for a third time was impossible.

Therefore, France entered the conflict resigned but determined. The idea of a compromise peace, of fighting for specific strategic or political goals short of total victory, was not seriously considered by any of the belligerent powers. As the war continued, month by bloody month, the atmosphere of unreality shaded off into the realm of the surreal. Annexationist demands, especially in Germany, increased in inverse proportion to the power to achieve them. For the French, this meant that, from the beginning, the war was fought in a peculiar psychological frame of mind. Faced with an enemy determined to fight, who occupied almost one-quarter of the national territory, and whose conditions for peace would have reduced France to the level of a third-rate power, rational military goals (a compromise peace with or without honor) were scratched from the vocabulary of soldiers and civilians existing in a complicity of madness, believing firmly that a war not won was a war lost.

These factors made it difficult for politicians and soldiers to get a firm grasp on the war, to stand back and assess the situation of France in the hard light of reality. Too often military thinking hardly rose above the level of the rather forced optimism of popular clichés like, *'On les aura.'* The Western Front became a wishing well into which men were dropped like so many coins destined to transform desires into reality.

But apart from its psychological handicaps, France was badly equipped to organize its war effort rationally. Like politicians of other countries, those of France had no experience of directing a long war, no fund of knowledge upon which they could draw when dealing with military questions. The tendency at the beginning of the war to separate political and military functions into water-tight categories became difficult to modify because ministries were weak and tended to defer to soldiers on military questions. For their part, soldiers in the early years of the war continued to assure politicians that the next offensive would bring a breakthrough into open warfare. Most believed that victory was a question of more cannon, better coordination of attacks, or, quite simply, *volonté*. However, to a great extent, this was not altogether the fault of the soldiers, as to suggest caution would have run counter to the official, if rather forced, mood of optimism.[47]

Joffre was by far the most influential of the French commanders. His political power grew out of the adulation bestowed by the public on the 'Victor of the Marne,' the fragile nature of parliamentary coalitions, and the desire, especially on the right, to insulate the high command from parliamentary interference. In this sense, Joffre's strength lay less in his ability to sway or influence the political leadership (he was a man of few words) than in the fact that he had transformed the *Grand Quartier Général* (GQG) into a fortress virtually impregnable to parliamentary assault. However, Joffre's failure to march to victory over the bodies of his troops, capped by an astonishing complaisancy in the face of the obvious German threat to Verdun in 1916,[48] gradually sapped his credibility and brought about his downfall.

The disappearance of Joffre did not facilitate the ability of French service chiefs to influence policy. On the contrary, the removal of the monolithic commander-in-chief allowed dissenting opinions in the forces to be heard at last. Republican skepticism and even, in some quarters, distrust of soldiers had returned with a vengeance. In 1917 French strategic choices swung wildly between the quick victory formula of Nivelle's *bataille de rupture* and Pétain's patient *attendre les chars et les américans.* Only when the Nivelle offensive had been shattered and the army was badly shaken by mutinies could Pétain's more realistic assessment gain the upper hand in policy making. Both he and Prime Minister Georges Clemenceau realized that France simply did not have the strength to break the German lines, at least not in 1917, and that continued attempts to do so before France was able to restore the morale of its army and build up and modernize its matériel would ultimately lead to defeat. However, Pétain imposed his views only with difficulty. A strong contingent of soldiers led by Foch complained that Pétain lacked fire, and managed to gain the ear of many people who found Pétain's methods dilatory and even defeatist. Even Clemenceau wavered in his support of Pétain in 1918. Foch's opposition certainly delayed Pétain's projected offensive into Alsace and Lorraine, an offensive which, if successful, might have strengthened France's position at the peace talks.[49]

In sum, it may be said that, Pétain apart, the high command did little to influence the political leadership toward militarily logical national goals. This stemmed in part from a *déformation professionelle*, the misplaced need to demonstrate aggressiveness and the belief that a patient and cautious strategy was somehow unsoldierly, and possibly even un-French. The poor civil-military relations of the prewar years also played a part, in so far as the soldiers, and especially Joffre, were almost obsessive in their desire to exclude deputies from the front, to withhold information, and so to prevent them from acquiring an informed view of the strategic situation.[50] But civilians must also shoulder some of the blame, for the repeated offensives offered the only strategic option which reflected the preconceptions of the politicians and the mood of the country.

Given its situation of inferiority, France should have sought from the beginning of the war to husband its resources, acquire allies, and adopt a defensive posture while building up its strength. It did not choose to do this, but instead looked to impose its will on the adversary, dislocate German attacks, and sap German power. The irony was that it was Germany which managed to impose its strategic will on France, albeit in a way unforeseen by German generals. In 1914, France's very weakness caused its military leaders to act with great boldness; nor did the absence of sufficient numbers of troops, adequately trained cadres, and artillery support dissuade French generals from persisting in their attacks. Verdun apart, Germany opted for a defensive strategy on the Western Front between the Marne and the final offensives of spring 1918, preferring to concentrate its efforts against Russia in the east. By their very passivity in the west, the Germans virtually forced the French to attack. As the war progressed, the French labored intensely to build up their offensive capabilities, especially in artillery and aircraft, and to perfect their supply system by turning increasingly to motorized transport. However, progress was slow, and the infantryman armed with little more than personal courage bore the brunt of the French offensives. German defensive tactics always managed to thwart French attacks despite sustained efforts made by French generals to restructure their forces for the offensive. Pétain was the first, indeed the only, commander to realize that the French Army was wasting away at a rate which would soon make France's major strategic goal – the avoidance of defeat – impossible to achieve. Therefore, from 1917, he sought to make the war into one of matériel rather than of men, and to await the substantial reinforcements promised by America's entry into the war.

The success of France's industrial mobilization has already been discussed. Despite a small industrial base, a largely artisan economic structure, and enemy occupation of at least half of the most industrially productive areas of France, the French war economy managed to supply not only its military needs, but also many of those of the AEF. Unlike Germany, France was free to purchase abroad what it could not manufacture at home. This was all the more reason for French soldiers to build up their strength before launching offensives like those of 1915, with inadequate support. French strategic choices appear to have been almost back to front. In the early years of the conflict, French generals commanded the manpower, but lacked the matériel to make the breakthrough. When, by 1917, the perspective of an overwhelming superiority in matériel was at last in sight, they discovered that their manpower had been squandered in ultimately useless offensives. Therefore, the Army was shrivelled and anaemic at the very moment when allied superiority in matériel began to shift decisively in their favor. Deprived of adequate numbers of fresh and well-trained troops, it became difficult in 1918 to transform fire power into offensive power.

To be fair to the generals, it must be remembered that almost no one foresaw the industrial nature of warfare in 1914. And even if they had, the conclusions would hardly have provided cause for comfort in the rue Saint-Dominique, the French war ministry. That the economic mobilization of France in the First World War was a truly remarkable achievement has come as a great surprise to historians. It must have astonished French soldiers. The war witnessed a revolutionary experiment in the mobilization of both human and industrial resources. Soldiers raised in the narrow operational traditions of Jomini or, like Joffre, in the little wars of Africa, may perhaps be pardoned for being overpowered by the sheer complexity of modern warfare. Secondly, it must also be born in mind that many of the weapons which, by 1918, had developed an awesome potential – tanks and aircraft in particular – were, in the early years of the war, flimsy and vulnerable and, to the untechnical eye, belonged more to the realm of Jules Verne than to that of the GQG. Nivelle, it is true, placed great faith in the crushing weight of the artillery. But Pétain strove to establish a more integrated battle order which combined artillery, tanks, infantry, and air support in proportions which, in theory at least, should have been capable eventually of breaking the trench stalemate.

Inter-allied cooperation during the war was very poor. Before the war, attempts by the French to coordinate a strategy with Russia ran up against a wall of secrecy. The French certainly hoped that Britain would join the fight against Germany – indeed, Joffre even modified his strategic plans to ease

British participation. However, the Allies struck upon no unified plan of operation, beyond placing the British Expeditionary Force (BEF) on the French left wing.[51] As the war progressed, little was done to coordinate the Allied war effort. There was general strategic agreement among the generals of both nations that the outcome of the war would be decided on the Western Front. Offensives were sometimes carried out to coincide more or less with those of allies. But, on the whole, each army fought its private war. That defense planning was parochial before the war was, perhaps, forgiveable given the rather vague nature of the *entente*. However, the failure to coordinate the war effort more fully, especially between allies fighting side by side, until the strong possibility of a German victory in 1918 forced them to establish a central reserve and a supreme Allied commander is almost incomprehensible. A long history of Anglo-French rivalry stimulated suspicion. Political leaders proved reluctant to have their troops commanded by generals of other nations. In this, the British were possibly at fault more than the French, for if there was to be a supreme commander, it could only be provided by France. However, Joffre's lackluster war record, the rivalries among French generals, and the intrusion of politics into the military sphere – most notably with *l'affaire Sarrail*[52] – hardly provided arguments in favor of coupling the British military machine behind a sputtering Gallic engine; nor did Lloyd George's transparent attempt to place Haig under French leadership reassure British generals about the intentions of their own political leaders. The French failed utterly to convince the Americans to intersperse their soldiers among those of France, a militarily logical option which ran up against American pride and political sensibilities. The Americans were given their own sector and fought for their own objectives, albeit under the overall direction of Foch. On the whole, however, unified direction was conspicuous by its absence on the Allied side.

It is doubtful that the French possessed a strategic plan for winning the war. Joffre's 'nibbling' strategy of attrition appears to have been a retrospective justification for the hammer blows at a German line which perversely refused to crack. The indirect approach through the Dardanelles failed through lack of planning and because Allied strength was overextended. It is difficult to see how the war could have been won elsewhere than on the Western Front. Most French generals recognized this. What they failed to appreciate, at least until 1917, was that the breakthrough was impossible. The war of attrition was working against France. In a real sense, it is impossible to see how France could have avoided putting its strength against German strength. The real tragedy, however, was that France applied this strategy in such a wasteful manner.

With the failure of the German offensive of 1914, the long-term odds favored the Allies. The industrial and manpower resources available to them, the naval blockade of Germany, and the strength of the defense over the attack meant that the Central Powers must eventually capitulate. However, by rushing events, by pressing home murderous offensives, Joffre almost handed over a victory which could come to him only in the fullness of time. Some of the political and psychological reasons for the absence of patience in the French high command have already been discussed. To these, one could add a distinct inability to envisage the war in global terms, the primacy of the tactical mind, and a fixation on events in a few square miles of Champagne or Flanders to the exclusion of all else.

From the early summer of 1917, Pétain adopted a more patient strategy which sought to increase the French advantage in matériel and await the considerable reserves promised by America's entry into the war. However, his was not a passive strategy. In two limited offensives at Verdun and Malmaison in the autumn of 1917, he massed overwhelming amounts of artillery, tanks, and planes against vulnerable salients in the German lines to achieve important tactical successes.[53] Under Pétain, the air corps was developed as a separate strategic arm. With Russia out of the war and a general German offensive looming in 1918, Pétain began to reorganize the French front into *zones profondes*. However, his efforts to introduce elasticity into French defense by fighting from the second position rather than from the front line horrified Clemenceau, who was unwilling to cede another inch of French soil to the invader, and Foch, who favoured counterattacks.[54] In the late summer of 1918, Pétain sought to hurl a major offensive into Alsace-Lorraine, where German defenses were weak. But again, his plans were stymied by Foch, who chose to pursue the retreating Germans.

Operational Effectiveness

Inter-arm cooperation in the French Army in 1914 was poor. This sprang from many sources. Rivalry among the various arms in the French Army had always been intense, and sometimes led to great bitterness, as in the Franco-Prussian War when infantry officers accused the artillery of being more interested in saving guns than in the protection and support of assaults. The artillery regarded itself as the army's elite arm. Most of its senior officers had passed through the prestigious Ecole Polytechnique, which offered a rigorous technical training far superior to the narrow professional courses dispensed at Saint-Cyr, where many of the infantry and cavalry officers were trained. Therefore, the army tended to be Balkanized in what was often referred to as *petites chapelles*; nor did the army have much chance to practice inter-arm cooperation. Training areas were few and too small for large-scale maneuvers. The army lacked telephones and failed to develop an effective spotter system using aircraft. In any case, the almost total absence of heavy artillery in the French Army in 1914 meant that German heavy batteries could punish French troops with little fear of retaliation.[55]

As the war progressed, the French gradually made up their deficiencies in heavy artillery so that by 1918 France matched, or perhaps even surpassed, the Germans in this area. The static nature of the fighting and the introduction of telephones and spotter aircraft facilitated cooperation between artillery and infantry. However, the French, like the British, held to rigid timetables for barrages, or, later, had the infantry advance behind a rolling barrage, rather than permit infantry officers to demand fire on request, as the Germans were doing by 1918. The problem of inter-arm cooperation was also partly solved by the decline of the French infantry, both in numbers and in quality, so that the artillery became the primary arm by 1917. By 1918 the air corps had also become a tactical arm in its own right. To this extent, the French could be said to be covering their deficiencies in infantry with their strength in artillery and aircraft. Pétain attempted to retrain his army for the offensive by stressing the importance of infantry–tank liaison as well as that between the artillery and aircraft. But these efforts were only partially successful. The French were never able to develop an integrated operational system as Ludendorff was to do in 1917–18. The infantry was called upon to attack with inadequate support in the war's opening years, and never seemed to adapt to the matériel renaissance of late 1917–18.

Following France's defeat in the Franco-Prussian War of 1870–71, the army took great pains to develop a general staff on the Prussian model. While the French staff was an enormous improvement over the old 'staff corps,' it never managed to develop the operational abilities of its German counterpart for several reasons. In the first place, the French general staff tended to be a bureaucratic machine rather than a 'brain.' Staff officers spent much time in routine administrative duties to the detriment of their operational skills. Secondly, the French tended to develop a 'picture' of enemy intentions and, too often, held to it even if German movements perversely failed to remain within the framework of French preconceptions. Lastly, French staff officers and commanders had little opportunity to hone their skills during peacetime. Neither army nor corps staff existed in peacetime, a condition imposed by insecure politicians, so that many duties had to be learned 'on the job.'[56]

When the war broke out, the French persisted with their own plans for an offensive in Alsace and Lorraine despite the gathering German menace on their left flank. The staff must certainly be given a great deal of credit for halting the retreat in August 1914, and taking advantage of German mistakes on the Marne in September. However, throughout the war, they persevered in their attempt to make an offensive work in the face of overwhelming evidence that this was impossible. They seldom exhibited great originality, content to copy German techniques which, by the time they were put into effect in the French Army, were already six months out of date and consequently easily countered. Like the British, the French command structure prevented any large degree of initiative on the part of subordinate commanders. Attacks were arranged according to a fixed timetable. Absence of initiative, which was built into the system, tightly choreographed attacks, and lack of communications often prevented commanders from exploiting local successes because the French machine lacked the flexibility to deviate from the pre-established plan and change the direction of an attack.[57]

Pétain's Directive 2 bis of December 30, 1917, attempted to introduce more flexibility into French operations, especially offensive operations, by stressing the advantages of surprise and the need to abandon fixed plans in favor of orders. However, opposition from commanders and staff officers used to a more methodical approach, the difficulties of training soldiers in new methods, and the pressures of the German offensives of the spring and summer of 1918 made those concepts difficult to apply. Pétain did have greater success in establishing a reserve of forty divisions in the summer of

1918 which allowed him to shift reinforcements to threatened points or to those which offered strategic opportunity.[58]

The French Army proved to be among the most technologically backward in Europe in 1914. Apart from the redoubtable 75-mm cannon, it was deficient in almost every other category of military hardware, but especially in heavy artillery, machine guns, and telephones. Even the Lebel rifle was cumbersome and lacked a magazine. The red and blue uniforms of the French Army had an unfortunate tendency to attract the attention of enemy riflemen. There were several reasons for this technological retardation, but a doctrine which exalted the *arme blanche* above the bullet was certainly less influential than many historians have suggested. Financial stringency, lack of firm direction at the top of the army, ministerial instability, confusion over tactical doctrine, the long debate over the merits of various artillery pieces in the years before the war, debates which were complicated by deep personality conflicts, and the bureaucratic nature of the selection process for even the most minor items of equipment, all contributed to the relative backwardness of the army in 1914.[59]

Not surprisingly, the technical evolution of the army quickened with the war. The artillery was the first to feel the effects, although more slowly than might be imagined. In 1918, 30 per cent of the French heavy artillery was still of the slow-firing de Bagne type, and only one-half of French divisions had actually received their new heavy guns.[60] Like their British counterparts, French officers were slow to evolve an operational doctrine which took account of the new matériel, relying on longer and longer preliminary bombardments before hurling infantry at the German lines, techniques which were too easily countered by the Germans, who simply increased the depth both of their positions and their dug-outs. In the opinion of British historian C. R. M. F. Crutwell, referring both to the British and the French high commands: 'The vastness of material and mechanical power . . . seemed to produce a kind of dull megalomania in which the ingenuity of execution was sacrificed to the intensity and elaboration of the preparation.'[61]

Until the summer of 1917, France made war essentially with its infantry. In the wake of the mutinies, Pétain sought to transform the war into one of matériel, both to spare the infantry and because he realized that the long-term advantage of the Allies lay in their industrial and technical superiority. He increased the production of rapid-fire artillery and made fuller use of tanks and aircraft. Far from using matériel to replace the infantry, Pétain sought to integrate the two into a unified operational system. He set up schools to teach commanders about the latest technical developments and how to employ them on the battlefield. However, his success did not match his aspirations. Retraining the infantry in combined operations was interrupted by the 1918 German offensives. The habit of tightly organized operations and fixed operation plans was too deeply ingrained to shake off easily. Many seemed to see matériel as a substitute, rather than as support, for the infantry, which saw its fighting qualities decline in the final months of the war.

On the whole, the French did not experience great logistical problems in 1914, although in the opening battles poor staff work meant that many of the roads became clogged. After that, the French were falling back on their bases and so had less difficulty than did the Germans, who often outdistanced their supplies. French communications were so poor that French officers had to rifle houses and schools near the battle zone to get telephones. The absence of an air-ground signalling system meant that too often the infantry lacked artillery support. The real failure of 1914, however, was that of intelligence. French intelligence failed to predict the great sweep of the Schlieffen Plan. This was in part because the Germans had changed their codes just prior to the war, blinding the French at the very moment when they needed the information.[62] However, unless the evidence presented by intelligence had been overwhelming, Joffre probably could not have been persuaded to abandon Plan XVII. French intelligence realized only belatedly that the Germans had placed reservists in the front lines in 1914, thus swelling the numbers of troops available for the flanking maneuver through Belgium.[63]

Once the war had settled down into a trench deadlock, it became easier to anticipate enemy action. The massing of troops in advance of an offensive could be picked out by air reconnaissance and aerial photography. French cryptography and communications intelligence also improved. On the Somme in the summer of 1916, the liaison between the Deuxième Bureau (intelligence) and the artillery was perfected to the point that some captured Germans believed that they had been betrayed.[64] In 1917, Pétain placed intelligence and operations under the same chief so as to better coordinate them. The Deuxième Bureau predicted the date and place of the German offensive of March 21, 1918, although they also believed Champagne to be menaced, causing Pétain to hold back troops to defend that front. The greatest intelligence lapse of the trench war was the failure to predict the German offensive on the Chemin des Dames on May 27, 1918, an attack which almost broke the French front wide open.[65] However, Foch's judicious use of intelligence allowed him to make more audacious attacks in the summer of 1918.

There were logistical failures, however, even in the static conditions of the trenches. The inability to support and supply attacks over ground which had been chewed up by artillery meant that many initially successful assaults failed due to lack of support. Also, on the human level, little trouble seems to have been taken over the material conditions of the troops. Food was poor, conditions in the rest areas primitive, and those in the trenches often appalling, factors which contributed to the mutinies of 1917. French medical services were such that France had the highest sickness rate of the three western belligerents.[66]

The French worked hard to increase mobility. When the war of movement was re-established by the German offensive of the spring and summer of 1918, the lack of roads and transport limited the numbers of reinforcements which the French could speed to a threatened sector to two or three divisions per day. However, in this respect they did much better than the Germans, who, having broken open the front, found that they lacked the mobility to exploit their tactical success. Thus Ludendorff's tactical success became a strategic defeat.[67]

Needless to say, for most of the war the French demonstrated a courageous but foolhardy persistence in attacking German positions which could be taken only at enormous costs. Despite Liddell Hart's view that the path to Berlin lay through the Bosphorus, it was difficult for France to apply its strength elsewhere than on the Western Front. By 1917, the futility of attempting to break the German lines had become apparent even to the French high command. When Pétain succeeded Nivelle as commander-in-chief in 1917, he sought to take advantage of increasing French superiority in artillery by concentrating massive fire power upon salients in the German lines. In this way he could inflict substantial casualties and occupy a few more kilometers of blistered earth, but he could not give a decisive turn to the war. However, Pétain did realize that technical advancements in artillery, tanks, and aircraft, together with the arrival of substantial American reinforcements, meant that the rupture of the Western Front was only a matter of time and careful planning. He worked to establish an operational base which would take account of these new developments. In this, he was largely successful, despite the lack of imagination of many French commanders unable to grasp the tactical implications of the new advances in matériel, opposition from men like Foch and Clemenceau, who equated Pétain's elasticity of defense with retreat, and the decline in the maneuverability of the French infantry. In the final analysis, French operational doctrine proved to be more sound than that of Germany. For all of the tactical brilliance of Ludendorff's offensives of March, May, and July 1918, they failed ultimately because the German Army lacked the operational capacity to sustain them. The French managed to parry the German blows and then pursue the enemy relentlessly until Germany sued for peace. Therefore, Pétain can be said to have placed France's strengths against those points where the German defense was at its most vulnerable.

Tactical Effectiveness

In 1914, France's strategic objective was to unhinge the German thrust through Belgium by striking into Lorraine and Alsace. Once the lines had jelled, the objective became the expulsion of the German armies from French soil. To accomplish these strategic objectives required an army trained to high standards of offensive warfare. The doctrine of the offensive was written into the pre-1914 regulations in strident terms and continued to dominate French thinking throughout the war. This was quite understandable. The pity was, not only did the French Army lack the tactical skills to succeed in its strategic goals, but also these *lacunae* weakened the French to the point that they very nearly forfeited the final victory.

The pre-1914 infantry regulations stressed rapidity of attack over order and method. In fact, the remarkable thing about the regulations (which were only published on April 20, 1914) was their refusal to take a firm position in the tactical debates of the day: 'In view of the polemics occasioned by recent wars, and in the absence of a well-established doctrine,' wrote French Lieutenant Colonel P. H. M. Lucas, 'it was probably thought advisable to reserve decision by publishing regulations which, instead of imposing settled rules of procedure, authorized full initiative.'[68]

Fire power and the importance of artillery liaison were talked about, but it was believed – in public, at least – that the attack would always succeed. That these regulations did not accurately reflect the realities of war as it was to be fought goes without saying. But regulations are merely words on a page. To take on life, they must be absorbed by competent and conscientious cadres and passed onto troops in training and maneuvers. This was not done.[69] Therefore, the early French operations consisted of poorly considered attacks, 'isolated brawls' in which the badly trained French came off second best against a more solidly prepared foe.

As the war progressed, the French recognized the need to make their attacks more methodical and deliberate. Rapidity was sacrificed to method, initiative to a list of set objectives and rigid timetables. As a consequence, French tactics became predictable and were easily countered. The lack of flexibility made the exploitation of initial success difficult, especially as many of the best officers and NCOs were killed. This was the tactical problem which constantly dogged the French Army throughout the war – how to reconcile method with surprise, speed of execution, and rapidity of exploitation. It was a problem which the army never successfully resolved.

The tactical system, or lack of one, in the French Army before 1914 reflected a confusion in the high command about the lessons of modern wars, as well as the absence of a group or institution capable of handing down a final verdict on these disputes which would be accepted throughout the army. The army lacked modern weapons, not because it disdained things like heavy artillery, but because for a variety of political, financial, and bureaucratic reasons they simply did not materialize. If the tactical regulations were vague in many areas, if they failed to be specific about the importance of heavy artillery, this was because they reflected the state of an army in the midst of a debate about tactics and armaments.[70]

The tragedy of the French Army was that its leaders were committed to an aggressive strategy which was beyond their tactical powers. French generals spent the war attempting to discover the right tactical combination which would deliver strategic success. Where rapidity of execution and courage had failed, the French increasingly attempted to substitute method and fire power. A preliminary artillery bombardment of increasing ferocity followed by waves of troops, it was hoped, would break through the German positions. The Germans replied by increasing the depth of their defenses, building up bunkers with interlocking fields of fire, and removing men from the front lines, choosing to resist in secondary positions beyond the range of French artillery. French countermeasures, like increasing the depth of attack formations and the power of the artillery, and introducing rolling barrages and counterbattery fire, were easily parried by the Germans, who simply increased the depth and strength of their defenses. Even when French soldiers managed to gain local successes, they were unable to exploit them due to the rigid pre-planning of attacks and to the efficiency of German infantry in the murderous business of trench warfare. Therefore, French advances quickly coagulated and little ground was gained despite substantial casualties. The French realized that their lack of operational flexibility, the inability to exploit rapidly an opportunity which had not been written into the attack plan, was at fault. Yet they never succeeded in reconciling flexibility with planning, despite repeated admonitions that they should do so. A note from the high command of November 1916 complained: 'We are surprised by success . . . [and] do not know how to take advantage of it.'[71]

Tactical ideas were certainly not lacking in the French Army. Some trace Ludendorff's successful infiltration tactics to a pamphlet written in 1915 by French Captain Paul Laffargue and captured by the Germans, entitled 'The Attack in Trench Warfare.' Laffargue argued that successive waves of troops should be replaced by deep penetration units, elite troops armed with automatic rifles and light machine guns, who, preceded by short, sharp artillery barrages, would bypass strongpoints and attempt to reach enemy artillery lines. It is possible that Laffargue's ideas influenced Nivelle. It appears certain that they influenced Ludendorff.[72]

Nivelle's 1917 *bataille de rupture* has often been dismissed as sheer folly, the product of a smooth public relations operation worked on a pair of nervous, even desperate, governments. However, this is to judge intentions by results. Many aspects of Nivelle's plan – rolling barrages and the bypassing of strongpoints – were to be applied with devastating success by Ludendorff a year later. At Verdun in 1916, Nivelle had already achieved impressive success with them; but in the conditions of 1917, they were doomed to failure for reasons which too often dogged the French war effort. A forced optimism in the GQG would tolerate no dissenting voices of caution, even when the Germans withdrew to fortified positions 30 kilometers to the rear. Nivelle had staked his future on the success of the operation, and those of his entourage of staff officers and subordinate commanders were bound up with that of their commander-in-chief. Consequently, they chose to ignore disturbing intelligence reports of new German defense methods which had transformed the first line into a lightly held web of listening posts and machine gun nests, and sited the second line – a 'battle zone' of three trench lines of 1,500 to 3,000 meters in depth – whenever possible on the reverse slope beyond the view of Allied observation and the reach of artillery. French enthusiasm reached down to unit level, where regiments vied with each other to have the fastest rolling barrage. Even when his plan of attack fell into German hands Nivelle was too committed, psychologically and politically, to withdraw.

When the French attacked on April 16, 1917, they fell in rows. The infantry could not follow 'the insane pace of the barrage.' Well-sited machine gun nests and strongpoints blasted the attackers from all sides, including the rear. The German planes massed to prevent the French from observing their positions, while at the same time directing devastating barrages from German batteries upon the exposed attackers. The *battaille de rupture* was discarded upon the rubbish heap of failed Allied offensives.[73]

The failure of the Nivelle offensive, followed by the mutinies, brought a sobering note of reality to French operations. In 1917, Pétain abandoned hopes for a breakthrough in favor of 'attacks with limited objectives, unleashed suddenly on a front wide enough to make full use of the numbers and various types of existing artillery.'[74] In other words, Pétain had inaugurated a real war of attrition relying upon matériel rather than manpower. In this respect, Pétain came closer than any other French general in devising an operational concept based upon the realities of the French situation – reorganizing the French army for offensive warfare, giving it all of the advantages which fire power, tanks, aircraft, and mobility could provide.

One of Pétain's major preoccupations was the strengthening of the French Air Force and its development into an effective tactical arm. Indeed, the evolution of the French Air Force since 1914, while spectacular, was uneven and had failed often to keep pace with German progress. At the beginning of the war, France counted 160 aircraft and 15 airships to 246 planes and 7 Zeppelins in Germany. Although the French Air Force was smaller than that of Germany, France led the world in aircraft technology and even had supplied the Royal Flying Corps with all of its 113 planes. The French rotary engines – the Gnome and Le Rhône – were considered the world's best, and even late into the war the Germans salvaged them from downed French aircraft to mount them on their fighters.

The early stages of the evolution of aircraft in the First World War are well known. Advantage in the air over the Western Front tilted between the enemies depending on the sophistication of the machines which each could produce. Observation planes attempted to devise more or less efficient ways to attack each other until, in the spring of 1915, the Germans introduced the Fokker El, a fighter which, though structurally weak and underpowered, had a Parabellum machine gun mounted on the cowling against which no Allied plane could contend. The winter of 1915–16 was the period of the 'Fokker scourge,' which was broken by the introduction of the Nieuport II Bébé fighter armed with a Lewis machine gun (which the French supplied to the British from May 1916), followed by the Nieuport 17. In the skies over Verdun, the French created the first truly large-scale fighter unit of the war – Les Cigognes (The Storks) – which remained the elite French fighter force until November 1918. However, French ascendency was destined to be brief. In the summer of 1916, the Germans brought out the Albatross. Although these planes were only marginally superior to the Nieuports, they were far better armed. The introduction of the Albatross III, combined with the organization of the Jasta or fighter wing modelled on the French Cigognes, meant that by early 1917, the Germans had again wrested air superiority from the Allies.[75]

In many respects, the French were quicker to see the potential of bombers than of fighters. This was encouraged by the trench deadlock and by the desire of politicians to strike at the German heartland. From September 1914, the high command envisaged a role for aircraft beyond intelligence gathering and artillery observation, arguing that planes could be used to bomb enemy artillery, railyards, and assembly points. By May 1915, the French had organized 12 bomber squadrons and carried out raids on Ludwigshafen and Karlsruhe. On June 8, 1915, Joffre ordered 50 squadrons of 10 planes each, of which 200 were to be for long-distance bombardment. Pressure in Parliament mounted for retaliatory raids on German cities, while private subscriptions were raised to manufacture fleets of bombers.

However, just as public hopes mounted, the creation of a strategic air force encountered a series of technical snags which retarded the development of bombers until the end of the war. The creation of an effective German fighter force made daylight bombing a costly business, while problems of navigation meant that bombers sent out on night missions might simply fail to find a target. Also, night flying required bombers to fly in loose formation so that bombing patterns were dispersed and ineffective. Bomb loads were too small to make a trip to Germany worthwhile, and manufacturers complained that bomber production was difficult and costly compared to that of fighters. To these technical problems were added political ones, for the government found that the bombing of German towns provoked diplomatic protests, while attacks on occupied French cities raised moral problems.[76]

When Pétain took command in the summer of 1917, the German Air Force was well in command over the Western Front. The Royal Flying Corps (RFC) especially had been decimated by German 'circuses' – fighter wings of two to four Jastas followed by mobile support systems which could be shifted along the lines to achieve local air superiority. The Germans also chose to fight on the strategic defensive, waiting for the Allies to attack them over their own territory rather than going in search of battle. This gave them at least two advantages. In the first place, Allied tactical doctrine required fighters to fly close protection for bombers and observation planes, and this greatly restricted their freedom of action. German fighters, on the other hand, roamed at will, seeking out vulnerable targets, lurking in ambush behind banks of clouds, and accepting battle only on their terms. Also, a disabled German pilot was often able, with the aid of the prevailing west winds, to glide back to his own airfield, or at least to come down in friendly territory, while a wounded Allied aircraft was almost always lost.

In 1917, the Germans had concentrated 1,680 planes against the British, while only 367 were needed to keep the French in check. Historian Alan Clark attributes this disproportionate allocation of force to the fact that the British were more aggressive flyers while the French, following a policy of creaming off their best aviators for elite units like Les Cigognes or Les Sportifs, had bled the remainder of *élan* and dash.[77] The truth is more prosaic. The Germans were able to hold the French with so few planes for the simple reason that, by late 1917, the French counted barely 500 modern aircraft of all types in working order.[78]

Pétain's priorities in the air war were two: first expand aircraft production which, by the admission of the under secretary of state for aviation Paul Dhé, was *en crise*. Secondly, he sought to devise a tactical doctrine for French aircraft so that they, like their German opponents, could become adjuncts of the infantry on the battlefield.

The first problem was the more difficult to resolve as the army had no direct control over aircraft production. The GQG continually placed orders for aircraft, but were plagued by poor organization of production, its essentially artisan character, and shoddy workmanship. The Spad XIII fighter and the Bréguet XIV bomber were excellent planes, but they were too often delivered without arms, and even without gas tanks, carburators, or radiators. The Spad biplane spent two days out of three in the repair shed, while the motor of the Spad monoplane was judged 'incapable d'un service sûr.' Pétain took up the question directly with Prime Minister Clemenceau, pointing out that France's situation would be 'grave' in 1918 unless ruthless action was taken. In November 1917, the government reorganized the production services. The numbers of aircraft began to increase, albeit slowly, hindered especially by the shortfall in the numbers of motors produced. By March 1918, the French, while not as well endowed with aircraft as the Germans, at least were able to make a respectable showing.[79]

Pétain's second priority was to establish a tactical doctrine. In 1917, the Germans had seen the need for cooperation between planes and ground commanders. Air intervention had helped to stem the British tank offensive at Cambrai in 1917, and the Germans began to integrate aircraft into their blitzkrieg tactics, which were to be unleashed on the Western Front in March 1918. On July 19, 1917, Pétain issued a *note* from his headquarters on the tactical use of aircraft which inaugurated a new departure in French thinking about the air arm. Henceforth, planes were to become auxiliaries of the infantry by attacking enemy machine gun nests, trenches, and batteries, as well as German planes assigned the same tasks. Bombers were to attack targets close behind the lines. The new offensive doctrine, together with the arrival of the Spad XIII, infused new life into an air force whose morale had gone flat due to neglect and a shortage of planes. Throughout the winter of 1917–18, GQG worked out defensive air tactics which would be used to counter the coming German offensive. Larger groups – *escadres* – composed of several *escadrilles* were organized and assigned the task of attacking enemy planes before coming to the support of the ground forces. The number of anti-aircraft batteries was increased and bombers dispatched to harass German rear areas day and night, a tactic whose effects were more psychological than actual, given light bomb loads and poor accuracy. Nevertheless, these changes added to Ludendorff's problems and especially helped to exhaust the German offensive on the Chemin des Dames in May 1918.[80]

Pétain's tactical concepts offered no less than a revolution for the French Army in 1917. They were realistic and sensible, and without his reorientation of methods and priorities, the French army may well not have lasted the pace. However, this is not to say that Pétain was entirely successful in imposing his views throughout the Army. On the contrary, his methods, especially the concept of 'elastic defense,' of giving ground to economize men, provoked a bitter controversy in the army and one which stretched behind the lines to the Palais Matignon, the residence of the French prime minister. In fact, the primary reason why the German attack on the Chemin des Dames in May 1918 met with stunning initial success was that French General Duchesne, against the directives of Pétain, had packed his front lines so that his troops fell within easy range of German artillery.

There are several reasons why Pétain found it so difficult to change French tactics at a stroke – some psychological, some related to the style of French command procedures, and some institutional. Psychologically, many Frenchmen, including Clemenceau, found it difficult to accept a doctrine which was prepared to surrender yet more French territory to the invader. To these people, every inch of French soil had been hallowed by the blood already shed to defend it. A tactic which stressed economy of force and flexibility encountered a mind set of men like Foch and war minister General

Pierre Roques, who denounced Pétain as men who had undergone a religious experience might dismiss the logical arguments of an unbeliever. Many took pride in a rather dogged, if foolish, determination to hold on to every inch of scarred earth as the quintessential expression of the French spirit of resistance. For them, the mud became more important than the lives of the men defending it. For Foch especially, Pétain's flexible defense came close to heresy, a betrayal of the faith in deliverance which could be brought about only by the offensive. The offensive became not so much a tactic as a mission, a sacred duty for Foch. For this reason, the debate over tactics in 1917–18 can almost be seen as a clash of wills between the pious, spiritual Foch, and the agnostic, pragmatic Pétain.[81]

The doctrinal difference between the French Army's two most important generals influenced the army's ability to respond to Pétain's reforms. Generals split into camps and rallied behind the doctrines of their champion. (It will come as no surprise that Duchesne fell into Foch's camp.) For this, the French command system was largely at fault. While German tactical doctrine evolved as part of an open discussion between the high command and junior officers in the field, French doctrine, even if based originally on practical experience (as was the case with Nivelle's offensive), quickly degenerated into deductive formulas handed down from on high, like a pastoral letter read from the pulpit, meant to apply in any situation. The enemy was treated as an abstraction rather than an intelligent adversary who might react with countermeasures of his own. Objections by field commanders that tactics might not work were treated in much the same way as the medieval church dealt with heresy. Dissent was equated with disloyalty, scepticism with cowardice. In this atmosphere, it became therefore quite natural that French officers chose sides based on personality or patronage, rather than considering the arguments on their own merits.[82]

With the high command in such disarray, Pétain's theories were, quite naturally, misunderstood or misapplied. Too many commanders assumed that the French had adopted a purely defensive posture based on fortifications and fire power. While some infantry units were retrained in the new concepts of defensive flexibility dear to the commander-in-chief, too many were transformed into escorts for the artillery, diminishing still further their tactical efficiency. In some sectors, gunners made up 60 per cent of front-line troops.[83] Pétain found the bureaucratic style of the French forces – the adherence to the plan, the absence of surprise, minute regulation of the employment of the infantry, the increasing emphasis on massive deployment of heavy guns to punch holes in enemy lines – difficult to break.

In the final analysis, it was easier to find reasons for not applying Pétain's doctrines than getting down to the task of retraining the army in maneuver and open warfare tactics. Commanders complained that they did not have enough time both to train their soldiers and to construct new positions 4 to 5 kilometers in the rear as Pétain's flexible defense required. Some argued that they covered areas of strategic importance which permitted no retreat. Foch complained that Pétain's plans to defend from the second position precluded any possibility of counterattack. And besides, to make flexible defense sound, Pétain had called for the creation of an Allied reserve of forty divisions which, in Foch's eyes, was totally unrealistic. Because opinion in the army was divided, and because Foch had the ear of Clemenceau on this question, Pétain found it difficult to impose his views throughout the army.[84] The result was the old story of a French army which could not be trained to common principles because no one could agree on what those principles should be.[85] For these reasons, the French infantry was unevenly prepared to resist the infiltration tactics of picked German troops in 1918.

In summary, it may be said that, until the summer of 1917, the French Army possessed neither the operational capabilities nor the fire power to make their tactics succeed. Pétain attempted to build up the ability to move rapidly and respond to new situations rather than adhere to a fixed plan. In this, he met with only partial success. However, his modifications made no small contribution to the ultimate victory of 1918.

Inter-arm liaison suffered the same fate as French tactical doctrine in general before 1914 – regulations speak of its importance, but the army seldom had a chance to put it into practice in maneuvers. Aviation was gradually employed during the war to aid in the coordination of artillery and infantry attacks. But French commanders preferred to centralize control of the battle to the extent that they forfeited the ability to take advantage of tactical opportunities. For instance, in the French Army, the artillery was controlled on the corps level, while the Germans gave it to the division. One of the consequences of this was that infantry commanders on the ground did not have the means to call up artillery support to respond to a particular situation.

Pétain went some way toward decentralizing control of the battle and introducing a new sense of reality into operational plans. He required staff officers to visit the front to get a better grasp of the difficulties faced by ground commanders. His Directive 2 bis of December 30, 1917, encouraged the substitution of orders for plans to allow the French more tactical flexibility. He stressed the importance of communications, especially of links between tanks and infantry, and artillery and aircraft. This directive followed by that of July 12, 1918, established, in the opinion of French historian Guy Pedroncini, 'the synthesis of the advantages of offensive procedures known or imaginable at that date.'[86] The use of tanks and aviation by the French was essential in halting Ludendorff's Champagne offensive of July 1918, while the employment of those two arms in liaison with the infantry produced impressive results in the counteroffensives of July 18, 1918. It is certain, however, that the lack of inter-arm training and the absence of command experience in combined arms operations, especially in a war of maneuver, caused the French attacks to lose momentum in the following days.

One of the great problems for the Allies was how to combine surprise with the need to build up sufficient reserves of manpower and artillery before an attack. With the increasing use of air reconnaissance, it became virtually impossible to camouflage preparations for an attack. The movement of troops in the rear, the stockpiling of large parks of matériel, the construction of extra communications trenches, all were indications that a major offensive was brewing. This allowed the Germans to move reserves close to the suspected point of attack and quickly staunch any local success. The tank and airplane offered the Allies the best hope of a surprise breakthrough. But again, the technical limitations of the tank together with the small numbers available meant that it was only used in penny packets until relatively late in the war. The Germans were usually able to blunt tank attacks effectively with artillery.

From September 1916, French directives stressed the importance of surprise and exploitation of success. However, the army was badly placed to realize either goal. The enormous casualty rates of the war's opening months, especially in the lower cadres, the poor record of inter-arm liaison, the near disastrous *laissez-aller* of the early offensives, forced the high command to turn to more rigorous regulation of attacks, to rely increasingly upon the heavy artillery to clear a path for the advancing infantry, and upon strict control of the advance at the highest levels. These methods often brought the French good initial success. But the reliance upon ponderous attack waves, the need to shift the position of the artillery forward to bombard targets in the German rear, the de-emphasis of initiative on the battalion, company, and platoon levels, all made the exploitation of success difficult.

The tactical system in the French Army suffered from poor unit cohesion. This was a problem of which the French had been aware before 1914, but the repeated admonitions that officers establish a rapport with and gain the confidence of their men seem to have had only a limited effect. The most common complaint heard against officers before 1914 was that they were distant, indifferent to their men, and had little contact with them. As far as this was true, it was more likely the result of a bureaucratic approach to military life, in which a great deal of an officer's time was spent in paperwork, rather than to an aristocratic *hauteur*, as some on the left claimed. While it is important not to exaggerate the distance between officers and men, it is certain that too little was done before 1914 to improve the life of the conscript, who tended to live in dilapidated barracks, exist on an unvaried menu of *rata* (a sort of vegetable stew), and have little provided for him in the way of amusements or healthy leisure activities.[87] The shortcomings of French NCOs have already been discussed at some length. Suffice it to add that when Joffre saw the roads strewn with abandoned equipment in August 1914, he immediately concluded that the cadres were not in control of their troops.[88]

The enormous casualties, especially of lower cadres, in the early months of the war could have done little to improve unit cohesion. Certainly, the decline in initiative which was almost quantifiable by 1917, if not earlier, can be put down in great part to the deaths of many of the best leaders on the unit level. This deprived the French Army of much of its capacity to adapt to new opportunities promised by advances in matériel by 1918.

The decline in the quality of cadres – and consequently in the relationships between officers and troops – was a contributory factor in the mutinies which broke out in the army in May 1917. Despite the attempts of many generals to blame left-wing agitators inspired by the Russian Revolution, the crisis was strictly a military one. Its most direct cause was the failure of the Nivelle offensive, coming on the heels of other costly failures. These were not revolts against the war. Rather, they were a protest caused by a lack of confidence in the high command's ability to deliver victory, a protest against a certain way of making war. The Nivelle offensive brought the frustrations of the 'ill-led and misused Poilu' boiling to the surface. Investigations revealed an indifference to the conditions of the common soldier which bordered on the criminal – virtually inedible rations, indescribable conditions in the trenches and uncomfortable ones behind the lines, infrequent and inequitable leave, slow and filthy leave trains, and extreme parsimony in decorations and promotions. The mutinies broke out behind the lines, especially in the depots, where men were in transit and where there were few personal links between officers and troops. Nevertheless, Pétain recognized that poor relations between officers and men had dangerously weakened cohesion in some units: 'The men like officers who *tutoyer* them, are familiar, friendly and who look after their welfare,' a Deuxième Bureau report of July 15, 1917 read. However, they 'disliked those who are arrogant or who hide in the face of danger.'[89] Pétain calmed the situation with an absolute minimum of repression, relying instead on a combination of better treatment and removing the menace of having to mount more futile offensives.[90] Nevertheless, he was always aware that the morale of the army remained fragile. His two offensives of autumn 1917 were carried out largely to restore faith in the army and to demonstrate that they could win when backed by massive amounts of matériel.

Poor training was a major failing of the French Army, both before and during the war. A French conscript spent his first months in basic training, but tended to receive little effective preparation after this. Many soldiers were absorbed into non-combatant positions, while others, locked into urban barracks, could do little more than drill. Indeed, when he first became prime minister in 1906, Clemenceau cut the annual training period for reservists from three weeks to two because, he claimed, they were not being trained. The dearth of training areas and the relatively small size of the camps limited the numbers of men who could be trained as well as the scale of maneuvers. This meant that senior officers and staff men had little experience in handling groups larger than a brigade. Annual maneuvers were more of a public relations exercise than a serious attempt to prepare the army for war. Soldiers were not allowed to dig in fields, so that instructions concerning field fortifications were relegated to the engineering manual, an important but seldom-read work. Attempts to hurry exercises, to get them over by a prescribed time, meant that mock attacks were rushed, infantrymen taking little trouble to develop the tactical use of terrain or fire and maneuver techniques. The nature of exercises meant that they often ended before the artillery, and especially the heavy artillery, could be deployed.[91]

As the war continued, it became only too obvious that French soldiers were not trained to the level of skills necessary to combat German superiority in trench fighting. Fortifications, camouflage, and the use of interlocking fire, machine guns, mortars, and hand grenades – flexibility and initiative in the trenches – were deficient in the army. Attack waves of men preceded by artillery barrages required little of the individual soldier except that he go forward. Regulations were issued which took account of this state of affairs, but they seemed to have had little influence, in part, perhaps, because they were often held to be secret and therefore did not percolate down to the training centers and unit level.

Verdun proved that the skill of the individual soldier was all-important. The depth of the killing ground, the loss of contact with command posts, meant that battle became an affair of small-unit operations. Pétain attempted to pull men out of the line for retraining in combined operations in the last months of 1917 and to prepare them for the war of maneuver which would become necessary with the expected German offensive in the spring. He set up centers where generals could study the latest German methods and digest the tactical implications of new weapons. Generals and staff officers were encouraged to visit the front to get a better feel for the realities of the battle area. However, the French Army was unevenly prepared when the German attack broke in 1918.[92] American troops trained by the French in 1917–18 complained that their instructors simply demonstrated set situations like how to organize a sector or relieve units in line. The soldiers themselves were simple spectators, never asked to practice the maneuver, nor taught to react to surprise attacks. Initiative, mobility, and surprise were absent from French training methods.[93]

French officers greatly underestimated the stress which modern war placed on both the logistical systems and the ability of men to fight for long periods without respite. The rapid exhaustion of artillery ammunition in the opening weeks of the war is well known. The French were not noticeably more shortsighted than other armies in underestimating the consumption of supplies, but rapid measures had to be taken to pull skilled workers out of uniform and return them to the factories to restart war production. French officers also failed to appreciate the stress which modern war places upon the fighting soldier. Early battle reports in 1914 speak of declining combat efficiency, of men simply exhausted from marching and countermarching, sleeping in the open air, and being inadequately supplied, before being hurled into battle.

Once the war settled down to a static war of trenches, it became far easier to support, although French officers deserve no special credit in foreseeing this state of affairs. The major need was, of course, artillery shells. At Verdun, massive numbers of trucks were mobilized to keep the battle supplied. The difficulty often was not to get the supplies to the battle area, but to move them into the forward zones. Too often, the only item which seemed to arrive in the trenches in any quantity was the ubiquitous *pinard*, or rough red wine.[94]

In 1914 the French emphasis on the tactical offensive did contain a certain, albeit specious, logic in that it recognized the greater manpower and industrial resources available to Germany, as well as the superior training and equipment of German forces. Therefore, it sought to overwhelm them with sudden attacks, which would throw the enemy off balance and cause confusion. Of course, the French possessed neither the operational doctrine, the artillery support, nor the tactical skills to permit this to succeed. The doctrine of the tactical offensive was one of weakness, almost desperation, not of blind overconfidence in French will power.[95]

The French remained wedded to the attack in 1915–16, even though Germany was obviously strongly entrenched. This was an unfortunate, not to say foolish, tactical choice when viewed in the cold light of day. In 1915, the French did attempt to attack the German lines in areas where there were no obstacles – forests or villages – because, especially in the early years of the war, French 75s were not powerful enough to eliminate opposition in these strong points. In 1917 Pétain launched limited offensives against vulnerable salients in the German lines using massed heavy artillery rather than risking infantry in great numbers. In defense of the French soldiers, it may be said that it was a question of attacking German strength or of not attacking at all, which they saw as an unacceptable option. By 1918 the French equalled the Germans in heavy artillery and aircraft, and had a considerable superiority in tanks. All of these were used with considerable effect in the offensives of 1917 and 1918. In preparation for the German onslaught of March 1918, Pétain attempted to transform the front line into a series of listening posts and machine gun nests designed to slow down the initial attack. By establishing the second position as the main line of resistance, he took the majority of French forces beyond the reach of German medium artillery and removed the threat of counterbattery fire to his own guns. However, even as late as May 1918, on the Chemin des Dames, the French were caught with their front positions packed with troops and, as a consequence, suffered high casualties and a substantial German advance. But even at its most developed stage in 1918, French defensive techniques still followed linear principles, while the Germans had largely abandoned trench lines for a defensive web of strong points and fortified shell holes. Although in many ways the *poilu* adjusted to trench warfare better than did his British counterpart, he never equalled his German enemy in skill. In such tactical categories as the use of natural cover and concealment, the positioning of machine guns, and the devolution of battle to regimental and battalion commander, the French proved slow to adapt.

Conclusion

In general, it can be said that the French Army in 1914 suffered from the absence of a system which paid close attention to all aspects of strategy, tactics, logistics, and armaments. The French adapted badly to the trench deadlock. The problem was in great part a psychological one, for it was difficult to adjust to a foreign army of occupation on French soil. Consequently, French commanders attempted to rush events, to force their way through the German lines even though their army was inadequately trained and supported. The general historical verdict on the French Army in the First World War is that it put in a courageous but unintelligent performance. This study does not disagree with that verdict. It has only sought to place the problems of the army in perspective and to demonstrate the political and technical context in which the war was fought, as well as the problems of managing and adapting a large bureaucratic machine to the changing conditions of war. The French generals are criticized for lacking a long-term perspective. However, in this they simply reflected the general impatience among the soldiers and politicians and in the country at large to push on to victory. A long-term view was a luxury until the summer of 1917. It might be more to the point to criticize the high command for lacking the courage to point out the military realities of the trench stalemate, for failing to make clear that, in the conditions which prevailed in the first three years of war, a breakthrough was impossible. Still, it must not be forgotten that, although the Germans proved to be the most adaptable soldiers on the Western Front, they lost the war nevertheless. France was victorious thanks largely to its courage, its allies, its industry and, lastly, to Pétain, the true architect of victory. France fielded the best army on the Allied side in the First World War. The major charge which can be laid against the French generals is that the price they paid for victory was too high.

Notes

1 Abel Ferry, *Les carnet secrets d'Abel Ferry* (Paris, 1957), p. 64.
2 See Philip Bankwitz, *Maxime Weygand and Civil-Military Relations in France* (Cambridge, Mass., 1967).
3 Jere Clemens King, *Generals and Politicians: Conflict Between France's High Command, Parliament, and Government, 1914–1918* (Berkeley and Los Angeles, 1951).
4 J. Monteilhet, *Les institutions militaire de la France* (Paris 1932); R. D. Challener, *The French Theory of the Nation in Arms* (New York, 1955).
5 Eugene Weber, *The Nationalist Revival in France* (Berkeley and Los Angeles, 1959).
6 King, *Generals and Politicians*, p. 16.
7 Theodore Zeldin, *France, 1848–1945* (Oxford, 1973), Vol. 1, pp. 574–7.
8 King, *Generals and Politicians*, pp. 3–4, 45–7.
9 Douglas Porch, *The March to the Marne, The French Army 1871–1914* (Cambridge, 1981), p. 227.
10 Ibid., pp. 237–41.
11 Ibid., p. 242.
12 Ibid., p. 243–4.
13 P. Banquet, *Souvenirs d'un directeur d'artillerie* (Paris, 1932), p. 41.
14 Robert O. Paxton, 'Organization of the War Effort in France, 1914–1918,' unpublished paper delivered at Princeton University, January 1984, p. 2.
15 Francois Caron, *An Economic History of Modern France* (New York, 1979), pp. 244–5.
16 Ibid., p. 173.
17 Ibid., pp. 144, 175, 245.
18 Banquet, *Souvenirs*, p. 38; J. Challeat, *L'artillerie de terre en France pendant un siècle* (Paris, 1935), Vol. 2, *1880–1910*, p. 388.
19 *Archives historique de la guerre, Chateau de Vincennes*, 7N, p. 107.
20 Porch, *Marne*, p. 242.
21 Paxton, 'Organization,' p. 5.
22 Caron, *Economic History*, pp. 244–8.
23 Proch, *Marne*, pp. 202–3, 244.
24 Guy Pedroncini, *Pétain, général en chef, 1917–1918* (Paris, 1974), p. 188.
25 Porch, *Marne*, p. 167.
26 Christopher Andrew and A. S. Kanya-Forstner, *France Overseas, The Great War and the Climax of Imperial Expansion* (London, 1981), pp. 134–6.
27 Ibid., p. 140.
28 Marc Michel, *L'appel l'Afrique, contributions et réactions à l'éffort de querre en AOF, 1914–19* (Paris, 1982).

29 Porch, *Marne*, pp. 101, 218–19, 242.
30 Ibid., pp. 196–200.
31 S. R. Williamson, 'Joffre Re-shapes French Strategy, 1911–1913', in Paul Kennedy (ed.), *The War Plans of the Great Powers* (Boston, 1979), p. 144.
32 See D. Stevenson, *French War Aims against Germany, 1914–1919* (New York, 1982).
33 George H. Cassar, *The French and the Dardanelles* (London, 1971); Jan Karl Tanenbaum, *General Maurice Sarrail, 1856–1929: The French Army and Left-wing Politics* (Chapel Hill, N.C., 1974).
34 Pedroncini, *Pétain*, pp. 110–12, 246–7.
35 Ibid., p. 429.
36 Porch, *Marne*, p. 228.
37 Ibid., pp. 216–18.
38 Ibid., p. 224.
39 H. Contamine, *La revanche* (Paris, 1957), p. 129.
40 P. Lucas, *The Evolution of Tactical Ideas in the French and German Armies during the War, 1914–1918* (Paris, 1923), translated for US Army War College, 1925, typescript p. 40.
41 André Kaspi, *Le temps des américains, 1917–18*, (Paris, 1976), pp. 24, 124.
42 Arthur Marder, *From Dreadnaught to Scapa Flow* (London, 1961–70), Vol. 1, *The Road to War*, pp. 116–17.
43 Ibid., pp. 304–9.
44 Ibid., Vol. 2, *The War Years to the Eve of Jutland*, pp. 335–41.
45 Ibid., Vol. 5, *Victory and Aftermath, January 1918–June 1919*, pp. 20–7.
46 David Watson, *Georges Clemenceau: A Political Biography* (London, 1974), p. 225.
47 Corelli Barnett, *The Swordbearers* (London, 1964), p. 203.
48 Alistair Horne, *The Price of Glory, Verdun 1916* (London, 1978).
49 Pedroncini, *Pétain*, p. 429.
50 King, *Generals and Politicians*, pp. 36–64.
51 Porch, *Marne*, pp. 228–9.
52 Tanenbaum, *Sarrail*, ch. 4.
53 Pedroncini, *Pétain*, p. 109.
54 Ibid., pp. 213, 218, 246–7.
55 Porch, *Marne*, pp. 193–6, 200–2, 234–5, 241–2.
56 Ibid., pp. 220–3.
57 Lucas, *The Evolution*, p. 68.
58 Pedroncini, *Pétain*, pp. 294, 408–9.
59 Porch, *Marne*, ch. 11.
60 Pedroncini, *Pétain*, p. 291.
61 C. Crutwell, *A History of the Great War, 1914–18* (London, 1936), p. 260.
62 Christopher Andrew, 'Dechiffrement et diplomatie; Le cabinet noir du Quai d'Orsay sous la Troisième République,' *Rélations internationales*, vol. 3, no. 5 (1976).
63 Joffre, *Mémoires*, (Paris, 1932), Vol. 1, pp. 148–9.
64 Lucas, *The Evolution*, p. 88.
65 Pedroncini, *Pétain*, pp. 288–9.
66 Barnett, *Swordbearers*, p. 201.
67 Pedroncini, *Pétain*, p. 285.
68 Lucas, *The Evolution*, p. 15.
69 Porch, *Marne*, pp. 222–3.
70 Ibid., chs. 11 and 12.
71 Ibid., p. 94.

72 Timothy T. Lupfer, *The Dynamics of Doctrine: The Changes in German Tactical Doctrine during the First World War* (Fort Leavenworth, Kans., July 1981), pp. 38–9.
73 Ibid., p. 35.
74 Barnett, *Swordbearers*, p. 203.
75 Alan Clark, *Aces High: The War in the Air over the Western Front, 1914–1918* (New York, 1973), pp. 24–5, 27, 39–45.
76 Philippe Bernard, 'A propos de la stratégie aérienne pendant la première guerre mondiale,' *Revue d'histoire moderne et contemporaine* (1969), pp. 358–63.
77 Clark, *Aces High*, p. 161.
78 Pedroncini, *Pétain*, p. 207.
79 Ibid., pp. 60, 207–8.
80 Ibid., pp. 59, 208–10.
81 B. H. Liddel Hart, *Foch: The Man of Orleans* (Boston 1932), pp. 454–6.
82 Lupfer, *Dynamics*, pp. 55–7.
83 Barnett, *Swordbearers*, p. 253.
84 Pedroncini, *Pétain*, pp. 211–12.
85 Barnett, *Swordbearers*, pp. 263–4.
86 Pedroncini, *Pétain*, p. 409.
87 Porch, *Marne*, pp. 125–8, 131–3, 177–8.
88 Joffre, *Memoires*, Vol. 1, p. 101.
89 Guy Pedroncini, *Les mutineries de 1917* (Paris, 1967), p. 250.
90 Pedroncini, *Pétain*, p. 28.
91 Porch, *Marne*, pp. 193–6, 204, 234.
92 Barnett, *Swordbearers*, p. 259.
93 Kaspi, *Le temps*, pp. 178–9.
94 Pedroncini, *Mutineries*, 241–2.
95 Porch, *Marne*, pp. 225–8.

[7]

Japan, 1914–18

IAN NISH
The London School of Economics and Political Science

Introduction

With the Restoration of imperial authority in Japan in 1868, the emperor assumed supreme command over both the army and the navy. Although these forces were not yet constituted, the principle of imperial authority was established at the outset. In the atmosphere of the Restoration the Japanese army, which had existed in the form of clan forces from time immemorial, was speedily brought into line with European armies. The professional warrior class (samurai), though not excluded from service in the new national army, often chose to seek other occupations, after being pensioned off. The army was to become a conscript one, drawn from males of every class, though conscription did not in practice affect all classes equally. Active service became obligatory for all aged over 20 and lasted for three years. Service with the reserve was compulsory for those who had completed their stint with the colors and lasted over four years. The army in 1914 exceeded half a million men.

By his prerogative the emperor had to appoint the minister of war, who was responsible for military administration (*gunsei*), and the chief of the general staff, who was responsible for military command (*gunrei*). The latter had by convention the right of direct access to the throne and was therefore separate from, and independent of, the civilian ministers of state. It was already the practice before 1914 for the minister of war (as also the minister of marine) not to be a civilian. Training was arranged through the staff college, the officers cadet school, and the various preparatory schools related to artillery, engineering, infantry, and cavalry, to the last of which special attention was given in the period down to 1914.

Immediately after the Meiji Restoration, the army and navy were controlled by one department; but in 1872 they were separated into independent departments of government. To give the navy a boost, the government, in the following year, employed British instructors on the staff of the Naval Academy set up in Tokyo. The Naval Academy subsequently moved to Etajima in the Inland Sea, while the Naval War College came to be located at

Tsukiji, Tokyo. The emperor appointed both the minister of marine and the chief of the naval general staff who, as in the case of the army, had the right of direct access to the throne. The dockyard at Yokosuka had been established before the Restoration in 1864, while the major naval arsenal at Kure was set up in 1874. It was perhaps natural that Japan should concentrate on expansion of the army with its older traditions rather than the 'new navy,' despite pleas to the contrary.

For various reasons the Meiji government gave the army a higher priority than the navy. First, an army based on conscript service was more vital for protection of the emperor and public order in the unstable 1870s. Second, it was much cheaper to operate an army than to build up a modern navy with ships imported from overseas. From 1894 this situation changed as Japan increasingly aspired to an international role. Thanks to the massive indemnity which Japan obtained from China in 1895, the navy made great strides thereafter. Inevitably intense inter-service rivalry developed from this time. There were naturally differences between the army and the navy. The personnel of the navy required a technical expertise, and promotion had to reflect this professionalism rather than feudal clan considerations. By contrast, the army – or at least the infantry – tended to be more traditionalist in approach.

There were also cultural differences between Japan and other countries which shaped the effectiveness of their armed services. The first of these was loyalty to the emperor as commander-in-chief and devotion to the imperial system. The Meiji constitution of 1889 may have been vague on the demarcation between the ministry and the general staff but there was no dispute over the loyalty of the servicemen of that generation. The soldier was obligated to give his life for the emperor or the country, a duty instilled by the Emperor Meiji's precepts to soldiers and sailors. It was not only that life was not regarded as something worth preserving in itself, as *seppuku* (or *harakiri*) showed; it was also the dogma that the Japanese soldier must never allow himself to be taken alive by an enemy or made a prisoner of war. It was ignoble and cowardly and a betrayal of the group to which he belonged, whether platoon, company, regiment, or nation. Hence the Japanese soldiers' code of no surrender to the enemy.

Then again there were certain well-established aspects of martial fervor in Japan. At least in the army there were traditional values and practices which can be traced back to the samurai and can be linked to *Bushido*, the way of the warrior. The Japanese Army clung to the mystique of military élan, which required infantrymen to advance and not retreat, and declined to consider fall-back positions. The code promised glory to anyone who distinguished himself on the field of battle or who showed self-sacrifice. Thus, the ordinary soldier was prepared to tolerate a relatively harsh regime, sometimes entailing cruel discipline and harsh conditions of great deprivation, and often involving corporal punishment, as was the custom in Japan before 1914.

The special characteristics of Japan's effort during the First World War require particular attention. Japan fought on the Allied side from the end of August 1914 onwards. Itō Masanori, in one of the standard textbooks about the history of Japanese defense, discusses the special characteristics of Japan's contributions to the world war of 1914–18. These included the attack on the German base in China at Tsingtao, combined with the occupation of various islands in Nanyō (sometimes called Micronesia); the operations in the Mediterranean Sea, when a force of three cruisers and twelve newly built destroyers was in 1917 sent to the aid of the Allies in what was described as 'the highest duty assigned to Japan'; and finally the expedition against the Bolsheviks in Siberia from 1918 onwards.[1] It will be observed that these operations were largely dependent on the navy.

It is perhaps more important to record occasions when Japan was asked to contribute and declined to do so. The requests made by Japan's allies were as follows:

(1) to send land forces to the Eastern Front;
(2) to send land forces to the Western Front;
(3) to send naval forces to the Mediterranean;
(4) to send a cruiser force to the American Atlantic coast;
(5) to send an expedition to the Gulf of Aden or the Red Sea.[2]

It should be understood that these Allied requests were presented over the course of the war, made in a haphazard way, sometimes official, sometimes unofficial, and were on the whole not pursued if they were once rejected by Japan. Rejection was not invariably total. Military supplies were sold on a large scale to the Russians for use on the Eastern Front, but men were not sent. Even when a compromise solution was reached with the Americans over sending troops to Siberia in 1918, the Japanese troops were to be confined strictly to eastern Siberia, and there was no question of sending them to European Russia. So far as the Western Front was concerned, there was no thought of sending land forces. On the other hand, in return for promises of a political kind from the Allies in January 1917, Japan did agree to assist with the patrolling of the Mediterranean (despite disagreements between the Cabinet and the naval general staff). Some Japanese vessels emerged into the Atlantic after the armistice in November 1918. But, on the whole, the Japanese wanted to avoid extending the range of their naval forces beyond the Mediterranean and to confine the activities of their land forces to the Far East.

Japan's military and naval effectiveness was not fully tested in combat experience during the First World War and, in view of the limited scale of its operations, conclusions about effectiveness are hard to draw. Japanese observers were very few on the battlefronts of Europe; Japan, therefore, tended to miss out on military developments which were taking place in the campaigns there.

Political Effectiveness

In the period under review Japanese military organizations had the same difficulties in obtaining a regular share of the national budget as were experienced in other states, but in some respects their task was easier. Japan was still a poor country in 1914. Militarily it had won a high reputation by its victory over Russia, but it had emerged from the war without an indemnity and with a great deal of new territory which required intensive investment. When Japan turned to the international money market, it discovered that its credit was not unlimited. International bankers seem to have taken the view that Japan had no great natural resources and few profitable industries and that it had incurred too heavy a foreign debt during the Russian war. This meant that the financial position after 1905 was one of stringency and that the armed services had to compete for scarce resources.

In general the military organizations were well placed to exert influence politically – and financially. In the twenty years from 1898 to 1918, the prime minister of Japan was a general or admiral six times, extending over thirteen years, and a civilian five times, extending over five and one-half years. This was not a predominance of military government but a reflection of the fact that those who had to appoint prime ministers found it more attractive to appoint military leaders rather than the bosses of the nascent political parties. These 'military' prime ministers were under pressure from two sides: from the military side asking for increased budgets and from the Diet seeking to cut budgets and often to question military-naval expenditure. Inevitably the army and navy became increasingly involved in politics and in the lobbying which that entailed.

The military had both constitutional and extra-constitutional powers. Their constitutional power lay in the right of direct access to the emperor which was enjoyed by generals and admirals. They had an extra-constitutional power through the body of the emperor's advisers – the *Genrō*, or Elder Statesmen, which included three with a military background (Yamagata, Ōyama, and, till 1902, Saigō). In addition there was the convention that the war and navy ministers had to be appointed respectively from generals and admirals on the active list.[3]

Such was in brief the balance of political power affecting the army and navy in the decade after 1912. If the Japanese fighting services had good political cards up their sleeves compared to those of other countries, there were on the other hand some things which told against them. The most important of these was competition between them which had existed since Japan came into being as a modern state. The army derived its leadership from the Chōshū clan, while the navy drew to a large extent on the Satsuma clan. These clans were rivals and, while their monopolistic power over high office was declining as the services expanded, clan power was still one vital factor affecting promotions around 1914.[4] Moreover political power had in the preceding four decades been dominated by Chōshū personalities, and it was one of the grievances of the navy that the army had benefited disproportionately therefrom.

A subsidiary point of difficulty was that the National Defense plan drawn up in 1907 had pointed to Russia as the likely adversary of the army, while the United States was the enemy contemplated by the navy. It was not that war with either was thought to be imminent; these countries were chosen for budgetary purposes in order to enable estimates to be made by the services of the cost of out-building their nearest rivals.[5]

The budgetary position during the war was much affected by what had gone before in the political crisis of 1912–13. In the summer of 1912 the war minister, General Uehara, had demanded that the army be increased by two divisions so that the newly acquired colony of Korea could be adequately garrisoned. When the Cabinet and the minister failed to reach a compromise, Uehara resigned and brought down the ministry. When the successor ministry was set up, the navy refused to nominate a navy minister without assurances that its position would be maintained *pari passu* with the army. The next Cabinet, formed in February 1913, was a Satsuma Cabinet led by Admiral Yamamoto which disallowed the two-division army expansion and threatened to sanction a substantial expansion of the navy. It was, however, forced to resign by the Siemens scandal, in which senior naval officers were implicated for taking bribes. While Yamamoto was not personally involved, he chose to resign; and the navy came under a cloud for a while as the war in Europe began.

The debates of 1914–18 were not about the war effort; they were about *kokubō*, or national defense. As we have seen, Japan's main contribution to the war effort was made by the efforts of its navy, and even the army's operations could not have been carried out without naval support. An important newcomer, Admiral Katō Tomosaburō, came to power as navy minister in 1915 committed to the idea of an eight-eight fleet, but he adopted a mild line of approach, suggesting that an increase in the size of the navy was part of the logic of the great war. The Cabinet accepted in principle a program for an eight-four fleet, bearing in mind the prosperity that war had brought to the Japanese economy and to exports of war matériel in particular. When the Terauchi ministry came into power, it was necessary to hold a general election early in 1917 in which one of the political parties, the Seiyūkai, obtained an overwhelming majority. This did not affect the government but it made it necessary for the army and navy to lobby with the party leaders in competition with one another. While the war minister argued for an eighteen-year expansion program for the army, Katō asked for approval to start work on two additional cruisers and thus create an eight-six fleet. Eventually the party obtained safeguards over the proposals for the increased taxation which was inevitably required and the arms expansion plan funded by tax increases was passed by the Diet. Financial constraints, however, meant that both the army and the navy had to be content with less than they desired. Fortunately the entry of the United States into the war in April 1917 took some of the fire out of the naval crisis because the United States, against whom Japan had been building, now became an ally and invited naval cooperation in the defense of the eastern Pacific. Moreover the newly constructed wartime alliance had convinced Washington of the need for destroyer construction. Accordingly Admiral Katō may have been relieved to report to the Diet in 1918 that he would prefer to see how the naval situation developed globally before making decisions about further expansion.[6] On a more practical plane, Japan's Megata mission to the United States to ask for economic cooperation including steel exports for naval shipbuilding was unsuccessful, and it is doubtful if the yards could have fulfilled an enhanced shipbuilding programme. The rhetoric of arms expansion continued, but caution prevailed.

When the political party Cabinet under Prime Minister Hara took office in September 1918, Japan was in confusion, with widespread rice riots. This brought home to the army and navy that a conflict between them for scarce resources was out of date. The newcomer ministers for the army and the navy conceded to Hara that they would shelve their expansion plans for the time being in the national interest. The budget was introduced without tax increases for defense purposes. With the end of the war and the rumors that new international institutions would put pressure on governments to bring about armament reduction, the problem changed. But Hara met the armed services halfway by giving assurances and even long-term commitments for arms expansion, initially favoring the navy and thereafter the army. Even this undertaking was subject to review internationally as happened at the Washington Conference of 1921.[7]

In general, budgeting for military-naval expenditure had a very high priority in Japan. The politicians were ready to tighten the nation's belt and impose further taxation if they were persuaded of the need for such expenditure. There were debates at all levels about the security problem. Possibly the opposition to defense expenditure was more muted in Japan than elsewhere.

By 1914 armament industries and shipbuilding yards had been established in Japan for a decade. The basic industry was Yawata Ironworks, set up in 1899; but Japan was weak in natural resources and was dependent on imports, especially from Korea and Manchuria. Japan benefited from its association with Hanyehping enterprises in central China. Army requirements were supplied in the main by the Ōsaka military arsenal and the Wakamatsu government iron foundry. Naval requirements were met by the Kure naval steel foundry or the Japan steel works, a company financed partly by Vickers Armstrong and partly by Japanese private companies, possibly with help from the Japanese government. On the shipbuilding side, Japan's weakness was shown up in 1917, when its supplies of steel were cut off by the United States.[8]

A frequent complaint in the army was that its weakness was in matériel not personnel. In 1914 many troops were still armed with out-of-date rifles (the so-called thirtieth-year model), which were of doubtful value as combat weapons, led to accusations of bad marksmanship by Japanese troops, and were certainly no match for those manufactured in Europe at the time. Needless to say, the Japanese tried to avoid imports wherever possible and were by 1914 largely able to meet their own needs, except for the building of destroyers and aircraft.

The conscription system operated in Japan. Apart from such *causes célèbres* as the issue of the two divisions to Korea, there were no problems about the quantity of recruits. The number of those trying to avoid being conscripted was small, but steps had to be taken in 1914 to prevent abuses on the part of students whose service was postponed. A number of young men who, though not bona fide students, had managed to evade service by keeping their names on the books of a college (which they may possibly never even have entered), thereby became eligible.

As regards quality, the standard of intelligence of recruits was high, and they were enthusiastic and ambitious. Health and physique were good.

Training was intense; and the fortitude shown by Japanese troops in Manchuria in 1904–5 was a testimony to their high quality. Some observers expressed the view that the Japanese troops were (as fighting matériel) as formidable as troops of any other nation.

Strategic Effectiveness

In Japan's supreme experience of war, the war with Russia in 1904, the Japanese had boasted of the degree of coordination which had been achieved between the civil and military arms of government. It is most strongly expressed in the Japanese cabinet's report to the emperor on 8 April 1905: 'After the start of her war against Russia, our country took the initiative as a result of achieving *perfect coordination in diplomacy and military strategy*.'[9] The same notion is also adopted by two recent scholars to some extent:

> In the quest for empire that commenced in earnest during the closing decade of the 19th century, the Meiji oligarchy consistently and brilliantly coordinated the military capabilities of the nation in the conduct of foreign affairs. During these years, moreover, military planning and policies always remained subordinated to political leadership.[10]

> The Japanese oligarchs, as the decision-making group, showed these outstanding capabilities in the war against Russia: realism and flexibility in the formulation and execution of policy, the ability to maintain, on the whole, good coordination between civilian government and military authorities, and the ability to resist pressure.[11]

Professor Okamoto, the latter of these two authors, while admitting that one major reason for victory in 1905 was the successful coordination between Japanese civilian and military leaders in the policy-making process, asks how effective this coordination was in reality. I have myself suggested that there was less perfection and coordination than might be imagined. In the run-up to the war in 1903 and 1904 there were significant tensions at various levels: there were the tensions of a fundamental kind between the army and the navy over strategy; there were major disagreements among the ministers and among the *genrō*; and consensus could only be achieved with difficulty and without much compromise through the offices of the extra-constitutional agency, the *genrō*. Yet, even if reconciliation was less perfect than government statements alleged, it is nonetheless significant that 'perfect coordination' was claimed.

In 1903, restraint was advocated from two quarters: the Elder Statesmen, especially Marquis Itō, and the navy. It was not that the navy was opposed to the taking of Korea in general or to the army's plan for a continental expedition to Korea in particular. It did, however, insist that Japan should try to ensure command of the seas beforehand. The navy was determined not to be taken for granted. There was a long history of army-navy tension, of which this was only the latest example. The army, because of its dependence on the navy for transports to convey troops to Korea and Manchuria and for naval vessels to escort them there, had to wait until the Navy declared the moment right for starting the operation. Meanwhile the Foreign Ministry had to spin out the negotiations.[12]

In the 1914–18 period there were often attempts to reach consensus between the civilian and military leaders in Japan so that there should be a consistency between strategic means and political ends. It can be seen in two episodes: the confusion over the Twenty-one Demands imposed on China in 1915, and the decision to delay the military intervention in Siberia in 1918 until the agreement of the United States had been obtained. The latter case is worth further study later. The former will be pursued here.

After Japanese armies had occupied the Tsingtao leased territory, there was much discussion in Japan about the administrative requirements on which it would have to insist. Eventually a package of terms which went down in history as the Twenty-one Demands was devised and presented to the Chinese president on 18 January 1915. These demands were coordinated by the Foreign Ministry and prepared by Koike Chozo, a senior official, under the influence of and after consultation with the military. Professor Nomura Otojiro has published a letter dated 20 August 1914 from General Akashi Motojiro, vice chief of the general staff, to General Terauchi Masatake, governor general of Korea and one of the leaders of the military faction in Japan, which, he claims, anticipates in many ways the Twenty-one Demands. It argues that the instability of China was a danger to the peace of the Far East and calls upon the Japanese government to come to some definite understanding with China on the subject: 'our aim is not limited to the leased territory of Tsingtao and the Shantung railway alone. There is no reason why all pending questions with China cannot be sorted out at this juncture.'[13] Would it not be opportune to secure recognition of the definite responsibilities of the Tokyo government for these matters from China? If it is true that the military had a role in initiating the approach which resulted in the Twenty-one Demands, it is also true that the military contributed much advice behind the scenes leading to the formulation of the demands. While it would be wrong to think that the military was the sole factor in this diplomatic initiative, there is evidence that it had the dominant voice. Although it is nowhere spelt out in so many words, Japan seems to have had two over-riding goals during the period of the First World War: to keep on the best possible terms with old and new allies, and to pursue ambitions on the Asian mainland. Over the Twenty-one Demands it was the second of these goals which came to the fore, though in attaining its ends Japan had to make concessions to China under pressure from other countries.

The leaders of the army and navy were generally able to communicate with the political leadership regarding militarily logical goals through direct representations, through lobbying, and through propaganda. They were able to influence but not to dictate the decisions. The political leadership had to take account of a wider range of considerations than did the service leaders, i.e., the costs of the proposal and the need to avoid alienating international opinion. A good example of this is the Siberian Intervention of 1918, where there was in the army a strong interventionist group which was for six months held in check. In discussions in the *Gaikō Chōsakai* (Advisory Council on Foreign Relations), which had by 1918 become one of the important decision-making bodies, a cautious group of politicians (with some army participation) decided that they did not favor intervention unless they received the advance approval of the United States.

In the 1914–18 period Japan had been asked for military-naval aid by its allies on many occasions and would, other things being equal, have wished to respond to these calls on political grounds in order to improve its slightly flawed international image. In fact, because of considerations of force strength and structure, Japan eventually turned them down. It would be instructive – but not, alas, feasible here – to consider the individual requests and the internal mechanisms in Japan which led to their being rejected. We shall, however, consider in detail one of these instances where the Japanese finally agreed to meet the requests of their European allies, the case of naval assistance in the Mediterranean Sea.

In January 1917, because of the large losses incurred as a result of the German submarine campaign in the Atlantic and the declarations regarding unrestricted submarine warfare, Britain (and France) asked on three occasions for Japan to send a squadron to the Mediterranean. Japan replied that, since Britain had made it clear at the start of the war that the role of the Japanese Navy should be regarded as limited to the eastern seas, its request to send a force to the Mediterranean seemed to be very illogical. However, Rear Admiral Akiyama Saneyuki, returned from a world tour as an emissary of the naval general staff, argued strongly in favor of sending a squadron to the Mediterranean on the ground that, though there would be danger and possibly casualties, it would contribute to a greater understanding of naval techniques and technology and lead to the improvement of weaponry. But there was a strong group in the general staff who opposed this course on the ground that 'for Japan to operate in a war zone which is of no direct interest to the empire will not only cause disaster to her ships but also put at risk the valuable bulwark (of the state).'[14] They argued that despite all the 'academic benefits,' it was futile to operate in such a remote war zone regardless of the security of Japan itself which was the whole purpose of the navy's existence. By sending a force to the Mediterranean, Japan would be leaving its home islands undefended and vulnerable.

After further calls for increased inter-Allied cooperation, the Japanese came round to favoring the British request. Admiral Shimamura Hayao, the chief of the naval general staff, who was not reconciled to this outcome, took the view that

> it is necessary to lay down new vessels straight away as replacements for the squadron sent to the Mediterranean.
>
> I am thinking not just of sinkings or unforeseen accidents but, if we are able to operate actively in the Mediterranean, it will mean a substantial reduction of our capacity.[15]

Again there is the evident anxiety here that an expedition to European waters would leave Japan vulnerable in home waters. Nonetheless, on 10 February the Cabinet accepted Britain's request on the lines of the navy minister's recommendation. The navy organized two squadrons, the first consisting of two ships to go to the Capetown station, the second to the Mediterranean station. In April a further special squadron was sent to Australia and New Zealand; but it was only held there till the end of 1917. The Capetown and Mediterranean squadrons served for two years; and it was not until August 1919 that they were disestablished.

An important change in national policy had been made for political reasons. This had shown up divisions within the navy between those willing to comply (*hakensetsu*) and those opposing (*hantaisetsu*). In general, it was part of the worldwide naval debate between the alternatives of concentration and expansion. In the Japanese context the naval general staff argued that the force left over after the ships were dispersed beyond Singapore was not adequate in size to cope with the 'Anglo-Saxon naval giants.'[16] They appear only to have agreed to it on condition that it would strengthen their navy's case for new shipbuilding targets.

This acquiescence, of course, did not mean that the Japanese Cabinet was meekly submissive to the Allied requests. Japan responded to Britain that the Diet could only be convinced of the merits of sending such a large slice of its fleet if it received assurances of something tangible in return: an immediate promise by the Allies to support Japan's claims to former German possessions which it then occupied. On 14 February Britain acceded 'with pleasure' to Japan's claims to the disposal of Germany's rights and possessions in islands north of the equator at any peace conference. Unofficially Britain thought that Japan had acquired considerable war gains at a relatively low price. The French and Russians followed suit and gave the inter-Allied guarantees which Japan had required. Such was the political price to be paid for a greater Japanese naval contribution.[17]

The Japanese squadron under Rear Admiral Satō Tetsutarō in the light cruiser *Akashi* reached the naval base of Malta in April 1917. It consisted of eight of the new destroyers which had been built with great speed in Japanese yards at the start of the war. At the first Allied naval conference it was agreed unanimously that the Japanese should be used for escort duties to protect Mediterranean convoys against submarine attack. The *Akashi* was replaced by the cruiser *Izumo* and the *Nisshin*; and four more destroyers were added to the expedition. The Japanese commander placed himself at the disposal of the British. By an exceptional procedure two British trawlers and two destroyers were given over to the Japanese for the duration of the war and were manned by Japanese crews. The losses which those who were oppposed to cooperating (the *hantaisetsu* party) had foreseen did not take place. Only the destroyer *Sasaki* was torpedoed and, because of delays in refitting, remained out of action for most of the war.[18]

Itō Masanori, the naval historian, is probably reflecting a Japanese naval view when he writes that in the Mediterranean operations the Allies had given the Imperial Japanese Navy their highest responsibility during the war: the protection of 750,000 Allied soldiers.[19]

Japan's allies in the 1914–18 war were Britain, because of the Anglo-Japanese alliance of 1902; France and Russia, by virtue of the Declaration of London; Russia, by the Russo-Japanese alliance of 1916; and the United States, since it joined the wartime coalition in 1917.[20] Japan did not integrate its strategy with its allies in that it was not represented at Allied War

Councils, though it did send senior officers, both army and navy, to Europe in order to inspect the Allied campaigns. Japan's war effort was so disparate with those of the other Allies that it would be far-fetched to speak of coordination or integration.

The British alliance in particular was going through a bad patch during the war years. All alliances have their ups and downs, but the British felt that the Japanese had been disloyal to the alliance in some respects and spoke of the alliance as 'the present hollow friendship.' The two allies were operating in different strategic areas and, apart from naval cooperation in the early months and after 1917, there was little scope for integrating strategic objectives.[21]

On the Japanese side, it chose to pursue its own national objectives in declaring war against Germany, for so long as the outcome of the war was uncertain there was a perhaps understandable desire among Japanese to distance themselves from their allies. Yamagata, the most senior Chōshū general, was suspicious of too great an attachment to Britain and sought to spread Japan's commitments. It was he and his faction which took Japan into its alliance with tsarist Russia in July 1916. Yet it was a difficult time for many Japanese Army officers who had been trained by Germans, had many friends there, and looked to them for strategic effectiveness. It was a case of divided loyalties which only the outcome of the battle resolved.

The war started with a diplomatic disagreement between Japan and its prime ally, Britain, over the latter's suspicions about Japan's future intentions towards China. When Japan declared war on Germany on 23 August, therefore, this news was not ecstatically received in London. Since one of Japan's objectives was to drive Germany from East Asia, it was natural that Japan should attack the German-leased territory of Tsingtao. After a naval blockade of the port, troops landed on 2 September at Lungkow on Chinese territory well beyond the German base. Meanwhile a British expeditionary force arrived at Laoshan Bay close to the German lease on 24 September. The arrangement was that the British force, which contributed only 1,650 men to the force, should operate under the Japanese commander-in-chief. With whatever good grace Tokyo accepted Britain's cooperation in the expedition, the military authorities on the spot did not welcome British interference since their commanders had of course to arrange for food, horses, and fodder for the British troops. Moreover they cannot have been unaware that one of the purposes of Britain's 'presence' was to act as a watchdog over Japanese activities. Doubtless at one level the strategic objectives of Japan and Britain were the same, that is, to force the surrender of the Germans at Tsingtao, but at other levels their strategic objectives were probably widely different and there was no hope of ironing out the inconsistencies.[22]

The other instance of Allied activity which is worth examining is the Siberian intervention of 1918. After the Bolshevik Revolution, Japan's European allies urged upon it the necessity of safeguarding the vast Allied supplies which were to be found in warehouses in Vladivostok and preventing them from falling into Bolshevik hands. They would have been happy to give Japan a free hand, but the Wilson administration would not agree, and the Japanese leaders declined to send an expedition to the area of the Amur basin unless they were invited to do so by the United States. After lengthy discussions, the United States and Japan reached an agreement (without really consulting their European allies) to undertake an inter-Allied expedition on 2 August.

Intervention forces were sent to Vladivostok in September. Within a month there were major Allied disagreements about numbers. An arbitrary figure of 7,000 from each of the Allies had been specified by the United States, although it bore little relationship to the actual numbers required for the vastness of Siberia. Indeed Britain, France, and Italy had earlier urged that Japan be allowed to send a force far larger than the stipulated 7,000. During the negotiations with Washington, Japan had avoided committing itself over the numbers to be sent and the zones which would be covered by operations.

Despite the initial Japanese distaste for a joint intervention, they finally agreed to it. However, once the expedition had begun, they showed a spirit of independence by dispatching a force of 70,000 men as against the contingents sent by Britain, France, and the United States of 7,000 men each. By the time the Japanese were left alone to face the Bolsheviks after the withdrawal of the Allied contingents, they extended their operations to Sakhalin off the coast of the Maritime Provinces.[23]

There was no meeting of minds between Japan and the United States and no real consultation with other members of the Alliance. Japan wanted a free hand; the United States wanted to keep Japan on a leash. The inevitable result was that the negotiations became for the Japanese an exercise in obfuscation. They publicly accepted the substance of the American guidelines while making considerable reservations by way of private explanations to Washington. In these circumstances there could hardly have been an effective integration of strategic objectives. This point is touched on by Professor Morley in what is still the most authoritative study in English on this subject:

> [In the first week of July 1918] the Japanese had repeatedly insisted that [they] could not operate effectively beyond the Amur basin. But would Japan be willing to operate even there if the purpose were restricted solely to aiding the Czechoslovaks [as the Americans wanted]? What the American officials did not know was that their proposal was to force Japan to a decision about the long-standing plans of the military interventionists for a large-scale independent expedition to Siberia.[24]

It goes without saying that political agreements of this kind made in advance of military actions very often do not hold good when they come to be tested. Sometimes when the inadequacies of these agreements are discovered, they can be overcome by practical arrangements between commanders on the ground. In the case of the Siberian Intervention, the gap between Japan and the United States in particular was so great that there was little scope for one side inducing the other to adopt consistent strategic objectives. It was a classic example of muddled aims and conflicting policies where the friction grew and grew the longer the international action continued.

Operational Effectiveness

We have earlier discussed integration between the military and civilians. Here we have to discuss integration between the army and the navy. We may summarize the position by saying that the Japanese armed services were not adequately integrated in the 1914–18 period because of two factors, clan jealousies and professional pride. There had always been a resentment on the part of the Satsuma-based navy against the Chōshū-based army, which had hitherto held a largely undisputed dominance. The first breakthrough by the navy was the appointment of Admiral Yamamoto as prime minister in 1913 and, while his ministry was shortlived, it was a shot across the bows of Chōshū superiority. Professional pride was also a factor acting against integration. During the war of 1904–5, that factor had been overcome among other things by the intervention of the Elder Statesmen (*genrō*). In the aftermath of the war, the *genrō* began to play a less prominent part in affairs just at the time when the army and navy were becoming more overt in their demands from politicians. The governments of the day tended to temporize rather than coordinate the policies of the armed services by the creation of an effective inter-service committee.

There was of course some coordinating machinery. During the Sino-Japanese and Russo-Japanese wars, the *Dai-Hon'ei* (Imperial General Headquarters) had been set up. But it was a wartime device and, strictly speaking, could only be established after a declaration of war had been issued by the emperor. With the return of peace the *Dai-Hon'ei* lapsed.[25] There was sufficient willingness to cooperate to allow the general staffs of both services in 1907 to come together to formulate the *Teikoku Kokubō Hōshin* (imperial defense policy), but in the implementation of that policy, the army did not follow the navy in its desire to prepare the way for war with the United States.

When Japan declared war in 1914 no *Dai-Hon'ei* was created. Instead the government relied on the *Bōmu Kaigi* (Council of Defense Affairs), which had been set up in April 1914 after the military budgeting crises of the previous years. It was indeed a body to reconcile the needs of the army and navy but, as it worked out, it became a device to avoid civilian embarrassment over budgeting rather than a device to coordinate strategic thinking. Japan went through the war without anything like Britain's Committee of Imperial Defence. It could be said that the needs of Japan in the First World War did not warrant the creation of a special body for the purpose.[26]

When the general staffs came together to revise their National Defense Policy in 1918 there was no permanent mechanism created to monitor army-navy tensions. There was reluctance to tamper with the concept of an autonomous service, acting independently and responsible to the emperor alone. This scheme of things was to persist for the next quarter century.[27] At the same time there had to be army-navy coordination for the operations at Tsingtao and Siberia.

Flexibility depends on the mental attitudes of individuals. It is necessary therefore to take a look at the training of the Japanese officer corps. In our period, the potential officer would have to go through either the Military Academy (*Rikugun Shikan Gakkō*) or the Naval Academy (*Kaigun Gakkō*), which were the only channels for entry. From the age of 13 onwards he might have attended a preparatory college (*Yōnen Gakkō*). Entry to all was difficult and the colleges tended to become elitist. Following graduation, an officer could, after spending some years in service, apply for admission to the staff colleges (*Rikugun-Kaigun Daigakkō*).

The Japanese officer corps had both strengths and weaknesses. It was intensely loyal and patriotic and gallant. The officers were single-minded: they were devoted students of their profession to the exclusion of outside interests. On maneuvers and in action, as both the war with Russia and the rigorous and punishing campaign against Tsingtao showed, they had great endurance and displayed much bravery. Naval officers whose experience included cruises overseas tended to be more internationalist in outlook and were, as befitted members of a technical service, perhaps more scientific and rationalist in their approach.

The weaknesses were that army officers tended to be narrow and poorly informed, having lived during their training a claustrophobic existence excluding outside interests. In preparing for a military career, they had from a young age been cocooned and removed from ordinary society. Ingrown and narrow-minded, they developed a dogmatic self-confidence in their own breed. They tended to be poor linguists and were not greatly influenced by forces outside Japan. There are, of course, many distinguished exceptions to this, more on the navy than the army side. Even on the navy side, however, one expert writes of a 'dearth of creative leadership.'[28]

In both cases there was the factor of *seishin kyōiku* (moral or spirit education). It tended to make the Japanese believe that they had a special quality so that, even if they were numerically inferior to an adversary and their equipment less adequate, they could yet survive in a struggle. This tended to place a premium on military decisions based on gambles and deflect them from drawing up situation reports based on logic. This was surely not a healthy trend since it placed decision making on a non-intellectual basis.

Moral education has many aspects: morale, discipline, fighting spirit, and so on. It was observed in both the army and the navy but was especially to be found in army units and colleges. It was equivalent to inculcating the military virtues from Japan's feudal past. It appears to have started in the Meiji period (1868–1911) with the cultivation of old clan loyalties, the so-called *Bushidō* code. During the period of Taishō Democracy (1912–25), which covers the period of this essay, army commanders were particularly worried about the influences present in a changing Japanese society and the possibility that socialist and anarchist ideas would spread to the troops by way of newspapers and pamphlets. However, spiritual education was still on a small scale compared to the late 1930s.[29] For the present it implied reverence for the emperor and what might be called the moral code of the soldier: loyalty to the group or the team and willingness to sacrifice one's life for the emperor and the service, that is, the notion that a soldier should not be taken alive as a prisoner of war.

This brings us back to the question of whether Japan's army and navy, with their narrow training, were mobile and flexible in their responses. This question is part of a broader, controversial debate on which vast treatises can be, and have been, written: are the Japanese as a people original or imitative? My own instinct is to think that they are a bit of both. My reaction to the question of mobility and flexibility is much the same: the Japanese Army and

Navy could be eminently flexible at times and equally inflexible at other times. This means that I treat with skepticism the contemporary assessment of Britain's military attaché in Tokyo in the embassy annual report for 1912 when he writes: 'From a military point of view, his [the army officer's] most conspicuous failing is the national one – that of a lack of originality, coupled with slowness in arriving at a decision.'[30] Foreign observers were prone to make assertions of this kind, which one is reluctant to reject out of hand because they were judgments of contemporaries who had a unique chance to look at the Japanese scene. However, such stereotypes – and references to 'national characteristics' – should be accepted only with reserve. Perhaps there was an outward appearance of stability and cohesion which may have suggested immobility to the outsider, but it was a doubtful conclusion. At the military academies cadets were told to be mobile and flexible. Many of them turned out like that and were so as junior officers.

Nevertheless there was a lot of deadwood at the top. Since promotion was largely on a seniority basis rather than on merit or brilliance, it would have been surprising if it had been otherwise. One illustration of this is the Japanese attitude towards cavalry. The war with Russia had in large measure been a cavalry war. Many army leaders were wedded to the idea of equestrian skills. Indeed one of the branches of the service in which spectacular improvement was made between 1904 and 1914 was the cavalry. The horses had been greatly improved in physique, while the riders had made great progress in their horsemanship. Cavalry officers were jealous of the encroachments of others. Captain Malcolm Kennedy, who went out to Japan from the Western Front in 1917, tells an interesting story about Major General Yoshibashi:

> Horrified by the newly issued cavalry training manual (1920), which did away with massed cavalry charges and decreed that something in the nature of mounted infantry tactics would be more appropriate under modern conditions, the old gentleman protested to the General Staff and urged reconsideration. His recommendations went unheeded, so he disembowelled himself in the traditional warrior manner, by way of stressing his conviction that the contemplated changes would be disastrous for Japan.[31]

It was of course hard for the cavalry in any country to adapt to new circumstances. Perhaps there is a sense in which the Japanese Army, with its strong traditions and its respect for elders, was slower than others to make the necessary transition. On the more general point of flexibility we may leave the last word to Captain Kennedy. He reports:

> When late in 1917 I arrived in Japan for the first time and saw Japanese troops on parade and in training, I noted that they were still armed with much the same weapons, and employed much the same tactics, as had been in use in the British and other Western armies in what seemed those far-off days of August 1914.[32]

It might be concluded from this that the Japanese Army was slow and backward, immobile and inflexible. Yet the truth was that there were considerable budgetary constraints. When staff members went on tours of the

European battlefields, as they did in great numbers, they were not particularly positive in the lessons they drew. Those who had ideas for innovation found that these were in most cases ruled out because of limitations on military-naval expenditure.[33]

In order to illustrate the capacity of the Japanese military to adopt technology available at the time, we may cite the case of applying aviation to the conduct of war. Considerable steps had been taken by the various European nations by 1914. The Japanese seem to have reacted slowly: as a subject of military study, aeronautics was still in its infancy compared to foreign countries. The army evidently reacted more slowly than the navy. In 1913 the army had five planes: a Bleriot, a Farman, a Wright, a Grade, and one designed by Captain Tokugawa. An 'aeronautical establishment' was built at Tokorozawa. Yet by 1911 the navy had extended the period of training at Etajima Naval College to three years and four months to allow for the teaching of aeronautics, a new discipline. By the time the operations against Tsingtao took place in 1914, aircraft from the navy bombed ships in the harbor, the wireless station, army camps, and so on. At the end of the war, when the various European agents came to induce Japan to buy wartime aircraft, it was the navy which again showed most interest.[34] Under the influence of Admiral Yamamoto Isoroku (later of Pearl Harbor fame), special testing grounds and training sites were set up at Kasumigaura, north-east of Tokyo. If the field of aeronautics is anything to judge by, it would appear that the Japanese were ready to adjust to new technology which had to be imported in this case from overseas.

There is a sense in which the Japanese were aware of backwardness in their technology. That was allegedly one of the reasons why they declined to send troops to the Western Front during the war years. Because they did not take up the invitation, they did not pick up the new skills which developed so fast under war conditions. So, as Captain Kennedy observed in 1917, the Japanese fell progressively behind. In the supporting activities which any army has to supply, the Japanese experience was patchy, sometimes successful, sometimes unsuccessful.

The use of intelligence was well developed in Japan. The Japanese felt that they had to make up for their inferiority in numbers and equipment by exploiting the lessons of intelligence.[35] While we know of the individual exploits of intelligence officers, we understandably know less of the specific use to which the information they supplied was put at Imperial Headquarters. Yet it would appear that during the Russian war Japanese intelligence men were resourceful and enterprising: they produced good information on China and on Russian strength in the Far East; they exploited imaginatively not just the military weaknesses of their enemy but also its political weaknesses; they exploited not just its weaknesses at the front but also the unpopularity of the regimes at home, especially the opposition in Finland and Poland to the Russian policies of assimilation.[36]

During the war of 1914–18, the Japanese made good use of intelligence during the campaign against Tsingtao. When we come to the Siberian campaign of 1918, Japan's intelligence preparations were as thorough as they had been during the war with Russia in 1904, when it had agents in Siberia,

Manchuria, Korea, and China. Japan's aim was to prevent the spread of Bolshevism to East Asia, and the spread of the contagion thence to the Japanese islands themselves, so the Japanese Army and Navy had a strong motive in promoting this intelligence work. In January 1918 the army sent Major General Nakajima Masatake, a Russian linguist, to Vladivostok with the object of building up a network of anti-Bolshevik sympathisers. Even though the Siberian intervention was still some months off, intelligence agents were circulating in north China, Mongolia, and especially the Amur basin in order to maintain relations with all the resistance groups led by Semenov, Khorvat, and Kolchak. These military-political functions continued to be an area of great importance down to the end of the Siberian intervention in 1922.[37]

Other military support systems presented a mixed picture. Japanese Army and Navy medical services were first-rate. The Japanese Red Cross Society was probably better organized and more generously supported than in any other country.

Communications and transportation, on the other hand, were areas where the Japanese were inferior. The engineers who were responsible for both had good enough bridging equipment but there was an absence of reliable bridges in Japan, Korea, and Manchuria, the main areas for army operations, and this made the use of heavy trucks and tanks virtually impossible. Mechanical transport was relatively scarce and could only be realistically employed in towns in Japan. Wireless, which was also an engineer's responsibility, was very much in its infancy in the army. Signaling was also weak. The Japanese had an unshakeable faith (derived from the Russian war) in the field telephone to the exclusion of semaphore.

Using communication in its wider sense, the Japanese services believed in fighting wars in secret. They had not encouraged military attachés and journalists to go to the front in 1904. Because of the British alliance, Britain was rather favored and knew more about the Japanese forces in the 1900s and 1910s than any other power. During the war of 1914–18, the Japanese did not disseminate their actions and ideas unduly. Thus, a recent book has told us that 'the Japanese naval units occupied Ponape, Truk, Palau and Angaur in the Carolines and Saipan in the Marianas by October 1914. The Japanese naval headquarters announced only the capture of the tiny Jaluit atoll in the Marshalls.'[38] If this information is true, it is a remarkable instance of reticence. There was in any case a good deal of secretiveness on the part of the Japanese forces and the navy and army ministries. When Japanese newspapermen got hold of good stories of Japanese action, they often had to face a rigorous press censorship which was applied to quite trivial aspects of military actions. We do not know enough about the motives for this but it may have been the result of the military's intense professionalism, or the attitude that military operations were not the business of the general public.

Tactical Effectiveness

It is a little hard to generalize about tactical effectiveness on the basis merely of the Tsingtao campaign or the Siberian expedition. There was probably adequate integration of infantry, cavalry, and artillery; but integration still appears to have presented many problems at the tactical level. There were rivalries between various sectors of the army. Some units had a bad reputation. Thus, the Ōsaka regiments were sometimes held to be less dedicated, supposedly on the ground that those troops who came from an urban and industrial background were less fit and less obedient than those from farming backgrounds. It would seem that, while there was a great patriotism overall in the army and navy, there could also be intense competitiveness between units.

Generalization is difficult over Japan's tactical conceptions, which emphasized surprise and a rapid exploitation of opportunities. In general the Japanese in their training placed great emphasis on surprise attack, that is, attack at a moment or locale inconvenient for the enemy. There are many instances of night attack during the war with Russia and the campaign in Tsingtao. On the other hand, Japanese set-piece attacks at maneuvers revolved around the regimental flag, which was carried prominently.[39] There are probably social reasons which explain this paradox.

Morale was not a major problem because the calibre of soldiers and sailors was high. Only the flower of the nation was chosen during the examination for conscripts. They were chosen for good health and physique. After training they showed remarkable qualities of stamina and endurance under adverse conditions. The siege of Port Arthur in 1904–5 and the battle of Mukden were fought under hostile weather conditions. So too was the advance against Tsingtao in 1914.[40] The willingness of the conscript army to accept hardship was remarkable. In a pre-mechanized age of warfare the Japanese soldier could be relied on to march great distances carrying a full pack (of an unnecessarily burdensome kind) without demur.

Training in the army and navy inculcated ideas of teamwork which came naturally to most Japanese. Cohesion at the unit level was not a problem. The Japanese are used to a corporate leadership and corporate decision making in civilian life. There is every reason to believe that this applied equally in the context of the army and the navy.

While there is a good deal of conflicting data and sentimentalism about relations between officers, NCOs, and enlisted personnel, the burden of evidence tends to suggest that relations between them were better than in other armies and navies.[41] By and large, Japanese officers, being intensely professional and having often risen from the ranks, were conscientious in attending to the needs of their men. In the main, this was reciprocated by loyalty on the part of the enlisted men. It would appear that at this level there was a good deal of mutual respect.[42]

Training in the army seems to have been directed at this stage of Japan's development towards the attack. The military academy dogma which was uppermost was: 'There's no parry like a thrust.' As in the big battles of the Russo-Japanese war, the emphasis was on advance and attack, regardless of casualties. Fear of loss of life was not a major constraint on military decision making. At the annual grand maneuvers generally held in the autumn, the organizers concentrated on advances which culminated in a charge under circumstances which were unrealistic in the warfare of the First World War.

By contrast defensive tactics were hardly taught. The wars with China (1894) and Russia (1904) had not suggested the need for defense. It was therefore highly doubtful how the Japanese armies would react if and when they were up against a superior enemy and were compelled to adopt defensive tactics.[43]

The Japanese Army in 1914–18 was still fighting with the methods which had proved successful in 1904–5 against Russia. Since it had no experience of fighting on the Western Front, it had scarcely updated its weapons from the previous war and still employed the tactics applicable to it.

Notes

1 Itō Masanori, *Kokubōshi* (Tokyo, 1941), ch. 5.
2 W. R. Braisted, *The United States Navy in the Pacific, 1909–22* (Austin, Tex., 1971), pp. 305, 336.
3 S. Okamoto, *The Japanese Oligarchy and the Russo-Japanese War* (New York, 1970), pp. 33–40; J. B. Crowley, 'Japan's Military Foreign Policies,' in J. W. Morley, *Japan's Foreign Policy, 1868–1941* (New York, 1974), pp. 26–8.
4 This view about the residual power of the clans is disputed, e.g., by S. Asada, 'The Japanese Navy and the United States,' in Dorothy Borg and S. Okamoto, *Pearl Harbor as History* (New York, 1973), p. 225.
5 Tsunoda Jun, *Manshū Mondai to Kokubō Hōshin* (Tokyo, 1967), pp. 700–11.
6 Hora Tomio, *Dai 1-ji Sekai Taisen* (Tokyo, 1966), pp. 63–4; *Yamamoto Gombei to Kaigun* (Tokyo, 1966), pp. 409–11.
7 R. Dingman, *Power in the Pacific, 1914–22* (Chicago, 1976), pp. 48–63; Bōeichō Senshishitsu, *Dai Hon'ei: Kaigunbu - Rengō Kantai*, Vol. 1 (Tokyo, 1975), pp. 195–203.
8 The standard work is Kobayashi Ushisaburō, *Military Industries of Japan* (New York, 1922).
9 *Nihon Gaikō Nempyō narabi ni Shūyō Bunsho*, Vol. 1 (Tokyo: Gaimushō), pp. 234–6, Cabinet resolution on reconciling strategy and diplomacy during the Russo-Japanese war, 8 April 1905, approved by the emperor, 10 April.
10 Crowley, 'Japan's Military Foreign Policy,' p. 20.
11 S. Okamoto, *Russo-Japanese War*, pp. 228–9.
12 I. H. Nish, 'The Army, the Navy, and the Outbreak of the War with Russia, 1904,' in *Proceedings of the British Association of Japanese Studies*, forthcoming; *Yamamoto to Kaigun*, pp. 143–9.
13 Nomura Otojiro, *Kindai Nihon Seiji Gaikoshi no Kenkyū* (Tokyo, 1982), pp. 205–8, esp. 205.
14 'Taishō 4-nen naishi 9-nen Seneki Kaigun Senshi Furoki,' in Boeicho Senshishitsu; *Dai Hon'ei*, Vol. 1, p. 149.
15 Ibid.
16 Dingman, *Power in the Pacific*, p. 58.
17 I. H. Nish, *Alliance in Decline* (London, 1972), pp. 207–9.
18 Itō, *Kokubōshi*, pp. 387–90.
19 Ibid., pp. 390–2. Hora, *Sekai Taisen*, p. 125, takes a less glorious view, claiming that the Mediterranean squadron was described as *yatoware kantai*, thereby implying that it was like a mercenary squadron.
20 See I. H. Nish, *Japanese Foreign Policy, 1869–1942: Kasumigaseki to Miyakezaka* (London, 1977), for further details.
21 Nish, *Alliance in Decline*, ch. 10.
22 Ibid., pp. 132–40.

23 Hora, *Sekai Taisen*, pp. 243–61; see also Morley, *Japan's Foreign Policy*.
24 Morley, *Thrust into Siberia*, p. 264.
25 Morimatsu Toshio, *Dai Hon'ei* (Tokyo, 1979). See also Ikeda Kiyoshi, in Nish, *Anglo-Japanese Alienation* (Cambridge, 1982), pp. 125–6.
26 *Yamamoto to Kaigun*, pp. 408–10.
27 *Dai Hon'ei*, Vol. 1, pp. 163–5.
28 M. R. Peattie, *Ishiwara Kanji and Japan's Confrontation with the West* (Princeton, N.J., 1975), ch. 1;. On 'the dearth of creative leadership,' see Asada, in Borg and Okamoto, *Pearl Harbor as History*, p. 226.
29 Splendidly analyzed in Kumagai Teruhisa, 'Nihon Riku-Kaigun no Seishin Kyōiku,' in *Gunji Shigaku*, vol. 16 (1980), pp. 66–72; M. D. Kennedy, *Some Aspects of Japan and Her Defence Forces* (London, 1928), p. 153 ff.
30 'Annual Report on Japan for the Year 1912,' para. 317, in Sir C. Greene to Sir E. Grey, 1 January 1913, in British Foreign Office 410/69[10232].
31 M. D. Kennedy, *The Estrangement of Great Britain and Japan* (Manchester, 1969), p. 8.
32 Ibid., p. 6.
33 See the recommendations of Admiral Akiyama Saneyuki in *Dai Hon'ei*. Vol. 1, p. 148.
34 Hora, *Sekai Taisen*, pp. 102–5, suggests that the army was just as active as the navy in pursuit of aeronautics.
35 Nish, 'Japanese Intelligence and the Approach of the Russo-Japanese War,' in C. Andrews and D. Dilks (eds.), *The Missing Dimension* (London, 1984), pp. 17–32.
36 Major sources are Shimanuki Shigefushi, *Senryaku: Nichi-Ro Sensō* (Tokyo, 1979), and Kurobane Shigeru, *Nichi-Ro Sensō to Akashi Kosaku* (Tokyo, 1976).
37 Morley, *Thrust into Siberia*, pp. 67–9.
38 M. R. Peattie and R. H. Myers (eds.), *Japanese Colonial Empire, 1895–1945* (Princeton, N.J., 1984), p. 181.
39 Kennedy, *Japan's Defence Forces*, p. 160.
40 Hora, *Sekai Taisen*, pp. 95–7.
41 General Staff, India, *Japanese Military Forces*, New Delhi: October 1942, 4864/D/6/GSI.
42 Kennedy, *Japan's Defence Forces*, pp. 140–2.
43 Ibid., pp. 158–9.

[8]

Imperial Russia's Forces at War

DAVID R. JONES
Dalhousie University

Introduction

For the professionals of any nation's armed forces, the challenge of battle traditionally has been the only true test of their troops' effectiveness. Yet some crude equation of effectiveness with victory tells us very little. An army may wage war skillfully and even successfully, but victory may elude its grasp thanks to any number of diplomatic, political, social, or other factors. The true 'combat effectiveness' of any military establishment thus must be judged in a broad political-diplomatic-strategic context. Only then can one examine how soldiers deal with concrete situations, often unforeseen, within a network of constraints over which they have often little or no control. Of course, one may argue that the professionals *should* have foreseen both the situations and the constraints. Even so, history shows that wars have a nasty habit of taking unexpected turns that few would have predicted beforehand.

For a political leadership, on the other hand, the real test of their forces' effectiveness may be the extent to which they deter wars. Therefore the peacetime relations between the military and their political masters may be fraught with tensions about the armed forces' ultimate purpose, tensions that do much to shape the army that eventually enters a conflict. Similarly, the virtues demanded of commanders in peace may be very different from those needed on the battlefield. It seems fair to suggest that the longer the period of prewar peace, the larger will be the number of 'managers' among commanders at all levels; and while such managers may prove disappointing leaders once hostilities commence, in peace their fiscal, bureaucratic, and political abilities will be highly prized, not least by their civilian counterparts.

These considerations must be borne in mind when examining Imperial Russia's efforts in the First World World War. So too must the particular constraints imposed on Russia's leadership by geographical, social, political, and other factors. Yet while recognizing such problems, until recently many historians have persisted in regarding the story as one of almost unbroken bumbling, corruption, and defeat. For even those taking a more balanced view, 'Russia's failure to carry the war through to victory in 1917 is often read retroactively to mean that she achieved little and was a negligible quantity prior to it.'[1] This judgment has seemed justified by the destruction of General A. V. Samsonov's Second Army at Tannenberg, the shell shortage and Great Retreat of 1915, and the regime's collapse in February 1917. German military historians too, as Dennis Showalter recently pointed out, have portrayed the kaiser's army as a virtual equivalent of 'The Gang that Couldn't Shoot Straight.' However, he notes these views only 'integrate perfectly with the images of the Russian army developed by Norman Stone or Allan Wildman, in fiction above all by Alexander Solzhenitsyn: a force so comically or tragically inefficient that even the semi-modern German army ultimately had no trouble winning a decisive victory.'[2]

Given this revision of the traditional estimates of the Germans' military efficiency, a similar reassessment of Russia's war effort seems in order. And in all fairness, one must admit that many Russian problems were not unique. Before 1914, all the Great Powers had planned for a short conflict, had underestimated the demands that would be made for shells and other weapons, and had wasted much effort on preparing their cumbersome (in terms of the transport needed) cavalry for mobile battles that seldom materialized. The year 1915 was one of shell shortages for all the warring nations as they scrambled to mobilize their resources. As for incompetent generals, one glance at the carnage of the Western Front should dispel the myth that tsarist Russia had a monopoly on dunderheads. Russia may have faced particular political, social, and economic difficulties in handling these difficulties, but the Russians themselves were Europe-wide in scope.

Apart from all this, accounts of Russia's wartime ineffectiveness ignore or discount both the major successes won by Russian arms and the areas of efficiency that the war economy had demonstrated by late 1916. During the autumn of 1914, for example, the August disaster in East Prussia was balanced by a string of victories over the Austro-Hungarians in Galicia. True, by June–July 1915 the Imperial Army seemed on its last legs. Yet only a year later it had recovered sufficiently to score a brilliant victory on the Southwest Front that surpassed any thus far won by its allies. In addition, this victory also demonstrated that some Russian generals were capable of learning the lessons of trench warfare at the operational and tactical levels. As in other armies, technology lagged behind the concepts of mobile warfare developed before 1914 by theorists like A. A. Neznamov. Nonetheless, some of the tsar's commanders continued to show remarkable innovative abilities right up to the eve of the February Revolution of 1917 (e.g., the Matau Operation of December 1916–January 1917). In the meantime, as Stone points out, Russia's industries had been mobilized and had expanded their production levels to provide sufficient arms and munitions for further offensives.[3]

True, major difficulties remained in areas such as rail communications (and hence the distribution of foodstuffs and other supplies), inflation, and military manpower. Even so, in early 1917 the tsar's armies were in better shape materially than they had been in August 1914. However, when the long-smoldering fires of political and social discontent burst into flames at the end of February, the chaos of revolution quickly reduced the value of past successes to nought. As a result, the armed forces' capability for effective combat fell so low that Lenin's Soviet regime had no choice but to begin demobilizing the old army in December 1917, and to accept the humiliating Treaty of Brest-Litovsk in March 1918.

All this suggests a somewhat more complex story than the oft-told tale of corruption, incompetence, out-right treason, and continuous failure. Indeed, in many respects this tale corresponds more closely to what Stone called the 'demonology of 1917' than it does to historical fact.[4] The roots of this legend are to be found rather in the polemics and propaganda of Russia's wartime domestic politics, and its strength in the subsequent repetition of these charges by so many Red and emigré White authorities in the years that followed.[5] Even so, during the war internal factors had a major impact on the Imperial Army's capabilities and so they too must be a concern of this study.

One also must remember that the capabilities of the Imperial armed forces fluctuated considerably over the three and a half years under investigation. The army that mobilized in 1914 was not the one that collapsed in 1917. In terms of command, the headquarters or *Stavka* that Nicholas II oversaw in 1916 was considerably more effective than that presided over earlier by the Grand Duke Nikolai Nikolaevich. Similarly, although demands for more war material continued unabated throughout the conflict, acute shortages existed only in mid-1915, and even then they were exaggerated by generals seeking excuses for their defeats. All in all, four distinct periods, each of which represents a separate political-strategic and operational-tactical context, must be noted.[6] These are, in brief:

(1) *July 1914 to April 1915,* during which Russia's peacetime armies are efficiently mobilized, suffer initial disasters in East Prussia, fight the Germans to a standstill in Poland, conquer Austrian Galicia, threaten Hungary with invasion, and brilliantly repel a Turkish offensive in the Caucasus. Domestically, this is a period of political truce and industrial 'business as usual.'

(2) *April-May to August 1915,* during which a successful German attempt to relieve the desperate Austro-Hungarians in Galicia, combined with the Russians' munitions shortages, poor tactics, and inept leadership, forces the tsar's armies from Galicia and most of Russian Poland. The Great Retreat and the mobilization of industry at home are used by the political opposition as an occasion to force major concessions from Nicholas II. He responds by establishing the special councils to run the war effort, personally assuming the supreme command, and proroguing the State Duma, or parliament. These moves coincide with a stabilization of the European Front and further victories in the Caucasus.

(3) *August-September 1915 to February-March 1917.* Under the new *Stavka*, progress in reordering the shattered armies is so rapid that by December 1915 the Russians can launch a limited counterattack against the Austrians on the Styrpa and, by the spring of 1916, can contemplate more ambitious

operations. These include a major attack against the Germans at Lake Noroch in March and A. A. Brusilov's June offensive on the Southwest Front. Despite the disastrous Rumanian campaign that follows, both Brusilov's victory and those on the Caucasian Front demonstrate that the army's capabilities have been restored. This judgment seems strikingly confirmed by the Mitau Operation, the first battle of 1917. With supplies at long last reaching adequate levels, the prospects seem good for the upcoming campaign.

However, other factors negate these gains. As noted, problems continue to plague the transport, and especially the vital rail, system. These lead to temporary food and fuel shortages in industrial centers. Amplified by rumor, such shortages combine with anger over wages and inflation to fuel growing discontent and more frequent strikes. The army's demands for men meanwhile force the call-up of older reservists, whose reliability in the face of civil unrest is less than perfect. And the political opposition, having lost its battle in 1915, concentrates on an underground propaganda campaign to discredit the regime. Stories of the treason of the German-born empress and the court, and of Rasputin's alleged influence over thoroughly corrupt and talentless ministers, do much to destroy the government's credibility at both the front and the rear.

(4) *February-March 1917 to March 1918.* All these factors combine at the end of February to provoke riots and mutinies in Petrograd that bring down the tsarist regime. Fearing civil war, the high command throws its support behind a provisional government. However this lacks real authority and the process of revolution demoralizes the armed forces, eventually destroying their effectiveness. After October, the victorious Bolsheviks face these problems by concluding an armistice, demobilizing the old army, and building their own Red Army on a volunteer basis. While some units see action against the Germans in late February 1918, their inability to halt the advancing enemy compels Lenin's government to accept the harsh terms imposed by the Central Powers at Brest-Litovsk on 3 March 1918. This ends Russia's formal participation in the First World War.

Political Effectiveness

An analysis of a military-naval establishment's political effectiveness must first examine its position within a nation's political-social structure. In this regard, the imperial Russian armed forces may be considered exceptionally fortunate. Thanks to a unique mixture of political-strategic, economic, and demographic factors, the military has had an immense impact on the history and evolution of the Great Russian state, of its government, and of its society. From the days of Kievan Rus and Muscovy on, the real security problems posed by Eurasian geography meant that most Russians have accepted military leadership as one of their rulers' most vital functions and large armies as unpleasant, expensive, but unavoidable necessities. Military service was never popular, but it was a recognized if onerous duty. In addition, it was one that long had offered an ambitious peasant or artisan a path to social advancement.[7]

Another recurring theme is the technological backwardness of Russia. The need to match more advanced enemies – first the Mongol-Tatars to the east and south, and then the European neighbors to the west – forced the Russian state into a series of basic reforms. The most militarily significant were those of Ivan III in the 1470s, Ivan IV in the 1550s to 1560s, Peter I in the early 1700s, and Alexander II in the 1860s to 1870s. On each occasion, the process involved not just the military establishment *per se*, but entailed profound social, economic, and administrative changes for the state as a whole. Thus the reforms of Peter I began with the army, but quickly embraced all aspects of a civil administration whose primary task was to support and maintain his modernized armed forces.[8]

This interrelationship has meant that military men often were cast in the roles of innovators and reformers. Equally important, many professional soldiers have been drawn into the actual work of the civil administration. In the late 1840s, for instance, ten of Nicholas I's thirteen ministers had served as officers in the army or fleet; in the early 1900s, General of Infantry P. L. Lob'ko filled the post of state controller; and throughout the imperial period (1721–1917) numerous officers can be found staffing lesser administrative offices at every level.[9] This was one way in which, as Wildman puts it, the 'army as a whole gave structure and substance to the empire.'[10]

Originally this mixing of civil and military functions also reflected the fact that until the early 1800s the officers made up the largest available reservoir of trained state servants. Yet its continuation for another century involved other factors as well. One of the most important was the faith that most tsars had in the virtues nourished by military service. They themselves usually had had extensive military training, and they frequently had greater trust in their military than in their civil servants. In fact, the bonds between the monarchy and its military establishment were 'far more than protective and physical ties – the bond was moral and spiritual as well.'[11] For above all others, the church included, the army was the institution that had built the Russian state, guaranteed its integrity, and preserved its social and political system. Under its sovereign and commander-in-chief, it stood on guard against the empire's 'external' and 'internal' enemies, and so maintained Russia among the ranks of the Great Powers.[12]

In 1906 the Fundamental Laws created a parliament, or State Duma, and so turned the Russian empire into a quasi-parliamentary monarchy or, as it was known, a 'limited autocracy.' Yet by these same laws the emperor remained 'the supreme commander of all the armies and fleets' who 'personally directs all military matters.'[13] More important still, Nicholas II saw these responsibilities as being much more than the formal and ceremonial ones assumed by his English cousins. In 1902 he indicated his intention of leading his armies in any European war, in 1904 he contemplated personally commanding his Manchurian armies, in 1906 he reserved military and naval affairs from the new Duma's competence, and in 1915 he finally took charge of the war at *Stavka*.[14] Meanwhile, the military had remained strongly represented in his immediate Court.[15] For all these reasons, his administration recognized that the needs of the army and fleet should have the highest priority.

Beyond the limits of 'official society,' during the decade before 1904 a growing gap had been evident between the military and most of 'unofficial society.' Although this worried thoughtful soldiers of the day, their duties in repressing a mounting strike movement and peasant disorders left them ill equipped to combat the growing anti-military sentiments of much of Russia's intelligentsia and middle class.[16] But with the establishment of the Duma, many of the latter saw themselves as sharing responsibility for the nation's welfare. This, along with an increased sense of German hostility, brought an upsurge of nationalist and pan-Slavist sentiment among many of the Octobrist and Cadet radicals of 1904.[17] As moderate liberals, they still remained determined to wrest further political concessions from Nicholas II, but they also set themselves the task of acting as the true guardians of Russia's honor and power. In 1907 this group – led by men like A. I. Guchkov and M. V. Rodzianko – gained control of the Third Duma and immediately placed military and naval reform at the top of the agenda.[18]

We also should note that at every level, family and social ties connected professional military and naval men with members of both 'official' and 'unofficial' society, revolutionaries included. As a result of all these factors, after 1907 the defense establishment could count on considerable support for its programs within both the Cabinet and the Duma. But if 'society' in general backed their efforts, that word had a very limited sense in the Russia of the day. In this context, 'society' denotes the thin, educated, and Westernized stratum of the population that had developed over the two centries since Peter I. Beneath it remained the overwhelming mass of the peasantry and lower urban classes. Since their representation in the Third and Fourth Dumas remained small, their direct influence on the imperial regime's defense (and other) policies was negligible. Only with the creation of soviets in the early spring of 1917 could these classes give weight to their views.[19]

This distinction between 'society' and the masses who provided the generals' cannon fodder is especially important when discussing war aims. All in all, little disagreement existed between the regime and 'society' over the goals Russia sought in the conflict. Yet the defeats of 1915, and the strain placed on the empire's social fabric by the intensified war effort, made a separate peace objectively appear as an ever more sensible policy. Indeed, many educated Russians professed to believe that the German-born empress and her supposedly germanophile supporters – the infamous 'dark forces' – were pursuing this course as a means of avoiding political concessions. Documentary evidence, and particularly the tsar's and tsarina's private correspondence, have since revealed that they were as committed as their critics to a 'war to a victorious conclusion.' But convictions aside, any unilateral move to end the war was an 'untakeable decision.' Apart from risking the empire's position as a Great Power, an attempt to do so probably would have sparked a *coup d'état* by an outraged 'society,' civil and military alike. Once the regime fell and popular soviets appeared, this changed. Then 'society's' efforts to pursue the old war aims led first to the 'April Days,' and in the end drew the masses to the program of Lenin's Bolsheviks. Perhaps better than any other, the issue of peace illustrates the gulf between the 'two Russias' that went to war in 1914. In a narrower sense, it also demonstrates the constraints that even an autocrat faces from the differing aspirations of the various social classes on which his war effort depends.[20]

Nonetheless, before 1914 there was a general commitment to defense on the part of all those involved in the formation of state policy. We might therefore expect the military and naval planners to have pushed through their programs with relative ease. However a number of factors inhibited their effectiveness. First, despite prewar conditions of economic expansion, resources remained limited. Secondly, even when levels of funding were sufficient, the services had great difficulties in absorbing or expending those funds. Often this reflected a need to carry out preliminary work before beginning a program, or to outfit plants to produce new weapons. Yet effective defense spending was hampered as well by bureaucratic inefficiency, occasional cases of corruption, military-naval rivalries, and, in the War Ministry, the conflicting demands of different branches of the army.[21]

This last was complicated still further by the heterogeneous nature of the higher officer corps. Stone's description of a high command irreconcilably split into conservative, patrician supporters of the Grand Duke Nikolai Nikolaevich and the reform-minded and socially humble praetorians led by War Minister V. A. Sukhomlinov is oversimplified. So too is Solzhenitsyn's view of two officer corps. Neither explains, for example, the innovativeness of Brusilov, a noble cavalryman who never attended the Staff Academy but who showed a greater capacity for adaption than did any of that institution's celebrated 'Young Turk' professors of 1907–9.[22] Even so, both views do serve to underline the fact that the high command was riven by divergent service and personal loyalties, and that basic differences of opinion existed about the reforms and programs being implemented with the monies available. Worse still, these inter- and intra-service rivalries quickly became enmeshed in the general political polemics that gripped Russia after 1906.

Although Nicholas II had exempted military-naval affairs from direct parliamentary influence, the Octobrists of the Third Duma resolved to use their budgetary powers to influence the course of military reform. For this purpose they established a military commission to review proposals of the war and naval ministers. Yet while they were sincere nationalists, Guchkov and his colleagues also sought to undercut the tsar's hold on the armed forces by making the Duma a second and equal symbol of patriotism, and hence an object of military loyalty. At first the Duma's commission worked in unison with officials of both ministries. Then in 1908 a number of contentious issues convinced Nicholas II that he must abolish Grand Duke Nikolai's Council of State Defense and reassert his own authority. His agent was Sukhomlinov. He was appointed first as chief of the general staff, and in 1909 as war minister, with orders to reduce the Duma's interference to the limits foreseen by the Fundamental Laws. Being clearly the tsar's man, Sukhomlinov naturally became the target of liberal scorn. His recently discredited rival, Grand Duke Nikolai, meanwhile began acquiring an undeserved reputation as a military genius and closet political reformer. Further, the army's intra-service rivalries now were of national political significance, a fact that did much to confuse and delay the cause of military reform.[23]

As head of the recentralized War Ministry, Sukhomlinov consolidated his authority by concentrating all powers still more tightly in his own hands. This meant preventing any official within the ministry, and particularly the traditionally powerful Chief of the General Staff, from emerging as a potential rival. This is one explanation for the rapid turnover of these chiefs in the immediate prewar period. During 1909 to 1914, the General Staff had four chiefs, as many as Prussia/Germany had had in the previous fifty-three years. This weakened the authority of the minister's foremost deputy, and to some extent retarded, as N. N. Golovin argued, 'the work of preparing the country for war.'[24] Others charge as well that the men chosen were either too junior or were talentless nonentities,[25] a judgment the wartime careers of Ya. G. Zhilinskii and N. N. Yanushkevich seem to justify. Yet here we should remember that the virtues needed in peacetime are not necessarily those of a field commander. Thus Zhilinskii, who moved on to command the vital Warsaw Military District and, in 1914, the Northwest Front, had a not undistinguished record; A. Z. Myshleavskii continued his career as a successful administrator within the War Ministry; and the relatively young Yanushkevich – dismissed by Stone as a mere 'clerk'[26] – was an expert on wartime supply whose ideas were incorporated into the field regulations of 1914.[27] All therefore fall into the category of peacetime managers who, to a surprising degree, possessed qualities needed during their tenures as chief. Nonetheless, whatever bureaucratic strength and other advantages Sukhomlinov gained from these frequent repostings, the process itself promoted instability within the ministry and provided ammunition for his critics.

Such criticism, the basis for the bad press Sulkhomlinov still receives,[28] was inevitable. During 1907–8 Guchkov and the Octobrists had successfully expanded their influence with the central naval and military administrations. Armed with the tsar's brief, the new minister set out to disrupt their network of unofficial contacts. He instituted a series of promotions and reassignments that involved dispersing the French-influenced 'Young Turk' reformers at the General Staff Academy.[29] The process culminated with the dismissal of Deputy War Minister A. A. Polivanov in 1912. Sukhomlinov himself had held aloof from the Duma and left all routine contacts to Polivanov. This move thus deprived the deputies of one of their most useful contacts.[30] Meanwhile other policies, such as the use of gendarmes to keep watch on officers' loyalty, won Sukhomlinov few political friends outside of the Court.[31] He himself was remarkably uncommunicative, even with his subordinates, and seemed indifferent to criticism. Frustrated, the Duma became increasingly receptive to requests from the Naval Ministry, whose officials proved more cooperative and politically sensitive.[32]

The outbreak of war in July 1914 put a moratorium on domestic political strife. All educated Russians, a few germanophiles and revolutionary extremists excluded, enthusiastically embraced the empire's war aims and accepted the righteousness of its cause. But the prewar divisions reemerged in early 1915 over whether the emperor or the Duma would provide political leadership to the war effort, and so take credit for an eventual victory. As noted above, this led to a political crisis that Nicholas II ended in August by departing for *Stavka* as Supreme Commander-in-Chief. In banishing Nikolai

Nikolaevich, the liberals' new-found ally, to the Caucasus, the tsar sought to reduce the impact of domestic politics on the field armies.[33]

Whatever success he achieved, it was short-lived. Deprived of a political victory that had seemed within its grasp, the liberal deposition redoubled its efforts to win major concessions before a general Allied victory left the monarchy more entrenched than ever. In the underground 'onslaught against the autocracy'[34] that followed, the opposition paid special attention to the armed forces. From late 1915 to early 1917 junior officers and the rank and file were subjected to a vicious propaganda barrage, both in the rear and in the war zone. There it was conducted by liberal and revolutionary activists, many of whom worked in the vast network of bath houses, delousing stations, canteens, and hospital trains established by the Duma and the so-called Voluntary Organizations.[35] Meanwhile some Duma leaders devoted themselves to winning over members of the high command. Here Guchkov's famous letter to Chief of Staff M. V. Alekseev is only the most glaring example.[36]

It remains impossible to determine to what degree these efforts were coordinated by the opposition. If any leader stands out, it is Guchkov. Indeed, the letter just mentioned was only a small part of his extensive activities. By late 1916 these included trying to win influential sections of the officer corps for a court *coup d'état*.[37] A group of Moscow liberals devised a similar plan. It collapsed, however, when Grand Duke Nikolai Nikolaevich refused to lead the *coup* on the grounds that it would not have army support.[38] Even so, all these efforts helped to lower the army's morale, fuel popular discontent in the rear, and divide Russia's small military, political, and managerial elite. By discrediting the tsar and his government, the opposition made it difficult for men of talent to serve without being tarred as appointees of Rasputin. However, the real victory came during the February Revolution. Fearing civil war, most senior officers abandoned Nicholas II to support the Duma and its provisional government. They then were deeply embittered when it too lost control of events, the revolutionary tide engulfed the armed forces, and the latter's combat effectiveness disintegrated. In its turn, this bitterness did much damage to White hopes in the civil war that followed.[39]

Having sketched the place of the armed forces in late Imperial Russia and its politics, we can examine the effectiveness with which they operated within this context. One major indicator is their success in competing with other interests for the resources available. Although figures on imperial defense spending are almost as debated as those for today's Soviet Union, one fact is clear: the commitment of Russian governments to their military has ensured the latter a regular, and usually a substantial share of the nation's funds. In 1680, the earliest year for which a rudimentary budget is available, some 60 per cent was devoted to defense.[40] By 1725, after Peter I's reorganization of the army and creation of a fleet, 6,541,000 (71.6 per cent) out of an estimated 9,140,900 rubles went to maintain them.[41] Again, from 1781 to 1796 they consumed an average of 40.7 per cent of the state's annual expenditures.[42]

As Table 8.1 indicates, after 1860 industrialization allowed a lowering of

Table 8.1 Russian Defense Budgets, 1855–1913 (in millions of contemporary rubles)

Year	*Adminis-tration*	*Health and education*	*Defense*[a]	*Total budget*	*Defense as % of total*
1885	194	23	240	866	27.7
1888	207	21	249	888	28.0
1891	247	26	296	962	30.8
1894	250	30	331	1,084	30.5
1896	295	31	347	1,361	25.5
1900	326	46	483	1,889	25.6
1903	391	52	436	2,072	21.0
1907	443	57	570	2,496	22.8
1910	536	101	588	2,592	21.5
1913	583	154	970	3,383	28.7

[a] Does *not* include expenditures on final goods and services, interest on the state debt, and expenditures on subsidies to state and private concerns. Although other sources use slightly varied figures, the differences are insignificant (e.g., a total of 2,597, not 2,592, for 1910).

Source: Paul R. Gregory, *Russian National Income, 1885–1913* (Cambridge, 1982), p. 252, table F. 1.

such averages. This reflects both the state's more diverse interests and a growth in the overall revenues available to the state from an expanding national income. During the years 1900 to 1913, the latter rose by over 80 per cent. Along with foreign loans, this permitted a 93 per cent increase in the size of state budgets.[43] In normal conditions this meant an annual defense expenditure of 25 to 31 per cent. Interestingly enough, these figures correspond closely to the Central Intelligence Agency's estimate of 28 to 32 per cent of Soviet budgets during the early 1970s.[44]

Such figures demonstrate the consistency with which the Russian state has supported its armed forces. Yet as Tables 8.2 and 8.3 indicate, they do not tell the whole story. Apart front the regular budgetary estimates, the tsarist government used loans to raise substantial funds for 'exceptional' expenditures. Over 1904 to 1906, some 3,260 million rubles of income fell into this category. Of these, 2,260 million rubles were quickly spent, largely on suppressing disorders and on railroad construction.[45]

Later, as Table 8.3 illustrates, railway building retained its place as the top priority, with military and naval expansion replacing maintenance of order as the second. Table 8.1 therefore actually understates the real sums allotted to defense. If regular and exceptional expenditures are totaled, then during the five years 1909–13 roughly one-third of the state's funding was absorbed by the army and fleet. In fact, according to Finance Minister V. N. Kokovtsov these outlays really amounted to 43 per cent of total governmental expenditure during the years 1909–10.[46]

Such exceptional funding went mainly to the services as capital grants for particular programs: the 'small' naval program of 1908–1909, the army reorganization of 1910, and the 'Grand Program' of 1914. For the first two, defense had received some 700 million rubles by 1914, and the third foresaw

Table 8.2 Analysis of Russian Defense Expenditures, 1909–12 (in millions of rubles)

	1909	*1910*	*1911*	*1912*	*1913*	*Total 1909–13*
Direct Defenses[a]						
Expenditure	565.59	597.64	618.73	703.95	825.95	3,311.86
war ministry	473.37	484.91	497.77	527.87	581.10	2,562.02
naval ministry	92.22	112.73	120.96	176.08	244.85	746.84
Total regular budget	2,451.42	2,473.16	2,536.00	2,721.76	3,094.25	13,276.59
Total exceptional budget	156.13	23.50	309.69	449.30	288.67	1,327.29
Total expenditures	2,607.55	2,596.66	2,845.69	3,171.06	3,382.92	14,603.88

[a] Exceptional funds excluded from military and naval figures.

Source A. L. Sidorov, *Finansovoe polozhenie Rossii v gody pervoi mirovoi voiny (1914–1917)* (Moscow, 1966), p. 47.

spending 140 million yearly on the ground forces – quite apart from an extra capital investment of 432 million rubles over the three-year period ending in 1917. Meanwhile the navy had received 800 million rubles in 1913 for fleet expansion, largely in the Black Sea.[47] According to estimates of German official historians, this meant that by 1913 to 1914 the Russian army received more money than their own – which understandably worried German planners when they considered their prospects in any conflict after the Grand Program had borne fruit.[48]

These developments meant that by 1913 the average Russian saw 50 per cent more of the income appropriated for current defense spending than did the average Englishman, and this even though the Russian's income was only 27 per cent of the Englishman's.[49] Further, as Table 8.1 indicates, this concentration on defense occurred at the expense of public health and educational programs, which in the long run could have had a major impact on Russia's military potential. Within the government, Kokovsov as early as 1908 had noted the dangers inherent in the state's growing debt, even though he insisted that it would be a mistake 'to propose that we seek in our regular budget sufficient funds to cover both the progressive growth of spending in all our civil departments and a further increase in expenditures on state defense.'[50] Outside of the Council of Ministers, others were still more concerned. Thus in 1909 an influential publicist, Prince G. N. Trubetskoi, openly warned that Russia's resources were insufficient for it to meet its military commitments, especially as conceived by its pessimistic generals and ambitious admirals. In the view of this and other commentators, an attempt to meet these commitments risked undermining the economy and bankrupting the treasury.[51] Yet as Kokovtsov's statement indicates, the government was determined to make precisely this effort. So too was the Octobrist-controlled Third Duma. At times, particularly after Russia's humiliation

Table 8.3 Analysis of Government Expenditures, 1913

	Millions of rubles	%
Regular budget expenditures		
War and naval ministries	825.9	26.7
Railways	586.9	19.0
Payments on loans	424.4	13.7
Alcohol monopoly	235.0	7.6
Remaining expenditures	1,022.0	33.0
Total	3,094.2	100.0
Total exceptional expenditures	288.67	—
On army and fleet	127.3	—
On railway construction	133.8	—

Source: Sidorov, *Finansovoe polozhenie Rossii*, p. 43.

during the Bosnian crisis of 1908–9, it even offered the service chiefs larger credits than requested.[52]

This last was not always a blessing. Even if the Duma appropriated large sums for the war and naval ministries, these might remain unused by the time of the next year's budget estimates. Good reasons, such as the lead times required for perfecting designs or equipping plants, often existed to explain this situation. Nonetheless, it usually brought charges of mismanagement, if not of outright corruption. Issues of military-naval funding and procurement thus became issues of domestic politics and the debates involved at times seriously impaired the relevant minister's credibility.[53] Still worse were the impressions created by competition between the ground forces and fleet for the resources available. Until 1908, the navy's bad performance in the Russo-Japanese War of 1904–5, as well as the army's domination of Grand Duke Nikolai's Council of State Defense, ensured that the fleet stayed starved of funding for its ambitious rebuilding programs. After that matters improved thanks to the emperor's personal interventions, Sukhomlinov's growing unpopularity, and Naval Minister I. K. Grigorovich's own successful courtship of the Duma. As Table 8.2 indicates, after 1909 the navy's credit increased proportionally at a faster rate than did the army's. However, if indecision over whether to strengthen the Baltic or the Black Sea Fleet hampered the effective use of these funds by naval men, there is little reason to argue that the ground forces lacked needed funding, or that any such starvation explains the problems of materiel they faced in 1915.[54]

Charges of mismanagement and corruption increased in volume during the war. However, the general commitment of Russian 'society' to the struggle ensured that every sinew was strained to support the armed forces. This massive effort involved state plants, foreign suppliers, prominent domestic industrialists, and the small enterprises organized under the 'Voluntary Organizations' and Guchkov's 'War Industries Committees.' Yet competition between these varied agencies, both for funding and for the associated credit of having overcome the shortages of 1915, lowered the effectiveness with which money was spent and further split the nation's educated elite.[55]

Even so, during 1915 the state spent 25.7 million rubles on the war, a figure that had risen to 58.4 million by 1917.[56]

The government financed these vast outlays by raising direct and indirect taxes, by internal and foreign loans, by prohibiting exchanges in gold, and by a massive growth in the circulation of paper currency (from 1,530,000 rubles on 1 July 1914 to 17,175,000 rubles on 1 October 1917).[57] The immediate results were rapid inflation and a massive increase in the government's debt, as well as considerable bickering with the Allies – especially with Britian, 'Russia's banker' – over how loans would be secured and credits spent. Nonetheless, monies were raised. As a result, Russia's prewar debt doubled over the years 1914–17, increasing by a total of 8 billion gold rubles. Neither consequence had a direct impact on the combat effectiveness of the armed forces as such. Yet in the long run, the inflation and associated economic consequences contributed to the internal unrest that sparked the February Revolution, and Russian indebtedness – largely to Britain – created suspicions that hardly helped inter-Allied relations.[58]

Even if the armed forces did receive sufficient funding, one must still consider the judgment, as I. Maevskii puts it, that Imperial Russia proved 'incapable at the existing stage of industrial development of meeting the demands of modern war.'[59] The above mentioned problems at the home front – inflation, low wages, fuel and food shortages, and a deteriorating railway network – seemed sufficient proof of this fact to contemporaries. At the front, this opinion appeared equally comfirmed by stories of criminal shortages of rifles and shells that critics blamed for the Great Retreat and near collapse of the field armies in mid-1915.[60] Since this latter allegation is a benchmark by which Imperial Russia's military effectiveness often is judged, the production and supply of shells will receive particular attention below.

Many writers blame these and other shortages on Sukhomlinov's mismanaging of the funds allotted to his ministry, and on its artillery department for stubbornly refusing to recognize the unexpectedly large number of shells consumed by modern battle.[61] However, Stone has argued convincingly that before 1914 his 'administration fell victim to development-economics rather that corruption, or mismanagement.'[62] The real problems were whether or not Russia should develop specialized and expensive domestic war industries in peacetime, and whether the War Ministry could not find private domestic producers to provide war matériel at prices competitive with those of the state plants or foreign suppliers.

Here aviation is a case in point. Given the empire's reputation for technological backwardness and military conservatism, it is surprising to find that in 1914, the Russian air services – with some 244 combat aircraft – were the world's second largest.[63] Even so, critics charged that Sukhomlinov's ministry should have built up a still stronger force by following the Naval Ministry's example. The latter had concentrated on importing aircraft (largely from France), rather than on promoting and investing in domestic firms. However, the War Ministry's foresight was strikingly vindicated when four Russian companies, Shetinin, Lebedev, Dux, and Anatra, proved capable of supplying 80 per cent of the 222 machines a month the air services estimated they needed in 1915–16.[64] By 1917 the production of airframes had risen still further, from a monthly average of 37 in mid-1914 to 352 for twelve different firms.[65] By then transport difficulties and their own needs had limited the Allies' willingness to provide Russia with combat-capable aircraft. This domestic supply thus was vital, even if its utility was impaired by a much lower output of motors. Unfortunately the War Ministry had less success in this area. By the end of 1916 Russian plants could produce only 110 to 150 aero engines, which considerably raised their importance in discussions of inter-Allied aid.[66]

With regard to guns, shells and most other types of materiel, the War Ministry had adopted a different course than that for aviation. In fact, the ministry's support of the small, newly established private air industry was exceptional. The opinion of Russia's industrialists held by most officials in the War Ministry's technical supply agencies was expressed best by General A. A. Manikovskii of the Artillery Department. In his field, he later wrote, 'all the negative qualities of Russia's industry emerged in spades – bureaucratic red tape, intellectual sluggishness on the part of management, and an ignorance that verged on illiteracy on the part of the labor force.'[67] Apart from this, private suppliers usually expected large advances, frequently failed to produce on time, and were also much more expensive. Once they became involved in war production, their price for a 3-inch shell rose to 14.25 rubles, as compared to 6.40 rubles for one from a state plant. Again, while the latter charged from 3,000 to 6,000 rubles for a field gun, private industry demanded 7,000 to 12,000 rubles.[68] The War Ministry thus understandably sought to avoid relying on Russia's private capitalists.

An obvious alternative was to expand the state's own system of defense production. Under pressure of war, steps were taken to do just this. By 1916, for example, the Artillery Department planned to build 37 more state plants.[69] Yet before prolonged fighting had made such expansion an obvious necessity, this same department had preferred to prepare for the expected short conflict by stockpiling guns and shells. These it obtained from existing Russian state factories or from abroad. As Stone points out, this was far from being a uniquely Russian practice and, at the time, it made good economic sense. For a factory to produce 20,000 fuses daily would cost the War Ministry 41 million rubles, but in peacetime the factory would lie largely idle. For the same price, on the other hand, the Artillery Department could add 2 million shells to its existing reserves.[70] Since, in the words of the introduction to the 'Grand Program' of 1914, 'the present political and economic circumstances of Russia's main neighbors rule out the possibility of a long war,' this stockpiling seemed the only responsible course.[71]

On the basis of experience in the Russo-Japanese War, the ministry's artillery experts believed that 1,000 rounds per gun would suffice for any European conflict. (France, however, had reserves of 1,400 to 2,000 shells, and Germany of 3,000 per gun.) The Russians therefore maintained peacetime reserves of just under 7 million shells of various types (see Table 8.4). As matters turned out, this meant that in 1914, the Russians had for each gun an amount of shells equivalent to its expenditure in ten days during an offensive in 1916. Furthermore, in 1914 these reserves were to be mobilized in artillery parks over a period of 480 days, and supplemented by the production of three

Table 8.4 Artillery Shell Reserves, July (August) 1914

Type of munitions	*No. by regulations*	*No. actually available*	*Shortage (−) or surplus (+)*
Shells for 76-mm guns	6,216,300	6,422,605	+206,305
Shells for 107-mm heavy guns, 122-mm and 152-mm howitzers	767,200	571,731	−185,469
Total	6,983,500	7,004,336	+20,836

Source: I. I. Rostunov, *Russkii front pervoi mirovoi voint* (Moscow: 'Nauka,' 1976), p. 98.

state plants at a rate of only 500,000 per month after war broke out.[72] The Artillery Department had considered following France and raising its reserves to 2,000 shells per gun, but as Manikovskii noted, this would have required an additional 130 million rubles, while a level of 3,000 per gun would have cost twice that much. 'No Minister of War,' he insisted, 'even one having the full support of the Duma, could expect such appropriations to be granted at the time.' He also pointed out that there were technical limitations on the size of the reserves that could be maintained: the larger the reserve, the longer it took to renew it, and so the greater was its deterioration in storage.[73]

Such problems aside, the estimates of the Russians, French, and Germans were all woefully inadequate. Yet in the Russian case, the munitions shortage that developed in 1915 was compounded by another factor. For this the artillerists' prewar policies did bear partial responsibility. In 1910 they joined the Grand Duke Nikolai's clique and other groups of the high command in opposing Yu. N. Danilov's and Sukhomlinov's proposed abandoning of the out-dated Polish fortresses. This opposition victory resulted in the expenditure of vast sums from prewar appropriations on rebuilding and rearming these positions. This diverted funds from reorganizing the field artillery (from 8-gun to 6-gun batteries) and from developing the light, high-trajectory field howitzers that proved so useful in trench warfare. Worse still, it affected the shell reserves as well. During the great crisis of 1915, a time when the field armies clamored for shells and heavy guns, the two captured fortresses of Kovno and Novogeorgievsk alone netted the Germans 3,000 artillery pieces and close to 2 million shells. So while the shortages of 1915 were real enough, their effects were magnified by the legacy of the prewar opposition to reform, as well as by inadequate tactical preparations on the battlefield and *Stavka*'s mishandling of the stocks available.[74]

The story of the rifle shortage is similar. Before the war, the War Ministry estimated it needed on hand 4,210,582 7.2-mm Mosin M-1891 and 348,421 10.67-mm Berdankas. This gave a total of 4,559,003 rifles for the men to be mobilized, and for maintaining a reserve. In addition, 700,000 then were to be added annually by the increased production of state rifle works. With stocks at the required levels, orders came to sell off 450,000 older models to officers as hunting guns. Nonetheless, as of 20 July (2 August) 1914 4,290,350 Mosin and 362,019 Berdankas, for a total of 4,652,369, were available.[75]

However, according to Manikovskii, the armies' real needs during three years of war reached 5,000,000 on completion of mobilization, 5,500,000 for men called up later, and 7,200,000 over three years to cover losses and wastage.[76]

As for machine guns, the mobilization plan envisaged a machine gun platoon (8 weapons) being attached to each infantry regiment and each cavalry division. Allowing for a 10 per cent wartime reserve, this meant a total of 4,990 guns that would be further supplemented during hostilities by the production of some 500 annually. The number (4,157) available when war broke out was insufficient, although the authorities had expected to acquire the remaining 833 over the next four to five months (at a rate of 200 monthly). They also anticipated a very low (about 40 per month) wartime rate of loss.[77] The first battles demonstrated clearly that these numbers were inadequate, even for a short conflict. Realizing this, the Artillery Department acted on its own initiative as early as September 1914 to increase sharply the production of new machine guns. Due to timely action, in 1915 its works provided 350 weapons a month and were preparing to supply 1,000 in 1916.[78]

The story was much the same with regard to artillery. As Table 8.5 indicates, by 20 July (2 August) 1914 the number of guns in service still fell slightly short of those called for by the mobilization plan: 7,650 light guns instead of 7,821, and 7,903 heavy pieces rather than 8,085.[79] On the basis of slightly different figures, Stone points out that in 1914 the Germans actually had fewer guns than the Russians. He argues that the former were 'incontestably superior to their enemies only in one area – high-trajectory artillery – and even here their superiority was greatly over-rated.'[80] The real problem for Russia, of course, was that many of its weapons, and especially the heavy guns, remained cooped up in the over-aged Polish fortresses. Wildman therefore quite correctly follows Manikovskii and Golovin in insisting that the real comparison should be made between Russian and German field units. Seen from this viewpoint, a Russian infantry division comprised six 8-gun batteries of 76-mm field guns, and two 6-gun batteries of 122-mm light howitzers (60 guns in all), against a German division's nine batteries (72 guns) of light field guns, three batteries of light howitzers, and two of 152-mm guns. This gave a German division over a twofold advantage, and left only 164 heavy weapons available to Russian field forces. These were the 152-mm weapons, organized into two detached formations as a strategic reserve for the whole field army.[81]

Space does not permit the examination of all aspects of military equipment (pontoons and engineering equipment, telephone and telegraph apparatuses, uniforms, boots, rations, forage, and so on). The point is that in all these areas, what deficiencies existed between the quantities on hand and those stipulated as necessary in 1914 were minimal. One more example, that of small arms ammunition, highlights the situation. Estimating that in Japanese war each rifle had used 820 bullets, in 1906 the Mobilization Committee of the Main Administration of the General Staff set the equation for peacetime reserves at 1,000 bullets per rifle and 75,000 (300 belts) per machine gun. This gave an overall total of 3,346,000,000 cartridges. As the government found the cost prohibitive, the General Staff lowered its figure to 2,829,000,000.

Table 8.5 Artillery Stocks, July (August) 1914

	Number required by plan			*Number on hand*		
	With troops	*In reserve*	*Total*	*With troops*	*In reserve*	*Total*
Light Weapons						
76-mm field guns	5,480	781	6,271	5,588	677	6,265
76-mm horse guns	434	61	495	390	17	407
76-mm mountain guns	424	57	481	408	32	440
122-mm Howitzers	510	74	584	516	22	538
All light guns	6,848	973	7,821	6,902	748	7,650
Heavy Weapons						
107-mm guns	76	8	84	76	4	80
152-mm howitzers	164	16	108	164	9	173
All heavy guns	24	24	264	240	13	253
Total Of All Guns	7,088	997	8,085	7,142	761	7,903

Source: Rostunov, *Russkii front*, p. 97.

Despite the efforts of the War Ministry, by mid-1914 the existing stock contained only 2,446,000,000 cartridges, leaving a shortfall of 383,000,000. This is perhaps the most outstanding case of 'unpreparedness,' and one of the few where fiscal constraints forced the ministry to reduce its original plans. Indeed, within the context of norms as set before 1914, this case appears to be an exception on both counts.[82]

From the vantage of 1915, the figures for prewar stocks clearly were woefully inadequate in comparison with the demands of modern warfare. They also make Sukhomlinov's announcement in the spring of 1914 that 'Russia is ready' appear as empty bravado or a grisly joke.[83] From that vantage Wildman's charge of the 'criminal underestimation of the expenditure of bullets and shells' gains substance, as do the sneers of General N. N. Golovin about the War Ministry's 'unscientific' approach and general mismanagement of its resources.[84] Yet such charges, as well as suggestions that Russia was too backward to build a modern army,[85] miss the point. True, fiscal restraints did prevent ambitious admirals from building the navy of their dreams and did limit the stocks of small arms ammunition available in 1914. However, most of the shortages revealed at the front resulted from planners' faulty estimates rather than from a lack of funding or economic backwardness. In part these flawed estimates reflected divisions within the high command over issues like the Polish fortresses or utility of reserve divisions, but another factor was of greater significance: the widely-held belief that a future war could only be of brief duration.[86]

In this context Sukhomlinov's pronouncement reflected a confidence felt by most of Russia's professional soldiers in mid-1914. Since 1906 they seemingly had rebuilt their army and either acquired, or were on the verge of acquiring, the matériel they *anticipated* a new war would require. If much remained to be done, they took comfort in the 'Grand Program.' Aimed at making Russia the predominant military power in Europe by 1917, it had been launched that June.[87] It would fund raising the annual contingent of recruits, who would serve three rather than two years, by 585,000 men, and so provide an army of 122.5 (rather than 114.5) divisions. In terms of matériel, the number of field guns would increase to 8,358, organized at least into the more efficient 6-gun batteries. Division also would field 12 (not 6) howitzers, and now 4 heavy field guns as well. Beyond this, the rail system was to be improved and stocks of munitions still further built up.[88] Small wonder indeed that Helmuth von Moltke, Chief of the German General Staff, watched the Russian army with growing gloom and insisted 'that the balance of force was inevitably and irreversibly turning against the Second Reich.'[89]

Evidence that demands for munitions would outpace prewar expectations came quickly. As early as 10 (23) August 1914, after Rennenkampf's First Army had seen only four days of fighting, the supply chief of the Northwestern Front reported 'an enormous expenditure of 3-inch ammunition.' Noting that the army commander had requested 108,000 shrapnel and 17,100 ordinary shells, as well as 56,000,000 cartridges, he said he had sent his 'last reserves' (2,000 ordinary and 9,000 shrapnel shells, and 7,000 rifle rounds). He therefore requested assistance 'in expediting at earliest, supplies of ammunition to make up what has been used.'[90] By that month's end, similar calls had arrived from the Southeastern Front's supply officer as well. 'Heavy fighting is taking place along the whole front,' he wired on 28 August (10 September); 'the expenditure of ammunition is enormous; soon the stock will be completely exhausted. Immediate supply is necessary; the situation is critical.'[91] Repeated pleas from the fronts, echoed by similar appeals from both Chief of Staff Yanushkevich and Grand Duke Nikolai, quickly alerted Petrograd to the need for action to sustain even a short conflict.[92]

There supply questions were handled by agencies – in particular the war and naval ministries – that initially underwent little structual change. Having received a vote of confidence from the Duma, the Council of Ministers governed by means of emergency powers provided under Article 87 of the Fundamental Laws.[93] These should have given the government sufficient authority in state finance, censorship, and other spheres to wage the expected brief war. In terms of mobilizing industry, the relevant statute – the Law on the Period of Preparation for War of 1913 – indicated merely that state-owned enterprises were to be given 'technical guidance' to ensure that they 'developed full productivity.'[94] The actual supervision of army supply was left in general to the War Ministry, and in particular to its Main Administration of the General Staff (GUGSh). Headed after Yanushkevich's departure for *Stavka* by General M. A. Beliaev, GUGSh was charged with 'unifying the activities of all the main supply administrations to achieve the complete and appropriate provision of all forms of supplies to the active army.'[95] As for weapons and munitions *per se*, the most important of these administrations was the Artillery Department.

Deteriorating relations between *Stavka* and the War Ministry quickly isolated GUGSh both from the realities of the front and from any influence on strategic or operational planning. This partly accounts for the skepticism with which GUGSh and the ministry at first greeted pleas for increased munitions and other supplies. In the Artillery Department, this skepticism was fueled by other factors, the artillerists' traditional disdain for the infantry included. They now suspected, for instance, that infantrymen wasted shells and that the artillery, thanks to Sukhomlinov's policies, had become too dominated by the infantry.[96] These officials especially resented the shells expended to support the allegedly useless second-line divisions. They also quite rightly noted that the infantry was doing little to counter German fire by tactical defensive measures; and having demonstrated that *Stavka* was mishandling the shells that were available, these officials not unnaturally believed that headquarters was deliberately exaggerating the shortages both to explain its own failures and as part of Nikolai Nikolaevich's vendetta against Sukhomlinov.[97] For its part, *Stavka* could not provide details of shell expenditure and those received from front and army staffs often contradicted each other. Further, inspections of the fronts frequently demonstrated unexpected stocks. So when the War Ministry found *Stavka* could account for only a third of the 5 million shells shipped by the end of 1914, the Artillery Department concluded that some 3 million rounds must remain.[98] Yet its officials themselves were not free from blame. Aside from their prejudices, they themselves had been proponents of both the wasteful 8-gun batteries and the Polish fortresses, whose commanders now hoarded large stocks of much-needed guns and shells, some seemingly being concealed from *Stavka* for fear of losing them.[99]

During the initial fighting the problem was largely one of delivering the peacetime stocks on time. This was overcome, as even the critical Golovin admits, thanks to 'the energetic measures of the Artillery Department.'[100] These ensured that by early December 1914 the 112 'light parks' listed in the mobilization plan had reached the front with full stocks of munitions. However, by that time he insists experience had demonstrated that each 76-mm gun needed 300 rounds a month, which entailed assigning 50 parks with some 1.5 million rounds a month to the field army – 'a task [that] was beyond the power of the Artillery Department.' Thus in December only 12 parks 'could be relied upon to contain a month's supply.' After this, he argues, Russia's unpreparedness for manufacturing munitions, the 'catastrophic decrease' in prewar stockpiles, and bureaucratic inefficiency combined to bring disaster.[101]

However Petrograd (as St. Petersburg had been renamed) had recognized the problem of meeting the ever increasing demands of the front. During August and September a series of laws had established special committees to coordinate wartime transport, to stockpile matériel needed by the army and fleet, and to distribute fuel.[102] Despite their suspicions and prejudices, by September officials of the Main Artillery Department or Administration had taken steps to increase the production and supply of munitions to compensate for the unexpectedly high consumption of ammunition.

A statute of 7 (20) September had reorganized this agency. Under a 'special chief,' it was to be responsible for 'completely guaranteeing the state's needs' in armaments and munitions through the efforts of both public and private firms. For this purpose it had three basic sections for administrative, economic, and technical affairs.[103] However, the artillerists still treated requests from the front with considerable skepticism. And even when they acted, their orders had to pass through the ministry's Military Council. Conscious of civilian criticism of military accounting practices and still expecting a short conflict, the Council's senior generals in September reduced the Artillery Department's order for 2 million shells to 800,000. Indeed, they approved these only on the grounds that their noise would raise the troops' morale. The upshot was that during this period, orders were not placed for even the 5 million rounds per year that Russia could produce.[104]

As the autumn wore on, even the most optimistic military officials came to accept that the conflict would be protracted. Yet the Artillery Department's distrust of Russian industrialists, and the latter's higher prices, caused the ministry to turn to foreign firms first. Given the French Army's demands on that nation's industries, the Russians presented British and American companies with large orders for both rifles and munitions. By November 1914, the Vickers firm already had received an advance of 41 million rubles.[105] Other efforts aimed at promoting full production at Russia's state works. As a result, the Artillery Department expressed confidence that by 1 (14) May 1915, some 1,936,000 rounds would be available (see Table 8.6), and reported by early 1915 that a total of 14,000,000 had been ordered abroad.[106] To oversee these transactions, purchasing commissions were established abroad. In January 1915 a Russian Government Commission began work in London, and similar bodies eventually appeared in France, the United States, Italy, and Japan.[107] Within the War Ministry itself, on 15 (28) February 1915 a decree set up the Special Administrative Commission on Artillery, chaired by Grand Duke Sergei Mikhailovich, to provide tighter central control.[108]

Despite these efforts, considerable confusion continued to plague Russian ordering procedures. This sprang both from the continued rivalry between *Stavka* and the ministry, and from Allied, especially British, interference in the ordering processes. In February 1915, Britain's Lord Kitchener offered his good services directly to *Stavka* and not the ministry in obtaining an additional 10 million rounds from America. Grand Duke Sergei opposed this order on the grounds that Kitchener would do better to expedite Russia's orders in Britain rather than place a new series at double the price in the United States. Nonetheless, *Stavka* accepted this offer behind his back. The Artillery Department first got wind of the deal when the British attaché, Lt. Colonel Alfred Knox, called to obtain the appropriate blueprints two months later.[109] Such confusion was annoying enough, but worse was to come when the foreign firms bitterly disappointed Russian expectations. In 1915 domestic production amounted to 11.2 million shells, but imports yielded only an additional 1.3 million. More indicative still, by November 1916 only 7.1 million of 40.5 million shells ordered abroad had reached Russia.[110]

The story was the same with rifles. After hesitation caused by worries over mixing calibers, the War Ministry placed large orders with three American firms: 1.8 million from Westinghouse, 1.5 million from Remington, and 300,000 from Winchester. These were to begin arriving in batches of 100,000 a month in mid-1915, rising to 200,000 a month in mid-1916. Yet again, such hopes were illusory: by February (March) 1917 only 216,000 Westinghouse, 180,000 Remington, and 27,000 Winchester guns had arrived.[111] Meanwhile

Table 8.6 Expected Available Shells, Spring and Autumn, 1915 (in thousands of rounds)

Type of shell	*Russian production*	*Vickers*	*American production*
By 1 (14) May			
76-mm shrapnel	820	490	275
76-mm high explosive	146	100	75
Total	966	590	350
By 1 (14) September			
76-mm shrapnel	950	400	250
76-mm high explosive	315	225	350
Total	1,265	625	600
Grand total	2,231	1,215	950

Source: N. Stone, *The Eastern Front, 1914–1917* (London, 1975), p. 151.

Russian production had provided an additional 278,000 rifles by 31 December 1914, and 860,000 more throughout 1915, a year in which some 200,000 a month probably were required.[112] As a result of such shortfalls, by June 1915 the shell reserve for field guns fell to under 200 rounds each while in training units in July, five men shared two rifles.[113] In the long run, Allied aid did do much to provide the machinery needed to expand Russia's war industries. Even so, their short-term experiences left bitter memories among Russian military men. Further, as A. A. Sidorov notes, this reliance on foreign suppliers distracted the War Ministry's attention from the more difficult task of creating an industrial base to reduce the empire's dependence on such imports.[114]

Nevertheless, given the unexpected expenditure of all types of matériel in 1914 and early 1915, it is questionable if any other course was open to the government. Initially it had hoped that the administrative reforms just noted would satisfy *Stavka*'s demands. But as the case cited above indicated, Grand Duke Sergei's short-lived commission lacked the authority to deal with the real problems of supply, and it did little to smooth relations between front and rear. Meanwhile the government, using Article 87, continued to strengthen its controls over fuel, food, and forage through various committees. Despite this, in the spring of 1915 *Stavka*'s hysterical complaints of shortages continued to grow in volume as the armies retreated. As a result, the need for a more powerful agency became painfully evident.[115]

In May 1915 Nikolai Nikloaevich, supported by Duma President Rodzianko, urged Nicholas to create a single powerful agency to solve the supply crises by 'immediately drawing all the country's vital forces into the work' and supervising all orders abroad.[116] A prototype body, with War Minister Sukhomlinov as chairman, held its first meetings on 14 (27) and 18 (31) May 1915. Unfortunately bureaucratic jealousies, the renewed aspirations of the Duma's liberal opposition (now organized as the Progressive Bloc), the demands of Russia's great industrialists and those of the smaller concerns represented by Guchkov's War Industries Committees, and the

Table 8.7 Estimated Growth Rate of the Russian Economy, 1913–17

Year	Growth rate
1913	100.0
1914	101.2
1915	113.7
1916	121.5
1917	77.3

Source: A. A. Sidorov, *Ekonomicheskoe polozhenie Rossii v grody pervoi mirovoi voiny* (Moscow, 1973), p. 350.

intrigues of *Stavka* all worked to delay matters. As a result, a really effective agency to mobilize the economy for a war of attrition officially appeared only on 17 (30) August. Then the tsar approved a law setting up the Special Conference for the Discussion and Coordinations of Measures for State Defense, usually known simply as the Special Council for Defense. Four similar but more specialized bodies followed. These dealt with fuel, transport, provisions, and refugees. Yet as Figure 8.1 demonstrates, the first was by far the most powerful and took the lead in guiding the economic expansion that followed.[117]

This growth was achieved mainly through a concentration of capital in the larger existing firms rather than through the efforts of the small producers of the War Industries Committees and of the Municipal (Zemgor) organizations. It thus resulted in the rapid expansion of large-scale production reflected in the growth rates in Table 8.7, which led to tremendous increases in the amounts of war materiel reaching the front.

By 1917, the output of shells had increased by 2,000 per cent, of artillery by 1,000 per cent, and of rifles by 1,100 per cent. To put it differently, by September 1916 Russian plants were producing 2.9 million shells a month, a rate which left the Bolsheviks with a shell reserve of 18 million in November 1917. As for artillery, during the war Russian plants turned out 20,000 light field guns while only 5,625 were received from abroad. By 1917 domestic production rose to 900 a month. At that time Russia was providing 100 per cent of its howitzers and three-quarters of its heavy artillery.[118] While it still lagged behind its enemies slightly in these last two regards (see Table 8.8), by the war's end *Stavka* could count on a considerable superiority in field artillery. The output of small arms ammunition also had grown, reaching 1.482 billion a year in 1916. If the total domestic production from August 1914 is added to the 2.5 million rounds purchased and 400 million captured over this same period, Golovin estimates that the army received some 9.5 billion cartridges. As for machine guns, the 75,946 acquired during the conflict did not meet *Stavka*'s optimum requirements, but the ammunition being received was fully sufficient for the weapons available.[119]

Similar figures exist in almost every area of essential supplies. The number of telephones, for instance, rose from 10,000 in 1914 to 50,000 in 1916. Meanwhile Russia's five major automobile works, supplemented by imports and the output of smaller shops, had equipped the armies with 5,300 cars,

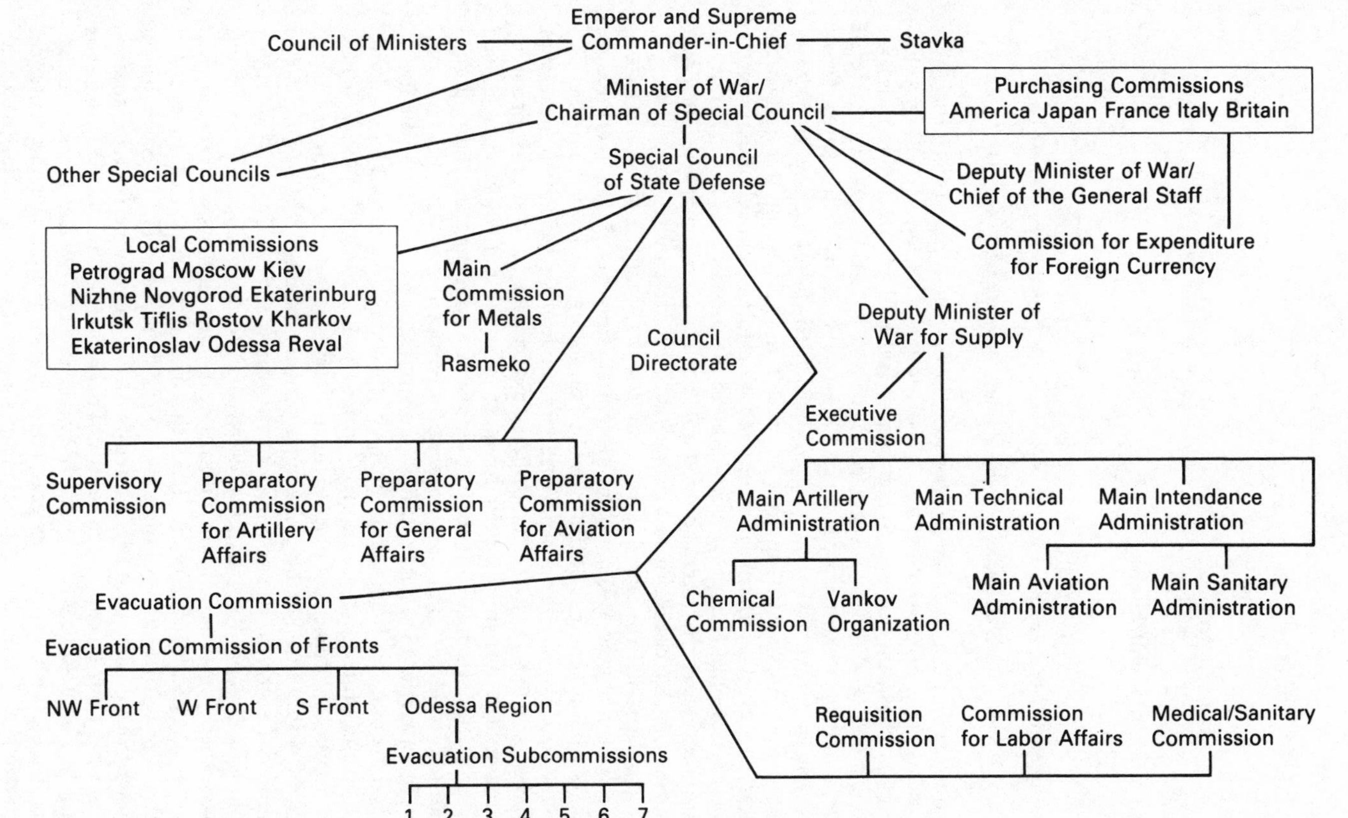

Figure 8.1 Structure of the special conference for State Defense, 1915–17
Source: Adapted from Ya. M. Bukshpan, Voenno-khoziaistvennaia politika (Moscow, 1929).

Table 8.8 Balance of Forces on the Eastern European Front October 1917 (Caucasus Excluded)

	Russia	*Austro-Germans*[a]
Infantry (bayonets)	2,116,700	1,178,600
Cavalry (sabers)	110,600	39,000
Field, horse, and mountain guns	6,730	4,170
Light howitzers	1,226	1,690
Heavy guns	1,139	2,230

[a] By this time, of course, some German units had been transferred to the Western Front.

Source: E. Barsukov, 'Russkaia artillery v mirvoi voine,' *Voennaia Mysl'* no. 7 (1939), p. 65.

1,350 motorcycles, and 3,500 bicycles by 1 (14) January 1916. In that year they produced another 6,800 cars, 1,700 motorcycles, and 8,800 bicycles. While even these increases did not meet *Stavka*'s optimum demands (for 19,300, 13,600, and 9,300, respectively), they are particularly indicative of the war economy's growing potential.[120] On the basis of such figures, Stone argues that by January 1917 Russia enjoyed a 'considerable superiority not only in men, but also in matériel.'[121] Some may consider this judgment exaggerated, but the fact that it can be made seriously in itself illustrates the effectiveness of both the special councils and of Russian industry. However, these impressive results were achieved only at the cost of a massive effort that did much to create conditions of domestic discontent and revolt.

One paradox of Imperial Russia's war effort is that if both enemies and allies alike underrated its economic potential, they both also overrated its ability to fuel a 'Russian steamroller' with almost unlimited numbers of peasant conscripts. Yet for a variety of reasons, it was precisely in the area of manpower that by late 1916, the military authorities faced their most acute problems and demonstrated their greatest political ineffectiveness. In part these difficulties sprang from the problems of imposing the modified conscription law of 1874 on a vast population comprised of Slav peasants and numerous other diverse nationalities. During the war, however, the inefficiency of military officials and the incomprehension of civil bureaucrats further compounded the situation. The net result was that by 1917, Russia faced a manpower crisis that neither the military nor the government seemed capable of resolving. Further, the steps already taken to do so in the end contributed directly to the downfall of the tsarist regime.

While space does not permit a detailed investigation of all the issues involved, their general contours will suffice for our discussion. According to data of the Ministry of War, in 1853 the Imperial Army had entered the Crimean War with a strength of some 1,112,000 men.[122] The overwhelming majority of these had been conscripted from the peasant serfs, state peasantry, and other commoners, both rural and urban, who paid the hated head or poll tax. Since 1834 they had been obligated to serve twenty years, a reduction of the earlier twenty-five-year term, but still a virtual life sentence. Along with the often brutal conditions of service life, this goes far to explain the average Russian's traditional dislike of rendering service personally. The government meanwhile had to maintain a massive professional army, a very costly proposition in both the state's human and fiscal resources. Worse still, the war of 1853–6 demonstrated that despite the heroism of Sevastopol's defenders, this force's effectiveness in combat was far from satisfactory.[123]

Military considerations played a significant role in the reforms instituted by Alexander II after 1856.[124] The measures reorganizing the armed forces culminated in the law on military service of 1874, termed by Wildman as 'the most radical social measure of the reform era' (after the emancipation of the serfs in 1861).[125] Inspired by the concept of 'the nation in arms,' which many believed lay behind the German-Prussian victories of 1864–71, War Minister D. A. Miliutin and his colleagues sought to transplant this model into a modernizing Russian empire. According to Alexander II's manifesto on conscription of 1 (13) January 1874, 'the strength of the State does not depend exclusively on the number of its troops, but is based chiefly on the moral and intellectual qualities of the army, which can be fully developed only on condition that the defense of the country has become the common task of the people, and when all, without distinction of rank or class, unite in that sacred cause.'[126] The law itself reiterated this patriotic sentiment by declaring defense of throne and country to be 'the sacred duty of every Russian subject.'[127] In this manner, the third element of the military's trinity – 'Faith, Tsar, and Fatherland' – was given more modern definition. However the first two remained as before. As late as 1912, new field regulations considered the empire's polyglot troops to be 'Christ-loving' defenders of the tsar and Orthodoxy.[128]

This juxtaposition illustrates the major obstacle inhibiting the creation of a true 'nation in arms' within Russian reality of that day. True, after 1905 at least 20 per cent of the adult males of most major social groups (peasant householders, factory workers, artisans, small proprietors, merchants of the first two guilds, tradesmen, lower officials, and so on) had passed through military or naval service and returned to civilian life.[129] This experience may have taught them much, but not necessarily the sense of modern nationalism that many reformers had hoped this 'national university' would instill. Here Wildman is probably correct in concluding that the reform 'was based on a concept that conflicted too much with the mores of society at large to create the hoped-for sense of enterprise shared by soldier and officer alike. The legacy of serfdom, driven out of the front door, filtered back through all the side doors and windows.'[130]

As Wildman points out, Miliutin had designed his legislation on the model of Prussian reformers like Gneisenau and Scharnhorst, and with the expectation that educational and other measures would create in Russia feelings of civic responsibility similar to those found in Germany.[131] These did not appear, and even the literacy courses for peasant recruits, stipulated in the law of 1874, received a low priority at best before 1905. Older officers had little time or talent for such work, while their younger colleagues frequently were overburdened by other duties and, from the 1880s on, hampered by economic restraints. During this same period, society's growing anti-military sentiments made an officer's career less and less attractive for an educated youth. Interestingly enough the rise in nationalist spirit after 1907 saw a parallel rise in the officer's role as educator of the masses, even if the old army never achieved the goals set by Miliutin and colleagues.[132]

In this regard, the army's difficulties were complicated still further by the educational exemptions of the conscription statute of 1874. Whole categories of educated professionals (i.e., teachers, doctors, and veterinarians) were freed completely. Further, the normal term of service was reduced to six months for those with university degrees, and to eighteen months for graduates from gymnasiums. The educated also had the option of taking officer training as a 'volunteer' for one year (after 1912, two years). After this, they entered the reserves as a *praporshchik*, or ensign. Wildman quite rightly describes them as 'incorrigible civilians in uniform and an awkward presence in the military environment.'[133] In addition, they had little impact on the mass of worker and peasant commoners that comprised the army's rank and file.[134]

The split between these two Russias – the educated 'society' and the peasant-worker masses – has been noted. It was especially evident in July (August) 1914. All observers noted that educated Russia greeted the news of war with outbursts of patriotic fervor, and many assumed the lower orders shared this sentiment. Yet as numerous contemporary sources attest, in many places the peasants answered the call-up with riots and drinking bouts that recalled the fatalistic send-offs given recruits entering the old army of Nicholas I.[135] General Golovin nonetheless remained convinced that the formula 'For Faith, Tsar and Fatherland' was 'for the bulk of the common people in 1914, the voicing of a kind of national ritual.' He maintains that in comparison with the West, Russian patriotism was of 'a much more primitive sort.'[136] The disorders he explains 'by the crude simplicity of the mass of the Russian people,' but he insists that among them (unlike the numerous intellectuals who sought safer work with the voluntary organizations), 96 per cent of those called up reported for duty.[137]

Nonetheless, other observers were less sanguine. Golovin himself quotes Colonel B. A. Engelhardt, a member of the Duma's Military Commission, to the effect that 'the Russian peasant served unwillingly.'[138] Again, General Yu. N. Danilov insisted that the 'people proved that they were unprepared psychologically for war. Most of the people – the peasants – scarcely understood why they were going to war . . . [and] answered the call because they were accustomed to doing everything that the government ordered them to do. They passively bore their cross with patience until the final ordeal arrived.'[139] Here Wildman's analysis probably approaches the truth. While admitting that peasant soldiers frequently had mystical veneration of the tsar's person, he considers the view that this equalled patriotism to be 'a gross miscalculation.' Pointing out that peasantries in general feel little 'identification with the goals of the larger society or with such abstractions as the nation, the state, or the empire,' he argues that their veneration of the ruler did not carry over to the army. This institution, like the rest of the state's 'hierarchy of authority, . . . [was] fundamentally alien and illegitimate' to members of this class. Treating the war as fatalistically as he treated a natural castrophe, and knowing 'that to resist the military obligation could only mean his ruin,' Wildman's peasant recruits submitted to the tsar's will and prayed to the Saints for their protection.[140]

One might argue as well that high levels of illiteracy among the rank and file made it difficult to imbue the army with any sense of purpose, especially during a total war such as that which developed after 1914. According to the census of 1897, only 20 per cent of the population had a primary school education, and only 1.1 per cent had attended secondary schools or universities.[141] These levels had risen by 1914, but even so they remained very low by British, French, or German standards. Yet the rapid spread in 1917 of revolutionary ideas, in which agitational pamphlets and party newspapers played a major role, suggests that illiteracy itself is no barrier to successful propaganda. Rather it seems that the *ideas* of 1917 – the promises of peace and land – struck chords within the common soldier's psyche that the Turkish Straits could not touch.[142] Here too the gulf between the two Russias hindered official efforts. Indeed, even such a popular orator as War Minister A. F. Kerenskii often used language in ways the peasant soldiers misunderstood. When he urged troops on the Southwestern Front in 1917 to fulfill their 'duty' (*dolg*) to the revolution, some soldiers asked their officer if this meant that they owed a greater debt (*dolg*) in taxes.[143] In view of this, Nicholas II's efforts to rally the army during 1915–16 by exploiting the mysticism attached to his person may have displayed more political insight than historians have hitherto realized.[144]

The above discussion may suggest that the human material available to Russian generals was of dubious military quality. Yet these same peasant soldiers had fought with Peter at Poltava in 1709, won Frederick the Great's grudging respect at Zorndorf in 1758, followed Suvorov across the Alps in 1799, repulsed Napoleon in 1812, and eventually stormed Plevna in 1877. Even when the Russians left a field without victory, foreigners remained impressed with their qualities and the power they gave their superiors. Thus a British observer in Manchuria during 1904–5 noted that while recent defeats might 'make the Russian Army appear greatly inferior to what it really is; . . . taken as a whole, [it] is distinctly a good one.'[145] Further, the upsurge of resistance to the French invaders during the Patriotic War of 1812 suggests that some 'primitive' patriotism might well exist, at least during defensive struggles. And as the battles of 1914–16 demonstrated, even 'unwilling' peasant conscripts frequently could display a prowess that the above quasi-sociological analyses would seem to belie.

Possible reasons for this apparent contradiction will be considered later. For the moment, let us return to the conscription law itself and the quantitative aspects of the manpower issue. To begin with, despite the principle of the universality of military service, the figures cited above suggest that only about one-fifth of those eligible actually entered the ranks. Apart from educational exemptions, the statute contained a series of other articles that freed Finns, Central Asians, married men, only sons, frequently Jews, and so on.[146] As a consequence, the army inducted only a portion of those physically fit and otherwise suitable. In 1874 the recruit contingent therefore numbered only 150,000, a figure that rose to 235,000 in the 1880s, 320,000 by 1900, and 450,000 in 1906. It was to be raised to 585,000 by the 'Grand Program' of 1914, but even this represented merely a third of the men available.[147]

The reason for such deliberate shortfalls is obvious: the army simply lacked the ability to absorb and support greater numbers. There were limits to the number of recruits it could house, equip, and feed with the resources available, and train with the existing officers and NCOs. To some extent this consideration inhibited all armies. But in Russia, vast distances and other factors raise these administrative and *intendentstvo* (clothing, food, fodder, etc.) costs still further. As Stone points out, in the 1870s supply consumed more than 100 million rubles, and administration some 19 million rubles, of the army's annual budgets of some 172 million rubles, and by 1913–14 these categories consumed 450 out of 580 million rubles.[148] Military men thus had to reckon that the more men they trained, the fewer funds would be available for capital investment in munitions, artillery, or other items. In April 1909, the War Ministry estimated that it cost 350 rubles per annum to support each enlisted man.[149] Since everyone foresaw a short war, neither the War Ministry's Main Staff (*Glavnyi Shtab*) nor the Military Districts' recruiting offices ever imagined that one day Russia would need all eligible conscripts in the various categories as established in 1874.

In accord with the conscription law, the annual contingent was selected from all males who had turned 21 by 1 October of a given year. After exemptions had been granted, the required number of recruits were drawn by lot. During the 1870s to 1880s, this meant that some 48 per cent were exempted and 25 per cent freed by the lottery. The government sought to maintain a peacetime army of some 800,000 permanent cadres and conscripts, backed by roughly 550,000 reservists. This large standing force seemed justified by Russia's vast distances and still underdeveloped transport system, factors that hampered a rapid mobilization of the reserve. Since training the often illiterate peasant soldiers allegedly required more time than did that of the more educated West Europeans, Russian conscripts served longer. The law of 1874 set the period of active service at five years (for the infantry and artillery), as compared to Prussia's three, and that of service in the active reserve (*zapas*) at nine. The reservist then passed into the *opolchenie*, often called the militia or territorial army in Western works, until the age (before 1906) of 38.[150]

Young men who escaped direct service also were enrolled in this territorial force. The standing army and reserves proper both comprised fighting units that immediately took the field. The *opolchnie*, on the other hand, was to form a pool for replacements once the reserves had been exhausted, and to provide a basis for forming territorial units for rear service. These duties corresponded to two classifications of militiamen (*ratniki opolcheniia*), divided on the basis of family situation and of age. The first category or *razraid* contained ex-reservists, aged 39 to 43, and provided the active army's first-line replacement.

By law the reservists proper were obligated to up to two periods of annual training. These were not to last longer than six weeks. In fact, the periods usually were considerably shorter because of limited funds. Those with three full years of active service normally were recalled once a year for two weeks, and those with less active service, twice a year for three weeks. As for the territorial *ratniki*, they received no official training whatsoever. In addition, they were not considered attached to any particular unit. When called up in wartime, they entered a common pool in their respective military districts. There they received rudimentary training before receiving their assignments.[151]

After 1874 changes were introduced into the periods of active and reserve service. In 1888 the War Ministry sought to cut costs and increase the wartime pool of reserves by reducing active service to four years while increasing time in the reserves to eighteen years. Again, in 1906 it cut the active term back to three and that in the reserve to fifteen, but added five years to service in the *opolchenie* (to age 43).[152] By 1 (14) April 1909 the ministry reported that the army, border guards, and Corps of Gendarmes contained 1,348,769 men. This figure represents 1.8 per cent of the empire's male population, Finland included. Sukhomlinov then sought to raise his service's strength by a reorganization. By 1910 this had raised battalions in the wartime field armies from 1,110 to 1,252 by reducing the wartime reserve battalions from 671 to 560; but if this measure cut expenses and improved the quality of the reserves, it did not affect the actual conscription procedure.[153]

This was changed by the new Law on Military Service of 1912. Its provisions retained a three-year term for those inducted into the infantry and foot artillery, four years for the horse artillery and other branches, and five years for the navy. The corresponding terms of reserve service were fifteen, thirteen, and five years, respectively, and 43 was retained as the cut-off age for the *opolchenie*. The statute also removed educational distinctions that had divided volunteers into two groups in terms of service. Now both categories served for two years, although this term might be reduced by four to six months if they passed an officer's qualifying exam.[154]

In addition, in that year a new mobilization plan took effect that incorporated new and seemingly sound military principles. It was worked out by Sukhomlinov's protege and Chief of the General Staff's Mobilization Section, General A. S. Lukomskii. As a result, a large number of units, with their staffs and equipment, were redeployed in the empire's interior to accord with the pattern of population densities. Earlier they had been concentrated in frontier military districts and with war, brought up to strength with reservists from the interior. Now units would reach full strength in their new quarters and move by rail to their points of concentration as combat-ready entities. Kept effective by trial mobilizations in the immediate prewar years, Lukhomskii's plan deserves much of the credit for the smooth and rapid concentration of the tsar's forces in 1914. However the complexity of the scheme was such that during the July Crisis, the generals feared a partial mobilization against Austria would hopelessly confuse any later, full mobilization in response to subsequent German actions. They therefore pressed Nicholas II for a full mobilization, even though few doubted that this would make war inevitable. In this sense, then, military effectiveness in a technical regard diminished the government's ability to use its armed forces as a flexible instrument for deterrence.[155]

In some ways this is true of the 'Grand Program' that Nicholas II approved on 24 June (7 July) 1914. Its impact on future manpower was outlined earlier in a law of 1 (14) May 1914, which ordered an increase in the army's strength of 11,592 officers and 466,178 enlisted men.[156] Along with the intended increases in armaments noted above, this undoubtedly alarmed German planners and played a part in their insistence on forcing a decision during the Sarajevo crisis.[157] Here too, one might argue, the military's very success in obtaining resources for expanding its forces helped bring about the very situation that the political leadership sought to avoid.

Since the 'Grand Program' never took effect, war found Russia with an army that numbered, as of 1 (14) January, 40,238 officers and 1,145,244 men.[158] The addition of border guards and the Corps of Gendarmes presumably explains the figure of 1,423,000 given by early Soviet statisticans as the army's strength on the eve of the mobilization.[159] In any case, at this time Russia still trained only 25 per cent of its eligible males, as compared to Germany's 52 and France's 80 per cent.[160] The thought of the remaining untapped millions fuelled dreams and nightmares of 'the Russian steamroller.' These visions seemed confirmed by the mobilization of 3,115,000 reservists on 18 (31) July, 800,000 first-class militiamen on 22 July (4 August), a further 300,000 territorials on 22 September (5 October), and the 715,000 drawn from the annual recruit contingent on 1 (14) October. With the 200,000 additional first-class territorials inducted in November, Golovin estimates that 6,553,000 Russians had been enrolled by the end of 1914.[161]

There is considerable confusion about the total mobilized by October 1917, and about the casualties suffered by that date. In large part this results from the difficulties the War Ministry's main staff had in keeping accurate records in both areas. Comprised of five sections, it functioned as the army's personnel and statistical office. In explaining its failure to keep abreast of events, Stone insists that it 'was run, almost by definition, by incompetents, who had failed to make a career in anything other than this department, which was regarded as a waste-paper-basket.' He maintains that the real problem was that its 'few dozen dim-witted officers' continued routine record-keeping until the immensity of the numbers involved overwhelmed them and they 'could produce nothing beyond enlightened guess-work.'[162] This judgment is unduly harsh to the overworked and understaffed officials involved. Like everyone else, they too had prepared for a short conflict. Further, throughout the war's first year *Stavka*'s vendetta with the ministry, along with the vastness of the front and chaos of the Great Retreat, made serious statistical work impossible. Although some of these difficulties disappeared in August 1915 with Nikolai Nikolaevich, by that time the damage was done and, as Stone puts it, the *Glavnyi Shtab* 'succumbed.'[163]

In discussing the numbers mobilized, Golovin used statistics published by Soviet experts in the 1920s. He gives a figure of 15,378,000, which he rounds to 15.5 million, recruited by 1 (14) October 1917 (see Table 8.9). This is slightly higher than the figures of his Soviet contemporaries, who gave estimates of just over 15 million.[164] Their figures match the data provided to Knox in October 1917 by the General Staff's Mobilization Section, which set the number at 15,150,000, as well as the estimate made in the autumn of 1917 by Russia's last War Minister, General A. I. Verkhovskii.[165] Stone, on the other hand, has reviewed more recent studies and concludes that a little over 14 million were inducted out of a total population of 180 million.[166] This corresponds to the Council of State figure provided by members of the

Table 8.9 Estimated Numbers Called Up, 1914–1917 (in thousands)

	To 31 Dec. 1914	*To 31 Dec. 1915*	*To 31 Dec. 1916*	*To 1 Oct. 1917*
Unmobilized strength, 1914	1,423	1,423	1,423	1,423
Reservist	3,115	3,115	3,115	3,115
1st class territorials:				
From reserve	400	400	400	400
No previous regular service	900	2,385	2,705	2,705
2nd Class territorials	—	1,325	3,045	3,075
Recruits	715	2,952	3,860	3,860
Re-examined men	—	—	100	4,460
Total	6,553	11,600	14,648	15,378

Source: N. N. Golovin, *Vonnye usiliia Rossii v mirovoi voine*, 2 vols. (Paris, 1939), Vol. 1, pp. 95–6.

defense of 14.5 million by November 1916.[167] Stone also puts his figure into perspective by noting that it represents fewer men than those conscripted in Germany from a population of 65 million and only slightly more than in France from its 40 million inhabitants.[168] So clearly, the 'steamroller' had failed to arrive.

Worse still, the imperial military system lacked either the will or the means, or both, to draw on its remaining reserves. This explains the manpower crisis that emerged at the end of 1916, when the government contemplated the problem of maintaining the army's strength if hostilities continued beyond the campaign of 1917. When the conflict began, the active army contained the conscripts of the years 1911, 1912, and 1913. It was fleshed out by reservists (about 2.8 million, according to Stone) who had passed through the ranks between 1904 and 1910. They were supported by Cossacks and various territorial units, who guarded bridges, depots, and so on, in the rear. All in all, the mobilization of July 1914 affected some 4.5 million (Stone) to 4.7 million (Golovin) men, territorials evidently being excluded. Of that number, Golovin estimates that 3.5 million formed the field army.[169] However, casualties were much higher than expected, perhaps averaging 300,000 to 400,000 a month over the course of the war.[170] In the first months, losses were even higher. Golovin maintains that the field army would have reached full strength only after 1 October, but estimates that by that time losses had reduced its numbers to 2.7 million, and to 2 million by 1 December 1914.[171]

Casualty figures are even more debated than the above. The figures available range from below 4 million to 11 million. The arguments need not be rehashed here, but Stone probably is right in accepting recent Soviet figures from 7 million to 7.5 million, from which he draws the monthly average given above. By 1917 this total included the 2.4 million prisoners-of-war claimed by the Central Powers, and probably some 1.6 million to 1.85 million killed in action or dead of wounds. Of the total losses, the army suffered some 4 million killed, missing, prisoners, and wounded between

August 1914 and December 1915. Official reports put the field army's strength at 3.85 million men in that January, its losses by 1 September at a minimum of 2.4 million, and the number of replacements reaching it by that date only 2.3 million.[172]

Since casualties far surpassed prewar expectations, the authorities quickly found themselves desperately searching for new sources from which to replenish the army. Although figures again vary, the basic groups available are listed in Table 8.9. The first obvious choice was the trained reserve, men who had served in the fifteen annual contingents of 1896 to 1910, inclusive. They should have yielded 5 million men, but in fact it is doubtful if more than 3,115,000 actually entered the ranks, mainly as a result of the initial mobilization. The next available categories were the territorial *ratniki*, first class, that is, older men who had passed into the militia from the reserves or younger men who had escaped regular service by lot. According to Golovin, 400,000 of each group were called up on 22 July (4 August), the fifth day of mobilization; another 500,000 later in 1914; 1,485,000 in 1915; and 320,000 in 1916.[173] In all, these two groups may have given the armed forces 3 million men over two and a half years. Yet most of this vast reservoir 'was frittered away in 1915 faster than it was being tapped' and, as the figures illustrate, by 1916 the well was running dry.[174]

Another obvious source of replenishment were the annual recruit contingents of 20-year-olds who became liable each October. Although officially set at 550,000 men, during the war the authorities took all those available. By mid-1915 they also moved to anticipate forthcoming contingents up to 1918. By the year's end they had secured passage of a new law affecting those of 1919 as well. Another law of October 1915 meanwhile had permitted a reexamination of past exemptions, but bureaucratic problems so hampered the process that this netted only some 200,000 to 250,000 additional recruits.[175]

This left the regime with the territorial militia, second class, as its last resource. In order to draw on it, a new law was rushed through the Duma in August 1915, which underlined Russian 'society's' commitment to the war. However, the division between 'society' and the masses became immediately clear when the first 900,000 men [20- to 24-year-old breadwinners only] were conscripted for front-line duty in September, and two more age groups followed in October. When officials attempted to raise these levies, their efforts sparked riots in numerous centers throughout the empire. As Stone points out, here the real limits on Russia's attempt to create a nation-in-arms by conscription are glaringly obvious: 'the government rightly feared that, if they [the recruiting-sergeants] became more [efficient], it would be swept away in a tide of popular indignation.'[176] This fear, the lack of records in many district offices, the demands of industrialists for exemptions for their workers in towns where records existed, and numerous other bureaucratic and social obstacles, explain why this category – which presumably included two-thirds of Russia's males – in the end provided just over 3 million men for the armed forces.[177]

By 1916 the government faced a manpower crisis of major proportions. Attempts to extend conscription to previously exempt non-Russians led to riots and, in Central Asia, a native uprising of serious proportions.[178] Meanwhile the call-ups of 25 March (7 April), 25 August (7 September), and 20 September (3 October) had embraced the remaining militiamen, first class, and made liable those of the second class aged 27 to 37. On 25 October (7 November), a last draft of 350,000 second-class *ratniki*, aged 38 to 40, joined the colors. With the 150,000 first-class over 40-year-olds taken in October, these family men were crowded into the large, under-officered training battalions that made up Russia's rear garrisons in early 1917. As such,, they played a significant role – especially in Petrograd – in the February Revolution.[179]

These over-age restless conscripts were clear evidence that 'the giant Russian 'steamroller' was running out of fuel.'[180] Recognizing the extent of this problem, the authorities with some trepidation prepared to attempt to dip further into the second-class *opolchenie*. Meanwhile *Stavka* sought to underplay the problem to the Allies. Indeed, on one occasion it even ordered the General Staff to draw up a false set of statistics for the British attaché Knox.[181] Yet this discussion of the problem of rank-and-file combatants should not distract attention from three interrelated and equally important aspects of the manpower issue: those of technically competent personnel, non-commissioned officers, and officers proper.

The first category obviously affected the others. Given the educational levels noted above, the pool from which to draw command personnel of all types was strictly limited. At the same time, one should not assume Russia was technologically ignorant. Although educated 'society' might comprise a thin stratum at the top of the social edifice, within it many had become increasingly fascinated by technology and its applications during the prewar decade. This in some ways contrasts to the intellgentsia's oft-cited loss of interest in politics after 1907, and it found its expression in adherence to the technocratic ideas espoused by D. I. Mendeleev, V. I. Grinevetskii, and others. In a more practical form, it is evident in the enthusiasm with which many Russian youths embraced aviation after 1909–10.[182] At a lower level, continuing industrialization also meant a growing working class with the technical skills needed for modern battle.[183]

Even so, the numbers of both groups remained small by West European standards. This, along with the traditional dislike of the soldier's profession felt by many Russians of all classes, meant the armed forces faced chronic shortages of both officers and NCOs. Thus April 1914, despite recent measures to make military careers more attractive and an upsurge of nationalism since 1908, found the army 3,380 officers short. The situation with regard to NCOs was equally disturbing. In 1903, according to General A. Rediger, Germany had an average of 12 re-enlisted NCOs serving with each company in peacetime, and France had six (corporals excluded). Russia, on the other hand, had only two. This placed it below even similarly multinational or peasant-based European armies. Thus Italy (corporals excluded) and Austria-Hungary each had three such regulars per company.[184] Golovin suggests this was the case in 1914. If so, it is striking evidence that despite the planning of measures after 1907 for the creation of the necessary cadres of long-service regulars, very little had been achieved in practice. For in 1903 the War Ministry had reported that the army contained only 12,109, or only 46 per cent, of the 23,943 re-enlisted professionals it required.[185]

This failure to provide the basis for a real NCO class within the service was the major failure of Miliutin's reforms. Surprisingly, there has been very little scholarly investigation of this vital element of the tsarist army. A number of factors seem to explain the continuing shortage: the lack of a numerous artisan and petty bourgeois stratum, as well as of an independent self-sufficient class of peasant landowners; the low pay and lack of prestige associated with non-commissioned service; the traditions of society that until recently had been semi-feudal; and so on. Thus unlike their counterparts in Britain or Germany, tsarist NCOs generally lacked special traditions and institutions (i.e., their own messes). For the most part, they were appointed from literate and preferably rural conscripts as needed, although some did receive special instruction in training commands in the military districts. As noted, while the authorities had long recognized the need for change, by 1914 little had been done. The Imperial Army still relied mainly on the company sergeant-major, backed by one or two regular senior sergeants and their conscript juniors, to ensure that the ranks maintained at least the appearance of discipline and reached minimal standards of competence – a situation that naturally increased the burden on the junior officers.[186]

The ensuing conflict then quickly exhausted the number of regular NCOs that did exist, especially in the infantry. Again surprisingly, the new mobilization plan introduced in 1909–10 had made no distinction between NCO and ordinary combatant reservist. The replacement of NCOs therefore proved particularly difficult, especially since opposition from the front commanders prevented the transfer of those in cavalry regiments to the sorely pressed infantry. In an effort to replace them and provide for an expanding field army, the War Ministry established special 'training companies' in reserve units for men with experience at the front. Although initially this effort gave 'completely unsatisfactory results,' by the end of 1916 one such company usually existed in each of the 162 'training battalions' set up to train the flood of wartime conscripts. Nonetheless, at that time the armed forces were still woefully short of NCOs who could link the masses of mobilized conscripts to their officers.[187]

Worse still, by 1917 the nature of the officer corps itself had changed drastically. According to data of the War Ministry, the 40,590 peacetime regulars were supplemented by 20,740 reservists. According to General Yuri Danilov, Sukhomlinov's recent reform of the volunteer system had actually reduced the number of reservists by keeping volunteers longer with the ranks. In any case, the number available fell short of requirements and emergency measures – the recall of over 1,000 retirees, the enlistment of qualified Allied and Slav citizens, and reassignment of students at the Staff Academy – gave only a handful more. In addition, close to 3,000 soldiers with the appropriate educations received immediate promotions, a measure that further increased the pressure on the NCO cadres. In all, this provided the wartime army of 1914 with a total of roughly 70,000 commissioned personnel, but the power of modern weapons, abetted by the desire of many regulars to win fame and promotion by feats of glory, quickly decimated their ranks. *Stavka* tried to reduce their vulnerability by recommending that officers cover or remove their epaulets, and that they carry rifles rather than sabers and pistols. Even so, by July 1915 officer casualties may have numbered some 60,000. Many of these, however, returned to their units after recovering from wounds.[188]

Nonetheless, by that time the army's officer cadres had dropped to around 40,000 effectives.[189] The import of these figures is clear from General Alekseev's letter of August 1915 to Polivanov, Sukhomlinov's recent replacement as War Minister. Noting that some units in vital sectors of the front had lost half of their officers, he expressed fears for the army's future.[190] However, worse was to come. By September some sources maintain that it was rare for over a dozen officers to be found in front-line regiments, and in December of that year the War Minister reported an overall shortage of 15,777. Apart from lowering the combat effectiveness of the field armies, this situation also hindered the training of the recruits in the training battalions, from which they were expected to emerge as soldiers after a mere six weeks.[191]

As with munitions, the empire's mobilization for total war did much to solve this particular aspect of the manpower issue. Throughout the conflict's first year, the War Ministry had to satisfy itself with appealing to educated Russia for officer volunteers. Many youths satisfied their patriotism instead with service in the hospital and rear support network that the Duma and 'Voluntary Organizations' of Zemgor established and operated with lavish government subsidies. In this way they remained exempt from military service. Meanwhile the Council of Ministers, partly because its members 'resented the waste of talented men on the army, partly because they feared what the educated classes would do if the State leaned on them,' had refused to permit the mobilization of university students until the end of 1915.[192] After that matters improved, and by 1916 the army had 80,000 officers. All in all, the War Ministry reported as of 1 (14) January, that since April 1914 the number of serving officers had risen to 145,916, that 62,847 had been lost, but that command vacancies had been reduced to a mere 226.[193] Other sources give slightly higher figures. These maintain that by May 1917 the army still contained some 133,000 commissioned ranks, and that since July 1914 107,000 had been killed, wounded, captured, or reported missing.[194] And of course, all these figures exclude the fleet, which in 1917 had some 7,000 commissioned ranks.[195]

While figures are as unreliable here as in other aspects of the manpower issue, it is safe to agree with Peter Kenez that (at least) 170,000 young Russians were commissioned during the war, of whom perhaps 130,000 entered service as ensigns.[196] While a number, especially from 1915 on, were soldiers promoted from the ranks, the overwhelming majority were graduates of accelerated courses in regular military schools, or products of the newly established four-month ensign schools. The first also turned out infantry officers in four months, but devoted eight months to training specialists for other branches. In all, the military schools gave the army a reported 18,999 officers in 1915, a figure that grew somewhat over the next year. By the end of 1915, on the other hand, there were 34 ensign schools, with 200 to 400 students each, that by 1916 could provide annually as many as

40,000 men fit for positions as senior warrant or junior commissioned officer positions. The admission requirements for these latter were lower than for the accelerated officer courses, but under pressure of events, even the accelerated courses drastically lowered both their educational and their social standards.[197]

In these ways the War Ministry managed to meet the army's need for commanders, but it did so only at the cost of drastically changing the nature of its officer corps, especially at the lower and middle levels. By 1917, only some 10 per cent of the pre-1914 regulars remained with the army, and many of these held staff positions far removed from the troops.[198] This meant that at the regimental level, the great majority of officers were either wartime graduates or men promoted from the ranks (usually from another regiment).[199] Meanwhile, as the figures cited earlier indicate, the turnover of enlisted personnel had been even more stupendous. The Life Guards Grenadiers, for instance, had entered the conflict with 4,000 men, and seen 44,000 men pass through its ranks during the conflict's course. By early 1917, according to its official historian, it was comprised almost solely 'of young officers whose graduation had been hastened, line officers transferred to the regiment, soldiers called up from the reserves, and badly trained recruits.'[200]

The above analysis of the political effectiveness of the Imperial Army suggests a number of seemingly contradictory conclusions. On the one hand, official Russia remained willing and surprisingly able to supply the fiscal and matériel sinews of war. And while the well was just about dry, the army had continued to receive the necessary reinforcements, even if the quality often was far from satisfactory. On the other hand, the very efforts required demonstrated the limits of the prewar military and civil bureaucracies. By 1917 this was especially evident in the looming manpower crisis, but it was apparent as well in the problems still plaguing the railway system and the associated difficulties of supplying industrial centers with fuel and coal. In the armed forces proper, Stone is probably near the truth in arguing that 'the old army's structure' collapsed,[201] or rather was overwhelmed, in 1915. Nonetheless, enough talent remained both to rebuild it and win a series of stunning victories in 1916, and to mobilize the empire's economy for the production of the necessary matériel.

However, all these successes entailed substantial political costs and dangers. The fiscal effort brought inflation, the industrial mobilization brought underpaid overtime and shortages of consumer goods, and the military effort changed the army's composition and badly weakened its old ideals of service. By December 1916 there was ample evidence of low morale on both the home and war fronts.[202] This was not, of course, an exclusively Russian phenomenon, but it was particularly dangerous in the tsar's empire thanks to the ongoing political struggle between ruler and Duma. Although both were steadfast behind the Allied cause, influential elements of the Duma were determined to undermine the military's loyalty to the existing regime in their efforts to gain major political concessions. Indeed, some were prepared for a *coup d'état* if necessary. If by December 1916 these patriots had made some converts among senior regular officers, they undoubtedly had a much larger following among the wartime newcomers – and it was these who now mixed with the rapidly trained and often dispirited conscripts in the front-line trenches and rear training battalions. This situation did not make revolution inevitable but, as Wildman notes, the 'amalgam was a deadly combination, seriously undermining the Army's combat capacity and vastly increasing the danger in the eventuality of a political crisis.'[203]

Strategic Effectiveness

Despite disagreement over how and by whom the empire should be governed, by 1914 there remained considerable unanimity among the non-revolutionaries of the educated elite about Russia's political and strategic goals. First and foremost, all agreed that whatever the financial and economic burden, their state must retain its status as a Great Power. This in turn meant sustaining a vast military machine with the increasing complexity and expense of modern armaments. This explains the military's 'political' success in obtaining funds. More specifically, most politically concerned Russians saw this machine as necessary for maintaining regional balances in the Far East and along their sensitive, ethnically non-Russian Afghan-Persian-Caucasian frontier, as well as for preserving the Great Power balance in Europe proper.[204]

Some insisted this last could be guaranteed best by improving relations with the young German empire, but Berlin's growing assertiveness made this difficult. After 1894 most therefore favored instead the Franco-Russian alliance, and after 1908 a parallel entente with Great Britain. Yet from the Russian perspective, attention focused even more directly on the Balkans and Turkey. In these regions the empire's 'vital' interests seemed intimately involved in resisting German/Austro-Hungarian pressures on 'fellow Slavs,' and in guaranteeing navigation through the Turkish Straits, the lifeline of Russian commerce. They believed this would best be achieved by decisively neutralizing or destroying Ottoman power.[205]

This duality of focus divided Russian attention between the need to support its French ally and the pursuit of its own Balkan policies, and so during the war, between the German and Austrian (and later the Caucasian) Fronts. The divided focus thus influenced both St. Petersburg's prewar planning and *Stavka*'s subsequent conduct of operations until the collapse of 1917. Further, any discussion of this strategic aspect of the empire's war effort falls naturally into two broad categories.

First, there is the strategic-political sphere. This includes examining such questions as the degree to which planned strategic goals met Imperial Russia's political aspirations, to which they simultaneously fitted with and affected those of its allies, to which the military establishment influenced the political leadership to seek militarily logical strategic objectives, and to which the risks involved in a possible failure were justified by expected political-strategic gains. In its widest sense, this last can of course be extended to include the central political question of war and peace. Then secondly, judgments on these issues involve analysis of more narrowly strategic-military issues. Among these are the degree to which the objectives selected were consistent with the size and structure of the available forces, as well as with the nation's industrial base and logistical infrastructure, and the extent to which the Russians' strategic planning succeeded in pitting their strengths against their opponents' weaknesses.

As suggested above, in striving to maintain its Great Power status, Imperial Russia faced two separate but interrelated problems. In the first place, the rise of the German Empire as Europe's dominant land power threatened Russia from the west in a manner that was unimaginable before 1870. In 1873 D. A. Miliutin drew up the first plan for a war against an Austro-German coalition. This possibility became particularly likely after the Austro-German alliance of 1879. By 1880 General N. N. Obruchev, then Chief of the Russian General Staff, was reporting on further plans for a war with these two powers. Not only did Russia now face a double threat from the south and west, but the Hapsburg empire now replaced Turkey as the main threat to St. Petersburg's interests in the Balkans, interests that were inextricably tied to Russia's position as a Great Power.[206]

To counter this threat, in 1894 conservative Russia entered into an alliance with republican France. This aimed at placing Berlin as well in double jeopardy. Some continued to urge a conciliatory policy towards Germany as late as 1914. Yet that nation's open hostility during the Bosnian crisis of 1908–9, and the events of the Balkan Wars of 1912–13, convinced most patriotic Russians that their best hopes lay in preserving the French alliance in peacetime, and in ensuring their ally's survival during any conflict so as to prevent an eventual German-Austrian victory.[207]

This placed military planners under a peculiar burden, one which geographic and technical considerations made still more complex. Russia's immediate war aims and sentiments dictated an immediate strike southwest against Austria. Yet its longer range strategic considerations, as well as pressure from Paris, demanded a rapid offensive westward to prevent France from being overwhelmed by superior German forces, which would leave Russia isolated. To implement either or both such actions, Russia's troops had to concentrate in tsarist Poland, a region that formed a salient between East Prussia and Austrian Galicia. This meant that any sizeable force deployed forward there by Russia might well be cut off and destroyed by an Austro-German pincer. Such a threat was especially acute thanks to the tsarist empire's vast distances, lack of strategic railways, and consequently slow rates of mobilization. To prevent this eventuality, during the 1880s to 1890s the Russians constructed a chain of fortresses in central Poland, behind which the generals would deploy. Yet the French, who were providing substantial loans for railway construction, feared this meant they would be left in the lurch.

Haunted by contrary commitments and desires, Russian planners by 1900 already had divided their armies into two commands – a Northern Front against Germany and a Southwestern Front against Austria-Hungary. By 1902, in response to French pressure, they had agreed as well to simultaneous offensives against Germany and Austria. Their ally at first wanted these by the fifteenth day of the German mobilization, and later by the fourteenth. The Russians, arguing that by the fifteenth day they would have deployed

Table 8.10 Growth of Comparative Railway Networks, 1880–1914

State	*Length of railroads (in thousands of kilometers)* 1880	1 Jan. 1914	% Increase
France	26	51.0	93
Germany	23	58.4	155
European Russia	34	63.7	87

Source: I. I. Rostunov (ed.), *Istorii pervoi mirovoi voiny, 1914–1918*, 2 vols. (Moscow, 1975), Vol. l, p. 63.

only a fraction of their troops, resisted. But in 1906 St. Petersburg felt especially vulnerable thanks to defeats in the Far East and revolution at home. Russian planners therefore returned to the older, more defensive idea of concentrating their armies in a central position behind the dubious protection of the now outdated Polish fortresses. While these still offered some security of concentration and permitted the major blow to be struck either west or south, concentration there meant the tsar's armies could not take the offensive in less than six weeks, and probably not in less than two months.[208]

By 1909 German hostility and French pressure had made such a delay impossible. Furthermore, by that time it was clear that Berlin planned to strike first at France, not Russia. In addition, Russia's expanding railway network (see Table 8.10) made a more rapid mobilization and deployment more feasible than it had been a decade earlier. For these and other reasons, Sukhomlinov and Quartermaster General Yuri Danilov produced Plan No. 19. This recognized the need of forestalling a French disaster by a rapid Russian attack in the east. Yet since a drive into Central Germany would risk the pincers from East Prussia and Galicia, the main attack was to be directed against German forces in the northwest. Since Austria-Hungary would be slower to concentrate, Danilov proposed leaving only nine (of twenty-eight) army groups to hold Germany's ally. The other nineteen, divided among four armies, were to drive into the tactically difficult terrain of East Prussia. There they were to destroy the Germans' concentrations, and so divert reinforcement from the French front. To speed matters up, the Russian armies would concentrate well forward. This simultaneously would permit the razing rather than expensive reconstruction of the aged fortress system.[209]

In this spirit St. Petersburg promised France in 1911 to oppose Germany with 800,000 men by the fifteenth day, and to begin an offensive immediately afterwards. Meanwhile the new plan had aroused a storm of protest among Sukhomlinov's enemies in the Kiev and Warsaw Military Districts, the General Staff, and so on.[210] The debates need not concern us here, but they ended in the adoption of 'Plan No. 19 Altered' in May 1912. Its main varient foresaw that in the case of a German invasion of France, Russia would launch *simultaneous* offensives against East Prussia and Austria. However now only two armies (29.5 infantry divisions or 33 per cent of the mobilized forces) would strike the former while four armies (46.5 divisions or 52 per cent) would face the Austrians. As of 1913, the remaining 15 per cent were to be

Table 8.11 Anticipated Mobilization Schedule, 1914

	1st-line infantry divisions	*2nd-line infantry divisions*	*Cavalry divisions (2nd-line)*
Total by day 15	27	—	20
Additional by day 23	20.5–23	12	6
Additional by day 29	3–5	6	4
Additional by days 30 to 60	6.5–11.5	6	1.5
After day 60	Siberian troops become available		

Source: David R. Jones (ed.), *The Military-Naval Encyclopedia of Russia and the Soviet Union* (Gulf Breeze, Fla., 1978), Vol. I, p. 5.

allocated to the Sixth Army, based in St. Petersburg and guarding the Finnish Gulf, and to the Seventh Army, centered on Odessa and observing the Rumanians. Meanwhile the Baltic Fleet was to deploy behind the 'Central Position' mine fields to prevent a German sweep up the Finnish Gulf. Unfortunately for the Russian field armies, Sukhomlinov's opponents obtained retention of the expensive Polish fortresses, which henceforth consumed much of the available heavy artillery and relevant munitions.[211]

In August 1913 St. Petersburg informed the French General Staff that if Germany invaded France, Russia's armies would be more or less ready by the fifteenth day to launch an immediate offensive westwards. This would be directed against either East Prussia or Berlin, depending on the German deployments. Such was the plan that went into effect in 1914. Since then, many writers have blamed the subsequent disasters in East Prussia on its provisions. They argue that in order to assist France, the tsar's armies undertook premature offensives that were beyond their strength. Such critics point out that the mobilization schedule (Table 8.11) meant that by the fifteenth day Russia would have merely one-third of its strength available for initial operations. Thus Samsonov's Second Army advanced hurriedly, without one-fifth of its infantry, to its destruction at Tannenberg.[212]

In retrospect, this argument is not convincing. True, the plan was a compromise and therefore far from perfect. Its greatest long-term defect undoubtedly was the retention of the expensive Polish fortresses, but this only became evident in 1915. In August 1914, despite the weakening of Danilov's anticipated Prussian drive, the forces allocated to the First and Second armies (Table 8.12) should have been sufficient. The same is true of the Austrian front. There, in fact, the Russians did score impressive victories, even if their four armies there were not at full strength until the thirtieth day. Yet even if the plan was imperfect and hurried preparations for the offensives did create some confusion, the East Prussian disasters resulted more from poor leadership and the faulty coordination of the two armies at the front level than from fatal defects in prewar planning.[213]

In any case, this pull between two strategic directions had been implicit in Russian planning since 1870, and it had been codified in the actual war plans since 1900. By 1914, given the prevailing mood in Russian society (civil and military alike), the exigiencies of the French alliance, the Imperial Army's

Table 8.12 Forces Deployed on Eastern Front, August 1914

Fronts and Armies	*Infantry divisions*	*Cavalry divisions*	*Guns*
Northwestern Front			
Russian 1st Army	6.5	5.5	402
Russian 2nd Army	11.5[a]	3	702
Total	18[a]	8.5	1,104
German 8th Army	6.5	1	1,044
Southwestern Front			
Russian 4th Army	6.5	3.5	426
Russian 5th Army	8	3	516
Russian 3rd Army	12	3	685
Russian 4th Army	8	3	472
Total	34.5	12.5	2,099
Austrian 1st Army	9	2	480
Austrian 4th Army	9	2	474
Austrian 3rd Army	6	3	318
Woysch's Corps	2	—	72
Kummer's Corps	3	1	144
Kevis' Corps	8	3	366
Total	37	11	1,854
Total Russian	52.5	21	3,203
Total Central Powers	52	12	2,898

[a] Other sources give these figures as 11, 17.5, and 52, respectively.

Source: Rostunov, *Ruskii front*, p. 110.

offensive doctrine, and the immediate causes of the war, such a division of effort was inevitable. So too were the risks involved, though few – the Germans included – anticipated the stunning outcome of the first East Prussian campaign.[214] In theory, one may agree with D. C. B. Lieven that 'genuine joint Franco-Russian planning aided by a sensible grasp of the alliance's strategic position' would have convinced Paris to take a defensive stance until the Russians were prepared to commit their full forces, and that this might have occurred 'had Russian generals been able to infect their French counterparts with some of their much-despised defensive-mindedness.' That the Russians did not do so, he blames on a certain degree of 'muddle-headedness and lack of self-confidence' on their part; but to succeed in this, the Russian military would have had to rewrite their own doctrine, and have convinced the French to abandon theirs – and this at a time when all major armies stressed immediate offensives to win decisive victories in what was to be a brief, sharp war. This seemed the lesson of the much-studied Franco-Prussian conflict of 1870–71. Since the Russians shared this European-wide delusion, early offensives were inevitable.[215]

One must stress as well that most responsible civilian leaders fully agreed with the generals on the need for simultaneous offensives westwards and southwards to support the French and strike the despised Austrians. As noted, the nature of the imperial elite made civil-military conflicts in the normal sense unlikely in prewar decision making, and Nicholas II himself was involved in much of the planning. Further, although the data is scanty, Imperial Russia seems to have had an effective prewar intelligence system, especially in Austria; but though it scored a number of coups, the impact of its revelations on planning remains difficult to gauge.[216]

Once war began, the institutional military-strategic framework, and later the pressures of domestic politics, badly damaged and finally destroyed much of the existing military-civil unity. Even so, as late as 1917 few educated Russians objected to a strategy that strove to secure national goals in Galicia, the Balkans, the Turkish Straits, and the Caucasus. They also accepted that the necessities of alliance politics simultaneously demanded attacks to relieve German pressure on the French, British, and (after 1915) the Italians. Meanwhile Russia's wartime strategic planning had consistently accorded with these dual political imperatives and throughout remained integrated with that of the Western Allies. Although an expedition against the Straits never took place, in general the Russians proved repeatedly responsive to their allies' pleas. In March 1916, for example, they first launched the unsuccessful attack against the Germans at Lake Naroch in the north to relieve the pressure on Verdun, and then advanced the date of their June offensive on the Southwestern Front in reponse to a frantic Italian request in May. Again, they cooperated with the British against the Turks, supplied troops for the Allies' Salonika expedition, and even sent a brigade to France.[217]

In this planning process, the empire's political and military leaders shared responsibility for both the success and the failures, such as Rumania's disastrous entry into the war in August 1916.[218] Russia's military representatives – even the ill-starred Zhilinskii, who was transferred from his front command after Tannenberg to the post of military representative to Allied meetings in France – on the whole proved competent in defending their empire's interests during Allied planning sessions, but the Allies' desperate appeals frequently forced the high command to change its plans or divert forces from the weaker Austrians and Turks in order to launch assaults against the stronger and better entrenched Germans. While this at times may have impaired *Stavka*'s ability to oppose its strengths to enemy vulnerabilities, it more often reflected the constraints of coalition warfare than it did strategic blundering.[219]

All in all, Russia's allies had little cause for complaint before 1917 – a point deserving special emphasis given both the empire's practical reasons for seeking a separate peace after 1915, and the malicious rumors that many in court and government circles recommended just that course. In the end, the domestic costs of pursuing the conflict helped to destroy the empire, but continuation of the war was more a political than a military decision. Given the commitment found throughout both official and unofficial society to Russia's 'national' goals, a decision to withdraw was unthinkable.[220]

The tsarist military performance in the area of military-strategic effectiveness, at least initially, is much more open to criticism. The reforms introduced after 1908 had raised considerably the armed forces' combat potential, and those of the Great Program of 1914 would have done so still further.

However, as Europe lurched toward war in 1914, Russia lacked the institutional forms capable of providing effective strategic leadership and operational directions for field administration which would replace those of 1890 and incorporate the lesson of 1904–5.[221]

Military men had recognized the need to revamp the existing law as early as 1901. Yet it was only after a series of wargames and conferences that the General Staff finally began preparing a new draft in January 1913. Because of debate and opposition, the draft law still awaited the emperor's approval in the summer of 1914. Under the pressure of events, Sukhomlinov finally obtained Nicholas II's confirmation of its generally unmodified provisions only on 16 (29) July 1914, the day of Russia's first and quickly aborted mobilization.[222] Since this law was intended to crown all the military reforms of the prewar years, and since it is one of the most important and most criticized pieces of legislation approved by this monarch, it deserves special attention.

Nicholas II, much to the irritation of most politicians and some military men, had made clear his intention of serving personally as Supreme Commander-in-Chief since at least 1903.[223] The new Law on the Field Administration of the Army in Wartime therefore sought to establish the smooth functioning of both front and rear through his person. As Figure 8.2 shows, his immediate deputies would be the Chief of Staff at *Stavka*, for operational direction of the battlefields, and the War Minister in St. Petersburg, for the supervision of administrative, supply, and replenishment work at home. Apart from the sovereign himself, the War Minister also would serve as a direct link with the government through the Council of Ministers. Meanwhile, part of the General Staff would move to *Stavka* from the staff of the Supreme Commander, and part would continue its duties in the War Ministry. The Naval Ministry, with its own representative at *Stavka*, would provide leadership to the fleets, the direct, operational command of which lay in the hands of their commanders.[224]

The result should have been a relatively clear-cut system in which Nicholas's position as supreme military commander and supreme civil administrator unified the whole war effort. The law therefore granted the ruler as Supreme Commander-in-Chief, along with his *Stavka* and its agencies, complete civil as well as military authority in an extensive theater of operations. This last included the capital of St. Petersburg (now renamed Petrograd), and much of the country's industry, as well as a broad front zone stretching along Russia's western frontier. In the case of a retreat, this zone would move backwards with the front line to embrace still more of the empire. This meant that the Council of Ministers lost all effective authority in a vital region, the boundaries of which could change constantly, but which from the first included the capital. The possibilities for civil-military conflict of course were enormous; but acting on the assumption that the emperor would be Supreme Commander, those drafting the law did not trouble to define relations between that figure and his ministers, or give serious consideration to resolving disputes between the two.[225]

The simplicity of this system was fatally ruptured on 19 July (1 August) 1914. Then Nicholas II bowed to ministerial arguments and appointed Grand

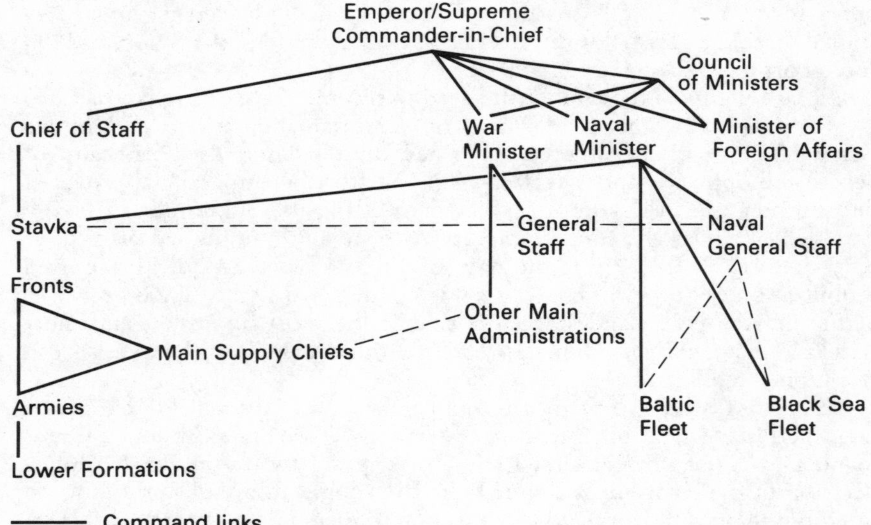

Figure 8.2 Proposed structure of High Command, July 1914
Source: D. R. Jones (ed.) *The Military-Naval Encyclopedia of Russia and the Soviet Union* (Gulf Breeze, Florida, 1980), II, p. 144.

Duke Nikolai as Supreme Commander.[226] While the ministers had some valid political concerns, their victory had a number of unfortunate results and created a much more complex system of command (see Figure 8.3). First, despite his presumed prestige, for the last six years the Grand Duke had been on the sidelines of planning and, in practice, during 1914–15 he showed himself to be a mediocre generalissimo.[227] Furthermore, the vendetta he and his supporters had waged against War Minister Sukhomlinov now continued and poisoned smooth relations between the field armies and their rear supply network.[228] Most important, under the new regulations Nikolai Nikolaevich became in fact a viceroy, responsible only to the emperor, over vast areas in the rear of the front.[229] By not assuming the post himself, Nicholas II had removed the linch-pin connecting the front to the supporting military and civil administrations of the rear. He did establish a Supreme Council, with its own chancellery, to serve this purpose under his personal headship. However both his own reluctance to interfere with Nikolai Nicolaevich and the latter's determination to preserve every iota of the authority granted him in his new post doomed this institution to a mere paper existence.[230]

The last body's impotence and *Stavka*'s consequent autonomy in effect deprived Russia of any supreme institution capable of providing political-strategic leadership to the whole defense effort. Although the Grand Duke seems to have aspired to this responsibility, his small headquarters staff (nine generals, thirty-six other officers, and twelve civilian officials), even as expanded by early 1915, showed itself incapable of enforcing effective

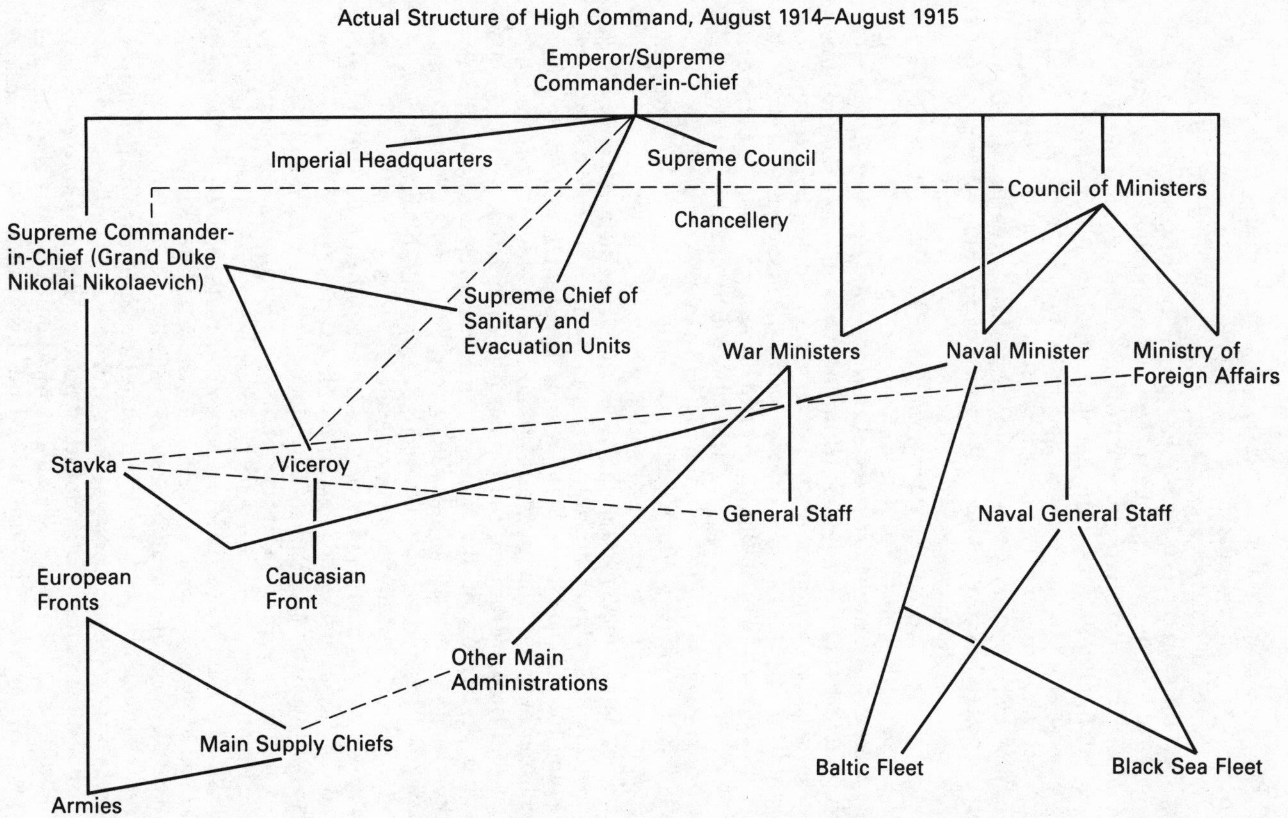

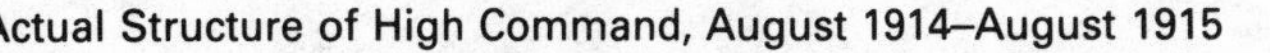

Figure 8.3 Administrative system and policy-making process: actual structure of High Command, August, 1914–August, 1915
Source: D. R. Jones (ed.) *The Military-Naval Encyclopedia of Russia and the Soviet Union* (Gulf Breeze, Florida, 1980), II, p. 153.

operational direction, let alone leadership in more complex spheres. In the meantime, despite his promises to work closely with the Council of Ministers, the Grand Duke's arrogance, along with *Stavka*'s ham-fisted abuse of the civil authority granted it by the law of 16 (29) July, led to a growing atmosphere of hostility and suspicion between headquarters and the government. This was especially highlighted by his refusal even to receive War Minister Sukhomlinov, his continuing efforts to discredit the latter, and his opposition to any attempt to create an institutional means of mediating conflicts between himself and the ministers as a whole. At the same time, he gave leaders of the Duma's liberal majority a warm reception that encouraged them to see Nikolai Nikolaevich as the key to obtaining long-desired domestic political concessions.[231]

Matters deteriorated rapidly during the Great Retreat of 1915. Then an hysterical *Stavka* first lost complete control over its armies' operations and blamed their defeats on the activities of German and Jewish spies.[232] It later complicated matters still further by instituting unnecessarily large and disorganized evacuation programs. As the retreat continued, headquarters pushed morale still lower by charging that its ineffectiveness stemmed from the treason and corruption of Sukhomlinov and his supporters. Even though the hated War Minister lost his position, relations between the ministers and *Stavka* had reached such a low point by July that even Polivanov, the Grand Duke's own man and new War Minister, was in despair.[233] At the same time, the *Stavka*-liberal alliance coincided with the recall of the Duma (for debate over the Special Councils) and military disaster to produce a major political crisis. As noted, Nicholas II resolved this in August-September by finally establishing the Special Councils to organize supply (Figure 8.1), restoring the linch-pin between front and rear by himself becoming Supreme Commander, and then proroguing the Duma. If the last action only drove the opposition underground, the first two measures restored coordination between *Stavka* and its political-military rear, guaranteed the field armies adequate matériel, and rapidly restored their combat capability.[234]

In sum, from the autumn of 1914 to August 1915 civil-military, or rather *Stavka*-government, relations had progressed to an all-time low. At the same time, confidence in *Stavka*'s professional military-strategic effectiveness had collapsed. Already by November-December 1914, the Grand Duke's headquarters had shown itself incapable of adequately controlling the Southwestern Front, and so ensuring a full concentration of effort against the Germans.[235] By June-July 1915 it had become virtually helpless in the face of the Central Powers' continued offensives, and the Grand Duke himself seemed on the verge of mental collapse. By refusing to withdraw much of its artillery and munitions from the Polish fortresses, *Stavka* had helped keep its field forces starved of the sinews of war. Seeking excuses, the Grand Duke and his subordinates dabbled in domestic politics and refused to cooperate with the official rear agencies responsible for the field armies' supplies and manpower. While a worried tsar looked on, his armies – lacking serious strategic direction – stumbled blindly towards collapse.[236]

This situation changed drastically in August-September 1915. With Nicholas II at *Stavka*, political-military friction again was reduced to a minimum and inter-Allied integration was assured. Under the tsar's calm supervision, Chief of Staff M. V. Alekseev restored order at the front. With the Austro-German offensive losing steam, *Stavka* halted the field armies' headlong retreat, established a stable front, and in 1916 again took the offensive. While the attack at Lake Naroch hardly pitted Russian strength against German weakness, it resulted more from Allied pressures than from Russian strategic planning. Similarly, the Rumanian campaign's disastrous results owed as much to inter-Allied diplomatic maneuvering as to faulty Russian decisions. Throughout the summer of 1916, this bickering delayed Rumania's entry into the fray while Brusilov's offensive was bringing startling victories. So by the time Rumania moved, the Central Powers had stabilized the front, the chance of decisively defeating Austria had been lost, and Russia found itself with a strategic liability rather than an asset.[237]

Nevertheless, the *Stavka* of Nicholas II and Alekseev was a vast improvement over that of the Grand Duke. On the whole, it gave the Russian field armies credible military-strategic guidance within the inter-Allied context. As just suggested, during 1916 this latter frequently disrupted Russian strategic planning. Apart from the Lake Naroch and Rumanian cases, Allied demands also limited the results Brusilov achieved on the Southwestern Front. In December 1915 an Allied conference had met at Chantilly. It had agreed that early 1916 would see offensives launched on the French, Italian, and Russian Fronts, so as to prevent the Central Powers from concentrating their forces. The Russians were to take the field by early June. In accord with this, a conference of front commanders, chaired by the tsar and Alekseev, agreed in early April 1916 that this would involve simultaneous attacks on all three (North, West, and Southwestern) fronts. In this manner they sought to oppose Russian numerical strength against a still technically superior enemy. However, apart from flaws in operational concepts and preparations, both the Allied and the Russian plans were forestalled by the German assault on Verdun and the Austrian onslaught in Italy. As noted above, these events forced the abortive attack at Lake Naroch and induced Brusilov to move before the other fronts, a fact that helped prevent his operational success from achieving strategic significance. Yet while the Russian plan was not realized, it does illustrate *Stavka*'s attempts to use its armies' assets as effectively as possible.[238]

In this period the force structure of these armies was consistent with the tasks envisaged. While generals like A. E. Evert continued to demand huge quantities of shells, their failures resulted more from faulty operational-tactical conceptions than matériel shortages. That this was the case reflects the improved supply situation brought about by the mobilization of Russia's industrial base. As described above, once plants evacuated from Poland during the Great Retreat were reestablished and others had reached full capacity, production expanded rapidly. Although hindered by the enemy's blockade, this base now was relatively invulnerable, had adequate raw materials and manpower, and had a surprisingly high degree of technical sophistication (as evidenced by the aviation industry's products). Thus by 1917 the troops were being fully supplied with the requisite matériel for the forthcoming campaign.[239]

By the end of 1916 the army's logistical infrastructure had improved immensely. Gone were the days when artillerists believed 420 shells per gun was a generous allocation (as in the First Army in 1914), or when generals, like Samsonov's staff, prepared a mere 10,415 hospital beds for a battle's casualties.[240] The army now was backed by a massive network of supply depots and sanitary hospital facilities. However, their operation remained hampered by the deficiencies of Russia's railway system, which had deteriorated badly under the pressure of war. As shown above, this system had expanded considerably before 1914. Even so, the empire remained sparsely served compared to other European nations. Whereas Germany had 10.7 and Austria-Hungary 6.7 kilometers of rail for every 100 square kilometers, European Russia had only 1.2.[241] Equally important, most Russian lines radiated out toward the frontiers from population centers. This left few north-south lateral lines that could move troops from front to front in wartime, a fact that hindered Alekseev's movement of strategic reserves during Brusilov's offensive in 1916.[242] Furthermore, the creation of a front zone by the law on field administration of 1914 had badly confused the management of the system: in the rear a line remained under the civilian ministry, but on approaching the front control passed to *Stavka*. During the retreat of 1915 this had caused considerable chaos. But again, with the departure of Nikolai Nikolaevich for the Caucasus that August, matters had improved. *Stavka* remained aware of continuing deficiencies, however, and by the end of 1916 measures were being prepared to help remedy the situation.[243]

The above analysis suggests that Imperial Russia's military establishment possessed a high degree of strategic competence. Unfortunately this was not apparent during the war's first thirteen months thanks to the split between front and rear imposed by the law on field administration of July 1914. During that period the complete ineffectiveness and arrogance of Nikolai Nikolaevich exacerbated an already difficult situation, which improved immediately once Nicholas II reunified the armies and their support structure by himself assuming the Supreme Command. After that, as in the prewar planning, the military demonstrated considerable skill in pursuing the empire's own strategic objectives while supporting its Western allies. True, the demands of coalition warfare sometimes meant that the former were seemingly sacrificed to the latter, a fact that on occasion caused much grumbling and some bitterness among Russians at all levels. Nonetheless, 'society' remained unified on the need to pursue the war, even if sharp divisions existed as to who should direct it. This made the conclusion of a separate peace an 'untakeable' decision. In the end, however, the revolutions of 1917 – to some degree a product of the empire's successful war effort – doomed the armed forces' strategic effectiveness as the field armies lost their capability for combat in the chaos of domestic radicalism.

Operational Effectiveness

The issues involved in this section are those discussed by Soviet writers when they refer to an 'operational' level of command. They consider that this level exists between the strategic and tactical levels, and that it involves entities such as fronts and army groups. They argue that such higher operational grouping first appeared in a planned manner when the regulations on field administration of 1914 instituted two 'fronts.' These had separate headquarters that maintained sections similar to those found at the Supreme Commander's *Stavka*. In the Soviet view, this event marked a major step forward in the development of the military 'art.'[244] Yet others disagree. Stone, for instance, believes that these fronts only reflected the fact that the army was 'fatally split' between the East Prussian and Galician operations. This provision of the 1914 law, he insists, was 'not an appreciation that affairs of command had become so complex that not only army commands, but also army group ones, were needed to administer land forces; it was rather a perception that the army had to be divided between irreconcilible tasks. The construction of these separate groups was . . . an almost insuperable hinderance to the evolution of coherent strategy.'[245]

Whatever the strategic problems raised by the creation of the new operational commands, Stone's judgment ignores some essential features of Russia's prewar planning. As outlined above, the 'fatal' split between possible opponents was probably inevitable given Imperial Russia's political-strategic goals and obligations. More important, the new level of command resulted just as much from developments in Russian doctrine, which in turn reflected the army's long experience in waging war over vast distances, as it did from a compromise forced on the army by faulty planning and strategic disagreements. The previous (1890) law on field administration had envisioned field armies as the largest operational groupings. These were to be logistically independent yet operationally subordinated to a supreme headquarters. However, as demonstrated in Manchuria in 1904–1905, during extended battles involving large combined formations this arrangement could lead to confusion between the armies involved, as well as between them and *Stavka*. The law of 1914 therefore deprived armies of their autonomy by introducing fronts as an intermediate agency for the coordination and control of battles that often were far distant from the supreme headquarters.[246]

The importance of these operational headquarters in the military's plans is evidenced by the fact that they – not *Stavka* – contained the highest officers charged with ensuring 'the supply to the armies of all their needs, and of organizing their general rear.' Such an official did so by means of a series of 'staging supply sections,' and he handled evacuation measures as well; but given *Stavka*'s overall powers of control, the absence of a 'supreme supply chief' there at first sight is surprising. This is especially so since no figure existed at headquarters with authority to unite the rear as a whole.[247]

This lacuna seems explained by two considerations. First, Russian planners expected a short, mobile war in which a front's responsibility for its own rear was required to provide the flexibility such a conflict demanded. And secondly, those drafting the law of 1914 had expected the War Minister and his ministry's network to organize the 'deep rear' for supply of the theater forces. As he was to be responsible to the emperor as Supreme Commander, the minister would in fact serve as supreme supply chief. So here was another assumption that had to be abandoned once Nikolai Nikolaevich, not Nicholas II, took charge at *Stavka*.[248]

In August 1914, then, the Russians set up a supreme headquarters that was to give overall strategic direction and coordination to the operations conducted by autonomous front commands. These in turn controlled two or more armies each. The large amount of authority granted the front commanders in their sphere reflected both past Russian experience and the widespread belief among European military men that a supreme commander could do little more than plan the overall order in which his troops would be committed. As in Leo Tolstoy's account of Borodino, events then took over while the commander-in-chief attempted to calmly await the evening action reports before drawing up his deployments for the next day. This attitude also helps explain the latitude granted by semi-autonomous front commanders like Zhilinskii to their army commanders. In part it also may lie behind the apparent passivity with which Samsonov oversaw the Second Army's destruction at Tannenberg.[249] As one scholar recently noted, one of the major lessons of 1914's first battles was the extent to which modern means of reconnaissance (i.e., aircraft rather than calvary) and communications (i.e., radios, telegraphs, and telephones rather than couriers) had increased both a senior commander's control over events and the pressures upon him.[250] That this came as a surprise is clear from the communications equipment supplied to the armies that went to war. The German armed forces reportedly had a total of forty wirelesses, and the Russians even fewer. As for Samsonov, he had a total of twenty-five telephones, a few Morse code machines, and a primitive Hughs teleprinter that produced 1,200 words an hour. And when it broke down, the unfortunate general was reduced to traveling about by horse in an attempt to follow events.[251]

Logistically, *Stavka* was to work through the War Minister while the front supply chiefs organized the immediate rears of their operational zones (Figure 8.2). To guarantee success in combined operations, the navy and (later) the air fleet had their own representatives at *Stavka*. At sea the fleets served as the operational entities for naval actions.[252] When a new Caucasian Front appeared in November 1914, this was entrusted to a separate, semi-autonomous headquarters – modelled on *Stavka* – headed by the viceroy. This left it dependent on the central headquarters only for decisions on major issues of policy, and the successes won in that theater suggest that the new structure *could* work effectively with a competent commander-in-chief.[253]

Despite later critics, it was also suited to the war envisaged by planners. Although roads usually remained primitive in Eastern Europe, railroads had considerably speeded up the mobilization process. At the same time, new logistical methods had liberated armies from strict reliance on prepared magazines and supply bases.[254] Therefore the Russians, like other Europeans, counted on taking the offensive quickly in a war of maneuver that was to be waged by mobile, combined-arms columns. In many ways the best, if also the most extreme, expression of such expectations is found in the work of General A. A. Neznamov. By 1912 he was arguing that any serious doctrine must be based on such factors as mass, fire power, and movement, and that operationally it must stress a mobile offensive. He believed that in any future conflict, victory would be gained from a series of battles or 'operations.' These would be linked by 'an operational line' or 'basic idea' that governed goals. They thus would form an inter-related series of forward leaps that could entail multi-corps and even multi-army actions, any of which might become 'today's battle of exhaustion.' To avoid this and gain victory, he taught that one must first define clearly the goals of the operations, and then prepare them carefully. Above all else one had to take care to establish and sustain the fire relationships between one's units on a battlefield that had become more disorganized than ever.[255]

The front structure obviously accommodated such operations. And theoretically at least, the Imperial Army's concept of combined-arms battle seemed equally suited to the modern battlefield. Both its tactical handbooks and the Field Regulations of 1912 recommended that armies move in mixed columns of infantry and cavalry. Supported by machine and field guns, these must be prepared at any moment to enter an 'encounter' or 'meeting' engagement directly from the march. Unfortunately branch rivalries – and especially the artillery's disdain for the infantry – frequently hampered the realization of the necessary cooperation between arms.[256]

There was another, still greater problem with such concepts of mobile warfare. In 1914, an army's mobility still remained limited by the speed with which men and horses could move under their own power once they left a railhead. In the best conditions, on good roads and in favorable weather, rested infantrymen could travel only some 2.6 miles (4.16 kilometers) an hour. For large operational formations, even daily moves of 10 miles (16 kilometers) had to be considered to be 'forced.' Cavalry naturally seemed to offer greater opportunities for maneuver, and European military men continued to value this arm. They had been particularly impressed by Jeb Stuart's deep raids during the American Civil War (1861–5). In 1904 the Russians had tried a similar strike against the Japanese with a mobile column under General P. I. Mishchenko. Again, before 1914 War Minister Sukhomlinov – a student of Stuart's raids – had contemplated a full-scale cavalry strike into Germany. Yet even such mounted columns could advance only 4.6 miles (7.6 km) per hour by alternate trotting and walking. Worse still, cavalry by itself lacked the weaponry to deal with even small infantry strong points. Yet if infantry and artillery were attached to form a mixed column, the cavalry's rate of movement again was reduced.[257]

Despite such drawbacks European generals, desperate to increase the mobility of their armies, insisted on maintaining large cavalry forces. In peacetime these consumed considerable funds that, in retrospect, might have been spent better elsewhere. Even so, cavalry retained a certain psychological effect. In the popular German mind, a Russian invasion of East Prussia entailed hordes of pillaging Cossacks. For this reason the First and Second armies began their campaign with a total of eight and a half cavalry divisions. In the event, they proved of little use, even for reconnaissance. For the most part, during the ensuing conflict Europe's cavalry divisions spent most of the war waiting for a breakthrough that never happened. However, the retention of this arm also meant that all European armies, Russia's included, wasted critical railway capacity on moving horses and providing them with the

Table 8.13 Horses and Forage Requirements, 1914–17

	No. of horses	Forage (tons) average/month	RR Cars Required average/month	average/day
1914	670,775 (1 Oct.)	556,993	53,057	1,768
1915	1,035,682 (1 Jan.)	758,089	72,199	2,407
1916	1,589,909 (1 Feb.)	1,589,909	110,997	3,700
1917	2,760,000 (1 Sept.)[a]	1,227,718	116,926	3,898

[a] If those of the 'voluntary public organizations' are included, by this date there were 3,164,000 horses in the theater of war.

Source: F. Shutnikov, 'Prodferazhnyi vopros v sovremennoi operations,' *Voennaia mysl'*, (1939), no. 10, p. 103.

bulky fodder they needed. Since the transport of a cavalry division (4,000 men and 12 guns) utilized 40 trains, the same number as an infantry division (16,000 men and 54 guns), the mobilization of Russia's 20 to 21 calvary divisions undoubtedly delayed the army's full concentration in 1914. Beyond this, the cavalry's horses needed 12 pounds of grain daily, even when not in action.[258] The burden this placed on Russia's already overworked rail network is obvious from Table 8.13 which details the increase of horses used in the war zone, the forage they consumed, and the railway cars needed to supply them.

When the above factors are considered in combination with the defensive power given infantry by machine guns, rapid-fire rifles and artillery, it becomes obvious that the mobile warfare of Neznamov and others would have to await the full-scale introduction of the internal combustion engine on the battlefield. Yet this did not necessarily make the operational structure of 'fronts' inappropriate. Indeed, the subsequent adoption of army groups by other countries suggests the opposite.[259] Nonetheless, the disaster suffered by Samsonov's Second Army in East Prussia in August (September) 1914 seems to support critics like Stone. Yet this defeat resulted from a number of factors. They include hasty preparation for the advance, poor intelligence, dismal communications, and inadequate logistical support, quite apart from Samsonov's own errors and General Zhilinskii's lamentable failure at coordinating his two East Prussian armies at the front level.[260] As pointed out earlier, during the Polish-East Prussian battles of late 1914, even *Stavka* proved incapable of forcing its will on the Southwestern Front, and so of ensuring a concentration of effort against the Germans.

Although this helplessness in part resulted form the freedom of action granted the fronts by the July law, it reached mammoth proportions during 1915 thanks as much to the incompetence of Nikolai Nikolaevich and his subordinates as to the front structure *per se*. In 1916 *Stavka*, now under Nicholas II and Alekseev, still at times had difficulty enforcing its orders on its subordinate commanders.[261] In spite of this, the new operational formula had been expanded by the creation of new 'fronts.' By 1917 they had proven their worth, both as agencies for conducting battle and for organizing the armed forces' logistical infrastructure, and since then have been an integral element in Russian doctrine.[262]

In analyzing the tsarist army's operational effectiveness, attention must be paid to the quality of commanders available in 1914. For if the army that marched to war was hindered by the fact that most of its regulations were new and its re-equipment program had just begun, the disasters of 1914–15 are fully explicable only in terms of faulty leadership at the operational (front, army), as well as the tactical level. Thus D. C. B. Lieven recently scored 'the relatively limited ability of most of the senior commanders' as 'a key Russian failing.'[263] Efforts to improve the calibre at this level had been implemented. These included the creation of a Supreme Credentials Commission in 1906 to ensure the qualifications of those receiving senior promotions, an order of that same year that regimental and higher commanders undertake further training in handling troops, and another of 1909 requiring all staff and general officers to participate in wargames. Yet these frequently floundered in execution thanks to the 'protectionism' inherent in any bureaucratic organization, as well as to the rivalries and personal jealousies that plagued the high command.[264]

As a result, critics maintain that in 1914 most senior Russian generals lacked practical experience in commanding troops. They also explain this flaw by both the nature of instruction received by junior officers in their regiments, and by the quality of higher military education. An attempt was made to improve the first in 1908 by raising the level of the winter discussions of tactics given regimental officers. However, the success of this measure differed widely from regiment to regiment; in some, critics charged, the sessions became excuses for drinking bouts, but in others they were taken seriously and involved lectures by staff officers. Thus, the quality of junior commanders undoubtedly varied greatly from arm to arm, and between different units of the same arm.[265] As for the lack of experience displayed by senior personnel, this usually is blamed on the early age at which candidates were selected for the staff college, the theoretical nature of many of that institution's courses, and the fact that many graduates later spent much of their time in positions of military administration, rather than in those of command. Reviewing the situation, one émigré writer sadly concluded that Russian generalship probably could have been improved only by 1920 to 1925, after the older generation had passed from the scene.[266]

For those sharing this view, ample evidence seems available from the criticisms that emerge from accounts of the prewar maneuvers and wargames. Each year the training activities in each military district officially culminated in large field exercises at that level both to demonstrate the quality of the troops and to assess the senior commanders' operational abilities. Before 1904 such maneuvers, especially those in the St. Petersburg Military District that the tsar attended, had had the reputation of being purely formal exercises that were staged for show rather than realism.[267] While this picture is unduly harsh, after the Manchurian campaign the War Ministry did recognize that such annual exercises were an excellent means of eradicating some of the defects revealed in operational command. Since earlier efforts had been hindered by limited funding, the ministry now budgeted considerably larger funds to permit the participation of more units, which again increased the problems faced by senior commanders.[268]

As John Bushnell notes, the utility of such maneuvers obviously depended on the quality of the officers involved. Maintaining that in some districts they continued to amount to 'little more than picnics,' he points out that senior district commanders often sought to avoid risking their reputations by participating, or that they arranged to avoid naming a winner to protect those that did take part. He also concludes that overall, these exercises clearly were 'so carelessly conducted' as to be 'worse than useless.'[269] In many respects, his judgment seems borne out by contemporary evaluations. Thus P. N. Krasnov, who took over command of the 10th Don Cossacks in late 1913 and quickly brought them up to his own high standards, complained that the comments following a divisional review praised all regiments equally and ignored the mistakes made by other regiments.[270] More telling still, the military press continued to chronicle recurring flaws in operational practice and command until the very eve of hostilities. Since these reflected on the quality of the army that entered battle in July 1914, they deserve attention here.

As described by émigré authorities like generals A. I. Denikin and V. M. Dragomirov, as well as contemporary critics, even after 1906 field exercises often remained set-piece affairs. Each side was assigned objectives that were so specific (i.e., what to attack or defend, and even in which direction to retreat) that the commanders were left with little or no room to display initiative. The units involved usually were prepositioned in their bivouac areas and moved off together. Even if one did have a detached point of departure, it normally reunited quickly with the main body. The latter moved rapidly along a narrow front to fulfill its assignments and make contact with the opponent. During the march, scouts were wasted in the first stages so that later reconnaissance was insufficient, the cavalry units sent on deep reconnaissance often disappeared, and communication or coordination with flanking detachments was generally nonexistent, thanks to the commanders' dislike of the trouble involved.

On reaching the battlefield, the forces involved rushed into battle with no attempts at close reconnaissance whatsoever. As a result, little attention was paid to picking suitable fire positions for either infantry or artillery; the latter usually remained in the same position throughout, and no effort was made to mask troop movements. Field fortifications were not constructed, and the troops consequently received no practice in assaulting entrenched positions. Equally disturbing, the artillery received little fire direction and the problem of keeping it supplied with shells was ignored. So too were the use of signals, engineers and medical services, as well as serious staff work and the advantages of night movement. As for supply, since the detachments supplied their own from caches that usually had been established in advance, commanders deviated from their preplanned march routes as little as possible. When victories were calculated, these were based almost solely on the numbers of troops involved rather than on their positioning, effective fire, and efficient supply.[271]

Field exercises conducted in this manner can hardly be considered serious maneuvers. Indeed, junior artillery officers sometimes were excused from attending on the grounds that they could learn nothing from the experience! As for the senior commanders, there was little here to test their capabilities. In retrospect, they have been largely judged by their performances in the series of wargames or command exercises held before 1914. Almost all accounts are generally grim. One exercise, organized in 1912 by Zhilinskii as Chief of the General Staff, reportedly scandalized that institution thanks to its absurdity. Another had been scheduled for senior commanders a year earlier and was to be held in the tsar's presence in the Winter Palace; but it had to be cancelled due to 'conflicts' between the participants, which most observers explain by the fear of risking their reputations. Most distressing of all, a series of exercises held by Sukhomlkinov in the Kiev Military District during April 1914 supposedly demonstrated the complete incompetence of most of those involved (and especially of Zhilinskii). The participants advanced armies too rapidly, made little attempt to coordinate their movements, paid little or no attention to problems of communications and supply, and planned attacks in grossly inappropriate conditions. Yet none of the participants was even officially criticized, let alone reprimanded or replaced.[272]

Such accounts, as well as the failure of many senior commanders during the first months of the war, would seem to justify the almost universally unfavorable judgments made of the Imperial Army's high command. Yet other considerations must temper this view. For example, accounts of the wargames come after Tannenberg, and usually aim at finding a culprit for that disaster. Instead, prewar operational capabilities must be considered within the context of the prevailing doctrine as established by Naznamov and others, and in relation to the events of the day. For example, whatever the fears of generals for their reputations, there were real conflicts in 1912 – the year when Danilov's new war plan was being debated and the fate of the Polish fortresses decided – that help explain reactions to Zhilinskii's games and the cancellation of those in the palace. Again, many of the criticisms made of commanders in the Kiev exercise are of actions that the day's doctrine demanded. As pointed out above, armies were expected to advance as rapidly as possible and to wage autonomous battles, often from the march. Further, that men who spent much of their time in peace as administrators or 'managers,' especially in an army where even regimental and more senior commanders had very broad 'economic' responsibilities, had some difficulty in realizing such doctrinal concepts in practice should occasion no surprise.[273] More remarkable, perhaps, is the fact that with war, some commanders – like P. K. Rennenkampf at Gumbinnen on 7 (20) August 1914 – did wage successful 'meeting' or 'encounter' engagements. Similarly, his colleagues on the Austrian front showed operational skills that were at least the equal of their opponents', once they had adjusted to the realities of the modern battlefield.[274]

As for the field maneuvers, other sources suggest that the above outline is at best distorted. Even the critics mentioned admit that some exercises, such as those held in the Kiev and Vilna military districts, were not without value. That even this grudging praise does not reflect the facts is clear from the informed and confidential reports of professional British observers. These frequently contradict head-on assertions that the deficiencies listed were universal. The report for 1908 on those in the St. Petersburg District, for example, does note that General Danilov advanced his 'blue corps' westward 'without sufficent information,' and that Baron Ashberg's 'red corps' failed in its attack thanks to poor communications (i.e., the use of mounted couriers rather than telephones) with his left wing. However it also congratulates Ashberg for the 'neat withdrawal of his detachments from a dangerous position' by night, maintains that the 'supply of blank ammunition was lavish,' and remarks that overall, the 'present state of training shows remarkable progress as compared with that before the war.' Other criticisms include the seemingly 'suicidal' deployment in the open of fourteen squadrons of 'red' cavalry, the lack of a use of signaling by the cavalry and of entrenchments by the infantry, and the umpires' willingness to favor the attack by permitting an advance 'before superiority of fire had been obtained.' On the positive side it listed the fact 'that a free hand was given to commanders and there was less restriction on the movements of the troops.' With regards to artillery the British observed an improvement in the close support of infantry with a few batteries being 'boldly advanced' for the final assault.[275]

One other aspect of this report deserves mention. This is the list of 'general principles' that 'Russian officers consider the experience of war demands . . . all training should . . . inculcate.' Briefly, these were: '(1) Concealment of troops from view and extension under fire. (2) Upkeep of communications between all parts of the force. (3) Development of independent action and initiative of the smallest units. (4) Insistence on the practice of offensive tactics.' If these objectives were not always realized in the exercise, the British had no doubt that they were taken seriously.[276]

Although the reports for 1909 to 1912 are generally less favorable and more supportive of the view of the critics, they nonetheless remain mixed in tone. In 1912, for instance, great attention is paid to the new, very detailed and stringent rules by which umpires were to judge the participants.[277] In 1913 British officers – who attended the maneuvers of the St. Petersburg, Kiev, and Moscow military districts, as well as those of the I Turkestan Corps – 'mention the umpiring as being well carried out,' except in Turkestan.[278] Both because of its timing and the criticism that appeared in the military press, the report for that year is especially interesting. None of the usual well-chronicled deficiencies are noted. Instead, both the regular infantry and cavalry receive high marks, as do the large number of reservists who participated in those of the Kiev district. The report again approvingly notes that 'the opposing commanders were said to have been given complete liberty of action.' It also comments favorably on Russian staff work, and in particular on the attention paid to communication, especially in Kiev; but in general, the report concludes that 'telephones have not been developed to an extraordinary extent in the Russian Army.'[279]

All this suggests that 'the old routine' was not as fully acceptable at the command level as Bushnell and others maintain.[280] True, in any organization as large and complex as the tsarist army, change took time; and little enough had passed since the defeats in Manchuria. Even so, if the war soon demonstrated that some commanders lacked the operational talents needed for war, it proved that others (i.e., Brusilov, A. M. Kaledin, and others) did not. Thus in July 1914, both commanders in East Prussia (Samsonov and Rennenkampf) seemed commendable choices. Both had had considerable experience in handling troops, were younger than their German counterparts (Max von Prittwitz and Paul von Hindenburg), had had recent combat experience in the Japanese War, and enjoyed the confidence of their subordinates. For these reasons, a noted British student of the 1914 campaign could only conclude sadly that both appeared 'to have deteriorated much' since 1905.[281]

While this judgment, informed by hindsight as it is, may be applicable to Samsonov, Rennenkampf arguably remained at least as effective a commander as did such British leaders as field marshals French and Haig.[282] Unfortunately the same is not true of the Northwest Front's commander, Zhilinskii, or worse still, of the Supreme Commander Nikolai Nikilaevich. In spite of the Grand Duke's continuing reputation as a commander of brilliance, the evidence suggests that he was a complete incompetent who 'never bothered about war plans, which had to be prepared on the spot by the general staff and served fresh, like an omelet by his cook.'[283] Even worse, during the Great Retreat of 1915 he panicked so badly that his wife worried openly that 'her husband would have a complete nervous breakdown.'[284] It is small wonder that the ministers complained that *Stavka* 'has apparently lost its head, and its directives are acquiring an hysterical character.'[285]

Russia's military leadership, apart from some of the generals on the Southwestern Front, must generally be given low marks for operational as well as strategic effectiveness during the war's first year. Furthermore, commanders of this calibre were hardly capable of accommodating themselves to the new realities of a conflict in which improved communications made central control vital, defensive fire power made most assaults costly failures, and real mobility remained a mirage. In this, of course, they were not alone among Europe's leaders. For the most part, after Tannenberg the Russians had held their own in the north, and won major victories in the south. This situation continued as long as the period of 'maneuver warfare,' as it is somewhat erroneously known, lasted on the Eastern Front. By April of 1915 the tsar's armies seemed poised in the Carpathians for a drive that threatened to force the Hapsburg empire from the conflict, and in the Caucasus they had brilliantly turned back a Turkish offensive. On the Western Front, meanwhile, the Germans were absorbing the lessons of the trench warfare brought on by the factors just mentioned. When they then resolved to send eight divisions eastwards to aid the desperate Austrians, they also sent these lessons. The result opened a new phase on the Eastern Front.[286]

The initial German success resulted largely from local factors. Their assault was launched on a relatively narrow front against two corps of the Russian Third Army. Thanks to incessant quarrels between *Stavka* and the two front commands, this army had been left undermanned, strategically isolated, and without reserves to defend a long front running from Cracow to the Carpathians. Furthermore, the two Russian corps involved comprised largely second-line troops who were badly entrenched. These factors, along with poor tactical leadership and a mishandling of what reserves were available at the operational and strategic levels, go far to explain both the Gorlice-Tarnov breakthrough and the subsequent Russian defeats over the next four months. Here Russia's poor railway network with its lack of lateral lines played a role, but as Stone points out, the problem was also the low quality of Russian railway troops. For July 1916, the Germans made much more effective use of these same lines to move 494 troop trains with 10 divisions, as well as 98 artillery trains, to stem the Russian breakthrough on the Styr. And in any case, once the front had caved in, *Stavka* lost complete control over events. This left the semi-autonomous fronts to manage without the coordination required by the Russian command structure, thus magnifying the impact of local disasters and furthering the spread of hysteria. For while the Central Powers did enjoy superiority in guns and shells, this was far from a sufficient cause for the Russian collapse. However once Russian generals had convinced themselves that it was, their operational and tactical effectiveness changed accordingly.[287]

When the front stabilized in a state of trench or 'position' warfare during the fall of 1915, Russian military men turned to the study of their own recent experiences and those on the Western Front. While many of their conclusions are discussed in the following section on tactics, some are properly operational in scope. Many of the tsar's generals ended by agreeing with Haig that only an offensive on a narrow front had any chance of breaking the stalemate. There a massive infantry assault, preceded by a stupendous artillery bombardment, theoretically would pierce the enemy's lines of trenches and allow the cavalry through to exploit the breakthrough. However, the effort required to concentrate sufficient artillery and infantry for the initial assault and to bring up the cavalry meant abandoning the element of surprise. This permitted the enemy to bring up its own reserves to stem any troops that managed to pass through its heavily fortified entrenchments. The end result usually was a new and costly stalemate. This the Russians learned from the XI Corps' attack on the Strypa in December 1915, and during the Lake Noroch operation of March 1916. This last, in which some 240,000 to 350,000 Russians launched themselves against 62,000 Germans, cost the Russian Northern and Western Fronts some 100,000 men, yet failed miserably. Although artillery support had been generous (about 1,000 guns with 200 rounds per day each), the enemy lines remained virtually intact. Nonetheless, the generals once again blamed an insufficiency of munitions for their problems, a position that seemed bound to doom the tsar's army to passivity.[288]

Obviously, this method of conducting operations meant opposing one's own strengths to the enemy's, who on the Russian front usually could amass a local superiority in materiel. On the Southwestern Front, however, matters were somewhat different. There A. A. Brusilov and some of his colleagues also had studied recent experience, and particularly the Seventh Army's failure of December 1915. As a result, Brusilov developed a new operational technique of striking with little artillery preparation (to achieve surprise) at several points along a broad front. When he became front commander in early 1916, the general at last received a chance to implement these ideas. At

Table 8.14 Force Levels on the Eastern Front, February-March 1916

Front	*Russian*	*Austro-German*	*Russian Superiority*
Northern	466,000	200,000	266,000
Western	754,000	420,000	334,000
Southwestern	512,000	441,000	71,000
Total	1,732,000	1,061,000	671,000

Source: L. Vetoshinkov, 'Brusilovskii proryv (Kratkii-operativno- stragicheskii ocherk), *Voennaia Mysl'*, no. 7, (1939), p. 71.

Stavka, Alekseev and other generals fully appreciated the strategic utility of coordinating the Allies' offensives in general, and those on their own fronts in particular. This would prevent the Central Powers from using their internal lines to defeat attacks individually, and so allow the Russians to take advantage of their superiority in men (see Table 8.14). The originality of Brusilov's conception lay in utilizing a number of tactical innovations to stage simultaneous assaults at several points along the same front.[289]

Stavka had understood from Brusilov's predecessor that his armies were incapable of offensive action. The plan presented by Alekseev therefore called for Evert's Western Front to launch the main attack towards Vilna, and for A. N. Kuropatkin's Northern Front to launch a secondary assault in the same direction. When Brusilov insisted his troops could join in and so pin down the enemy on the Southwestern Front as well, he received permission to proceed, but only on the understanding that *Stavka*'s artillery and troop reserves had been promised already to the other fronts. Nonetheless, he remained as optimistic as the other front commanders despite their greater numerical superiorities and stockpiles of materiel.[290]

With the general attack scheduled for the end of May, Brusilov issued his directives for the forthcoming assault. In accord with these, General Kaledin's Eighth Army was to deliver the major blow with three corps at Lutsk, along a front 22 kilometers in length; the Eleventh and Seventh armies were to make subsidiary attacks on smaller fronts (6 kilometers or less) in Tarnopol and Yazlovetsa; the Eleventh Army was to make a demonstration in the direction of Lvov; and the front's reserves were to be concentrated in the Rovno region. Great precautions were taken to ensure secrecy and hence surprise: leaves continued as usual; all engineering work took place at night, and then the results were carefully camouflaged; large underground bunkers were built to conceal the assault parties; and despite the dangers that a breakthrough might remain unexploited, there was no massing of large forces of cavalry. In addition, the date of the proposed attacks was revealed to a very small number of senior officers until the last moment. As a result, when Brusilov opened his offensive on 22 May (4 June), he achieved complete surprise and quickly ruptured the enemy lines.[291]

In this manner, the Russians found the key to breaking the deadlock of trench warfare at the operational-tactical level. Brusilov's success is all the more striking when compared to the defeat of the subsequent narrow-front assaults of Kuropatkin and Evert. As usual, these generals explained their failures by the lack of adequate artillery support and munitions. Yet Brusilov's guns had fired only some 250 rounds a day over two days of fighting. This was considerably fewer shells than those supplied to his colleagues, and a mere pittance compared to the 600 rounds being fired daily along the Somme.[292] Yet it was Brusilov who achieved the long-sought breakthrough thanks to his rejection of the new orthodoxy. Indeed, it is quite possible that his operational and tactical innovations might have remained untested if Russian generals had had the unlimited stocks of shells of which they dreamed.[293]

In the end, though, Brusilov's victory failed to win any operational-strategic advantages and ground to a halt in the bloody mud along the Stokhod. In part this resulted from Alekseev's hesitation to withdraw for his support the reserves of troops, guns, and munitions already assigned to the other fronts, and in part it reflected the Germans' efficient use of railways to rush reinforcements to the aid of the defeated Austrians. Furthermore, in the later stages of the summer campaign the Russians tended to return to the familiar but useless 'grand phalanx,' narrow-front battles favored by other commanders. Yet the main reason probably was that Brusilov still lacked the mobility with which to sustain and exploit his breakthrough. Concentrations of cavalry might have provided this, but their presence would have meant forfeiting the vital element of surprise; and even if the squadrons had galloped forward, the army would still be tied to its horse-drawn supply trains. Herein lay the paradox of trench warfare: for surprise one surrendered mobility, and vice versa. The internal combustion engine was to prove as important for logistical mobility as it was for combat. Until armies became motorized, operations would only rarely rise above the level of grand tactics.[294]

Nevertheless, if in late 1916 many generals still seemed wedded to phalanx-style battles like those on the Stokhod, the stunningly successful Mitau Operation of December 1916 to January 1917 demonstrated that the techniques of Brusilov were slowly gaining ground. Then units of General R. D. Radko-Dmitriev's Twelfth Army achieved a complete surprise before Riga by using *no* artillery preparation at all.[295] Equally indicative, by April 1917 Lt. Colonel A. Syromiatnikov had incorporated the lessons of this campaign into his lectures at the Staff Academy.[296] Meanwhile, 1916 had witnessed other proofs of Russian operational competence, the most notable being the storming of Erzurum on the Caucasian Front in February. Less significant but just as interesting were the actions waged along the Black Sea Coast of Lazistan. These had led to the capture of Trebizond in April 1916. In them the Russians had demonstrated fully their capability in land-sea combined operations and amphibious techniques.[297]

By the spring of 1917 Brusilov, now Supreme Commander-in-Chief, was preparing to test his methods in a general summer offensive; but while they again scored initial successes, by this time the army was too demoralized by revolution to sustain the tempo.[298] Despite this, on the basis of his earlier victory and the other successes won by Russian arms in 1916, one must conclude that the Imperial Army had within it commanders of sufficient intellectual flexibility to adapt themselves to the reality of modern war. When they were given their heads, they in turn provided excellent examples of operational effectiveness. That they were given such opportunities reflects the suitability of the front structure, which in the end also proved relatively efficient as a means of organizing the infrastructure of the immediate rear. To blame this structure or other more incidental factors for the earlier failures is to obscure the main point: unfortunately many Russian generals, whatever their managerial prowess in peacetime, proved to be either incompetent in war, or as obstinately conservative as their fellows elsewhere when faced with a long war of a type they had not anticipated.

Tactical Effectiveness

Many of the above factors are equally applicable to considerations of the tsarist army's tactical effectiveness in the First World War. During that conflict, the line between the operational and tactical 'arts' was frequently blurred to the point of being indistinguishable. By 1914 the army was preparing tactically for a mobile war in which advancing combined-arms (infantry, cavalry, and artillery) columns would employ formations suitable for entering battle directly from the march. In practice, however, the implementation of such tactics was hindered by a number of factors. Among these was the artillery's arrogance, the diverse training methods employed, and the uneven quality of junior officers who remained overburdened by the demands of their economic responsibilities.[299] As the British observers of the 1912 maneuvers noted, the 'Russian officer has many good qualities, but his lack of education and the poorness of his prospects are fatal at present to any great improvement.' For while many young officers were described as 'interested in their profession and keen,' there seemed few outlets for such ambitions. Their keenness therefore was dulled 'by the routine of a conscript army.'[300] Meanwhile, the army still lacked a 'unified military doctrine' as hot debates continued among its theoreticians over the nature of 'encounter' and other types of conflicts.[301]

Given these continuing problems, the troops who took the field in August 1914 were surprisingly ready to wage the type of tactical struggle evisaged by military planners. The latter naturally had defined this in terms of the prevailing operational concepts. As in that area, actual mobility often fell far short of the theoretical demands of tactical precepts. These had been reworked since 1905, encoded in such manuals as the Field Regulations of 1912, and were applied – with various degrees of success – in field exercises and maneuvers.[302] On such occasions, the infantry generally won good marks from foreign observers for both its physique and ability to carry out modern tactical drills.[303] Tactically, the cavalry won fewer plaudits, and in modern war it proved a disappointment. Unfortunately, Russia's generals – who like their confrères elsewhere often were ex-cavalrymen – long ignored the lessons of the conflict's first months.[304]

Apart from mobility, the tactical precepts and training of the tsar's forces in 1914 also emphasized the need for combining the traditional arms in battle. Much is often made of the traditionalists' professed belief in the power of the bayonet, allegedly as a replacement for fire power; but the axioms of the great

A. V. Suvorov and M. I. Dragimorov were used more as training aids, intended to instill a Russian martial spirit in peasant conscripts, than as serious expressions of tactical preference.[305] True, Russian (and other) theorists still had not comprehended the awesome power that modern weapons gave well-entrenched defenders, and the tsar's artillerists still resented having to work in close cooperation with the infantry. Nonetheless, almost all understood full well that fire power was a decisive factor. As Neznamov put it: 'Fire decides battles; the bayonet culminates the attack' – a judgment that almost every manual or writer echoed to some degree.[306]

Because of this recognition, during 1908 to 1914 Russian training emphasized marksmanship and the siting of fire-points to a degree never seen before in the Imperial Army. Similarly, all arms were becoming accustomed to new tactical formations that stressed the need for the troops to deploy rapidly from the march, often directly into battle. These were described in a series of new manuals that also recommended the troops drill in skirmish lines, make full use of cover, and develop initiative.[307] In this last regard, British officers were especially impressed by the training given scouts in the I Turkestan Corps.[308] By 1914 Russia's artillerymen, despite their frequent choices of exposed positions, had an excellent reputation for accuracy.[309] Others maintained that the infantrymen had become the best shots in Europe as well.[310] This claim was probably exaggerated, but the army as a whole was not badly prepared for a war of maneuver. This is evident from the victories of the Galician armies, and from the successes scored by the infantry of Rennenkampf's First Army in its first actions in East Prussia. Indeed, Soviet writers still cite the actions fought at Gumbinnen as models of encounter battles in this period.[311] More impressive still, the march formations of today's Soviet army are basically those practiced by the Imperial Army in 1914, with tanks and APCs replacing cavalry and infantry, respectively.[312]

Wedded to their belief in mobile war, most Russian commanders by the early spring of 1915 still had not recognized the need for acquiring new tactical skills. In this regard, the situation matched that described in the operational section above. When the German divisions moved eastwards to relieve the hard-pressed Austrians, they brought with them the costly tactical lessons of the more compact Western Front. These included the careful use of artillery, the need for close cooperation of the gunners with the infantry, and the utility of well prepared field fortifications. As pointed out, Russian artillerists had continued to consider themselves an elite and to disdain working closely with the infantry, which in turn had yet to learn the need for proper trenches. Although there had been a flurry of interest in trenches after the Manchurian campaign, this had waned with a reassertion of the doctrine of offensive mobility. While manuals continued to note their utility and officers were supposed to prepare the appropriate plans on maneuvers, in practice little was done to train the troops in their use.[313] In addition, the vast extent of the Eastern Front and the poorer railway communications already noted made the use of sufficient reserves tactically as well as operationally much more difficult. All sides in the east therefore tended to rely on thick front lines with little reserve backing, which made breakthroughs there much more difficult to handle. This the Germans demonstrated with their carefully organized assault at Gorlice in May, and in the subsequent battles of the spring and summer of 1915.[314]

At first Russian commanders at all levels proved slow in abandoning their preconceptions, but by autumn 1915, with the enemy finally stalled, they had begun to reassess their methods in the light of recent experiences. By July 1916 French and German handbooks had been translated for Russian use, and *Stavka* had issued new manuals on infantry combat and on attacking fortified zones. Now, as one émigré expert noted, each soldier was trained in a particular skill rather than as a jack-of-all-trades, and their commanders' initiative was severely limited. This was to ensure that they adhered closely to their roles in meticulously timed assaults made by waves of infantry, whose advance had been coordinated closely with the artillery's supporting bombardment. These waves were to strike the enemy's entrenchments in a narrow sector after a devastating barrage had supposedly smothered the enemy's defenses, break through to the rear, and so open the way for the cavalry.[315]

In general, the course of tactical change mirrored the operational developments outlined above. The majority of Russian commanders – men like N. I. Ivanov, A. E. Evert, and N. V. Russkii – had concluded that they must adopt this version of the German tactics, and that overwhelming artillery fire was an absolute requirement. For this they estimated that it was hopeless to attempt to move until up to a hundred light and heavy guns, each with a thousand rounds for a ten-day battle, could be concentrated on each kilometer of the sector of the assault.[316] Only then could it be struck successfully by the massed infantry. In this manner, of course, they also reiterated their belief that a shell shortage – not military incompetence at every level – lay behind recent disasters.[317]

Such tactics were tested in the series of bloody yet unsuccessful attacks that opened on the River Strypa in December 1915 and terminated on the Stokhod ten months later. These clearly demonstrated that such methods could not end the stalemate of trench warfare; for even if artillery-infantry cooperation could have been guaranteed, which in the earliest of these battles was never the case, even the most massive artillery preparation seldom destroyed the second or third lines of hostile trenches. Yet it so broke up the battleground as to impede the infantry's advance and make it subsequently impossible to bring up guns to support, or cavalry to exploit, any breakthrough. In addition, the efforts required to concentrate the necessary munitions and cavalry, let alone infantry, meant that real tactical as well as operational surprise became impossible. Therefore enemy reserves usually were in place well before the attack, which thus struck the strongest, rather than the weakest, section of his line. To solve this problem, the commanders mentioned could only call for still more shells and guns.[318]

As pointed out earlier, matters were viewed differently on the Southwestern Front. There, Brusilov and his colleagues recognized the need to regain the possibility of both operational and tactical surprise. The system that they worked out, and had an opportunity to implement when Brusilov replaced the aging Ivanov as front commander, was mutually consistent at these levels. To begin with, careful reconnaissance and observation took place along a broad front, which left the enemy doubtful over where the blow would fall. In the event, a number of blows came simultaneously in several sectors and aimed in several directions. Equally important, the initial attack was conducted by specially selected and carefully trained 'shock' or assault units. Having been familiarized with every detail of their objectives, they were secretly assembled in underground dug-outs on the eve of the offensive. Further, rigorous steps were taken to organize infantry-artillery cooperation at the tactical level. Officers were exchanged between units of the two arms, the artillerymen in the trenches serving as spotters. During the preparatory period, they selected and carefully registered targets in the opposing line. In this process aerial reconnaissance proved to be of considerable assistance. During the actual assault, the infantry advanced after a minimal but effective artillery preparation. On reaching the enemy lines, they by-passed his remaining strongpoints and so quickly overran even 'thick,' well-entrenched defensive lines. That they did so was thanks largely to the fact that they had achieved complete surprise. This meant that initially the stunned Austro-Germans blundered as much in using their available reserves in 1916 as the Russians had done in 1915.[319]

At the same time, this surprise resulted largely from the skillful use of camouflage and deception techniques, and from the fact that the enemy had not been alerted by any unusual concentrations of munitions or cavalry. Yet if the tactical and immediate operational benefits of this system were abundantly clear – indeed, within less than a year the Germans had adopted a similar system as their own preferred style of tactics – it failed to bring major operational-strategic results. Some blamed this on the fact that Brusilov struck with four extended fingers rather than a fist; that is, that no single assault had enough force to be decisive. Others once again blamed a lack of guns and shells.[320] Yet as already noted, it was a lack of cavalry to exploit the breakthrough, as well as the inability of the cumbersome supply and artillery columns of that day to keep pace with the advancing infantry, that eventually permitted the Germans to stem the flood and so robbed Brusilov's techniques of decisive strategic significance. As at the operational level, only the use of the internal-combustion engine for aircraft, tanks, and the trucks of supply columns could restore a mobility to the battlefield that was fully consistent with the warring nation's strategic objectives. Nonetheless, signs that Brusilov's system was finding wider use on other Russian fronts made the empire's prospects for 1917 seem much brighter.[321]

However in that year the army collapsed dramatically under the impact of domestic revolution. The consequent disintegration of its components in turn raises the issue of unit cohesion, an area in which the tsarist army usually has earned a low score. Stone has suggested that the 'old' army in fact collapsed during the disasters of 1915, and that the nucleus of a 'new' army began gestation on the Southwestern Front in 1916. In support of the first part of his thesis he cites considerable evidence concerning the low morale during the Great Retreat, the rising figures on desertion and illness, and the miserable conditions of service caused by chaos in the railways, the supply and evacuation networks, and the military administrative system in general. As other contributing factors he includes the chronic shortages in officers and

NCOs, the heavy losses suffered by both these categories in 1914 and early 1915, and the replacement of the conscript-regulars of 1914 by reservists and militiamen. Given the traditional distance between Russian officers and men, the reluctance to promote new officers from the ranks, and the general horror aroused by modern warfare, he notes that many wonder why signs of revolution did not break out among soldiers as early as December 1914. The army's 'structural' problems, he posits, were by then being reinforced by the common soldier's growing sense that his officers did not understand their business.[322] Moreover, as he, Wildman, and others demonstrate, such symptoms continued throughout 1916.[323]

Despite this catalogue of misfortune, these writers explain the army's continued existence and combat capability almost solely in terms of the harsh disciplinary measures imposed by senior and junior commanders.[324] Yet despite the effective use of such measures to meet similar signs of demoralization in other armies that did survive, this explanation is hardly convincing. As mentioned earlier, one Guards' regiment, for instance, began the war with 4,000 men, but by 1917 had had 44,000 men pass through its ranks. Yet until June of that year, it continued to be capable of combat. The existence of this and many similar units, as well as the success they scored in 1916, therefore seems to demand more sophisticated explanations.[325]

One recent study of the prewar tsarist army suggests that its basic unit, the regiment, in many ways replicated the peasant village. In this the soldier supposedly remained the toiler, and the officer the gentleman landlord or *barin*, in a world in which economic concerns and labor occupied much of the time of both.[326] While there is much to support this view, it still ignores other essential aspects of the regiment's nature. On joining it, the conscript and officer alike entered a 'family' with its own traditions, distinctive way of doing things, and corporate existence. Its connection with other similar units was based on particular instances of past glories, a common allegiance to the tsar and – despite religious diversity – the ideal of an orthodox empire. To some extent each soldier, although to a lesser degree than the officer, was drawn into this corporate entity.[327]

Given the vast turnover of personnel occasioned by the losses of 1914–16, as well as the general disillusionment and fatalism induced by such losses, the inculcating of such military traditions became much more difficult. Opposition propaganda, official stupidity and inefficiency, and all the other problems just enumerated undoubtedly hampered the process still further. Nonetheless, such traditional values seem to have combined with the individual soldier's sense of pride and his search for self-respect among his peers to a degree that sufficed to keep most regiments existing as cohesive fighting units into 1917. Here the oft-noted bonding of men who see action together, as well as the peasants' veneration for a tsar who made a point of being seen among his men, also probably played a part. However, in 1916 the liberal and radical opposition's propaganda began undermining both the soldier's traditional symbols of church and tsar. When this reached a crescendo after Nicholas II's abdication in early 1917, the regimental system collapsed – and with it the Imperial Army as a fighting organization.[328]

Tactically, the picture of the tsarist army's effectiveness parallels developments in the operational field. Before 1914 tactics were consistent with doctrine and the troops were receiving the appropriate training. True, the latter's efficacy varied from officer to officer, from unit to unit, and from military district to military district. Even so, during the war's initial campaigns (apart form Tannenburg) the troops gave a good account of themselves. Indeed, even during that operation the Russians showed considerable tactical skills, and the disaster's roots were more operational in nature. Nonetheless, until May 1915 actions on the Eastern Front supported the illusion that the war was still one of limited maneuver. This relieved Russian commanders of the need to recognize the bloody lessons being taught by defensive fire power on the Western Front. When the Germans demonstrated these at Gorlice-Tarnov in May 1915, the result was a catastrophe. By that autumn, however, the Russian commanders were reassessing their tactical concepts. While the majority adopted those then being used in France, on the Southwestern Front Brusilov and his colleagues demonstrated that some officers of the Imperial Army were capable of original operational-tactical thinking. The result was their stunning victory of 1916, and their precepts seemed destined to see wider application during the summer of 1917. Then, however, revolution undermined the army's capabilities, finally destroying the regimental system, and with it the old army. Nonetheless, before 1914 it had had a tactical system consistent with its perceived capabilities, and after 1915 it was developing one consistent with the new realities of modern war.

Conclusion

In summary, then, the story of the Imperial Russian Army's conduct of the First World War has been badly misrepresented. True, it had many failings in all the spheres under consideration; but these failings often were not unique, and frequently they are nôt those chronicled by historians. Politically and strategically, most educated Russians agreed on war aims and strategic objectives. They therefore provided their armed forces with adequate funding and, despite administrative inefficiency, created a war economy capable of providing the materiel for waging the struggle. Meanwhile, tsarist planners had developed an appropriate strategic-operational structure for the conduct of war, and an operational-tactical system consistent with the underlying doctrine of their day. These advantages were offset in 1914–15 by the conflict's unexpected duration, by an incompetent high command, by structural flaws within the empire's political and military systems, and by an inefficient military bureaucracy. By 1917 this last still had not solved the problems of shortages in manpower. In the end, such problems combined with domestic political opposition and economic strains to produce a revolution. Yet this should not obscure the fact that in 1916 the tsar's armed forces had shown remarkable powers of recovery and doctrinal innovation, or that in early 1917 they still remained a potent factor in the optimistic calculations of their Allies.[329]

Notes

1 Keith Neilson, *Strategy and Supply: The Anglo-Russian Alliance, 1914–17,* (London, 1984), p. 8.
2 Dennis E. Showalter, 'Even Generals Wet Their Pants: The First Three Weeks in East Prussia, August 1914,' *War and Society, vol. 2, no. 2 (September 1984), p. 63.*
3 Norman Stone, The Eastern Front, 1914–1918 (London, 1975), pp. 12–14, 210–11, 231, 282.
4 Ibid., p. 25.
5 Apart from General Nicholas N. Golovin's *The Russian Army in the World War* (New Haven, Conn., 1931) and his expanded *Voennyia usiliia Rossii v mirovoi voine* 2 vols. (Paris, 1939), see Sir Bernard Pares's famous *The Fall of the Russian Monarchy: A Study of the Evidence* (New York, 1961); Michael T. Florinsky, *The End of Imperial Russia* (New Haven, Conn., 1931); Vladimir Maevskii, *Na grani dvukh epokh* (Madrid, 1963); V. Semennikov, *Romanovy i germanskie vliianiia vo vremia mirovoi voiny* (Leningrad, 1929); and P. Berezov, *Sverzhenie dvuglavogo orla* (Moscow, 1967).
6 Apart from Stone, most general, Western-language accounts of Russian military operations are superficial at best. For a detailed, chronological military account, a student must turn to such works as A. A. Strokov, *Vooruzhennye sily i voennoe iskusstvo v pervoi mirovoi voine* (Moscow, 1974); I. I. Rostunov, *et al., Istoriia pervoi mirovoi voiny, 1914–1918,* 2 vols. (Moscow, 1975); and I. I. Rostunov, *Russkii front pervoi mirovoi voiny* (Moscow, 1976), all of which have good bibliographical references.
7 On the average Russian's attitude to military service, despite the chances of advancement it offered, see the perceptive comments of A. N. Drew in his *Russia: A Study* (London, 1918), pp. 107–9. A good general account of the peasants' relationship to military service remains John S. Curtiss, 'The Peasant and the Army,' in Wayne S. Vucinich (ed.), *The Peasant in Nineteenth-Century Russia* (Stanford, Calif., 1968), pp. 108–32.
8 George L. Yaney, *The Systematization of Russian Government: Social Evolution in the Domestic Administration of Imperial Russia, 1711–1905* (Urbana-Chicago, 1973), pp. 51–63.
9 David R. Jones, *Russian Military Traditions and the Soviet Military Establishment,* in K. M. Currie and G. Varhall (eds.), *The Soviet Union: What Lies Ahead? Military-Political Affairs in the 1980s* (Washington, D.C., 1985), p. 31; William C. Fuller, Jr., *Civil-Military Conflict in Imperial Russia, 1881–1914* (Princeton, N.J., 1985), pp. 17–18, 39, 45–6, 109–10, 161–2; Allen K. Wildman, *End of the Imperial Army: The Old Army and the Soldiers' Revolt (March-April 1917)* (Princeton, N.J., 1980), pp. 3–11.
10 Wildman, *End of the Imperial Army*, p. 10.
11 Ibid., p. 3.
12 For the importance of Russia's 'Great Power' status in the eyes of contemporaries, see the discussion in D. C. B. Lieven, *Russia and the Origins of the First World War* (New York, 1983), pp. 5 ff.
13 Professor Eltchaninow (Elchaninov), *La Regne de S. M. Nicolas II* (Paris, 1913), p. 71.
14 On Nicholas II's early expression of his intention of personally commanding his troops, see 'Dnevnik A. N. Kuropatkina,' *Krasnyi arhkiv* (1922), kn. 2, pp. 29–30, and E. Bing (ed.), *The Letters of Tsar Nicholas and Empress Marie* (London, 1937), p. 177. The question of Nicholas II's attitudes to his military responsibilities are treated extensively in David R. Jones, 'Nicholas II and the Supreme Command:

An Investigation of Motives,' in Study Group on the Russian Revolution, *Sbornik 11* (1985), pp. 47–83.

15 The military presence in the imperial court is clear from the official *Pridvornyi kalendar*, published annually in St. Petersburg, and from numerous memoirs such as General A. A. Mosolov, *At the Court of the Last Tsar* (London, 1935).

16 Apart from the sources cited in note 12, see 'Dnevnik Kuropatkina,' pp. 13, 40; A. N. Kuropatkin, *The Russian Army and the Japanese War*, 2 vols. (London, 1909), pp. 102–3; and E. I. Martynov, *Iz pechal'nogo opyta russko-iaponskoi voiny* (St. Petersburg, 1906), p. 9.

17 A. A. Kersnovskii, *Istoria russkoi armii*, 4 vols. (Belgrade, 1933–8), Vol. 3, p. 615; Lieven, *Russia and the Origins*, pp. 33–7, 75–6; Ben-Cion Pinchuk, *The Octobrists in the Third Duma, 1907–1912* (Seattle, 1974), p. 160, 177 ff.; Geoffrey A. Hosking, *The Russian Constitutional Experiment: Government and Duma, 1907–1914* (Cambridge, 1973), pp. 228–33. Also see E. Messner, 'Tsar i ofitser,' in S. Zavalishin (ed.), *Gosudar Imperator Nikolai II Aleksandrovich* (New York, 1968), pp. 176–7; and Jones, *Russian Military Traditions*, pp. 30–1.

18 On the Duma and defense, see Wildman, *End of the Imperial Army*, pp. 69–79; Fuller, *Civil-Military Conflict*, pp. 225–44; and Lieven, *Russia and the Origins*, pp. 51–7.

19 General support, of course, does not mean an absence of debate within either the Cabinet or 'society' about the exact levels of military funding. As Fuller (chs. 6–8) demonstrates, there were numerous issues apart from the budget that created 'military-civil' tensions (e.g., the use of the army internally).

20 Russia's wartime politics are analysed in Raymond Pearson, *The Russian Moderates and the Crisis of Tsarism, 1914–1918* (London, 1977); Robert Edelman, *Gentry Politics on the Eve of the Russian Revolution: The Nationalist Party, 1907–1917* (New Brunswick, N.J., 1980), pp. 202 ff.; Margarete Wolters, *Aussenpolitische Fragen vor der vierten Duma* (Hamburg, 1969), pp. 106 ff.; B. B. Grave, *K istorii klassovoi bor'by v Rossii v gody imperialisticheskoi voiny, iiul, 1914 g. - fevral, 1917 g.: Proletariat i burzhuaziia* (Leningrad, 1926); B. B. Grave, *Burzhaziia nakanune fevral'skoi revoliutsii* (Moscow, 1927); V. S. Diakin, *Russkaia burzhuaziia i tsarizm v gody pervoi mirovoi voiny, 1914–1917* (Leningrad, 1967); V. Ia. Laverychev, *Po tu storony barrikad (Iz istorii bor'by moskovskoi burzhuazii s revoliutsiei* (Moscow, 1967), pp. 109 ff.; E. D. Chermenskii, *IV Gosudarstvennaia duma i sverzhenie tsarizm v Rossi* (Moscow, 1976), pp. 68 ff.; V. I. Startsev, *Russkaia burzhuaziia i samoderzhavie v 1905–1917 gg. (Bor'ba vokrug 'otvetstvennogo ministerstva' i 'pravitel'stva doveriia')* (Leningrad, 1977), pp. 131 ff.; and G. Z. Ioffe, 'Verkhi' tsarskoi Rossii v ferral'sko - martovskie dni 1917g.,' *Istoricheskie zapiski* (Moscow, 1983), kn. 110, pp. 67–113.

21 Stone, *Eastern Front*, p. 29; and Fuller, *Civil-Military Conflict*, pp. 219–44.

22 Stone, *Eastern Front*, pp. 19–28. Also see his comments in 'The Historical Background of the Red Army,' in John Erickson and E. J. Feuchtwanger, *Soviet Military Power and Performance* (London, 1979), pp. 11–16.

23 On the Council of State Defense and the politics surrounding it, see David R. Jones, 'Central Military Administrative System and Policy-Making Process (before 1917),' in D. R. Jones (ed.), *The Military-Naval Encyclopedia of Russia and the Soviet Union* (Gulf Breeze, Fla., 1980), Vol. 2, pp. 128–37; and Michael Perrins, 'The Council for State Defense, 1905–1909: A Study in Russian Bureaucratic Politics,' *Slavonic and East European Review*, vol. 58 (July 1980), no. 3, pp. 371–98.

24 Golovin, *The Russian Army*, p. 13; and Stone, *Eastern Front*, p. 26.

25 Stone, *Eastern Front*, p. 26; and Wildman, *End of the Imperial Army*, pp. 69–70.

26 Stone, *Eastern Front*, p. 26.

27 See N. N. Yanushkevich, *Organizatsiia i rol' intendantstva v sovremennykh armiiakh na voine* (St. Petersburg, 1912).

28 For recent reassessments of Sukhomlinov, see Stone, *Eastern Front*, pp. 24 ff.; Wildman, *End of the Imperial Army*, pp. 67–8; C. D. Bellamy (1978) 'Sukhomilinov's Army Reforms, 1909–1915,' MA thesis, Kings College, University of London; and W. T. Wilfong (1977) 'Rebuilding the Russian Army, 1905–1914,' PhD dissertation, University of Indiana.

29 Wildman, *End of the Imperial Army*, pp. 68–9; and Stone, *Eastern Front*, pp. 25 ff.

30 Ben-Cion Pinchuk, *The Octobrists in the Third Duma, 1907–1912* (Seattle, 1974), pp. 187–8; and Fuller, *Civil-Military Conflict*, pp. 235–6, 243.

31 On this issue, the subsequent 'Miasoedov affair,' and the reactions of officers, see M. Grulev, *Zapiski generala-evreia* (Paris, 1930), pp. 245–6; A. I. Denikin, *Put' russkoge ofitsera* (New York, 1953), pp. 248–9, 278–9, 283; and *Staraia armiia*, 2 vols. (Paris, 1929–31), Vol. 1, pp. 149–50, Vol. 2, pp. 36–8.

32 Pinchuk, *The Octobrists*, pp. 191–2; and Edward R. Goldstein (1971), 'Military Aspects of Russian Industrialization: The Defense Industries, 1890–1917,' PhD dissertation, Case Western Reserve University, pp. 241 ff. Both stress Nicholas II's strong commitment to the navy as a major motivating force behind the prewar shipbuilding programs, but the latter makes it clear that the Duma only released the needed funds thanks to dissatisfaction with the War Ministry.

33 On the mood in 1914 see Lieven's analysis in *Russia and the Origins*, ch. 4, and Leopold Haimson's pessimistic 'The Problem of Social Stability in Urban Russia, 1905–1917,' *Slavic Review*, no. 4 (December 1964), pp. 619–42. The course of wartime politics is traced in the works cited in n. 20. Also see Stone, *Eastern Front*, ch. 9.

34 George Katkov, *Russia 1917: The February Revolution* (London, 1967), p. 153.

35 The 'Voluntary Organizations' were the Unions of Municipalities and of Zemstvos (i.e., the rural local councils). The two subsequently merged their administration into the Main Committee for the Supply of the Army, known as 'Zemgor.' In 1915 a third group appeared in the form of the War Industries Committees (WICs), whose national office was headed by Guchkov. These organizations competed with the central government's agencies and the Red Cross in establishing hospital trains, bath houses, etc., for the field armies, but they cooperated closely with the Duma (which had established its own hospital train service when war broke out).

36 For the text of Guchkov's letter, see V. P. Semennikov, *Monarkhiia pered krusheniem, 1914–1917. Bumagi Nikolaia II i drugie dokumenty* (Moscow, 1927), pp. 281–2.

37 On the so-called Guchkov Plot see Katkov, *Russia, 1917*, pp. 173–7, which follows S. P. Melgunov's classic *Na putiakh k dvortsovomu perevorotu, (Zagovory pered revoliutsiei 1917 goda)* (Paris, 1931), pp. 143 ff.

38 On Nikolai Nikolaevich and the Moscow plot, see A. I. Khatisov, 'U pokoleblennage trona . . . Iz istorii predrevoliutsionnykh dnei,' *Illiustrirovannaia Rossiia,* (Paris, 5 December 1931), no. 50 (343), pp. 1–4; and Katkov, *Russia, 1917*, pp. 215–17.

39 Wildman, *End of the Imperial Army*, pp. 107 ff.

40 See figures in George Vernadsky, *The Tsardom of Moscow, 1547–1685*, 2 vols. (New Haven, Conn., 1969), Vol. 1, p. 731; and P. N. Miliukov, *Gosudarstvennoe khoziaistvo Rossii v pervoi chetverti XVIII stoletiia i reforma Petra Velikago* (St. Petersburg, 1905), p. 76.

41 S. M. Troitskii, *Finansovaia politika russkogo absoliutizma v VIII veke* (Moscow, 1966), p. 224.

42 N. D. Chechulin, *Ocherki po istorii russkikh finansov v tsarstvovanie Ekateriny II* (St. Petersburg, 1906), p. 313.
43 Lieven, *Russia and the Origins*, p. 12; A. M. Podkolzin, *A Short Economic History of the USSR* (Moscow, 1968), p. 76; and George Vernadsky, *A Source Book for Russian History from Early Times to 1917*, 3 vols. (New Haven, Conn., 1972), Vol. 3, pp. 822–4.
44 Paul R. Gregory, *Russian National Income, 1885–1913* (Cambridge, 1982), p. 252; and Central Intelligence Agency, National Foreign Assessment Center, *The Soviet State Budget since 1965: A Research Paper*, ER77–10529 (Washington, D.C., December 1977), p. 17.
45 A. A. Sidorov, *Finansovoe polozhenie Rossii v gody pervoi mirovoi voiny, (1914–1917)* (Moscow, 1960), pp. 39, 43.
46 Ibid., p. 43.
47 Ibid., pp. 47–50; Vernadsky, *A Source Book*, Vol. 3, pp. 824–5; and Stone, *Eastern Front*, pp. 28–9.
48 Stone, *Eastern Front*, p. 29.
49 Lieven, *Russia and the Origins*, pp. 12–13; Vernadsky, *A Source Book*, Vol. 3, pp. 823–4; and A. P. Pogreginskii, *Gosudarstvennye finansy tsarkoi Rossii v epokhu imperializma* (Moscow, 1968), pp. 71–5.
50 Sidorov, *Finansovoe polozhenie rossii*, pp. 32–3.
51 He made this point in *Moskovskii ezhenedel'nik*, no. 44 (7 November 1909), and his argument is cited by Lieven, *Russia and the Origins*, p. 12.
52 See the sources listed in n. 17, especially Pinchuk, *The Octobrists*, pp. 65–6.
53 Ibid.; Fuller, *Civil-Military Conflict*, pp. 225–30. On Russia's military industries at this time, see Goldstein, 'Military Aspects,' chs. 4–5.
54 Pinchuk, *The Octobrists*, pp. 189–90.
55 Ibid., pp. 201 ff.
56 Podkolzin, *Economic History*, p. 79.
57 Ibid.
58 Stone, *Eastern Front*, ch. 9.
59 I. Maevskii, *Ekonimka russkoi promyshlennosti v usloviiakh pervoi mirovoi voiny* (Moscow, 1957), p. 63.
60 For *Stavka*'s excuses and the government's reactions see Michael Cherniavsky (ed.), *Prologue to Revolution: Notes of A. N. Iakhontov on the Secret Meetings of the Council of Ministers, 1915* (Englewood Cliffs, N.J., 1967), pp. 21–6, 36, 43.
61 Golovin, *Voennyia usiliia Rossii*, Vol. 2, pp. 24–7.
62 Stone, *Eastern Front*, p. 29.
63 P. D. Duz', *Istoriia vozdukhoplavaniia i aviatsii v SSSR. pervoi mirovoi voiny (1914–1918 gg.)* (Moscow, 1960), p. 10.
64 N. Kozlov, *Ocherk snabzheniia russkoi armii voennotekhnicheskim imushestvom* (Moscow, 1926), pp. 35 ff.
65 Duz', *Istoriia*, p. 209.
66 On engine production, see ibid., p. 232. With regard to imports, see the comments in Golovin, *The Russian Army*, pp. 149–50.
67 A. A. Manikovskii, *Boevoe snabzhenie russkoi armii v 1914–1918 gg.*, 3 vols. (Moscow, 1920–3), Vol. 3, p. 192.
68 Stone, *Eastern Front*, p. 196.
69 A. L. Sidorov, 'K voprosu o stroitel'stve kazennykh voennykh zavodov v Rossii v gody pervoi mirovoi voiny,' *Istoricheskie zapiski*, vol. 54. (1955), p. 161.
70 Ibid., p. 159; and Stone, *Eastern Front*, pp. 145–6.
71 A. M. Zaionchkovskii, *Podgotovka Rossii k mirovoi voine v mezhdunarodnom otnoshenii* (Moscow, 1926), p. 87.

72 Rostunov, *Russkii front*, pp. 96–8; Golovin, *Voennyia usiliia*, Vol. 1, pp. 54–69; Vol. 2, pp. 34–7; Stone, *Eastern Front*, pp. 145–6.
73 A. A. Mannikovskii, *Boevoe snabzhenie russkoi armiii v 1914–1918 gg.*, 3 vols. (Moscow, 1920–3), Vol. 3, p. 9.
74 Stone, *Eastern Front*, pp. 29–32, 147–9.
75 Mannikovskii, *Boevoe snabzhenie*, Vol. 1, pp. 25, 70–1, 84 ff.
76 Ibid., pp. 84–5.
77 Golovin, *Voennyia usiliia*, Vol. 2, pp. 12–13.
78 Ibid.
79 Rostunov, *Russkii front*, pp. 98–9.
80 Stone, *Eastern Front*, pp. 37–8.
81 Wildman, *End of the Imperial Army*, pp. 73–4; Mannikovskii, *Boevoe snabzhenie*, Vol. 3, pp. 215 ff.; Golovin, *Voennyia usiliia*, Vol. 1, pp. 54 ff. But Stone (*Eastern Front*, pp. 23–4, 29 ff.) does fully recognize the weaknesses of the prewar planning of Russia's artillerists.
82 See Rostunov, *Russkii front*, pp. 98–102; Golovin, *Voennyia usiliia*, Vol. 2, pp. 42 ff.; and Stone, *Eastern Front*, pp. 210–11, on matériel in general.
83 This announcement took the form of the unsigned article 'Rossiia khochet mira, no gotova voine,' which first appeared in *Birzheviia Vedomosti* and then was republished in *Rech'*, no. 57, p. 2, on 28 February (13 March) 1914. For more on Sukhomlinov's boast and its broader implications, see Lieven, *Russia and the Origins*, pp. 108 ff.
84 Wildman, *End of the Imperial Army*, p. 74; Golovin, *Voennyia usiliia*, Vol. 1, p. 26.
85 Wildman (*End of the Imperial Army*, chs. 1 and 2), along with writers like John Bushnell ('The Tsarist Officer Corps, 1881–1914: Customs, Duties, Inefficiency,' *The American Historical Review*, no. 4 [October 1981], pp. 753–80) and K. F. Shatsillo (*Rossiia pered pervoi mirovoi voinoi* [*Vooruzhennye sily tsarizma v 1905–1914gg.*] [Moscow, 1974], pp. 101–3), basically accepts that various forms of social and economic 'backwardness' made it difficult, if not impossible, for tsarist Russia to field an efficient, modernized army in 1914.
86 Stone, *Eastern Front*, p. 145.
87 Lieven, *Russia and the Origins*, p. 111; Stone, *Eastern Front*, pp. 35–6; and Rostunov, *Russkii front*, p. 59.
88 Shatsillo, *Rossiia*, pp. 97–100.
89 Showalter, 'Even Generals,' p. 62; and Stone, *Eastern Front*, pp. 38 ff.
90 Golovin, *Voennyia usiliia*, Vol. 2, pp. 35.
91 Ibid.
92 Ibid., p. 36.
93 Jones, 'Central Military,' p. 151.
94 Ibid., p. 152.
95 A. Kavtardze, 'Iz istorii russkogo general'nogo shtaba (avgust 1914 goda - mai 1918 goda)', *Voenno-istoricheskii zhurnal*, no. 3 (March 1976), p. 103.
96 Stone, *Eastern Front*, pp. 23–4, 146–7.
97 Ibid., pp. 149–50.
98 Ibid.
99 Ibid., pp. 148–9.
100 Golovin, *Voennyia usiliia*, Vol. 2, p. 36.
101 Ibid., pp. 36–7.
102 Jones, 'Central Military,' pp. 152–4.
103 Ibid., p. 154.
104 Stone, *Eastern Front*, p. 149.
105 Ibid., p. 150.

106 Ibid., pp. 151–2.
107 Jones, 'Central Military,' p. 154.
108 Ibid.
109 Stone, *Eastern Front*, pp. 155–6.
110 Ibid., p. 152.
111 Ibid.
112 Golovin, *Voennyia usiliia*, Vol. 2, pp. 6–7.
113 Ibid., pp. 7–8; Wildman, *End of the Imperial Army*, pp. 83–4; Stone, *Eastern Front*, pp. 144–5.
114 Sidorov, *Finansovoe*, ch. 1.
115 Jones, 'Central Military,' p. 155.
116 Ibid; A. Terne, 'Osoboe soveshchanie po oborone gosudarstva 1915–1916 gg.,' *Vozrozhdenie*, no. 188 (Paris, 1967), p. 67.
117 Jones, 'Central Military,' pp. 155, 157–9.
118 Stone, *Eastern Front*, pp. 210–11.
119 Ibid; Golovin, *Voennyia usiliia*, Vol. 2, pp. 12 ff.
120 Stone, *Eastern Front*, p. 210; Golovin, *Voennyia usiliia*, Vol. 2, pp. 42–6.
121 Stone, *Eastern Front*, p. 211.
122 Rostunov, *Russkii front*, p. 52.
123 Ibid. On the army before the Crimean War, see John S. Curtiss, *The Russian Army Under Nicholas I, 1825–1855* (Durham, N.C., 1965).
124 The case for a military imperative for the 'great reforms' is presented in A. J. Rieber, *The Politics of Autocracy* (The Hague, 1966), pp. 23–30.
125 Wildman, *End of the Imperial Army*, p. 125.
126 Quoted in Golovin, *Voennyia usiliia*, Vol. 1, p. 10.
127 Ibid. The best discussion of the preparation of this statute is Robert F. Bauman (1982), 'The Debates Over Universal Military Service in Russia, 1870–1874,' PhD dissertation, Yale University.
128 Vernadsky, *A Source Book*, Vol. 3, p. 819.
129 Wildman, *End of the Imperial Army*, pp. 26–7, 30; Rostunov, *Russkii front*, pp. 48–52; and Golovin, *Voennyia usiliia*, Vol. 1, pp. 16–20.
130 Wildman, *End of the Imperial Army*, p. 36.
131 Ibid., pp. 38–40.
132 On attempts to use the army to combat illiteracy see John Bushnel, 'Peasants in Uniform: The Tsarist Army as a Peasant Society,' *Journal of Social History*, vol. 13 (1980), pp. 565–6; and *Mutiny and Repression: Russian Soldiers in the Revolution of 1905–1906* (Bloomington, Ind., 1985), pp. 7–9.
133 Wildman, *End of the Imperial Army*, p. 28.
134 Ibid., pp. 28–9.
135 Ibid., pp. 76–80.
136 Golovin, *Voenyia usiliia*, Vol. 2, p. 124.
137 Ibid., p. 120.
138 Quoted in ibid., p. 119.
139 Yu. N. Danilov, *Rossiia v mirovoi voine, 1914–1915* (Berlin, 1924), pp. 111–12.
140 Wildman, *End of the Imperial Army*, pp. 36–8. His views receive support from the experiences of a French officer who had served six months in the Imperial Army in 1913; see Lieven, *Russia and the Origins*, pp. 113–14.
141 Golovin, *Voennyia usiliia*, Vol. 1, p. 41. However, according to the figures of one Soviet scholar, between 1907 and 1909 the literacy rate among conscripts averaged 63 per cent; A. G. Rashin, 'Gramotnost' i narodnoe obrazovanie v XIX i nachale XX v.,' *Istoricheskie zapiski*, vol. 37 (1951), p. 45.

142 This seems clear from the analysis in Wildman, *End of the Imperial Army*, pp. 332 ff., and from the multitude of other accounts of the 'revolutionizing' of the army.
143 Colonel 'Billy' Oliferov to the author in an interview in San Francisco, June 1968.
144 On the continuing personal magnetism excercised by the tsar see Wildman, *End of the Imperial Army*, p. 37; Lieven, *Russia and the Origins*, p. 114; P. N. Krasnov, 'Pamiati Imperatorskoi Russkoi Armii,' *Russkaia letopis*, vol. 1 (Paris, 1921), pp. 25–8, 55 ff.; and Krasnov's novel, *From Double-Headed Eagle to Red Flag* (London, 1928), pp. 96 ff.
145 Quoted in Neilson, *Strategy and Supply*, p. 8.
146 Stone, *Eastern Front*, p. 213; Golovin, *Voennyia usiliia*, Vol. 1, pp. 11–12, 32–8, 41–6. The exemptions granted national groups are detailed in Robert F. Baumann, 'Universal Military Service and the Russian Empire,' unpublished paper presented to a conference at Cornell University, September 1984.
147 Stone, *Eastern Front*, pp. 212–13; Rostunov, *Russkii front*, pp. 51–2, 58.
148 Stone, *Eastern Front*, p. 213; and Fuller, *Civil-Military Conflict*, pp. 47–74.
149 Rostunov, *Russkii front*, p. 52.
150 Ibid., pp. 46–7; Wildman, *End of the Imperial Army*, pp. 25–7; Golovin, *Voennyia usiliia*, Vol. 1, pp. 12–16; and Golovin, *The Russian Army*, pp. 3–7.
151 Golovin, *Voennyia usiliia*, Vol. 1, pp. 13–14.
152 Ibid., Vol. 1, pp. 34–8; Wildman, *End of the Imperial Army*, pp. 25–7; Rostunov, *Russkii front*, pp. 48–50.
153 On the reorganization of 1909–10, see Rostunov, *Russkii front*, pp. 52–8; and Shatsillo, *Rossiia*, pp. 43–9.
154 Golovin, *Voennyia usiliia*, Vol. 1, pp. 46–9; Wildman, *End of the Imperial Army*, pp. 27–8.
155 Wildman, *End of the Imperial Army*, pp. 66–7; Shatsillo, *Rossiia*, pp. 86–7. The problems caused by the rigidity of mobilization are well known and fully described in such studies of 1914 as Sidney B. Fay, *The Origins of the World War* (New York, 1930), Vol. 2, pp. 286 ff., 439 ff.
156 Rostunov, *Russkii front*, p. 58.
157 Stone, *Eastern Front*, pp. 42–3.
158 Rostunov, *Russkii front*, p. 58.
159 Central Statistics Department, *Rossiia v Mirovoi Voine 1914–1918* (Moscow, 1925), table 2.
160 Wildman, *End of the Imperial Army*, p. 23.
161 Golovin, *Voennyia usiliia*, Vol. 1, p. 81.
162 Stone, *Eastern Front*, p. 215.
163 Ibid.
164 *Rossiia v Mirovoi Voine*, table 2.
165 Both figures cited in Golovin, *Voennyia usiliia*, Vol. 1, p. 82.
166 Stone, *Eastern Front*, p. 213.
167 Golovin, *Voennyia usiliia*, Vol 1, p. 82.
168 Stone, *Eastern Front*, p. 213.
169 Golovin, *Voennyia usiliia*, Vol. 1, pp. 180–1.
170 Stone, *Eastern Front*, p. 215.
171 Golovin, *Voennyia usiliia*, Vol. 1, p. 181. On early losses also see Wildman, *End of the Imperial Army*, pp. 181–4.
172 Stone, *Eastern Front*, p. 215; Golovin, *Voennyia usiliia*, Vol. 1, ch. 5 on losses, and pp. 181–4 on strengths over time; Wildman, *End of the Imperial Army*, pp. 95–6.
173 Golovin, *Voennyia usiliia*, Vol. 1, pp. 75–8l.
174 Wildman, *End of the Imperial Army*, p. 96.
175 Ibid.; Stone, *Eastern Front*, pp. 215–17.

176 Stone, *Eastern Front*, p. 214.
177 Ibid., pp 216–17; Golovin, *Voennyia usiliia*, Vol. 1, pp. 80–2.
178 Wildman, *End of the Imperial Army*, pp. 97–9. There is a vast Soviet literature on the Central Asian uprisings, of which Z. D. Kastel'skaia, *Osnovnye predposylki vosstaniia 1916 goda v. Uzbekistane* (Moscow, 1972), and B. S. Suleimenov and V. Ya. Basin, *Vosstanie 1916 goda v Kazakhistane* (Alma-Ata, 1977), are typical. In English, see Edward D. Sokol, *The Revolt of 1916 in Russian Central Asia* (Baltimore, Md., 1954).
179 Wildman, *End of the Imperial Army*, pp. 99, 104. On the Petrograd garrison in particular, see B. M. Kochakov, 'Sostav petrogradskogo garnizona v 1917 goda,' *Uchenie zapiski LGU, No. 205: Iz istorii SSSR* (Leningrad, 1956), pp. 50–86.
180 Wildman, *End of the Imperial Army*, p. 99.
181 Ibid.
182 S. V. Utechin, 'Bolsheviks and Their Allies After 1917: The Ideological Pattern,' in S. Harcave (ed.), *Readings in Russian History*, 2 vols. (New York, 1962), Vol. 2, pp. 195–200.
183 See D. A. Garkavenko, 'Sotsial'nyi sostav vooruzhennykh sil Rossii v epokhy imperializma,' in I. I. Mints (ed.), *Revoliustionoe dvizhenie v russkoi armii v 1917 godu. Sbornik statei* (Moscow, 1981), pp. 30–45.
184 Peter Kenez, 'Changes in the Social Composition of the Officer Corps during World War I,' *Russian Review* (October 1972), p. 373; Golovin, *Voennyia usiliia*, Vol. l, p. 49.
185 Golovin, *Voennyia usiliia*, Vol. 1, p. 49. Also see Rostunov, *Russkii front*, p. 51, who suggests that in fact by 1909 the army was only 11 per cent short of NCOs.
186 Stone, *Eastern Front*, pp. 167; Bushnell, 'Peasants,' pp. 570–1, and *Mutiny and Repression*, pp. 17–18, 163–4.
187 Danilov, *Rossiia*, p. 247; Wildman, *End of the Imperial Army*, p. 125; Stone, *Eastern Front*, p. 166.
188 Kenez, 'Officer Corps,' p. 370–1; Danilov, *Rossiia*, p. 246; Stone, *Eastern Front*, p. 166.
189 Stone, *Eastern Front*, p. 217.
190 Letter of 3 (16) August, published in A. M. Zaionchkovskii, *Mirovaia voina* (Moscow, 1929), pp. 405–8.
191 Stone, *Eastern Front*, p. 166; Kenez, 'Officer Corps,' p. 373.
192 Stone, *Eastern Front*, p. 217.
193 Kenez, 'Officer Corps,' pp. 369, 373–4.
194 See figures and sources cited in David R. Jones, 'The Officers and the Soviets, 1917–1920,' in D. R. Jones, *The Soviet Armed Forces Review Annual 1: 1977* (Gulf Breeze, Fla., 1977), pp. 176, l83.
195 S. S. Khesin, *Oktiabr'skaia revoliutsiia i flot* (Moscow, 1971), pp. 23 ff., and his 'Lichnyi sostav russkogo flota v 1917 godu,' *Voenno-istoricheskii zhurnal* no. 11 (November 1965), pp. 99–104.
196 Kenez, 'Officer Corps,' p. 369. Other figures suggest 90,000 wartime officers and 130,000 ensigns; see N. V. Piatinskii, *Voennaia organizatsiia gosudarstvennoi oborony SSSR*, 2 vols. (Paris, 1932), Vol. 2, p. 14; and Golovin, *Voennyia usiliia*, Vol. 1, p. 160.
197 Kenez, 'Officer Corps,' pp. 371–2.
198 Ibid., pp. 374–5; Wildman, *End of the Imperial Army*, pp. 100–1; Golovin, *Voennyia usiliia*, Vol. 1, pp. 159–62; and General Chernavin, 'K voprosu ofitserskago sostava Russkoi armii k kontsu eia sushchestvovaniia,' *Voennyi Sbornik* (Belgrade, 1925), Vol. 5, p. 227.
199 On promotions from the ranks, see Stone, *Eastern Front*, pp. 166–7; Kenez,

'Officer Corps,' p. 371; and the comments in A. V. Gorbatov, *Years Off My Life* (London, 1964), p. 60.

200 F. V. Rusanov, *Leib-Gvardii Grenaderskii Polk (1760–1956)* (New York, 1960), p. 85.

201 Stone, *Eastern Front*, p. 166.

202 This issue is briefly reviewed by Wildman, *End of the Imperial Army*, pp. 105 ff.

203 Ibid., p. 107.

204 On this consensus, see Lieven, *Russia and the Origins*, pp. 5 ff.

205 Ibid., pp. 21 ff.

206 The evolution of Russia's war plans are outlined at length in A. M. Zaionchkovskii, *Podgotovka Rossii k imperialisticheskoi voine. Ocherki voennoi podgotovki i pervonachal'nykh planov* (Moscow, 1926); and most recently in Jack Snyder, *The Ideology of the Offensive: Military Decision Making and The Disasters of 1914* (Ithaca, N.Y., 1984), pp. 157–98.

207 Russian opinion on these issues is examined at length by Lieven, *Russia and the Origins*, pp. 8, 24–7, 105–6.

208 The considerations involved are examined in Rostunov, *Russkii front*, pp. 60–89; Snyder, *Ideology of the Offensive*, pp. 157–60; Stone, *Eastern Front*, pp. 32–3; and 'A' (War Plan, 1914), in Jones, *Military-Naval Encyclopedia of Russia and the Soviet Union* (Gulf Breeze, Fla., 1980), Vol. l, p. 4.

209 Rostunov, *Russkii front*, pp. 89–92; Snyder, *Ideology of the Offensive*, pp. 166–72; Stone, *Eastern Front*, pp. 33–4.

210 Snyder, *Ideology of the Offensive*, pp. 172–9; Stone, *Eastern Front*, p. 34.

211 Rostunov, *Russkii front*, pp. 92–5; Snyder, *Ideology of the Offensive*, pp. 197–81; Stone, *Eastern Front*, pp. 30–2; and Danilov, *Rossiia*, pp. 76 ff.

212 Stone, *Eastern Front*, p. 35; Lieven, *Russia and the Origins*, p. 106; Snyder, *Ideology of the Offensive*, pp. 181–8.

213 This is also the view of General Sir Edmund Ironside. Although he criticized the early date of the Russian offensive, he nonetheless concluded that the 'initial advance into East Prussia failed owing to bad leadership and bad administration (i.e., command and control)'; see his *Tannenberg: The First Thirty Days in East Prussia* (Edinburgh, 1933), p. 285.

214 Showalter, 'Even Generals,' *passim.*

215 Lieven, *Russia and the Origins*, p. 106. On the Russians' dedication to the offensive, see David R. Jones, *The Advanced Guard and Mobility in Russian and Soviet Military Thought and Practice*, 'SAFRA Papers,' no. 1 (Gulf Breeze, Fla., 1985), ch. 9.

216 See, for example, J. F. N. Bradley, 'The Russian Secret Service in the First World War,' *Soviet Studies* (1968–9), pp. 242–8; K. K. Zvonar'ev, *Agenturnaia razvedka*, Vol. 1: *Russkaia agenturnaia razvedka vsekh vidov do i vo vremia voiny 1914–1918 gg.* (Moscow, 1929); I. Bol'shakov, 'Russkai razvedka v pervoi mirovoi voine 1914–1918 godov,' *Voenno-istoricheskii zhurnal*, no. 5 (May 1964), pp. 44–8; and William C. Fuller, Jr., 'The Russian Empire,' in Ernest R. May (ed.), *Knowing One's Enemies: Intelligence Assessment Before the Two World Wars*, (Princeton, N.J., 1984), pp. 98–126. The major coup of the prewar period is discussed in M. Mil'shtein, 'Delo polkovnika Redlia,' *Voennoistoricheskii zhurnal*, no. 1 (January 1966), pp. 46–56.

217 Russian-Allied relations in general are covered in Barbara Jelavich, *St. Petersburg and Moscow: Tsarist and Soviet Foreign Policy, 1814–1974* (Bloomington, Ind., 1974), pp. 280–8; C. Jay Smith, *The Russian Struggle for Power: 1914–1918. A Study of Russian Foreign Policy during the First World War* (New York, 1956); V. A.

Emets, *Ocherki nveshnei politiki Rossii v period pervoi mirovoi voiny. Vziamootnosheniia Rossii s soiuznikami po voprosam vedeniia voiny* (Moscow, 1977); and the essays in A. Dallin, *et al.*, *Russian Diplomacy and Eastern Europe, 1914–1917* (New York, 1963).

218 On this issue see Arthur J. Rieber, 'Russian Diplomacy and Rumania,' in Dallin, *et al.*, *Russian Diplomacy*, pp. 269 ff., and V. A. Emets, 'Protivorechiia mezhdu Rossiei i soiuznikami po voprosu o vstuplenii Rumynii v voinu (1915–1916 gg.),' *Istoricheskie zapiski* (Moscow, 1956), kn. 56, pp. 52–90. On the disastrous Rumanian campaign that followed, see F. I. Vasil'ev, *Strategicheskii ocherk voiny 1914–1918 gg. Rumynskii front* (Moscow, 1922).

219 See discussions of operations mentioned in the references in n. 217, and the relevant sections of N. Valentinov, *Snosheniia s soiuznikami po voennym voprosam vo vremia voiny 1914–1918 gg.* (Moscow, 1920), ch. 1, which covers the period to the end of 1916.

220 Stone's comments (*Eastern Front*, pp. 218–19) are apposite here.

221 Jones, 'Central Military,' p. 143.

222 On the preparation and issuing of the new regulations, see Rostunov, *Russkii front*, pp. 112–13, and Danilov, *Rossiia*, pp. 51–2, 105 ff.

223 'Dnevnik A.N. Kuropatkina,' *Krasnyi Arhkiv* (Moscow, 1922), ch. 2, pp. 29–30. For the tsar's attitude in 1904–5, see E. Bing (ed.), *Letters to the Tsar Nicholas and the Empress Maria* (London, 1937), p. 177.

224 Jones, 'Central Military,' pp. 143–4; and Rostunov, *Russkii front*, pp. 113–14.

225 Jones, 'Central Military,' pp. 144–5; Daniel W. Graf, 'Military Rule behind the Russian Front, 1914–17: The Political Ramifications,' *Jahrbücher für Geschichte Osteuropas*, no. 3 (1974), pp. 390–2.

226 Yu. N. Danilov, *Velikii Kniaz Nikolai Nikolaevich* (Paris, 1930), pp. 104 ff.; Danilov, *Rossiia*, pp. 105 ff.; I. A. Blinov (ed.), 'Dnevnik generala Sukhomlinova,' *Dela i dni*, I, (Petrograd, 1920), no. 1, pp. 220-l; A. M. Spiridovich, pp. 89–90; V. N. Voeikov, *S tsarem i bez tsaria. Vospominaniia posledniago Dvortsovago Komendanta Gosudaria Imperatora Nikolaia II* (Helsingfors, 1936), pp. 89–90.

227 Danilov, *Velikii Kniaz*, pp. 102 ff.; and Jones, 'Nicholas II,' pp. 59–60.

228 Jones, 'Central Military,' pp. 150–1.

229 Ibid., pp. 149–50; Graf, *Reign of the Generals*, pp. 393 ff.

230 Jones, 'Central Military,' pp. 148–9; Jones, 'Nicholas II,' p. 60.

231 Jones, 'Central Military,' pp. 149–50; Graf, 'Military Rule,' pp. 403–9.

232 See, for example, R. R. McCormick, *With the Russian Army* (New York, 1915), p. 51, and the works cited on the 'Miasoedov affair' in n. 31 above. On the subsequent plight of Russia's Jewish population, see Katkov, *Russia, 1917*, pp. 55–62.

233 Cherniavsky, pp. 108–9, 120–1, 147–8.

234 Jones, 'Central Military,' pp. 157–8.

235 Stone, *Eastern Front*, pp. 94–6; and Rostunov, *Russkii front*, pp. 154 ff.

236 Jones, 'Central Military,' pp. 150, 155–6.

237 For the impression supposedly made by Nicholas II's calmness during the battles of August-September 1915, as noted by General Dubenskii, see 'Svetloi pamiati Gosudaria Imperatora Nikolaia Vtorogo,' *Vozrozhdenie*, no. 200 (August 1968), p. 60; and K. Popov, 'Bylli polkovodtsem Imperator Nikolai II?' *Voennaia byl'*, no. 43 (July 1960), pp. 2–4. For the details of General Alekseev's handling of the crisis, see I. Evseev, *Sventsianskii proryv (1915 g.). Voennye deistviia na vostochnom fronte mirovoi voiny v sentiabre-oktiabre 1915 g.* (Moscow, 1936), esp. pp. 13–21, 60–72. On the new Stavka, see Jones, 'Central Military,' pp. 157 ff.; Stone,

Eastern Front, pp. 187–93; Rostunov, *Russkii front*, pp. 144–5; and A. G. Kavtaradze's entry 'Stavka Verkhovnogo Glavnokomanduiushchego,' in *Sovetskaia istoricheskaia entsik - lopediia* (Moscow, 1971), Vol. 13, pp. 775–7.

238 Inter-Allied affairs are covered by references in nn. 217–19 above.

239 Stone, *Eastern Front*, pp. 210–11, 256, 270.

240 Ibid., p. 49.

241 Rostunov, *Istoriia pervoi mirovoi voiny*, Vol. 1, p. 63.

242 Stone, *Eastern Front*, pp. 133–5; Golovin, *Voennyia usiliia*, Vol. 2, pp. 104–10.

243 Jones, 'Central Military,' pp. 147–8; Golovin, *Voennyia usiliia*, Vol. 2, pp. 110–11.

244 V. A. Semenov, *Kratkii ocherk razvitiia sovetskogo operativnogo iskusstva* (Moscow, 1960), pp. 17–18.

245 Stone, *Eastern Front*, p. 35. Lieven *(Russia and the Origins*, p. 106) basically agrees.

246 D. Filat'ev, 'Nashe polozhenie o polevom upravlenii voisk,' *Izvestiia imp. Nikolaevskoi voennoi akademii*, no. 22 (1911), pp. 1035 ff.; Rostunov, *Russkii front*, pp. 114–15.

247 Ibid.; Jones, 'Central Military,' pp. 147–8.

248 Jones, 'Central Military,' pp. 147–48.

249 Showalter ('Even Generals,' pp. 68–72) demonstrates the impact of this attitude on the German command in the first stages of that campaign. His remarks seem to apply equally to the Russian commanders involved.

250 Ibid, p. 80.

251 Stone, *Eastern Front*, p. 51.

252 Jones, 'Central Military,' p. 144.

253 This front's organization is described in E. V. Maslovskii, *Mirovaia voina na Kavkazskom Fronte, 1914–1917 g. Strategicheskii ocherk* (Paris, 1933), pp. 20, 37, 137–40, 429–30, 438–43.

254 The best account of the state of military logistics in 1914 is Martin van Creveld's *Supplying War: Logistics from Wallenstein to Patton* (Cambridge, 1977), pp. 96–113. For the impact of this situation on the Russian Front, see Stone, *The Eastern Front*, pp. 44 ff.; and Showalter, 'Even Generals,' pp. 64–6.

255 The basic assumptions behind this version of an expected European conflict are outlined by Snyder, *Ideology*, pp. 15–18, 157–64; and S. P. Ivanov (ed.), *Nachal'nyi period voiny (Po opytu pervykh kampanii i operatsii vtoroi mirovoi voiny)* (Moscow, 1974), pp. 29–42.

256 Jones, *Advanced Guard*, pp. 67 ff.

257 Ibid., pp. 58–9.

258 On the feeding of livestock and the railways, see van Creveld, *Supplying War*, p. 111; Golovin, *Voennyia usiliia*, Vol. 2, p. 77; and Stone, *Eastern Front*, pp. 49–50, 134–5.

259 Semenov, *Kratkii ocherk*, p. 17; N. V. Ogarkov, *Vserda v gotovnosti k zashchite Otechestva* (Moscow, 1982), pp. 32–4.

260 See the discussion in Ironside, *Tannenberg*, ch. 9.

261 See, for example, Stone, *Eastern Front*, pp. 246 ff., and Rostunov, *Russkii front*, pp. 321 ff.

262 Semenov, *Kratkii ocherk*, pp. 22–4; Ogarkov, *Vserda*, pp. 33–4.

263 Lieven, *Russia and the Origins*, p. 111.

264 Jones, 'Central Military,' pp. 133–4; and Bushnell, 'The Tsarist Officer,' pp. 777–8.

265 John Bushnell, 'The Tsarist Army after the Russo-Japanese War: The View from the Field,' unpublished paper presented at symposium at Carlisle Barracks, Penna. (August 1982), p. 5.

266 Kersnovskii, *Istoriia*, Vol. 3, pp. 611–14. For a critique of the Academy see V. M. Dragomirov, 'Podgotovka russkom armii k velikoi voine,' *Voennyi sbornik*, Vol. 4 (Belgrade, 1923), pp. 100–1, as well as Colonel Shliakhtin's assessment 'Imperatorskaia Nikolaevskaia,' *Voennaia byl'*, no. 109 (March 1971), pp. 15–20.

267 Bushnell, 'The Tsarist Officer,' pp. 763–5; P. N. Krasnov, *From Double Eagle to Red Flag* (London, 1928), pp. 88 ff.

268 Deniken, *Staraia armiia*, Vol. 1, pp. 23–7; Dragomirov, 'Podgotovka,' p. 102.

269 Bushnell, 'The Tsarist Army,' p. 9.

270 P. N. Krasnov, *Nakanune voiny* (Paris, 1937), pp. 38–9, 53.

271 Denikin, *Staraia armiia*, Vol. 1, pp. 103 ff.; and *Put'*, pp. 245–6; Dragomirov, 'Podgotovka,' vol. 4 (1923), pp. 114–15; vol. 6 (1925), p. 70; L. Radus-Zenkovich, 'Nashi bol'shie manevry,' *Voennyi sbornik,* no. 6 (St. Petersburg, 1910), pp. 76–95; Kvetsinskii, 'Teknika organizatsii manevra,' *Voennyi sbornik*, no. 1 (1914), pp. 27 ff.; and Bushnell, 'The Tsarist Officer,' p. 778.

272 Danilov, *Rossiia*, pp. 99–105; Dragomirov, 'Podgotovka,' vol. 4 (1923), pp. 102–3; Bushnell, 'The Tsarist Army,' pp. 7–8.

273 The debates and prevailing doctrines are discussed in Jones, *Advanced Guard*, pp. 87–9; Stone, *Eastern Front*, pp. 30–5, 45; and Danilov, *Rossiia*, ch. 2.

274 A. A. Yamanov, *Vstrechny boi. Kn. 1: Operativno-takticheskoe issledovanie na voenno-istoricheskoi osnove* (Moscow, 1959), pp. 155–70.

275 Bushnell, 'The Tsarist Army,' p. 7, admits that the exercises carried out in the Vilna and Kiev military districts were exceptions to his overall gloomy picture of stagnation. The program for the maneuvers in these frontier districts for 1911 is outlined in the notes on 'Manoeuvres in 1911' and 'Summer Training,' *Journal of the Royal United Services Institute*, vol. 55 (June 1911), p. 809, and (July 1911), p. 950.

276 General Staff, War Office, *Report on Foreign Manoeuvres, 1908* (London, 1909), p. 153.

277 General Staff, War Office, *Report on Foreign Manoeuvres in 1912* (London, 1913), pp. 99–100.

278 General Staff, War Office, *Report on Foreign Manoeuvres in 1913* (London, 1914), pp. 79.

279 Ibid., pp. 78–9, 82.

280 Bushnell, 'The Tsarist Officer,' p. 778.

281 Ironside, *Tannenberg*, p. 26.

282 Rennenkampf's prewar career is assessed favorably, and not unfairly, in Jean Savant, *Epopée Russe. Campagne de l'armée Rennenkampf en Prusse-Orientale* (Paris, 1945), pp. 93–118.

283 A. D. Kalmykov, *Memoirs of a Russian Diplomat: Outposts of Empire, 1893–1917* (New Haven, Conn., 1971), p. 197.

284 Princess Cantacuzene, *Revolutionary Days: Recollections of Romanoffs and Bolsheviki, 1914–1917* (Boston, 1919), pp. 66–7.

285 Michael Cherniavsky (ed.), *Prologue to Revolution: Notes of A. N. Iakhontov on the Secret Meetings of the Council of Ministers, 1915,* (Englewood Cliffs, N.J., 1967), p. 36.

286 On the winter battles of 1914–15, see Stone, *Eastern Front*, ch. 5; and Rostunov, *Russkii front*, pp. 154–232.

287 On the collapse of the Russian front and the Great Retreat during April-August 1915, see Stone, *Eastern Front*, chs. 6–8, esp. pp. 133–4 on the railways. Also see Rostunov, *Russkii front*, pp. 233–62; and Danilov, *Rossiia*, chs. 15–17.

288 Rostunov, *Russkii front*, pp. 273–4, 286; Stone, *Eastern Front*, pp. 221–31.

289 On the operational background of the Brusilov offensive, see Semenov, *Kratkii*,

pp. 18–22; Rostunov, *Russkii front*, pp. 289–94; Stone, *Eastern Front*, pp. 224 ff.; and A. A. Brusilov, *Moi vospominaniia* (1946), pp. 178 ff.

290 Ibid., esp. Brusilov, *Moi vospominaniia*, pp. 184–91.

291 Brusilov, *Moi vospominaniia*, pp. 193–7, 255–9.

292 E. Z. Barsukov, 'Russkaia artilleriia v mirovoi voine,' *Voennaia mysl'*, no. 7 (1939), p. 66.

293 This is suggested by both the objections raised by his colleagues in April and by his own resort to a massive bombardment later in the 1916 campaign.

294 Rostunov, *Russkii front*, pp. 325–7; Stone, *Eastern Front*, pp. 255–63.

295 For a brief account, with bibliography, of the Mitau Operation, see 'Aa (Kurland), Battles on, 1916–1917,' in Jones, *Military-Naval Encyclopedia*, Vol. 1, pp. 25–6.

296 A. Syromiatnikov, *Nastyplenie i oborona v usloviiakh pozitsionnoi voiny* (Petrograd, 1917), pp. 94–9.

297 W. E. D. Allen and Paul Muratoff, *Caucasian Battlefields: A History of the Wars on the Turco-Caucasion Border, 1828–1921* (Cambridge, 1953), pp. 344–63; N. Novikov, *Operatsii flota protiv berega na Chernom more v 1914–1917 gg.* (Moscow, 1937), *passim.*

298 On the mood of the army at this time, see Marc Ferro's interesting analysis in 'The Russian Soldier in 1917: Undisciplined, Patriotic and Revolutionary,' *American Slavic and East European Review*, vol. 30 (1970), pp. 483–512.

299 Jones, *Advanced Guard*, pp. 87–9.

300 General Staff, War Office, *Report on Foreign Manoeuvres in 1912*, pp. 111–12.

301 On this issue, see the discussion in Peter von Wahlde (1966) 'Military Thought in Imperial Russia,' Ph.D. dissertation, University of Indiana, pp. 241 ff.

302 Jones, *Advanced Guard*, pp. 74–89.

303 For example, see General Staff, War Office, *Report on Foreign Manoeuvres in 1908*, p. 154; ibid. *1909*, p. 190; and ibid. *1913*, p. 79.

304 On the very limited role played by Russia's cavalry after 1914 see Alexis Wrangel, *The End of Chivalry: The Last Great Cavalary Battles, 1914–1918* (New York, 1982), *passim.*

305 This point is made in 'Voennye aforizmy M. I. Dragomirova, *Voenno-istoricheskii zhurnal*, no. 3 (March 1962), pp. 119–23. Also see Bruce W. Menning, 'The Army of D. A. Miliutin and M. I. Dragomirov,' unpublished paper presented at a conference at Cornell University (September 1984), pp. 17–19; and A. M. Zhigulev's modern collection of *Russkie voennyi poslovitsy i pogorovki* (Moscow, 1960), pp. 4–5.

306 A. A. Neznamov, *Tekushchie voennye voprosy* (St. Petersburg, 1909), p. 56.

307 Bushnell, 'The Tsarist Army,' pp. 2–6.

308 General Staff, War Office, *Report on Foreign Manoeuvres in 1913*, p. 79.

309 Stone, *Eastern Front*, pp. 23–4: General Staff, War Office, *Report on Foreign Manoeuvres in 1912*, pp. 107–8.

310 Stone, *Eastern Front*, pp. 29–31.

311 A. A. Yamanov, *Vstrechnyi boi*, pp. 155–70; N. G. Korsun and P. Kh. Kharkevich, 'Taktika russkoi armii v pervuiu mirovuiu voinu 1914–1918 gg.,' in D. V. Pankov (comp.), *Razvitie taktiki russkoi armii, XVIII v. - nachalo XX v. (Sbornik statei)* (Moscow, 1957), pp. 286–92.

312 C. Bellamy, 'Seventy Years On: Similarities between the Modern Soviet Army and Its Tsarist Predecessor,' *RUSI Journal of Defense Studies*, no. 9 (1979), p. 30; and Jones, *Advanced Guard*, pp. 2–3.

313 Bushnell, 'The Tsarist Army,' p. 3; General Staff, War Office, *Reports on Foreign Manoeuvres in 1908*, p. 154.

314 Stone, *Eastern Front*, pp. 128–38.
315 E. Messner and Iv. Eikhenbaum, *Velikaia Lutsk-Chernovitskaia pobeda 1916-go goda* (Buenos Aires, 1966), p. 4. Also see Stone, *Eastern Front*, pp. 222–3; and Korsun and Kharkevich, 'Taktika,' pp. 298–305.
316 Stone, *Eastern Front*, pp. 213–14; Messner and Eikhenbau, *Velikaia*, p. 3.
317 Korsun and Kharkevich, 'Taktika,' pp. 312–313; Stone, *Eastern Front*, p. 223.
318 Stone, *Eastern Front*, pp. 227–31, outlines these problems admirably, while the diagrams of trench systems presented by Korsun and Kharkevich ('Tatika,' p. 314) illustrate the dimensions of the problem.
319 The tactical preparation for this offensive is discussed in Korsun and Kharkevich, 'Taktika,' pp. 299–304; Stone *Eastern Front*, pp. 232–40; and Messner and Eikhenbaum, *Velikaia*, pp. 3–7.
320 See the discussion in Messner and Eikhenbaum, *Velikaia*, pp. 6–8; and Stone, *Eastern Front*, pp. 249 ff.; among others.
321 For such signs, see the Mitau Operation, discussed above, along with the work cited in n. 295; the discussion in A. Syromiatnikov, *Nastavlenie dlia bor'by za ukreplennye polosy*, Chast' II: *Deistviia artillerii pri proryve ukreplennoi polosy*, and Chast' III: *Deistviia artillerii pri oborone ukreplennoi polosy*; the publication of V. Kirei's, *Artilleriia oborony* (Izd. Armeiskogo Vestnika, 1917); and the appearance of Russia's first manual for combatting armor, the *Nastavlenie dlia bor'by s nepriiatel'skimi sukhoputnymi bronenostsami* (Tip. Stavka, 1917).
322 Stone, *Eastern Front*, pp. 166–71, 224–5.
323 Ibid.; Wildman, *End of the Imperial Army*, pp. 91–4, 106–7.
324 For example, Wildman, *End of the Imperial Army*, p. 107. The same assumption naturally underlies such Soviet studies as S. G. Kapshukov, *Bor'ba bol'shevistskoi partii za armiiu v period pervoi mirovoi voiny (1914 g. - mart 1917 g.)* (Moscow, 1957); and F. A. Shurygin, *Revoliutsionnoe dvizhenie soldatskikh mass severnogo fronta v 1917 godu* (Moscow, 1958), pp. 7–26; among others.
325 David R. Jones, 'The Imperial Russian Life Guards Grenadier Regiment, 1906–1917: The Disintegration of an Elite Unit,' *Military Affairs* (October 1969), pp. 289–301.
326 Bushnell, 'Peasants in Uniform,' pp. 567–70. Also see Bushnell, *Mutiny and Repression*, pp. 11–23.
327 Lieven, *Russia and the Origins*, pp. 113–14; Jones, 'The Imperial Russian Life Guards,' pp. 296–8. While such traditions were especially important in such elite units as the Guards, the cavalry, and the grenadiers, the regimental histories of line units demonstrate that similar traditions existed throughout the lowly infantry.
328 This is the conclusion to be drawn from Jones, 'The Imperial Life Guards,' pp. 298–300. A further examination of numerous other regimental histories suggests that the fate of the Life Guards Grenadiers was fairly typical.
329 Alfred W. F. Knox, *With the Russian Army, 1914–1917*, 2 vols. (London, 1921), Vol. 2, pp. 551–2; Rostunov, *Russkii front*, pp. 328–33. This also is evident from the ubiquitous manner in which the Russian question intruded into the discussions of Britain's Imperial War Cabinet in late 1916 to early 1917. See, for example, the *Millner Papers*, Docs. AE 52–3, 208-10; and War Cabinet Minutes (CAB 23/1) for meetings 2, 12, 22, 26, 29–33, 36–8, 40, 43, 47 (11 December 1916 through 29 January 1917), in the Public Record Office, London.

[9]

Military Effectiveness in the First World War

PAUL KENNEDY
Yale University

It will be clear by this stage that the First World War was not a conflict which, in the annals of history, is synonymous with military effectiveness. On the contrary, it has offered abundant evidence for a whole host of studies of military incompetence, whether in its psychological, tactical, or institutional aspects.[1] It bequeathed to posterity the searing image of millions of men engaged for years in a futile struggle through the mud to achieve niggling gains at immense cost. It discredited the professional military almost everywhere,[2] and the admirals fared little better. Within a short while after the 1919 settlement it was widely asserted that there had been no real winners; *everyone* had lost. Versailles had been a 'Carthaginian peace,' ultimately as dissatisfying to the victors as to the defeated. It has, understandably, been hard to get enthused about the military aspects of a conflict which, some seventy years later, is still being described as '*the* great seminal catastrophe of the century.'[3] Since the legend of the years 1914–18 is of near-universal *in*effectiveness, what possible lessons could be drawn from it – apart from the 1920s conclusion that such a war should be avoided in the future at all costs?

Yet as soon as that question about 'lessons' is posed, of course, the importance of the First World War for the study of military effectiveness becomes obvious. Because it was the first, all-out, mass industrialized coalition war of this century, it tested effectiveness at all levels – political, strategic, operational, and tactical – and usually found things wanting. For four years, many of the most talented and resourceful individuals on each side struggled to make their systems more effective, from the realm of grand strategy and civil-military relations to that of small-group tactics on the battlefield. Slowly, painstakingly, solutions to some of the problems began to emerge, the pace of improvements being very much affected by each belligerent's strengths and weaknesses in this sort of war. Yet, as the preceding chapters have shown, advances at one *level* of effectiveness could all too easily be vitiated by continuing failures at another: tactical incompetence could have repercussions upon strategy and politics; inadequacies of supply (e.g., shells) could severely affect operational outcomes; civil-military tensions could lead to one campaign gaining preference over another. Until one of the coalitions had a distinct superiority at all levels of military effectiveness, it was not possible to overcome the stalemate which was the First World War.

The fact that individual powers evidently found it more difficult (or easier) to achieve effectiveness at one level rather than another is itself good reason for further investigation; for such differentiation not only suggests important points for later analysts seeking to understand military effectiveness *as a whole*, but also gives strategic and political historians useful insights into the institutions and national proclivities of the individual belligerent states. To take perhaps the most obvious example: why were the British usually much more effective in handling the strategic, political, and diplomatic challenges thrown up by the war than in grappling with its tactical problems, whereas in the German case the opposite seems to have been true? Since it was precisely those imbalances in the different levels of military effectiveness which repeat themselves in the Second World War, a careful comparative scrutiny of such a problem (and others which have become evident) may permit useful conclusions to be drawn about the strong and weak elements in each country's respective military systems.

With that in mind, the comments which follow are intended to point toward some of the more general conclusions which may be drawn from the chapters above, rather than to offer a factually inclusive summary which allocates equal space to the performances of each of the seven powers. While there are also obvious practical reasons for such a decision,[4] the chief motive is to allow attention to be concentrated upon what turned out to be the key issues of military effectiveness in the First World War. For the same reasons, no space will be allocated to providing general background remarks (for example, on the prewar *mentalité* of the offensive, or on the fire power revolution of the late nineteenth century), since they will have already emerged from a reading of the preceding chapters.

Although the arrangement of those chapters has moved from the general conduct of the war to the particular handling of small-scale encounters on the battlefield – in other words, from the political and strategic levels of military effectiveness down to the operational and tactical – there is a strong case for *reversing* that order when it comes to summarizing the First World War experience as a whole. For it seems worth claiming that it was at the *tactical* level in this war (much more than in the 1939–45 conflict) that the critical problems occurred. The argument, very crudely, would run as follows: because soldiers simply could not break through a trench system, their generals' plans for campaign successes were stalemated on each side; these operational failures in turn impacted upon the strategic debate at the highest level, and thus upon the strategic options being considered by national policy makers; and these, *pari passu*, affected the consideration of ends versus means at the political level, the changing nature of civil-military relations, and the allocation of national resources. In a roughly similar (if less widespread way), the inability of the admiralties to find an effective way of dealing with the new tactical circumstances facing big ships at sea, or with the challenge posed by the U-boats to merchant shipping, had repercussions upon operational possibilities, strategic options, and political priorities.

This is not to say there were no exceptions to the above pattern. Many of the campaigns fought on the Eastern Front, in Serbia, in Mesopotamia, and in Palestine were *not* checked by tactical paralysis and did therefore lead to important strategic and political results. Stalemate in the trenches did not impact upon American civil-military relations or strategic priorities. The results of the battle of the Falklands were clear-cut enough, at all levels, even while those of Jutland were not. Nor was it the tactical level which always dictated events: the German Army's tactics in March-June 1918 were fine, but they were vitiated by strategic uncertainty at the top; the Zeebrugge Raid was tactically and operationally stunning, but of little strategic consequence. Yet as soon as one begins to list such exceptions, the larger point reemerges. The Falklands battle was decisive precisely because it was the last one fought between surface fleets by gunfire alone and without the cramping tactical effects induced by the mine, torpedo, submarine, and aircraft. The campaigning in eastern Europe and in the Near East could see spectacular breakthroughs occurring from time to time because the sheer distances involved had prevented the creation of a consolidated trench line and altered the critical balance between fire power and mobility. Moreover, the Americans did not suffer from the consequences of tactical stalemate because they were not in the war long enough and, by the time that Pershing's force was engaged, that stalemate was at last being overcome by the armies of both sides. For more than three years of the fighting, however, the major combatants had generally been frustrated by their armed forces' *in*effectiveness, which appeared all the more galling in the light of the prewar forecasts of a swift victory.

To a very large degree, in other words, it was impossible for the powers to achieve military effectiveness in the First World War without first finding a solution to a small but vital number of tactical problems: how to close with, and then overwhelm, the enemy's battlefleet; how to counter the attacks of the U-boats; how to open up a new strategic flank through amphibious operations; and – by far the most important of all – how to break into, and then out of, an enemy-held trench system.

Some of these problems need only be mentioned in passing here, since following early failures, they were held to be so intractable that further attempts to solve them were abandoned – and not taken up again until the Second World War itself. Thus, the possibilities of opening up a new flank by an amphibious landing on the enemy's shore were discarded, following the Gallipoli débâcle, so far as Britain was concerned; and that country was, in theory, the power to which peripheral operations should have come most naturally. For France, too, the inability of the Allied expeditionary forces to achieve a break-out from Salonika doomed any further amphibious ventures. Taking their cue, the Italian General Staff opposed all suggestions of a cross-Adriatic invasion after 1915, pointing to the tactical and operational difficulties. In the Baltic, the Germans did at least carry out the operations to the Aaland Islands and Finland in 1918, but overall very little was done compared with, say, the repeated invasions from the sea which had occurred in the Great Northern War. Apart from the Zeebrugge Raid, the North Sea was even more of a 'dead' area for amphibious operations. One reason for this neglect was the overwhelming distaste expressed by *all* the general staffs for committing their troops to watery ventures. A second, but associated, reason was the growing awareness that land power's mobility (railways) and punch (coastal defense guns, offshore minefields, machine guns) had reduced the advantages enjoyed by sea power; tactically and operationally, getting an army landed onto an enemy-held coast was now altogether more difficult than it had been in Nelson's day.[5]

A third reason was the general difficulty which surface warships, and therefore battlefleets, had in the presence of the newer weapons of the mine, torpedo, and submarine. For over three hundred years, the big-gunned ship had, tactically (and therefore operationally and strategically) dominated naval warfare; yet in the 1914–18 conflict admirals became wary of taking their massive Dreadnoughts into the North Sea or Adriatic out of a fear of being hit by torpedoes or mines. Because the surface naval war had become paralyzed (except for some exciting small-boat actions), the idea of carrying an invasion force across such dangerous waters was also excluded. Instead of trying to work out how to solve these practical difficulties, naval staffs everywhere tended to bemoan – but accept – such new, cramping conditions. As compared with the Second World War, therefore, surface actions and amphibious operations after 1915–16 were like the Sherlock Holmes story of the dog which should have barked in the night; the fact that it didn't happen is the most interesting aspect of all. And that it didn't happen, because of unsolved tactical and operational difficulties, precluded a whole number of strategic possibilities which were only opened again after 1940.

On the other hand, what turned out to be the two most important tactical challenges of the war, that is, the containment of the U-boats and the penetration of an enemy-held trench system, *were* solved, albeit slowly and at great cost. Doenitz's description of the tactical difficulties suddenly facing a U-boat commander when the Allied decision to convoy merchantmen was introduced can hardly be bettered; even to get close to the enemy's ships, the submarine had to expose itself to all manner of possible counterattacks. Since the convoys and their escorts now had the tactical advantage in the event of any encounter, the overall operation of bringing thirty or forty merchantmen across the Atlantic or through the Mediterranean was also successful; and thus the Allied strategy of preserving command of the sea was upheld. It is even more instructive why that change took so long in coming: because it was mentally difficult for senior naval officers, brought up in the traditions of the big-gun battlefleet, to grapple with the unanticipated forms of warfare and newer weapons systems; because there was little operational analysis, or 'feedback,' from those engaged in anti-submarine warfare (or from submariners); and because it was difficult for innovative junior officers, or even pushy politicians like Lloyd George, to influence the admiralties. Lacking an adequate staff system with an independent bent towards problem solving and in close contact with the practical realities at the 'cutting edge' of war, the navies of the Great Powers were poorly equipped to defeat the U-boat challenge. As in so many other instances, the acid test of military effectiveness was whether one could handle not the expected but the *unexpected* elements thrown up in war.

In such respects, the U-boat case offers many parallels to the problems which army commanders faced as they grappled with the unexpected tactical landscape of trench warfare after 1914. With the wisdom of retrospect, one can see that this conflict took place at a very particular period in the history of military technology and transport. In the first place, it occurred when the Industrial Revolution, through the railway system, had given armies the capacity to bring masses of men, guns, and shells to the rear of the battlefield, but had not yet discovered the means (e.g., trucks and transport aircraft) to convey those items *forward*. If anything, the use of millions of horses to carry munitions where the railways ceased to operate simply compounded this problem, since their fodder needs were so enormous. Secondly, it occurred at a time when those same quick-firing guns whose demand for shells drastically complicated logistics also made it impossible for infantry and cavalry to survive on top of the ground in the face of the vastly enhanced fire power, and *before* the internal-combustion engine solved that problem as well, through the development of tanks and armored personnel carriers. The firepower revolution meant that troops had to dig deep to survive; the transport conundrum meant that the more that defensive trench systems could be built up on an elaborate and massive scale (in western Europe and northern Italy), the more difficult it was to penetrate them. If one attempted to punch a hole through the first line by prolonged bombardments, one surrendered the element of surprise and allowed the enemy to reinforce the second and third lines of trenches. Any advance took the troops farther and farther away from their logistical supplies and rear commanders; fatigue merely compounded the problem. Whichever side moved forward had put itself *immediately* at a disadvantage. This was recognized to the extent that the experts called for the attacker to have a numerical superiority of, say three to one; but in many ways that added to the interacting problems of supply and mobility. What was needed was not a change of ratios, but a rethinking of battlefield tactics.

In terms of drawing tactical lessons from the conduct of this war, therefore, the most interesting campaigns may be neither the wide-ranging strikes of Allenby and Lettow-Vorbeck, nor the stalemated horrors of Gallipoli, Verdun, the Somme, and the Isonzo; but rather those of the Brusilov offensive, Riga, Cambrai, Caporetto, and the March-August 1918 struggle along the Western Front, since all of those gave evidence that at last the military staffs on each side were beginning to overcome the tactical paralysis of trench warfare and, in consequence, to open up once again both operational and strategic possibilities.

By no means, however, were these changes of approach uniform, even if they all had their roots in the battlefield experiences of certain officers who were actively seeking to overcome the stalemate. Although it was probably Captain Laffargue who was the first to argue for the more flexible use of small units of infantrymen and for much less reliance upon lengthy, mass bombardments, these ideas were never adopted as doctrine by the French Army, many elements of which remained attached to linear advances and (after

1917, to reduce casualties) a heavy weight of shell. As Professor Porch argues, 'Initiative, mobility, and surprise were absent from French training methods,' and much the same appears to have been true of the Italian Army until the very last months of the war; yet, without those qualities, it was impossible to imitate the fast-moving storm trooper tactics. By contrast, Brusilov and his staff seem to have been very successful in bringing together all the necessary ingredients – sharp, surprise bombardments at many places on the front, swift overrunning of the defender's lines, good coordination at all levels, and a commitment to keeping up the pressure – when they overwhelmed the Austro-Hungarian Army in September 1916. The real problems for the Russian military (apart from the overstraining of the society and economy in general) were: could Brusilov-like methods be adopted by the army as a whole, and, more important still, would they work so well against the formidable Germans, who were not only moving towards a loosening-up of their own offensive tactics but were also vastly improving their defensive battlefield techniques? By the end of that same year, the answers to those questions were becoming all too clear.

The British and German military organizations dealt with the newer tactical possibilities in very different ways. On the face of it, one might have thought that the former would have been the most advanced and enthusiastic in the search for improved battlefield tactics. They complained the loudest about the slaughter in the trenches. Their army had a lengthy 'small wars' tradition which emphasized mobility. They had produced, by late 1917, both an array of intelligent officers who were emphasizing flexible, small-unit attacks, and a sophisticated artillery support system. Under the urgings of Churchill and others, they were farthest ahead in the production of tanks – a revolutionary solution to the fire-power mobility problem, provided (as always) it was used in the proper way. Yet while improvements occurred at the divisional and regimental level, in a piecemeal fashion, the generally unimaginative and inflexible tone of the senior officer corps under Haig, plus the lack of adequate 'feedback loops' between front-line experiences and the staff at the rear, prevented the broad dissemination of the newer tactical doctrines. This is in glaring contrast to the Prussian General Staff under Ludendorff. Even if it is difficult to believe that the dissemination and discussion of new tactical ideas proceeded all the time as smoothly as has been portrayed in Lupfer's account,[6] it is nonetheless clear that this was a system which was both much more open to advice 'from below,' and much more capable of inculcating newer methods throughout the military organization as a whole. It remains to this day, therefore, an important example of how to get an army to change its battlefield techniques.

Most of the other elements in the measurement of tactical effectiveness flowed from, or sometimes necessarily preceded, this alteration in fighting habits. Intensive training, it has already been noted, was needed to accompany the newer methods; the latter also required a much less hierarchical set of relationships between officers, NCOs, and rankers, and an emphasis upon unit cohesion and mutual support. Not surprisingly, the *Stosstruppen* methods worked best among elite troops (like the Italian *Arditi*) or with forces whose social backgrounds did not cramp individualism (like the formidable

Australian Corps); even the Germans, who threw great efforts into training the newer methods, only managed to inculcate them into a select number of divisions by March 1918. All-arms integration, which obviously also required intensive training and tactical flexibility, was still chiefly related to an improved coordination of infantry and artillery, superior to the linear assaults of 1916; and there are only rare instances – the French offensive in Champagne in July 1918, or the British 'push' of August 8th, 1918 – in which infantry, artillery, tanks, and aircraft worked together. It was also scarcely surprising that those late examples of all-arms warfare fascinated the post-1919 students of battlefield tactics and stimulated the early *Blitzkrieg*-style theories of Fuller and Liddell Hart.

This change in the tactical nature of warfare clearly had an important impact upon 'morale.' Given the very high level of conscious and subconscious patriotic indoctrination in all of the combatant societies prior to 1914, it would require repeated evidence of the horrors and futility of warfare to cause disintegration. By that measure, it is easy to see why the US forces seemed so confident and strong when they first appeared on the Western Front; much less easy to understand why the Italians could be sent forward repeatedly into the Isonzo battles, and why the French could recover from the 1917 mutinies; and remarkable that the Russian Army did not disintegrate until 1917, and that the heterogeneous Habsburg Army fought until the bitter end. Loyalty, discipline, and fear of disgrace together provided an effective cement; local and regional ties and decent living conditions also helped. All that said, it seems clear also from the preceding chapters that high morale was much more likely to be achieved in small, specialized units and in all services where a sense of purpose and the rationality of fighting were preserved. Where an attack seemed evidently futile and suicidal, like Nivelle's offensive or the High Seas Fleet's intended operation of October 1918, unrest and disaffection occurred; where troops and sailors saw they had a chance of survival, and perhaps a victory, they always went forward. Such conclusions are not at all new; but they need to be re-learned in every war.

Operational effectiveness during the First World War was caught in a two-edged vice: on the one hand, potential operations were often constrained by considerations of policy, strategy, and geography; on the other, actual operations were all too frequently hampered, and undermined, by the tactical and technical problems mentioned earlier. One can think of literally dozens of successful operations in the Second World War which were both strategically relevant and tactically impressive. For the 1914–18 conflict, one scratches one's head to make up even a short list – the Falklands (perhaps), Tannenberg/Masurian Lakes, Lemberg, the German overrunning of Rumania in 1916, Caporetto (perhaps), Allenby's drive toward Jerusalem, and the combined Allied offensives of July-September 1918 on the Western Front. All of the other operations left something to be desired; many were unmitigated disasters.

The naval war was, operationally, anything other than a 'Great War at Sea,'[7] for the reasons given above. Geography had boxed in the German and Austro-Hungarian surface fleets, and allowed the Allies to retain command of the sea merely by staying on the strategic defensive. In view of their inferiority in battleship numbers, it would have been rash for the Central Powers to commit themselves to offensive naval operations. This mutual inertia was reinforced by the admirals' fear of the mine, torpedo, and submarine – probably much exaggerated, if one recalls the important battleship actions in the later war (Narvik, Matapan, *Bismark* Chase, North Cape) despite the great advances in submarine and aircraft technology. Policy and diplomacy were also important constraints. The Italians wanted to preserve their fleet intact as a bargaining chip at the end of the war (little wonder, then, that they had *no* operational doctrine!), and the same calculation prevailed in Paris and Vienna. For the kaiser and his admirals, it was also politically important not to let the High Seas Fleet be eliminated.

All this restricted main-fleet operations to a few chance encounters, such as the Dogger Bank and Jutland. Those clashes, like the land battles, suggested that operational expertise had not caught up with the new technology. Internal-combustion engines could drive opposing battlefleets toward (and away from) each other at a combined speed of nearly 50 knots, yet the admirals did not possess the 'command and control' technology to handle their own disparate squadrons, let alone follow the enemy's motives. Unlike trench warfare, however, there was little opportunity to test operational improvements among the battlefleets; and the focus of the naval struggle shifted increasingly toward the U-boat campaign against merchant shipping. Yet that was of its nature a very decentralized form of warfare, so that its operational success hung upon each side's tactical habits; when the Allies adopted the convoy, the U-boats' operational chances declined dramatically. Far from having the desired strategic effect of bringing Britain and France to their knees, the actions of the German submarines were the major factor in provoking the United States to enter the war, thereby sealing the Reich's fate.

Combined-service operations in this conflict were also caught in this vise, and thus conspicuous by their absence. Strategy and geography made them seem a distraction to most of the powers, engaged as they were in a land-based 'struggle for mastery in Europe.' Policy – in particular, the lack of cooperation (and, in most cases, sympathy) between the army and navy staffs – was a further constraint. Indeed, the one great Allied attempt at combined operations, Gallipoli, failed to overcome the many technical problems which such a complicated action would throw up, and thus became a glaring example of how *not* to conduct that sort of campaign.

Far from being unique, Gallipoli was but one of a number of operations conducted away from the standard European theaters – Kut, Tanga, and Salonika were others – which failed because too little account was taken of the necessary underpinnings for such long-distance strikes: intelligence, supply, communications, medical services, and so on. If any real lesson emerges from these campaigns, it is that what we might nowadays term 'out-of-area operations' were *not* cheap. Because such actions might involve an advance across hundreds of miles (compared with the hard-won 5 miles on the Western Front), good mobility and logistics were of the essence; but that in turn demanded a massive infrastructural investment – light railways, new roads, river steamers, telegraphs, and hundreds of thousands of mules and camels to transport men, munitions, tents, and field hospitals. At the end of the day, such operations were successful, and the careful planning which attended them paid off: the Russians blasted their way through the Caucasus; the British entered Baghdad, Jerusalem, and Damascus; German East Africa did eventually fall – but all at a cost. 'Sideshows,' in other words, made their own operational demands, which armies neglected at their peril.

Nevertheless, the fact remains that it was much harder to achieve operational effectiveness across the trench lines of the Western Front, northern Italy, and (in some places) along the Eastern Front, than anywhere else. Here circumstances restricted the chances for a successful operation in the most devastating way. For the tactical and technical reasons given above, one side began to lose its advantage as soon as it commenced an offensive against the other. The sheer difficulty of forcing a hole through an enemy trench system *4 miles wide* (and to do it in time to reach the other side before reinforcements were brought up) was such that all of the normally expected indicators of operational success could give no guarantee of victory. An army – say, Haig's before the Somme, or Falkenhayn's at Verdun – could possess enormous stocks of guns and ammunition, command dozens of fresh divisions, have good morale, supply transportation, and so on, and yet to no avail. Operation after operation was therefore closed down, following appalling casualties, with the front line changed by little more than a mile or two.

Even the more mobile and spectacular campaigns in the European theater eventually fizzled, or ended in disaster, because the technical and logistical problems proved insuperable. The fate of the Schlieffen Plan in August-September 1914 was an early example of that; for, as Professor Herwig shows, the faster that the leading German divisions moved, the farther they drew away from their supplies, and the more the advantage tilted toward the French. This sequence of events was repeated in March-June 1918, by which time, interestingly, the German Army had solved the tactical problem of how to break through an enemy trench system, but it then fell victim to Ludendorff's lack of strategic purpose, not to mention operational 'overstretch.' Exactly the same happened following those two other large-scale breakthroughs, the Brusilov offensive and Caporetto. Each, by using the elements of surprise, combined arms, and tactical flexibility, not only cleared a way through the enemy's trenches but then also advanced 20, 30, or even 40 miles beyond, driving the defenders back in confusion. Neither attacking army, however, had been properly prepared for a follow-up. The farther they advanced, the more they strained their supply systems. Plundering consumed the troops' energies. As the defending forces fell back, their lines shortened; and Allied reinforcements appeared. In fact, no European theater operation of the First World War – save perhaps the German counteroffensive campaigns of Tannenberg, the Polish salient (1915), and Rumania (1916) – saw the successful army fully achieving its aim before being bogged down along a new front line, which in turn needed to be built up; and even those three successes were actions intended to stabilize the front, not operations planned to bring a larger victory.

Since military operations did not normally lead to a decisive change in the battle lines, it was perhaps not surprising that various commanders began to redefine their strategic aim: instead of going for an unattainable breakthrough, they would aim instead at attrition, wearing down the enemy's forces until the magic moments arrived when they buckled under. This was, notoriously, Falkenhayn's intention at Verdun, and had been Joffre's in the previous year; it was increasingly the *raison d'être* behind the many battles of the Isonzo; and by 1916 British generals like Rawlinson had also come to see it as the only plausible strategic justification for what they were doing on the Western Front. However, this change brought fresh problems, which in turn could erode the prospects of biting off a chunk of enemy-held territory at a time. The first of these was the obvious effect upon soldiers' morale if they gained the impression that forthcoming attacks were merely part of an attrition strategy and not the 'big push' to end the war – witness here the unprintable Australian reactions to Haig's euphemisms about making 'methodological progress' in the Somme battles.[8] The second problem with this situational form of warfare was that even if an operation went better than expected, there had often been no preparations to exploit it. The British were probably the worst here – neither in the blowing-up of the Messines Ridge nor the tank attack at Cambrai had any follow-up plan been worked out – but this also occurred in most other armies except the German. Finally, a strategy of battlefield attrition always assumed that one's resources would ultimately prove superior, even while suffering the proportionately larger casualties that repeated offensives entailed; but that assumption rested upon factors (manpower reserves, industrial muscle, public morale) which front-line generals were not well equipped to measure objectively. That was the flaw in Joffre's and Falkenhayn's offensives, and in the falsely confident Russian assessments of early 1917; it was also evident, despite Lloyd George's objections, in Haig's own calculations. Ultimately, attrition warfare is likely to shift the focus of military effectiveness from the operational level to the strategical and political, as was the case with the Vietnam War.

Before moving to those levels, it may be worthwhile drawing attention to the very successful *defensive* campaigns of the First World War, since they include operational lessons not much studied by Western experts, whose image of this conflict is one of the repeated failed *offensives* of 1914–17 followed by a run of successful *offensives* in 1918. The French defense of Verdun owed much not simply to the fact that for once it was Germany that was launching attacks across Western Front trenches, but also to the clever defensive tactics used – digging deep, launching surprise counterattacks to regain lost trenches, rotating the French division frequently to preserve their morale, and so on. The Bulgarian defensive campaigns at Salonika would also repay closer study, as might the hand-to-mouth (and rather lucky) Turkish defense of the Dardanelles. However, the most impressive practitioners of defensive warfare were undoubtedly the Germans. In this respect, their frequent slashing counterattacks on the Eastern Front – usually to rescue their Austro-Hungarian ally from disaster – may be the less interesting if more spectacular examples, since they flowed rather naturally from the German advantages over Russia in terms of railway communications, heavy artillery, and field intelligence. Less well known was the massive *re-learning* effort in defensive, situational warfare undertaken by the German Army after

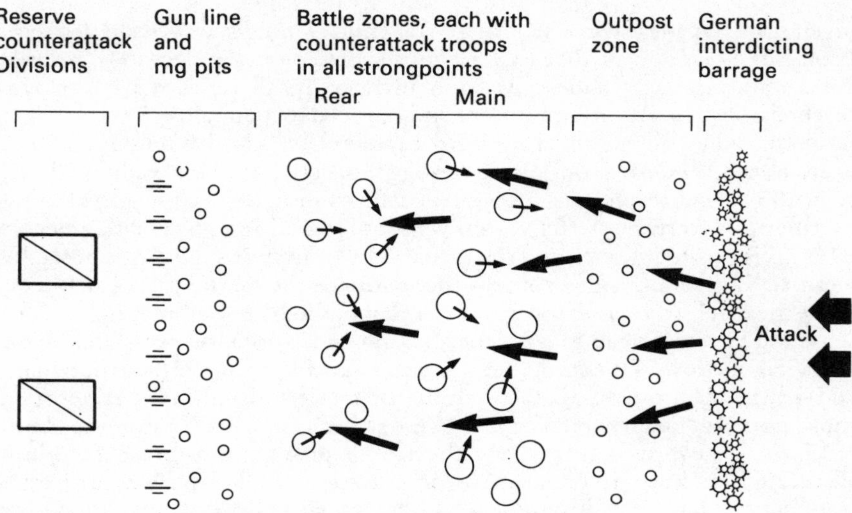

Figure 9.1 The German Defense in Depth, 1917–1918
Source: P. Griffith, *Forward into Battle: Fighting Tactics from Waterloo to Vietnam* (Chichester, Sussex, 1981), p. 78.

its heavy losses in the front trenches during the Somme bombardments. By abandoning formal trench *lines* in favour of the elastic defense of a much wider zone, with dozens of mutually supporting strongpoints behind the first scattered outposts, and with reserve divisions on call in the rear, the Germans made an Allied offensive on traditional lines more difficult than ever before (see Figure 9.1).

By inculcating this emphasis upon counterattack, moreover, the German Army could recover even from enemy surprise assaults if the latter once relaxed their pressure, as their famous *riposte* to the Cambrai tank operation amply demonstrated. Just how long that sort of warfare could have been continued, had Lundendorff not decided to switch to his own unlimited offensive campaign of March 1918 (and thus lose these operational advantages), is hard to guess. Yet that ought not to obscure the fact that, just as in the 1942–45 period, the German Army was remarkably good in conducting defensive warfare.

At the strategic level, however, the Teutonic genius for war peters out quickly. Before examining that deficiency, it may be worth looking at those countries which found it easier to be militarily effective in terms of strategy. Clearly, Japan had the lightest task; eliminating the German presence at Kiaochow and in Micronesia was not difficult operationally, and it fitted in nicely with Toyko's strategic aim of enhancing its own position in the Orient. At the same time, political prudence tempered territorial ambition, and the *Genro* (Elder Statesmen) made it clear that Japanese strategic decisions should not antagonize its allies unduly. Hence the retreat from the Twenty-One Demands upon China, the decision to send warships to the Mediterranean, and the waiting upon American approval of the Siberian intervention (even if the Japanese force sent there was much larger than Wilson desired). Professor Nish shows that each of those three strategic decisions aroused debate among the Japanese decision makers. In all cases, a balance was reached between national ambitions and the need to maintain the good will of powerful allies. Japan acted neither obsequiously (say, by sending a large army to the Western Front) nor over-aggressively (say, by invading China, as in 1937), and reaped the strategic benefit from it.

America's wartime strategy, too, was both logical and successful, given its 1917 decisions to intervene on the Allied side, to suppress the threat posed by German U-boats, and to compel the defeat of the German armed forces. Since the chief strategic threat at sea was that posed by the submarine, it made sense to redirect the US Navy's energies into anti-submarine warfare. It was also vital, in view of the strain the war was imposing upon the French, Italian, and British economies, to increase the financial and industrial support to those powers. Finally, although it had not been in Wilson's mind in April 1917, it was also wise to agree to the army's plan to commit an American Expeditionary Force to France. Any other theater would have been a distraction; *not* to send an AEF might well have given Ludendorff his hoped-for victory in June 1918. Compared with these basic matters, the issue of what section of the front the AEF should occupy and whether it should be an independent army even in its early stages were of much less strategic import. To some degree, the Americans were the beneficiaries of circumstance. Allied naval and land strategy had already been worked out, and they merely fitted into it; the defects in force size, equipment, and training caused by the very rapid expansion of the US Army were masked by borrowings from Allies and being given time (though not much) to learn about trench warfare; and they appeared on the Western Front just when the tactical deadlock had been unfrozen and Ludendorff had over-extended the capacities of his battle-weary armies. Operationally and tactically, when the American units went forward against German-held positions, they encountered the same difficulties as everyone else – as they would do again at the Kasserine Pass and in Normandy. Yet by August 1918 that did not matter. Despite the resistance of individual German units, the German line as a whole was breaking up and the Americans were ready with hundreds of thousands of fresh troops. That was an enviable strategic position to be in as the war whimpered to its close, even if it did not of itself guarantee the securing of Wilson's utopian dreams of a new world order.

For the other main belligerents, however, the strategic demands of the war were much more severe. In many cases, there was really very little choice, at least so far as the theater of war was concerned. France, for example, was like a man whose shoulder was being torn off by a savage beast; in such a life-and-death circumstance, it was predictable that Paris had little time for the naval war and was skeptical (and suspicious) of British operations in the Near East. Gallipoli, with its promise to strengthen Russia's strategic position, was another matter; but the French were not operationally equipped to ease the British difficulties there, and even less willing than Sir John French or Sir Douglas Haig to divert troops to that theater. The Italian campaign was, increasingly, an irrelevance for the French. Essentially, all that counted was the defeat of the German Army in the field, and France's war effort and armed forces were properly concentrated upon that end. On the other hand, Professor Porch is surely right to deplore France's habit of applying 'its strategy in such a wasteful manner' – in its rash Plan XVII of 1914, the even more disastrous assaults of 1915 and 1916, and Nivelle's folly of Spring 1917. Not only did this habit ignore the tactical-operational difficulties of bursting through a German trench system, but it was also strategic nonsense. Such assaults pitted French strength against even greater German strength; the more the French attacked, the faster they were running out of men. This was even more remarkable when one considers the French unwillingness to wait until the British had built up their own army. Only with the 1917 mutinies, followed by Pétain's decision to await 'the tanks and the Americans,' did France adopt a military strategy likely to bring victory rather than defeat.

Italy's strategy combined the French folly of repeated mass infantry offensives with the hubris of seeking to advance all the way to Vienna. Alternative strategies in the Balkans were abandoned, following the half-hearted Albanian venture of December 1915. Yet the task of driving along the unpromising route to Vienna reflected neither the Italian Army's tactical competence nor the country's infrastructural and industrial underdevelopment. All it did was to demoralize an already unhappy army, produce growing strains in Italian society, and (after the Caporetto disaster) make the country increasingly dependent upon its richer and more technologically advanced Western allies. The improvements in battlefield tactics and weapons coordination which were at last occurring in 1918 suggest that the Italian Army's experiences need not have been so bloody; they do not make the chosen strategy any more plausible.

Once the war had broken out, Russia's strategic options (like France's) were severely restricted by the fact that part of its territories was threatened by the most formidable army in the world. However, things were also complicated by the opportunities which beckoned on the Galician front against the far less formidable Austro-Hungarian Army (together with the need to give indirect support to the Serbs). They were complicated still further when Turkey entered the war, thereby opening up a southern, Caucasian front. In theory, the Russians would have done better to have concentrated even more upon these southern and southwestern opportunities and to have avoided, so far as was possible, mixing it with the Germans. Yet there were two compelling objections to that strategy. The first was the political dislike of withdrawing from Russian Poland and the Baltic states, whose peoples would most likely oppose any later return. The second was the needs of Russia's allies, which St. Petersburg took very seriously, perhaps too seriously considering the disasters of 1914, 1916, and 1917. Nonetheless, there *was* a logic in putting pressure upon the German Army so as to help preserve France, just as there was a case to be made, by summer 1916, for an offensive to divert some of the Austro-Hungarian forces from the Italian front. The Russian strategy of mobilizing millions of fresh recruits each season for renewed western offensives was thus a very plausible one. It foundered, alas, on the harsh realities of operational incompetence, plus an awful array of organizational and infrastructural deficiencies in such a mass, peasant-based army. Against the Austro-Hungarian and Turkish forces, the Russians were repeatedly successful, sometimes brilliantly so; but those strategic actions in the southwest would have just overstretched their system when the Germans would come crashing in, with great speed and devastating fire power, to roll the Russians back again. With some rare exceptions, facing the German Army seems to have paralyzed Russian commanders. Ignoring the stunning surprise tactics of the Brusilov offensive, losing the ingenuity displayed in the mountain campaigns against the Turks, Russian generals unimaginatively ordered their divisions forward against German-held positions, and watched them being slaughtered *en masse* in the marshes, or cut to pieces by explosively fast counterattacks. Losing heavily against the Germans was not a new element in Russian strategy, and one imagines that *Stavka* had gradually come to expect it; but by 1917 the new recruits were no longer the placid younger sons but the resentful second-category men (e.g., those who were the sole breadwinners in a family, and thus traditionally exempt from conscription). In such circumstances, repeating the offensive strategy of earlier years – however logical in terms of Allied cooperation – was fatal.

With regard to Russia's repeated military disasters since the Crimean War, that result was at least not unusual; but it is ironic to see that the homeland of Clausewitz, the elder Moltke, and Bismarck was also unable to formulate a coherent strategy in the 1914–18 conflict. That it was good at the tactical and operational levels of military effectiveness, whether fighting offensively or defensively, seems undoubted, and Professor Herwig's chapter also details the way in which it could re-train its forces at those levels. Its basic flaw, which it repeated even more spectacularly in 1941, was to opt for strategic courses of action which, while having a certain military logic to them, undermined rather than secured the nation's larger political goals. In overreaching itself to gain a victory in a specific campaign, it ran the risk of ensuring that it could never win the war as a whole.

It is true that the Germany of 1914 was a victim of geography, in a way that the United States, Japan, and Britain were not; but, as has been noted, France, Russia, and even Italy were also disadvantaged by their location (as were, even more so, Austria-Hungary and Turkey). Yet whereas the French, for example, enhanced their strategic effectiveness by clever alliance diplomacy, the German military mind preferred a quite different solution: escaping from their geopolitical bind by a bold offensive move which, while provocative to neutral Great Powers, would hopefully shatter their immediate foe and thus achieve the desired swift victory. Such a move might fail; and it might well bring another powerful nation into the enemy coalition. Convinced of its own military effectiveness, however, Berlin proved incapable of coldly weighing the balance of short-term versus long-term risk which was at the core of a truly Clausewitzian grand strategy.

The two most notorious German examples of making gratuitous enemies are, of course, the Schlieffen Plan and the 1917 decision to instigate unrestricted U-boat warfare. By the first action, Berlin brought not only Belgium into the war, but also Britain – and, in consequence, the British Empire and (for its own good reasons) Japan – as well as influencing Italy's future course of conduct. Britain's entry sealed the fate of the German overseas empire, and of its merchant marine. It brought enormous financial reserves, and later a great army, into the Allied camp. It neutralized the High Seas Fleet – which was the chief reason why the admirals began to favor using the submarine to carry out *guerre de course* (despite the fact, as Professor Nenninger points out, that the German navy really had very few boats to implement that strategy). The High Command's decision on unrestricted U-boat warfare (plus the Zimmermann Telegram) added to the list of Germany's foes the United States, by that time the industrial and financial powerhouse of the world, and a country also capable of producing a large, fresh army for war in Europe. Against the Dual Alliance of France and Russia, the Central Powers were somewhat superior in terms of industrial, economic muscle; with the British Empire and the United States becoming enemies, the balances shifted dramatically (even with Russia's demise) and made the German *bloc* decidedly inferior.[9] Such was the narrow view of 'strategy' that prevailed in Berlin that these larger points were never fully considered; nor, indeed, was there a forum in which to consider them, which may be the most significant negative lesson to draw from any study of German military effectiveness.

Strategic historians walk on very thin ice when they indulge in counterfactual and hypothetical arguments; but it seems plausible to claim that if the Central Powers had only been fighting against France, Russia, and Serbia, they would have had a very good chance of winning outright. Both on land and at sea, they would have been in a much better position. As it was, once the Germans had recovered from the logistical overextension which was the Schlieffen Plan, they learned to utilize their central lines of communication to gain a good degree of strategic flexibility. Correctly assessing the advantages of staying on the defensive in the West – confirmed by the futility of Falkenhayn's Verdun campaign – the High Command concentrated on an eastern offensive, where it could exploit the army's speed and fire power. With Russia's military collapse in 1917, that strategy seemed the correct one. Yet the cost, in manpower and to the German economy, of conducting *two* major wars at the same time was enormous; even the defensive strategy along the Western Front led to appalling casualties, especially at the Somme and Passchendaele battles. The improved defensive tactics described above slowed the bleeding, but did not stop the hemorrhage; hence the temptation to cut France and Britain off from their vital transatlantic supplies, whatever the risk, and, when that had failed, to raise the gambler's stakes even higher with Ludendorff's 'all or nothing' lunge of March 1918, before the odds swung even more against Germany. After four years of unremitting struggle, however, even the German war machine could not keep going much longer; it had done astonishingly well to have managed so long.

Impetuous youths have boasted of taking on 'the four corners of the earth in arms'; only the Germans have made a practice of it, twice in this century, and suffered the strategic and political consequences therefrom. This seems the more curious given the openness and flexible manner in which tactical and operational innovations were discussed by the German Army staff, and then refined by empirical experience.[10] Yet a similar form of free-ranging debate was never permitted at the level of grand strategy, nor was there a body like a Cabinet for considering the longer term political aims of the German nation. Why that was so cannot be examined further here. The traditional separation of the military and civilian spheres of government, the kaiser's role as 'supreme war lord,' the conservatives' fear that an open debate about war aims would open up a Pandora's box of critical opinions, and – last but not least – the militarists' dismissal of both Britain and the United States as ineffective, non-warrior societies, all no doubt form part of the explanation.

It is at the level of strategy, and its relationship with politics, that the British system looks superior. Britain's world position was, to use Beloff's phrase, 'more of a *tour de force* than that of her rivals.'[11] Since Britain was much more of an imperial, extra-European power than France, Italy, Austria-Hungary, Germany and, in the last resort, even Russia, it felt obligated to pay particular attention to preserving relations with the United States and Japan, to ensuring the unity of the empire, to cushioning its substantial interests in the Middle East, Africa, and the Indian sub-continent from the full reverberations of the war, and to keeping its unique place at the center of a liberal, cosmopolitan, trained empire resting upon delicate credit and supply arrangements. On the other hand, since Britain was also much more of a European power than the United States or Japan, it therefore felt compelled to commit a far greater proportion of its manpower and wealth to the preservation of the Continental military balance of power, despite the appalling costs. Finding the right strategic middle way between these two poles, and (again to quote Beloff) striking 'the correct balance between the immediate requirements of the war and the long-term prospects of the country and Empire'[12] was an extremely difficult task.

On the whole, the British managed it reasonably well. The Continental balance was upheld (barely); imperial interests were preserved, in some areas considerably enhanced; and relations with all of the Allied Great Powers were skillfully utilized to benefit Britain's complex strategic situation. Once again, there is no space here to investigate the reasons for this in detail. In part, it can be explained by the fact that the British had been engaged in such a strategic-diplomatic juggling act for a very long time, and had been forced to evolve decision-making structures (e.g., Cabinet sub-committees and the Committee of Imperial Defence) to deal with the working out of priorities. If one examined their handling of the Crimean War, they would look less impressive. This process was aided by a university training for the elite which emphasized 'judgement and facility in absorbing and rendering reliable opinions upon a complicated mass of factual material and devising a policy out of it.'[13] Finally, and less flatteringly, it was helped by the fortunate fact that Britain was an island; as the French often pointed out, if the British had had an enormous German army encamped only as short a distance from London as, say, Canterbury or Brighton, they also would have found it difficult to divert troops to Baghdad and Tanganyika. More specifically, though, the British Isles enclosed the North Sea, thus reducing the strategic effectiveness of the High Seas Fleet and giving the Allies an immense strategic flexibility if they could find the means to use it. All this helped to ensure the success of British war aims.

This does not mean there were no problems. On the contrary, civil-military relations were far more controversial during this war than in the 1939–45 conflict, to a large part because the strategic debate was far more divided and angry. The bitter memoirs of leading decision makers which appeared soon after the war, and the polemical writings of Liddell Hart and others, are clue enough that many participants felt that British strategy had been *in*effective. Seventy years later, the debate still rumbles on.[14]

Yet the more the subject is examined, the clearer it becomes that the problem was not about strategy so much as the *practical application* of that strategy; that is, tactics and operations. This was true, it has been argued above, for all the major combatants; but the British case offers such a superb example of this because in so many other areas (geographical position, supreme direction of the war, assessment of priorities, reserves of economic and diplomatic strength) it was so advantaged. Yet none of those factors would be enough if battles could not be won. Strategically, the 'Continental commitment' was the correct one; strategically, the strike at Gallipoli was brilliant in its promise; strategically, protecting the Allied sea routes was quite vital and rightly given high priority. However, the awful problem was that, however correct in theory, those strategies did not seem to work in practice. The Continental commitment, the peripheral strategy, the protection of merchant shipping, all seemed to be hopelessly flawed during the first three years of the war; only in 1917–18 was the corner turned.

Why? In the first place, it has to be said again that this weakness was common to all the Great Powers. For most of the war, *no one* knew how to break through a strongly held trench system; *no one* knew how to implement a large-scale amphibious operation; and *no one* knew how to deal with the U-boat menace. The refined Cabinet committee and decision-making system, so good at grand strategy, was ineffective here because 'judgement is useless unless the material is in the briefs, and for what was needed in military matters once the lines of trenches to the sea were complete, or at sea with the coming of the submarine, was not in the briefs.'[15] The split which had evolved between the civilian and military spheres of life in the Victorian political culture had meant that, while ministers were well equipped to deal with the political and diplomatic aspects of strategy, they paid little attention to military and naval details: *that* was for the experts. Yet neither the British Army nor the Royal Navy had, at this time, created an effective staff system to handle tactical and operational problems, to analyze empirical data, to experiment with new methods, and – most important of all – to encourage open discussion which would also include challenging received ideas about how best things were to be done. In this respect, the Prussian staff system was much more 'liberal' and 'forward thinking' than that in Britain and the other Western democracies, with the possible exception of the United States. Because Haig's army did not possess a system for the frequent re-examination of tactical methods and operational doctrine, improvements in battlefield technique came slowly and piecemeal. Because the Admiralty had closed minds toward convoy, only a combination of pressures, chiefly external, forced them to experiment with it. Because neither service was enthusiastic about combined operations, little was done about them. All this impacted upon strategic possibilities in a very decisive, if negative, way.

The preceding discussion of military effectiveness from a 'tactics-upwards' perspective also allows us to understand more clearly the place of *political* factors in the larger equation. The term *political* as used in these essays has actually referred to two separate if interrelated aspects, the first being the availability of financial, industrial, technological, and manpower resources for the pursuit of victory, and the second being the willingness of the nation at large, and their political representatives in particular, to keep on supporting the war effort. Obviously, the former aspect depended upon the latter – although there also were natural, absolute limits to a country's resources and manpower, if the war went on long enough. With a society which had overstrained itself, the level of morale both in the army and on the home front would become a vital factor in that country's continuing political-military effectiveness. Virtually all of the writers in this volume report upon the massive economic and manpower resources made available to the military organizations once the war commenced, but this is hardly surprising. Prewar animosities had stoked up military and naval arms races; the 'mood of 1914' was patriotic and belligerent; and extraordinary sacrifices seemed justified to ensure the expected swift, decisive victory. When the early offensives ground to a halt, it still seemed natural for each side to call for more intensive efforts, more conscripts, and more munitions, although this frequently produced bottlenecks and massive inefficiencies until new organizations were created to handle them. This slide towards the total mobilization of the economy and society was accelerated by the reports from the generals that the matériel requirements of the conflict – barbed wire, cement, trucks, machine guns, aircraft, artillery, and especially shells – were fantastically larger than their earlier calculations; in 1915, virtually every belligerent suffered a 'shell crisis.'

The consequence of this was that, from 1915 onwards, munitions production in all these countries soared, creating new industries and thousands of new factories. The historians of the individual war efforts have warmly praised such transformations,[16] yet the latter also are unsurprising. For all the laments of Liberals about the 'burden of armaments' prior to 1914, only a small proportion of national income (4 per cent, on average) was committed to that end. When 'total war' raised that figure to 25 or 33 per cent, it was inevitable that the output of armaments would rise dramatically. Given the powers of the modern bureaucratic state to float loans and raise taxes, there was no longer any internal fiscal impediment to sustaining a lengthy war, as had crippled eighteenth-century states. While to the shrinking band of traditional political economists this appeared to be mortgaging the nation's future, their voices were drowned out by patriotic assurance that the defeated enemy would pay. For the moment, all that was needed was to boost armaments production.

This in turn simply meant that fresh masses of guns, shells, and troops were heading to the front month after month, season after season – to be wasted and slaughtered and stalemated in the trenches because of the failure of the military organizations to solve the new tactical and operational challenges which the war had thrown up. In that sense, an ever costlier armaments stalemate was interacting with an ever bloodier operational (and therefore strategic) stalemate, so it was not surprising that generals grew baffled, politicians grew desperate, and the public grew ever more resentful as the arms output meant little; what was more critical was how long each economy and society could meet these unprecedented demands when the prospects of outright victory for either side seemed to be fading away. This was where the *coalition* aspect of the First World War became crucial. Austria-Hungary, despite its repeated defeats by Russia, could be rescued and propped up by Germany; Italy, after Caporetto, could be militarily reinforced by France and Britain; France and Italy could be economically helped by Britain, which in turn could be financially assisted by the United States; the American Expeditionary Force could obtain its tanks, aircraft, artillery, and machine guns from Britain and France; and the British merchant marine could transport these vast flows of men, munitions, grain, and coal.

None of the individual chapters in this collection, by their very nature, can sufficiently cover the *collective* balance of forces which, following years of stalemate and slaughter, eventually decided the war. Significantly, Russia was the one Allied power which could not be sustained by its partners, as France and Italy could be; unable to protect itself from the German war machine, suffering rampant inflation, with its transportation system breaking down, and its latest round of conscripts disaffected, the country could take no more. It is astonishing, in retrospect, how long it lasted.

Yet the German triumph here was short-lived. By the fourth year of campaigning, its own manpower stocks had been bled away (the army's size peaked in June 1917, then declined), and even its enormous industrial base had been overstrained by the demands of war. The Hindenburg Program had unbalanced the economy, produced high inflation, reclaimed workers from the army, and ruined agriculture (and thus food stocks). At the same time, the High Command's inept policies had brought into the conflict a new enemy, the United States, with a manufacturing output at least two and a half times that of Germany's shrinking economy, and with a massive manpower stock. It was in these unpromising circumstances – with industrial output down to 57 per cent of its 1913 figure, and the public grumbling at the lack of food – that Ludendorff launched his great offensive of March 1918. Tactically and operationally, it was extremely successful in its early stages, and extremely mobile compared with Verdun, the Somme, and Passchendaele; but as Ludendorff's armies lunged first in one direction and then in another, his supply lines became overextended and his casualties mounted. By contrast, American and British Empire reinforcements were at last giving the Allies the manpower superiority – and the flow of tanks, aircraft, trucks, and artillery giving them the fire power and mobility – to counterattack the German trenches and then to maintain a steady advance. Curiously, the German collapse occurred at just about the same time as the Turkish, Bulgarian, and Austro-Hungarian. In this coalition war, the entire coalition cracked together.

Even with all the detail we now possess, it is difficult to relate this story of relative military effectiveness to the state of civil-military relations in each of the combatant countries. In this enquiry, it is necessary to separate the United States and Japan immediately from the other Great Powers, for in neither country were civil-military relations a matter of deep political concern, possibly because war was not intense enough. That leaves for consideration two clusters of constitutional types: (1) the three liberal democracies of Britain, France, and Italy; and (2) the three autocracies, or semi-autocracies, of Germany, Austria-Hungary, and Russia. In all five examples covered in this volume – and, of course, in the Habsburg Empire, too[17] – the military leadership of the war was in frequent, and usually increasing, tension with civilian leaders and political assemblies. In the case of the western democracies, this tension primarily arose because the civilian governments, which *de jure* were in charge of the supreme direction of the war, feared that they had surrendered *de facto* control to Haig, Joffre, and Cadorna; that is, to generals who, unable to produce strategic successes, demanded ever larger sacrifices of men and munitions. As Dr. Gooch points out, while Lloyd George and Clemenceau eventually managed to re-assert civilian leadership, Italian politicians were less successful in controlling the *Comando Supremo*, even after the disaster at Caporetto.

In those societies where the monarchs were the military heads of the nation, and in which civilian interference in military affairs was not permitted, the tensions were somewhat different. In the first half of the war, as in the other belligerent states, domestic criticism was directed at the incompetence of the military organization to produce the promised victory, and was not greatly focused upon constitutional reform *per se* (although the Duma's rise in influence was obviously due to those twin discontents). With the strain of the war intensifying, and with the respective high commands calling for ever greater sacrifices from their populations without any evident sign of victory, it was predictable that cries would arise for a reform of the entire governing system, not to mention for social and economic compensations for the enhanced 'military participation ratio.' Many of the same internal pressures were arising in the western countries – Britain offers many examples of this[18] – but they could be more easily absorbed into the parliamentary democratic system than was the case in the military autocracies. More than that it is difficult to claim, since those powers which did collapse internally (Russia in 1917, Germany and Austria-Hungary in 1918) were also the societies which had overstretched themselves militarily, where transport and food supplies were breaking down, and where it was not possible to secure external aid. Public disenchantment at the political aspects of the war therefore interacted with public unrest at social and economic deprivation, to topple governments and to bring the war effort to a halt. This, in the audit of Mars, was the ultimate test of a Great Power's military effectiveness.

There are no easy lessons to be drawn from the experiences of the military organizations and societies which fought in the First World War – apart from such obvious platitudes as 'make sure you solve your tactical problems,' or 'don't overstrain the economy too far.' As this volume amply demonstrates, military effectiveness is a complicated, multi-layered phenomenon, and one that is unlikely to be attained by a few smart reforms here and there.

Excellence can be secured at one level, only to have the results dissipated at another – higher or lower – level. Being good at *all* levels is very rare indeed, especially in the early stages of a conflict that is being fought under new technological, economic, and geopolitical conditions; yet the evidence suggests that improvements can be made in the areas of identified weakness, if the system is flexible enough.

Clearly, not all elements which go to make up *national* military effectiveness can be improved upon by the military organizations alone. The geographical location of a country, whether favorable or unfavorable to the conflict under way, is unchangeable. A backward, poorly educated peasant society cannot be transformed overnight by the order of a High Command suddenly realizing that it needs hundreds of thousands of trained technicians. Weapons systems cannot be swiftly produced, if the necessary raw materials or industrial infrastructure is lacking. Certain forms of warfare may be impossible, or at least very difficult, due to the political culture of the country in question. Military organizations which try to deal with *those* issues are likely to suffer Ludendorff's fate. On the other hand, while themselves understanding how such larger political, socio-economic, and geographical factors are likely to restrict certain strategic aims, the military *can* and should inform the civilian leadership of the implications of those constrictions, in order to allow a reassessment to be made of the nation's political war aims. If an enemy cannot be defeated with the resources in hand and by the strategies available, the military ought to say so; and the political leadership should then consider seriously the alternatives to outright victory. When Clausewitz argued that the military point of view had to be subordinated to the political, because 'policy is the intelligent faculty, war only the instrument,' this also encompassed circumstances in which 'policy' would be intelligent enough to win a war or to wind one down. If the military organization has done its best up to that point of political decision, no one need reprove it.

That leads to the final, elemental point. More than anything else, the military organization ought to strive to get its own house in order before criticising outside factors. This is an easy thing to say; at this moment, Washington and other Western capitals are surrounded by politicians, scholars, and 'think tanks' preaching the need for the reform of the military. If the preceding chapters are any guide, it is that that endeavour, too, is a complex, multi-layered one, going all the way down from improving bureaucratic, inter-service structures to producing well-trained and motivated soldiers who know how to *fight* and who have the right weapons to do so. That means building into the military organization at various levels some sort of self-questioning, problem-solving facility in order to deal with the as yet unforeseen difficulties which *will* arise. Perhaps it is impossible for any service training to inculcate what one scholar has termed 'that rare kind of imagination which enables men to plan not just for the exploitation of the existing state of their art but for its future developments also.' Yet if the organization shrinks from encouraging 'imagination – the ability to see facts afresh without professional blinkers,'[19] it is unlikely to maintain its military effectiveness for long – or even to be very effective in the first place.

Notes

1 I am thinking here not only of N. Dixon's *On the Psychology of Military Incompetence* (New York, 1976), but also of the images of the senior officers which have come from the war literature of Blunden, Graves, and Remarque, of, 'Oh, What a Lovely War,' of Solzhenitsyn's *August 1914*, and so on.
2 D. C. Watt, *Too Serious a Business* (London, 1975), is the most relevant work here.
3 G. Kennan, *The Decline of Bismarck's European Order* (Princeton, N.J., 1979), p. 3.
4 It would be absurd, for example, to devote equal space to all seven navies, or to comment as much upon Japanese Army tactics as upon German.
5 For a development of this argument, see P. M. Kennedy, *The Rise and Fall of British Naval Mastery* (London and New York, 1976), chs. 7 and 9.
6 T. T. Lupfer, 'The Dynamics of Doctrine: The Changes in German Tactical Doctrine during the First World War,' *Leavenworth Papers*, no. 4 (July 1981).
7 The unthinking title of R. Hough's patriotic offering, *The Great War at Sea, 1914–1918* (Oxford, 1983), which blithely assumes the continued influence of sea power without ever appreciating that the major problem for the British was that the old navalist doctrines were not working in this war.
8 B. H. Liddell Hart, *History of the First World War* (London, 1970), pp. 326–7.
9 See the relevant figures in P. Kennedy, 'The First World War and the International Power System,' *International Security*, vol. 9, no. 1, pp. 7–40.
10 Apart from Lupfer, 'Dynamics of Doctrine,' see also W. Murray, *The Change in the European Balance of Power, 1938–1939* (Princeton, N.J., 1984), pp. 338 ff.
11 M. Beloff, *Imperial Sunset*, Vol. I, *Britain's Liberal Empire, 1897–1921* (London, 1969), p. 180. Beloff's superb work asks many penetrating questions about effectiveness in the larger sense; there is no equivalent study for the other nations.
12 Ibid., pp. 176 ff.
13 Ibid., p. 179.
14 The debate is summarized in H. Strachan, 'The British Way in Warfare Revisited,' *Historical Journal*, vol. 26, no. 2 (1983), pp. 447–61.
15 Beloff, *Imperial Sunset*, p. 179.
16 See, for some example, C. Barnett, *The Collapse of British Power* (New York, 1972), pp. 113 ff., for Britain; N. Stone *The Eastern Front, 1914–1917* (London, 1975), esp. ch. 9, for Russia; and W. H. McNeill, *The Pursuit of Power* (Oxford, 1983), pp. 318 ff., for France.
17 A. J. May, *The Passing of the Habsburg Monarchy, 1914–1918*, 2 vols. (Philadelphia, 1966), is the most detailed account; but see also R. A. Kann, *A History of the Habsburg Empire, 1526–1918* (Berkeley, 1974), ch. 9.
18 See A. Marwick, *The Deluge: British Society and the First World War* (Harmondsworth, Mddsx., 1967).
19 Beloff, *Imperial Sunset*, p. 179.

Index